KIERKEGAARD'S
INTERNATIONAL RECEPTION

TOME I: NORTHERN AND WESTERN EUROPE

Kierkegaard Research: Sources, Reception and Resources
Volume 8, Tome I

Kierkegaard Research: Sources, Reception and Resources
is a publication of the Søren Kierkegaard Research Centre

This volume was published with the generous financial support
of the Danish Agency for Science, Technology and Innovation

Kierkegaard's International Reception

Tome I: Northern and Western Europe

Edited by
JON STEWART

ASHGATE

Published by
Ashgate Publishing Limited
Wey Court East
Union Road
Farnham
Surrey GU9 7PT
England

Ashgate Publishing Company
Suite 420
101 Cherry Street
Burlington, VT 05401-4405
USA

www.ashgate.com

British Library Cataloguing in Publication Data
Kierkegaard's international reception
  Tome 1: Northern and Western Europe. –
(Kierkegaard research : sources, reception and resources ; v. 8)
  1. Kierkegaard, Soren, 1813–1855
  I. Stewart, Jon (Jon Bartley)
  198.9

Library of Congress Cataloging-in-Publication Data
Kierkegaard's international reception / edited by Jon Stewart.
Tome 1: Northern and Western Europe.
  p. cm. (Kierkegaard research ; v. 8)
  Includes bibliographical references and index.
  ISBN 978-0-7546-6496-3 (hardcover : alk. paper)
  1. Kierkegaard, Soren, 1813–1855. I. Stewart, Jon.

198'.9–dc22

ISBN 978-0-7546-6496-3

Cover design by Katalin Nun.

Mixed Sources
Product group from well-managed
forests and other controlled sources
www.fsc.org Cert no. SGS-COC-2482
FSC © 1996 Forest Stewardship Council

Printed and bound in Great Britain by
TJ International Ltd, Padstow, Cornwall

Contents

List of Contributors

Vilhjálmur Árnason, Department of Philosophy, University of Iceland, Main Building, 101 Reykjavik, Iceland.

Thor Arvid Dyrerud, Forlaget Press, Kongensgate 2, 0153 Oslo, Norway.

Jonna Hjertström-Lappalainen, Filosofiska institutionen, Stockholms universitet, 106 91 Stockholm, Sweden.

Lars-Erik Hjertström-Lappalainen, Filosofiska institutionen, Stockholms universitet, 106 91 Stockholm, Sweden.

Janne Kylliäinen, University of Helsinki, Department of Philosophy, P.O. Box 9 (Siltavuorenpenger 20 A), 00014, Finland.

Heiko Schulz, Department of Theology, University of Duisburg-Essen, Universitätsstr. 12, 45117 Essen, Germany.

Jon Stewart, Søren Kierkegaard Research Centre, Farvergade 27D, 1463 Copenhagen K, Denmark.

George Pattison, Christ Church, Oxford OX1 1DP, England.

Steen Tullberg, Søren Kierkegaard Research Centre, Farvergade 27 D, 1463 Copenhagen K, Denmark.

Karl Verstrynge, Vrije Universiteit Brussel, Vakgroep Wijsbegeerte en Moraalwetenschappen Pleinlaan 2, 1050 Brussels, Belgium.

Preface

Although Kierkegaard's reception was initially more or less limited to Scandinavia, it has for a long time now been a highly international affair. As his writings became translated into the different languages, his reputation spread, and he became read more and more by people ever more distant from his native Denmark. While in Scandinavia, the attack on the Church in the last years of his life became something of a *cause célèbre*, which contributed to the immediate reception of his thought, later many different aspects of his work became the object of serious scholarly investigation well beyond the original northern borders. As his reputation grew, he became co-opted into a number of different philosophical, religious, and literary movements in different contexts throughout the world. The three tomes of the present volume attempt to record the history of this reception according to national and linguistic categories. Later volumes in this series will explore the different lines of reception according to specific traditions and fields, for example, theology, philosophy, and literature.

The three tomes of this volume are thus divided along geographical lines. Tome I covers the reception of Kierkegaard in Northern and Western Europe. The articles on Denmark, Norway, Sweden, Finland, and Iceland can be said to trace Kierkegaard's influence in its more or less native Nordic, Protestant context. Since the authors in these countries (with the exception of Finland) were not dependent on translations or other intermediaries, this represents the earliest tradition of Kierkegaard reception. The early German translations of his works opened the door for the next phase of the reception by allowing it to expand beyond the borders of the Nordic countries. The articles in the section on Western Europe trace Kierkegaard's influence in Great Britain, the Netherlands and Flanders, Germany and Austria, and France. All of these countries and linguistic groups have their own extensive tradition of Kierkegaard reception.

Tome II covers the Kierkegaard reception in Southern, Central and Eastern Europe. The first set of articles, under the rubric "Southern Europe," covers his reception in a Catholic context in Portugal, Spain, and Italy. The next group covers the rather heterogeneous group of countries (bound loosely by their former affiliation with the Habsburg Empire) designated as central Europe: Hungary, the Czech Republic, Slovakia, and Poland. Finally, the Orthodox countries are represented with articles on Russia, Bulgaria, Serbia and Montenegro, Macedonia, and Romania.

Tome III is the most geographically diverse, covering the Near East, Asia, Australia and the Americas. The section on the Near East features pioneering articles on Kierkegaard reception in Israel, Turkey, Iran, and the Arab world. The next section dubbed "Asia and Australia" features articles on the long and rich traditions of Kierkegaard research in Japan and Korea along with the more recent ones in

China and Australia. A final section is dedicated to the Americas with articles on Canada, the United States, hispanophone South America, Mexico, and Brazil.

In the planning of this volume, an attempt was made to identify the leading Kierkegaard scholars in the individual countries and solicit the articles from them. The goal was to include as many articles as possible, even when the country in question had a relatively limited reception. The authors were instructed to give a representative overview of the history of the Kierkegaard reception in their respective countries in a way that was objective and easily comprehensible for the international reader. In this sense the volume is conceived as a kind of reference work. The authors were encouraged to present and argue for a critical thesis about the development of Kierkegaard studies in their countries, but they were at the same time enjoined to refrain from using the article to engage in personal polemics.

The articles are intended to be instructive for both the local and the international reader. The local reader can use them to learn about the Kierkegaard reception in his or her own country and will find specific bibliographical references in his or her own language. By contrast, the international reader can by means of these articles gain a quick overview of the reception in the different countries in a way that makes it easy to compare and contrast it with the reception in his or her own country. Further, in the main text and the bibliographies, the titles and bibliographical references are generally in English so that the reader can gain a sense of the content of the individual works without necessarily needing to know the local language.

A quick glance at the material presented in this volume will convince the attentive reader of the absurdity of insisting on absolute divisions in the subject matter along national or linguistic lines. There is invariably a degree of overlap due to a number of factors. There is linguistic ambiguity since large languages such as French, German, and English are spoken in several countries. There is also national ambiguity in countries like the former Yugoslavia or the Soviet Union, which, while representing a national unity, contained within their borders several different languages and ethnic groups. Moreover, as is the case with these countries, borders change historically, and thus different national identities come and go; for example, in the case of the Czechs, who were once part of the Habsburg Empire, Bohemia, Czechoslovakia and now the Czech Republic. Moreover, some Kierkegaard scholars are difficult to pin down unambiguously since they have a complex national identity and as a result have had influence in different traditions of reception for different reasons. For example, the famous scholar Gregor Malantschuk was born in the Ukraine, which at the time was the Soviet Union; he had a Polish passport during the Second World War, and he emigrated to Denmark where he became a Danish citizen. Similarly the expatriate Russian philosopher Lev Shestov had as much influence on the French Kierkegaard reception as on the Russian.

Finally, in our modern, global world of the twenty-first century, it is becoming more and more difficult to talk about Kierkegaard research along nationalist lines. While there are, to be sure, still isolated local or national groups of Kierkegaard scholars in some places, the mainstream has in recent years become a genuinely international. Scholars from all over the world travel to the regular conferences at St. Olaf College and the Søren Kierkegaard Research Centre in Copenhagen. They publish their works regularly in the international journals such as *Kierkegaardiana*, the *International Kierkegaard Commentary*, and the *Kierkegaard Studies Yearbook*. It is not uncommon today for scholars to travel abroad to teach or give papers, and to write books and articles in a foreign language, published at a foreign publishing house, with the result being that they come to obtain a scholarly profile virtually independent of their home country. In this sense, Kierkegaard research is becoming more and more of an international dialogue which largely transcends national borders. For this reason, the present volume is of particular importance since it documents the development of the national traditions of Kierkegaard research at the same time as they are disappearing.

However, the internationalization of Kierkegaard research in recent years has paradoxically led to a rise in the national consciousness of Kierkegaard scholars. While formerly many researchers occupied with Kierkegaard felt isolated even in their own countries, now they have more and more come into contact with their fellow countrymen, often oddly, at international conferences. The result has been the unprecedented growth of national Kierkegaard societies and ambitious new translation projects of Kierkegaard's works into the different languages. This has been fostered by the cooperation of the international institutes such as the Søren Kierkegaard Research Centre and the Hong-Kierkegaard Library. There has thus been a parallel development that follows both national and international lines.

Acknowledgements

This volume has been several years in the making and owes its existence to the selfless help of a number of institutions. A generous grant from the Danish Agency for Science, Technology and Innovation has made this series possible. The Søren Kierkegaard Research Centre at the University of Copenhagen continues in its capacity as the host institute for the project. I would like to extend my deepest gratitude to the kind staff at Ashgate Publishing for their gracious support of the series.

Many individuals have also helped in the production of this work in many different capacities. I would like to thank Tonny Aagaard Olesen, Ingrid Basso, Camilla Brudin Borg, Andrew Burgess, Daniel Conway, István Czakó, Takahiro Hirabayashi, Lisa Hoelle, Finn Gredal Jensen, Darío González, Min-Ho Lee, Cynthia Lund, David Possen, Richard Purkarthofer, Joel Rasmussen, Heiko Schulz, and Brian Söderquist for their invaluable suggestions, their bibliographical and editorial help. I would like to thank Bjarne Laurberg Olsen for his tireless assistance in support of this project. I am particularly grateful to Katalin Nun for her colossal efforts in the editing and formatting of these articles as well as her tremendous bibliographical work.

I am deeply grateful to the authors of this volume who have kindly set aside valuable research time to work on the articles presented here. For their patience with the slow production of this volume and for the many sacrifices they doubtless had to make to find time to write these articles, I say thank you very much. Kierkegaard studies owes you all a great debt of thanks.

List of Abbreviations

BA   *The Book on Adler*, trans. by Howard V. Hong and Edna H. Hong,
        Princeton: Princeton University Press 1998.

C   *The Crisis and a Crisis in the Life of an Actress*, trans. by Howard V.
        Hong and Edna H. Hong, Princeton: Princeton University Press 1997.

CA   *The Concept of Anxiety*, trans. by Reidar Thomte in collaboration with
        Albert B. Anderson, Princeton: Princeton University Press 1980.

CD   *Christian Discourses*, trans. by Howard V. Hong and Edna H. Hong,
        Princeton: Princeton University Press 1997.

CI   *The Concept of Irony*, trans. by Howard V. Hong and Edna H. Hong,
        Princeton: Princeton University Press 1989.

CIC   *The Concept of Irony*, trans. with an Introduction and Notes by Lee M.
        Capel, London: Collins 1966.

COR   *The Corsair Affair; Articles Related to the Writings*, trans. by Howard V.
        Hong and Edna H. Hong, Princeton: Princeton University Press 1982.

CUP1   *Concluding Unscientific Postscript*, vol. 1, trans. by Howard V. Hong
        and Edna H. Hong, Princeton: Princeton University Press 1982.

CUP2   *Concluding Unscientific Postscript*, vol. 2, trans. by Howard V. Hong
        and Edna H. Hong, Princeton: Princeton University Press 1982.

EO1   *Either/Or*, Part I, trans. by Howard V. Hong and Edna H. Hong,
        Princeton: Princeton University Press 1987.

EO2   *Either/Or*, Part II, trans. by Howard V. Hong and Edna H. Hong,
        Princeton: Princeton University Press 1987.

EOP   *Either/Or*, trans. by Alastair Hannay, Harmondsworth: Penguin Books
        1992.

EPW   *Early Polemical Writings*, among others: *From the Papers of One Still
        Living; Articles from Student Days; The Battle Between the Old and
        the New Soap-Cellars*, trans. by Julia Watkin, Princeton: Princeton
        University Press 1990.

EUD   *Eighteen Upbuilding Discourses*, trans. by Howard V. Hong and Edna
        H. Hong, Princeton: Princeton University Press 1990.

FSE   *For Self-Examination*, trans. by Howard V. Hong and Edna H. Hong,
        Princeton: Princeton University Press 1990.

FT   *Fear and Trembling*, trans. by Howard V. Hong and Edna H. Hong,
          Princeton: Princeton University Press 1983.

FTP   *Fear and Trembling*, trans. by Alastair Hannay, Harmondsworth:
          Penguin Books 1985.

JC   *Johannes Climacus, or De omnibus dubitandum est*, trans. by Howard V.
          Hong and Edna H. Hong, Princeton: Princeton University Press 1985.

JFY   *Judge for Yourself!*, trans. by Howard V. Hong and Edna H. Hong,
          Princeton: Princeton University Press 1990.

JP   *Søren Kierkegaard's Journals and Papers*, vols. 1–6, ed. and trans. by
          Howard V. Hong and Edna H. Hong, assisted by Gregor Malantschuk
          (vol. 7, Index and Composite Collation), Bloomington and London:
          Indiana University Press 1967–78.

KAC   *Kierkegaard's Attack upon "Christendom," 1854–1855*, trans. by Walter
          Lowrie, Princeton: Princeton University Press 1944.

KJN   *Kierkegaard's Journals and Notebooks*, vols. 1–11, ed. by Niels Jørgen
          Cappelørn, Alastair Hannay, David Kangas, Bruce H. Kirmmse, George
          Pattison, Vanessa Rumble and K. Brian Söderquist, Princeton and
          Oxford: Princeton University Press 2007ff.

LD   *Letters and Documents*, trans. by Henrik Rosenmeier, Princeton:
          Princeton University Press 1978 (A translation of *B&A*).

LR   *A Literary Review*, trans. by Alastair Hannay, Harmondsworth: Penguin
          Books 2001.

M   *The Moment and Late Writings*, trans. by Howard V. Hong and Edna H.
          Hong, Princeton: Princeton University Press 1998.

P   *Prefaces / Writing Sampler*, trans. by Todd W. Nichol, Princeton:
          Princeton University Press 1997.

PC   *Practice in Christianity*, trans. by Howard V. Hong and Edna H. Hong,
          Princeton: Princeton University Press 1991.

PF   *Philosophical Fragments*, trans. by Howard V. Hong and Edna H. Hong,
          Princeton: Princeton University Press 1985.

PJ   *Papers and Journals: A Selection*, trans. by Alastair Hannay,
          Harmondsworth: Penguin Books 1996.

PLR   *Prefaces: Light Reading for Certain Classes as the Occasion May Require*,
          trans. by William McDonald, Tallahassee: Florida State University Press 1989.

PLS   *Concluding Unscientific Postscript*, trans. by David F. Swenson and Walter Lowrie, Princeton: Princeton University Press 1941.

PV   *The Point of View* including *On My Work as an Author*, *The Point of View for My Work as an Author*, and *Armed Neutrality*, trans. by Howard V. Hong and Edna H. Hong, Princeton: Princeton University Press 1998.

PVL   *The Point of View for My Work as an Author* including *On My Work as an Author*, trans. by Walter Lowrie. New York and London: Oxford University Press 1939.

R   *Repetition*, trans. by Howard V. Hong and Edna H. Hong, Princeton: Princeton University Press 1983.

SBL   *Notes of Schelling's Berlin Lectures*, trans. by Howard V. Hong and Edna H. Hong, Princeton: Princeton University Press 1989.

SLW   *Stages on Life's Way*, trans. by Howard V. Hong and Edna H. Hong, Princeton: Princeton University Press 1988.

SUD   *The Sickness unto Death*, trans. by Howard V. Hong and Edna H. Hong, Princeton: Princeton University Press 1980.

SUDP   *The Sickness unto Death*, trans. by Alastair Hannay, London and New York: Penguin Books 1989.

TA   *Two Ages: The Age of Revolution and the Present Age. A Literary Review*, trans. by Howard V. Hong and Edna H. Hong, Princeton: Princeton University Press 1978.

TD   *Three Discourses on Imagined Occasions*, trans. by Howard V. Hong and Edna H. Hong, Princeton: Princeton University Press 1993.

UD   *Upbuilding Discourses in Various Spirits*, trans. by Howard V. Hong and Edna H. Hong, Princeton: Princeton University Press 1993.

WA   *Without Authority* including *The Lily in the Field and the Bird of the Air, Two Ethical-Religious Essays, Three Discourses at the Communion on Fridays, An Upbuilding Discourse, Two Discourses at the Communion on Fridays*, trans. by Howard V. Hong and Edna H. Hong, Princeton: Princeton University Press 1997.

WL   *Works of Love*, trans. by Howard V. Hong and Edna H. Hong, Princeton: Princeton University Press 1995.

PART I

Northern Europe

Denmark:

The Permanent Reception—150 Years of Reading Kierkegaard

Steen Tullberg

I. Introduction

The criticism and research on H.C. Andersen's fairy tales and other works follow two main roads with several side paths. The one runs through his fairy tale life, while the other seeks out his works directly, although it is almost impossible to keep the two tracks separate from each other given that Andersen clearly made use of material from his own life and produced a colossal documentation right from the beginning in the form of diaries, correspondence and autobiographies. Thus his life has been used to understand his works, and the fairy tales have been used to understand his life in reciprocal elucidations especially in the traditional genre "life and works," as one says in English, where the tradition is strong....[1]

What Torben Brostrøm writes here about "the long line" in the literature on H.C. Andersen holds true almost to the letter for Danish research on Søren Kierkegaard. This perhaps implies that the two authors had more in common than they themselves thought, but also that in research at any time there is a certain spirit of the age, which the scholarly issues are, if not subordinate to, then in any case colored by. Danish research traditions on Kierkegaard and Andersen are, moreover, equally old; both of them begin in earnest with Georg Brandes' sympathetic and critical readings and have also since then had many common representatives.

Completeness is a hazardous ambition, when one seeks to cover almost any given aspect of the Kierkegaard reception, and to want to present the entire Danish reception is a straightforwardly desperate undertaking. Søren Kierkegaard is such an integrated part of Danish culture that the scope and depth of his influence and significance is impossible to survey exhaustively. While his other great contemporary, N.F.S. Grundtvig's life's work resulted concretely and visibly in innumerable schools, societies, and movements, Kierkegaard's influence has been of a more indirect kind. A recent statement that "personalities like H.C. Andersen, Søren Kierkegaard and Niels Bohr [constitute] an inescapable, albeit often unconscious,

---

[1] Torben Brostrøm, "Den lange linje," afterword to the third edition of Eigil Nyborg, *Den indre linje i H.C. Andersens eventyr—en psykologisk studie*, Copenhagen: Gyldendal 2005, p. 215.

ballast for every Dane's attempt at a more theoretical grasp of life and the world,"
should be believed—and this characterization appears in a treatise on something as
(apparently) remote from Kierkegaard studies as biosemiotics.[2]

Fully aware of the subject matter's overwhelming scope, the present investigation,
which immediately recognizes its debt to previous studies on the history of reception,
is an attempt at a representative presentation of the history of Danish Kierkegaard
studies with emphasis on scholarly research and with occasional reference to the
contemporary background in which it is situated: the intellectual and perhaps political
and ideological circumstances, which in every epoch play a role in the treatment
of such a central and lionized authorship as Kierkegaard's. I have attempted, to
the degree possible, to present the material in a neutral fashion instead of giving a
critical discussion of it. The study proceeds chronologically, dwelling at times on
the various editions of the collected works and of the journals and papers, which
constitute an important foil for the character and degree of detail in the research.

The chronological divisions are essentially made following the three wars, which
have so decidedly put their stamp on the intellectual life of the twentieth century,
and which especially constitute a split within Kierkegaard research: the two World
Wars and the Cold War. At the risk of insisting too strongly on this perspective of
the wars, one could also use it for the first period of this study, namely the time from
Kierkegaard's death to the First World War. The lost war to Prussia in 1864 not only
fertilized the soil for the new Danish *belles lettres*, which with time arose in its wake,
but the mood of defeat also constituted the mental background for the beginning of
Kierkegaard research. On the one hand, it was during this period that Georg Brandes
(1842–1927) extricated himself from an early and profound Kierkegaard influence
and took aim at a career as critic and source of inspiration for the so-called "modern
breakthrough." On the other hand, it was at this time that the bishop of Aalborg,
Peter Christian Kierkegaard (1805–88), began to read his brother's literary *Nachlaß*
and decided to publish this material, which proved absolutely decisive for later
research. One recalls involuntarily the expression, "What is lost outwardly will be
won inwardly."[3]

II. The Beginning of Kierkegaard Research (ca. 1860–90)

A. Faith and Knowledge

The 1860s were the stage for what has been called the faith and knowledge debate.
This debate had a brief precursor in Kierkegaard's own time, namely in 1849–50
in connection with the publication of H.L. Martensen's *Christian Dogmatics*; it
has reemerged with greater or lesser force in the Danish history of ideas several

---

[2]   Jesper Hoffmeyer, *Biosemiotik. En afhandling om livets tegn og tegnenes liv*,
Charlottenlund: Ries Forlag 2005, p. 417.

[3]   This saying comes from the founder of the Heath Society, Enrico Dalgas (1828–94)
and refers to the cultivation of the heath areas in Jutland, which began after the defeat in 1864.
The inward movement has also a symbolic expression in the fact that Dalgas' son, the author
Ernesto Dalgas (1871–99), was strongly influenced by Kierkegaard.

times since.[4] The main figure in the conflict was the former student and friend of Kierkegaard, the professor of philosophy Rasmus Nielsen (1809–84), who, from the one side, was attacked by a young Georg Brandes and the philosopher Hans Brøchner (1820–75), and, from the other, by Bishop Hans Lassen Martensen (1808–84).[5] Although Søren Kierkegaard at that time played a, to be sure, decisive, albeit only indirect role, for the different positions, I will not enter into the details of the debate here, but will merely underscore a few main lines with significance for Kierkegaard research later on.[6]

In 1864 and 1866 Rasmus Nielsen published a two-volume work, *The Logic of Fundamental Ideas*,[7] where he argued that faith and knowledge represented two distinct, absolutely heterogeneous entities, which nonetheless (or, according to Nielsen, precisely for this reason) can be contained in one and the same consciousness without contradiction.[8] Nielsen's thought up to that point had, albeit in a way that was somewhat out of context, made use of Kierkegaard's ideas of subjectivity and specifically underscored the human being's religious and intellectual consciousness as two separate spheres. Here he goes a step further and claims (in a polemic against Kierkegaard), that the religious also has its universal side, which anchors

---

[4]   Most recently in connection with the case about the pastor Thorkild Grosbøll from 2003. Cf. his book from the same year, *En sten i skoen—Et essay om civilisation og kristendom*, Frederiksberg: Forlaget Anis 2003.

[5]   The main works in the conflict were, in chronological order: Rasmus Nielsen, *Grundideernes Logik*, vols. 1–2, Copenhagen: Den Gyldendalske Boghandling 1864 and 1866; Georg Brandes, *Dualismen i vor nyeste Philosophie*, Copenhagen: Gyldendal 1866; Hans Lassen Martensen, *Om Tro og Viden, et Lejlighedsskrift*, Copenhagen: C.A. Reitzel 1867; Rasmus Nielsen, *Om Hindringer og Betingelser for det aandelige Liv i Nutiden*, Copenhagen: Den Gyldendalske Boghandling 1868; Hans Brøchner, *Problemet om Tro og Viden, en historisk-kritisk Afhandling*, Copenhagen: P.G. Philipsens Forlag 1868; R. Nielsen, *Hr. Prof. Brøchners filosofiske Kritik gjennemset*, Copenhagen: Den Gyldendalske Boghandling and H. Brøchner, *Et Svar til Professor R. Nielsen*, Copenhagen: P.G. Philipsens Forlag 1868. Not directly relevant for the debate itself but offshoots of it are Hans Brøchner, *Om det Religiøse i dets Enhed med det Humane*, Copenhagen: P.G. Philipsens Forlag 1869 and Rasmus Nielsen, *Religionsphilosophie*, Copenhagen: Den Gyldendalske Boghandling 1869.

[6]   For a detailed account, see Habib C. Malik, "The 'Tro and Viden' Controversy, Or the Rise and Demise of 'Pseudo-Kierkegaard,' " in *Receiving Søren Kierkegaard. The Early Impact and Transmission of His Thought*, Washington, D.C.: Catholic University of America Press 1997, pp. 171–210. In his work, *Biskop H.L. Martensen. Hans Liv, Udvikling og Arbejde* (Copenhagen: G.E.C. Gad 1932, pp. 325–406), Skat Arilden also has a thorough chapter on "Striden om Tro og Viden." See also Aage Kabell, *Kierkegaardstudiet i Norden*, Copenhagen: Hagerup 1948, pp. 78ff. Kabell has, moreover, an account of the earliest discussions about Kierkegaard from the time around the attack on the Church and in the wake of his death, pp. 49ff.

[7]   Rasmus Nielsen, *Grundideernes Logik*, vols. 1–2, Copenhagen: Den Gyldendalske Boghandling 1864. In fact, this is a torso, since Nielsen in the foreword to the first volume of the book ambitiously (and in a wholly Hegelian spirit) announces, "this work is only a small part of a larger whole—hardly two-thirds of the first one-ninth of the entire logic"(!)

[8]   This view is already found in Rasmus Nielsen's *Philosophisk Propædeutik i Grundtræk*, Copenhagen: Gyldendalske Boghandling 1857, p. 77.

the personal appropriation in the community. However, it was primarily Nielsen's simultaneous use of an absolute epistemological heterogeneity and a conscious unity, which evoked protests. In his debut work as author, *Dualism in Our Most Recent Philosophy* from 1866, Nielsen's former student Georg Brandes criticizes his former teacher for in reality operating with an absolute dualism, which, for example, overlooks the in principle irreconcilable biblical and scientific statements about the creation. According to Brandes, it is Kierkegaard who lies behind the radical dualism, and Nielsen's attempt to harmonize the conflicting elements is described as a fusion of Kierkegaard's *The Moment* and H.C. Ørsted's *The Spirit in Nature:* "The entire doctrine consisted essentially in the fact that one took Kierkegaard's *The Moment* in the one hand and Ørsted's *The Spirit in Nature* in the other, put them together and mixed them into one."[9] A mixture of this kind is, however, an intellectual absurdity, and Brandes is of the opinion that the result is that Ørsted disappears, and only Kierkegaard remains—and Kierkegaard has even said what Nielsen says, in a much better way.

Bishop H.L. Martensen also entered the debate—on behalf of the Church and dogmatic theology—with a short book, *On Faith and Knowledge* (1867). Martensen also lumps Nielsen's principle of heterogeneity together with Kierkegaard and interprets Nielsen's philosophy from a historical perspective as "a concordance" between Hegel and Kierkegaard; however, according to Martensen's view, Kierkegaard comes out the worst from this agreement. Kierkegaard's passionate existential effort undergoes a distortion in Nielsen: "It may be asked whether anything is more suitable to weaken, enfeeble and paralyze that which must be regarded as the reality of *religious* activity of the so-called 'individual' than the concordance and collegial system of R. Nielsen."[10] This, however, does not mean that Martensen approves of Kierkegaard's position, which is designated as fundamentally "antisocial." Precisely Kierkegaard's overemphasis on what is subjective-Socratic excludes the good from having significance not only for the life of the individual person but also for the life of society and existence as a whole.[11] Concerning Christianity, Martensen's most essential disagreement with Kierkegaard is in the conception of God, which in Kierkegaard, as a result of his exaggerations in the direction of the subjective, has a corresponding deficiency in the objective and is replaced by the doctrine of the paradox. Kierkegaard's conception of God then remains something abstract and logical instead of something ethical, and his views of God's eternity and unchangeability are, according to Martensen, borrowed from Greek thought rather than connected with the Revelation.

A criticism of Rasmus Nielsen from the opposite side comes from the left Hegelian Hans Brøchner, who, of those involved in the discussion, goes to work most extensively in his treatment of Kierkegaard and his presence in Nielsen's thought.

---

[9]   Brandes, *Dualismen i vor nyeste Philosophie*, p. 67.

[10]   Martensen, *Om Tro og Viden, et Lejlighedsskrift*, pp. 133–4.

[11]   Martensen also issued this criticism of Kierkegaard's alleged acosmism in the foreword to *Den christelige Dogmatik*, Copenhagen: C.A. Reitzel 1849, pp. IIf. Kierkegaard is not mentioned by name, but the criticism is unambiguously directed against him; cf. the commentary in *SKS* K22, p. 190.

Brøchner's analysis appears in his book, *The Problem of Faith and Knowledge, a Historical-Critical Treatise* from 1868. Here Nielsen and Kierkegaard are presented in a new constellation in the history of philosophy. While Brandes and Martensen describe Nielsen's endeavor as an (impossible) attempt to unite Kierkegaard with, respectively, Ørsted and Hegel, Brøchner points primarily to Kierkegaard's (and then Nielsen's) relation to Ludwig Feuerbach.[12] Feuerbach is the most significant representative of the protest, which, from the side of philosophy, is directed against the speculative reconciliation of religion and philosophy. But while Kierkegaard, according to Brøchner, is in agreement with Feuerbach in claiming that there is an opposition between religion's practical standpoint and science's theoretical one, he disagrees on the foundation and application of this opposition. Kierkegaard distinguishes between religion and philosophy in the interest of religion (in contrast to the atheist, Feuerbach). By ascribing to faith and knowledge their own spheres and by subordinating knowledge to faith, Kierkegaard makes possible their unification in the same consciousness. Brøchner regards as well and good this attempt to resolve the issue, which is expressed, among other places, in Kierkegaard's doctrine of the paradox, although he thinks it is not without destructive consequences for "the certainty of all knowledge." Moreover, according to Brøchner, it is an unfortunate implication of Kierkegaard's view that it allows the ethical to disappear in "a religiosity which is abstract and lacking reality." Rasmus Nielsen's view, by contrast, does not enjoy Brøchner's respect; it is described as derived from Kierkegaard's view and is lacking any independent value. What is of value in Nielsen's thought is due to Kierkegaard, but while in Kierkegaard knowledge is subordinated to faith in a clear and consistent manner, Nielsen with his absolute heterogeneity is too unclear and ends, according to Brøchner, in a dualism, which leads to "the inevitable self-dissolution of consciousness."[13]

Hard-pressed, Rasmus Nielsen defended himself on a few occasions against the criticism. Against Brandes and Martensen he argues, for example, that the appearance of two heterogeneous principles in one and the same consciousness cannot be explained but is an "*absolute mystery*."[14] The designation "mystery" for the unity of faith and knowledge occupies hereafter a central place in Nielsen's thought, for example, in his long work, *Philosophy of Religion* from 1869.[15] It is

[12]   Brøchner was not the first one, as Malik claims (*Receiving Søren Kierkegaard*, pp. 190–1), who places Kierkegaard in connection with Feuerbach. The first one was C.F. Christens in his article, "En Parallel mellem to af den nyere Tids Philosopher," in *For Literatur og Kritik*, vols. 1–6, ed. by L. Helweg, Odense: Fyens Stifts Literære Selskab, vol. 3, 1845, pp. 1–17. Kierkegaard is, however, not mentioned here by name, but is merely called "X." But there can be no doubt that Kierkegaard is the referent since Christens refers directly to, among other things, *Either/Or, Fear and Trembling* and *Philosophical Fragments*.
[13]   Brøchner, *Problemet om Tro og Viden, en historisk-kritisk Afhandling*, pp. 6–7.
[14]   Rasmus Nielsen, *Om "Den gode Villie" som Magt i Videnskaben*, Copenhagen: Gyldendal 1867, p. 33. Nielsen's launching of "the mystery" set off an extended criticism from Sophus Heegaard (1835–84), who had previously taken up a position very close to Nielsen's; cf. P.S.V. Heegaard, *Professor R. Nielsens Lære om Tro og Viden*, Copenhagen: Den Gyldendalske Boghandling 1867.
[15]   Rasmus Nielsen, *Religionsphilosophie*, Copenhagen: Gyldendal 1869.

an interesting question whether one can ultimately regard Nielsen's "mystery" not only as a defense against the criticism of his logic but also as a replacement for, or response to, Kierkegaard's concept of the paradox.[16] The paradox was a problem for Kierkegaard's immediate posterity, and almost everyone involved in the debate about faith and knowledge criticizes the notion of the paradox in one way or another.[17] This constant element in the debate is an early testimony of one of the central points of controversy in Kierkegaard research, which also will be a main theme in the account below.[18] Martensen's demonstration of Kierkegaard's profound dependence on Greek philosophy and the consequences of this for his understanding of Christianity is, furthermore, an issue which now and again emerges in Kierkegaard studies (explored by, among others, A.B. Drachmann). Similarly, Brøchner's criticism of Kierkegaard's abstract-religious annulling of the ethical is later taken up with renewed energy by Georg Brandes and Harald Høffding.[19]

What is of further interest is that one of the results of the controversy was that Rasmus Nielsen moved in a more marked Grundtvigian direction (although, to be sure, Grundtvig had been a part of Nielsen's intellectual baggage from the start). During the entire debate he was supported by the Grundtvigians, for example, in the Grundtvigian journal *Dansk Kirketidende*, whose editor Niels Lindberg (1829–86) was a personal friend of Nielsen. It has been suggested (by the literary scholar Vilhelm Andersen),[20] that Rasmus Nielsen's efforts aimed at a greater unification of Kierkegaard and Grundtvig. Malik comments on this in his history of reception: "if so, he would be the first to

---

[16]   It should be emphasized that Nielsen did not himself have a concept of the paradox and likewise did not explicitly juxtapose his concept of "the mystery" to Kierkegaard's paradox. In his philosophy of religion Nielsen criticizes Kierkegaard's separation of the "what" of faith and the "how" of faith for ending up in "the well-known sophism of subjectivity, that everyone becomes blessed through his faith." By placing all weight on the subject's "how" one becomes worked up in passion and unceasingly runs one's head against the paradox; cf. *Religionsphilosophie*, p. 57.

[17]   It was presumably first A.F. Schiødte (pastor in Århus), who attempted to defend Kierkegaard's idea of the paradox, but this only happened some time after the faith and knowledge debate had died out; cf. A.F. Schiødte, *Om de dialektiske Grundbegreber hos Søren Kierkegaard*, Copenhagen: Axel Schiødte 1874. Schiødte is also critical of Rasmus Nielsen: "R. Nielsen's entire appropriation of Søren Kierkegaard is a complete misunderstanding" (ibid., p. IV). Cf. also Malik, *Receiving Søren Kierkegaard*, pp. 204–5.

[18]   Malik believes that the whole debate can in a certain sense be regarded in light of the concept of the paradox. He explains the age's rejection of the idea of the paradox as follows: "For an age desperately striving after rational clarity, comprehensive wholeness, and harmonious unities in every field of human endeavor, and among the fields themselves, the Kierkegaardian paradox, with its defiance of reason and its suggestion of absurdity, was anathema. Nobody wanted it." ibid., p. 210.

[19]   Brøchner's follow-up to the faith and knowledge debate, *Om det Religiøse i dets Enhed med det Humane*, is even more expressly anti-Kierkegaardian and takes up especially (cf. the title) Kierkegaard's separation of the paradoxical religiousness and the ethical (where the ethical is merely a transitional link), see, for example, p. 41n and pp. 42–3.

[20]   Vilhelm Andersen, *Det nittende Aarhundredes første Halvdel*, in *Illustreret dansk Litteraturhistorie*, vols. 1–4, ed. by Carl S. Petersen and Vilhelm Andersen, Copenhagen: 1924–34, vol. 3, 1924, p. 712.

have taken on a challenge that Danish culture has been attempting unsuccessfully to meet ever since. The proposed combination is close to impossible."[21] Precisely this challenge—the question of the possibility or impossibility of the unification of Kierkegaard and Grundtvig—will be taken up at the end of the present article.

B. The Edition: *Af Søren Kierkegaards Efterladte Papirer (1869–81)*

The debate about faith and knowledge concluded for the most part in the same year that the first volume of *Af Søren Kierkegaards Efterladte Papirer* appeared. With the publication of this source material the seed was planted for the scholarly study of Kierkegaard, and the history of the edition is in itself, to use the words of Aage Kabell, "an odd chapter in Kierkegaard research."[22]

The tale of Kierkegaard's literary *Nachlaß* is a complicated story of packets and bags full of carefully described papers, which after a stormy life, first in a few apartments in Copenhagen, then to a bishop's residence in North Jutland, ultimately made its way to the Royal Library, where they are today among the most carefully guarded materials.[23] After Kierkegaard's death in November 1855, his rebellious nephew Henrik Lund (1825–89) saw himself called to act as the literary executor of the estate. He shortly thereafter (in December 1855–January 1856) made the first registration of the posthumous papers, partly an overview, "The Order of the Papers," partly a catalogue, "List of the Manuscripts." Lund thought that the publication of the materials would be done by Kierkegaard's lifelong friend Emil Boesen, but Boesen declined. After some correspondence, P.C. Kierkegaard received the material in his bishop's residence in Aalborg presumably at the end of May 1857.[24] At the end of 1859 P.C. Kierkegaard published *The Point of View for My Activity as an Author*,

---

21   Malik, *Receiving Søren Kierkegaard*, p. 197.

22   Kabell, *Kierkegaardstudiet i Norden*, p. 121.

23   Cf. the preface to Niels Jørgen Cappelørn, Joakim Garff and Johnny Kondrup, *Skriftbilleder. Søren Kierkegaards journaler, notesbøger, hæfter, ark, lapper og strimler*, Copenhagen: G.E.C. Gad 1996, p. 7. (English translation: *Written Images. Søren Kierkegaard's Journals, Notebooks, Booklets, Sheets, Scraps, and Slips of Paper*, trans. by Bruce H. Kirmmse, Princeton and Oxford: Princeton University Press 1997, p. 7.) The following information is primarily taken from this book.

24   Ibid., p. 22, both editions: where it is mentioned (without any reference to a source) that the arrival of the material in Aalborg took place sometime "at the beginning of 1858," but according to a newly found letter from May 19, 1857 from Henrik Lund's father, the merchant Johan Christian Lund, to P.C. Kierkegaard, Kierkegaard's literary *Nachlaß* was packed up in two crates and sent already at the end of May 1857, that is, a year earlier than previously assumed. The letter also makes clear that J.C. Lund and Henrik Lund had the view that Kierkegaard had appointed Henrik Lund to take care of Kierkegaard's papers. J.C. Lund writes to P.C. Kierkegaard: "I would like to ask you to give his manuscripts your best attention, something which I probably do not even have to mention, *but since as you know he had requested Henrik to do this*, and since I urgently dissuaded him from this, the matter itself lies very close to my heart. I strongly believe that they contain some interesting things based on the quick impression that I received from some of them while packing them; it is possible that there is a precious treasure in the material respect if it is taken care of in the correct way" (my emphasis). Cf. Finn Gredal Jensen, "To genfundne breve. Fra J.C. Lund til

which he found in manuscript form among the papers. But then it took a further six years before he again took up the work of publishing the materials. When he finally decided that there should be a registration of the material, he allied himself for this purpose with the jurist and former newspaper editor H.P. Barfod (1834–92), who in February 1865 moved into the bishop's residence and immediately set about the work. Along the way Barfod made a few finds, among others, the entry about Kierkegaard's father cursing God, but also a little octavo page, which contained Kierkegaard's intention with respect to his literary *Nachlaß*. From this it is clear that Kierkegaard had designated Rasmus Nielsen to be in charge of the publication of his manuscripts, journals, etc. Even if Barfod and P.C. Kierkegaard had the right not to regard this as Kierkegaard's final literary will, it doubtless provoked a minor crisis in the editorial work—and ten years later a minor crisis in the relation between P.C. Kierkegaard and Rasmus Nielsen, when the latter was made aware of the discovery of the page in question.[25] At the beginning of November 1865 Barfod finished his catalogue of Kierkegaard's posthumous papers ("Catalogue of the Papers Found After the Death of *Søren Aabye Kierkegaard*"), a work which he had bound and ceremoniously gave to P.C. Kierkegaard on the ten-year anniversary of Kierkegaard's death, on November 11, 1865.[26]

In the fall of 1867 Barfod received the green light to work on Kierkegaard's literary *Nachlaß*, and on December 13, 1869 the publication of *Af Søren Kierkegaards efterladte Papirer* began with the first of what would ultimately be eight volumes (with the first being a double volume). Barfod, however, only published the first four volumes himself. After the publication, in the spring of 1877, of the journals from 1847, a volume which had been under way for several years presumably due to Barfod's fatigue, the young German secondary-school teacher Hermann Gottsched (b. 1849) was brought on board. In 1879–81 he, with Barfod as his assistant, edited the last five volumes.[27] Gottsched thus appears to be a considerably more effective editor than Barfod, but one must keep in mind that the complexity of the material is considerably greater for the earlier years. Moreover there is the fact that Gottsched did not carry out, in anywhere near the same quantity as Barfod, the time-intensive

---

P.C. Kierkegaard og fra Regine Schlegel til Henrik Lund," *Danske Studier*, Copenhagen: C.A. Reitzel 2005, pp. 194–200.

[25]   Rasmus Nielsen had, however, already contributed to Kierkegaard research with his publication of *S. Kierkegaard's Bladartikler, med Bilag samlede efter Forfatterens Død, udgivne som Supplement til hans øvrige Skrifter*, Copenhagen: C.A. Reitzel 1857.

[26]   The catalogue contains 472 numbers, which up until number 382 keeps pace with the numbers in Henrik Lund's catalogue (which in Barfod is number 473). In contrast to Lund, Barfod included everything in his catalogue, with the exception of certain things (shorter articles and letters), which lay in Bishop Kierkegaard's "hiding places." Cf. *Skriftbilleder*, p. 44 (*Written Images*, p. 44).

[27]   The year of publication for the individual volumes and the periods in Kierkegaard's life which they cover are as follows: vols. 1–2 (vol. 1, 1833–38; vol. 2, 1839–43) published in 1869, vol. 3 (1844–46) in 1872, vol. 4 (1847) in 1877, vols. 5–7 (vol. 5, 1848; vol. 6, 1849; vol. 7, 1850) all published in 1880 and vols. 8–9 (vol. 8, 1851–53; vol. 9, 1854–55) both published in 1881.

work of writing elucidating notes, and finally the two last volumes only included around 50% (in contrast to the former 85–90%) of the journal entries.

For posterity Barfod has been regarded as a problematic editor, primarily due to his heavy-handed treatment of the original material. Moreover, he was regarded by some people at the time as indiscreet both regarding the publication of Kierkegaard's allegedly private papers at all, but also when these entries discussed people who were still alive. The first criticism—Barfod's slapdash editorial practice—was noted by the editors of the *Efterladte Papirer*'s heir, *Søren Kierkegaards Papirer* (1909–48) (more on this later). The second criticism was to a large degree closely connected to the age and died out relatively quickly, making room for a recognition of the value of the material which Barfod presented.[28]

In the foreword to the first volume, Barfod gives an account of the general point of view which lies at the foundation for the selection and ordering of the entries. The idea of the edition is to create "a collection of material, an archive, ordered as much as possible, of loose often not even mutually continuous supplements *for a future portrayal of Søren Kierkegaard's story,*" and as for this goal Barfod found it most natural to organize the material "*according to the chronology.*"[29] (Barfod's emphasis). This organization of the material, its fundamental determination as a biographical source and the accompanying chronological principle of organization meant, for example, that the presentation of the *Journal JJ* and the first of the 36 NB journals took on a fragmentary and split-up character, and that the letters, loose pages, and unpublished polemical articles were interspersed between each other in a chronological series. In order to further give the edition its dramatic character as a biographical source Barfod began, with the third volume, to group material under headings such as "The Polemic with Heiberg" and "*The Corsair* and Goldschmidt." The desire to put the material in chronological order left Barfod with a problem since far from all of Kierkegaard's entries are dated. This same problem would appear again for the editors of *Søren Kierkegaards Papirer* (*Papirer*), but Barfod "solves" it by keeping first to the entries of a personal nature, which are relatively easy to date, and second to the entries which can be placed against the background of the content of thought and that contained allusions to contemporary events. However, he omits a great deal of material which is connected with Kierkegaard's studies and drafts and outlines to planned works (material that in the *Papirer* is placed in the groups B and C).

Barfod, as mentioned, included in the edition explanatory notes which, among other things, were conceived as an anticipation of the charge of indiscretion, a kind of counterweight to Kierkegaard's polemics or unflattering discussions of people who were still living. In the case of, for example, M.A. Goldschmidt, this concerned references to and quotations from passages in the journals *The Corsair*

---

[28]   The negative reception of the first volume is described in *Skriftbilleder* (pp. 53ff.; *Written Images*, pp. 53ff.), and in Kabell, *Kierkegaardstudiet i Norden*, pp. 128ff. For an account of the positive reception of Gottsched's first volume, see *Skriftbilleder*, pp. 69–70 (*Written Images*, pp. 67ff.)

[29]   *Af Søren Kierkegaards Efterladte Papirer*, vols. 1–9, ed. by H.P. Barfod and H. Gottsched, Copenhagen: C.A. Reitzel, vol. 1, 1869 (1833–43), p. XI.

and *North and South*, so that Kierkegaard's crass criticism of Goldschmidt did not stand entirely isolated and without comment. This sympathetic and reader-friendly feature of the edition is emphasized further by the useful memoirs of Kierkegaard's early schoolmates and friends of youth, which Barfod collected and included in his introductory "Notes" to the first volume. The initiative of collecting testimonies about Kierkegaard in time spawned various contributions, which constitute important psychological material and a corrective and supplement to Kierkegaard's own autobiographical statements. One of the most important of the documents is Hans Brøchner's "Recollections of Søren Kierkegaard," which was written around the beginning of the year 1872 and was published after the death of the author in Edvard and Georg Brandes' journal, *Det nittende Aarhundrede*, in March 1877 (by Brøchner's student Harald Høffding).[30]

C. Georg Brandes

When Georg Brandes wrote his book about Kierkegaard, which appeared in 1877, he had had, since Brøchner's death in 1875, the latter's handwritten memoirs about Kierkegaard at his disposal. Moreover, the papers up until 1846 had been published, and when Brandes republished his book in 1880, he could say with great satisfaction that the diaries which had been published in the interim confirmed all of his suspicions. The book not only rests on a solid study of the available sources but is at the same time the culmination of a passionate occupation with Kierkegaard, which dates back to Brandes' earliest youth and which takes the form of him increasingly distancing himself from the religious and the Christian elements in Kierkegaard's authorship. It has been claimed (by the literary scholar Paul V. Rubow), that Brandes' relation to Kierkegaard "is the most serious in his entire intellectual life." Evidence for this claim can be found in many places in Brandes' diary kept during his youth, where he, for example, asks himself if Kierkegaard is not "Denmark's or the world's greatest man," and asserts that "Kierkegaard is the only human being, before whose greatness I feel like nothing."[31] At the same time Brandes nourishes from the outset a suspicion about something fundamentally unhealthy in Kierkegaard, and at times he doubts "whether Kierkegaard's Christianity is really the historical Christianity and not much more a conceptually accommodated Christianity." Through the 1860s his skepticism gains in strength, and in his contribution in the aforementioned debate about faith and knowledge it is characteristic that Brandes is only interested in Rasmus Nielsen's doctrine to the extent that it is Kierkegaardian—here Brandes struggles against ideas which he himself had long praised. Under the influence of, among others, the French literary historian Hippolyte Taine's positivism and the

---

[30]   The most recent and most complete collection of recollections about Kierkegaard is Bruce H. Kirmmse, *Søren Kierkegaard truffet. Et liv set af hans samtidige*, Copenhagen: C.A. Reitzel 1996 (in English as *Encounters with Kierkegaard. A Life as Seen by His Contemporaries*, Princeton: Princeton University Press 1996). This work is more than double the size of its immediate predecessor, Steen Johansen, *Erindringer om Kierkegaard*, Copenhagen: Hasselbach 1980.
[31]   Cf. Paul V. Rubow, *Georg Brandes' Briller*, Copenhagen: Levin & Munksgaard 1932, pp. 101ff.

English philosopher John Stuart Mill's thought, Brandes in the meantime steers clear of Kierkegaard's thought, without, however, being able to wrench himself free from the structure in Kierkegaard's thinking. In the epoch-making lectures of 1871–72, *Main Currents of European Literature*, in Danish *Hovedstrømninger i det 19de Aarhundredes Litteratur*, one thus senses Kierkegaard's polemical works from 1854–55 as the deepest matrix of the first part, *Emigrant Literature*, the composition of which, moreover, recalls the first part of *Either/Or*. In the second volume, *The Romantic School in Germany*, Kierkegaard takes on an even larger role, and Brandes' attack on the Romantics is at the same time a criticism of Kierkegaard.[32]

Søren Kierkegaard. A Critical Exposition in Outline from 1877 was therefore in many ways prepared in the first two volumes of *Main Currents*. The book is generally recognized as one of Brandes' best, and he was himself of the opinion that it was the finest work that he had produced with respect to psychology. This evaluation is found in the famous letter to Friedrich Nietzsche from January 11, 1888, where Brandes introduces the German philosopher to Kierkegaard in the following manner:

> *Es giebt ein nordischer Schriftsteller, dessen Werk Sie interessieren würde, wenn sie nur übersetzt wären, Sören Kierkegaard; er lebte 1813–55 und ist meiner Ansicht nach einer der tiefsten Psychologen, die es überhaupt giebt. Ein Büchlein, das ich über ihn geschrieben habe (übersetzt Leipzig 1879) giebt keine hinreichende Vorstellung von seinem Genie, denn dies Buch ist eine Art von Streitschrift, geschrieben um seinen Einfluss zu hemmen. Es ist wohl aber in psychologischer Hinsicht entschieden das feinste, was ich veröffentlicht habe.*[33]

What still makes the book a pleasure to read to this very day is the fact that Brandes' presentation is to the same high degree artistically conceived and executed as it psychologically penetrates its subject. It is introduced by an overture, which presents us with four pictures of Kierkegaard—as walking, riding, discussing, and writing—in a lively, suggestive language, and Brandes strews throughout the book descriptions of dramatic and evocative situations from Kierkegaard's life. The book's stylistic stamp reflects to this degree its genesis, since it was originally conceived as four lectures, but it is primarily an artistic choice.[34] It contains 28 chapters, which can be divided into four well-defined sections, and is composed around three facts of a higher order: Kierkegaard's father, his engagement with Regine Olsen, and the *Corsair* affair. When Brandes in an exceptional case mentions other biographical facts, they are almost always introduced under these three and are organized in their

---

[32]   Ibid., p. 128; pp. 134ff.

[33]   Cf. *Correspondance de Georg Brandes*, vols. 1–4, ed. by Paul Krüger, Copenhagen: Rosenkilde & Bagger 1952–66, vol. 3 (1966), p. 448.

[34]   Alongside the book's artistic ambitions—and of course its biographical ones—there also exist, according to Johnny Kondrup, a set of methodological ambitions, which are rooted in Brandes' consciousness of the fact that with his book he opens a new field of research for literary scholarship. Kierkegaard's work, according to Brandes, is only understandable via the biographical method and technique (the historical-genetic view), which he demonstrates in his book. It was the book about Kierkegaard, which actually made biography into a genre in Danish literary research. Cf. Johnny Kondrup, *Livsværker. Studier i dansk litterær biografi*, Valby: Amadeus 1986, pp. 110–11.

mutual connection with them. Each of the three basic facts carries the book's first, second, and fourth section, while the third section represents a more systematic introduction to Kierkegaard's philosophy.[35]

In the first six chapters of the book Brandes gives an account of Kierkegaard's childhood and adolescence, which under his father's determining influence is described as an early warping of an originally healthy nature. As a reaction to the unnatural external effects, Kierkegaard's inward nature develops in a corresponding manner. He learns to express his real thoughts under masks. On the one side an inward space of dissimulation and mystification is created, which Brandes regards as a condition for the later pseudonymous authorship, and on the other side there grows a secret and unhealthy arrogance, which Brandes conceives as the beginning of Kierkegaard's later doctrine of the religious exception. To what degree Kierkegaard's well-known melancholy was inherited or a result of his father's upbringing is less clear in Brandes' presentation, but it is presumed, along with Kierkegaard's physical weakness, to lie behind his sharp and humorous words. The melancholy manifested itself, moreover, according to Brandes in the area of sexuality, presumably as impotence, and prevented Kierkegaard from marrying. Kierkegaard's qualities are derived from the two "basic drives," which also constitute the key to his authorship: *piety*, the unhealthy fruit of his upbringing, and *disdain*, which arises in combination with the inherited drive to opposition and the talent for ridicule and mockery.

In chapter 7 Brandes demonstrates the presence of these two basic drives in *From the Papers of One Still Living* and then in chapters 8–15 goes on to demonstrate the close connection between life and work for the early authorship. At the center stands the story of the engagement, the event which, according to Brandes, concentrates the productive forces in Kierkegaard's mind and gives his imagination a direction. The engagement is conceived as a guiding thread which can be followed through several works and describes a movement from the relationship between Clavigo and Marie Beaumarchais in "Silhouttes" to "The Tragic in Ancient Drama Reflected in the Tragic of Modern Drama" to Judge Wilhelm's letters until it finally takes on religious dimensions and reaches the category of the paradox in *Fear and Trembling* (Abraham and Isaac).[36] When Kierkegaard has come so far that he catches sight of Abraham just opposite himself, he believes he has reached the paradox of faith, which the age has forgotten. But Brandes objects that Kierkegaard's enthusiasm for the father of faith is not faith in itself but rather personal inwardness or passion, and that

---

[35]   Here I follow Kondrup's division and rely much of the way on his thorough analysis of the book. See also Johnny Kondrup, "Keine hinreichende Vorstellung von seinem Genie. Strategien in der negativen Kierkegaardrezeption von Georg Brandes," *Kierkegaardiana*, vol. 18, 1996, pp. 148–72.

[36]   The background for the paradox is, in other words, the many rewritings of the sufferings of the engagement episode, and Brandes' "biographism" does not then dwell on the external forms of the events in order to find them again in the works, but rather reveals the heart of the matter, given that Kierkegaard's imagination reworks the events. The works should, according to Brandes, be regarded as active moments in Kierkegaard's process of self-knowing and development and not mere reflections of his mental state. Cf. Kondrup, *Livsværker. Studier i dansk litterær biografi*, pp. 95–6.

the meeting therefore does not take place in the special category of "the Christian," but in the general category of "the individual." Kierkegaard's mistake in confusing inwardness with faith comes from being in love with the paradox as phenomenon, a, in Brandes' view, sick desire to drive thought, in all areas, out beyond its limits and into the irrational. Brandes' consistent attempt to link Kierkegaard's life and work is seen in this section again on the methodical level, since the opinions and experiences of the pseudonyms are treated as if they were Kierkegaard's own, which Brandes justifies, among other things, with reference to the many passages from the *Efterladte Papirer* which have flowed into the pseudonymous works.

The longest continuous section in the book is chapters 16–21, which break with the strict historical method to give a systematic account of Kierkegaard's so-called stage theory, and for this purpose Brandes makes use of especially *Either/Or*, *Stages on Life's Way*, and the *Concluding Unscientific Postscript*. Brandes' most important critical point claims that Kierkegaard does not do justice to his own middle stage, the ethical. The defense of ethics and marriage in the second part of *Either/Or* builds, according to Brandes, not on any independent ethics, but is supported by an external authority, Christianity, whereby the ethical is reduced to a province of the religious without any value of its own. The reason for this is biographical: Kierkegaard is split (due to his original healthy nature and unhealthy upbringing) and forced out into mutually hostile extremes. In his personality there is only room for a demonized, aesthetic attraction and the pure, religious spirituality, but not for the healthy, natural intermediary position. And while the religious works are "baptized," that is, the expression for a pious bowing before a ruling ideology (Christianity), the aesthetic works, by contrast, are an expression of unbaptized passions and are thus to be understood as eruptions of natural passions, which Christianity has made taboo and repressed.[37]

Between the third and the fourth section, chapter 22 stands isolated. It takes up Kierkegaard's relation to the natural and historical sciences, which awakens Brandes' deepest opposition. Here one notices most clearly Brandes' goal of conjuring away Kierkegaard's influence (cf. the letter to Nietzsche), and his main conclusion here is that Kierkegaard was an angry opponent of modern humanity and tolerance. After this the historical method is taken up again in chapters 23–38, which treat the period from the mid 1840s until 1855 and take as their point of departure the *Corsair* affair and the attack on the Church, two events, which, according to Brandes, are related as presupposition and consequence, when one regards them from the perspective of their effect on Kierkegaard's mind. With the help of the journals and works, Brandes elucidates the various moments in the process, at the conclusion of which Kierkegaard himself stands as a Christian martyr—indeed, almost like Christ himself—and the *Corsair* virtually as the Antichrist. Here the process is described as a change in Kierkegaard's conception of the essence of Christianity—while he previously regarded religion from the intellectual side (as a

---

[37]   This undeniably recalls Freud's division of the mind into the id and the superego, and according to Kondrup, the family resemblance between Brandes and the father of psychoanalysis is also clear, among other things, in their coining of the essential relations between the key factors: nature, censure, distortion and interpretation. See ibid., pp. 100–1.

paradox), now its passionate side comes forth (its practical character). The paradox thus yields, to this extent, to passion.[38] The process also changes Kierkegaard's view of "Christendom," in that he perceives hypocrisy as a fundamental power in a society which calls itself Christian. Brandes draws attention to the fact that the attacks on lukewarmness, indolence, cowardice, etc. already appeared in the 1840s, but come to full expression after Mynster's death. In this way the attack on the Church can be seen as a continuation of the *Corsair* affair, and the last decade of Kierkegaard's life is thus, according to Brandes, like the time after the engagement story, a process of learning and development. The incitement in both cases was an event, and the tools of the process in both cases were the journals and works,[39] but while the first process was allowed to run its course to the end, the second was interrupted prematurely by Kierkegaard's death. Brandes thinks that Kierkegaard's relation to the ruling ideology at the time of his death was in a consistent line, the natural end point of which would be a break with the Christian orthodoxy which he was raised in. The journal *The Moment* even signals, according to Brandes, Kierkegaard's movement "out into the daylight," and the attack on the Church would stand in the future as his "actual and decisive achievement" and presumably will contribute to "the separation of Church and state, which the development of centuries ever more urgently demands."[40]

What Brandes arrives at in the end, is thus a position which can without hesitation be called "Brandesian." In other words, Brandes tries in his book to conjure up a forerunner of his own criticism of Christianity—he tries (in Johnny Kondrup's words) to work out his own spiritual physiognomy from the Kierkegaardian features.[41] There is a double polemic in the book, on the one side, an attempt to weaken Kierkegaard's position due to its fundamental distance from Brandes' own secular humanism, and, on the other side, a mobilizing of Kierkegaard as someone belonging to the same party and with the same opinion in the relation to the Church. As a reader, one notices in decisive places in the presentation Brandes' personal passion for distinguishing

---

[38]   Jørgen Bonde Jensen finds in Brandes' description of this movement a parallel to Joakim Garff's biographical Kierkegaard analysis in *"Den Søvnløse." Kierkegaard læst æstetisk/biografisk* (Copenhagen: C.A. Reitzel 1995), where Garff "identifies Kierkegaard's religious doings with his aesthetic actions, and in the figure of the insomniac sees Kierkegaard himself, who anticipates martyrdom." Cf. Jørgen Bonde Jensen, "Vel desværre vor største Mand. Georg Brandes om Søren Kierkegaard," in his *Jeg er kun en Digter. Om Søren Kierkegaard som skribent*, Copenhagen: Babette 1996, pp. 173–4.

[39]   As Brandes allerede already formulates it in his introduction, Kierkegaard spoke "not only with his contemporaries but also with himself with the help of his pen." See *Søren Kierkegaard. En kritisk Fremstilling i Grundrids*, Copenhagen: Gyldendal 1877, quoted from Georg Brandes, *Samlede Skrifter*, vols. 1–18, Copenhagen: Gyldendal 1899–1910, vol. 2 (1899), p. 252.

[40]   Brandes, *Samlede Skrifter*, vol. 2, p. 403.

[41]   See Kondrup, *Livsværker. Studier i dansk litterær biografi*, p. 105. Kondrup believes further that this characteristic of finding oneself again in the person one writes a biography about is wholly necessary for the genre—a biographer who does not possess the drive to put himself in the position of the object of his study, lacks an important presupposition for understanding the person he is describing. The growing point of the understanding is lacking.

what is relevant and valuable in Kierkegaard's knowledge from what is outdated and particular, and what is valuable for Brandes is almost always identical with the foundation upon which he builds not only his treatment of Kierkegaard but also the better part of his own authorship: the idea of personality. The enduring thing in Kierkegaard was the discovery of the individual, and what did not endure was faith in general and Christianity in particular. Here Brandes touches on one of the decisive questions that can be posed to the authorship, but which only with time (after the First World War) came to the forefront of research: is Kierkegaard a spokesman for the principle of personality—or its critic?[42]

Georg Brandes' open declaration of enmity against Christian orthodoxy—his "free-thinking"—was already prominent in the lectures on *Emigrant Literature* and remained an important element both in Brandes' own life and in the movement of cultural radicalism which he founded. With this background it is not surprising that the period's strongest reactions to the book on Kierkegaard came from the theological and ecclesiastical camp, but also non-theological reviewers locked onto—and still firmly lock onto—the book's general direction and what was conceived as artifices in Brandes' presentation.[43] In spite of this—or perhaps for this very reason—the research spread out like rings in the water from Brandes' work, which, together with the edition of the *Efterladte Papirer*, are the main works in the period from 1860 to 1890. Both in Denmark and in Germany the book was decisive for the intellectual left's conception of Kierkegaard.[44]

---

[42]   Cf. Jørgen K. Bukdahl, "Søren Kierkegaard—personlighedsprincippets forkæmper— eller undergraver?" *Exil*, no. 1, 1968, pp. 27–31. He compares Brandes' and K. Olesen Larsen's Kierkegaard interpretations.

[43]   See Malik, *Receiving Søren Kierkegaard*, pp. 255ff., who emphasizes the anti-Jewish reactions, and Kabell, *Kierkegaardstudiet i Norden*, pp. 118ff. Concerning the criticism from the theological camp, Brandes was subsequently of the opinion that theologians should not "appear as glowing followers of S.K.; it is and becomes always comical and nothing other than comical to want to be K.'s defender from the perspective of theology, which he has exploded, and from the perspective of the State Church which he mocked." Quoted from Kabell, *Kierkegaardstudiet i Norden*, p. 121. Jørgen Bonde Jensen can also later claim that Brandes' book has preserved its power over peoples' minds until today, far beyond just the circle of free thinkers and the leftist radicals, and that one can even from the theological camp feel attracted to the book, "insofar as it gives an account of the absurdity in the Christian view which led to the confrontation with the Church. An unholy alliance can arise." See Jensen, *Jeg er kun en Digter*, p. 172. For a critical overview of Brandes' book, see also, for example, Malik, *Receiving Søren Kierkegaard*, pp. 246ff. and Aage Henriksen, who states: "From... erroneous premises Brandes consistently drew fallacious conclusions," and he concludes, "what his [Brandes'] book has lost in truth it has gained in beauty." See Aage Henriksen, *Methods and Results of Kierkegaard Studies in Scandinavia. A Historical and Critical Survey*, Copenhagen: Munksgaard 1951 (*Publications of the Kierkegaard Society*, vol. 1), pp. 29–30.

[44]   In Jørgen Bonde Jensen's estimation, this has been true in Denmark all the way up to and including Peter Thielst's book from 1994, *Livet forstås baglæns—men må leves forlæns* (Copenhagen: Gyldendal 1994) which is called a "welfare-edition" of Kierkegaard. See Jørgen Bonde Jensen, *Jeg er kun en Digter*, p. 169.

III. Kierkegaard Around the Turn of the Century (1890–1920)

> In a characteristic, but clear manner, the nineteenth century demarcates the scene for the
> voluminous literature on K[ierkegaard], which was to see the light in the twentieth century:
> partly by running through the most subjective positions, partly with verbose preparations
> in the most objective of all undertaking, dry editorial work.[45]

After the "modern breakthrough" inspired by Georg Brandes in the 1870s, there
followed a, in many ways turbulent, decade, which at the time was experienced
as a kind of spiritual collapse. For later ages the spiritual life of the 1890s had,
however, just as much the character of a "spiritual breakthrough" with a reaction to
Brandesianism's positivism and naturalism as negative point of departure and a new
emphasis on the inner, symbolic, and dreamlike as the positive driving force. This
turning inward was primarily a literary and artistic phenomenon, and even if one
can speak of a climate far more receptive for Kierkegaardian thoughts than in the
previous decades, what is at issue in the first instance is an affinity to the spirit of the
age more than a marked surge of interest in Kierkegaard. The Kierkegaard literature
of the age reflects, in part, that the impulse from Brandes was still alive, but required
a philosophical supplement and deepening (Harald Høffding), in part, the endeavors
of the new liberal theology to distinguish the essentially Christian doctrine from the
less essential orthodox dogmas, which propel Kierkegaard as a Christian thinker
into focus (Niels Teisen). Finally, the need for easier access to Kierkegaard's works
became apparent. A codification of the entire authorship had been sought since
Kierkegaard's death and was introduced at the beginning of the twentieth century with
the edition, *Søren Kierkegaards Samlede Værker* (1901–06), which was followed
up by a large new edition of the journals and papers, *Søren Kierkegaards Papirer*
(1909–48). The "dry editorial work" in the form of, respectively, Kierkegaard's
works and posthumous writings was undertaken by, amongst others, two brothers, the
philologist J.L. Heiberg and the doctor P.A. Heiberg, the latter of which introduced a
series of compact psychological portraits of Kierkegaard during the period. Another
editor of the *Samlede Værker*, the philologist A.B. Drachmann, moreover, delivered
at this time a small but weighty contribution to making Kierkegaard's presentation
of Christianity problematic.

A. Harald Høffding, Niels Teisen, A.B. Drachmann, and P.A. Heiberg

Like Georg Brandes, Harald Høffding (1843–1931) participated in the 1860s debate
about faith and knowledge and continued hereafter with a gold medal treatise and
a *Habilitation* thesis strongly under the influence of Kierkegaard, whose writings
had—as was the case with Brandes—led him to an early religious crisis. As professor
of philosophy, he published in 1894–95 *A History of Modern Philosophy*,[46] and
one of the preliminary studies for this work was his book, *Søren Kierkegaard as a
Philosopher* from 1892.

---

[45]   Kabell, *Kierkegaardstudiet i Norden*, p. 170.
[46]   Harald Høffding, *Den nyere Filosofis Historie*, vols. 1–2, Copenhagen: Philipsen
1894–95.

In his treatment of Kierkegaard, Høffding makes a remark (in connection with *Repetition*) about the fact that Kierkegaard's rich poetic apparatus expands at the cost of the concept and thought, but, moreover, it suffices for him to refer to Brandes for a treatment of the literary dimension. Instead he focuses on Kierkegaard's fundamental philosophical thinking, and the book consists of an account of Kierkegaard's epistemology and ethics, including the doctrine of stages. It begins with a personally stamped section about Høffding's path to and from Kierkegaard, which is followed by a philosophical-historical placement of Kierkegaard against the background of the Romantic-speculative philosophy of religion (Schleiermacher) and Kierkegaard's older contemporaries (Heiberg, Martensen, Sibbern, and Poul Martin Møller). In a section about Kierkegaard's personality, Høffding, moreover, moderates Brandes' emphasis on the significance of individual events for Kierkegaard's intellectual development, and Brandes' idea that piety and disdain should be his fundamental passions is rejected to the advantage of an emphasis on melancholy as the decisive element in Kierkegaard's personality. Otherwise, there are several similarities between Brandes and Høffding, among other things, in their polemic against Kierkegaard's tendency towards asceticism, his view of women and in their rejection of the Christian view of faith, which, for Høffding, is one-sidedly and eschatologically determined by the expectation of the world's imminent destruction. What fundamentally distinguishes Høffding and Kierkegaard is therefore to a large extent the difference in principle between a monistic and a dualist world-view. It runs like a red thread through the presentation that if Kierkegaard had not been inhibited by his Christian dogmatics, his thought would have had more directly a universal significance; as counterweight, Høffding thinks that a translation or process of separation must be undertaken before Kierkegaard's thoughts can come to play the role for humanity which they deserve.[47]

The most characteristic (and the longest) section of the book is then, not surprisingly, an analysis of Kierkegaard's ethics, which is seen in close connection with his psychology, because the relation between ethics and psychology, according to Høffding, in an exemplary manner makes clear the idiosyncratic character of a thinker. At the outset he undertakes a typical division of thinkers into two basic categories: those who strive for unity, continuity, and connections, and those who claim radical transitions, differences, and sharp limits between various fields. The first group emphasize "the relation of quantity" (the successive transitions, the degrees of difference), and the other group focuses on "the difference of quality" (the distinction, the disjunction). Kierkegaard, with his notion of "the leap" and "the qualitative dialectic," decidedly belongs to the latter group. At the same time there is the odd thing with Kierkegaard, that he, as a psychological genius, possesses the ability to see the greatest oppositions and the finest of mental nuances in context, which reveals a living drive for knowledge and a desire to think in terms of continuity. Høffding regards Kierkegaard's emphasis on the irrational and the sudden jolt or leap, seen most clearly in the doctrine of the paradox, as an expression of the fact that this drive to know has been disappointed; but this is still what characterizes

---

[47]   Cf. Harald Høffding, *Søren Kierkegaard som Filosof*, Copenhagen: Philipsen 1892, p. 70.

Kierkegaard. A thinker is only great within his category if he has a strong tendency in the opposite direction—only with a strong drive toward continuity is the break and discontinuity discovered and felt. The fact that Kierkegaard as a psychologist hangs on to context as far as he can, but as an ethicist posits the leap and the jolt of decision evokes Høffding's criticism. In this way ethics annuls psychology. Regardless of how far Kierkegaard emphasizes the task of psychology as that of seeking the possibilities for the new conditions, the successive and quantitative approaches, there comes, with respect to ethics, a point where the genuine ethically meaningful decision takes place, and a qualitatively new one is posited which does not find its explanation in what preceded it. The simultaneous recognition of the insights of psychology and the claim of its total independence from ethics is, for Høffding, a contradiction because one thereby operates with possibilities which are not possibilities for, or approaches to, anything—the psychological understanding becomes useless and even illusory with respect to ethics. The long section about Kierkegaard's ethics continues after this as an analysis of the doctrine of stages with a philosophical pointing out (in line with Brandes) that the ethical stage has no independent value in Kierkegaard, but in reality is religious and ascetic. With this Høffding has not only criticized Kierkegaard but also placed himself in opposition to the two categories of thought. His own relation to Kierkegaard as an intellectual type is concentrated in the statement that the humane ethicist (Høffding) stands vis-à-vis the ascete (Kierkegaard) just as the chemist stands vis-à-vis the alchemist: "He admires the energy, endurance, passion and the many new and profound thoughts, which are produced during the lonely work, but he wishes all of these noble forces to be applied in the service of other ends."[48]

By way of conclusion, Høffding's book includes an analysis of Kierkegaard's religious development in the years 1847–55. The main result is that the concluding attack on the Church should not be seen as a mistaken development or slip from Kierkegaard's earlier authorship but rather represents a logical extension of it: the outward struggle against the state Church was simply a continuation of the inner struggle (carried out in the diaries) against the political and religious authorities, which had begun at Easter 1848.[49] Høffding's view of the attack on the Church is stamped with sympathy; he admires Kierkegaard's consistency and honesty and regards *The Moment* as a journal on the level with Plato's dialogues and Pascal's provincial letters. But there can hardly be any doubt that this sympathy also has to do with Høffding's own past as a failed student of theology and his distancing himself from the Christianity of the time. The emphasis on the merits of humanism and the problems involved in the theologians' reconciliation with Kierkegaard is expressed

---

[48]   Ibid., p. 124.

[49]   The same theme was treated with the opposite result by the historian of literature and religion Hans Sophus Vodskov (1846–1910) in his article "En Krise i Søren Kierkegaards Liv," in his *Spredte Studier*, Copenhagen: Gyldendal 1884, pp. 1–30 (originally published in *Illustreret Tidende*, nos. 1128–30, 1881). Both Høffding and Vodskov use as their main source the final volumes of *Efterladte Papirer*, which appeared in 1880–81 and cover the period from 1848 to 1855. See also Henriksen, *Methods and Results of Kierkegaard Studies in Scandinavia*, pp. 35ff.

in the following manner: "He led some people to seek a more inward deepening in Christianity (as they conceive it), others he led away from it, owing to the principle of personal truth."[50]

Høffding's dig at the theologians should be seen, among other things, against the background of the Swedish theologian Waldemar Rudin's book, *Søren Kierkegaard's Person and Authorship* (1880),[51] which was written as a reaction to Brandes and was the first work (after that of the German Albert Bärthold) to take Kierkegaard's self-analysis in *The Point of View for My Activity as an Author* as reliable. The book, which one-sidedly emphasizes the edifying aspect of the authorship, was long regarded in church circles as without rival the best thing written about Kierkegaard as a Christian thinker.

At the end of the nineteenth century there was in Denmark a rising number of theologians and religious thinkers, who from a related fundamental recognition of Kierkegaard, although not in complete agreement with him, sought independently to take a position on the authorship, among others the historian of religion Peter Andreas Rosenberg (1858–1935), the Grundtvigian Carl Koch (1860–1925), and the pastor Christian Jensen (1873–1949).[52] I will briefly emphasize the theologian and author of works on the philosophy of religion Niels Teisen (1851–1916), who is not necessarily more important or independent than the others but represents a characteristic method which points toward the larger interpreters from the tradition of liberal theology. Moreover, in reading Teisen, one understands better why his generation of Christian thinkers could come to terms with Kierkegaard, who had been regarded a very dubious figure by the older generation.[53]

By 1884 Niels Teisen had written *Brief Contribution in the Case Between S. Kierkegaard and H. L. Martensen*[54] and published the piece *For Consideration Concerning Prof. Høffding's Book on S Kierkegaard* (1893),[55] whose main ideas were developed ten years later in the book *Søren Kierkegaard's Significance as a Christian Thinker* (1903). While Høffding does not adequately examine or straightforwardly ignores Kierkegaard's dogmatic presuppositions, Teisen sheds light on precisely this side of the matter, and he does so by distinguishing, not as Kierkegaard does, Christianity from Christendom but rather between Christianity and "orthodoxy." Teisen does not have much sympathy for the "dead uprightness of orthodoxy,"[56] and his recognition of Kierkegaard for the most part concerns the fact that he, due to his consistency, demonstrated the impossibility of orthodox theology

---

[50]   Høffding, *Søren Kierkegaard som Filosof*, p. 159.

[51]   Waldemar Rudin, *Sören Kierkegaards person och författerskap*, Uppsala: A. Nilsson 1880.

[52]   One can read about these authors in Henriksen, *Methods and Results of Kierkegaard Studies in Scandinavia*, pp. 49ff. and Kabell, *Kierkegaardstudiet i Norden*, pp. 141ff.

[53]   Cf. Kabell, *Kierkegaardstudiet i Norden*, p. 149.

[54]   Niels Teisen, *Kort Indlæg i Sagen mellem S. Kierkegaard og H. L. Martensen*, Copenhagen: Karl Schønbergs Forlag 1884.

[55]   Niels Teisen, *Til Overvejelse i Anledning af Prof. Høffdings Bog om S. Kierkegaard*, Odense: Milo'ske Boghandels Forlag 1893.

[56]   Niels Teisen, *Om Søren Kierkegaard's Betydning som kristelig Tænker*, Copenhagen: J. Frimodt 1903, p. 106.

and (without knowing it himself) cleared the ground for a far milder, lighter, and more compassionate form of Christianity.

Kierkegaard is praised by Teisen for his emphasis on the ethical-practical aspect of faith, and by underscoring appropriation, "to become and be a Christian in spirit and truth,"[57] he has in a penetrating manner worked in the direction of inward deepening in Christian life. With respect to dogmatics, Kierkegaard's merit is somewhat backward: in his uncritical acceptance and personal reworking of a series of traditional dogmas, especially the question of the nature of human beings (the doctrine of sin) and Christ (the doctrine of the God-man), he has become caught in absurdities and self-contradictions. Here Teisen draws on the account in *Philosophical Fragments*, whose consistently carried out train of thought ends in an account of the Christian's duty to die from the world and reject his ability to grasp the paradox—a consequence which Teisen fully recognizes but with the addition that Kierkegaard thereby (indirectly and unconsciously) has proven the absurdity of orthodox theology. The thought of Christ as the paradox can, according to Teisen, be traced back to the Athanasian doctrine of the simultaneous existence of a divine and a human nature in Christ (the doctrine of two natures). Similarly, Kierkegaard is claimed to have inherited Augustine's doctrine of sin, according to which human nature is completely corrupted by sin and an absolute difference is placed between God and man.[58] These two main results of Teisen's argumentation—Kierkegaard's taking over Augustine's conception of sin and his dependence on Athanasius for the notion of the paradox—are essentially what points forward to the great analyses of liberal theology in the works of the Swede Torsten Bohlin and Eduard Geismar after the First World War.[59]

Both the period's secular humanists and Christian thinkers thus attempted to distinguish what was valuable from what was antiquated in Kierkegaard. When it was a question of his conception of Christianity, the result is somewhat surprising: Kierkegaard's Christianity was more palatable for the former than for the latter. The humanists said: if there is anything to Christianity at all, then it must be more or less as Kierkegaard says. By contrast, the church people, for understandable reasons, resisted Kierkegaard's view of Christianity and (if they did not wholly reject Kierkegaard) sought partly to separate off the anti-ecclesiastical elements, partly to interpret Kierkegaard as a "cleanser," a station along the way to a new Christianity.

A new angle on Kierkegaard's conception of Christianity was given in a short treatise by the classical philologist Anders Bjørn Drachmann (1860–1935) from 1911. The article was originally a lecture from 1903, which presumably arose in connection with Drachmann's work with the edition of *Philosophical Fragments* in

---

[57]   Ibid., p. 4.

[58]   Teisen has only disdain for the dogmatic elements; he speaks about "these hopeless doctrines with their more or less scandalous consequences" and "this deadlock of irreconcilable concepts," which fortunately only theologians have any knowledge of—"if even they do." Cf. ibid., p. 64; p. 73; p. 63.

[59]   Teisen further shares with Bohlin the juxtaposition of Kierkegaard with the Swedish professor of philosophy and aesthetics Pontus Wikner (1837–88).

the first edition of the *Samlede Værker*. This work should be mentioned not least of all since it has been especially important for theologians.[60]

Drachmann's main point in "Paganism and Christianity in Søren Kierkegaard" is the deep dependency of the understanding of Christianity on the Socratic in Kierkegaard. Christianity, in the account given in the *Fragments* is, according to Drachmann, determined by the Socratic in the sense that the Socratic is what sets the norm: "*the decisive Christian determination is not developed by Christianity itself* (for this is only possible by a *historical* investigation), *but only by Christianity in connection with the Socratic; and it is Christianity which must be determined by the Socratic*, not vice versa."[61] Drachmann finds that this relation appears again in all of Kierkegaard's dogmatic definitions, for example, of sin, which, as the direct opposite of faith, is an intellectualistic construction. This is also true of the doctrine of Christ, from which there is nothing more left than the presumably ahistorical claim that he, Jesus, is the son of God. It is also true of the concept of community, which is rejected not due to Kierkegaard's Christian presuppositions but due to his Socratic ones. Only the absolute paradox is kept free. The Trinity is not discussed, and the Holy Spirit seems to lie outside Kierkegaard's circle of concepts, and he crosses out the entire real content of Christianity. Drachmann believes himself to be in opposition to the more widespread conception of Kierkegaard's understanding of Christianity (sc. Teisen's) as being in agreement with and determined by orthodoxy. If one wants to attack Kierkegaard's notion of Christianity, one must therefore attack the Socratic principles of individualism, religious equality and freedom, which are both the archenemy of positive religion and also indispensable for it. The higher a positive religion stands, the more it must distance itself from the authority in the religious—without, however, wholly abandoning it—and emphasize the internal, inwardness, and appropriation.[62]

---

[60]   Drachmann has elsewhere (see *Tilskueren*, 1912, pp. 149–50; pp. 152–3) told of how Georg Brandes was present at the lecture and allegedly said that the significance of Kierkegaard's presentation of Christianity lay in the fact that "if there were any meaning to the whole thing, then it would have to be the way Kierkegaard said it," quoted from Rubow, *Georg Brandes' Briller*, pp. 163–4.

[61]   A.B. Drachmann, "Hedenskab og Christendom hos Søren Kierkegaard," in *Udvalgte Afhandlinger*, Copenhagen: Gyldendal 1911, p. 132.

[62]   Torsten Bohlin in his extensive investigation (*Kierkegaards dogmatiska Åskådning i dess historiska Sammanhang*, Stockholm: Svenska Kyrkans Diakonistyrelsens Förlag 1925) in a commentary on Drachmann, thinks that Socrates and the Socratic do *not* have significance for Kierkegaard's Christian view. Bohlin in the first instance virtually turns Drachmann's interpretation on its head by saying that Drachmann interprets the Socratic in a broader fashion than there is historical evidence for, when he equates it with inwardness and appropriation. In this way there is no longer any reason to regard the Socratic as something which lies *outside* Christianity and in this principle to see ancient paganism's decisive influence on Kierkegaard's understanding of Christianity (cf. ibid., p. 57n). When Bohlin later interprets the Socratic in Kierkegaard as a symbol for the apex of the natural human and philosophical development, whose main axiom is that the human being is in possession of natural conditions for reaching the truth, he must, however, confess that Kierkegaard does not explicitly juxtapose Christianity and the Socratic in the *Fragments*, which he ascribes to the formal nature of the *Fragments* where the presentation is given in the form of a pure thought experiment.

The young doctor and later assistant archivist at the Rigsarkivet, Peter Andreas Heiberg (1864–1926), in the foreword to *Contribution to a Psychological Picture of Søren Kierkegaard in his Childhood and Adolescence* from 1895, notes that in the previous contributions (both Danish and foreign) to understanding Kierkegaard as an author, historical person, and human being, there is a striking tendency to judge him personally and to make the issue into a personal matter. In Heiberg himself, who became the driving force in the publication of the new edition of the journals and papers, one finds a completely different kind of reticence with the subjective evaluations. His lifelong occupation with, and great fidelity to, Kierkegaard's text finds expression here in his first book in the admission that its content is "in fact mostly quotations." Heiberg's books in a sense lie in a direct continuity with one another and can be seen under one rubric as a careful, text-near account of Kierkegaard's religious development from 1835 until 1852; compare the titles, *An Episode in the Youth of Søren Kierkegaard* (1912), *A Segment of the Religious Development of Søren Kierkegaard from June 1 1835 to May 19 1838* (1918), and *The Religious Development of Søren Kierkegaard. Psychological Microscopy* (1925).[63] The main conclusion is that this development can be described as a story of healing, a thesis with which Heiberg stands virtually alone in the research. Already in the first short book from 1895 one senses the later editor of the *Papirer*, in that Heiberg avails himself of both published and unpublished sources and in this connection issues a criticism of H.P. Barfod, whose main service as editor, according to Heiberg, is his catalogue of the manuscripts, which, however, reveals that his editorial work was indefensible, arbitrary, and lacking in plan and thought.[64] The book takes as its point of departure the testimony about the student Kierkegaard, which his principal Michael Nielsen made in 1830, and the further main theme is Kierkegaard's melancholy and its meaning, which Heiberg treats with a theretofore unseen thoroughness.

B. The Editions: Søren Kierkegaards Samlede Værker (1901–06 and 1920–36)

P.A. Heiberg's elder brother, professor of classical philology Johan Ludvig Heiberg (1854–1928), published in the years 1901–06, together with his fellow philologist, A.B. Drachmann, and the Egyptologist and chief librarian at the Royal Library, Hans Ostenfeld Lange (1863–1943) the edition, *Søren Kierkegaards Samlede Værker* (*SV1*) in fourteen volumes with modern Latin font (antikva). The division of labor among the three was that H.O. Lange was responsible for the edifying part of the authorship, while Heiberg edited the aesthetic/literary works and Drachmann the philosophical ones.

---

[63]   P.A. Heiberg, *En Episode i Søren Kierkegaards Ungdomsliv*, Copenhagen and Kristiania: Gyldendal 1912; P.A. Heiberg, *Et Segment af Søren Kierkegaards religiøse Udvikling 1835 1. juni til 1838 19. maj. Psykologisk Studie*, Copenhagen and Kristiania: Gyldendal 1918; P.A. Heiberg, *Søren Kierkegaards religiøse Udvikling. Psykologisk Mikroskopi*, Copenhagen: Gyldendal 1925.
[64]   P.A. Heiberg, *Bidrag til et psykologisk Billede af Søren Kierkegaard i Barndom og Ungdom*, Copenhagen: Otto B. Wroblewski 1895, p. 130.

The edition did not include any foreword in the strict sense, but A.B. Drachmann, in the article "Textual Criticism, applied to S. Kierkegaard's Writings,"[65] described the editorial principles and presented examples in the text in order "to show that the work which was done with the new edition of Kierkegaard, is not without fruit also for a common reader, who is only concerned with having a comprehensible text without stains and distortions."[66] Not surprisingly given their background and training, the editors made use of the methodology of classical philology, which means that the point of departure is found in the fact that one is not in possession of the original manuscript but instead of a long series of surviving variant texts which are placed alongside one another and from which one then attempts to reconstruct the original from which they stem. One thus builds on the surviving variant texts and not variants of the genesis of the text (drafts, outlines, and the clean copy), which, in Kierkegaard's case, means that the editors not only made use of Kierkegaard's own first editions but also his second editions. This "*letzter Hand*" principle—that is, to publish the text which Kierkegaard last wanted—is, however, supplemented by the sporadic use of Kierkegaard's manuscripts, from which the editors have taken expressions and formulations and placed them into the text of their edition.

In the more scholarly second edition (*SV2*), which was published by the same editors in the years 1920–36, the philological principles were changed to a certain degree. Here the edition moved more and more in the direction of the "*erster Hand*" principle, which means that the editors were far more amenable to correcting the first editions based on readings from the manuscripts, a praxis based on a (neoRomantic hermeneutical) idea about what must have been Kierkegaard's original intention.[67] In relation to *SV1*, which was conceived as a popular edition or "*folkeudgave*," *SV2* is not, however, essentially improved when it is a question of commentaries or explanatory notes, even if in the postscript to the last volume of *SV1* the editors write that the "elucidating notes beneath the text are only a first foundation to a real commentary; to approach even some degree of completeness in this regard must be the task of the future."[68] By contrast, *SV2* was accompanied by an index of persons and an index of subjects by A. Ibsen and a terminological index by J. Himmelstrup (vol. XV). A typographical curiosum is to be found in the fact that the editors of the *SV2* edition chose to imitate the first edition's gothic letters (fraktur), which perhaps

---

[65]   A.B. Drachmann, "Textkritik, anvendt paa S. Kierkegaards Skrifter," in *Udvalgte Afhandlinger*, Copenhagen: Gyldendal 1911, pp. 154–74 (originally published in *Dania*, 1903). J.L. Heiberg, moreover, reflected on some issues concerning the publication of *Either/ Or* in the article "Textkritiske Bemærkninger til 'Enten—Eller,' " *Danske Studier*, 1911, pp. 46–50.

[66]   Drachmann, *Udvalgte Afhandlinger*, p. 174.

[67]   In both cases (*SV1* and *SV2*) a text was created which in its order is wholly in accordance with the age's text-philological tradition, but which from the perspective of modern text-philological principles is synthetic and contaminated; a situation which was only remedied with the new historical-critical edition, *Søren Kierkegaards Skrifter* (1997–). See "Indledning," in *SKS* K1, Copenhagen 1997, pp. 7ff. Cf. also Niels Jørgen Cappelørn, "Søren Kierkegaards Skrifter i ny udgave," *Kulturbrev*, no. 9, 1996, pp. 20–39.

[68]   *SV1* XIV, 377. For a thorough criticism of the commentary praxis of the *Samlede Værker*, see Kabell, *Kierkegaardstudiet i Norden*, pp. 158ff.

can be regarded as an expression of the new national-historical consciousness in the wake of the First World War (one can, for example, think of the revival of a phenomenon such as Scandinavism during this same period).

The editions of the *Samlede Værker* doubtless improved the access to Kierkegaard's writings, but with respect to its historical effect, it did not have the same significance as the large new edition of the *Papirer*, which will be treated immediately below. The reason for this is, among other things, that a large number of Kierkegaard's writings during this period were published as individual works, which rendered further editions superfluous.[69]

C. The Edition: Søren Kierkegaards Papirer (1909–48)

Søren Kierkegaards Papirer edited by P.A. Heiberg, V. Kuhr and (from 1926) E. Torsting appeared in the years 1909–48 in 20 volumes (numbered I–XI 3) and was reprinted by Niels Thulstrup in a photomechanical reproduction with two supplement volumes (XII–XIII) in 1968–70. Moreover, Thulstrup's improved edition also included (in 1975–78) a three-volume *Index* (XIV–XVI) created by Niels Jørgen Cappelørn.[70] The monumental edition (referred to in the following simply as the *Papirer*) is a rare thing in the Danish context and represents a unique philological effort, which right from the beginning commanded respect even beyond the country's borders. The edition was welcomed from the publication of the first volume in 1909 as a worthy and much needed successor to its predecessor, Barfod and Gottsched's *Af Søren Kierkegaards Efterladte Papirer*.

The first edition of *Søren Kierkegaards Papirer* appeared in the years 1909–48 at the following pace (with the period covered in parentheses): volume I, 1909 (covering the period 1831 – January 27, 1837), volume II, 1910 (January 27, 1837 – June 2, 1840), volume III, 1911 (June 2, 1840 – November 20, 1842), volume IV, 1912 (November 20, 1842 – March 1844), volume V, 1913 (March – December 1844), volume VI, 1914 (December 1844 – December 2, 1845), volume VII 1–2, 1915–16 (December 2, 1845 – January 24, 1847), volume VIII 1–2, 1917–18 (January 24, 1847 – May 15, 1848), volume IX, 1920 (May 15, 1848 – January 2, 1849), volume X 1–6, 1924–34[71] (January 2, 1849 – November 2, 1853) and volume XI 1–3, 1936–38–48 (November 2, 1853 – September 25, 1855).

In the report from the Carlsberg Foundation for 1907–08, under point 30, one reads: granted "500 crowns to Professor A.B. Drachmann, Professor J.L. Heiberg and chief librarian H.O. Lange for the publication of volume 1 of S. K.'s posthumous

---

[69]   Ibid., pp. 209–10.

[70]   Peter Andreas Heiberg (1864–1926), physician and archivist at Rigsarkivet from 1917; Victor Kuhr (1882–1948) cand.mag. 1908, senior lecturer 1916, and professor of philosophy from 1918 at the University of Copenhagen; Einer Torsting (1893–1951), cand.scient. in mathematics 1917, headmaster of Ordrup Secondary School from 1933; Niels Thulstrup (1924–88), cand.theol. 1950, professor of systematic theology from 1968 at the University of Copenhagen; Niels Jørgen Cappelørn (b. 1945), cand.theol. 1977, director of the Søren Kierkegaard Research Centre since 1994.

[71]   *Pap.* X–1 (1924). *Pap.* X–2 (1926). *Pap.* X–3 (1927). *Pap.* X–4 (1929). *Pap.* X–5 (1932). *Pap.* X–6 (1934).

papers by assistant archivist P.A. Heiberg." The idea for the edition was that of P.A. Heiberg (the brother of J.L. Heiberg), who, together with his colleague Victor Kuhr in the preface (dated September 1909) to the first volume, reported that all of the decisions of principle concerning questions about the edition's plan, character and external form, along with the treatment of the text, have been made in consultation with the three mentioned editors of *Samlede Værker*.[72] The *Papirer* was therefore, right from the beginning, projected as a natural and carefully thought-through continuation of the first edition of Kierkegaard's published works with the awareness of the necessity of a corresponding complete corpus of non-printed Kierkegaard material.

The history of the publication of the edition decisively reflects the events of the twentieth century, for instance, the economic recession and crisis in the wake of the First World War. Up until 1919 one volume per year was regularly produced, but the ninth volume was delayed, when the price index rose from 100 crowns in 1913 to 306 crowns in 1919, without their being any corresponding increase in the grant and subsidies from the Carlsberg Foundation. The production costs thus rose just as the price of the books themselves (9 crowns in 1913, 18 crowns in 1918 and 36 crowns in 1920), and in addition to the economic misery the survival of the edition was threatened by P.A. Heiberg's failing health. When volume X–3 appeared in 1927, P.A. Heiberg was dead (July 1, 1926), and at the beginning of the volume there appears an obituary by Victor Kuhr. Einer Torsting came on board with volume X–2. The events surrounding and during the Second World War are also reflected in the history of the edition. Under Kuhr and Torsting's editorship during this period, the volumes were published more or less regularly every other year until volume XI–2, which was published in 1938. The last volume, XI–3, was markedly delayed due to the war—the First World War's economic decline was repeated, and in addition there came sickness, and when the two editors during the occupation went underground, work on the edition stopped entirely. In the reports of the Carlsberg Foundation from 1940 to 1945 the normal rubric for the *Papirer* edition is not to be seen. Only when the entire collection of Kierkegaard's manuscripts, which during the war had been evacuated from the University Library, after the Liberation was brought from their temporary protective hiding place in Esrum Cloister to the Royal Library, was the work resumed. Therefore the final volume appeared as late as 1948.[73]

The preface to the first volume of *Søren Kierkegaards Papirer* begins with the following declaration:

---

[72]   *Pap.* I, p. xxii.

[73]   The economically wearisome history of the edition, in its dry numbers, can be divided into three parts. In the first decade 4,188 printed pages were published with the support of the Carlsberg Foundation in the sum of 14,050 Danish crowns. The reading public had to pay 50,373 Danish crowns for the 500 copies. In the second decade 2,146 pages were published with a support of 36,403.61 crowns, with the reading public paying 33,000 crowns. In the third decade 2,714 pages were published with a support of 54,324.26 crowns, which cost the reading public a mere 25,000 crowns. These numbers, which speak for themselves and testify to the generosity of the Carlsberg Foundation, along with the factual information in the foregoing are taken from Kabell, *Kierkegaardstudiet i Norden*, pp. 201ff.

The goal of the edition is to give a Søren Kierkegaard diplomatarium, consisting of:
1) Everything which exists in the public domain or in private possession, or can be proved to have existed of *literary* Søren Kierkegaard manuscripts.
2) Everything which exists in the public domain or in private possession of documents and materials concerning S. K., his parents and ancestors.

The intention of the edition was first to produce "a series of volumes with the literary manuscripts with the exception of letters, insofar as these are not taken up in S. K.'s journals, then letters from, to and about S. K. and finally documents and materials."[74] The preface goes on to describe the material, which was made the foundation of the edition, with the University Library's collection of Søren Kierkegaard's papers as the primary source. It then describes the two catalogues of the material, which were made by Henrik Lund in 1855–56 and by H.P. Barfod in 1865. Then, it describes the material's partially defective condition due to Barfod's cutting, pasting, writing on the manuscripts, crossing-out, and corrections with an eye to sending the manuscripts themselves directly to the typesetters, which he used as the basis for his edition of the *Efterladte Papirer*; and finally it describes the ordering of the material.

As is clear from the overview of the edition (in parentheses), just as was the case with Barfod's edition, there lies an overarching chronological principle at the bottom of the organization of the material. But in addition to this there also comes a systematic principle which supplements a strict chronological ordering of the entries with a thematic one. The editors ground this with "the very nature of the material" and divide the entries into three main groups according to their content: "one group with the character of diary entries (including everything from exclamations torn out of context and notes to a continuous travel diary)—one group related to the development of the authorship in one form or another (including everything from short treatises and newspaper articles to large works)—one group related to Kierkegaard's studies and readings (including everything from short aphoristic entries to entire notebooks and verbose excerpts)."[75] These groups are then dubbed A, B, and C, and within the group C a further division, with respect to content, is introduced: "Theologica, Philosophica and Æsthetica." With this division of material according to theme and with the abandoning of a strict chronological principle, the editors were confronted with a special problem when it came to the placement of Kierkegaard's undated entries. They chose here to try to order the undated entries with the dated entries by estimating the date of the undated ones based on internal and external criteria, albeit with the following reservation:

> But although we thus believe, in any case concerning most of the undated entries, to have been able to put them in the place in the chronological series, where they more or less belong or might have belonged, it must be expressly emphasized that the silently undertaken chronological ordering in this edition, as soon as the meaning of the chronological should be stressed, cannot be taken as something finally decided, but only as a preliminary hypothesis, which it is reasonable to assume in many cases will be able to be improved upon.[76]

---

[74]   *Pap.* I, p. vii.
[75]   Ibid., p. x.
[76]   Ibid., pp. xii–xiii.

It is especially this last point, the undated entries' forced chronology, that are the focus of the few critical statements made about this edition in the contemporary reception. The first thorough position-taking and evaluation of the *Papirer* was, however, long in coming and can with some justice be said to be Henning Fenger's *Kierkegaard, The Myths and Their Origins* from 1976. One can suspect that this is due to the fact that editions which stretch over decades generally only come into their own and can be seen in overview and used critically and deeply when they exist as a finished whole. The *Papirer* has in time received a reputation for being difficult to work with due to the enormous material's unclear organization and the problematic chronology of the undated material. It seems, moreover, to presuppose that one has read the entire edition in order to find one's way around in the text, and in this context the importance of the *Index* can hardly be overestimated in making the use of this edition easier.

In opposition to its predecessor, the *Papirer* was received, as mentioned, in a predominantly positive manner at the time. The delicate problem of the mention in Kierkegaard's journal entries of people who were still alive, which offended many people with the publication of the first volume of *Efterladte Papirer*, had fallen away in more than one sense. Further, the question of principle about the right to publish Kierkegaard's papers only had a weak echo, specifically in a curious little piece by the consultant and master of forestry Ernst Heilmann entitled *Søren Kierkegaard's hitherto Suppressed Last Will concerning his Posthumous Writings*. Heilmann brings up the existence of the loose scrap of paper, in which Kierkegaard hands over to Professor Rasmus Nielsen the responsibility for publishing the posthumous papers. He further publishes in this context the correspondence between P.C. Kierkegaard and Rasmus Nielsen from ten years after the discovery of Kierkegaard's will. One can be in doubt as to exactly what point Heilmann wants to make, but the pamphlet's concluding demand borders on a threat: "I must now direct a demand to the gentlemen Mr. Archival Assistant Heiberg and cand. mag. Kuhr, namely, keep yourselves away from any critical revision of Søren Kierkegaard's literary posthumous writings, but let us receive a true reproduction of it; *nothing added, nothing repressed.*"[77]

In a double book review from January 1913 of Valdemar Ammundsen's *Søren Kierkegaard's Adolescence* and the fourth volume of *Papirer*, the literary scholar Hans Brix notes that the edition is moving forward well, "and the last volume to appear is just as outstandingly well done as the foregoing ones."[78] At the same time he praises Ammundsen's industry in his presentation of Kierkegaard's family relations, youth, and adolescence, and for having dug up material "where such material was lacking." However, he fails to note that precisely Ammundsen's book to some degree demonstrates the shortcomings of the first three published volumes of the *Papirer.* Namely, Ammundsen avails himself of material which is only registered but not fully reproduced in the edition.[79] This concerns especially material from the

---

[77]   Ernst Heilmann, *Søren Kierkegaards hidtil fortiede testamentariske Villie angaaende hans literære Efterladenskaber*, Copenhagen: Bertelsens Boghandel 1909, p. 7.

[78]   Feature article in *Politiken*, January 16, 1913.

[79]   Cf. Valdemar Ammundsen, *Søren Kierkegaards Ungdom. Hans Slægt og hans religiøse Udvikling*, Copenhagen: Københavns Universitet 1912, pp. 86ff.

first volume's section C, and one can imagine that afterwards the editors cast a side glance at Ammundsen's book since, in contrast to the first three volumes, from the fourth volume onward everything in this group is reproduced *in extenso*.[80] In addition to Ammundsen's indirect revelation about the shortcomings of the edition, the few critical points, which were mentioned at the beginning, were concerned, as noted, with the editors' dating of the undated material. Carl Weltzer, for example, doubted the dating of *Pap.* I A 331 (*SKS* 17, 202ff., CC:13),[81] and Frithiof Brandt wanted to move the dating of "The Battle between the Old and the New Soap Cellars," *Pap.* II B 1–21 (*SKS* 17, 280ff., DD:208), forward from 1838 to somewhere between July 1839 and spring 1840.[82] Finally, P.A. Heiberg does not shrink from correcting himself with regard to the dating, by arguing for switching the order of *Pap.* I A 114 and 116.[83]

The edition of the *Papirer*—with its substantially increased number of entries from Kierkegaard's younger years (compared to its predecessor)—spawned right from the beginning one detailed investigation after another of his youth and its secrets. Already A.B. Drachmann, with his two long book reviews of the edition's two first volumes in *Tilskueren,* or *The Spectator,* from February 1910 and March 1911, followed one of the most stubbornly returning themes in Kierkegaard research, namely, the dating and interpretation of *Pap.* II A 802–7. These six entries are known as "the earthquake" and stand out as an especially emphathic concentration of what was decisive for Kierkegaard's spiritual and intellectual development. In the first decades of the edition these entries were examined every which way by, in addition to Drachmann, among others, V. Ammundsen, P.A. Heiberg, Hans Ellekilde, and the aforementioned F. Brandt. The line, however, reaches back to Brandes and can be drawn all the way up through the twentieth century, right up to the most recent present with Grethe Kjær's elaboration of the traditional interpretation and Poul Behrendt's surprising new view of the matter.[84]

A more speculative direction was launched with P.A. Heiberg's book from 1912, *An Episode in the Youth of Søren Kierkegaard,* which contains the infamous thesis about Kierkegaard's alleged visit to a bordello.[85] Heiberg argues for such a visit

---

[80]   This is also implied in the preface to the supplement volumes to the second enlarged edition; see *Pap.* XII, p. i.

[81]   Carl Weltzer, *Peter og Søren Kierkegaard,* Copenhagen: Gad 1936, p. 52.

[82]   Frithiof Brandt, *Den unge Søren Kierkegaard. En række nye Bidrag,* Copenhagen: Levin & Munksgaard 1929, pp. 420–1.

[83]   P.A. Heiberg, *Et Segment af Søren Kierkegaards religiøse Udvikling 1835 1. Juni til 1838 19. Maj. Psykologisk Studie,* p. 89.

[84]   See Grethe Kjær, *Søren Kierkegaards seks optegnelser om Den Store Jordrystelse,* Copenhagen: C.A. Reitzel 1983; Poul Behrendt, "An Essay in the Art of Writing Posthumous Papers: The Great Earthquake Revisited," *Kierkegaard Studies. Yearbook,* 2003, pp. 48–109. Poul Behrendt criticizes the traditional biographical reading of the earthquake entries, which typically have been dated to 1838–39. Instead, he reads them "pseudonymously," as fiction, and connects them, among other things, with the first draft of the so-called inserted pieces in "Guilty/Not Guilty" in *Stages on Life's Way* (1845).

[85]   The book is the first in Heiberg's and Kuhr's series of *Kierkegaard-Studier,* which, however, only managed to produce two further volumes, namely, Heiberg's next book, *Et*

based on a "slip" of 30 days (in the spring of 1836) in the, according to Heiberg, otherwise so easily demonstrable chronology of the young Kierkegaard's entries. During this period he believes such a visit took place—along with Kierkegaard (1) having received three numbers of the journal *Humoristiske Intelligentsblade* from Reitzel, (2) having had repaired a pair of black trousers, (3) having had sown a new black coat for 36 rix-dollars, 4 marks and 8 schillings and (4) having helped his father to work out a list of residents for the property Nytorv nr. 2. Henning Fenger, the man behind the ironic point-by-point account of Heiberg's theory, emphasizes this book as an expression for his suspicion that Heiberg perhaps not only extracts his research from the papers, but can be thought to arrange the entries in the *Papirer*, so that there is room for such a bordello visit.[86] Below I will later give a more detailed account of Fenger's criticism of the *Papirer* as well as of the edition's further history of publication and significance for research.

IV. The Years Between the Wars (1920–40)

After a relatively peaceful nineteenth century, the twentieth century began with a World War, which was to be the greatest catastrophe theretofore in the self-understanding of Western man. The First World War was a watershed which divided people's consciousness into a marked before and after. In the words of George Orwell, with one blow the war changed "the entire spirit and tempo of life; people received a new view of life which was reflected in their political behavior, their customs, architecture, literature and everything else." More than anything else the war contributed to hurling Western man from the pedestal of civilization, upon which he had set himself and from which he was able to rise up over nature and the rest of the planet. In light of what happened since, the World War became in memory yet another "heart of darkness"—a prism for some of the darker sides of modernization and Enlightenment, the negative side of secularization, individualization and technological progress...where the nineteenth century was hubris, the twentieth was nemesis. There were no few chestnuts to pull out of the fire afterwards. Culture's traditional self-portrait in a golden frame, which presented an offensive and global entrepreneur in a pact with God and progress, was replaced by the reflection in a broken mirror of a defensive and uncertain human being. The relation between the sexes and the generations fell out of balance, and Western man stood to lose the final reference to the divine. While previous human beings could not do anything wrong in their own eyes, now they could not do anything right.[87]

Interest in Søren Kierkegaard's authorship experienced its first great blooming in the time around the First World War and against the background of the history of

---

Segment af Søren Kierkegaards religiøse Udvikling, and Victor Kuhr's *Modsigelsens Grundsætning*, Copenhagen and Kristiania: Gyldendal 1915. The series has primarily served to demonstrate the two editors' view of how the new edition of the *Papirer* could be used as a tool for research.

[86]   Cf. Henning Fenger, *Kierkegaard-Myter og Kierkegaard-Kilder. 9 kildekritiske studier i de kierkegaardske papirer, breve og aktstykker*, Odense: Odense Universitetsforlag 1976, p. 53. (English translation, *Kierkegaard: The Myths and their Origins*, trans. by George C. Schoolfield, New Haven and London: Yale University Press 1980, p. 57.)

[87]   Henrik Jensen, *Ofrets århundrede*, Copenhagen: Samleren 1998, p. 9.

consciousness sketched in the quotation. In Denmark, which was neutral in the war, the break was not nearly as violent as that in central Europe, and the result of the war's unmasking of the dissolution of values was seen here later and in a less radical manner than in the central European metropolises. But the ground swell reached the country, generally in the form of economic and political crises, new departures in science and art and peripherally in the form of criticism of old ideas in local and specific contexts. A marked example of such a criticism, which to such a high degree was also a conflict of generations, was the theological movement *Tidehverv*. Since much of this movement's inspiration and self-understanding was built on Kierkegaard's thoughts, the early *Tidehverv* also constituted a shift within Danish Kierkegaard research.

In Denmark throughout the 1920s a new variant of the old conflict between faith and knowledge played itself out, which in many ways gathered and strengthened the opposition between the radicalism of the 1870s and the symbolism of the 1890s. This so-called "life-view debate" has, in the first instance, its background in the compromising of rational, scientific civilization which the war had brought about. The relation of strength between science and religion was for a time inverted, but the first great wave of the new religiosity, which in this decade poured down on the Western world, to a large extent bypassed the Danish National Evangelical Lutheran Church, which was not able to meet the age's longing for a Christianity with the religious experience as its center (as expressed, for example, in the German historian of religion Rudolf Otto's classic book *Das Heilige* from 1917). In the debate about life-view there was, on the one side, a newly awakened attention for Kierkegaard's thoughts in line with a strong interest for oriental religions, theosophy, spiritualism, and various forms of liberal theology and philosophy of life. The other side of the debate was represented especially by radical cultural critics, socialists, social democrats and Darwinists. When the debate culminated in the middle of the 1920s, it involved many of the age's leading cultural personalities and the better part of the period's outstanding authors and poets, for example, Georg Brandes, Henning Kehler, Harald Høffding, Johannes V. Jensen, Sophus Claussen, Hans Kirk, Otto Gelsted, Johannes Jørgensen, Ludvig Holstein, Harald Bergstedt, and especially Helge Rode, whose book *The Square with the Green Trees* from 1924 is one of the debate's main turning points.[88] Among the authors who were specifically occupied with Kierkegaard at this time, were, for example, the journalist and author Christian Reventlow (1867–1954), who in *Letters from Purgatory* (1924) has Buddhism, Christianity and Kierkegaard show the way to salvation.[89] But there were also other people from Kierkegaard studies, such as J.L. Heiberg, H.O. Lange, and Eduard Geismar, who played a role.[90] With the transition from "the roaring '20s" to the crisis-struck 1930s, the debate about life-view died

---

[88]   Helge Rode, *Pladsen med de grønne Træer: Den religiøse Strømning i Nutidens Aandsliv*, Copenhagen: Gyldendal 1924.
[89]   Chr. Reventlow, *Breve fra Skærsilden,* Copenhagen: H. Aschehoug & Co. 1924.
[90]   One can read about this in Jesper Vaczy Kragh, *Kampen om livsanskuelse*, Odense: Syddansk Universitetsforlag 2005.

out, the spirit of the age became radicalized, and the theology of *Tidehverv* is an example of this radicalism.

A. Theology

With respect to the period between the wars, it is natural to begin with the theological Kierkegaard reception; this is due to the odd fact that it is here that one most clearly senses the intellectual-historical slide in the wake of the war. The new age (or modernity) made itself felt in Kierkegaard research in the most striking way in the theological reception and was given with *Tidehverv*'s relation to the age's "theology of crisis," dialectical theology and its criticism of liberal theology. The movement from liberal theology to dialectical theology anticipated a (slow) movement in Kierkegaard research generally from a psychologically, historically, biographically oriented approach to a more distinct concept-analytic reception and is thus an exponent of a development which sooner or later came to play a role in most of the other areas of life and scholarship.[91]

Tidehverv arose in the middle of the 1920s as a working community around the journal of the same name (which first appeared in 1926). The movement's leading figures had grown up in the Christian student movement, Danmarks kristelige Studenterforbund, and well into the 1920s were associated with it. This movement's main representatives from the older generation counted, among others, the later bishop of Haderslev Valdemar Ammundsen (1875–1936), the professor of ethics Eduard Geismar, (1871–1939) and the head librarian H.O. Lange (1863–1943). Ammundsen and Geismar introduced the study of Kierkegaard into the student movement, while Lange, as noted, was a collaborator on the first edition of Kierkegaard's *Samlede Værker* (1900–06). The Christian student movement arose primarily as a reaction to Georg Brandes' attack on Christianity and Christian values and regarded it as its task to restore the old synthesis of Christianity and culture, which cultural radicalism had dissolved. *Tidehverv*'s critical encounter with the student movement was in the first line a criticism of this mixing together of culture and Christianity, which had developed into a rather bizarre cultivation of personality and a religiosity and preaching stamped by feeling and experience. In a certain sense it was a criticism entirely in line with Brandes' "modern breakthrough" and his struggle against bourgeois-Christian monstrosity; but the criticism here took place, so to speak, internally, in the Christian camp itself. And while Brandes was right in regarding Kierkegaard as the main critic of his own naturalistic conception of human beings, *Tidehverv* saw in Kierkegaard an ally in the struggle against modern naturalism, which in their eyes ignored human freedom and responsibility. As a counterweight to the Christian student movement's naïve sentimentalizing of Christianity, the pious mimicking, the sexual fright, and the false harmony between grace and nature, faith and reason, church and culture, the young people in *Tidehverv* were inspired

---

[91] The field of art stands out as the earliest and clearest distillation of this development with the marked transitions from naturalism to phenomena such as jugendstil and symbolism to the abstract, expressionistic and non-figurative art, within the sphere of music from the tonal to the atonal music. In theology one has also talked about Karl Barth's commentary on the Letter to the Romans as a kind of "theological expressionism."

by contemporary theologians such as Karl Barth and Rudolf Bultmann, but also by authors such as Dostoevsky and Sigrid Undset with their clear realistic, non-idealized, life-like portrayals of everyday experience. Moreover, they also drew on Friedrich Nietzsche's attack on religiousness; theologians and authors such as Martin Luther, Thomas Kingo (1634–1703), Grundtvig (1783–1872), Otto Møller (1831–1915), and Jakob Knudsen (1858–1917) likewise belonged to the basic readings for the movement. However, the most important impulses came from, as noted, Søren Kierkegaard's authorship, and a substantial part of the conflict between the movement's "leaders" and the breakaways from *Tidehverv* came to expression in the struggle between Eduard Geismar's and Kristoffer Olesen Larsen's understanding of Kierkegaard, a conflict, which began in the 1920s and came to full expression at the beginning of the 1930s with lasting significance for Danish Kierkegaard reception and, moreover, with far-reaching personal consequences especially for Geismar.[92]

If one wishes to understand the basic difference in the approach to and interpretation of Kierkegaard which Geismar and Olesen Larsen represented, one might, as a start and painting with a wide brush, be tempted to trace the difference back to the two main claims from the *Concluding Unscientific Postscript:* "Subjectivity is the truth" and "Subjectivity is the untruth," which designates two banners under which the two kinds of reception operate. In other words, the question of whether Kierkegaard is an advocate or opponent of the principle of personality for the first time becomes completely clear. Generally speaking, Geismar is a theologian of mediation, who with an idealist thought structure seeks to meet halfway the age's biological, naturalist development of thought in order to build a bridge between the individual, the Church, and "the modern breakthrough," which he only believes to be possible with a Christian foundation and with Kierkegaard as the point of orientation. In a conscious polemic against Geismar, K. Olesen Larsen (1899–1964), who in the 1920s was Geismar's student and in 1924 wrote a prize essay on Kierkegaard's relation to Hegel, a competition which was overseen and judged by, among others, Geismar,[93] worked out his interpretation of Kierkegaard. In opposition to Geismar's

---

[92]   Subsequently Geismar was to a large extent on a side track in Danish theology, but also the people of *Tidehverv* had their careers threatened as a result of their radicality and had a difficult time finding appointments as pastors.

[93]   K. Olesen Larsen, *En Fremstilling og Vurdering af Søren Kierkegaards Lære om Paradokset og denne Læres etiske Konsekvenser under særlig Hensyntagen til Forholdet mellem Hegel og Kierkegaard*, Copenhagen 1923 (unpublished, located in the K. Olesen Larsen archive at The Royal Library, no. 4.1 in the catalogue); evaluated in *Festskrift udgivet af Københavns Universitet November 1924*, pp. 125–7 (the judges were Geismar, J. Oskar Andersen and Niels Munk Plum). In Torben Bramming's books, *Tidehvervs historie* (Frederiksberg: Anis 1993) and *Livsmod på Guds ord: Studier i Kristoffer Olesen Larsens eksistensteologi og tid* (Frederiksberg: Anis 1999) there is conflicting information about this treatise. In the first of these Bramming states correctly that the treatise is from 1923, while in the work from 1999 he states that it was written during Olesen Larsen's stay at Borch's College (from 1928) and, moreover, was lost in the archives of the Royal Library. The latter is not correct, but here Bramming is to be somewhat excused since it turns out that the treatise was found among Olesen Larsen's posthumous papers in September 1999 and subsequently

psychological, experiential and more harmonized interpretation, Olesen Larsen emphasizes the radicalism in Kierkegaard's work and places decisive weight on the notion of the paradox. His main objection is that Geismar makes Kierkegaard harmless and replaces consciousness of sin through the feeling of helplessness and decisiveness in the moment with self-reflecting striving.

If one wants to go deeper into the issue, it is appropriate to orient the account around the concept of the paradox and the predicate "intellectualism" typical of the age, which was especially associated with the interpretation of the Climacean writings and specifically, *Philosophical Fragments*, which is a problematic work for liberal theology and a central text for dialectical theology and related movements.[94] In this context one can introduce the Swedish theologian Torsten Bohlin, who in his extensive studies of Kierkegaard from the period (1918 and 1925), based on a comparative analysis of the concepts of sin and faith in the *Fragments* and the *Postscript* and in *The Concept of Anxiety* and *The Sickness unto Death* identifies two, for him, in principle irreconcilable strands in Kierkegaard's authorship, which strikingly recall the two strands which dominated the theological history of reception in the first half of the twentieth century: a *religious experiential* line and a *paradox* line.[95] While Kierkegaard, according to Bohlin, in the two first mentioned works makes sin into a condition with the basis in hereditary sin and stamps the concept of sin in an intellectualist direction, he strongly emphasizes in the two other works the character of sin as an act of freedom and will and polemicizes against the view of sin as a condition. The concept of sin in the *Fragments* and *Postscript* is therefore not oriented by the personal experience of sin and grace, but is, by contrast, a construction and a result of the doctrine of Christ as the absolute paradox, which is again due to the polemic against Hegel's understanding of Christianity. Therefore,

---

reached the library where it now figures as packet 4.1 (in the index of records on p. 13) in the K. Olesen Larsen archive. Concerning the treatise's relation to Geismar's Kierkegaard interpretation, Bramming writes in the first round (1993, p. 28), that the gold medal treatise "was written wholly in agreement with Geismar's view of Kierkegaard," while in the second round (1999, p. 10) it is added less confidently that the treatise "is said" to be stamped by Geismar's influence. If one now reads the treatise (and it should be emphasized that there has only been talk of partial reading) in the light of the later conflict between Olesen Larsen and Geismar, then it is in fact possible to register a certain ambivalence in Olesen Larsen's evaluation of his teacher's understanding of Kierkegaard. To be sure, Olesen Larsen emphasizes again and again that it is not possible to imitate Kierkegaard, before one has separated the life-denying and ascetic elements (particularly in his last writings), but at the same time the fulcrum of the entire treatise is such a fundamentally positive evaluation of the paradox that it points away from Geismar (Børge Diderichsen touches on this in his introduction to *Søren Kierkegaard læst af K. Olesen Larsen*, vols. 1–2, Copenhagen: Gad 1966, vol. 1, p. 10). Moreover, the treatise stands out as an exceedingly interesting period piece and deserves an independent treatment. Perhaps a topic for a thesis for a student of theology?

[94]   See Heiko Schulz, "Rezeptionsgeschichtliche Brocken oder die *Brocken* in der deutschen Rezeption," *Kierkegaard Studies. Yearbook*, 2004, pp. 404–5, which, however, problematizes this in relation to the early Barth and points out that it is rather the writings from the attack on the Church which Barth draws on in his commentary to the Letter to the Romans from 1922.

[95]   Bohlin, *Kierkegaards dogmatiska Åskådning i dess historiska Sammanhang*.

Kierkegaard's Christology, which he, according to Bohlin, directly took over from the traditional Athanasian two-nature doctrine (cf. Teisen), has had a retroactive effect on his doctrine of sin. He was himself not conscious of the contradictory nature of his account of the concept of sin, and the liberal theologian Bohlin argues that Kierkegaard's "real" conception of sin is to be found on the path of religious experience.[96]

One finds an interpretation of Kierkegaard in line with this in Geismar, who in addition to Bohlin's books drew especially on the books of P.A. Heiberg.[97] In a review of Bohlin's work, Geismar, however, criticizes the claimed parallelism in the concept of sin and faith. Geismar can agree with the stamp of the concept of faith as "anti-intellectualist intellectualism," but he thinks that the concept of sin in Kierkegaard *must* be derived from his own religious experiences. The Augustinian conception of sin is, for him, the originary and *primus motor* in his entire conception of Christ. Rather than the concept of sin being paradoxically stamped, the paradox is construed in order to defend the concept of sin. Geismar builds the argument for this in part by tracing the issue back to the different pseudonyms; he asks, why should the pseudonyms be in agreement with each other? He also builds his argument in part by ordering according to rank Kierkegaard's writings, according to which Kierkegaard himself appears most purely in the Christian discourses, then in the anti-Climacean writings, and then in the diaries and finally in the (other) pseudonymous writings. When, therefore, Johannes Climacus in the *Fragments* apparently derives the Augustinian consciousness of sin from the paradox, this should not be seen as an opposition to Kierkegaard's own experience-bound train of thought, but from Climacus' specific view: to ensure a qualitative difference between human and Christian religiosity. That the movement of thought in the *Fragments* is supposed to go from the paradox to the consciousness of sin, is moreover only a mistaken appearance, according to Geismar, who, however, does not manage to argue for this based on the *Fragments* itself. Further, Geismar objects to Bohlin's claim that the

---

[96]   Ibid., pp. 205–24; pp. 256–98.

[97]   In his overview of the history of the research, Aage Henriksen believes that it is the merit of Geismar at such an early point in time to have presented the insights of Bohlin and Heiberg in a popular form, although he has a problematic way of bringing two so different researchers under one hat. Thus Heiberg is the only scholar who has the view that Kierkegaard's life is a long ascent to religious faith (a story of a healing culminating in June 1852), while Bohlin, as implied, regards something in Kierkegaard as religious, but much else (especially in the later work) as intellectualist, unChristian and unLutheran. When there arises a conflict between the views of Heiberg and Bohlin, Geismar chooses typically the latter's side, but attempts to save as much as possible of Kierkegaard's person and work for a healthy church life and Christian life. Cf. Henriksen, *Methods and Results of Kierkegaard Studies in Scandinavia*, pp. 152ff. The claim that Heiberg is the sole researcher who regards Kierkegaard's religious development as a story of healing is true enough, but nonetheless it has a striking parallel in Olesen Larsen's conception of Kierkegaard's universe of concepts as serving the function of illuminating a single problem: how to *become* a Christian. Thus Olesen Larsen in fact also exempts the psychologically oriented Heiberg from his otherwise all-encompassing polemic. Cf. Holger Jepsen, "En Kierkegaard parafrase," *Dansk Udsyn*, vol. 48, 1968, p. 371.

Fragments seems to make impossible an organic transition between the old and the new life by emphasizing that Climacus himself illustrates the matter with an image of a slow, painful, organic process,[98] and elaborates on his position towards the alleged intellectualism of the concept of faith and sin in the *Fragments* and the *Postscript*. Again Geismar is forced to distinguish between Climacus and Kierkegaard, since Climacus as a humorist and admirer of Socrates with Hegelian presuppositions seeks to undermine Hegel's notorious intellectualism. That there really is a question of an intellectual knowledge of truth in the *Fragments*, is immediately clear from this, but Kierkegaard did not himself share these presuppositions, which the definition of sin and faith in *The Sickness unto Death* shows. By also including in the analysis *Practice in Christianity*, Geismar "saves" the concept of faith's interwoven motif of religiosity and paradox with the assumption that the paradox from the beginning in the *Fragments* must be a thought project which is played out against Hegel by Climacus, but Kierkegaard himself later uses it polemically against Martensen "in the sense that it only for a cheap apologetics needs to be determined that Christianity was the paradox, whereas faith in general does not have the paradox as its object."[99]

That Kierkegaard is thought to have let Climacus adapt himself to Hegel's linguistic usage in order that the opposition to Hegel could be expressed in a Hegelian manner, is something that Geismar also takes up in his extensive study *Søren Kierkegaard. His Life and Authorship* (1926–28),[100] which is, without rival, the period's most read book on Kierkegaard. The subtitle of the work is characteristic and an expression of the biographical approach which constituted the foundation of Geismar's understanding of Kierkegaard, an approach which has fundamental problems with the exclusivity of the notion of the paradox and thus, for example, the *Fragments* as a fully valid expression of Kierkegaard's personal religious life. The deepest thing in Kierkegaard's nature and life work one finds, according to Geismar, in his separation of the religious from the impossible intellectualism, which has stamped the Church for centuries. This is seen, among other things, in the fact that he expressly fought against the view that Christianity is a doctrine or a result, or that faith is a form of knowing. If a form of intellectualism nonetheless crept into Kierkegaard's conception of Christianity, it is due to the energy with which he isolated the revelation in Christ from all other forms of religiosity. Geismar explains this double view by imagining that the philosophical writings (especially the *Fragments* and the *Postscript*) do not themselves portray Christianity but construct its concept and clarify the road to Christianity.

Geismar mentions *Tidehverv* at the end of his long work and recognizes that he has disappointed the people involved in this journal ("these gadflies") in their struggle against the handed-down Christianity. Where he above all feels himself separated from them is in the fact that they reduce religiousness A to nothing at all: "This must derive from the fact that they do not sense how far-reaching this is. If

---

98   Cf. *SKS* 4, 240.
99   Eduard Geismar, "Omkring Søren Kierkegaard," *Teologisk Tidsskrift*, series 4, vol. 6, 1925, pp. 292–339, see pp. 315–16.
100   Eduard Geismar, *Søren Kierkegaard. Hans Livsudvikling og Forfatterskab*, vols. 1–2, Copenhagen: G.E.C. Gad 1926–28.

the richness and humility of the Christian life rests on the intense tension between religiousness A and religiousness B, then the whole thing disappears from reality, if the one pole is theoretically eliminated; and then the result is that life becomes wholly without reality; not even the task of raising one's children is a task which one is obliged to fulfill before God."[101]

In a series of continuous articles in *Tidehverv* from the end of 1932 and the beginning of 1933 with the title, "Something about the Decision in the Moment," K. Olesen Larsen unfolds the above mentioned thoroughgoing criticism of his former teacher, who on his side responded in a slightly offended tone. Olesen Larsen takes his point of departure in the issue of the *Fragments* and the *Postscript* and sets about investigating Johannes Climacus' presuppositions in order to show how they give the moment decisive significance, and vice versa under what presuppositions the moment does *not* receive significance—namely under Geismar's (pseudoHegelian) presuppositions: "Professor Geismar has with heavy hand cut Kierkegaard's thoughts off as soon as they come in the neighborhood of the absolute decision. Since the absolute decision in the moment—to use Professor Geismar's expression of the reformulation in existence—is present in every thought, then Kierkegaard's thoughts lose, with the help of the professor, not only all significance but also every justified demand for interest from the side of the existing human being."[102] I cannot here give a more detailed account of the polemic and the views involved,[103] but to show the continuity in Olesen Larsen's Kierkegaard interpretation and his

---

[101]   Ibid., p. VI; p. 113.

[102]   K. Olesen Larsen, "Noget om Afgørelsen i Øjeblikket," in *Søren Kierkegaard læst af K. Olesen Larsen*, vol. 1 (*Artikler fra Tidehverv*), p. 24.

[103]   Jens Holger Schjørring in his study on reception believes that polemic has had fateful significance for Kierkegaard research in Denmark—all of Olesen Larsen's opponents commit in principle the same mistake (cf. the pastor Johannes Nordentoft's well-known characterization in 1930 of the basic position of *Tidehverv*: "God is everything, I am nothing—and you are an idiot"). The question is whether Olesen Larsen's existence-theological interpretation or translation of Kierkegaard does not lead to a polemic monotony. Schjørring emphasizes the hopeless impression that the conflict between Geismar and Olesen Larsen makes and illustrates it with the doctor Hedvig Reinhard (1865–1952), who was associated with *Tidehverv* and who was Geismar's house doctor and had him as pastoral carer, but who after the conflict no longer mentions him among the significant Kierkegaard scholars (in contrast to, for example, P.A. Heiberg and Hjalmar Helweg). Schjørring poses the question why Geismar held firmly to his Kierkegaard interpretation instead of merely carrying on the selective line chosen by him, a consideration which plays a role for the theological thinking's response to the European cultural crisis. Geismar's later cultural criticism went unnoticed in Denmark because he stood as a failed Kierkegaard scholar. When his flank had fallen, *Tidehverv* continued its anti-ecclesiastical line and doubtless won a victory over, for example, a phenomenon such as the Oxford movement in the mid 1930s, while Geismar at that point was working with far more difficult problems surrounding the German struggle of the Church and national socialism, which he was for the most part alone with in Denmark. In this perspective one can, according to Schjørring, ask whether *Tidehverv's* victory was not a Pyhrric victory. Cf. Jens Holger Schjørring, "Kierkegaard und die dänische Theologie der zwanziger und dreißiger Jahre," *Die Rezeption Søren Kierkegaards in der deutschen und dänischen Philosophie und Theologie. Vorträge des Kolloquiums am 22. und 23. März 1982*, ed. by Heinrich Anz, Munich et al:

intense focus on the paradox, I can mention a longer, text-near account from the posthumously published "Posthumous Works," which give an account of the rise of the notion of the paradox in Kierkegaard's works, in part from the papers and in part in the *Fragments* and the *Postscript*, ending in a fundamental distinction between Christianity and existential philosophy.[104] The *Fragments* is understood in this context both from the work's relation to the tendency of the authorship and as the logical extension of the issue, which presents itself in the papers and the earlier works up until this point in the authorship: the systematic-abstract relation between the absolute philosophy, speculation, and Christianity as revelation. What is decisive, for Olesen Larsen, is that the paradox is determined as a limit concept, which the understanding cannot get past. Christianity is not some *doctrine* about the paradox but *is* the paradox. Climacus shows precisely the consequences and impossiblity of attempting to understand Christianity and at the same time raises the questions on a new level, that of existence. At the level of existence, Christianity is not a question of philosophy but a historical fact; it is not a conveying of knowledge, but an existence communication. Faith is therefore not construed from the paradox but arises in the fortunate encounter with it; its object is not a teaching, but the teacher, and it is therefore not some new piece of knowledge but an existential act. In Kierkegaard's words, the understanding stumbles in the paradoxical passion upon the paradox and must either be offended or put itself aside and make room for faith. On the other hand, the paradox is not a sacrifice of the understanding, but (with a characteristic formulation by Olesen Larsen) "is a manner of speaking to faith." This means that the problem is not intellectual but existential, and Climacus therefore makes possible in the *Fragments* the discovery of the category of existence, which is cashed out in full in the *Postscript's* criticism of "the system."

When Olesen Larsen treats the previous research, he emphasizes its lack of understanding of the paradox as a limit concept, and the intellectualism, which the better part of the research found in the *Fragments*, Olesen Larsen finds in the research. He divides the previous misunderstandings into a rationalist group (partly, humanist rationalism, for example, A.B. Drachmann, and, partly, a theological supernaturalism, for example, Barth and Diem) and an apologetic, pietistic group (Geismar). The rationalist misunderstanding, both in the humanist and orthodox form, operates with two spheres of knowing, for which reason the object of faith in the first case becomes a doctrine, which is to be obtained by sacrificing the understanding, while in the second case it happens by way of a miracle, the Holy Spirit's arbitrary intervention. For the humane view, both faith and offense are intellectually determined because it limits itself to an intellectual theory that God has existed in time, and for the supernaturalist the very same fact becomes a short sum total of the entire orthodox

---

Fink 1983 (*Text & Kontext*, Sonderreihe, vol. 15), (*Kopenhagener Kolloquien zur deutschen Literatur*, vol. 7), pp. 171–85.

[104]   The article, "Om Paradoxbegrebet—III. belyst ud fra Smulerne og Efterskriften" was presumably written around 1955, when it was published in an abbreviated version in *Symposion Kierkegaardianum, Orbis Litterarum*, tome X, fasc. 1–2, Copenhagen: Munksgaard 1955, pp. 130–47. Cf. Olesen Larsen, *Søren Kierkegaard læst af K. Olesen Larsen*, vol. 1, pp. 249–50.

dogmatics. The apologetic, pietistic interpretation, according to Olesen Larsen, also replaces the possibility of offense with a *sacrificium intellectus*, and likewise here the paradox is not conceived as a limit concept because the individual with the deepening in the human existence's weakness, uncertainty and blame is brought so close to the paradox that it with only a short leap in the course of thought, called the personal choice, finds itself in the sphere of the paradox.

This account should give an impression of how consistently and honestly Olesen Larsen is in his interpretation of Kierkegaard, but also how close he is in his word choice to Kierkegaard's own terminology. When he criticizes previous interpretations of the *Fragments* for having merely "photographed" the work's systematic course of thought,[105] it must be said, that his own method of close reading cannot wholly unfairly be characterized as a kind of Kierkegaard philology[106] or even a paraphrase of Kierkegaard.[107] I have treated this aspect of the reception in such detail due to the fact that *Tidehverv* was the point of departure for several of the following epochs' most significant Danish theologians, and Olesen Larsen's existence-theological reading of Kierkegaard would prove, with respect to theology, to be the most influential in the period. It constitutes an independent line in the research, which has continued all the way up to the most recent times. This is not without irony since Olesen Larsen did not want to be a Kierkegaard *researcher* but merely to read him existentially. The conflict between a religious experiential line and a paradox line appears, moreover, at regular intervals in Danish theology and reached its high point in the 1950s and 1960s in connection with Olesen Larsen's controversy with K.E. Løgstrup in the conflict about Kierkegaard—seen by many as the most important theological debate in the history of the Danish church in the twentieth century.[108]

B. Personal History and Psychology

It was claimed by way of introduction that the theological Kierkegaard reception was an early exponent of a general European movement in the history of spirit from a subjective, personality-oriented culture to a more factual, objectively concentrated condition of spirit. The period between the wars, however, was in Denmark with regard to the Kierkegaard literature, primarily biographically oriented and quantitatively characterized by a massive overrepresentation of psychological and

---

[105]   Olesen Larsen, *Søren Kierkegaard læst af K. Olesen Larsen*, vol. 2 (*Efterladte Arbejder*), p. 37; p. 49.

[106]   H.C. Wind, "Die Rezeption Kierkegaards in der neueren dänischen Theologie," in *Die Rezeption Søren Kierkegaards in der deutschen und dänischen Philosophie und Theologie. Vorträge des Kolloquiums am 22. und 23. März 1982*, ed. by Heinrich Anz, p. 195. The term "philology" here must almost be conceived as synonymous with "text-near" or "text-faithful."

[107]   Jepsen, "En Kierkegaard parafrase," pp. 370–84.

[108]   See Bramming, *Livsmod på Guds ord. Studier i Kristoffer Olesen Larsens eksistensteologi og tid*, p. 7. This book, moreover, contains an introductory account of Olesen Larsen's personal background and the contemporary culture and literature which he was shaped by.

personal-historical research. This is clear from the two long overviews of the history of research, which Aage Kabell (1920–81) and Aage Henriksen (b. 1921) published after the Second World War. Kabell's (1948) and Henriksen's (1951) works were answers to a prize competition in Nordic philology with the title "The History of the Study of Søren Kierkegaard. A Historical and Critical Account of its Phases in the Danish, Norwegian and Swedish Research" which was announced by the University of Copenhagen in 1944. One of the most striking things with these studies on reception is that Aage Henriksen does not even mention *Tidehverv*, and Aage Kabell only *en passant* makes room for K. Olesen Larsen. K.L. Aastrup therefore once claimed that "Danish Church history between the wars [is] the history of *Tidehverv*. It is *Tidehverv* which has stamped the period and determined the issues."[109] This is undeniably correct, and with this claim it must only be noted that the significance of K. Olesen Larsen's efforts in Kierkegaard research does not give Kabell and Henriksen occasion for a closer examination.[110] *Tidehverv*'s and K. Olesen Larsen's significance seems thus only to become evident outside the narrowly theological circles later, namely, in the intellectual climate after the war stamped by existentialism.[111] This can also be due to the fact that K. Olesen Larsen never actually published a work on Kierkegaard, but most often wrote his articles with a point of departure in other peoples' Kierkegaard interpretations.[112]

---

[109]   Quoted from *Den danske kirkes historie*, vols. 1–8, ed. by Hal Koch et al., Copenhagen: Gyldendalske Boghandel 1950–66, vol. 8, 1966, p. 181.

[110]   Another person who is passed over in Kabell's and Henriksen's studies (although Kabell regrets this in a brief comment in his index of names), is the theologian, librarian, and author Anders Gemmer (1889–1951). At a very early point in time Gemmer published a book together with the German August Messer about Kierkegaard and Karl Barth (see Anders Gemmer and August Messer, *Søren Kierkegaard und Karl Barth*, Stuttgart: Strecker & Schröder 1925), in which Gemmer authored the section on Kierkegaard and Messer the section on Barth. Gemmer is interested in Kierkegaard from the perspective of the philosophy of religion, and he is, to the best of my knowledge, the only one who in the Danish context at this time put Kierkegaard in connection with the age's (the first few decades of the 1900s) neoKantian philosophy of values. Gemmer can, for example, criticize Kierkegaard for confusing the concepts of value and actuality with his ideas about the absolute paradox, just as he criticizes the branch of research (for example, Hirsch and Valter Lindström), which fundamentally emphasizes the unity in Kierkegaard's work. It is therefore not surprising that his evaluation of Torsten Bohlin's analyses is more positive. Cf. Anders Gemmer, "Ufordøjet Kierkegaard," in his *Filosofisk Potpourri: Ti Afhandlinger*, Copenhagen: Munskgaard 1949, pp. 75–85. See also Anders Gemmer, *Søren Kierkegaards Livsfilosofi. En kritisk Gennemgang*, Odense: A.C. Normanns Forlag 1944.

[111]   As late as 1967 the newspaper *Information* could present Jørgen K. Bukdahl's review of the church historian Leif Grane's anthology about the central contributions in *Tidehverv* with the words: "the important and influential—but rather unknown to the general public—ecclesiastical movement *Tidehverv*." Cf. "Det klassiske Tidehverv," *Information*, July 10, 1967 (republished in Jørgen K. Bukdahl, *Frihed og frigørelse. Filosofi—Teologi—Kulturdebat. Artikler og essays 1956–1979*, Århus: Aros 1980, pp. 127–34). See also Leif Grane's introduction to his (ed.), *Tidehverv. En antologi*, Copenhagen: Gyldendal 1967, p. 9.

[112]   This is perhaps more then a mere coincidence since Olesen Larsen presumably had a decisive need for the views of others as the point of departure for and contrast to his own

When one goes to Aage Henriksen, one is presented with a typology of the research in the period from 1909 to 1949 in two main groups, respectively the psychological-historical research with the subgroups "reflexive" (P.A. Heiberg), "social" and "biological" psychology (the latter two we would today call nature and nurture), along with the substantially more scanty philosophical and theological research divided into Kierkegaard's relation to the humanistic and the theological tradition. In addition, the period's two great biographers are treated, Eduard Geismar's six-volume work from 1926–28 and Johannes Hohlenberg's two books from 1940 and 1948. Aage Kabell's less systematic but more comprehensive overview also emphasizes other subjective holistic conceptions of Kierkegaard, different from those treated in Hohlenberg's and Geismar's, and also, Bohlin's, Emanuel Hirsch's, and Troels Frederik Troels-Lund's. At the most general level Aage Henriksen divides Scandinavian Kierkegaard research on the basis of the two editions of the journals and papers, which results in two well-defined periods of time, respectively 1869–1909 and 1909–49, which in addition are equally long. The editions of the journals and papers thus constitute, in Henriksen's perspective, epochs of research, and one can ask whether this division does not color the history of reception in a biographical direction.[113] Or the other way around, whether it to too great an extent lets the age's dominant biographical orientation determine the split in epochs. In this connection the question is further whether it is correct at all that the journals and papers should be regarded as a biographical resource with privileged information about Kierkegaard's private life.[114]

---

ideas. Cf. Vibeke Olesen Larsen's and Tage Wilhjelm's preface to *Søren Kierkegaard læst af K. Olesen Larsen.*

[113]   Cf. Finn Hauberg Mortensen, "Kierkegaard in Scandinavia—A History of Radical Reception," in *Kierkegaard Revisited,* ed. by Niels Jørgen Cappelørn and Jon Stewart, Berlin and New York: Walter de Gruyter 1997 (*Kierkegaard Studies. Monograph Series,* vol. 1), p. 419.

[114]   A few examples of different evaluations of the character of the papers should be mentioned. In an article entitled "The Retrospective Understanding of Søren Kierkegaard's Total Production" (in *Kierkegaard. Rescources and Results,* ed. by Alastair McKinnon, Montreal: Wilfrid Laurier University Press 1982, pp. 18–38) Niels Jørgen Cappelørn makes use of extracts from the journals as sources for his attempt to achieve an integrated understanding of Kierkegaard's collected literary production. One of his theses is that the journals are not independent of this production but are a constitutive part of it, and Cappelørn—just like Bohlin and Brandes—argues for the inestimable value of the journal entries in the understanding of the complete train of thought's source in, for example, current events in Kierkegaard's time or through his reading of certain books. Cappelørn emphasizes in this context that the information from the journals in respect to Kierkegaard's universe of concepts is in fact more reliable than when it is a matter of tracing his biography due to Kierkegaard's express poetic disposition. The poetic dimension is such a vital part of Kierkegaard's personality that the authorship for just this reason cannot be understood in isolation from the personality—Kierkegaard's life *is* in this sense his production, something which he in *Papirer* VIII–1 A 424 (*JP* 5, 6078) foresees the consequences of: "And this is why the time will come when not only my writings but my whole life, the intriguing secret of the whole machinery, will be studied and studied." (Cf. ibid., pp. 18ff.) Joakim Garff believes that by giving the journals a special status with respect to Kierkegaard's biography, one overlooks the fact that Kierkegaard in his pseudonymous

Whatever the case, the trace of the edition and the continuation of the large new edition of the papers is an important road marker in the period's constantly growing stream of books about Kierkegaard. The *Papirer*, with the publication of the individual volumes, was (as noted, generally positively) reviewed and commented upon in newspaper articles, feature articles, and journals both domestically and abroad. Hans Brix was from the beginning convinced of the necessity of the edition in light of the shortcomings of its predecessor. The first volume "documents with its content its justification, just as the precision of the edition seems extraordinary."[115] Future researchers will have at their disposal "a complete body of material of enormous volume." But Brix is more reserved in his evaluation of the significance of the edition for research: "To be a Kierkegaardian will, if possible, require to an even greater extent a man's life, and for detailed research the widest fields now lay open. On what is central in S. Kierkegaard's life, by contrast, one can hardly cast any new light." This prophecy and specifically its first part about the edition of the *Papirer* having opened up for more or less near-sighted and hair-splitting detailed studies of Kierkegaard's life, came to be true. This, however, is hardly due to the new material that the *Papirer* brought to light but rather to the dominant subjective-biographically oriented spirit of the age.

Now, specialized studies on Kierkegaard's life are not the same as specialized studies on the *Papirer*; in fact, one is tempted to count many of the psychological and personal-historical studies to the category of "that which precisely is *not* found in the *Papirer*." Frithiof Brandt (1892–1968) can be introduced as a witness to the special seduction which lies in the occupation with Kierkegaard's papers. He was an initiator of a very comprehensive literature on Kierkegaard's personal appearance and his mental constitution, which culminated in Rikard Magnussen's double work, *Søren Kierkegaard seen from the Outside* (dedicated to Brandt) and *The Exceptional Cross* from 1942.[116] Brandt's contribution to this verbose branch of the research is *The Young Søren Kierkegaard* from 1929,[117] where he, by way of introduction, mentions Kierkegaard's journals as the main source for understanding him. The journals help us, according to Brandt, to get to know Kierkegaard from the inside,

---

authorship, on the strength of the pseudonymity, allows himself to be more private than in the journals, where he from the start stands out more as a poet and stamps the entries' "reality content" literarily (a view which Garff also finds in the author Martin A. Hansen. Cf. "'...da er der en, der nikker i Smug nær dig.' Om at fornemme det fremmedes medvirken i teksten—et kierkegaardsk kætterbrev," *PS. Om Martin A. Hansens korrespondance med kredsen omkring Heretica*, ed. by Anders Thyrring Andersen, Copenhagen: Gyldendal 2005, pp. 148–64). Thus when Henning Fenger (see *Kierkegaard-Myter og Kierkegaard-Kilder* (*Kierkegaard: The Myths and their Origins*)) demythologizes entries and reveals their fictional context in order to unmask the "real" Kierkegaard, he overlooks, according to Garff, that "mythologizing and fiction are constitutive features of Kierkegaard's (self-)staging and to this extent fail to show the 'real' Kierkegaard." Cf. Garff, *Den Søvnløse*, p. 30n.

[115]   See the feature article in *Politiken*, November 13, 1909.

[116]   Rikard Magnussen, *Søren Kierkegaard, set udefra*, Copenhagen: Ejnar Munksgaard 1942 and *Det særlige Kors. Efterskrift til Bogen: Søren Kierkegaard, set udefra*, Copenhagen: Ejnar Munksgaard 1942.

[117]   Brandt, *Den unge Søren Kierkegaard*.

as he was, at one with himself, but the journals give no information about how he was in the eyes of others: "Most people interested in Kierkegaard have certainly felt the difficulty of seeing him from the outside. How was he face to face? What impression did one receive of his nature and character? How did he move about in daily life, and how was he in personal interaction?"[118] It is here as if the interest in the inner switches over to an interest in the outer—from what supposedly is found in the *Papirer*, to exactly what is not found in the *Papirer*. This tendency to seek the reality behind the text is perhaps especially striking with regard to the periods where the papers are the most important and often the only source on Kierkegaard's life and thought. There can hardly be any doubt that the *Papirer's* many entries have attracted special attention with regard to the years before the beginning of the actual authorship, 1833–43, and the years immediately up to the outbreak of the attack on the Church in 1854. Regarding the interest in Kierkegaard's outward appearance, his possible disability, it is, apart from the common human curiosity for such things, without doubt also the special interest in phrenology, physiognomy, and eugenics of the 1920s and 1930s which is at work.[119]

Brandt's book, which at the beginning awakened enthusiastic reviews by, among others, Eduard Geismar,[120] set off a minor literary dispute between the author, who was a professor of philosophy, and the aforementioned Hans Brix (1870–1961). While the theological debate played itself out in the more or less peripheral *Tidehverv*, the literary debate attained a much larger public through feature articles and debate pieces in the months of January–March 1930 in the newspaper *Nationaltidende*. This whole kind of research is for better or worse very Danish—*also* because the presuppositions for personal-historical and similar investigations are naturally most obviously present in a Danish context. Brandt vs. Brix is worth mentioning not so much due to the substance of the matter and the arguments—this is frankly often absent—but because the controversy both continues and sharpens the biographical and psychological inheritance from Brandes and anticipates a few things which have caused debate in the most recent times. It concerns the ever rummaging general picture of Kierkegaard—who he *really* was and how much we dare deduce from detailed knowledge to general statements about his person and relation to the contemporary age (the danger of speculation). Or vice versa, to what degree the detailed study is dominated by the picture which one, as a researcher, has of Kierkegaard beforehand (the danger of bias). One only needs a little sidestep before a researcher becomes a producer of legends. Moreover, it is a question of the literary scholars' objections to large parts of the research, whether it be biographical, psychological, personal-historical, philosophical, or theological—the question of the texts' literarity and the relation between fiction and reality. The literary scholar Aage Henriksen, for

---

[118]   Ibid., p. 1.

[119]   See, for example, Lene Koch, *Racehygiejne i Danmark 1920–56*, Copenhagen: Gyldendal 1996.

[120]   Cf. his article about the book, in *Berlingske Tidende*, December, 12, 1929, where he writes: "A fortunate find of a new clue—an iron discipline in following the clue—an extraordinary ability to see—have together created one of the masterpieces of Danish literary history."

example, in his history of the research constantly keeps a careful eye on researchers who undertake a biographical application of a passage in Kierkegaard's texts without first having investigated the literary context and thus make themselves guilty of underestimating the modern aesthetic conception that the work is what is central. The placing of literature with a basis in life side by side with literature with a basis in another literature and finally with (the, according to Brandt, most outstanding) literature branded by the personality makes Brandt, according to Henriksen, guilty of this underestimation: "Where Brandt uses remarks, notes, and poetical works to place Kierkegaard in a human environment, his critics try to understand the same parts of the text separately, in their literary setting. Behind these differences in the trend of the interpretation, there is no different intention but a difference in the view of literature."[121]

Brandt's book has its point of departure in his "discovery" of the fact that Henrik Hertz's *Stemninger og Tilstande* (1839) is a key novel, whose characters are based on living contemporary models. Kierkegaard is thus identified with the character "the translator," and Hertz's description of a symposium shares, according to Brandt, the external circumstances with the scene in "In vino veritas"—apart from the host of the banquet, who in reality was Kierkegaard, which is documented by a restaurant bill of 235 rix-dollars. Further, it is argued that Poul Martin Møller modelled his Ahasverus Fragments (1836–37) on Kierkegaard as type, and that the critic P.L. Møller is Johannes the seducer. The statement that Johannes is a "marked" (*mærket*) individual, leads Brandt in this connection to consult the Danish dictionary, *Ordbog over det danske Sprog*, where "*mærket*" is explained with the examples of having red hair or being a hunchback.

The newspaper dispute with Hans Brix concerned primarily the general view of literature (the relation "*Dichtung und Wahrheit*") and also to what extent H.C. Andersen gave a malicious caricature of Kierkegaard as a parrot in *The Galoshes of Fortune* (1838), whether Kierkegaard's voice was shrill or meek, and finally Kierkegaard's disability, his "prematurely old" appearance. "The strongly animated debate,"[122] which was also enriched with contributions by, among others, the actor Robert Schmidt and the clerk H.G. Olrik, had as one of its critical points an outline drawing which Brandt believed was a portrait of Kierkegaard. The drawing had been theretofore overlooked, and, it was claimed, supports Hertz's portrait in *Stemninger og Tilstande* and the suspicion of Kierkegaard's "premature old age" and makes it believable that he had inherited the form of his cranium from his father rather than his mother. To this Brix replies that for "the cranium problem to be able to be discussed with sufficient thoroughness and effect, the three relevant skulls had to be procured. The analysis of such things based on a portrait is in my view as a rule a rather arid sport."[123] Without following this line of Kierkegaard research in detail,[124]

---

[121]   Henriksen, *Methods and Results of Kierkegaard Studies in Scandinavia*, p. 97.
[122]   See *Nationaltidende*, February 2, 1930.
[123]   See *Nationaltidende*, February 12, 1930.
[124]   In the wake of Brandt there comes, among others, Knud Jensenius, who uses the same method of finding living models for Kierkegaard's figures. The young melancholy man at the banquet in *Stages* is thus Hans Brøchner (cf. Knud Jensenius, "Det unge Menneske hos Søren

which, as noted, was brought into full bloom with the two books by the sculptor Rikard Magnussen, where Kierkegaard's melancholy and suffering are traced back to his outward deformities, there is, however, the wrinkle that the discussion about Kierkegaard's appearance apparently did not want to come to an end and reached a quite entertaining climax at the beginning of the 1940s when Brandt brought into the discussion a theretofore unknown porcelain figure of Kierkegaard, and the theologian and later social-democratic minister of culture Julius Bomholt (1896–1969) suggested deciding once and for all the chatter about Kierkegaard's supposed hunchback and the form of his cranium by simply opening Kierkegaard's grave![125]

But also in studies in the field of psychology one finds again the age's occupation with, if one will, physiognomy (or, as Henriksen calls it, biology), a certain positivistic desire to classify and categorize. By far the main part of the age's psychological or psychiatric studies of Kierkegaard makes use of a pathologizing vocabulary and follows, in the words of Kresten Nordentoft, the route laid out by Brandes: to study Kierkegaard as a psychological case, not as a psychologist.[126] To this end, people often make use of Ernst Kretschmer's typology (from *Körperbau und Charakter* (1921) and *Geniale Menschen* (1929)), which operates with, among other things, two fundamental human types, the "cyklotome," which in body is small and fat (pyknic) and of mind unbalanced, and the "schizotyme," in body tall and thin (asthenic or leptosomatic) and of mind fanatical. The former can, with an overdevelopment of his disposition, be prone to develop manic-depressive psychosis, while the latter is disposed to schizophrenia.[127] Hjalmar Helweg (1886–1960), one of the age's most important and influential Danish psychiatrists, makes use of this typology in his extensive *Søren Kierkegaard – A Psychiatric-Psychological Study* (1933).[128] Helweg diagnoses Kierkegaard (and his whole family) as suffering from manic-depressive psychosis of an endogenous origin beginning in 1835 and lasting for life. This affliction appears, as noted, primarily in people of a pyknic stature and syntonic (that is, emotional, open and immediate) nature; however, in Kierkegaard's case the typology must be taken with the qualification that, judging from everything, he was an asthenic type, but presumably developed pyknic characteristics as a result of illness and weakness. Psychologically, everything points to schizoid characteristics, but we find syntonic elements such as extroverted affectedness, longing for human contact and compassion for the sufferings of others. The mixture gave the manic-

---

Kierkegaard," *Nordisk Tidsskrift 1930*, pp. 340ff.). The extensive *Nogle Kierkegaardstudier. "De tre store Ideer"* (Copenhagen: Nyt Nordisk Forlag/Arnold Busck 1932) further follows Brandt (and the tradition from P.A. Heiberg and the German scholar Emanuel Hirsch by investigating especially Kierkegaard's youth) and tries to place the three figures (Faust, Don Juan, and the wandering Jew) in Kierkegaard's individual history in order from there to shed light back on the figures: thus we see their shadows in his production.

[125]   See *Social-Demokraten*, September 10, 1942; cf. also Kabell, *Kierkegaardstudiet i Norden*, p. 300.

[126]   Kresten Nordentoft, *Kierkegaards psykologi*, Copenhagen: Hans Reitzels Forlag 1972, p. 20.

[127]   Cf. Kabell, *Kierkegaardstudiet i Norden*, p. 254.

[128]   Hjalmar Helweg, *Søren Kierkegaard – en psykiatrisk-psykologisk studie*, Copenhagen: H. Hagerups Forlag 1933.

depression an atypical course in Kierkegaard (there were not as, for example, with Grundtvig acute limited attacks with healthy intermediary periods), and Helweg describes it with the help of the diaries and the published writings as the ebb and flow of the mind. The course of the disease is interpreted, in other words, as playing a determining role for the works. The classic problem concerning Kierkegaard's apparently disproportionate pattern of reaction to this or that should not be ascribed (as P.A. Heiberg does) to violent oversensitivity or (as Geismar does) to our lacking knowledge of the decisive events in his life. In this way the problem is presented in a mistaken manner; a "secret note" is not the explanation, but, by contrast, Kierkegaard's ignorance of the illness which he had and which made him transfer the causes to unfortunate circumstances or regrettable outward events. Concretely, Helweg interprets, for example, the outbreak of joy on May 19, 1838 at 10:30 am[129] as a result of the illness' oscillation of mood and as determinant for Kierkegaard's religious direction. The attack on the Church is seen not as a manifestation of the disease but as the psychological consequence of its effect on his mind and development.[130] The sole thing which is not under the influence of the illness, according to Helweg, is Kierkegaard's unique reflection; light cannot be shed on the act of thinking itself by psychiatry. According to Aage Henriksen, this confuses things considerably, for how can one distinguish clearly between the mental elements—depression, mania, and reflection and their respective influence—when the mind must be assumed to function as a whole?[131]

At the same time as Helweg, the doctor and psychiatrist Ib Ostenfeld (1902– 95) made his debut in book form with the short psychological study *The Anxiety Concept in Søren Kierkegaard: The Concept of Anxiety* (1933). The book does not conceive of itself as a Kierkegaard biography or pathography but attempts with a free presentation of the contents of *The Concept of Anxiety* to reflect the light that Kierkegaard casts on the concept of anxiety back on to himself in order to "contribute to a clarification concerning his own odd person."[132] Without taking a position on Helweg's contemporary book, Ostenfeld, in contrast to Helweg, thinks that Kierkegaard's conception of anxiety is not grounded in his own experience. However, the description of the demonic is regarded as a veiled autobiographical element: "in the demonic [Kierkegaard] has described his own psychopathic temperament, as it was disposed from the hand of nature and further solidified through his childhood and initial years of development. Later in life other external and internal factors came to dominate in his mental life, but the demonic was always in the background,

---

[129]   Cf. *SKS* 17, 254–5 / *JP* 5324.
[130]   Helweg, *Søren Kierkegaard. En psykiatrisk-psykologisk studie*, pp. 117–18; p. 305.
[131]   The Swede John Björkheim, like Helweg, uses Kretschmer's typology, but thinks, contrary to Helweg, that Kierkegaard primarily belonged to the schizotyme and not the cyklotyme type. Cf. John Björkheim, *Søren Kierkegaard i psykologisk betydning*, Uppsala: Nyblooms Forlag 1942. In his characterization of Kierkegaard, Helweg relies on Victor Kuhr's book, *Grundtræk af en Karakterologi* (Copenhagen: Gyldendal 1934), which in several points recalls the basic idea of Kretschmer, cf. Kabell, *Kierkegaardstudiet i Norden*, p. 261.
[132]   Ib Ostenfeld, *Angst-Begrebet i Søren Kierkegaard: Begrebet Angest*, Copenhagen: G.E.C. Gad 1933, p. 7.

as given by nature."[133] The most important thing about the investigation, according to Ostenfeld, is that it draws attention to the characterological dimension and to what is determined by temperament in Kierkegaard, and since Ostenfeld also understands *The Concept of Anxiety* as a literary whole, before he begins his analysis, his investigation enjoys Henriksen's confidence.[134]

---

[133]   Ibid., p. 108.

[134]   In an analysis of Helweg and Ostenfeld's books, Aage Kabell criticizes both authors for lacking an eye for dogmatics in their treatment of Kierkegaard. To this extent this is a criticism in line with Henriksen; here it is merely the dogmatic frame and not the literary frame, which is sought. Moreover, Frithiof Brandt is quoted by Kabell for a review of Helweg's book in *Ugeskrift for Læger* (1934, 700a): "In summary, one can say that what Heiberg traces under the name of 'religious development,' is the same thing that Helweg traces under the designation 'the development of afflictions of the mind.' " According to Kabell, one could have expected an outcry from the ecclesiastical and Christian side as reaction to especially Helweg's book, but this did not come: "In order to understand this failure to react, one must recall the special constitution of the twentieth century's Lutheran Christianity in general and the conception of sin in particular. [Henning] Kehler speaks offhandedly of Kierkegaard's 'exaggerated views about sin and guilt'; Alfred Th. Jørgensen believes that K.'s constant expanding on and calling forth of the feeling of sin and suffering is a regrettable situation, 'which again shows how mentally deranged he was.' Even if Helweg apparently did not know Teisen and only a little of Bohlin, his work is determined by the interpretation of Christianity which also comes from these theologians. When he presents the oppressing and crushing feeling of sin as something which people should rather avoid, then he in no way wants to do away with Christianity. On the contrary, he had the year previous (1932) just like his friend Schou written a guide for theologians (*On Pastoral Care*). In Helweg's book everything is prepared for a view of the manic-depressive psychosis as scapegoat in the general theological attempts at reconciliation vis-à-vis S.K. And in Geismar's considerations of Helweg in the 'Teologisk Tidsskrift' in 1933 one sees that Geismar in his time has taken the possibility into consideration, but if he had used it, 'then those who attack me for having clipped the claws off of K., would have claimed that I had taken the sting out of his attack on the Church by declaring him mentally ill' (302)." Geismar does not doubt the correctness of Helweg's portrayal of Kierkegaard's illness, which on the contrary is a confirmation of his assumption of a crookedness or one-sidedness in Kierkegaard; however, he has a few lines' reservation about not forgetting that the experience of the unutterable can just as well be an encounter with God as an illness. This was, according to Kabell, the only protest from the theological camp (cf. Kabell, *Kierkegaardstudiet i Norden*, pp. 257ff.), which is quite surprising. Especially from the side of *Tidehverv* one could expect a protest against making Kierkegaard into someone ill, but in a series of articles by the doctor Hedvig Reinhard, which went on for several numbers in *Tidehverv* from the fall of 1938 until 1940(!), one perhaps receives an answer for why the movement's Kierkegaard experts did not feel the urge to respond. Reinhard here goes through P.A. Heiberg's and Hjalmar Helweg's Kierkegaard books, from an evaluation of these two scholars as the only ones of quality in Denmark, and she at one point determines that Kierkegaard and his father may well have suffered from a manic-depressive psychosis, but that the illness in their case was not an illness in the ordinary sense. With a choice of words taken directly from the heart of dialectical theology she writes that both in the father and in the son the illness was present in changed form "as *something completely different*." Cf. "Søren Kierkegaard," *Tidehverv*, no. 3, 1939, p. 34.

A few of the period's other books can also be treated briefly. The jurist Jens Himmelstrup (1890–1967) with his *Søren Kierkegaard's View of Socrates* (1924)[135] places himself in the slipstream of the humanistic tradition from the literary historian Vilhelm Andersen. While Vilhelm Andersen (1864–1953) attempted, among other things, to distinguish between "Kierkegaard and Socrates" and "Kierkegaard and Plato" and contrasted Kierkegaard as a type with the poet and critic Johan Ludvig Heiberg (1791–1860) by—somewhat à la Høffding—having the two represent respectively the philosophy of discontinuity and continuity in the Platonic period of the nineteenth century,[136] Himmelstrup's angle is much narrower since he investigates the development in Kierkegaard's view of Socrates from the earliest reflections on the "Roman" form of mentality in 1837 up to 1855. The development is described as moving from cold negativity (irony) to infinite humanity with the year of the dissertation 1841 as the great turning point. Many, especially German, scholars were subsequently skeptical about Himmelstrup's work. Their critique concerned the thesis about the year 1841 as the time when a radical change in the view of Socrates took place, and the claim that Kierkegaard had a Hegelian standpoint around the time of the writing of the dissertation (Hirsch thinks, for example, that Kierkegaard in the dissertation uses Socrates against Hegel, so that the individual in his faith in God can find a defense against speculation—the figure of Socrates does not undergo a change but a deepening in the course of the authorship.) In Himmelstrup's treatise and in the discussion which followed, people agreed that Kierkegaard found his way to the Greeks with Hegel as guide, but there is no agreement on the extent of his dependence on Hegel. Aage Henriksen therefore in his account of the history of the research calls for the need for an investigation of Kierkegaard's debt to Hegel—the researchers had until then treated more peripheral problems in this connection, as if the main questions were already decided: the question of the indirect communication and the relation to Hegel.[137] Himmelstrup later made valuable contributions to Kierkegaard research with his *Terminological Index* (1936) to the second edition

---

[135]   Jens Himmelstrup, *Søren Kierkegaards Opfattelse af Sokrates*, Copenhagen: Arnold Busck 1924.
[136]   The Platonic period in Danish intellectual life borders, according to Andersen, on the one side with a Homeric period (Oehlenschläger–Thorvaldsen) and on the other side with an Alexandrian period (Georg Brandes–Julius Lange). See Vilhelm Andersen, "Søren Kierkegaard," in *Tider og Typer af dansk Aands Historie*, vols. 1–4, Copenhagen: Gyldendal 1907–16, vol. 2, pp. 65–108. Preben Lilhav's *Kierkegaards valg* (Copenhagen: Forlaget SICANA 2003) is the most recent example of the placing of Kierkegaard in a Platonic tradition. Lilhav follows what he regards as a neglected Plato–Goethe track in the early journals, including a possible mystical set of issues in the young Kierkegaard, who is supposed to have had an experience of "God's death" (evidence of which can be found in, among other places, the "earthquake" entries). Kierkegaard's relation to Plato and pietism and Christian mysticism has also been treated by Marie Mikulová Thulstrup, for example in *Kierkegaard og pietismen*, Copenhagen: Munksgaard 1967 (*Søren Kierkegaards Selskabets Populære Skrifter*, vol. 13); *Kierkegaard, Platons skuen og kristendommen*, Copenhagen; Munksgaard 1970 (*Søren Kierkegaards Selskabets Populære Skrifter*, vol. 15); and in *Kierkegaard i kristenlivets historie*, Copenhagen: C.A. Reitzel 1991.
[137]   Cf. Henriksen, *Methods and Results of Kierkegaard Studies in Scandinavia*, pp. 136–7.

of *Søren Kierkegaards Samlede Værker* (1920–36) and with his *International Bibliography* (1962).

The theologian Julius Schousboe (1886–1960) takes up an appropriate theme in connection with Kierkegaard in *On the Concept of Humor in Søren Kierkegaard* (1925),[138] but the general evaluation of the work is that it is confused and tautological since it partly transfers the entire set of issues to Kierkegaard's person and seeks to describe him against the background of the concept of humor, but also describes the concept of humor against the background of Søren Kierkegaard, and partly ascribes to humor too many definitions, so that it comes to remind one of "the word *Schnur* in the dictionary."[139] Thus the work begins with a general definition of humor, which is followed by a determination of humor as a form of communication, then as an element in temperament and character (Kierkegaard's personal humor), as life view, as *confinium* to the religious, and finally as incognito for the religious.[140]

A work with far greater impact and significance for the biographical study of Kierkegaard is Frithiof Brandt's and Else Rammel's (later Thorkelin) *Søren Kierkegaard and Money* (1935),[141] which is based on thorough source studies of Kierkegaard's private finances. The main result of the book is that, in contrast to the traditional picture of Kierkegaard (spread by Brandes, who presumably was relying on Troels Frederik Troels-Lund) as someone who lived in accordance to the Lutheran command not to take interest from his capital, he had significant private expenditures, was meticulous in money matters and only used a limited amount on charity. Kierkegaard's Christianity and finances do not, according to Brandt (the actual author of the book) cast any light on each other, but it nonetheless means that the picture of Kierkegaard as an idealist collapses and that one must take seriously his own words about not being a Christian. It is, in other words, a well-established part of the general picture of Kierkegaard which is challenged here. The quite violent reactions that the book occasioned, shows this, and Aage Kabell gives a detailed account of them in his history of reception.[142] Kabell for his part concludes thus: "The canonization of our great philosopher, which took place at the turn of the century and especially by the theologians was driven out into pure legend, has shown itself to stand in a misrelation to the truth."[143] Kabell is thinking here of, among others, Geismar, who was one of those who most stubbornly maintained the picture of Kierkegaard as an idealist in money matters, but also of the pastor Carl Weltzer, whose negative reaction to Brandt and Rammel's book is regarded the most interesting with his insistence on Kierkegaard as a charitable person, a view which also runs though Weltzer's book the following year, entitled *Peter and Søren*

―――――――――

[138]   Julius Schousboe, *Om Begrebet Humor hos Søren Kierkegaard*, Copenhagen: Arnold Busck 1925.
[139]   Cf. *SKS* 2, 45 / *EO1*, 36.
[140]   Henriksen, *Methods and Results of Kierkegaard Studies in Scandinavia*, pp. 139–40; Kabell, *Kierkegaardstudiet i Norden*, p. 238.
[141]   Frithiof Brandt and Else Rammel, *Søren Kierkegaard og pengene*, Copenhagen: Munksgaard 1935.
[142]   Ibid., pp. 307ff.
[143]   Ibid., pp. 312–13.

Kierkegaard (1936).[144] The reactions to the book extend from this kind of rejection to relief (for example, Henning Kehler, who writes, "the new cleaned picture of Kierkegaard...is free from all characteristics which point in the direction of a pedantic asceticism"), consternation (for example, Chr. Rimestad, who calls it "consternating reading") and a revaluation of Kierkegaard (for example, Sven Clausen, who after a certain initial admiration for Kierkegaard in several places speaks of "the pathetic self-pity, with which S. K. destroyed his large inheritance on luxurious living") to a poorly hidden malicious pleasure, as, for example in the author Johannes V. Jensen (1873–1950), who with raised voice writes: "It is a cut at the very root. Not since Svantevit was brought down and worms and mice swarmed out has a better work been done."[145]

Finally a few books should be mentioned by the painter, writer, and Buddhist Johannes Hohlenberg (1881–1960). In March 1938 H. Hagerup's Publishing House announced a competition for the best Danish biography which in 1941 was won by Hohlenberg with the at the time widely disseminated and translated *Søren Kierkegaard* (1940). The book, among other things, makes a front against the theologians, for example, Barth, whose understanding, according to Hohlenberg, is in conflict with Kierkegaard's actual form and type of spirit. But it is primarily a criticism of the realism of the Brandes' line, which is charged with taking uncritically what they tangibly see before their own eyes, which in reality is a lack of fantasy (Hohlenberg lumps this approach with what he calls John Stuart Mill's "spectator's philosophy"). Against Brandes' view of personality as an analyzable chemical connection, consisting of vitriol, sugar, and other elements, Hohlenberg describes the personality not as a combination of properties but as the force which selects and groups these, just as the poet chooses the words from which he makes his poem; the properties are the material through which the personality expresses itself. The basis is a Romantic principle of the creative and independent spirit, a notion that the individual is an autonomous existence and a microcosmic unit, which in a constant evolution strives to bring the world to ever greater consciousness of the way to complete the work of creation. Kierkegaard's life is thus a revelation of a personality, which is successful in forming his fate in his own image, a prearranged fate, which only for a naive understanding is determined by external factors: it is the intellect, the genius, which determines the work, not external fate or private conflict. With this train of thought Hohlenberg, who has also written about more or less

---

[144]   Carl Weltzer, *Peter og Søren Kierkegaard*, Copenhagen: Gad 1936.

[145]   See Werner Svendsen's Preface to Frithiof Brandt and Else Rammel, *Søren Kierkegaard og pengene*, Copenhagen: Spektrum 1993 [Copenhagen: Levin & Munksgaard 1935], pp. 7–12. Poul Behrendt's review in *Weekendavisen* is an example that the book as late as 1993 was considered an undetonated bomb under most of Kierkegaard research ("Sørens fars penge," *Weekendavisen*, November, 5, 1993). In his book, *Kierkegaards København* (Copenhagen: Politikens Forlag 2004), Peter Tudvad by contrast draws attention to the fact that Brandt's and Rammel's account of Kierkegaard's (lack of) charitable action is based on an account book, which testifies only to the fact that Kierkegaard's servant had *carte blanche* to use the housefold money. What Kierkegaard in addition to this gave to charity is unknown, but Tudvad has found several pieces of evidence indicating that it was a considerable amount; cf. ibid., pp. 370ff.

exotic themes such as the pyramid at Cheops, Nostradamus, Kaspar Hauser, Faust, Yoga, etc., distrusts and is indeed hostile towards biographical research which is based on the assumption of causal connections in the mental sphere. All the external circumstances nonetheless appear in his biography because the genius must be assumed to have chosen his circumstances in a prenatal existence from an evaluation about whether they would harm or help his effect—nevertheless he does not write, for example, that Kierkegaard chose to be manic-depressive, but that he suffered from this disease.[146] In Hohlenberg the sympathy is entirely on Kierkegaard's side. His book is if not a biography of a saint then that of a hero, and Kierkegaard's enemies are Hohlenberg's enemies, for example, he takes over wholly uncritically Kierkegaard's criticism of Hegel and wholeheartedly defends the philosopher's (in the wake of Brandt and Rammel's book) much debated extravagence.

In Hohlenberg's second book about Kierkegaard, *The Path of the Lonely One* (1948),[147] the object of his treatment is the works and not the person. This book was written as a supplement to his first book, in that it treats that which there was not room for in the biography, where so much of the work was treated as was necessary for the understanding of the biography. By contrast, the new book takes as much of the biographical as is indispensable for an understanding of the work. The book fills, according to Hohlenberg, a lack in Danish Kierkegaard literature, which up until then had been lacking a presentation of the content of ideas and mutual relations of Kierkegaard's writings and had far too much been interested in peripheral issues such as "the question of whether Kierkegaard in his youth was a boozer or not, his relation to his family and to money, and whether he was schizoid or manic-depressive, hunchbacked, crooked or stooping—questions which clearly have their interest, but nonetheless are not what one who wishes to get to know Kierkegaard's work and gain an impression of their significance, in the first instance seeks information about."[148] Hohlenberg regarded this book as better than his biography, an evaluation which was shared by Aage Henriksen, who was otherwise quite skeptical about

---

[146]   This mystical, prenatal principle is brought to full development in the following description of Kierkegaard's birth: "Thus everything was prepared to receive the child that was expected. But the child for his part looked at the matter differently and had his own plans with what was going on. He knew the old man's melancholy and the complusive thoughts instilled in him, and knew precisely what powers were at work in choosing him as father, and to what he would use the inheritance that could be expected after his death. He knew that the spiritual atmosphere that surrounded him by letting himself be born in the family was exactly what he needed if his thoughts were to receive the necessary acuity and power, and that the inhibitions and difficulties he would face were exactly what was needed to keep him on the correct path. He also figured that the upbringing he would receive was best suited to stretching the bow so hard that the arrow could have the correct speed. At the same time he had an eye on the fortune—had perhaps in the right moment whispered in the father's ear a word about holding on to the Royal bonds. And when he has assured himself that everything was in order, that both the spiritual and the material weapons which he was to use were present and certain, he did not wait long, but let himself be born exactly four months later, on May 5." See Johannes Hohlenberg, *Søren Kierkegaard*, Copenhagen: H. Hagerup 1940, pp. 33–4.

[147]   Hohlenberg, *Den Ensommes Vej*, Copenhagen: H. Hagerup 1948.

[148]   Ibid., p. 8.

Hohlenberg's first book, but who (somewhat surprisingly) thinks that *The Path of the Lonely One* is the age's best introduction to Kierkegaard's production. The only thing that should be noted in this context is that the relation between Hohlenberg's two books describes a shift of interest in Kierkegaard's authorship, which comes forth at just this point in time: from the man to the work.

V. The Post-War Years (1945–68)

A. Background—the Trace of the Editions

During the German occupation of Danmark (1940–45) it was much more the historical and nationally oriented N.F.S. Grundtvig, who, with his emphasis on the commonality of the people, was mobilized to strengthen (especially) the inward opposition against the occupying power than the "individualistic" Kierkegaard. This happened, among other things, through the famous Grundtvig lectures at the University of Copenhagen in the fall of 1940 given by the church historian and politician Hal Koch (1904–63). The widespread anti-German mood was even directed directly against Kierkegaard, for example by the jurist and author Sven Clausen (1893–1961), who in the final years of the war published a selection of feature articles from the 1930s and 1940s, three of which were about Kierkegaard. Here he writes:

> If there is not an outward line from Kierkegaard's arrogance, Brandes' aristocratic spirit and Nietzsche's megalomania to the misfortunes which now befall millions, then there is in any case an inner family resemblance, and an outward connection is far from excluded. Compared to what I like, Kierkegaard lies like a dangerous reef under the surface in Danish intellectual life, and one must be allowed to put a sea marker on the spot. The entire passion, haste work, ruthlessness (towards Mr. Schlegel, his brother, the pastors, the bishop, Goldschmidt, Regine), the unbending logic from twisted presuppositions, the locking out of the outside world, the misanthropy, anti-Semitism (because he had a falling out with a Jew which he had brought upon himself), the desire to speculation, the lack of self-irony and much else—all this strikes me as being distinctly German. The entire house stands ready for anyone who has offended against his surroundings—it is very easy to move inside of it and be an intellectual aristocrat. Everything is there except for the heating. It is freezing cold.[149]

This harsh evaluation, which was supplemented, among other things, by a decided mud-slinging at *Either/Or*, fell, according to Aage Kabell, like rain during a drought.[150] Nonetheless it was after the war and especially in the 1950s that the interest in Kierkegaard experienced a second great renaissance. Some of the period's headlines are existentialism, demythologizing, and cultural criticism, and politically, culturally and socially it was stamped by a movement from the country to the city: the dismantling of the old peasant society, which took its beginning in the period between the wars, and the construction of the welfare state, which achieved its fully instrumentalized form in the course of the 1960s.

---

[149]   Sven Clausen, *Udvalgte Tvangstanker*, Copenhagen: Gyldendal 1945, pp. 153–4.
[150]   Kabell, *Kierkegaardstudiet i Norden*, p. 314.

The jubilee years 1955 and 1963 are the immediate high points during this period, but at the symbolic level the years 1948 and 1968 stand out as turning points in Kierkegaard studies. In 1948 the large first edition of the *Papirer* was finally complete, an event which coincided with a fundamental new emphasis on the systematic-critical interpretation of the works rather than the relation between life and work. The Danish Søren Kierkegaard Society was created in the same year as a sign of and motor for the dawning internationalization of Kierkegaard research. 1948 was also the year when K.E. Løgstrup and K. Olesen Larsen discovered their mutual disagreement about Kierkegaard, a debate which culminated in the year of student protest 1968 with Løgstrup's book *Confrontation with Kierkegaard*.[151] In what follows an account will be given of the main lines of these events.

The old discussion about the justification of publishing Kierkegaard's journals and papers and the concomitant argument that he could have burned them if he had not wished them to be known to posterity, received new life as late as 1959 and a new twist with Jørgen Bukdahl's article "Kierkegaard-Addiction" in the journal *Danish Vision* (*Dansk Udsyn*). Here he writes in the introduction:

> One can sometimes wonder if it would not have been best that Kierkegaard's journals and papers and letters had been burned, such that he only affected people through the writings which he wrote for the public. These works appear as a collected whole, which, from the dissertation to *The Moment*, in a broad and full manner exhaustively covers his intention, if they are read with thoughtfulness and understanding. The journals and papers do not add anything new to this, but give us, through the diaries, the personal background, the many reflections—which are preliminary exercises to decisive passages in the published works—along with, naturally, a whole series of considerations which do not appear in the published works. But at the same time they have contributed to derailing Kierkegaard research from occupying itself with the works alone, their context, their universe of concepts, and have led to an occupation with S. K. as a person, his *privatissima*, his psychological constitution, his family, his fiancée, etc., and for the most part scholars have gone on the hunt after what he wanted to be silent about...the debate about his person is almost everywhere connected to the account of his intention; not least of all in the Danish Kierkegaard literature, whose in any case quantitatively largest contribution to research concerns more the person than a systematic study of the works.[152]

The author and philosopher Villy Sørensen (1929–2001), in his commentary to this passage in Bukdahl, thought that it would have been a shame for Kierkegaard if his papers had been burned, because—with the exception of the entries from his youth—they were doubtless written for posterity. To be sure, Bukdahl is, according to Sørensen, the right person to ironize about the superficial Kierkegaard literature, but he is not the right person to wish that the posthumous papers had been burned, for he himself had made exceptional use of them in his book *Søren Kierkegaard and the Common Man* (see below).[153]

---

[151]   K.E. Løgstrup, *Opgør med Kierkegaard*, Copenhagen: Gyldendal 1968.
[152]   Jørgen Bukdahl, "Kierkegaard-Narkomani—omkring den psykologiske kierkegaard-forskning," in *Dansk Udsyn*, ed. by Askov Højskole (Vejen), 1959, p. 360.
[153]   Villy Sørensen, "Søren Kierkegaard og det folkelige," in his *Mellem Fortid og Fremtid—kronikker og kommentarer*, Copenhagen: Gyldendal 1969, p. 103. Villy Sørensen

That the journal-fixated, psychological, and personal-historical Kierkegaard research, which Bukdahl was so tired of, was overrepresented in Danish Kierkegaard literature at this time, is confirmed by the foregoing section. If one now jumps barely a half century forward in time to Joakim Garff's extensive biography *SAK* (2000), one finds in the introduction the claim that the biographical reading of Kierkegaard has been so disliked that for decades one has almost attempted "a systematic exorcism of the man from his work."[154] The background for this claim should be sought in the paradigm shift within literary scholarship, which Garff (b. 1960) is a contemporary with, namely new criticism, which made its arrival at the universities in the 1950s and 1960s, and which insists on a sharp distinction between author and work.[155] In the context of Kierkegaard studies Niels Thulstrup, in his continuation of Henriksen's and Kabell's overviews, can in 1954 claim that there is a tendency in the research in the direction of a historical-analytic work, a more work-internal methodology than found in the often dilettante biographical studies,[156] whose weaknesses F.J. Billeskov Jansen had already pointed out in 1949:

> The researcher risks that the very discovery of the biographical source restrains him and directs his glance backwards; it becomes the genesis of the text which interests him the most, and he believes that his job is done when he has demonstrated the connection between life and book. He then easily forgets the work's own existence as a whole, which rests in itself, and he blocks the way for the systematic interpretation.[157]

In other words, it is as if the first edition of the *Papirer* was completed (in 1948), just as the biographical methodology was gradually being brought into discredit. Before the significance of this for the period's Kierkegaard literature is treated, the *Papirer*'s further history of publication will be briefly sketched.

The primary actor in this context is the aforementioned Niels Thulstrup (1924–88), who was the *primus motor* in the creation of the Søren Kierkegaard Society, which was founded on May 4, 1948.[158] As a student of theology he had, in an article in the *Berlingske Aftenavis* on February 10, 1948, made some concrete reflections about

---

is himself an exponent of a special kind of reception of the *Papirer*, since the encounter with especially the first few volumes of Kierkegaard's papers has inspired his own form of diary. Cf. Villy Sørensen, *Talt— et interview ved Finn Hauberg Mortensen*, Copenhagen: Gyldendal 2002, p. 136.

[154]   Joakim Garff, *SAK Søren Aabye Kierkegaard. En biografi*, Copenhagen: Gad 2000, p. xv. (English translation, *Søren Kierkegaard. A Biography*, trans. by Bruce H. Kirmmse, Princeton and Oxford: Princeton Univesity Press 2005, p. xx.)

[155]   The main Danish work in new criticism is Johan Fjord Jensen, *Den ny kritik*, Copenhagen: Berlingske Forlag 1962.

[156]   Niels Thulstrup, "Kierkegaard-Studiet i Skandinavien 1945–52, *Edda* (Oslo), 1954, pp. 79–122.

[157]   F.J. Billeskov Jansen, *Hvordan skal vi studere Søren Kierkegaard?* Copenhagen: Faaborg 1949 (*Søren Kierkegaard Selskabets Populære Skrifter*, vol. 1), p. 28.

[158]   One can read about the history of the Society in Joakim Garff and Tonny Aagaard Olesen, "Episoder af Søren Kierkegaard Selskabets historie," in *Studier i Stadier. Søren Kierkegaard Selskabets 50-års Jubilæum*, ed. by Joakim Garrf, Tonny Aagaard Olesen and Pia Søltoft, Copenhagen: C.A. Reitzel 1998, pp. 195ff.

what task a "Kierkegaard Community" might have. Here he mentions, among other things, the need for a bibliographical overview of the large body of Kierkegaard literature, which already by that time had been published along with the fact that for the new edition of the papers "it would be highly desirable if there could be a well-organized index volume."[159] The twentieth and final volume of the *Papirer* was published in early fall of 1948, but with the completion of the edition it was clear that new tasks were in the waiting primarily due to two things: the edition's omission of letters to and from Kierkegaard as well as the problem of orienting oneself in the enormous mass of text. In The Søren Kierkegaard Society's annual report for 1951 it is written: "From Gyldendal's Publishing House a commitment has been given about an advance payment for the preliminary work on the organization of the text for 'Søren Kierkegaard: Letters and Documents' along with the creation of an index volume to S.K.'s papers. These two tasks have been entrusted by the Society's Board to the secretary, Niels Thulstrup, to carry out."[160] While *Breve og Aktstykker vedrørende Søren Kierkegaard* appeared in 1953, containing 21 different documents from Kierkegaard's baptism certificate to his will, 312 letters and notes to and from Kierkegaard along with a preliminary series of dedications from Kierkegaard's hand,[161] the index volume left people waiting. It was conceived as an analogue to the more than 500-page person and subject index, which A. Ibsen had made for the second edition of the *Samlede Værker*, but in the first instance it received only a skimpy forerunner in the Finnish Kierkegaard scholar Kalle Sorainen's 90-page photocopied index of names in A4-format, which in the Society's newsletter, *Meddelelser,* for the fall of 1952, no. 1, was offered on a subscription basis for members of the Society. Niels Thulstrup's work on the index resulted in a trial index which appeared at the same time as the publication of the ninth volume of the journal *Kierkegaardiana* in 1959, and contained some "Instructional Remarks," where it is explained that he and his wife, Marie Mikulová Thulstrup, at that time had created slips of paper for a person and subject index consisting of 70,000 references to *Søren Kierkegaards Papirer*. This provisional index would suffice for some time, and the project was not mentioned again until 1968—the year that witnessed the photomechanical reproduction of the *Papirer* under the joint administration of The Søren Kierkegaard Society and The Danish Society for Language and Literature.

In the preface to the "Second enlarged edition" one could read: "The printed volumes are followed by supplement volumes, which contain corrections and additions to the texts along with heretofore unpublished entries (from section C) from Søren Kierkegaard's hand. The final supplement volumes contain a person and subject index for the entire edition, created by M. Mikulová Thulstrup and the

---

[159]   Quotation from ibid, p. 197.
[160]   Quotation from ibid, p. 289.
[161]   That Thulstrup's overview of Kierkegaard's dedications was not complete—and could not have been since many dedications were still unknown—is demonstrated by Gert Posselt; see his "Kierkegaard som boggiver," *Tekstspejle. Om Søren Kierkegaard som bogtilrettelægger, boggiver og bogsamler*, ed. by Niels Jørgen Cappelørn, Bent Rohde, and Gert Posselt, Esbjerg: Rosendahl 2002, pp. 73ff.

editor [sc. Niels Thulstrup]."[162] In 1968–69 the photomechanical reproduction of the twenty original volumes appeared, with one volume being published per month, and in 1969–70 the two supplement volumes were published, containing mainly excerpts and lecture notes and book notes, which the first edition of the *Papirer* had omitted. The second edition of *Søren Kierkegaards Papirer* was, however, only completed when Niels Jørgen Cappelørn, who had worked on the material of the "Mistakes and Corrections" in the supplement volume XIII, and to whom the demanding work had been entrusted to go through the Thulstrups' collected small slips of paper, had conceived anew, reworked, and expanded the person and subject index to around 140,000 references in the *Index* in 1978.[163]

At the beginning of the 1960s Thulstrup and Villy Sørensen were asked by the publishing house Gyldendal if they would take it upon themselves to publish a third edition of the *Samlede Værker*, a request which was motivated by the 150-year anniversary of Kierkegaard's birth in 1963. Their conditions were, however, unsatisfactory (since the publishing house wanted to publish one volume per month!), and the project was instead taken over by the author Peter P. Rohde (1902–78), who under serious pressure for time managed to keep to the production plan, although this was not without consequences with respect to quality. The edition (1962–64) was—in line with its predecessor—conceived as a popular edition or "*folkeudgave.*"[164] It was based on the text of the second edition and was accompanied by a reprint of Himmelstrup's terminological index and an expanded apparatus of notes; it subsequently became, without comparison, the most widely used edition in Denmark, since it was cheap and, moreover, in time appeared as a paperback. Peter P. Rohde also published, parallel to the third edition of the collected works, a four-volume selection of Kierkegaard's diaries (1961–64).[165] In addition to these editions, one of the research's most used tools saw the light of day at this time in the form of the auction catalogue of Kierkegaard's book collection. *The Auctioneer's Sales Record of the Library of Søren Kierkegaard* appeared with a bilingual introduction (Danish and English) in 1967, the work of the art historian H.P. Rohde (1915–2005), who also wrote an introductory essay, "Søren Kierkegaard as Book Collector." The auction catalogue contains almost 3,000 entries (including the appendices of books not in the catalogue) and is a significant improvement over its immediate predecessor, Niels Thulstrup's reprint of the original list of books

---

[162]   *Pap.* I, p. xxiii.

[163]   For information about this section, see also *Studier i Stadier*, ed. by Joakim Garff, et al., pp. 289–92.

[164]   Cf. Peter P. Rohde's Preface to *Søren Kierkegaards Samlede Værker*, vols. 1–19, 3rd ed., Copenhagen: Gyldendal 1962, vol. 1, p. 7.

[165]   Further F.J. Billeskov Jansen published in 1950 the distinguished, commentated, *Værker i Udvalg med Indledninger og Tekstforklaringer*, vols. 1–4, Copenhagen: Gyldendal 1950. One should also mention a wrecked project like H. Hagerup's Publishing House's jubilee edition for the 100-year anniversary of the publication of the *Postscript* (1946), although only two volumes saw the light of day. What is interesting is that this edition relied, as its philological principle, on the first printings of Kierkegaard's works, and in this point anticipated *Søren Kierkegaards Skrifter* (Copenhagen: Gad 1997ff.). Moreover, it was accompanied with a facsimile of the original editions' title pages.

from 1856, *Catalogue of the Library of Søren Kierkegaard* (*Katalog over Søren Kierkegaards Bibliotek*) (1957).[166]

Of important editions of individual works by Kierkegaard during this period, one can mention, among others, Villy Sørensen's edition of *The Concept of Anxiety* (1960), Thulstrup's edition of *Fear and Trembling* (1961; 2nd edition 1983), P.G. Lindhardt's edition of *The Moment no. 1–10, What Christ Judges...and The Changelessness of God* (1961), Gregor Malantschuk's editions of *Repetition* (1961), *On My Activity as a Writer* and *The Point of View of My Activity as a Writer* (1963). and *Armed Neutrality* (1965). The journal *Kierkegaardiana* was, moreover, launched in 1955 and has since then functioned as one of the most important testing grounds for new research with a mixture of longer scholarly articles, thorough book reviews of the most recent Kierkegaard literature, and bibliographic overviews.[167] Finally, an institutional addition beyond The Søren Kierkegaard Society can be mentioned. In affiliation with the Teologisk Laboratorium at the University of Copenhagen, the "Søren Kierkegaard Library" was created in 1965. Its daily director was Niels Thulstrup. In 1969 the library became the framework for an independent Søren Kierkegaard Institute, and under Thulstrup's leadership, scholars worked here in the first half of the 1970s on a gigantic Kierkegaard encyclopedia, which was planned to appear in English in ten volumes, and which had dozens of Danish and foreign contributors affiliated with it. The project, which was conceived as an ambitious expansion of Himmelstrup's terminological reference work, was never completed. But in the project's offshoot, the sixteen volumes of *Bibliotheca Kierkegaardiana*, which the Thulstrups published in the years 1978–88, some of this material was published.

B. Theology and Philosophy

In our overview of the theological and philosophical Kierkegaard reception in the period after the war, it will be necessary for the sake of clarity to take up again the main emphasis of the previous section on the Climacean writings and namely the *Philosophical Fragments*, which is still the work that marks the fork in the road.

The theologian and principal of the folk high school Askov, Knud Hansen (1898–1996), published in 1954 *Poet of the Idea*, which contains a longer chapter entitled "The Concept of Faith in *Philosophical Fragments*."[168] Knud Hansen takes up the challenge from A.B. Drachmann and admits that if one conceives the issue of the *Fragments* to be a question of the relation between philosophy and theology, then the Socratic is the decisive dimension. But the point is lacking in Drachmann,

---

[166]   One can read about Kierkegaard as a book collector in Niels Jørgen Cappelørn, "Søren Kierkegaard som bogkøber og bogsamler" in *Tekstspejle*, ed. by Niels Jørgen Cappelørn et al., pp. 105ff.

[167]   Tonny Aagaard Olesen runs through ("Index with a Short Historical Survey," *Kierkegaardiana*, vol. 21, 2000, pp. 201–27) the history of the journal and gives an overview of the contents of the first 20 volumes. See also *Studier i Stadier*, ed. by Joakim Garff, et al., pp. 266ff.

[168]   Knud Hansen, *Søren Kierkegaard. Ideens Digter*, Copenhagen: Gyldendal 1954, see pp. 258–76 (originally published, *Dansk Teologisk Tidsskrift*, vol. 14, 1951, pp. 34–57).

for even though one has to search long in both philosophy and theology for an all-conquering logic like that of the *Fragments*, it is not logical considerations which led Kierkegaard to the paradox as the Christian form of life, but a much more passionate motivation. Precisely passion and not the Socratic is decisive for Kierkegaard's position on the church dogmas, and Hansen speaks in several places of the paradox as something which "electrifies" the understanding and changes it into a passion, which strives against its own destruction. In extension of this, Kierkegaard's concept of faith is conceived as "a passionate high tension, a kind of intellectual ecstasy,"[169] a concept of faith, which, according to Knud Hansen, is as far from The New Testament as from the objective concept of faith which Kierkegaard criticizes and which has more of an affinity with the conception of an ecstasy of feelings like that of the mystics of the late Middle Ages than with Jesus of Nazareth.

Another central, but not well-explored theme is taken up by the Professor of Systematic Theology Søren Holm (1901–71) in his work *Søren Kierkegaard's Philosophy of History* (1952). The broader topic is Kierkegaard's determination of the relation between Christianity and history, and in his introduction Holm gives an account of the problem in the philosophy of religion from Lessing to Strauss and argues, with an allusion to Anselm of Canterbury, that the real title of the *Fragments* should have been "The Essence of Christianity or Why God Became Man." To this end he investigates the accounts in the compact "Interlude."[170] What is, however, equally interesting is his controversial interpretation of the paradox (the God-man) in the *Fragments*, the *Postscript*, and *Practice in Christianity*. According to Holm, it is in these works, to an increasing degree, a problem of whether the event of Christ only exists to faith, but not in the world of empirical knowledge: is "this fact" or "the absolute fact" for Kierkegaard a real event or an outward fact in line with all other historical events—or merely a paradoxical formulation of the concept which should be maintained in passion, *as if* the event really took place? Holm is here inclined to assume that Kierkegaard's Christology should be interpreted in the direction of the fictional (cf. Vaihinger's *Philosophie des Als Ob*), and hardly any other interpretation has led to such categorical rejections.[171]

---

[169]   Hansen, *Søren Kierkegaard. Ideens Digter*, p. 276.
[170]   Søren Holm, *Søren Kierkegaards Historiefilosofi*, Copenhagen: Nyt Nordisk Forlag/Arnold Busck 1952, pp. 31–47. The "Interlude" is, moreover, treated in Johannes Sløk's *Forsynstanken. Et forsøg paa en dogmatisk Begrebsbestemmelse*, Hjørring: Expres–Trykkeriets Forlag 1947, pp. 94ff; See also Johannes Sløk, *Kierkegaard—humanismens tænker*, Copenhagen: Hans Reitzel 1978, pp. 143–159; Paul Müller, "Tvivlens former og deres rolle i erkendelsen af det historiske," *Dansk Teologisk Tidsskrift*, vol. 37, 1974, pp. 177–216; Flemming Harrits, "Grammatik des Glaubens oder Zwischenspiel über den Begriff der Geschichte. Zeit und Geschichte bei Søren Kierkegaard und Walter Benjamin," *Kierkegaardiana*, vol. 18, 1996, pp. 82–99; H.C. Wind, "Kierkegaard og det historiske," in *Kierkegaard og...hovedtemaer i forfatterskabet*, Århus: Philosophia 2001, pp. 25–39.
[171]   See, for example, Johannes Sløk, "Tre Kierkegaard-tolkninger," *Kierkegaardiana*, vol. 1, 1955, pp. 89–101, see pp. 90ff.; Paul Müller, *Meddelelsesdialektikken i Søren Kierkegaard's Philosophiske Smuler*, Copenhagen: Institut for Religionshistorie 1979, p. 38; and Jørgen K. Bukdahl, "Grundtvig og Kierkegaard," in his *Om Søren Kierkegaard—artikler i udvalg ved Jan Lindhardt*, Copenhagen: C.A. Reitzel 1981, p. 11.

In his overview of the history of the research, "The Study of Kierkegaard in Scandinavia 1945–52," Niels Thulstrup dedicates a longer criticism to Søren Holm's book. Thulstrup emphasizes first and foremost that Holm has been too selective in his choice of Kierkegaard's works. Had he introduced into his investigation, in addition to the pseudonymous writings, the "genuine" non-pseudonymous writings and especially the *Papirer*, a fictional interpretation of Kierkegaard's Christology would quickly have proven impossible. In the same overview article, Thulstrup, moreover, rejects Knud Hansen's definition of Kierkegaard's concept of faith as "an ecstasy of the understanding," incidentally without further argumentation, and raises the fundamental criticism of Hansen's interpretation of the *Fragments* that he "just as little as most of the others has noted that *Philosophical Fragments* is built up as a parody of Hegelian speculation, which allows the concepts to develop out of each other."[172] On the 100-year anniversary of Kierkegaard's death, Thulstrup published a commentary edition of the *Fragments*, which in its introduction claims that while the great philosophical and theological works of the period between the wars made it an obvious matter to emphasize the investigation of Kierkegaard's historical and principled relations to other thinkers and to philosophical, theological, and literary directions and schools, there is now (sc. in 1955) a tendency to abstract from that kind of research and instead to concentrate on the systematic elucidation of the authorship: "*Man will jetzt fast ausschliesslich Begriffsanalysen vornehmen und die Struktur der Gedankenkomplexe darlegen, ohne dabei irgend welche besondere Rücksicht auf die speziellen Voraussetzungen Kierkegaards zu nehmen.*"[173] As a counterweight to this approach, which, according to Thulstrup, prioritizes in an unfortunate manner the extensive Kierkegaard research higher than Kierkegaard's own literary, philosophical, and theological presuppositions, he then subsequently undertakes a thorough investigation of possible sources and polemical and contemporary references in a piece of text from the first chapter of the *Fragments*.[174] Thulstrup's purely practical rationale for being able to undertake such a historical opening and contextualization of Kierkegaard's text is that at that point in time one was, as noted, in fact in possession of complete editions of Kierkegaard's *Samlede Værker* along with a terminological index (1920–36), as well as his *Papirer* (1909–48) and *Breve og Aktstykker* (1953–54). Moreover, he here formulates a desire to develop in the context of an edition a much demanded practice of commentary.

Both in the introduction to Thulstrup's edition of *Philosophical Fragments* (1955) and later in his book *Kierkegaard's Relation to Hegel* (1967), one of the main points is that the *Fragments*, with its experimental manner of presentation, would make impossible Hegel's claimed reconciliation of Christian faith and speculative knowing, but that the two thinkers' point of departure and views at the same time

---

[172]   Thulstrup, "Kierkegaard–Studiet i Skandinavien 1945–52—en kritisk Oversigt," pp. 101–5; p. 117.
[173]   Niels Thulstrup, "Die historische Methode in der Kierkegaard–Forschung—durch ein Beispiel beleuchtet," *Symposion Kierkegaardianum, Orbis Litterarum*, tome X, fasc. 1–2, p. 280.
[174]   This is about note 1, *SKS* 4, 219.

are not only different but utterly irreconcilable.[175] Thulstrup in his role of editor of the *Papirer* is, like P.A. Heiberg, in a situation where he can make use of theretofore unpublished material. In his book on Kierkegaard and Hegel it is the material from the C section which can be called Thulstrup's specialty—material that a few years later was published as volumes XII and XIII, and which contain, among other things, dogmatic and philosophical explanations of Erdmann, Martensen and Marheineke, Schelling's lectures on the *Philosophie der Offenbarung* along with excepts from Werder's lectures on logic and Hegel's aesthetics. But, in addition, Thulstrup makes use of his familiarity with the *Papirer* to follow his theme out into every corner and cranny of the edition, and he has an eye for the fact that the entries in the sections A (the journal entries) and C (the entries related to Kierkegaard's studies and readings) are relatively fewer in the period of time in which Kierkegaard's works were pouring forth in earnest, 1842–46—a period when the entries under B (preliminary drafts to the authorship) for the same reason explode—while the journals' correspondingly swell in the pause in the publications from the fall of 1851 to the end of 1854, when the attack on the Church begins.[176]

Gregor Malantschuk (1902–78), who was born in the Ukraine and came to Denmark in 1934 via Germany, where he studied under Geismar, played a major role in Danish Kierkegaard research, especially due to his personal influence on various later scholars.[177] As a striking example of the tendency criticized by Thulstrup to exclusively undertake text-immanent, conceptual analyses of Kierkegaard's works,

[175] See, for example, Niels Thulstrup, *Kierkegaards Forhold til Hegel og til den spekulative Idealisme indtil 1846*, Copenhagen: Gyldendal 1967, pp. 308–13. (English Translation: *Kierkegaard's Relation to Hegel*, trans. by George L. Stengren, Princeton: Princeton University Press 1980, pp. 358–65.) For Thulstrup's overview of the research, see *Søren Kierkegaard: Philosophiske Smuler*, ed. by Niels Thulstrup, Copenhagen: C.A. Reitzel 1955, pp. XXXVIIff. Only with Jon Stewart's book from 2003 can Kierkegaard's relation to Hegel be said to be investigated from top to bottom. In *Kierkegaard's Relations to Hegel Reconsidered* (Cambridge and New York: Cambridge University Press 2003) Stewart shows to what a high degree Kierkegaard's negative criticism was directed more against Danish Hegelians such as Heiberg, Adler, and Martensen than against Hegel himself.

[176] This relation is made clear statistically and graphically in an article from 1982 by Niels Jørgen Cappelørn and Alastair McKinnon. By precisely calculating Kierkegaard's productivity in word units per quarter year during the period 1834 to 1855, they have managed to bring about a clear picture of the frequency in Kierkegaard's work tempo for both the published writings and the papers. From this it is clear that the journals—with a notable exception in the year 1853—were used most extensively in the period immediately prior to the outbreak of the attack on the Church; see Niels Jørgen Cappelørn and Alastair McKinnon, "Kierkegaard's Literary Production by Quarterly Rates," *Danske Studier*, 1982, pp. 21–34. The graphic presentation of Kierkegaard's constant high productivity shows that it is problematic—if not straightforwardly impossible—to speak of manic-depressive ups and downs in Kierkegaard's life.

[177] Two of his students, Niels Jørgen Cappelørn and Paul Müller, published in 1980 a collection of articles, *Frihed og Eksistens* (Copenhagen: C.A. Reitzel), and in the preface give a description of the difficult circumstances which Malantschuk grew up in and lived under as well as his reputation as a teacher.

one should name his *Kierkegaard's Thought* (1968).[178] Malantschuk, in contrast to
much of the older research, emphasizes the unity and not the dualities or oppositions
in Kierkegaard. For him the authorship is a continuous whole and its progression is
a gradual development from an original objective orientation towards a conscious
concentration on the reality of the subject in the unfolding of Kierkegaard's "dialectical
method." It is, for example, characteristic for this approach that the *Papirer* are
viewed as a kind of work-in-progress which show us the man or thinker in transit, and
that the *Fragments* is seen in continuation with not only the contemporary *Concept
of Anxiety*, but also *Johannes Climacus or De omnibus dubitandum est*, whose
main character is Johannes Climacus, the dialectician and main pseudonym,[179] who,
according to Malantschuk, until that point had steered the authorship's course from
behind the stage. "From *De omnibus dubitandum est* we know how Climacus during
his exercises in the dialectic either began from below to come to 'the higher thought'
or from above, that is, from this 'higher thought' in order to go back to the lower
positions."[180] This methodology explains, according to Malantschuk, the relation
between *Philosophical Fragments* and *The Concept of Anxiety*.[181] In the *Fragments*
the higher thought breaks into the human life's context, while the direction in *The
Concept of Anxiety* is just the opposite and can be characterized as an upward climb,
from the person's guilt gradually up to the person's confrontation with Christianity.
When therefore Torsten Bohlin (in his analysis of the concept of sin) points out that
the two works go back to different points of departure, he is certainly correct in his
analysis but not in his conclusion: the double point of departure is not due to an error
in thought, but expresses the fine and well-considered dialectic with which the two
works supplement each other.[182] Malantschuk has also provided descriptions and
explanations of concepts, for example to the English edition, *Søren Kierkegaard's
Journals and Papers* (ed. and trans. by Howard V. Hong and Edna H. Hong

---

[178]   Gregor Malantschuk, *Dialektik og Eksistens hos Søren Kierkegaard*, Copenhagen:
Hans Reitzel 1968. (English translation: *Kierkegaard's Thought*, trans. by Howard V. Hong,
Princeton University Press 1971.)
[179]   For treatments of the pseudonym Johannes Climacus, see, for example, *Philosophiske
Smuler*, ed. by Niels Thulstrup, pp. XXXIV–XXXV; Birgit Bertung, "Johannes Climacus—og
Kierkegaard. Kommunikation og pseudonymitet," *Kierkegaard pseudonymitet*, ed. by Birgit
Bertung et al., Copenhagen: C.A. Reitzel 1993, pp. 33–45; Pia Søltoft, "The Unhappy Lover
of Subjectivity: Is the Pseudonym Johannes Climacus an Unequivocal Figure?" *Kierkegaard
Studies. Yearbook*, 1996, pp. 255–76.
[180]   Gregor Malantschuk, *Dialektik og Eksistens hos Søren Kierkegaard*, Copenhagen:
Hans Reitzel 1968, p. 233ff. (*Kierkegaard's Thought*, pp. 243ff.)
[181]   See also Gregor Malantschuk, *Frihedens Problem i Kierkegaards Begrebet Angest*,
Copenhagen: Hans Reitzel 1971.
[182]   In his review of Malantschuk's book, N.H. Søe is far from convinced that Malantschuk
really responds to Bohlin's analysis of the tension between the two conceptions of sin in
Philosophical Fragments and *The Concept of Anxiety*, and refers to Thulstrup's edition of
Philosophiske Smuler, p. 150; p. 176, see *Kierkegaardiana*, vol. 7, 1968, pp. 198–9.

(1967–78)).[183] In his book *Fra Individ til den Enkelte* (1978) he seeks to elucidate Kierkegaard's entire authorship from the movement given in the title.[184]

C. Controversy about Kierkegaard

One of the postwar period's leading theologians and Kierkegaard experts, Johannes Sløk (1916–2001), can be quoted for the following brief anecdote, which captures well the relation between the main actors in the controversy about Kierkegaard, which played itself out in the 1950s and 1960s, and which indirectly set the agenda for most Kierkegaard research in the few decades after 1968:

> Around 1950 Løgstrup had come into conflict with *Tidehverv*, which he originally had a positive disposition towards, especially concerning *Tidehverv's* conception of Kierkegaard, and that means automatically Olesen Larsen. Then there was a big meeting in Fårup vicarage with N.O. Jensen, where the matter was to be discussed. Everyone gathered in the hospitable rooms, and Olesen Larsen began to set forth his views about Kierkegaard in a lecture. When Olesen Larsen gave a lecture, the conventional norms for time for such things were temporarily suspended. Therefore, he went on and on; every presupposition, point and consequence had to be mentioned. Being the in all respects honest person, that Løgstrup was, he began by taking extensive notes in his pocketbook. This went on until two hours had passed; then he smacked his book closed, put down his pencil and the rest of the time stared in the air. He had become tired. Finally Olesen Larsen stopped; we were supposed to have lunch, and then the discussion was supposed to take place. It didn't take place. Løgstrup refused to say a word. There could be no question of discussing things. Under those circumstances! It was close to being embarrassing, or with the boredom that nothing came of it. Then I began speaking—and attacked Olesen Larsen, brought out all of the objections and views *ad nauseum* which I knew Løgstrup had in mind. There arose a lively discussion between Olesen Larsen and me, or Løgstrup in my person. Olesen Larsen was in the situation priceless. He understood immediately the point and not only grasped it but enjoyed it. And I was successful in taking over Løgstrup's role of getting Olesen Larsen to destroy Løgstrup's views right down the line—at the same time he looked at me with fire in his eyes. I do not know how many of the others present understood the wonderful subtlety of the situation.[185]

In the theological Kierkegaard reception up until that point there had been, with few exceptions, a more or less express apologetic disposition, often in an attempt to annex Kierkegaard, to bring him over to one's side by distinguishing the essential from the inessential or by magnifying a single concept or a part of the authorship as the central one. With K.E. Løgstrup we receive a decided *Confrontation with Kierkegaard* (1968), which by way of introduction only admits to being "interested in what is the tendency and consequence of his conception of Christianity and not

---

[183]   Grethe Kjær and Paul Müller later published a Danish pendant from Malantschuk's *Nachlaß*; see Malantschuk, *Nøglebegreber i Søren Kierkegaards tænkning*, Copenhagen: C.A. Reizel 1993.
[184]   Gregor Malantschuk, *Fra Individ til den Enkelte*, Copenhagen: C.A. Reizel 1978. (English translation: *Kierkegaard's Concept of Existence*, trans. by Howard V. and Edna V. Hong, Milwaukee: Marquette University Press 2003.)
[185]   Johannes Sløk, *Mig og Godot*, Viby J.: Centrum 1986, pp. 102–3.

in what he—also—said....What I leave aside I leave to those people who are certain
that he is the sole Church father and read him for their own edification."[186]

The background to Løgstrup's confrontation with Kierkegaard, which was thus
different from the controversy between Geismar and Olesen Larsen in the 1920s and
1930s in that it concerned if Kierkegaard was right at all, rather than to what degree
he was right,[187] therefore in actuality lasted for years and dates all the way back to
1948, when Løgstrup together with Sløk (who at that time was not yet a professor)
was giving a course at Aarhus University on the *Concluding Unscientific Postscript*.
Torben Bramming renders in his book on the history of *Tidehverv* an oral account, by
dr. theol. Søren Nordentoft (1927–99), who was Olesen Larsen's nephew, and who
attended the class in 1948. According to Nordentoft, it became clear in the course
of the class that Sløk and Løgstrup, who had both expected that they were going to
be in agreement in their views on Kierkegaard, had diverging views. Olesen Larsen
was then called in as impartial arbitrator, and he agreed with Sløk's understanding
of Kierkegaard.[188]

In the following years Løgstrup was a guest professor in Berlin, where he worked
out his anti-Kierkegaardian position in a lecture series, which was later brought
together in a book, which is the background for the controversy that played itself
out in *Tidehverv* in the 1950s: *Kierkegaard und Heideggers Existenzanalyse und
ihr Verhältnis zur Verkündigung* (1950). Løgstrup attacked Kierkegaard's (and
thus Olesen Larsen's) conception of neighbor love, as it comes to expression in
the *Postscript* and *Works of Love*, since he criticizes it for being: "an ingeniously
thought out system of assurances for keeping another person away from oneself."[189]
Kierkegaard was, according to Løgstrup, a life-denying pietist, for whom neighbor
love concerned solely helping one's neighbor to love God, a view which he shared
with his friend Knud Hansen, who, in the period 1951–52 in a series of articles in
Tidehverv, *Højskolebladet*, and *Heretica*, attacked Kierkegaard and especially the
last part of the authorship, the attack on the Church.[190] The conflict between Olesen

---

[186]   Knud Ejler Løgstrup, *Opgør med Kierkegaard*, Copenhagen: Gyldendal 1968, p.
9. (The first chapter of the book, "Kristendom uden den historiske Jesus," was originally
published in German, in *Orbis Litterarum*, vol. 18, 1963, pp. 101–12.)
[187]   Geismar was, moreover, Løgstrup's firm supporter, and Løgstrup thanks Geismar in
the preface to his dissertation; see Løgstrup, *Den erkendelsesteoretiske Konflikt mellem den
transcendental-filosofiske Idealisme og Teologien*, Copenhagen: Samlerens Forlag 1942.
[188]   Cf. Bramming, *Tidehvervs historie*, p. 77.
[189]   *Tidehverv*, May–June, 1955, pp. 59–60.
[190]   Cf. Knud Hansen, "Søren Kierkegaards Kristendomsforståelse," *Heretica*, no. 1,
1951, pp. 83–107; Knud Hansen, "Søren Kierkegaards angreb på kirken," *Højskolebladet*,
no. 5, 1952, pp. 45–7; and "Den absolutte fordring," *Tidehverv*, nos. 9–10, 1951, pp. 82–92
(with a response from K. Olesen Larsen in the article "Den uendelige fordring og kærligheden
til næsten," *Tidehverv*, no. 1, 1952, pp. 4–9; no. 2, 1952, pp. 13–20; nos. 3–4, 1952,
pp. 29–39; and no. 5, 1952, p. 44–56). See also the above on Hansen's criticism of
Kierkegaard's understanding of Christianity as more stamped by the mysticism of the late
Middle Ages or Manichaeism than by the New Testament. Løgstrup, Knud Hansen and others
from *Tidehverv* in connection with their cultural criticism after the war came into contact with
the *Heretica* circle, represented especially by the poets Martin A. Hansen (1909–55), Ole

Larsen and Løgstrup has precisely this as one of its main points, the question of the double command of love. For Olesen Larsen the command to love one's neighbor is included in the command to love God, while, put coarsely, just the opposite is the case for Løgstrup: the first part of the command, that we should love God, is contained in the second, that we should love our neighbor. Therefore, Jesus in his teaching can, according to Løgstrup, be understood in a purely human manner, which is one of the main points in his breakthrough book *The Ethical Demand* (1956).[191]

That is also the case in *Confrontation with Kierkegaard*, which begins with something which had certainly been noted and treated in earlier reception, but not in the same thorough manner and with the same strength as here, namely the question of to what extent Kierkegaard's Christianity is a Christianity without the historical Jesus. Using the *Fragments* as his point of departure, Løgstrup argues that the Christian message in Kierkegaard is derived from the paradoxical without reference to what Jesus' earthly life and historical life consisted of. The only thing that we are told is that the god of love for humans assumed the humble form of a servant, but apart from his freedom from worry, his unmarried civil status, and his lack of property, he could not in any decisive manner be distinguished from other human beings. In continuation of this, the *occasion* for faith becomes a problem, that is, how could a decision about faith or offense even come up at all when the god has made himself unrecognizable in the form of a servant, and neither in words, acts nor way of life is there anything which occasions the questions of who he was. By also including *Practice in Christianity*, Løgstrup comes to the conclusion that in Kierkegaard one is only placed in a decision between faith and offense by the miracle and by Jesus' own claim to be God—a claim which the better part of the expert knowledge, moreover, doubts the historical truth of. Løgstrup then develops his alternative to Kierkegaard's view when he emphasizes that an understanding of Christianity, which includes the historical Jesus, implies that even if the divine in the

---

Wivel (1921–2004) and Thorkild Bjørnvig (1918–2004). *Heretica's* cultural criticism was like that of *Tidehverv* directed against the "superstition" of the intellect, materialism, and progress. This fundamental skepticism about the cultural phenomena, which bore the stamp of welfare ideology led progressive-minded contemporaries to give the people of *Heretica* the nickname "the athletes of anxiety." The key words, which *Heretica* shared with parts of *Tidehverv*, were *transformation* and *redemption* of man. *Heretica* blamed, in extension of Løgstrup's criticism of Kierkegaard, *Tidehverv* for driving a "doomed theology" and stood on Løgstrup's side of the conflict. Cf. Bramming, *Tidehvervs historie*, p. 78.

[191]   The conflict between Olesen Larsen and Løgstrup (and Knud Hansen) can be formulated (as in, for example, Løgstrup, *Den etiske fordring*, Copenhagen: Gyldendal 1956) as a question about to what degree the ethical demand has a constant empirical content or not. Løgstrup believes that the demand has a determinate content since it intends to take care of that part of the other's life, which is given to us. For Olesen Larsen the demand is absolute, that is, without content and impossible to fulfill, a point of view which makes Løgstrup point to the agreement between *Tidehverv* and the dominant, "valuefree" positivism. In Hans Hauge's extensive Løgstrup dissertation he also makes the point that Løgstrup constantly confronts Kant (epistemologically, ethically, and aesthetically), and that he sees in Olesen Larsen's theology an existence-theological variant of Kant's ethics. Cf. Hans Hauge, *K.E. Løgstrup—en moderne profet*, Copenhagen: Spektrum 1992, see, for example, p. 247.

life of Jesus could not be immediately known, it is not unknowable or paradoxical in the absolute sense that it is for Kierkegaard. On the contrary, just the opposite is the case: since human existence and the world in which Jesus lived is God's, and God's power is present *in the fact* that Jesus exists, but therefore as an obvious consequence also in *what* he lives, says and does, "the only non-paradoxical life is the life of Jesus of Nazareth. Everything is here straightforward and obvious. What is paradoxical is how the life that everyone else lives could come about."[192]

In his further treatment of Kierkegaard's version of paradoxicality, Løgstrup examines more closely the Socratic element in the *Fragments*. With his claim that not the truth but also the condition for truth is given to the individual, and that as soon as this is given, everything is again Socratic, Kierkegaard anticipates the objection that the appropriation of the truth cannot be personal. Løgstrup, however, finds the determination of the Christian, which the Socratic alternative gives rise to, untenable because it means that the human being is not responsible for his untruth. To be sure, Kierkegaard nuances his claim by saying that when the human being is without the condition for understanding the truth, this is not revelant because he is created without the condition but because he has deprived himself of it. But this thought is, according to Løgstrup tendentially irreconcilable with the paradoxicality because the life which the human being has deprived himself of the condition for understanding, must be the truth of a life, which is given, and not, by contrast, the life which arises out of paradoxicality, which is the life of God, and a truth, which only comes into existence for the sake of sin. Løgstrup concludes, "the existence in faith for Kierkegaard does not consist in one, as forgiven, consummating the life to which the human being was created. By contrast, it consists in following the god in the unknowable love's suffering."[193]

How much Løgstrup otherwise sticks to the *Fragments* in his criticism of Kierkegaard is also evident in *Creation and Destruction* (1978), where he, wholly in agreement with Drachmann, finds it odd, "that the religion, which for Kierkegaard

---

[192]   Løgstrup, *Opgør med Kierkegaard*, p. 22. Villy Sørensen expresses this by saying that "precisely the Kierkegaardian basic ideas about God's human existence are used by Løgstrup about human beings' human existence." Cf. Villy Sørensen, "Løgstrups opgør med Kierkegaard," in *Mellem Fortid og Fremtid—kronikker og kommentarer*, pp. 122–3.

[193]   Løgstrup, *Opgør med Kierkegaard*, p. 33. Arne Grøn is one of those who has brought Løgstrup's thinking and especially his talk about the sovereign manifestations of life close to Kierkegaard by a close reading of *Works of Love*. In the article "Suverænitet og negativitet" Grøn criticizes, among others, Løgstrup's unargued joint reading of the *Fragments* and *Practice in Christianity*, and claims that Løgstrup overlooks the fact that already from the *Fragments* one can read that the story of the Passion belongs to the paradoxicality. Moreover, Grøn emphasizes that there is no talk of a nuancing when Kierkegaard says that the human being deprives himself of the condition he is created with—that is namely the claim of the *Fragments*. See "Suverænitet og negativitet—Løgstrups opgør med Kierkegaard," *Kredsen*, vol. 60, no. 2, 1994, pp. 32–51. For a criticism of Løgstrup's claim that Kierkegaard in his understanding of Christianity does not take his point of departure in Jesus' words and actions but in the paradox, see further the references in Joakim Garff, *"Den Søvnløse"—Kierkegaard læst æstetisk/biografisk*, Copenhagen: C.A. Reitzel 1995, p. 190n.

at the same time is different from faith in the god in time and constitutes a horizon of understanding for it, is not the god of creation, but Socrates' religiosity."[194]

D. Aesthetics

Georg Brandes was—also on this point—the first one, in spite of his biographical approach, to take seriously not only Kierkegaard's system of pseudonyms but also the aesthetic works, but with regard to a real aesthetic reading as such his efforts remained only preliminary. However, in the 1950s three books appeared with this focus: F.J. Billeskov Jansen's *Søren Kierkegaard's Literary Art* (1951), Aage Henriksen's *Kierkegaard's Novels* (1954), and Villy Sørensen's *Poets and Demons* (1959).

Billeskov Jansen (1907–2002) endeavors to investigate the little-explored literary art in Kierkegaard, which is not the same thing as "clipping quotations from the works in order to put them together in accordance with the categories of rhetoric or style,"[195] but in taking his books one at a time, interpreting their meaning and then getting clear about in what literary form of expression this meaning appears. The investigation dwells on the forms of composition and the kinds of style within Kierkegaard's various genres, beginning with the aesthetic works (*Either/Or* and *Stages on Life's Way*), continuing with the philosophical-theological main works (*Repetition, Fear and Trembling, The Concept of Anxiety* as well as the Climacean and Anti-Climacean writings), and concluding with the edifying authorship and the writings from the attack on the Church. He thus talks about "unraveling the authorship in a new way."[196] In extension of the German interpreters' (among others Walther Rehm) placement of Kierkegaard in the tradition from Jena Romanticism and Hegelianism, Billeskov Jansen, moreover, does a lot to track down Kierkegaard's literary sources.

---

[194]   Løgstrup, *Skabelse og tilintetgørelse—religionsfilosofiske betragtninger* (vol. 4 (1978), in his *Metafysik*, vols. 1–4, Copenhagen: Gyldendal 1976–84), pp. 259–60. On this and the ambiguous nature of the Socrates figure in Kierkegaard, see Arne Grøn, "Sokrates og Smulerne," *Filosofiske Studier*, vol. 15, 1995, pp. 97–107. That Løgstrup *also* held Kierkegaard in high esteem is perhaps not so clear from the previous, but in *Slagmark* (no. 42, 2005), which is dedicated to Løgstrup in connection with the 100-year anniversary of his birth, a theretofore unpublished and undated Løgstrup manuscript was brought to light with the title "Det filosofiske jerntæppe." Here Løgstrup reflects on the lack of dialogue between existentialism on the European continent and logical empiricism in the Anglo-Saxon world. The goal is to bring forth a dialogue between these two main streams by showing a common field of problems in spite of the shifting directions, and here Kierkegaard occupies a central place because he, behind the relation between nihilism and relativism raises the question of whether a human being can exist at all without metaphysics, at the same time that the thought must be subordinated to existence if it is to be kept alive as a fundamental philosophical thought (cf. the editorial preface, p. 8). In the same number Svend Andersen takes up *Opgør med Kierkegaard* in the article " 'I umiddelbarheden begynder det'—Løgstrups opgør med Kierkegaard" (pp. 63–76).

[195]   F.J. Billeskov Jansen, *Søren Kierkegaards litterære Kunst*, Copenhagen: Rosenkilde & Bagger 1951, p. 10.

[196]   Ibid., p. 11.

Billeskov Jansen's second chapter bears the title "The Great Novel Works," in which he places the aesthetic writings (*Either/Or* and *Stages on Life's Way* are called "life-view novels") in connection to Goethe's *Wilhelm Meister* novels and the German Romantics' numerous offerings for a *Bildungsroman* with Goethe as the model. This is connected to Aage Henriksen's treatise *Kierkegaard's Novels*. The book acknowledges its debt to the new criticism, which claims the unity and independence of a poetic work vis-à-vis the associating research but which is above all born from the lack of investigation of the aesthetic wholes in Kierkegaard's works, which Henriksen pointed out in his account of the history of the research. To this extent it is the problem of pseudonymity that he raises, and the book has, in its humble format, as its goal to contribute to the solution of this problem by "temporarily getting it out of the way; by respecting the integrity of the pseudonyms during an analysis of some of their books, one must be able to obtain material for judging their independence and their mutual relations."[197] To this end "The Diary of a Seducer" (from *Either/Or*), *Repetition* and "Guilty/Not Guilty" (from *Stages on Life's Way*) are treated, texts which, according to Henriksen, occupy a special place among Kierkegaard's pseudonymous works due to their epic form.

In Villy Sørensen's epoch-making philosophical aesthetics *Poets and Demons*,[198] Henriksen's characterization of the epic sequences in Kierkegaard's work as being novels is rejected. The epic sequences are, by contrast, illustrations of philosophical conceptual development:

> A work of art is, according to its essence, a fictional creation of symbols—and the external difficulties which arise in such an endeavor can very well be symbols of internal difficulties; Kierkegaard's "novels" are conceptual poetry: their "idea" is not derived from the artistic sequence but determine it, such that they do not display an artistic structure, but a philosophical system of concepts. This distinction does not constitute an evaluation; it is beyond discussion that Kierkegaard's poetic creations of thought are more significant works than the great majority of novels of his time—but one owes it to Kierkegaard to keep the categories distinct from one another.[199]

Sørensen's book thus distinguishes itself from the two others by not so much explicating Kierkegaard's aesthetics but rather by using him for his own aesthetics, in part from the perspective of a criticism of Kierkegaard's sharp distinction between the ethical and the aesthetic (between realizing oneself and formulating oneself), partly from the perspective of a more principled distinction between art and philosophy, and it is introduced with a characterization of the relation between (the poet) Hans Christian Andersen and (the philosopher) Søren Kierkegaard. The

---

[197]   Henriksen, *Kierkegaards Romaner*, pp. 7–8.
[198]   The intense debate in the most recent years about the Danish literary "modernism–construction" has Villy Sørensen's *Digtere og Dæmoner: fortolkninger og vurderinger* (Copenhagen: Gyldendal 1959) as one of its most essential fulcrums. The most important articles are collected in the book *Modernismen til debat*, ed. by Anne Borup, Morten Lassen and Jon Helt Haarder, Copenhagen: Gyldendal and Odense: Syddansk Universitetsforlag 2005.
[199]   Sørensen, *Digtere og Dæmoner*, p. 25.

book interprets and applies thereafter central Kierkegaardian categories to modern novels, for "Kierkegaard's abstract categories are visible in every major work of art, most clearly in the abstract work of art. Art confirms the Kierkegaardian philosophy, and thereby reconciles the aesthetic with the 'dogmatic,' the accidental with the essential. And this reconciliation is another name for 'repetition.'"[200] In Sørensen's interpretation, the Danish poet Harald Kidde (1878–1918) is presented as the "poet of recollection," Thomas Mann (1875–1955) as the "poet of the Fall," while the Austrian Hermann Broch (1886–1951) is interpreted and evaluated as the "poet of repetition."[201]

Villy Sørensen is, in his double capacity of philosopher and author of *belles lettres*, also a representative of the branch of Kierkegaard reception which includes the poets, and which perhaps in a special sense can be called intellectually related to Kierkegaard. While Villy Sørensen explicitly and critically uses Kierkegaard, in the case of most of the other poets one can speak not so much of an influence that can be directly documented but rather one which concerns a deeper, more ingenious, and general linguistic (especially humoristic) and philosophical inspiration.[202] I will not explore further this important strand (Kierkegaard as "the authors' author"[203]) which deserves an investigation of its own; the list is long and includes outstanding postwar authors such as Martin A. Hansen (1909–55), Suzanne Brøgger (b. 1944), and Henrik Stangerup (1937–98).[204]

---

[200]   Ibid., p. 35.

[201]   In one of the most penetrating of the contemporary reviews of *Digtere og Dæmoner*, Jørgen K. Bukdahl sees that one of the book's main presuppositions is Kierkegaard's (or Vigilius Haufniensis') *The Concept of Anxiety* (which Sørensen also published a few years later), and how its basic concept is a special fusion of dogmatics and psychology: "The philosopher Villy Sørensen has learned from dogmatics to speak about 'the Fall' and from psychology to speak about 'the trauma.' These two ways of speaking are blended together in one special sørensenesque, dogmatic-psychological manner of speaking, when the original sin in *Digtere og Dæmoner* is called 'the eternal trauma'....Villy Sørensen's entire book builds on the identification of biology and ontology,—of the original sin and trauma." Cf. Jørgen K. Bukdahl, "Om ontologi og biologi," in his *Frihed og frigørelse. Filosofi—Teologi— Kulturdebat. Artikler og essays 1956–1979*, Århus: Aros 1980, pp. 37–41.

[202]   Finn Hauberg Mortensen, in his history of reception, has reflected on this and operates with a modernistic phase in the Kierkegaard reception, which includes authors who otherwise are not occupied explicitly with Kierkegaard, for example, Tom Kristensen (1893–1974), Klaus Rifbjerg (b. 1931), and Henrik Nordbrandt (b. 1945). See Finn Hauberg Mortensen, "Kierkegaard in Scandinavia—A History of Radical Reception," in *Kierkegaard Revisited*, ed. by Niels Jørgen Cappelørn and Jon Stewart, Berlin and New York: Walter de Gruyter 1997 (*Kierkegaard Studies. Monograph Series*, vol. 1), pp. 433ff.

[203]   *SKS* 7, 571. *SKS* 22, 386 / *JP* 6547.

[204]   For Villy Sørensen's Kierkegaard reception, see also Peter Fink, "Enten og Eller," in *Både frem og tilbage. Portræt af Villy Sørensens forfatterskab*, ed. by Marianne Barlyng and Jørgen Bonde Jensen, Hellerup: Spring 2002 (*Springs Forfatterskabsportrætter*), pp. 377–87. On Martin A. Hansen and Kierkegaard, see, for example, Thorkild Bjørnvig, *Kains Alter. Martin A. Hansens Digtning og Tænkning*, Copenhagen: Gyldendal 1964, passim; Gitte Wernaa Butin, "Lindormens Skrig—Dæmoni og Skrift hos Martin A. Hansen og Søren Kierkegaard," in *Arvesyndens skønne Rose. Punktnedslag i Martin A. Hansens digtning*, ed.

E. Popular Works

It was also in the postwar years that popular publications about Kierkegaard seriously gathered speed. It can be difficult to explain precisely what characterizes these works, but a personal engagement and a prioritization of presentation to a popular audience rather than documentation in a scholarly manner is characteristic. Not only the fact that in a Kierkegaard context this is seemingly a special Danish phenomenon, makes it imperative to give a brief account here, but some of these works also maintain a high standard and, moreover, quantitatively are often far more widely disseminated than the scholarly works. That there is not necessarily a breach between serious research and popular publications is further clear from the various publications in the series *Søren Kierkegaard Selskabets Populære Skrifter* (which began in 1949), of which many are written by recognized scholars (for example, Billeskov Jansen, Malantschuk, N.H. Søe, and Søren Holm).

To this genre belong the innumerable introductions to Kierkegaard, which also in the most recent times constitutes a major part of the literature with respect to pure volume; here one can mention, for example, Peter P. Rohde's *A Genius in a Small Town* from 1956 (republished in 1962 as a supplement volume to the 3ʳᵈ edition of the *Samlede Værker*).[205] Villads Christensen (1883–1969) has, moreover, with a whole series of books in the period, made a name for himself as a popular author, for example, *Søren Kierkegaard's View of the Book* (1950), *Søren Kierkegaard's Path of Christianity* (1955), *Søren Kierkegaard in Light of Shakespeare's Hamlet* (1960), *Søren Kierkegaard and Frederiksberg* (1959), *Søren Kierkegaard's Motives for the Attack on the Church* (1959), *Søren Kierkegaard. What is Central in his View of Life* (1963), *The Peripatetic Søren Kierkegaard* (1965), and *The Kierkegaard Drama* (1967).[206]

---

by David Bugge, Copenhagen: Gad 2002, pp. 53–71; and the articles by Joakim Garff, Anders Kingo and Hans Vium Mikkelsen, in *PS. Om Martin A. Hansens korrespondance med kredsen omkring Heretica*, ed. by Anders Thyrring Andersen, Copenhagen: Gyldendal 2005, pp. 148–98. See also Suzanne Brøgger, "Kierkegaard adieu," *Den pebrede susen. Flydende fragmenter og fixeringer*, Copenhagen: Rhodos 1986, pp. 216–32; Henrik Stangerup, "Kierkegaard hed han. Parodisk bidrag til halvfjerdsernes ideologikritik" and Roger Poole, "Kierkegaard er vor tids filosof," in *Fangelejrens frie halvdel*, Copenhagen: Berlingske Forlag 1979, pp. 51–9 and pp. 61–73 respectively; Roger Poole and Henrik Stangerup, *Dansemesteren. Sider af Søren Kierkegaard*, Copenhagen: Gyldendal 1985, especially pp. 225–30; Søren Peter Hansen, "Kærlighed, identitet og skæbne. Kierkegaard og Stangerup," in *Denne slyngelagtige eftertid. Tekster om Søren Kierkegaard*, vols. 1–3, ed. by Finn Frandsen and Ole Morsing, Århus: Slagmark 1995, pp. 513–40. With respect to Sørensen and Brøgger, there was an original youthful enthusiasm for Kierkegaard, which was replaced by an increasing critical distance, while the movement is the other way around in the case of Henrik Stangerup.

205   Peter P. Rohde, *Et geni i en Købstad. Et essay om Søren Kierkegaard*, Oslo: det Norske studentersamfunds kulturutvalg 1956 (Copenhagen: Gyldendal 1962).

206   Villads Christensen, *Søren Kierkegaards Syn paa Bogen*, Copenhagen: Scripta 1950; *Søren Kierkegaards Vej til Kristendommen*, Copenhagen: Munksgaards Forlag 1955; *Søren Kierkegaard i lys af Shakespeares Hamlet*, Copenhagen: Rosenkilde & Bagger 1960; *Søren Kierkegaard og Frederiksberg*, Copenhagen: Rosenkilde & Bagger 1959; *Søren Kierkegaards Motiver til Kirkekampen*, Copenhagen: Einar Munksgaard 1959; *Søren Kierkegaard. Det*

As an outstanding example of the combination of insight and passion, one can emphasize Jørgen Bukdahl's *Søren Kierkegaard and the Common Man* (1961) (a book which was published as numbers 9–10 in *Søren Kierkegaard Selskabets Populære Skrifter* and has been republished a few times, in 1970 and 1996).[207] Jørgen Bukdahl (1896–1982) describes Kierkegaard's growing out from under the influence of, among others, Henrik Steffens' Herderian emphasis on folk life's anonymous spiritual life in myths and folksongs along with the environment which he was exposed to through his home (where, among others, the Grundtvigian Jacob Christian Lindberg was a regular guest). The original philosophical problem of the inner self-determination was suddenly raised, according to Bukdahl, in the new historical situation at the beginning of the nineteenth century as a decisive and wholly unphilosophical problem for the common man, partly under the influence of the peasant reforms and the French Revolution's ideas of freedom and equality, partly—and especially—as a result of the beginning of the new spiritual movements, which were a nationwide anti-authoritarian revolt against the priesthood and the civil servant class or against what Kierkegaard called "the educated" ["*de dannede*"]. The inner self-determination, Kierkegaard's true subjectivity or existence as opposed to bad individualism, has as a basic presupposition a popular originality, which the humanistic *Bildung* veils, and it is this that places his talk about the individual in decisive connection with the category of "the common man." In opposition to the manipulating "intermediaries" (the teachers, the journalists, and in time the pastors), Kierkegaard wrote from a sincere heart for the common man, especially in the period up until the year of revolution 1848, when he took more directly the side of the common human being against the educated and the bourgeoisie. Bukdahl thus demonstrates a line from the *Corsair* controversy to the attack on the Church with its direct appeal to the ordinary man and makes it clear to what a high degree Kierkegaard's action had a social goal.

VI. Kierkegaard after Løgstrup—from Marxism to Postmodernism (1968–89)

A. Love, Continuity, and the Attack on the Church

Løgstrup's criticism of Kierkegaard was massively opposed but nonetheless set the agenda for the next few decades of Danish Kierkegaard research.[208] In 1972 Kresten

---

centrale i hans Livssyn , Copenhagen: Gads Forlag 1963; *Peripatetikeren Søren Kierkegaard*, Copenhagen: Graabrødre Torv's Forlag 1965; and *Kierkegaard-Dramaet*, Copenhagen: Nyt Nordisk Forlag Arnold Busck 1967. For a brief account of these, see Niels Thulstrup, "Scandinavia," in *Kierkegaard Research*, ed. by Niels Thulstrup and Marie Mikulová Thulstrup, Copenhagen: C.A. Reitzel 1987 (*Bibliotheca Kierkegaardiana*, vol. 15), pp. 173–98, see pp. 190–1. Engaged popularizers such as Emanuel Skjoldager (1913–84) and Johannes Møllehave (b. 1937) should also be mentioned.

[207]   Jørgen Bukdahl, *Søren Kierkegaard og den menige mand*, Copenhagen: Munksgaard 1961.

[208]   See, for example, Anders Moe Rasmussen, "Kierkegaards eksistenstænkning som idealismekritik—en analyse af Johannes Sløks Kierkegaard-tolkning," *Philosophia*, vol. 17,

Nordentoft can claim that the renaissance which Kierkegaard's thought experienced in the twentieth century is on the decline, and in H.C. Wind's study of reception, from 1983, the point is made that Løgstrup's criticism has weakened interest in Kierkegaard and especially the existence-theological interpretation of Kierkegaard in Denmark: "*Løgstrups Auseinandersetzung mit Kierkegaard [hat] m.E. die Wirkung gehabt, daß die Stimme Kierkegaards in der theologischen Öffentlichkeit heute nahezu verstummt ist; und wo sie vernehmbar ist, mit unverkennbaren Nachklängen der radikalen Kritik Løgstrups.*"[209] Several of the most important studies from the 1970s are more or less conscious attempts to correct Løgstrup, and the criticism typically concerns the fact that he is too occupied with a certain Kierkegaard interpretation (K. Olesen Larsen's), and moreover in his alternative to Kierkegaard is very close to what Kierkegaard *also* said, especially in *Works of Love*.

Johannes Sløk's *Kierkegaard – a Proponent of Humanism* from 1978 can perhaps already in its title be suspected of wanting to take the sting out of not only Løgstrup's interpretation of Kierkegaard but also Knud Hansen's related one.[210] In opposition to Knud Hansen, for whom Kierkegaard's understanding of passion remains a solipsistic affair, Sløk interprets passion not only in its immediate appearance but in its developed form as love and therefore as an interpersonal phenomenon. This interpretation builds on the central claim in the *Fragments* that "the ultimate potentiation of every passion is always to will its own downfall," which at first refers to the understanding's or the intellect's paradox, but immediately after this receives its parallel in the sphere of love: "A person lives undisturbed in himself, and then awakens the paradox of self-love as love for another, for one missing. (Self-love is the ground or goes to the ground in all love)."[211] The at first isolated passion is thus transformed by being developed into an interpersonal passion, and the love which lies at bottom demands for its development that it be destroyed as preferential love. This law of the development or transformation of love—from self-love to preferential love to neighbor love—lies behind *Works of Love*, and Kierkegaard is therefore, in Sløk's interpretation, not so much the poet of the idea as the poet of inclusive love.[212]

This emphasis on Kierkegaard as a theologian and philosopher of love and passion is new in relation to Sløk's earlier works on Kierkegaard, that is, in relation to his analysis of Kierkegaard's philosophy of history and freedom in the book from 1947, *The Concept of Providence*,[213] and the anthropological conceptual structure and its appearance in the stage theory in *Die Anthropologie Kierkegaards* (1954).

---

nos. 3–4, 1988, pp. 129–30.

[209]   H.C. Wind, "Die Rezeption Kierkegaards in der neueren dänischen Theologie," in *Die Rezeption Søren Kierkegaards in der deutschen und dänischen Philosophie und Theologie. Vorträge des Kolloquiums am 22. und 23 März 1982*, ed. by Heinrich Anz, p. 188.

[210]   Johannes Sløk, *Humanismens tænker*, Copenhagen: Hans Reitzel 1978.

[211]   *SKS* 4, 243, 244 / *PF*, 37, 39.

[212]   The formulation is Jørgen K. Bukdahl's, see Bukdahl, *Om Søren Kierkegaard*, p. 159. Cf. also Sløk, *Humanismens tænker*, pp. 116ff.

[213]   Johannes Sløk, "Kierkegaards Bestemmelse af Incommensurabilitetens tvetydige Perspektiv," in *Forsynstanken. Et Forsøg paa en dogmatisk Begrebsbestemmelse*, Hjørring: Expres-Trykkeriets Forlag 1947, pp. 92–135.

As noted, one senses Løgstrup's agenda as the unspoken background here, but it is at least as important to see this and the period's other important Kierkegaard studies against the background of the 1970s' interest in psychoanalysis and, especially, the dominant university Marxism, which Jørgen K. Bukdahl (1936–79) as few others had an eye for. Bukdahl notes in his long article "Kierkegaard between Ideology and Utopia I–II" (1976–77) that "Marx in the decade since the students' rebellion at the end of the 1960s has inherited the place which Kierkegaard had occupied in the 1940s and 1950s as the most authentic critic of a ruling bourgeois mentality."[214] In the article "Kierkegaard used in a Marxist age" (1978) he subsequently treats Sløk's book along with Kresten Nordentoft's *Søren Kierkegaard. Contribution to the Criticism of Bourgeois Self-Absorption* (1977)[215] and reads these works as efforts to make more precise and to mobilize Kierkegaard as a supplement and criticism of Marxist situation analysis. Moreover, he praises them for being both thorough and generally comprehensible: "Both authors have from preceding in-depth studies of the collected Kierkegaard oeuvre made an outstanding presentation in their desire to make Kierkegaard relevant in a Marxist age."[216] Concerning Nordentoft (1938–82), this refers to his extensive studies on, respectively, Kierkegaard's individual and social psychology, *Kierkegaard's Psychology* (1972) and *"What does the Fire Chief Say?" Kierkegaard's Confrontation With His Times* (1973), the first of which distinguishes itself as being the first systematic account of Kierkegaard as a psychological thinker and not a psychological case.[217] At the end of *Kierkegaard's Psychology* there is a long analysis of *Works of Love*, which similar to (and anticipating) Sløk's interpretation, places decisive weight on Kierkegaard's claim that love is "at bottom," which brings

---

[214]   Jørgen K. Bukdahl, "Kierkegaard mellem ideologi og utopi I–II," in *Om Søren Kierkegaard*, p. 100.
[215]   Kresten Nordentoft, *Søren Kierkegaard. Bidrag til kritikken af den borgerlige selvoptagethed*, Copenhagen: Dansk Universitets Presse 1977.
[216]   Jørgen K. Bukdahl, "Kierkegaard brugt i en marxistisk tid," in *Om Søren Kierkegaard*, p. 147.
[217]   Kresten Nordentoft, *Kierkegaards psykologi*, Copenhagen: Hans Reitzels Forlag 1972 (English translation: *Kierkegaard's Psychology*, trans. by Bruce Kirmmse, Pittsburgh, Pennsylvania: Duquesne University Press 1978), and *"Hvad siger Brand-Majoren?" Kierkegaards opgør med sin samtid*, Copenhagen: G.E.C. Gad 1973. In addition to the aforementioned Helweg and Ostenfeld, the psychoanalyst Sigurd Næsgaard's *En Psykoanalyse af Søren Kierkegaard* (Odense: Psykoanalystisk Forlag 1950), can be counted to the tradition of personal diagnosis; in his book Kierkegaard is exposed to the entire Freudian music with the ego, superego, Oedipus complex, etc. At the same time as Nordentoft, Ib Ostenfeld published a book with an (almost) identical title, *Søren Kierkegaards Psykologi* (Copenhagen: Rhodos 1972), and with the subtitle *Undersøgelse og Indlevelse*. This book ends with a refutation of Helweg's book from 1933. In a somewhat different direction, the Jung-inspired consciousness researcher and historian of ideas Jes Bertelsen (b. 1946) has analyzed and applied Kierkegaard's thought, for example, in *Kategori og afgørelse. Strukturer i Kierkegaards tænkning*, Viborg: Nørhaven Bogtrykkeri 1972; and in the dissertation *Ouroboros. En undersøgelse af selvets struktur*, Copenhagen: Borgen 1974. In the latter, Kierkegaard's thoughts about passion function as a frame for Jung's theory of complex and his concept of mental energy since Kierkegaard's philosophical thinking, according to Bertelsen, can be seen as "a gigantic attempt to introduce and analyze the concept of energy in the context of existential philosophy," p. 11.

Kierkegaard close to Løgstrup's talk of the "precultural" sovereign manifestations of life.[218]

But Sløk and Nordentoft can also be brought in when discussing the disputed question of the continuity or lack thereof in Kierkegaard's authorship—a question which especially must be raised when the attack (or storm) on the Church is to be treated. Nordentoft sketches in the introduction to *"What does the Fire Chief Say?"* previous interpretations of the attack on the Church as, for example, "the departure theory" and "the theory of admission" and, in his own analysis of the matter, is of the opinion that Kierkegaard carried out a double bookkeeping during the period: he says one thing in his articles, for example, the generous use of the threats of hell, and something else in his "private diary," where it is clear that he does not believe in eternal damnation.[219] Sløk also analyzes the attack on the Church thoroughly and uses the papers as the point of departure in his *When Kierkegaard was Silent. From Authorship to Attack on the Church* from 1980. Here he claims a more fundamental lack of inner continuity since he finds two, objectively, independent lines of development in Kierkegaard: one which goes from treating the person's possibility of being able to establish himself as a single human being in personal self-determination and self-responsibility in the context of society, to treating a total heterogeneousness with the existing order; and another which takes place in Kierkegaard's own theological conceptual determinations and describes the transition from regarding Christianity from the perspective of Jesus as God's becoming-historical to emphasizing Jesus as a model for a way of life. The strange thing is now, according to Sløk, that Kierkegaard does not himself see that there are here two distinct lines of development, and this is clear from the fact that in his journal entries they converge into a single thing. Kierkegaard's attack on the State Church is the many considerations put into action, legitimated by the ingenius authorship which he can claim to have behind him. Kierkegaard thus feels that his attack on the Church is in logical agreement with his authorship, while Sløk's analyses show that there is a contradiction between the authorship, on the one hand, and the journals and the articles related to the attack on the Church, on the other.[220] A few years later Sløk began to doubt the validity of his conclusion—without, however, wanting to retract his analysis. In *Kierkegaard's Universe. A New Guide to the Genius* from 1983 he writes by way of conclusion:

---

[218]   Nordentoft's analysis of *Works of Love* has moreover inspired Paul Müller's close reading of the same book in *Kristendom, etik og majeutik i Søren Kierkegaards "Kjerlighedens Gjerninger,"* Copenhagen: Institut for Religionshistorie 1976 (*Skrifter udgivet af Københavns Universitets Institut for Religionshistorie,* vol. 1).

[219]   This makes Joakim Garff in *"Den Søvnløse"* from 1995 accuse Nordentoft of insisting on a firm caesura between "the private person Kierkegaard" and "the author and thinker of the same name" (ibid., p. 352n). Garff with his bio-graphical reading opts for the theory that there is consistency and continuity between the foregoing authorship and the attack on the Church—albeit not precisely Kierkegaard's own conception of the continuity and consistency. This is grounded in, among other things, another and more articulated view of the papers than Nordentoft, who cannot really be said to have any principled view about them.

[220]   Johannes Sløk, *Da Kierkegaard tav. Fra forfatterskab til kirkestorm,* Copenhagen: Hans Reitzel 1980, pp. 122–3.

In *When Kierkegaard was Silent* I tried to pursue the theory that Kierkegaard actually changed views, and in the iconoclastic articles was another than in the authorship proper. Here [in *Kierkegaard's Universe*] I have tried to pursue the opposite theory, that as a superior and exceedingly calculating strategist he planned the iconoclastic articles so that in their entirety they became a corrective to the existing state of things—and that they therefore do not in themselves express the truth.

Therefore it isn't I who have changed views from one book to the other. I have merely tried to advance the two theories in their respective volumes.[221]

B. Source Criticism and Demythologizing

One book which in many ways stands alone in Kierkegaard research and on several points anticipates the new edition *Søren Kierkegaards Skrifter* (*SKS*), is the literary scholar Henning Fenger's *Kierkegaard: The Myths and their Origins* from 1976. For this reason it will be presented in a bit more detail here. Henning Fenger (1921–85) undertakes a wide-ranging criticism of Kierkegaard research's uncritical relation to the source material, which has been presented so far, and he presents a sharp criticism of the *Papirer* edition and its editors. His style is polemical and ironic, and the words of praise are limited for the most part to an admiration of the hard work and the monumentality of the edition. But even the editorial work's "Sisyphean task" has, according to Fenger, a dubious quality of being performed by scholars with a decided theological, philosophical, and philological background, and he misses especially the historians who could competently oversee a responsible edition of the papers from Kierkegaard's youth. What is worse is that the entire edition's original intention of being a Søren Kierkegaard diplomatarium, as was stated in the foreword to the first volume from 1909, is not only not fulfilled, but in itself is an all too comprehensive ambition, which per definition causes confusion. Fenger criticizes among other things the unclear talk of "literary" Kierkegaard manuscripts and "letters from Kierkegaard" which constitute a special problem, because the editors have not reflected about the possibility that these letters might be fictional. He concludes: "the edition of Heiberg and Kuhr, its plan and division into parts, is unclear and imprecise from the very start."[222] Fenger virtually comes to defend H.P. Barfod's heavy-handed treatment of the original manuscripts, which made the *Papirer* dependent upon the *Efterladte Papirer*, Barfod's catalogue, and his transcription of the original manuscripts as source for the edition. In this context Fenger finds condescending Heiberg's and Kuhr's rough treatment of Barfod and his age's view of the practice of editing. Concerning the *Papirer*'s editorial principles, with its putting aside the strict chronological organization of the material to the advantage of the thematic-systematic principle in the groups A, B, and C, and within the C group a further division into Theologica, Philosophica, and Æsthetica, "the editors have succeeded in creating a perfect and absolute chaos, concerning which—without malice—one

---

[221]   Johannes Sløk, *Kierkegaards univers. En ny guide til geniet*, Viby J.: Centrum 1983, pp. 127–8. (*Kierkegaard's Universe. A New Guide to the Genius*, trans. by Kenneth Tindall, Copenhagen: The Danish Cultural Institute 1994, p. 155.)
[222]   Fenger, *Kierkegaard-Myter og Kierkegaard-Kilder*, p. 47. (*Kierkegaard: The Myths and their Origins*, p. 48.)

can use Kierkegaard's own words: 'discursive discussions and incomprehensible commentaries concerning the category of higher lunacy' (II A 808)."[223] While H.P. Barfod at least laid his cards on the table and admitted his own helplessness and lack of consistency with regard to Kierkegaard's actual discontinuous and problematic entries, the editors of the *Papirer* allowed the respect for the interdependency or the accidental connection among the entries to outweigh the respect for the chronological sequence, which in Fenger's eyes is misleading. It is hopeless to force the complexity in Kierkegaard's entries, especially in the papers from his youth, into an order of this kind. Therefore, with respect to these entries, according to Fenger, it would have been more honest, "if one had chosen either to publish the twelve books, or folders, from before the time of the journals—the twelve items described by Barfod, with the addition of the random papers—or to have opted for the following principle: dated entries in one section, undated ones in another."[224] Fenger's main criticism of the *Papirer* culminates in a quotation of the words of the editors about their practice of placing the undated entries together with the dated ones, "The most important passage in Heiberg and Kuhr's long preface," which is reproduced unaltered in the second edition. With an introductory address to the editors' officialese style of writing and P.A. Heiberg's arrangement of the undated entries so that they fit with his theory of the ups and downs of Kierkegaard's religious development, Fenger comments as follows on this practice:

> Translated into everyday language, this means that they stuck in the numerous undated slips where they believed they could aptly be used to support the concept of Kierkegaard they already had! It is astonishing, putting it mildly, that in the *Papirer*'s second edition (a photographic reproduction, of course) no attention was paid to the editors' own express opinion concerning the chronology's altogether doubtful value. It is high time that a team of experts be given the task of identifying, that is, dating and placing, the papers of the young Kierkegaard. In Annelise Garde, Denmark possesses a skillful graphologist, and the Royal Library has at its disposal both experts and technical equipment to aid in the identification of paper, watermarks, types of ink, and so forth. Of course, we shall never attain absolute accuracy in determining when Kierkegaard wrote what, but we can certainly not afford the reputation of putting up with the results of Heiberg and Kuhr.[225]

Not even the *Papirer*'s descriptions of the manuscripts which are found at the back of each volume and which before Fenger were not criticized for anything more than being superfluous, escape his criticism. By comparing the original manuscripts—in this case the many small pieces of paper which constitute the *Journal FF*—with the editors' information about them, Fenger resents that the reader only with great difficulty can deduce from the descriptions of the manuscripts that two entries, which are not printed one after another in fact appear on the front and back side of the same piece of paper. He rounds off his criticism of the philological side of the edition by

---

[223]   Fenger, *Kierkegaard-Myter og Kierkegaard-Kilder*, p. 48. (*Kierkegaard: The Myths and their Origins*, p. 50.)
[224]   Fenger, *Kierkegaard-Myter og Kierkegaard-Kilder*, p. 49. (*Kierkegaard: The Myths and their Origins*, p. 50.)
[225]   Fenger, *Kierkegaard-Myter og Kierkegaard-Kilder*, p. 49. (*Kierkegaard: The Myths and their Origins*, p. 51.)

requesting that the editors of Søren Kierkegaard's papers be pedantic. Pedantry is not only a virtue but a *must*. Moreover, he suggests that a scholarly edition present on the left side a photographic reproduction of the many different loose papers and on the right side descriptions and commentaries. "We must be able to afford it, after all. We have only one Kierkegaard."[226]

In addition to this, Fenger, in the second longest chapter in the book—the longest treats the relation between P.L. Møller, H.P. Holst, and Kierkegaard until 1843—interprets the famous entries from Gilleleje in the summer of 1835, including the letter to P.W. Lund (*Pap.* I A 72). Against Kuhr and Heiberg and Niels Thulstrup, he raises doubt about to what extent the entries refer to real events, and is instead of the opinion that they are literary drafts of a novel in the form of letters, which Kierkegaard, under the influence of Blicher, was allegedly working on during this period. The letter to Lund is thus fictional, with a fictional dating, and was presumably written at the end of 1836. Fenger argues for his theory of a project about a novel in the form of letters based on the undated entry *Pap.* II A 46, which he calls "The absolutely central entry, the 'matchless discovery' and 'the secret note,' " with the implication being that Kierkegaard at some point was working on a text with the working title "Letters."[227]

Fenger dedicates a special chapter to Niels Thulstrup's book on Kierkegaard's relation to Hegel. Here he pays special critical attention to Thulstrup's understanding of Kierkegaard's disposition towards Hegelian philosophy in the entries from his youth as a process of clarification, which came to an end around the time of the publication of *Either/Or*. Fenger, by contrast, believes the years 1835–43 represent a great fermentation and only with the *Concluding Unscientific Postscript* does he see a clarification in relation to Hegel. Fenger relies on his analyses of the sources, including the understanding of the Gilleleje entries as fictional—and it does not do

---

[226] Fenger, *Kierkegaard-Myter og Kierkegaard-Kilder*, p. 50. (*Kierkegaard: The Myths and their Origins*, p. 53.) In the new scholarly edition of *Søren Kierkegaards Skrifter* the editors have taken into account much of Fenger's criticism of the *Papirer*—although there have not been sufficient financial resources to publish a photographic reproduction of every one of Kierkegaard's numerous small scraps of paper. In an article from 1994 Joakim Garff sketches the perspectives for a new electronic edition and, on the same occasion, runs through older and newer editions of Kierkegaard's writings, including *Søren Kierkegaards Papirer.* Garff agrees with Fenger's problematization of the *Papirer*'s organization of the material and notes that a new group of editors should take on the task of reorganizing and thereby reconstructing the material's original chronology. In addition, the article points especially to two critical points; these concern the *Papirer* editors' lack of sense for the graphic signals of the manuscripts, among others, the numerous and often very important marginal additions, as well as the organization of the B section, which is supposed to make possible insight into the genesis of Kierkegaard's works, but which, according to Garff, is carried out in such a backwards manner that the material more or less loses its value. Joakim Garff, "Fra bog til bits," *Bogens Verden*, no. 6, 1994, pp. 332–3.

[227] Fenger, *Kierkegaard-Myter og Kierkegaard-Kilder*, p. 87 (*Kierkegaard: The Myths and their Origins*, p. 102.) In the new edition, *SKS*, the editors have in part agreed with Fenger's theory since the entries *Pap.* I A 72–81 are taken together as a single entry (AA:12), cf. *SKS* 17, 18ff.

that Thulstrup uses fictional material in a line with actual letters and diary entries, which, according to Fenger, should have been clear to Thulstrup already in 1953, when he published *Breve og Aktstykker.*[228] Also the unfinished philosophical novella *Johannes Climacus or De omnibus dubitandum est* (*Pap.* IV B 1), which Fenger believes the research has exploited in the crassest manner as a biographical source, is brought into the argumentation against Thulstrup. Here Fenger disputes, on the one hand, the dating of the work, in that he distinguishes between the working it out and the actual written composition, and, on the other hand, the open, definitive break with Hegel and Heiberg, which Thulstrup reads in it.[229]

C. Communication Theory (Paul Müller)

An important aspect of Kierkegaard's authorship, to which he himself ascribes great significance but which for a long time had been unfairly treated in the research, is his theory of communication. In several studies, Paul Müller (1940–92) remedies this and treats it in, among other place, his *The Dialectics of Communication in Søren Kierkegaard's Philosophical Fragments* (1979).[230] In a text-near interpretation with constant awareness of the question of the work's indirect, respectively direct form of communication, Müller reaches the conclusion that *the necessity of offense* determines the entire constellation of issues surrounding the dialectic of communication in the *Fragments*. While the Socratic self-deepening and recollection asks the question about the appropriation of the truth without stumbling upon offense and thus without suffering, the same question is not answered without precisely offense and suffering by faith. The difference is found in the revelation, which for the dialectic of communication means that the god first communicates himself indirectly by becoming human, but with his own statement about being the god at the same time makes the communication direct. When the paradox is posited, the believer must repeat the direct communication, but at the same time take care that the communication for the sake of freedom is converted into indirect communication, so that the self-activity and appropriation in which faith lives, comes about. The

[228]   Fenger, *Kierkegaard-Myter og Kierkegaard-Kilder*, p. 110. (*Kierkegaard: The Myths and their Origins*, p. 133.)

[229]   Fenger, *Kierkegaard-Myter og Kierkegaard-Kilder*, pp. 116ff. (*Kierkegaard: The Myths and their Origins*, pp. 142ff.) *De omnibus dubitandum est* is also the motto for Fenger's own book, and this "source criticism's answer to Sherlock Holmes" (Joakim Garff) was appropriately reviewed under the title "Afmytologisering af Kierkegaard" by Johannes Sløk, who in this article (in *Dansk Teologisk Tidsskrift*, vol. 40, 1977, pp. 120–7) in the essentials praises Fenger for his elegant, sometimes a bit too elegant, style and precise accounts, but ends with "mischievousness": twice Fenger refers to Kierkegaard's talk of "leaping out on 70,000 fathoms" (see ibid., p. 8; p. 142), but Sløk would very much like to know where Kierkegaard mentions this; to be sure, Kierkegaard speaks in many places of flowing or lying "out there on 70,000 fathoms," but leaping?! "This is a Kierkegaard myth, which is due solely to Kierkegaard scholars, who continue to repeat it without even thinking about it" (ibid., p. 127).

[230]   Paul Müller, *Meddelelsesdialektikken i Søren Kierkegaard's Philosophiske Smuler*, Copenhagen: Institut for Religionshistorie 1979.

paradox is thus alone in communicating itself, while its witnesses can merely draw attention to it. Moreover, "God's communication of himself and the communication about him...is not without a point of connection, even if the point of connection, with regard to what is Christian, does not exist without the inevitable fact of offense."[231]

D. Fin de siècle

With Paul Müller's focus on the theory of communication we have reached the 1980s and 1990s, when the study of Kierkegaard, on the back of Løgstrup's influential criticism and university Marxism's marginalization of Kierkegaard as a bourgeois philosopher and an ideologue of accommodation, experienced a renewed interest and several characteristic new directions. Postmodernism's embracing of Kierkegaard has many aspects and seems to be connected with a striking similarity in the spirit of the age from the preceding century's fin-de-siècle culture. In his book about Vienna in the period from 1890 to 1920 Steen Beck (b. 1958) writes about this similarity:

> In the fin-de-siècle culture's sometimes melancholic and sometimes aggressively self-certain consciousness of destruction and transition and seeking for values and identity on the premises of individualization we find our own postmodern condition. Just as they did then, we are searching today with the feeling of having to construct and make up our identity in a world where there is no longer any center, which can further a cultural formation of identity. In this situation it is not so surprising that a thinker such as Søren Kierkegaard, the philosopher of the individual and irony par excellence, is studied more than ever.[232]

The transition from the 1970s to the 1980s can be described from a perspective of consciousness, and with consequences for especially art, as a relatively abrupt transition from a primarily progress—and process—oriented (historical) thinking to an experience of an ambiguous world liberated from all abstract filters. Here in opposition to modernism's functionalist aesthetics and puritan linguistic form, there rules in a broad sense a play of appearances: manifoldness, irreconcilability, and (sex) differences appear, the ornament, the decoration, and the tableau are cultivated. Kierkegaard's labyrinthine authorship with its clever setting the stage and complicated system of pseudonyms, its richness in images, and manifoldness of stylized figures appears anew with an obvious relation to a series of (typically postmodern) concepts such as, for example, parade, ceremony, show, theater, side stage, mirage, mask, mirrors that mirror mirrors, ruins, etc. To the extent that it makes any sense at all to operate with the opposition of modern–postmodern, one can say that where modernism broke down the surviving forms, postmodernism

---

[231]   Müller, *Meddelelsesdialektikken i Søren Kierkegaard's Philosophiske Smuler*, p. 76. For the concept of offense, see also Niels Jørgen Cappelørn, "Et forsøg på en bestemmelse af begrebet forargelse hos Søren Kierkegaard," *Dansk Teologisk Tidsskrift*, vol. 38, 1975, pp. 197–229; and Poul Lübcke, "Guds og verdens visdom—troen og forargelsen hos Kierkegaard, Mynster og Martensen," *Filosofiske Studier*, vol. 14, 1994, pp. 131–95.
[232]   Steen Beck, *Mændene uden Egenskaber: køn og kunst i århundredeskiftets Wien*, Copenhagen: Museum Tusculanum 1997, p. 8.

quotes them.[233] This is then transfered to Kierkegaard research, which a superficial observation can already perceive in the titles of the books and articles which are produced: Kierkegaard's own texts are allowed to speak more than ever before; he is simply quoted (or paraphrased) to an entirely different extent than was ever the case before. In the age's literary and aesthetic readings the text's own rhetorical, maieutic, and seductive strategy directly becomes the object of investigation and often without any foregoing philosophical account. Careful attention is paid to how Kierkegaard says something and not only to what he says. In the same way the role of the reader comes into focus, which presumably is related to the character of the reading as "firstness" in relation to (derived) interpretations of a more abstract, philosophical kind.[234] Isak Winkel Holm has grounded the literary turn in Danish Kierkegaard research with words that almost sound like an echo of K. Olesen Larsen in his time, although from an entirely different perspective:

> In Denmark there is an unfortunate tradition of giving a *summary* rather than *reading* Kierkegaard. Probably due to the market's insatiable need for simplified accounts, large parts of Kierkegaard literature offer some, moreover, often wonderful accounts of the stage theory and related concepts, almost always ordered nicely from the works' chronological series. This kind of presentation of Kierkegaard's philosophy attempts to unravel his existence-philosophical doctrines from the text's impenetrable windings and present them in a language that is easy to understand. The ambition is to liberate the philosophical meaning from its refractory material—which is precisely what Kierkegaard expressly and constantly says that one cannot do.[235]

In addition to the literary readings there are also sex-related readings in the wake of the 1970s' women's movement. Few authors or philosophers have been occupied so intensively with falling in love, seduction, marriage, the inscrutable ways of desire, and the oppositions between men and women as Kierkegaard.[236] Existentialism's and existence theology's emphasis on inwardness and the related problems of the relation of the inner and the outer, the lack of mediation between the subject and the outside world, opens at this time for a revival of the philosophy of subjectivity.[237] The emphasis on existence instead of consciousness in the long run fails to suppress the fact that consciousness cannot without further ado be separated from the external world, and that there essentially belongs to the subject its understanding of itself

---

[233]   See also Beck, *Mændene uden Egenskaber*, p. 11.

[234]   Cf. Niels Gunder Hansen, "Dialog mellem læsere. Fænomenologi versus kognitivisme," *Kritik*, no. 172, 2004, p. 15.

[235]   Isak Winkel Holm, *Tanken i billedet. Kierkegaards poetik*, Copenhagen: Gyldendal 1998, p. 318.

[236]   Birgit Bertung (b. 1932) has especially been occupied with this aspect of the authorship. See for example, *Om Kierkegaard, kvinder og kærlighed—en studie i Søren Kierkegaards kvindesyn*, Copenhagen: C.A. Reitzel 1987. Gregor Malantschuk was presumably the first person in Kierkegaard research to take up the challenge from the 1970s' feminism for an investigation. He does this in his *Den kontroversielle Kierkegaard* (Copenhagen: Vinten 1976), which is also concerned with the political and social aspects of Kierkegaard's thought.

[237]   Cf. Wind, "Die Rezeption Kierkegaards in der neueren dänischen Theologie," pp. 207–8.

as something "external," an object in the world. Kierkegaard's relational thinking is introduced into this context and read anew with a view towards its significance for the theory of subjectivity, but also interpretations of the dependence of the self-relation on the relation to the other and its consequences for ethics becomes a dominant tendency.

The main interest in Kierkegaard during this period thus circles around concepts such as aesthetics, irony, sex, subjectivity, and ethics. In addition there is a renewed interest in the biographical study and a marked interested in Kierkegaard's edifying authorship, which in the 1990s came into focus to an extent theretofore unseen. This was primarily a matter for theologians, but the other fields have attracted both philosophers, theologians, and—especially—literary scholars. The last couple of decades of Kierkegaard research are on the whole stamped by a revival and variation of themes, which makes a complete or even a more or less representative account impossible. In what follows I will therefore attempt to shed light on individual points in the most recent Kierkegaard research with an emphasis on what is thematically new, and since much of this was hatched in the 1980s, but only brought to full development in longer books and treatises in the following decade, we will go straight to the literature of the1990s, albeit with a detour to the somewhat unwieldy question about the political use of Kierkegaard, which took on a new relevance with the fall of the Berlin wall and the end of the Cold War.

Excursus: Kierkegaard and Democracy—A Historical Sketch

In the final decades of the nineteenth century Denmark was politically stamped by a bitter constitutional struggle, whose main combatants were, on the one side, the conservative prime minister J.B.S. Estrup (1825–1913), who governed the country in the years 1885–94 with provisional finance bills against the majority of the voters, and on the other side, the opposition with especially the party, Venstre, and the political radicals in the circle around the Brandes brothers in the leading role. One important position was occupied by the important political journalist Viggo Hørup (1841–1902), who in 1884 together with Edvard Brandes (1847–1931) founded the newspaper *Politiken*. In the context of Kierkegaard reception, it is interesting that in his youth Hørup was greatly occupied with Kierkegaard, and (according to Brandes' obituary for Hørup) at a festive gathering on New Year's Eve 1871 at the home of the author Holger Drachmann, he is said to have given an enthusiastic speech about "the man, to whom we owe everything, who has taught us to love the disdained, the poor and humble, and who has given us ideals we would like to be true to: Søren Kierkegaard."[238] The, if one will, journalistic Kierkegaard reception took on a new dimension in 1904, when *Politiken* received a "nephew" in the form of *Ekstrabladet*, whose first editor, Frejlif Olsen (1868–1936), went back to Kierkegaard's attack on the Church and adopted his hatred for the clergy and his institutional criticism for the newspaper's anti-authoritarian and anticlerical line. This line has characterized

---

[238]   Cf. Georg Brandes, "Viggo Hørup," in *Samlede Skrifter*, vols. 1–4, 2nd ed., Copenhagen: Gyldendals 1919–20, vol. 3, p. 223.

Ekstrabladet ever since, above all in the 1960s and 1970s during the time of the legendary editor Victor Andreasen (1920–2000).[239]

The attack on the Church in 1855 was also an inspiration for socialist and radical agitators later in the nineteenth century. For example, the literary critic C.E. Jensen (1865–1927), and the social-democratic politician and editor F.J. Borgbjerg (1866–1936), in their extensive work from 1904 on the history of the workers' movement, gave the following positive evaluation of Kierkegaard's efforts in the last year of his life:

> *The Moment* set a deep division in people's consciousness; it enforced a mistrust of the State Church, which was later never extinguished, and hence a mistrust of those in power, who creep in hiding behind the walls of the church. By the sharp emphasis of Christianity's absolute irreconcilability with this world, Kierkegaard, moreover, gave the unclear free thinkers a strong push to abandon faith and place themselves on the ground of science. His thundering speech to the individual awakened a theretofore unknown feeling of personal responsibility. As conservative or, more correctly, life-denying as his course of thought may have been, it nonetheless received significance both for social and spiritual progress.[240]

The impulses from Kierkegaard's attack on the State Church thus penetrated (presumably via Brandes) deep into the political groups, which otherwise shared neither goal nor life view with him. This, however, did not change the general picture of Kierkegaard as someone who right up to the period between the wars marked a fork in the road between, on the one side, cultural radicalism and the workers' movement, and theology and the Church on the other. In the period between the wars, cultural radicalism stood in an entirely different situation, and after the death of Brandes and Høffding, they were no longer conceived as provocateurs by the ecclesiastical camp, among other things due to a less narrow-minded, feeling-oriented religiosity, but also due to *Tidehverv*. Danish cultural anticlericalism in the 1930s no longer invoked Kierkegaard but was to a much larger degree allied with left socialism. Further the Social Democrats (who were in power without interruption from 1929) and Det Radikale Venstre changed their Church policy in the direction of an orientation towards the Danish National Evangelical Lutheran Church. A continuation of the late Kierkegaard criticism of the Church was by and large muted. *Tidehverv*, to be sure, made capital of him in their protest against clericalism, but without bringing the polemic into the context of a general criticism of the Danish National Evangelical Lutheran Church.[241]

---

[239]   Cf. the anthology *Den kulturradikale udfordring*, Copenhagen: Tiderne Skifter 2001, p. 32; pp. 223–4 (with articles from, among others, Ebbe Kløvedal Reich and Jan Lindhardt). See also Sven Ove Gade, *Ulanen. En biografi om Victor Andreasen*, Copenhagen: Gyldendal 2002.

[240]   C.E. Jensen and F.J. Borgbjerg, *Socialdemokratiets Aarhundrede*, vols. 1–2, Copenhagen: Christiansen 1904, p. 150 (the entire section on Kierkegaard is found on pp. 142–50).

[241]   Cf. Jens Holger Schjørring, "Kierkegaard und die dänische Theologie der zwanziger und dreißiger Jahre," in *Die Rezeption Søren Kierkegaards in der deutschen und dänischen Philosophie und Theologie. Vorträge des Kolloquiums am 22. und 23. März 1982*, pp. 171–85.

The postwar period's and especially the 1960s' dramatic rise in welfare gave cultural radicalism a new front in the form of the spreading "pop culture," which had a sharp critic in, for example, the architect Poul Henningsen (1894–1967). Henningsen was regarded as Georg Brandes' most talented successor, but in Henningsen his forerunner's wrestling with and respect for Kierkegaard seems to have completely disappeared. On occasion of the publication of the pocketbook edition of Kierkegaard's *Samlede Værker* (*SV3*), he writes in a feature article with the title "From Golden Age to Panduro" in *Politiken* on April 1, 1963:

> It has been emphasized as a bright spot of hope in the midst of the pop age that Søren Kierkegaard as a pocketbook has almost become a best seller. This makes me anxious. For whatever philosophers and specialists can get out of Kierkegaard, I think that ordinary people—and it is them that are important in a democracy—will not be able to squeeze one drop of intellectual nourishment out of him. He can make one's bookshelf more beautiful, but it is my serious hope that no one will read him.[242]

This worry on behalf of ordinary people has its counterpart in, for example, Jørgen Bukdahl's *Søren Kierkegaard and the Common Man*, which, as we have already seen, demonstrates to what a high degree Kierkegaard had something to offer to the common man. When cultural radicalism and its spiritual heir, new radicalism, at this time—during the construction of the welfare state—had problems with Kierkegaard, it should be seen in the light of his alleged political indifference. From a political perspective, Kierkegaard, as noted, was no longer interesting as a critic of the Church, but instead his many statements about only wanting to change the person "inwardly" and let everything external stand untouched became a stumbling block for the age's leading intellectuals, who stood behind the welfare reforms. The issue was treated by Jørgen K. Bukdahl (the son of Jørgen Bukdahl) in a series of articles entitled "The folk high school and new radicalism" from 1965. Bukdahl traces Kierkegaard's rejection of social and political reforms back to his radical separation of the inner and the outer. The understanding of this separation is, according to Bukdahl, "the salient point in any Kierkegaard research." He writes further:

> Is the "inward" synonymous with the intense experience and inwardness to which one can retreat in indifference for the social-political environment? Or is the "inward" not a mental space at all where one can live in self-indulgent inwardness? Is it not rather—as I would like to understand Kierkegaard's texts—a direction of the will, namely a willingness to takes one's situation, including the political and social conditions, "seriously" as one's own?[243]

---

[242]   "Fra guldalder til Panduro," quotation from Poul Henningsen, *Kulturkritik*, vols. 1–4, ed. by Carl Erik Bay and Olav Harsløf, Copenhagen: Rhodos 1973–79, vol. 4 (*1956–57*), p. 119. Against the same background and in the same style the illustrator and author Hans Bendix (1898–1984) describes how Kierkegaard "today puts our culturally infected public into an ecstatic impotence." Cf. "Om at skille sig af med bøger," *Politiken*, December 18, 1965.
[243]   Jørgen K. Bukdahl, "Højskolen og nyradikalismen III: Forkundskaber for eksistensen," in his *Frihed og frigørelse*, p. 95.

In the context Bukdahl writes this critically with Knud Hansen in mind, but he also mentions Villy Sørensen ("the person most conscious of the problems and least dogmatic of the new radicals"). Villy Sørensen shares features with much traditional cultural radicalism, but constitutes at many points a corrective to it, for example, on the strength of his positive view of the value of religious and mythological symbols as knowledge and on the strength of his far more nuanced view of Kierkegaard. Sørensen stands out as one of the period's foremost spokesmen for (the idea behind) the welfare state and, on the whole, one of the most important thinkers of democracy in Denmark, but precisely when the issue concerns the relation to democracy and its possible content, he also has substantial objections to Kierkegaard. This is best treated by skipping forward to the new political situation after the fall of the Berlin wall.[244]

In 1990 the editor Henning Fonsmark (1926–2006) published his grand critical analysis of the Danish welfare model, *The History of the Danish Utopia*.[245] The book is a fierce analysis of the construction—and exaggeration—of the Danes' highly praised welfare democracy, whose "utopia," according to Fonsmark, consists in the fact that it is encumbered by the economic disadvantage that it can only be kept going by the uninterrupted incurring of debts. In Fonsmark's interpretation the patronizing Danish welfare state is an ideological fusion of Grundtvig and Marx, but in the book's postscript Kierkegaard is introduced into the discussion. This takes place against the background of Johannes Sløk's *This Society!* (1989),[246] which seeks to explicate and make topical Kierkegaard's criticism of democracy from the perspective of an express dissatisfaction with the obviousness and self-satisfaction with which democracy today is made into the sole sacred form of government. According to Sløk, Kierkegaard is, from a certain perspective, in an eminent sense a political thinker, and when Kierkegaard/Sløk reject democracy as a form of government, it is because of the "human fear" and the levelling of differences, which, according to them, is attached to the very essence of democracy, and by making the individuals into "masses" gives them fewer and fewer possibilities to be "private" or "themselves" as individuals. Sløk's alternative to democracy is not dictatorship but enlightened despotism or preferably an anarchic community, where the concept of power is done away with. He is aware that Kierkegaard himself did not use the word "anarchy," but he nonetheless interprets Kierkegaard's attack on

---

[244]   Here I leave out the important relation between Kierkegaard and Karl Marx, which is treated in several places in Villy Sørensen, but also in Knud Hansen, Jørgen K. Bukdahl and Kresten Nordentoft (see also section VI.A). The essence of the issue is, as it is presented by, for example, Kresten Nordentoft, *"Hvad siger Brand-Majoren?" Kierkegaards opgør med sin samtid*, Copenhagen: G.E.C. Gad 1973, that the two supplement one another: the critic of the age Kierkegaard, presents the occasion and the invitation to a dialogue with the critic of society Marx, and the possibility of dialogue lies first and foremost in the relation between the (social)psychologist Kierkegaard and the critic of ideology Marx. However, it is important to emphasize that the age's (the 1960s) attempt to bring Kierkegaard into dialogue with Marx, took place on Marx's premises: Kierkegaard not only can but *must* be supplemented by Marx.

[245]   Henning Fonsmark, *Historien om den danske utopi*, Copenhagen: Gyldendal 1990.

[246]   Johannes Sløk, *Det her samfund!*, Viby J.: Centrum 1989.

the Church in this direction and ascribes to him a view of the Christian Church in the original Lutheran sense as an anarchic model.

When Henning Fonsmark, from his side, uses Sløk/Kierkegaard, it is not to reject democracy but to sharpen his own criticism of the negative effects of democratic government. In addition, there is a polemic against a "qualitative" conception of democracy, which in its time was carried out by Hal Koch in a discussion with the legal positivist Alf Ross (cf. the books *What is Democracy?* from 1945, *Why Democracy?* from 1946, and *Nordic Democracy* from 1949)[247] along with Villy Sørensen's conception of democracy which is related to Koch's and, among other things, is based on a criticism of Kierkegaard's view that all people (in spite of all outward differences) are equal with respect to the most important things in life. Villy Sørensen expresses his criticism of Kierkegaard on this point in a very strong manner and, for example (in a comment to *Tidehverv*'s Børge Diderichsen in 1963) juxtaposes "Søren Kierkegaard and the children who worked themselves to death in the English factories at the same time as he was writing *Works of Love*."[248]

The point here is that, according to Sørensen, it does not make sense to demand a Kierkegaardian struggle for existence of a human being, unless certain social and material presuppositions have been fulfilled. Sørensen can thus, on the one hand, recognize Jørgen Bukdahl's indication of the social view in Kierkegaard's attack on the Church, but at the same time criticize the fact that the social in Kierkegaard is exclusively regarded as an "external spectacle": if the social is the goal, then "it is strange that the existentially concerned person is worried so little about it along the way—especially when the goal is never really achieved!" For Villy Sørensen, the point of the welfare state (in its correct form) is that the person is to be liberated for a spiritual life, that which Kierkegaard is interested in, and the fact that Kierkegaard's works have found such great currency in our time (and only in our time, that is, after the Second World War) suggests, according to Sørensen, that precisely the social development has made the existential issue more urgent. Put differently:

> when Kierkegaard is understood better in our time than in his own, the reason is that the development has proven him correct—and proven him incorrect in his view of the development. Only when society no longer places substantial obstacles in the way of the individual's free unfolding, is it possible for the individual to regard the entire social sphere as something inessential—and to conceive it with the same indifference as Kierkegaard himself did.[249]

Villy Sørensen carries this criticism further in a negative interpretation of the 1990s' great interest in Kierkegaard since, according to him, it suggests a spirit of the age which refuses to recognize the both/and of reality, its aggregate nature and

---

[247]   Hal Koch, *Hvad er Demokrati?*, Copenhagen: Gyldendal 1945; Alf Ross, *Hvorfor Demokrati?*, Copenhagen: Munksgaard 1946 and *Nordisk Demokrati*, ed. by Hal Koch and Alf Ross, Copenhagen: Westermann 1949.

[248]   Cf. *Vindrosen*, no. 6, 1963, p. 501.

[249]   Villy Sørensen, "Den abstrakte eksistens," in *Mellem fortid og fremtid—Kronikker og kommentarer*, p. 115.

compromises. The self-realizing individual in the market-based society imagines—just like Kierkegaard's esthete and ultimately like Kierkegaard himself—that he can take a short-cut from the personal reality to the religious sphere of existence (Sørensen calls it "the source of values" or "the force") by evading the common social-ethical reality—which is left to the market. When one in this manner runs across the social and does not want to know about its conflicts and compromises, it is, according to Sørensen, only logical that one ends up, like Kierkegaard, with "a rather cramped form of Christianity: the cultivation of the paradox."[250] Here one recognizes a criticism in the tradition from Brandes and Høffding, for whom Kierkegaard in reality neglected the ethical stage.[251]

Villy Sørensen's double criticism of contemporary society and Kierkegaard points to another example of a political neoliberal use of Kierkegaard in the wake of the collapse of communism, namely the Venstre politician and current prime minister (from 2001) Anders Fogh Rasmussen's *From the Social State to the Minimal State* (1993),[252] which likewise uses Kierkegaard (in Sløk's version) in his criticism of the welfare state's "slave morality" and flight from responsibility. In the political context, one should also mention the *Tidehverv* pastor and member of parliament for the Dansk Folkeparti, Søren Krarup (b. 1937), who in a long series of books has used Kierkegaard in his criticism of the welfare state's human rights-cultivating "democratism" (in among others, the book of the same name from 1968). The entire political and social conception of a human being as a function of society or a political- and class-determined being is decisively contradicted, according to Krarup, by Christianity and by Kierkegaard. In the postscript to the second edition of *The Modern Debacle 1789–1984* from 2001 (first edition 1984), Krarup further criticizes "Georg Brandes' misrepresentation of Søren Kierkegaard," a misrepresentation, which, according to Krarup, is again dominant in Denmark with Peter Thielst and Joakim Garff as heirs. Instead he emphasizes the Kierkegaard interpretations of K. Olesen Larsen and Anders Kingo.[253]

---

[250]   Cf. *Med Villy i midten—28 vidnesbyrd om Villy Sørensen*, ed. by Suzanne Brøgger, Erling Groth et al., Copenhagen: Gyldendal 2004, pp. 314–15.

[251]   In the postscript to the second edition of his detailed analysis of Jesus from 1993, Villy Sørensen gives his own account of the relation between the ethical and the religious in a criticism of Kierkegaard's *Fear and Trembling*. Sørensen writes in his conclusion: "If Jesus—as the gospels imply—broke with his family in order to follow his calling, it is an example of what in Kierkegaard is called an absolute duty towards God—and a better example than Kierkegaard's own in *Fear and Trembling*: Abraham who receives the command from Yahweh to sacrifice his son and obeys. The two examples show precisely the distance between the god of power, who demands blind obedience, and a god who is a 'father' to all human beings so that one's duties are not limited to one's closest family. Jesus' religiosity was not a 'suspension of the ethical,' but a sharpening of it, so that the difference between the ethical and the special religious is—that the religious is the special ethical." *Jesus og Kristus*, Copenhagen: Gyldendal 1993, p. 256.

[252]   Anders Fogh Rasmussen, *Fra socialstat til minimalstat*, Copenhagen: Samleren 1993.

[253]   Søren Krarup, *Det moderne sammenbrud 1789–1984*, Copenhagen: Gyldendal 1984. 2nd ed. 2001, see pp. 17–22; pp. 82–93; pp. 220–4. A chapter from the first edition of *Det*

VII. Kierkegaard in the Most Recent Times (1989–2005)

A. Literary Readings

In the last decade Kierkegaard, as mentioned, has been the object of literary readings, a displacement of attention from the epistemological to the rhetorical, or, if one will, from the categorical to the discursive (from *what* to *how*).

A main representative is Joakim Garff's *"The Insomniac"* from 1995,[254] which wants to "demonstrate the authorship's inner oppositions from its own presuppositions and reveal intended oppositions' unintended merging"—a deconstructive reading, which is supplemented by a reconstructive, diachronous movement, in that the authorship is read as a continuous text "against the grain of and in spite of the guidelines which Kierkegaard himself gave for the correct reading."[255] In this way Garff succeeds in combining a text-immanent reading of the individual works with an understanding of the whole of the course of the authorship. It is important for Garff to show the presence of the aesthetic in the religious, but also the divergence of the inner and the outer, the fluctuation between maieutic and action along with the (mis)relation between image (*billede*) and model (*forbillede*) is treated. As an example of the desire to let Kierkegaard's visible-making rhetoric negate his philosophical intention, one can mention the analysis of the *Fragments*. Here Garff is attentive to the "subtext," which in many places in a dialogue with an imagined reader is revealed as the New Testament narrative. When Climacus, for example, describes the forms of appearance of offense, it is, according to Garff, clear that the presentation to a greater extent draws on and stems from the narrative, which the project has as a silent reference, than the project itself. The philosophical intention is thus undercut when the absence of a distinguishing sign of God is filled out with the underlying narrative's distinguishing sign, which also shows itself in the use of erotic metaphors, foreign to the project's epistemological intention. Climacus' unmasking of the New Testament Jesus figure to the "absolute paradox," and an unperceivable object for "faith's autopsy" is moreover an expression for and consequence of an iconoclasm, which at the same time explains why almost no textual figures appear except a few exceptionally stylized ones. The presence of

---

moderne Sammenbrud about Georg Brandes and Kierkegaard printed in *Information* on March 26, 1984 set off an exchange of opinions between Krarup and the Brandes biographer Jørgen Knudsen, which demonstrates how much ideological dynamite there still is in (the judgment of) Brandes' book on Kierkegaard. See Søren Krarup, "Den store modstander," *Information*, March 26, 1984; Jørgen Knudsen, "Subjektiviteten der er sandhed—partiskheden der gør dum," *Information*, April, 3, 1984; Søren Krarup, "Brandes og det moderne sammenbrud," *Information*, April 11, 1984; Jørgen Knudsen, "Selvudfoldelse og gentagelsestvang," *Information*, April 30, 1984; and Søren Krarup, "Den kulturradikale illusion," *Information*, May 7, 1984.

[254]   Joakim Garff, *"Den Søvnløse". Kierkegaard læst æstetisk/biografisk*, Copenhagen: C.A. Reitzel 1995.

[255]   Ibid., p. 11.

presence [*nærværets præsens*] should not be lost in the picture's representation as he writes.[256]

As a more traditional oppositional piece to Garff, one can mention Anders Kingo's book *The Theology of Analogy*, also from 1995. Kingo (b. 1955) accuses Garff of writing from "the perspective of observation" and for searching for the interpretive key to the authorship, somewhat like the liberal theologians sought for the historical Jesus. Kingo's own reading is neither philosophical, psychological nor aesthetic, but places itself in the tradition of K. Olesen Larsen's systematic-theological interpretation. The Climacus writings occupy in this tradition a special place and constitute for Kingo the basis for the correct categorial understanding of Kierkegaard, in that Kierkegaard's use of concepts is precisely regarded as conditioned by the category and not vice versa. Kingo's concept of analogy is derived from the absolute paradox, and Kierkegaard is given credit for an analogy thinking, which is neither classical nor modern, since he "wants out of the analogy of deception and forward to the paradox's own analogy: the analogy, which paradoxically is no analogy."[257]

Another work, whose main points are to be briefly discussed, is Lars Erslev Andersen's *Beyond Irony* (1995).[258] Here Kierkegaard is placed in a modern text-theoretical context, which makes his texts into a kind of anticipation of Derrida's critiques. Kierkegaard's discourse finds itself, according to Erslev Andersen (b. 1956), on the border between a kind of text which seeks to win back an original meaning in the text, and a pragmatic text form, whose radical challenge is that there are no texts. This intermediary position characterizes Kierkegaard's special openness for the mobility of existence and language. The concept of "the moment" therefore becomes, for Erslev Andersen, a key figure, because it precisely has this diffuse instantaneousness, openness, and movement within itself. With support in Derrida's notion of a trace's movement in a game of difference, delay, and postponement—what Derrida calls *différance*—Erslev Andersen defines "the moment" as a figure for nonpresence, seeing that it shows itself as a determinable chasm, distance, or an intermediary space. The openness of indeterminacy Erslev Andersen sees as

---

[256]   Ibid., pp. 179–95; p. 404.

[257]   Cf. Anders Kingo, *Analogiens teologi. En dogmatisk studie over dialektikken i Søren Kierkegaards opbyggelige og pseudonyme forfatterskab*, Copenhagen: Gad 1995, p. 157. For a thorough critical account of Kingo's work, see Søren Bruun's review in *Kierkegaardiana*, vol. 18, 1996, pp. 230–8; and Arne Grøn, "Kierkegaards forudsætning," *Dansk Teologisk Tidsskrift*, vol. 58, 1995, pp. 267–90. On the Garff–Kingo opposition—and a possible overcoming of this opposition—see also Bo Kampmann Walther, *Øjeblik og tavshed—Læsninger i Søren Kierkegaards forfatterskab*, Odense: Odense Universitetsforlag 2002, pp. 20ff. Walther, in his investigations of the metaphor of the moment, also takes up the *Fragments*, whose repeated attempts to anchor the Christian ideality in the in principle imperceptable and uninterpretable in his account points to a feeling of homelessness or gnosis conditioned by modernity. See ibid., p. 187.

[258]   Lars Erslev Andersen, *Hinsides ironi. Fire essays om Søren Kierkegaard*, Aalborg: Nordisk Sommeruniversitet 1995.

something positive, namely, as a possibility for a Barthes-inspired pact between text and reader.[259]

Isak Winkel Holm's work *Thought in the Image. Kierkegaard's poetics* (1998) should also be mentioned. When Joakim Garff in *"The Insomniac"* wanted to examine the Kierkegaardian text's own "aesthetic," the concept of aesthetics took on the meaning of rhetoric with a conscious distancing of the theoretical "doctrine of the beautiful," a distancing which one also finds in Garff's, Poul Erik Tøjner's and Jørgen Dehs' *Kierkegaard's Asethetics* (1995), which by way of introduction draws attention to the fact that what in their book is treated as the aesthetic, is what Kierkegaard develops *"with* his work and *in* his work." Therefore, there is no talk of "an overview of the statements about art and aesthetic questions, which are found here and there in the authorship and the posthumous papers."[260] Winkel Holm (b. 1965) distinguishes himself from this tradition of aesthetic Kierkegaard readings by precisely using the concept of aesthetics in its theoretical sense, and the seeking out of the authorship's aesthetic-theoretic statements, which Garff, Tøjner and Dehs decline to do, he undertakes with the result that he can ascertain that Kierkegaard actually did not have an aesthetics, or more precisely, the aesthetics which Kierkegaard had was a copied form of the age's idealist aesthetics. The interesting thing now is that underneath the traditional art-theoretical statements there hides another more independent aesthetic theory, which is the treatise's discovery and main concern. "Kierkegaard's poetics" thus refers to the concrete experiences which Kierkegaard had as an author, a poetics which does not constitute any "explicit construction of a theory" but "rather an implicit poetological layer in the text, which must be meticulously laid bare with a hermeneutical excavation."[261] Central in the investigation stands "the collision between warm images and dry concepts," and Winkel Holm distinguishes here among four positions in the conception of Kierkegaard's literary images: the reductive (Villy Sørensen), the harmonizing (Billeskov Jansen), the contextualizing (Jørgen Dehs and George Pattison), and finally the problematizing (Garff and Adorno), while Winkel Holm's own approach is described as related to the contextualizing and the problematizing without really properly belonging to either of them.[262]

Lasse Horne Kjældgaard (b. 1974) in his *Between One Another* (2001)[263] has investigated the relation between tableau and narrative in Kierkegaard's pseudonymous writings against the background of especially Lessing's famous

---

[259]   My account is indebted to Walther, *Øjeblik og tavshed* , pp. 20–1, who also points to H.C. Wind's comparisons of Kierkegaard with Derrida. (See H.C. Wind, *Religion og kommunikation: teologisk hermeneuik*, Århus: Aarhus Universitetsforlag 1987.)

[260]   Joakim Garff, Poul Erik Tøjner and Jørgen Dehs, *Kierkegaards æstetik*, Copenhagen: Samlerens Bogklub 1995, pp. 7–8. Jørgen Dehs must, however, be exempted in this context since he, in several articles, places Kierkegaard's criticism of the aesthetics of the beautiful in connection with Kant's theory of the sublime.

[261]   Isak Winkel Holm, *Tanken i billedet. Kierkegaards poetik*, Copenhagen: Gyldendal 1998, p. 12.

[262]   Ibid., pp. 41ff.

[263]   Lasse Horne Kjældgaard, *Mellemhverandre: tableau og fortælling i Søren Kierkegaards pseudonyme skrifter*, Hellerup: Spring 2001.

treatise *Laokoon*, but Kjældgaard's interest is not exclusively aesthetic since he insists that aesthetic readings of Kierkegaard's writings must go hand-in-hand with historical readings. With this double view he establishes, among other things, a cultural-historical connection between the tableaus in the pseudonymous writings and the fascination with the tableau in the rest of the culture of the time—a connection which one with Kjældgaard's own book as an example is tempted to see repeated in the history of reception. Kjældgaard's book can be regarded as an expression of a new historicism in Kierkegaard research, which, among other things, is directed towards a contextualizing of the authorship. This endeavor will presumably find a further foothold in pace with the publication of *Søren Kierkegaards Skrifter*, whose commentaries make easier the access to Kierkegaard's literary, philosophical, and theological contemporaries.

B. Theory of Subjectivity and Ethics

The uncovering of the poetological, rhetorical, and metaphorical dimensions in Kierkegaard's work serves to show an ambiguity and complexity in the authorship, which traditional research has not been sufficiently attentive to.[264] Arne Grøn's treatise *Subjectivity and Negativity. Kierkegaard* (1997)[265] joins with its attention to Kierkegaard's special "phenomenological" method (the analysis of consciousness' various movements, positions, and figures) the textually oriented procedure, but, further, distinguishes itself from the critical, literary approach by a penetrating, almost meditative style, (re)presenting Kierkegaard's position as a thinker of subjectivity. Grøn (b. 1952) takes his point of departure in Johannes Climacus' statement from the *Concluding Unscientific Postscript* that the religious categories belong to the theory of subjectivity, but he hesitates to call his approach a reconstruction of a *theory*. When Kierkegaard can be categorized under the rubric of what one broadly calls "the philosophy of the subject," it should be modified since this designation above all refers to the key position of the subject in the thought from Descartes to Husserl, while Kierkegaard's position is thematically related to a far older tradition, where the individual is seen from a religious perspective, more precisely, in the light of the possibility of salvation and perdition. The book is clearly stamped with motifs which are associated with the influential, polemically determined readings of Kierkegaard, for example, Adorno's claim about the "objectless inwardness" and Løgstrup's rejection of Kierkegaard's understanding of the love of the neighbor as a way of keeping the neighbour at a distance. Grøn shows, by contrast, how one can read in Kierkegaard an experience-oriented and socially mediated concept of subjectivity, which acquits him of the charges of abstract individualism and for having a decisionistic ethics. On the contrary, the constitution of the individual in Kierkegaard is build on a dialogical principle, and Grøn makes use, above all of *The Sickness unto Death* in his account, a book which functions as the "*Grundtext*"

---

[264]   See also Walther, *Øjeblik og tavshed—Læsninger i Søren Kierkegaards forfatterskab*, and Jacob Bøggild, *Ironiens tænker: Tænkningens ironi. Kierkegaard læst retorisk*, Copenhagen: Museum Tusculanum 2002.

[265]   Arne Grøn, *Subjektivitet og negativitet: Kierkegaard*, Copenhagen: Gyldendal 1997.

for Grøn's treatise and is called Kierkegaard's "philosophical and theological main work" with its exemplary analysis of his understanding of subjectivity.

The dialogical or intersubjective element in Kierkegaard's thought is also in focus in more recent attempts to rehabilitate Kierkegaard as an ethical thinker. In Pia Søltoft's treatise *Ethics of Dizziness* (2000)[266] the dialogue-philosophical challenge of Martin Buber (*I and Thou*, 1923) and Emmanuel Lévinas (*Totality and Infinity*, 1961) is taken up critically as a prelude to an interpretation of Kierkegaard's various tentative efforts and definitions of the relation between subjectivity and intersubjectivity.[267] While for Søltoft (b. 1963) it is not only Buber's and Lévinas' criticism of Kierkegaard which is interesting but just as much their broader criticism of the entire Cartesian tradition's determination of subjectivity, the situation is just the opposite in Klaus Wivel (b. 1971). In his *Next to Nothing. A Jewish Criticism of Søren Kierkegaard* (1999) he goes through Lévinas' and Franz Rosenzweig's (*The Star of Redemption*, 1921) criticism with a different conclusion. The two Jewish thinkers' interpretation of Kierkegaard's Christianity as unethical and selfish and his philosophy, with all its consistency, as a justification of violence and terrorism is read into Kierkegaard's own works (*Fear and Trembling* and *Works of Love*) in order to seek an answer to the background for such harsh claims. Wivel argues that Kierkegaard is far from being the spokesman for the individual that he has been turned into: "In his thought the individual constitutes merely a name, a dash—and it is the Christian's mission to realize and continually struggle against the self-deception that he is something in himself."[268]

C. Kierkegaard with No End in Sight

The explosive growth in Danish literature on Kierkegaard in the 1990s is paralleled by a corresponding growth in international research. In 1996 Ole Morsing saw the need to publish a "book about the books," which covers Danish Kierkegaard literature in the 1990s (a stack of books 54.7 centimeters high and weighing 12.3 kg) featuring the entire spectrum from introductions and "Kierkegaard for children and young people" to the most recent presentation of "Søren Kierkegaard's secret" and his view of "the woman" and "womanhood," to some of the long treatises, which we have examined above.[269] After Morsing's efforts to get a hold

---

[266]   Pia Søltoft, *Svimmelhedens Etik. Om forholdet mellem den enkelte og den anden hos Buber, Lévinas og især Kierkegaard*, Copenhagen: Gads Forlag 2000.

[267]   A similar undertaking is found in Wenche Marit Quist, *Den enkelte og det mellemmenneskelige—den etiske betydning af det mellemmenneskelige forhold hos Søren Kierkegaard*, Copenhagen: C.A. Reitzel 2000.

[268]   Klaus Wivel, *Næsten Intet. En jødisk kritik af Søren Kierkegaard*, Copenhagen: C.A. Reitzel 1999, pp. 11–12. In addition to Søltoft and Wivel, the theologian and philosopher Peter Kemp (b. 1937) has also been occupied with the relation between Lévinas and Kierkegaard. See, for example, Peter Kemp, "Sprogets etik: fra Lévinas til Kierkegaard," in *Denne Slyngelagtige Eftertid. Tekster om Søren Kierkegaard*, vols. 1–3, ed. by Finn Frandsen and Ole Morsing, Århus: Slagmark 1995, vol. 2, pp. 315–47.

[269]   Ole Morsing, *Sprækker til det uendelige? Søren Kierkegaard i 1990'erne—en bog om bøgerne*, Århus: Slagmark 1996. The books in question are: Peter Thielst, *Livet forstås*

on the wide range of literature, the tempo and number of Kierkegaard-related publications has in no way diminished.²⁷⁰ In this context one should also mention the discussion about whether central Kierkegaard texts should be "translated" into modern Danish, since Danes today find themselves in the awkward situation that Kierkegaard's Golden Age language is often more inaccessible than, for example, a modern English translation (there has been a similar debate about H.C. Andersen).²⁷¹

An institutional expression for the profound new interest and a further stimulation for scholarly work on Kierkegaard can be seen in the foundation of the Søren Kierkegaard Research Centre (SKC) in Copenhagen in 1994. The Centre was established with a grant from the Danish National Research Foundation (on the initiative of Niels Jørgen Cappelørn) with two main objectives: (1) to promote Kierkegaard research nationally and internationally from both literary, theological and philosophical perspectives, and (2) to create a complete new edition of everything that has survived from Søren Kierkegaard's hand. The new historical-critical edition, *Søren Kierkegaards Skrifter*, will come to consist in 55 volumes, 28 with Kierkegaard's texts and 27 with philological accounts of the texts and explanatory notes—at present (spring 2008) 39 of the 55 volumes have appeared. Since the beginning, the Centre has permanently housed around 30 people—including the commentators and philologists working on the new edition—from numerous countries who work on a wide range of research and translation projects. The Centre also produces the two international publication series, the *Kierkegaard Studies. Yearbook* and the *Kierkegaard Studies. Monograph Series* (Berlin/New York).

In a situation of this kind, it is somewhat artificial to isolate the special Danish reception from the international reception (indeed, if this has ever made any sense). However, a debate should be mentioned that took place in the summer of 2004 which, with its impact in the printed media, demonstrates how much explosiveness there still is in the Danish context in the nation's only truly internationally recognized thinker. In a long article in the newspaper *Information* on July 24–5, 2004, the philosopher Peter Tudvad (b. 1966) attacked Joakim Garff's widely recognized and prize-winning biography from 2000, *SAK. Søren Aabye Kierkegaard. A Biography*, under the title "SAK—an Unscholarly Biography about Søren A. Kierkegaard."²⁷² The criticism, which was not just aimed at Garff but at the entire "research tradition he builds on,"

baglæns, men må leves forlæns, Copenhagen: Gyldendal 1994; Jens Estrup, *Vælg dig Selv. En bog om Søren Kierkegaard til unge*, Copenhagen: C.A. Reitzel 1995; Leif Bork Hansen, *Søren Kierkegaards hemmelighed og eksistensdialektik*, Copenhagen: C.A. Reitzel 1994; Birgit Bertung, *Kierkegaard, kristendom og konsekvens. Søren Kierkegaard læst logisk*, Copenhagen: C.A. Reitzel 1994.

²⁷⁰   As a most recent offshoot one can mention that Kierkegaard is now also used in modern theories on leadership in business; cf. Kirstine Andersen, *Kierkegaard og ledelse*, Copenhagen: Frydenlund 2004.

²⁷¹   An attempt to modernize Kierkegaard's Danish has been done in the collection of texts *Lykkens dør går udad. Søren Kierkegaard-tekster på nudansk*, ed. by Peter Thielst, Copenhagen: Gyldendal 1995.

²⁷²   Peter Tudvad, "SAK—en uvidenskabelig biografi om Søren A. Kierkegaard," *Information*, July 24–5, 2004. Garff's biography was honored with both the Georg Brandes

concerns generally the lack of use of primary sources, Garff's reliance on secondary literature as source material (sometimes even without referencing this literature), and the portrayal of Kierkegaard (as a dandy) which the biography, according to Tudvad, gives. One after another Tudvad critically reviews the presentation of the so-called Jutland journey, Kierkegaard's relations to the carpenter Strube, to the rector of the Borgerdydsskole Michael Nielsen, the Freudian interpretation of Kierkegaard's use of the signature "Farinelli," Kierkegaard's alleged tight-fistedness in giving alms, and some linguistic misunderstandings. Tudvad ends by condemning *SAK* for being "botched, plagiarized, sloppy, methodologically inconsistent, overinterpreted and containing inadequate knowledge of then contemporary life."

It was both a recognition of Tudvad's impressive archival work, which also came to expression in his topographical monograph, published the same summer, *Kierkegaard's Copenhagen* (2004),[273] and the general sense of a lack of fit between the premises and the concluding judgment about *SAK* and its author that spawned one article after the next in the Danish newspapers in the weeks (and indeed months) that followed.[274] Joakim Garff himself replied in an article entitled "The Price of Popularization" in *Politiken* on August 7, where he rejects having presented and launched *SAK* as a scholarly biography and argues that Tudvad has misunderstood the biography genre, which is to be conceived more as a narrative than as a "scholarly" presentation in the source-critical sense.[275] The subsequent debate, which involved researchers, writers, newspaper readers, and all kinds of laymen, had, in addition, as an inevitable element on its agenda the question of how much an author's picture of Kierkegaard is determined by his or her own psychology, but also a return of the more fundamental question of principle about the correctness and meaning of a biographical approach to an author like Kierkegaard, along with the larger question of what kind of scholarship the field of history should undertake. Even 150 years after his death Søren Kierkegaard seems to be more present than ever.[276]

---

prize and *Weekendavisen*'s literature prize. Tudvad had issued his criticism before (in 2001), but only with the article in *Information* did the debate take off.

[273] Peter Tudvad, *Kierkegaards København*, Copenhagen: Politiken 2004.

[274] In the lead article on July 28, in *Berlingske Tidende* a clear statement about the matter was even demanded of Niels Jørgen Cappelørn, who in his capacity as director of the Søren Kierkegaard Research Centre and the employer of both Garff and Tudvad, was expected to publicly take a position on this conflict between colleagues—and when Cappelørn made his statement in, among other places, *Jyllands-Posten* on July 30, the debate quickly took a turn in the direction of how scholarly milieus generally tackle internal controversies. The Tudvad–Garff affair was revived again in August 2005, when the professor of philosophy M.G. Piety, on occasion of the English translation of *SAK*, repeated Tudvad's criticism of the book. The following Danish debate ended with Peter Tudvad resigning from his position as commentator at the Centre.

[275] Joakim Garff, "Formidlingens pris," *Politiken*, August 7, 2004.

[276] One can also think of the media attention that was created when *Regine Olsens dagbog* was published in 2001. The diary was billed as a sensational newly discovered manuscript, which had for a long time been in the private property of a Dane formerly living abroad, whose grandfather in the fall of 1896 had bought a book about the Danish King Christian the Second, which contained the unimpressive manuscript of the diary. The diary paints a picture

D. Kierkegaard and Grundtvig—an Old Opposition in a New Dialogue

> One would have to look for a long time to find a starker contrast than these two Dioskuri in
> Danish culture. The one, naive in the deepest sense of the word, the other nothing but self-
> reflection and calculation, the one creative, the other wholly self-indulgent, the one wholly
> extroverted, vigorous, generous to the tips of his fingers, the other occupied with a single
> thing, himself, such that he conceived of himself as a demand on the environment.[277]

The historian of religion Vilhelms Grønbech's comparison of Grundtvig and
Kierkegaard in the book *The Struggle for Man* from 1930 is probably the strongest
expression of the view that the two great Danish theologians and intellectual
personalities of the nineteenth century were irreconcilable opposites. It is clear from
the quotation where Grønbech's own sympathies lie. While Kierkegaard, according
to Grønbech, turns his view backward and sings a requiem for a decrepit culture,
Grundtvig looks forward to a new realm beyond Protestantism and Catholicism—
while Kierkegaard plays to the heart's lonely song, Grundtvig writes poetry which
enjoins the modern world's split to a common song and points forward to a new
culture and a humanity, which "will choose society instead of isolation, demand the
choir and the march instead of moods at sunset, preferring life instead of observation
and enjoyment of life."[278]

There can hardly be any doubt that in the midst of the cultural struggle between
the wars, one felt a more urgent demand to take clear sides in the Grundtvig–
Kierkegaard debate than was the case in the less radicalized period that followed,
but one does not need to introduce special historical circumstances to explain
the widespread conception of the two as antagonists. The difference seems to
immediately jump out at one—Grundtvig thinks in social categories such as
the congregation and the people, while Kierkegaard speaks of the individual.
Grundtvig's Christianity is tied to history and the nation, while Kierkegaard's is
tied to the moment and the paradox. Grundtvig operates with an idea of growth and
regards the human and the Christian as continuous, while Kierkegaard develops
the category of the leap and makes sharp distinctions, etc. Moreover, their mutual
criticism is well-documented, namely in Kierkegaard's texts. His critical account
of Grundtvig's theory of the Church in the *Concluding Unscientific Postscript*
is well known.[279] Less well known perhaps are his many critical statements and
caricatured portraits of Grundtvig in the journals. Only relatively late has research

---

of Regine Olsen in the years 1840–41 as a naive, but intelligent high bourgeois daughter and
gives the impression that it was she and not Søren Kierkegaard, who took the initiative in
breaking off their engagement. Later (in September 2004) the author and journalist Flemming
Christian Nielsen confessed to being the author of this fiction, which was allegedly written on
a beach in Tunisia.

[277]   Vilhelm Grønbech, *Kampen om Mennesket*, Copenhagen and Oslo: Jespersen og Pios
Forlag 1930, p. 186.

[278]   Ibid., p. 202. Grønbech (1873–1948) exerted a great influence on the spiritual life of
the period between the wars (and later on the period of the student revolts), and in his work
one finds a picture of Kierkegaard which recalls, for example, Knud Hansen's (or the other
way around—Hansen was in his youth a zealous auditor at Grønbech's lectures).

[279]   See *SKS* 7, 41ff. / *CUP1*, 34ff.

begun to seriously occupy itself with the possible points of commonality in the efforts of the two men. As Hellmut Toftdahl pointed out in 1969, works about the Kierkegaard–Grundtvig relation that had appeared up until that time were of such a character that at best one reached the point that the two were antipodes with very few points of contact. Toftdahl asks, "How is this possible? They were after all contemporaries, albeit not the same age, and they moved in the same circles and were both educated theologians."[280]

Toftdahl's own book *Kierkegaard first—and then Grundtvig* is an energetic attempt to present and elucidate the relation between "Kierkegaard's Christianity" and "Grundtvig's religion" and has its natural gravitational pull in Kierkegaard's final attack on the Church, which in the Danish context has a precedent in precisely Grundtvig's critical attack on the professor of theology H.N. Clausen in *The Retort of the Church* (1825).[281] Typical of the times (1969), Toftdahl attempts, by way of conclusion, to evaluate Grundtvig and Kierkegaard from a modern complex of problems concerning alienation, and his conclusion is (cf. the title of the book) that "if the Grundtvigian humanism is to survive into the future, it must be emphasized that *no* commonality can today be established at the cost of the urge to reflection; that the road to Grundtvig passes through Kierkegaard's process of individuation: Kierkegaard first—and then Grundtvig."[282]

The significance of Kierkegaard's articles in the attack on the Church for Grundtvig's sermons in the church year 1854–55 was later taken up by P.G. Lindhardt in *Confrontation. The Sermons of Grundtvig 1854–55 against the Background of*

[280]   Hellmut Toftdahl, *Kierkegaard først—og Grundtvig så*, Copenhagen: Nyt Nordisk Forlag 1969, p. 8. Of the comparative analyses of Grundtvig and Kierkegaard before Toftdahl's the following can be mentioned (in addition to Vilhelm Grønbech's), Fredrik Jungersen, *Dansk Protestantisme ved S. Kjerkegaard, N.F.S. Grundtvig og R. Nielsen: Ti Foredrag holdte paa Borchs Kollegium*, Copenhagen: Karl Schønbergs Forlag 1873; Henrik Scharling, *Menneskehed og Christendom i deres historiske Udvikling: En Fremstilling af Historiens Philosophi*, vol. 1–2, Copenhagen 1872–74, see vol. 2, pp. 274–308; Carl Koch, *Grundtvigske Toner: Studier og Betragtninger*, Copenhagen: Det Schønbergske Forlag 1925, see pp. 7–37; Johannes Hohlenberg, *Den Ensommes Vej*, Copenhagen: H. Hagerup 1948, see pp. 253–74; Carl Weltzer, *Grundtvig og Søren Kierkegaard*, Copenhagen: Gyldendal 1952; Søren Holm, *Grundtvig und Kierkegaard*, Copenhagen: Nyt Nordisk Forlag Arnold Busck and Tübingen: Katzmann 1956; and *Kontroverse um Kierkegaard und Grundtvig*, vols. 1–3, ed. by K.E. Løgstrup and Götz Harbsmeier, Munich: Ch. Kaiser and Göttingen: Vandenhoeck & Ruprecht 1966–72. Hellmut Toftdahl in the same year as the publication of his book delivered a critical and objective overview of the most important comparative studies in the article, "Debatten om Grundtvig og Kierkegaard. En kritisk gennemgang," *Grundtvig-Studier*, Copenhagen: Grundtvig-Selskabet 1969, pp. 47–86. See also Hellmut Toftdahl, "Grundtvig og Søren Kierkegaard," *Grundtvig-Studier*, Copenhagen: Grundtvig-Selskabet 1973, pp. 30–49.
[281]   N.F.S. Grundtvig, *Kirkens Gienmæle,* Copenhagen: Den Wahlske Boghandlings Forlag 1825.
[282]   Toftdahl, "Debatten om Grundtvig og Kierkegaard. En kritisk gennemgang," p. 201. See also Jørgen Bukdahl's section "Kirkekamp og broderstrid. Grundtvig og Kierkegaard," in *Tordenvejret og gentagelsen*, Copenhagen: Gyldendal 1974, pp. 48ff., which takes its point of departure in Toftdahl's book.

Kierkegaard's Attack on the Danish Church and the "Official" Christianity (1974).[283]
The more or less hidden dialogue between the two is, moreover, treated in a long essay
by F.J. Billeskov Jansen in *Grundtvig and Kierkegaard – with Nine other Essays on
the History of Ideas* (1990).[284] Susan Roed takes up a comparison on another point
in *The Tree of Pamve* (1988), where Kierkegaard and Grundtvig (and Karen Blixen)
are analyzed from the assumption of an incipient (mental) crisis which gives rise to
their enormous productivity in a movement from chaos to cosmos (the framework
is art's catharsis effect and the religious world's special "rite-de-passage" structure).
Aage Henriksen in *The One and Only* (2004) treats the significance of the moment
of transformation in Kierkegaard's and Grundtvig's (and Goethe's) respective love
stories.[285]

A special phenomenon called *Tidehverv* Grundtvigianism merits consideration
because it demonstrates that what appears irreconcilable in scholarly discussion can
sometimes thrive in practice. The central figure of the *Tidehverv* Grundtvigians was the
folk high school man and parish pastor Kaj Thaning (1904–94), who was educated in
dialectical theology and shaped by the early *Tidehverv*, and who, in one of Grundtvig
research's most controversial treatises, *Man First: Grundtvig's Confrontation
with Himself*,[286] attempted to interpret Grundtvig as a secularizing theologian and
thereby make him palatable for the Kierkegaardian *Tiderhverv* theology. *Tidehverv*
Grundtvigianism enjoyed wide dissemination among the Church's pastors and
bishops in the second half of the twentieth century, and the movement was gathered
around the now defunct Grundtvig convention (*Grundtvigs konvent*), which is not
to be confused with the Grundtvig work convention (*Grundtvigs arbejdskonvent*),
founded in 1980, which consists of students and followers of K.E. Løgstrup.[287]

The comparative efforts and practical approaches mentioned here have,
however, not been able to remove the impression of a cultural gap and a research

---

[283]   P.G. Lindhardt, *Konfrontation. Grundtvigs prædikener 1854–55 på baggrund af
Kierkegaards angreb på den danske kirke og den "officielle" kristendom,* Copenhagen:
Akademisk forlag 1974. Grundtvig's taking a position on Kierkegaard is, in addition, found
in *Den christelige Børnelærdom*, Copenhagen: Karl Schønberg 1868, which was originally
a series of treatises, published in the years 1855–61 in *Kirkelig Samler. Et Tidsskrift til
christelig Oplysning*, vols. 1–7, ed. by Chr. M. Kragballe, Copenhagen: Ditlewsens Enke
1855–62.
[284]   F.J. Billeskov Jansen, *Grundtvig og Kierkegaard—med ni andre åndshistoriske
essays,* Copenhagen: C.A. Reitzel 1990. See also Otto Bertelsen, *Dialogen mellem Grundtvig
og Kierkegaard*, Copenhagen: C.A. Reitzel 1990 and Emanuel Skjoldager, *Hvorfor blev
Søren Kierkegaard ikke Grundtvigianer*, Copenhagen: C.A. Reitzel 1977 (*Søren Kierkegaard
Selskabets Populære Skrifter*, vol. 16).
[285]   Cf. Susan Roed, "Vejen fra kaos til kosmos—tre ekp.: Grundtvig, Kierkegaard og
Blixen," in *Pamves træ—om krise, kunst og religiøsitet*, Århus: Philosophia 1988, pp. 53–74
and Aage Henriksen, "Teologi og erfaring. Om Søren Kierkegaard, Grundtvig og Goethe," in
Den eneste ene og andre essays, Copenhagen: Gyldendal 2004, pp. 93–107.
[286]   Kaj Thaning, *Menneske først: Grundtvigs opgør med sig selv*, vols. 1–3, Copenhagen:
Gyldendal 1963.
[287]   Cf. also Jes Fabricius Møller, *Grundtvigianisme i det 20. århundrede*, Copenhagen:
Vartov 2005, pp. 144–5.

which either has a difficult time seeing anything other than fundamental differences between Grundtvig and Kierkegaard or with a comparison that has been colored by which authorship has been closer to the disposition of the researcher. This problem is possibly just as insurmountable as the two authorships—and especially Grundtvig's—are vast. But recently the framework for a renewed dialogue has been created in the form of a cooperative agreement between the Grundtvig Academy and the Søren Kierkegaard Research Centre, which from February 2005 has had a common place of residence in the old Grundtvigian Parnassus, Vartov in Farvergade in Copenhagen. The initiative has spawned a number of seminars, which were begun in 2002 with an ambitious lecture series with lectures from people from cultural, ecclesiastical, theological, and political milieus. The goal of these seminars was "to make a dialogue possible—not least of all because the need for a solid counterweight to the age's historical loss of memory, general stultification and deplorable mental inertia has made it necessary."[288]

Of new research in the wake of the new cooperation one should mention a few articles by the Grundtvig scholar Anders Holm (b. 1973) and the Kierkegaard expert Niels Jørgen Cappelørn. Taking his point of departure in Kierkegaard's (or Climacus') criticism of Grundtvig in the *Postscript* and the two theologians' common historical background in the reaction to the rationalist Bible criticism, Anders Holm has discovered similarities between central Kierkegaardian concepts such as the moment, repetition, and contemporaneity, and fundamental thoughts in Grundtvig. Niels Jørgen Cappelørn, in an extensive, penetrating study, investigates the parallels in Grundtvig's and Kierkegaard's anthropology against the background of the Church Father Irenaeus' distinction between the image of God and the similitude of God.[289]

E. Status

As early as a half century ago the Norwegian theologian Per Lønning demonstrated a variegated manifold of Kierkegaard images in the reception—from modern subjectivist, who to be sure in practice was not entirely able to liberate himself from an authoritarian upbringing (Brandes, Schrempf, Segerstedt, Grønbech), to preacher of a genuine and pure Protestant Christianity (Ruttenbeck, Rudin, Voigt, Hirsch, Lindström), from a religious mystic (P.P. Jørgensen, Hejll, Herbert, Hohlenberg), to an ecclesiastically orthodox thinker with clear proclivities in the direction of Catholicism (Haecker, Lilienfeld, Dempf, Przywara, Roos), in

---

[288] Cf. *Grundtvig—Kierkegaard. En samtale på høje tid*, ed. by Henrik Wigh-Poulsen, Hans Grishauge, Niels Jørgen Cappelørn, Joakim Garff and Henning Nielsen, Copenhagen: Vartov 2002, p. 9.
[289] Cf. Anders Holm, "The Contemporary Grundtvig. An Addition to Climacus' Critique in *Concluding Unscientific Postscript*," *Kierkegaard Studies. Yearbook*, 2005, pp. 24–36 and Niels Jørgen Cappelørn, "Gudbilledlighed og syndefald: Aspekter af Grundtvigs og Kierkegaards menneskesyn på baggrund af Irenæus," *Grundtvig-Studier*, 2004, pp. 134–78.

addition to all of the numerous views which can be placed in the spaces between these conceptions.[290]

Lønning's analysis was undertaken at a point in time when existence theology and existentialism were seriously beginning to set the agenda in Kierkegaard research, an agenda which was only seriously challenged in the 1980s and 1990s with the introduction of deconstruction. From the 1850s up until our own times it is possible to show a wealth of Kierkegaard interpretations which, often to a much greater degree than Lønning found, are in conflict with one another: Kierkegaard has been interpreted as an anti-authoritarian critic of institutions, a kind of young rebel, as a late capitalist, bourgeois philosopher, as a defender of the individual in an impersonal mass society, as an ethicist interested in preserving society, as a life-denying pietist, as a humanist, as an anarchist, as a welfare philosopher, as a philosopher of personality or self-development, as a fundamentalist, as an anti-fundamentalist, etc. Even though these descriptions are more or less popular oscillations at the somewhat more stable research foundation, which has constituted the main line in this presentation, this kind of (ideological) annexation and rejection is presumably what above all distinguishes Danish reception from that in other countries. Kierkegaard in his home country—just like Grundtvig—has been pushed and pulled from virtually every side. Whether he constitutes a corrective to the status quo or has merely been made to conform to the spirit of the times, seems to be a question that remains open for every age.[291]

What characterizes Danish study of Kierkegaard at the moment is not that the traditional oppositions no longer exist—for, indeed, they do—but that they do not, as formerly, seem to stand as opposites, isolated from one another in wholly separate traditions and milieus or to be subordinated to a dominant paradigm, such as existentialism in its time. A greater exchange than ever before is taking place, and a broader spectrum of interpretive perspectives is at work simultaneously. As a good example of this new tendency towards a broad spectrum is, finally, *The Immortal*.[292] This book, which was published on November 11, 2005, the 150th anniversary of Kierkegaard's death, contains an overview of all of Kierkegaard's published authorship, work for work, written by scholars from the most diverse traditions and with the most diverse range of specializations. Thus, in this book one finds again most of the names from recent research which have been emphasized

---

[290]   Per Lønning, *Samtidighedens situation*, Oslo: Forlaget Land og Kirke 1954, p. 8.
[291]   Joakim Garff raised this question in a review of the journal *K&K 83* (formerly, *Kultur og Klasse*) in 1998, that is, at a time when the deconstructive reading of Kierkegaard had made wide inroads. In his conclusions he writes of the articles by Isak Winkel Holm, Jacob Bøggild, Bo Kampmann Walther, Michael Juul Therkelsen and Henrik Stampe Lund: "The five pieces in *K&K 83*, each in its own and together, display the presence of an entirely new way of dealing with Kierkegaard, which has been elegantly steered out of the jargon of authenticity. To what degree he on the same occasion has lost the function of a corrective and has become conformist to the spirit of the age, is an open question, but perhaps there is nowadays nothing to be a corrective to?" Cf. "Kierkegaard—i stykker," in *Studier i Stadier*, p. 364.
[292]   *Den udødelige. Kierkegaard læst værk for værk*, ed. by Tonny Aagaard Olesen and Pia Søltoft, Copenhagen: C.A. Reitzel 2005.

in the foregoing, along with a few entirely new ones, literally side by side. There is doubtless something typical of the age in this kind of pluralism, but it is difficult not to see the richness in it at the same time.

Translated by Jon Stewart

Bibliography

I. Danish Editions of Kierkegaard's Works

S. Kierkegaard's Bladartikler, med Bilag samlede efter Forfatterens Død, udgivne som Supplement til hans øvrige Skrifter, ed. by Rasmus Nielsen, Copenhagen: C.A. Reitzel 1857.

Af Søren Kierkegaards efterladte Papirer, ed. by H.P. Barfod and H. Gottsched, vols. 1–9, Copenhagen: C.A. Reitzel 1869–81.

Samlede Værker (SV1), ed. by A.B. Drachmann, J.L. Heiberg and H.O. Lange, vols. 1–14, Copenhagen: Gyldendalske Boghandels Forlag (F. Hegel & Søn) 1901–06.

Søren Kierkegaards Papirer (Papirer), vols. I–XI.3, ed. by P.A. Heiberg, V. Kuhr and E. Torsting, Copenhagen: Gyldendal 1909–48 (2nd enlarged ed., vols. I–XI.3 by Niels Thulstrup, vols. XII–XIII Supplement Volumes, ed. by Niels Thulstrup, vols. XIV–XVI Index by Niels Jørgen Cappelørn, Copenhagen: Gyldendal 1968–78).

Samlede Værker (SV2), 2nd ed., ed. by A.B. Drachmann, J.L. Heiberg and H.O. Lange, vols. 1–15, vol. 15 Index of Persons, Subject and Concepts by A. Ibsen and J. Himmelstrup, Copenhagen: Gyldendalske Boghandel 1920–36.

Stadier paa Livets Vei, Copenhagen: Hagerup 1945.

Philosophiske Smuler med afsluttende uvidenskabelig Efterskrift, Copenhagen: Hagerup 1946.

Værker i Udvalg, vols. 1–4, selected and ed. by F.J. Billeskov Jansen, Copenhagen: Gyldendal 1950.

Breve og Aktstykker vedrørende Søren Kierkegaard, ed. by Niels Thulstrup, vols. 1–2, Copenhagen: Munksgaard 1953–54.

Søren Kierkegaard: Philosophiske Smuler, ed. by Niels Thulstrup, Copenhagen: C.A. Reitzel 1955.

Begrebet Angest, ed. by Villy Sørensen, Copenhagen: Gyldendal 1960.

Frygt og Bæven, ed. by Niels Thulstrup, Copenhagen: Gyldendal 1961 (2nd revised ed., 1983).

Gjentagelsen. Et Forsøg i den experimenterende Psychologi af Constantin Constantius, ed. by Gregor Malantschuk, Copenhagen: Hans Reitzel 1961.

Øieblikket No. 1–10. Hvad Christus dømmer: Guds Uforanderlighed, introduced by P.G. Lindhardt, Copenhagen: Hans Reitzels Forlag 1961.

Søren Kierkegaards dagbøger, vols. 1–4, selected and ed. by Peter P. Rohde, Copenhagen: Thaning & Appel 1961–64.

Afsluttende uvidenskabelig Efterskrift, ed. by Niels Thulstrup, Copenhagen: Gyldendal 1962.

Samlede Værker (*SV3*), 3rd ed., ed. by Peter P. Rohde, vols. 1–19, vol. 20, Cumulative Index by Jens Himmelstrup, Copenhagen: Gyldendal 1962–64.

Om min Forfatter-Virksomhed; Synspunktet for min Forfatter-Virksomhed, ed. by G. Malantschuk, Copenhagen: Hans Reitzel 1963.

Den bevæbnede Neutralitet, ed. by Gregor Malantschuk, Copenhagen: Lohse 1965.

Søren Kierkegaards Skrifter (*SKS*), ed. by Niels Jørgen Cappelørn, Joakim Garff, Jette Knudsen, Johnny Kondrup, Alastair McKinnon and Finn Hauberg Mortensen, vols. 1–55 (*SKS* 1–10, 17–22 and K1–10, K17–22, 1997–2005), Copenhagen: Gads Forlag 1997ff.

II. Secondary Literature on Kierkegaard in Denmark

Ammundsen, Valdemar, *Søren Kierkegaards Ungdom. Hans Slægt og hans religiøse Udvikling*, Copenhagen: Københavns Universitet 1912.

Andersen, Anders Thyrring, "Forførelse, tavshed og uret. Kierkegaard-inspirationen i Martin A. Hansens 'Løgneren,' " *Spring*, no. 14, 1999, pp. 186–210.

— "Helten og Digteren. Polspænding, synsvinkelrelativisme og kristen dialektik i Martin A. Hansens Lykkelige Kristoffer og Søren Kierkegaards Frygt og Bæven," in *Arvesyndens skønne Rose. Punktnedslag i Martin A. Hansens digtning*, Copenhagen: Gad 2002, pp. 9–38.

Andersen, Kirstine, *Kierkegaard og ledelse*, Copenhagen: Frydenlund 2004.

Andersen, Lars Erslev, *Hinsides ironi. Fire essays om Søren Kierkegaard*, Aalborg: Nordisk Sommeruniversitet 1995.

Andersen, Svend, " 'I umiddelbarheden begynder det'—Løgstrups opgør med Kierkegaard," *Slagmark*, no. 42, 2005, pp. 63–76.

Andersen, Vilhelm, "Søren Kierkegaard," in *Tider og Typer af dansk Aands Historie*, vols. 1–2.2, Copenhagen: Gyldendal 1907–16, vol 2.2, pp. 65–108.

Andersen, Vilhelm and Carl S. Petersen, "Søren Kierkegaard," in *Illustreret dansk Litteraturhistorie*, vols. 1–4, Copenhagen: Gyldendal 1924–34, vol. 3, pp. 679–706.

Arildsen, Skat, *Biskop H.L. Martensen. Hans Liv, Udvikling og Arbejde*, Copenhagen: G.E.C. Gad 1932.

Beck, Steen, "Søren Kierkegaards teater," *Litteratur & Samfund*, vol. 45, 1989, pp. 45–70.

— *Mændene uden Egenskaber: køn og kunst i århundredeskiftets Wien*, Copenhagen: Museum Tusculanum 1997.

Behrendt, Poul, "Sørens fars penge," *Weekendavisen*, November 5, 1993.

— "An Essay in the Art of Writing Posthumous Papers: The Great Earthquake Revisited," *Kierkegaard Studies. Yearbook*, 2003, pp. 48–109.

— "Søren Kierkegaards fjorten dage. Kronologien bag vendepunktet i Søren Kierkegaards forfatterskab—i anledning af Tekstredegørelsen for *Afsluttende uvidenskabelig Efterskrift, SKS* K7," *Danske Studier*, 2003, pp. 173–204. (In English, see *Kierkegaard Studies. Yearbook*, 2004, pp. 536–64.)

— "En literair Anmeldelse," in *Den udødelige. Kierkegaard læst værk for værk*, ed. by Tonny Aagaard Olesen and Pia Søltoft, Copenhagen: C.A. Reitzel 2005, pp. 219–34.

Bendix, Hans, "Om at skille sig af med bøger," *Politiken*, December 18, 1965.

Bertelsen, Jes, *Kategori og afgørelse. Strukturer i Kierkegaards tænkning*, Viborg: Nørhaven Bogtrykkeri 1972.

— *Ouroboros. En undersøgelse af selvets struktur*, Viborg: Nørhaven Bogtrykkeri 1974.

Bertelsen, Otto, *Dialogen mellem Grundtvig og Kierkegaard*, Copenhagen: C.A. Reitzel 1990.

— *Søren Kierkegaard og de første grundtvigianere*, Copenhagen: C.A. Reitzel 1996.

Bertung, Birgit, "Har Søren Kierkegaard foregrebet Karen Blixens og Suzanne Brøggers kvindesyn?" *Kierkegaardiana*, vol. 13, 1984, pp. 72–83.

— *Om Kierkegaard, kvinder og og kærlighed—en studie i Søren Kierkegaards kvindesyn*, Copenhagen: C.A. Reitzel 1987.

— "Johannes Climacus—og Kierkegaard. Kommunikation og pseudonymitet," in *Kierkegaard pseudonymitet*, Copenhagen: C.A. Reitzel 1993, pp. 33–45.

— *Kierkegaard, kristendom og konsekvens. Søren Kierkegaard læst logisk*, Copenhagen: C.A. Reitzel 1994.

— "Bladartikler 1854–55 & Øieblikket," in *Den udødelige. Kierkegaard læst værk for værk*, ed. by Tonny Aagaard Olesen and Pia Søltoft, Copenhagen: C.A. Reitzel 2005, pp. 397–409.

Billeskov Jansen, F.J., *Hvordan skal vi studere Søren Kierkegaard?*, in *Søren Kierkegaard Selskabets Populære Skrifter I–II*, Copenhagen: Munksgaard 1949.

— *Studier i Søren Kierkegaards litterære Kunst*, Copenhagen: Rosenkilde & Bagger 1951.

— "Grundtvig og Kierkegaard," *Kredsen*, vol. 60, no. 2, 1994, pp. 7–31 (republished in his *Grundtvig og Kierkegaard—med ni åndshistoriske essays*, Copenhagen: C.A. Reitzel 1996, pp. 47–76).

Bjerg, Svend, *Århusteologerne. P.G. Lindhardt, K.E. Løgstrup, Regin Prenter og Johannes Sløk. Den store generation i det 20. århundredes danske teologi*, Copenhagen: Lindhardt & Ringhoff 1994.

Björkheim, John, *Søren Kierkegaard i psykologisk betydning*, Uppsala: Nybloms Förlag 1942.

Bjørnvig, Thorkild, *Kains Alter. Martin A. Hansens Digtning og Tænkning*, Copenhagen: Gyldendal 1964.

Bøggild, Jacob, "Chiasmens kors: korsets chiasmer. Om en kierkegaardsk tankefigur," in *K&K*, 1997, pp. 29–45.

— *Ironiens tænker—tænkningens ironi: Kierkegaard læst retorisk*, Copenhagen: Museum Tusculanum 2002.

— "Opbyggelige Taler i forskjellig Aand," in *Den udødelige. Kierkegaard læst værk for værk*, ed. by Tonny Aagaard Olesen and Pia Søltoft, Copenhagen: C.A. Reitzel 2005, pp. 235–52.

Böwadt, Pia Rose, "Kierkegaard og de suveræne livsytringer—portræt af et paradigmeskift," *Fønix*, vol. 20, 1996, pp. 66–75.

Bramming, Torben, *Tidehvervs historie*, Copenhagen: Anis 1993.

— *Livsmod på Guds ord. Studier i Kristoffer Olesen Larsens eksistensteologi og tid*, Copenhagen: Anis 1999.

Brandes, Georg, *Dualismen i vor nyeste Philosophie*, Copenhagen: Gyldendal 1866.

— *Søren Kierkegaard. En kritisk Fremstilling i Grundrids*, Copenhagen: Gyldendal 1877.

— "Søren Kierkegaard," in his *Mennesker og Værker i nyere europæisk Literatur*, Copenhagen: Gyldendalske Boghandels Forlag 1883, pp. 185–205.

— *Hovedstrømninger i det 19. Aarhundredes Literatur. Emigrantliteraturen, Den Romantiske Skole i Tyskland*, vol. 4 in *Samlede Skrifter*, vols. 1–18, Copenhagen: Gyldendal 1899–1910, pp. 220ff.; pp. 250ff; pp. 351ff.

— "Viggo Hørup," in *Samlede Skrifter*, 2nd ed., vols. 1–4, Copenhagen: Gyldendal 1919, vol. 3 pp. 223–6.

Brandt, Frithiof, *Den unge Søren Kierkegaard. En Række nye bidrag*, Copenhagen: Levins & Munksgaards Forlag 1929.

— "Den unge Søren Kierkegaard," *Nationaltidende*, January 28, 1930.

— "Den unge Søren Kierkegaard," *Nationaltidende*, February 5, 1930.

— "Til Prof. Hans Brix," *Nationaltidende*, February 11, 1930.

— "Papegøjen," *Nationaltidende*, February 21, 1930.

— "Svar til Professor Hans Brix," *Nationaltidende*, March 25, 1930.

— *Syv Kierkegaardstudier. Udgivet i anledning af forfatterens 70 aars fødselsdag den 23. maj 1962 ved Selskabet for Filosofi og Psykologi*, Copenhagen: Munksgaard 1962.

Brandt, Frithiof and Else Rammel, "Den unge Søren Kierkegaard—Nogle Bemærkninger til Professor Fr. Brandts Bog," *Nationaltidende*, January 23, 1930.

Brix, Hans, "S. Kierkegaard—H.C. Andersen. Svar til Prof. Frithiof Brandt," *Nationaltidende*, January 29, 1930.

— "Andersen—Kierkegaard," *Nationaltidende*, January 31, 1930.

— "Angaaende Prof. Brandts Bog," *Nationaltidende*, February 7, 1930.

— "Et Par Ord om Prof. Brandt og S. Kierkegaard," *Nationaltidende*, February 12, 1930.

— "Den røde og den hvide Rose," *Nationaltidende*, March 21, 1930.

— "P.L. Møller og Prof. F. Brandt," *Nationaltidende*, March 26, 1930.

— *Søren Kierkegaard og Pengene*, Copenhagen: Levin & Munksgaard 1935.

Brostrøm, Torben, "Den lange linje," postscript to the 3rd edition of Eigil Nyborg, *Den indre linje i H.C. Andersens eventyr—en psykologisk studie*, Copenhagen: Gyldendal 2005, p. 215.

Brøchner, Hans, *Et Svar til Professor R. Nielsen*, Copenhagen: P.G. Philipsens Forlag 1868.

— *Problemet om Tro og Viden, en historisk-kritisk Afhandling*, Copenhagen: P.G. Philipsens Forlag 1868.

— *Om det Religiøse i dets Enhed med det Humane*, Copenhagen: P.G. Philipsens Forlag 1869.

— *Erindringer om Søren Kierkegaard*, Copenhagen: Gyldendal 1953 (originally printed in *Det nittende Aarhundrede*, March 1877).

Brøgger, Suzanne, "Kierkegaard adieu," in her *Den pebrede susen. Flydende fragmenter og fixeringer*, Copenhagen: Rhodos 1986, pp. 216–32.

Bruun, Søren K., "The Concept of 'The Edifying' in Søren Kierkegaard's Authorship," *Kierkegaard Studies. Yearbook*, 1997, pp. 228–52.

— "Atten opbyggelige Taler," in *Den udødelige. Kierkegaard læst værk for værk*, ed. by Tonny Aagaard Olesen and Pia Søltoft, Copenhagen: C.A. Reitzel 2005, pp. 153–66.

Bukdahl, Jørgen, "Tordenvejret og Gjentagelsen, omkring Kierkegaardlitteraturen," in *Dansk Udsyn*, Kolding: Askov Højskole 1956, pp. 3–24.

— "Kierkegaard-Narkomani—omkring den psykologiske kierkegaardforskning," in *Dansk Udsyn*, Kolding: Askov Højskole 1959, pp. 360–76.

— *Søren Kierkegaard og den menige mand*, in *Søren Kierkegaard Selskabets Populære Skrifter*, vols. 9–10, Copenhagen: Munksgaard 1961.

— "Kast dit brød på vandet...Omkring et Kierkegaardsår," *Dansk Udsyn*, vol. 42, Kolding: Askov Højskole 1962, pp. 331–47.

— "Kirkekamp og broderstrid. Grundtvig og Kierkegaard," in *Tordenvejret og gentagelsen*, Copenhagen: Gyldendal 1974, pp. 48–73 (republished in *Kierkegaardiana*, vol. 9, 1974, pp. 196–219).

— "Tordenvejret og gentagelsen. Omkring Kierkegaards forlovelse og dens følger," in *Tordenvejret og gentagelsen*, Copenhagen: Gyldendal 1974, pp. 155–76.

Bukdahl, Jørgen K., " 'Indrømmelsen.' Dens plads i Søren Kierkegaards kristendomsforståelse og vækkelsesaktion," *Dansk teologisk Tidsskrift*, vol. 26, 1963, pp. 96–124.

— "Søren Kierkegaard—personlighedsprincippets forkæmper—eller undergraver?" *Exil*, no. 1, 1968, pp. 27–31.

— "Kierkegaard mellem ideologi og utopi, I–II. Problemer og perspektiver i de senere års marxistisk inspirerede Kierkegaard-læsning," *Dansk teologisk Tidsskrift*, vol. 29, 1976, pp. 258–84 and *Dansk teologisk Tidsskrift*, vol. 40, 1977, pp. 31–56.

— *Frihed og frigørelse. Filosofi—Teologi—Kulturdebat. Artikler og essays 1956–1979*, Århus: Aros 1980, see pp. 37–41; pp. 79–99.

— *Om Søren Kierkegaard. Artikler i udvalg ved Jan Lindhardt*, Copenhagen: C.A. Reitzel 1981.

— *I den teologiske kreds. Artikler og afhandlinger*, ed. by Hans Hauge et al., Århus: Arkona 1981.

Butin, Gitte Wernaa, "Lindormens Skrig—Dæmoni og Skrift hos Martin A. Hansen og Søren Kierkegaard," in *Arvesyndens skønne Rose. Punktnedslag i Martin A. Hansens digtning*, Copenhagen: Gad 2002, pp. 53–71.

Cappelørn, Niels Jørgen, "The Retrospective Understanding of Søren Kierkegaard's Total Production," in *Kierkegaard. Resources and Results*, ed. by Alastair McKinnon, Montreal: Wilfrid Laurier University Press 1982, pp. 18–38.

— "Gennem fortvivlelse og forargelse til troen," in *Studier i Stadier. Søren Kierkegaard Selskabets 50-års Jubilæum*, ed. by Joakim Garff, Tonny Aagaard Olesen and Pia Søltoft, Copenhagen: C.A. Reitzel 1998, pp. 136–52.

— "Et forsøg på en bestemmelse af begrebet forargelse hos Søren Kierkegaard," *Dansk teologisk Tidsskrift*, vol. 38, 1975, pp. 197–229.

— "Søren Kierkegaards Skrifter i ny udgave," *Kulturbrev* (published by The Ministry of Education), vol. 9, 1996, pp. 20–39.

— "Kierkegaard som bogkøber og bogsamler," in *Tekstspejle: om Søren Kierkegaard som bogtilrettelægger, boggiver og bogsamler*, Esbjerg: Rosendahl 2002, pp. 105–215.

— "Gudbilledlighed og syndefald: Aspekter af Grundtvigs og Kierkegaards menneskesyn på baggrund af Irenæus," in *Grundtvig-Studier*, ed. by Grundtvig–Selskabet, Copenhagen, 2004, pp. 134–78.

— " 'Ypperstepræsten'—'Tolderen'—'Synderinden' and 'To Taler ved Altergangen om Fredagen,' " in *Den udødelige. Kierkegaard læst værk for værk*, ed. by Tonny Aagaard Olesen and Pia Søltoft, Copenhagen: C.A. Reitzel 2005, pp. 329–50.

Cappelørn, Niels Jørgen, Joakim Garff and Johnny Kondrup, *Skriftbilleder. Søren Kierkegaards journaler, notesbøger, hæfter, ark, lapper og strimler*, Copenhagen: Gad 1996.

Cappelørn, Niels Jørgen and Alastair McKinnon, "The Period of Composition of Kierkegaard's Published Works," *Kierkegaardiana*, vol. 9, 1974, pp. 133–46.

Cappelørn, Niels Jørgen and Bent Rohde, "Kierkegaard som bogproducent, tilrettelægger og forlægger," in *Tekstspejle: om Søren Kierkegaard som bogtilrettelægger, boggiver og bogsamler*, Esbjerg: Rosendahl 2002, pp. 9–64.

Christensen, Villads, *Søren Kierkegaard i sit Bedekammer*, Copenhagen: G.E.C. Gad 1937.

— *Søren Kierkegaards Syn paa Bogen*, Copenhagen: Scripta 1950.

— *Søren Kierkegaards Vej til Kristendommen*, Copenhagen: C.A. Reitzel 1955 (*Søren Kierkegaard Selskabets Populære Skrifter*, vol. 5).

— *Søren Kierkegaard og Frederiksberg*, Copenhagen: Rosenkilde & Bagger 1959.

— *Søren Kierkegaards Motiver til Kirkekampen*, Copenhagen: C.A. Reitzel 1959 (*Søren Kierkegaard Selskabets Populære Skrifter*, vol. 8).

— *Søren Kierkegaard i lys af Shakespeares Hamlet*, Copenhagen: Rosenkilde & Bagger 1960.

— *Søren Kierkegaard. Det centrale i hans Livssyn*, Copenhagen: Gad 1963.

— *Peripatetikeren Søren Kierkegaard*, Copenhagen: Graabrødre Torvs Forlag 1965.

— *Kierkegaard-Dramaet*, Copenhagen: Nyt Nordisk Forlag/Arnold Busck 1967.

Clausen, Sven, *Udvalgte Tvangstanker*, Copenhagen: Gyldendal 1945.

Damgaard, Iben, "Frygt og Bæven," in *Den udødelige. Kierkegaard læst værk for værk*, ed. by Tonny Aagaard Olesen and Pia Søltoft, Copenhagen: C.A. Reitzel 2005, pp. 87–104.

Dehs, Jørgen, " 'Ikke Phantasiens kunstrige Væven, men Tankens Gysen.' Kierkegaard og bruddet med idealismens æstetik," *Slagmark*, vol. 4, 1985, pp. 46–59.

— "Den tabte verden," in Poul Erik Tøjner, Joakim Garff and Jørgen Dehs, *Kierkegaards æstetik*, Copenhagen: Gyldendal 1995, pp. 127–67.

— "Kierkegaard og æstetikken," in *Kunst og æstetik*, ed. by Stig Brøgger and Otto Jul Pedersen, Copenhagen: Det Kgl. Danske Kunstakademi 1996, pp. 231–50.

— "Uendeliggørelsen af den æstetiske sfære," in *Studier i Stadier. Søren Kierkegaard Selskabets 50-års Jubilæum*, ed. by Joakim Garff, Tonny Aagaard Olesen and Pia Søltoft, Copenhagen: C.A. Reitzel 1998, pp. 29–40.

Drachmann, A.B., "Hedenskab og Christendom hos Søren Kierkegaard," in his *Udvalgte Afhandlinger*, Copenhagen: Gyldendal 1911, pp. 124–40.

— "Textkritik, anvendt paa S. Kierkegaards Skrifter," in *Udvalgte Afhandlinger*, Copenhagen: Gyldendal 1911, pp. 154–74.

Ellekilde, Hans, "Studier over Kierkegaards Ungdomsliv. 'Den store Jordrystelse,' " in *Danske Studier*, Copenhagen: C.A. Reitzel 1916, pp. 1–44.

Estrup, Jens, *Vælg dig selv. En bog om Søren Kierkegaard til unge*, Copenhagen: Assistens Kirkegårds Formidlingscenter 1994.

Fenger, Henning, *Kierkegaard-Myter og Kierkegaard-Kilder. 9 kildekritiske studier i de kierkegaardske papirer, breve og aktstykker*, Odense: Odense Universitetsforlag 1976.

Fink, Peter, "Enten og eller. Villy Sørensens forhold til Søren Kierkegaard," in *Både frem og tilbage: portræt af Villy Sørensens forfatterskab*, ed. by Marianne Barlyng and Jørgen Bonde Jensen, Hellerup: Spring 2002, pp. 377–87.

Fonsmark, Henning, *Historien om den danske utopi*, Copenhagen: Gyldendal 1990.

Gade, Sven Ove, *Ulanen. En biografi om Victor Andreasen*, Copenhagen: Gyldendal 2002.

Garde, Annelise, "Grafologisk undersøgelse af Søren Kierkegaards håndskrift i årene 1831–1855," *Kierkegaardiana*, vol. 10, 1977, pp. 200–38.

Garff, Joakim, "Fra bog til bits. Om ældre, nyere og kommende udgaver af Søren Kierkegaards skrifter," in *Bogens verden*, Copenhagen: Det Kongelige Bibliotek 1994, pp. 329–36.

— *"Den Søvnløse." Kierkegaard læst æstetisk/biografisk*, Copenhagen: C.A. Reitzel 1995.

— "Forfatternes forfatter," in Poul Erik Tøjner, Joakim Garff and Jørgen Dehs, *Kierkegaards æstetik*, Copenhagen: Gyldendal 1995, pp. 69–126.

— "Bagved Øiet ligger Sjælen som et Mørke," in *Studier i Stadier. Søren Kierkegaard Selskabets 50-års Jubilæum*, ed. by Joakim Garff, Tonny Aagaard Olesen and Pia Søltoft, Copenhagen: C.A. Reitzel 1998, pp. 12–28.

— "Kierkegaard—i stykker," in *Studier i Stadier. Søren Kierkegaard Selskabets 50-års Jubilæum*, ed. by Joakim Garff, Tonny Aagaard Olesen and Pia Søltoft, Copenhagen: C.A. Reitzel 1998, pp. 361–4.

— *SAK Søren Aabye Kierkegaard. En biografi*, Copenhagen: Gad 2000.

— " 'What did I find? Not my I.' On Kierkegaard's Journals and the Pseudonymous Autography," *Kierkegaard Studies. Yearbook*, 2003, pp. 110–24.

— "Formidlingens pris," *Politiken*, August 7, 2004.

— " '...da er der en, der nikker i Smug nær dig.' Om at fornemme det fremmedes medvirken i teksten—et kierkegaardsk kætterbrev," in *PS. Om Martin A. Hansens korrespondance med kredsen omkring Heretica*, ed. by Anders Thyrring Andersen, Copenhagen: Gyldendal 2005, pp. 148–64.

— "Om min Forfatter-Virksomhed og Synspunktet for min Forfatter-Virksomhed," in *Den udødelige. Kierkegaard læst værk for værk*, ed. by Tonny Aagaard Olesen and Pia Søltoft, Copenhagen: C.A. Reitzel 2005, pp. 363–80.

Garff, Joakim and Tonny Aagaard Olesen, "Episoder af Søren Kierkegaard Selskabets historie," in *Studier i Stadier. Søren Kierkegaard Selskabets 50-års Jubilæum*, ed. by Joakim Garff, Tonny Aagaard Olesen and Pia Søltoft, Copenhagen: C.A. Reitzel 1998, pp. 195–255.

Geismar, Eduard, "Omkring Kierkegaard. I. Torsten Bohlin. II. P.A. Heiberg," in *Teologisk Tidsskrift*, 4th series, vol. 6, 1925, pp. 292–339; vol. 8, 1927, pp. 177–200.

— *Søren Kierkegaard. Hans Livsudvikling og Forfattervirksomhed I–II*, Copenhagen: G.E.C. Gad 1926–28.

— "Den unge Søren Kierkegaard," in *Berlingske Tidende*, December 12, 1929.

Gemmer, Anders, *Søren Kierkegaards Livsfilosofi. En kritisk Gennemgang*, Odense: A.C. Normanns Forlag 1944.

— "Ufordøjet Kierkegaard," in *Filosofisk Potpourri*, Copenhagen: Munksgaard 1949, pp. 75–85.

Gemmer, Anders and August Messer, *Søren Kierkegaard und Karl Barth*, Stuttgart: Verlag Strecker & Schröder 1925.

Grane, Leif, *Tidehverv. En antologi*, Copenhagen: Gyldendal 1967.

Grundtvig, N.F.S., "Om en christelig Skilsmisse fra Folke-Kirken," *Dansk Kirketidende*, 1855, vol. 49, pp. 793–805.

— "Det Ny Testamentes Christendom!," *Kirkelig Samler*, vol. 2, 1856, pp. 1–14.

— "Det christelige, aandelige og evige Liv," *Kirkelig Samler*, vol. 3, 1857, pp. 97–114.

— *Den christelige Børnelærdom*, Copenhagen: Karl Schønberg 1868.

— *Vartovs-Prædikener 1839–1860*, Copenhagen: Gyldendal 1924, pp. 363–4.

Grøn, Arne, *Begrebet angst hos Søren Kierkegaard*, Copenhagen: Gyldendal 1994.

— "Suverænitet og negativitet. Løgstrups opgør med Kierkegaard," *Kredsen*, vol. 60, no. 2, 1994, pp. 32–51.

— "Kierkegaards forudsætning," *Dansk Teologisk Tidsskrift*, vol. 58, 1995, pp. 267–90.

— "Sokrates og 'Smulerne,' " *Filosofiske Studier*, vol. 15 (Copenhagen: Filosofisk Institut), 1995, pp. 97–107.

— "Kierkegaards Phänomenologie?" *Kierkegaard Studies. Yearbook*, 1996, pp. 91–116.

— *Subjektivitet og negativitet: Kierkegaard*, Copenhagen: Gyldendal 1997.

— " 'Anden' etik," in *Studier i Stadier. Søren Kierkegaard Selskabets 50-års Jubilæum*, ed. by Joakim Garff, Tonny Aagaard Olesen and Pia Søltoft, Copenhagen: C.A. Reitzel 1998, pp. 75–88.

— "Kjerlighedens Gjerninger," in *Den udødelige. Kierkegaard læst værk for værk*, ed. by Tonny Aagaard Olesen and Pia Søltoft, Copenhagen: C.A. Reitzel 2005, pp. 253–68.

Grønbech, Vilhelm, "Kierkegaard og Grundtvig," in *Kampen om Mennesket*, Copenhagen: Jespersen og Pios Forlag 1930, pp. 184–202.

Hansen, Knud, "Den absolutte fordring," *Tidehverv*, nos. 9–10, 1951.

— "Om begrebet Tro i 'Filosofiske Smuler,' " *Dansk Teologisk Tidsskrift*, vol. 14, 1951, pp. 34–57.

— "Søren Kierkegaards Kristendomsforståelse," *Heretica*, vol. 4, 1951, pp. 83–107.

— "Søren Kierkegaards angreb på kirken," *Højskolebladet*, no. 5, 1952, pp. 45–7.

— *Søren Kierkegaard. Ideens Digter*, Copenhagen: Gyldendal 1954.

— "Søren Kierkegaard og nutiden," in his *Revolutionær samvittighed. Udvalgte taler og essays om Karl Marx og Søren Kierkegaard*, Copenhagen: Gyldendal 1965, pp. 89–173.

Hansen, Leif Bork, *Søren Kierkegaards hemmelighed og eksistensdialektik*, Copenhagen: C.A. Reitzel 1994.

— "En mislighed i *Efterskriften* og dens konsekvenser," in *Studier i Stadier. Søren Kierkegaard Selskabets 50-års Jubilæum*, ed. by Joakim Garff, Tonny Aagaard Olesen and Pia Søltoft, Copenhagen: C.A. Reitzel 1998, pp. 165–75.

— "Til Selvprøvelse & Dømmer selv!" in *Den udødelige. Kierkegaard læst værk for værk*, ed. by Tonny Aagaard Olesen and Pia Søltoft, Copenhagen: C.A. Reitzel 2005, pp. 381–96.

Hansen, Søren Peter, "Kærlighed, identitet og skæbne. Kierkegaard og Stangerup," in *Denne slyngelagtige eftertid. Tekster om Søren Kierkegaard*, vols. 1–3, ed. by Finn Frandsen and Ole Morsing, Århus: Slagmark 1995, vol. 3, pp. 513–40.

Harrits, Flemming, "Grammatik des Glaubens oder Zwischenspiel über den Begriff der Geschichte. Zeit und Geschichte bei Søren Kierkegaard und Walther Benjamin," *Kierkegaardiana*, vol. 18, 1996, pp. 82–99.

Hauge, Hans, *K.E. Løgstrup. En moderne profet*, Copenhagen: Spektrum 1992.

Heegaard, P.S.V., *Professor R. Nielsens Lære om Tro og Viden*, Copenhagen: Den Gyldendalske Boghandling (F. Fegel) 1867.

Heiberg, J.L., "Textkritiske Bemærkninger til 'Enten—Eller,' " in *Danske Studier*, Copen-hagen: C.A. Reitzel 1911, pp. 46–50.

Heiberg, P.A., *Bidrag til et psykologisk Billede af Søren Kierkegaard i Barndom og Ungdom. Af trykte og utrykte Kilder*, Copenhagen: Otto B. Wroblewski 1895.

— *Nogle Bidrag til Enten-Eller's Tilblivelseshistorie*, Copenhagen: Tillge's Boghandel 1910 (*Studier fra Sprog- og Oldtidsforskning udgivne af Det Philologisk-Historiske Samfund*, vol. 82).

— *En Episode i Søren Kierkegaards Ungdomsliv*, Copenhagen og Kristiania: Gyldendal 1912.

— *Et Segment af Søren Kierkegaards religiøse Udvikling 1835 1. juni til 1838 19. maj. Psykologisk Studie*, Copenhagen og Kristiania: Gyldendal 1918.

— *Søren Kierkegaards religiøse Udvikling. Psykologisk Mikroskopi*, Copenhagen: Gyldendal 1925.

Heilmann, Ernst, *Søren Kierkegaards hidtil fortiede testamentariske Villie angaaende hans literære Efterladenskaber*, Copenhagen: Bertelsens Boghandel 1909.

Helweg, Hjalmar, *Søren Kierkegaard. En psykiatrisk-psykologisk studie*, Copen-hagen: H. Hagerup 1933.

Henningsen, Poul, "Fra guldalder til Panduro," in *Poul Henningsen. Kulturkritik*, ed. by Carl Erik Bay and Olav Harsløf, vol. 4, 1956–67), Copenhagen: Rhodos 1973, p. 119 (originally, *Politiken*, April 1, 1963).

Henriksen, Aage, *Kierkegaards Romaner*, Copenhagen: Gyldendal 1954.

— "Kærlighedens forvandlingsformer," in *Litterært testamente. Seks kapitler om kærlighed*, Copenhagen: Gyldendal 1998, pp. 7–35.

— "Teologi og erfaring. Om Søren Kierkegaard, Grundtvig og Goethe," in *Den eneste ene—og andre essays*, Copenhagen: Gyldendal 2004, pp. 93–107.

Himmelstrup, Jens, *Søren Kierkegaards Opfattelse af Sokrates. En Studie i dansk Filosofis Historie*, Copenhagen: Arnold Busck 1924.

— "Terminologisk Register til Søren Kierkegaards Samlede Værker," in *Søren Kierkegaards Samlede Værker*, 2nd ed., Copenhagen: Gyldendal 1920–36, vols. 1–15, pp. 509–770.

— " 'Den store Jordrystelse,' Lidt dansk Historik i Hovedlinier," *Kierkegaardiana*, vol. 4, 1962, pp. 18–27.

Høffding, Harald, *Søren Kierkegaard som Filosof*, Copenhagen: Philipsen 1892.

— "Søren Kierkegaard," in *Danske Filosofer*, Copenhagen: Gyldendal 1909, pp. 147–74.

— "Pascal og Kierkegaard," *Tilskueren*, vol. 40, 1923, pp. 412–34 (republished in *Religiøse Tanketyper*, Copenhagen: Gyldendal 1927, pp. 70–97).

Hoffmeyer, Jesper, *Biosemiotik. En afhandling om livets tegn og tegnenes liv*, Charlottenlund: Ries Forlag 2005, p. 417.

Hohlenberg, Johannes, *Søren Kierkegaard*, Copenhagen: H. Hagerup 1940.

— *Den Ensommes Vej*, Copenhagen: H. Hagerup 1948.

Holm, Anders, "The Contemporary Grundtvig: An Addition to Climacus' Critique in *Concluding Unscientific Postscript*," *Kierkegaard Studies. Yearbook*, 2005, pp. 24–36.

Holm, Isak Winkel, "Poesiens Himmelbrev," in *Studier i Stadier. Søren Kierkegaard Selskabets 50-års Jubilæum*, ed. by Joakim Garff, Tonny Aagaard Olesen and Pia Søltoft, Copenhagen: C.A. Reitzel 1998, pp. 41–58.

— *Tanken i billedet. Søren Kierkegaards poetik*, Copenhagen: Gyldendal 1998.

Holm, Søren, *Søren Kierkegaards Historiefilosofi*, Copenhagen: Nyt Nordisk Forlag/ Arnold Busck 1952.

— *Græciteten*, Copenhagen: Munksgaard 1964 (*Søren Kierkegaard Selskabets Populære Skrifter*, vol. 11).

Ibsen, A., "Sag- og Fofatterregister til Søren Kierkegaards Samlede Værker," in *Søren Kierkegaards Samlede Værker*, vols. 1–15, 2nd ed., Copenhagen: Gyldendal 1920–36, vol. 15, pp. 1–507.

Jensen, Finn Gredal, "To genfundne breve. Fra J.C. Lund til P.C. Kierkegaard og fra Regine Schlegel til Henrik Lund," in *Danske Studier*, Copenhagen: C.A. Reitzel 2005, pp. 194–200.

Jensen, Henrik, *Ofrets århundrede*, Copenhagen: Samleren 1998, see p. 9.

Jensen, Johan Fjord, *Den ny kritik*, Copenhagen: Berlingske Forlag 1962.

Jensen, Jørgen Bonde, *Jeg er kun en Digter. Om Søren Kierkegaard som skribent*, Copenhagen: Babette 1996.

Jensenius, Knud, "Det unge Menneske hos Søren Kierkegaard," *Nordisk Tidsskrift*, 1930, pp. 340ff.

— *Nogle Kierkegaardstudier. "De tre store Ideer,"* Copenhagen: Nyt Nordisk Forlag/Arnold Busck 1932.

Jepsen, Holger, "En Kierkegaard parafrase," *Dansk Udsyn*, vol. 48, 1968, pp. 370–84.

Johansen, Steen (ed.) *Erindringer om Søren Kierkegaard*, Copenhagen: Hasselbalch 1955 (augmented edition 1980).

Jørgensen, P.P., *H P Kofoed-Hansen med særligt Henblik til Søren Kierkegaard. Bidrag til Belysning af aandskulturelle Strømninger i det 19. Aarhundredes Danmark*, Copenhagen and Kristiania: Gyldendal 1920.

Jungersen, Fredrik, *Dansk Protestantisme ved S. Kjerkegaard, N.F.S. Grundtvig og R. Nielsen: Ti Foredrag holdte paa Borchs Kollegium*, Copenhagen: Karl Schønbergs Forlag 1873.

Kanding, Viggo, "Tvende ethisk-religieuse Smaa-Afhandlinger" in *Den udødelige. Kierkegaard læst værk for værk*, ed. by Tonny Aagaard Olesen and Pia Søltoft, Copenhagen: C.A. Reitzel 2005, pp. 303–10.

Kemp, Peter, *Lévinas*, Copenhagen: Anis 1992, see pp. 66–74.

— "Sprogets etik: fra Lévinas til Kierkegaard," in *Denne slyngelagtige eftertid. Tekster om Søren Kierkegaard*, vols. 1–3, ed. by Finn Frandsen and Ole Morsing, Århus: Slagmark 1995, vol. 2, pp. 315–47.

Kingo, Anders, *Den opbyggelige tale. En systematisk-teologisk studie over Søren Kierkegaards opbyggelige forfatterskab*, Copenhagen: G.E.C. Gad 1987.

— *Den pseudonyme tale. En studie over eksistensanalysens kategori i Søren Kierkegaards forfatterskab*, Copenhagen: G.E.C. Gad 1988.

— *Analogiens teologi. En dogmatisk studie over dialektikken i Søren Kierkegaards opbyggelige og pseudonyme forfatterskab*, Copenhagen: G.E.C. Gad 1995.

— "Gives der en teleologisk suspension af alle stadier?" in *Studier i Stadier. Søren Kierkegaard Selskabets 50-års Jubilæum*, ed. by Joakim Garff, Tonny Aagaard Olesen and Pia Søltoft, Copenhagen: C.A. Reitzel 1998, pp. 176–94.

— "Åndsfællesskab. Om ligheder og forskelle i Martin A. Hansens og Søren Kierkegaards tænkning," in *PS. Om Martin A. Hansens korrespondance med kredsen omkring Heretica*, ed. by Anders Thyrring Andersen, Copenhagen: Gyldendal 2005, pp. 165–77.

—"Indøvelse i Christendom," in *Den udødelige. Kierkegaard læst værk for værk*, ed. by Tonny Aagaard Olesen and Pia Søltoft, Copenhagen: C.A. Reitzel 2005, pp. 351–62.

Kjældgaard, Lasse Horne, *Mellemhverandre. Tableau og fortælling i Søren Kierkegaards pseudonyme skrifter*, Hellerup: Forlaget Spring 2001.

Kjær, Grethe, *Søren Kierkegaards seks optegnelser om Den Store Jordrystelse*, Copenhagen: C.A. Reitzel 1983.

Klercke, Kirsten, "Philosophiske Smuler," in *Den udødelige. Kierkegaard læst værk for værk*, ed. by Tonny Aagaard Olesen and Pia Søltoft, Copenhagen: C.A. Reitzel 2005, pp. 105–18.

Knudsen, Jørgen, "Selvudfoldelse og gentagelsestvang," *Information*, April 30, 1984.

— "Subjektiviteten der er sandhed—partiskheden der gør dum," *Information*, April 3, 1984.

— *Georg Brandes. Frigørelsens vej, 1842–77*, Copenhagen: Gyldendal 1985, pp. 55–67, pp. 413–20.

Koch, Carl, *Søren Kierkegaard. Tre Foredrag*, Copenhagen: Karl Schønbergs Forlag 1898.

Koch, Carl Henrik, *Den danske idealisme 1800–1880*, vol. 4 in *Den danske filosofis historie*, vols. 1–4, ed. by Steen Ebbesen and Carl Henrik Koch, Copenhagen: Gyldendal 2004, see pp. 299–360.

Koch, Hal, *Hvad er Demokrati?*, Copenhagen: Gyldendal 1945.

Koch, Hal and Alf Ross (ed.), *Nordisk Demokrati*, Copenhagen: Westermann 1949.

Koch, Lene, *Racehygiejne i Danmark 1920–56*, Copenhagen: Gyldendal 1996.

Kondrup, Johnny, *Livsværker. Studier i dansk litterær biografi*, Copenhagen: Amadeus 1986, pp. 55–134.

— "Kierkegaard og Brandes," in *Kierkegaard inspiration. En antologi*, ed. by Birgit Bertung, Paul Müller, Fritz Norlan and Julia Watkin, Copenhagen: C.A. Reitzel 1991 (*Søren Kierkegaard Selskabets Populære Skrifter 20*), pp. 70–81.

— "Keine hinreichende Vorstellung von seinem Genie. Strategien in der negativen Kierkegaardrezeption von Georg Brandes," *Kierkegaardiana*, vol. 18, 1996, pp. 148–72.

— "Tekstkritiske retningslinjer for *Søren Kierkegaards Skrifter*, med særligt henblik på de trykte skrifter," *Kierkegaard Studies. Yearbook*, 1996, pp. 427–54.

Kondrup, Johnny and Jette Knudsen, "Tekstkritiske retningslinjer for *Søren Kierkegaards Skrifter* (*SKS*), med særligt henblik på journaler og papirer," *Kierkegaard Studies. Yearbook*, 1997, pp. 306–35.

Kragh, Jesper Vaczy, *Kampen om livsanskuelse*, Odense: Syddansk Universitetsforlag 2005.

Krarup, Søren, *Demokratisme*, Copenhagen: Gyldendal 1968.

— *Det moderne sammenbrud 1789–1984*, 2nd ed., Copenhagen: Gyldendal 2001 [1984], see pp. 17–22; pp. 82–93; pp. 220–4.

— "Den store modstander," *Information*, March 26, 1984.

— "Brandes og det moderne sammenbrud," *Information*, April 11, 1984.

— "Den kulturradikale illusion," *Information*, May 7, 1984.

— "Den anti-autoritære Kierkegaard," *Det tavse flertal. Konservative essays*, Copenhagen: Tidehverv 1987, pp. 9–28.

— "Søren Kierkegaard i dansk åndsliv," in *Dansk kultur*, Copenhagen: Spektrum 1993, pp. 64–86.

Kretschmer, Ernst, *Körperbau und Charakter. Untersuchungen zum Konstitutions problem und zur Lehre von den Temperamenten*, Berlin: Verlag von Julius Springer 1921.

— *Geniale Menschen*, Berlin: Verlag von Julius Springer 1929.

Kühle, Sejr, *Søren Kierkegaards Barndom og Ungdom*, Copenhagen: Aschehoug Dansk Forlag 1950.

Kuhr, Victor, *Modsigelsens Grundsætning*, Copenhagen and Kristiania: Gyldendal 1915.

— *Grundtræk af en Karakterologi*, Copenhagen: Gyldendal 1934.

Larsen, A.C., *Samvittighed og Videnskab*, Copenhagen: C.A. Reitzel 1865.

Lilhav, Preben, *Kierkegaards valg*, Risskov: Forlaget SICANA 2003.

Lindhardt, P.G., *Søren Kierkegaards angreb paa folkekirken*, Aarhus: Forlaget Aros 1955.

— "Kierkegaard og Grundtvig," in *Præsteforeningens Blad*, vol. 47, 1957, pp. 697–706.

— "Subjektiviteten er sandheden—en kierkegaardsk maxime i dansk teologi," *Kierkegaardiana*, vol. 5, 1964, pp. 33–51.

— *Den danske kirkes historie*, vol. 8, Copenhagen: Gyldendal 1966.

Lindhardt, P.G. (ed.), *Konfrontation. Grundtvigs prædikener i kirkeåret 1854–55 på baggrund af Kierkegaards angreb på den danske kirke og den "officielle" kristendom*, Copenhagen: Akademisk Forlag 1974.

Lindhardt, P.G. (ed.), *Regeneration. Grundtvigs prædikener i kirkeåret 1855–56*, Copenhagen: Akademisk Forlag 1977.

Lübcke, Poul, "Guds og verdens visdom. Troen og forargelsen hos Kierkegaard, Mynster og Martensen," *Filosofiske Studier*, vol. 14, 1994, pp. 131–95.

Løgstrup, K.E., "Forkyndelsens Kategori og Embede med særligt Henblik paa Problemstillingen hos Luther og Kierkegaard," *Tidehverv*, vol. 24, 1950, pp. 14–26.

—*Kierkegaard und Heideggers Existenzanalyse und ihr Verhältnis zur Verkündigung*, Berlin: Blaschker 1950 (*Breviarium litterarum*, vol. 3).

— "Opgør med Kierkegaards 'Kærlighedens Gerninger,' " *Tidehverv*, vols. 5–6, 1955, pp. 52–60.

— "Opgør med Kierkegaard," in *Festskrift til N.H. Søe 29. november 1965*, Copenhagen: Gad 1965, pp. 97–111.

— *Kunst og Etik*, Copenhagen: Gyldendal 1966, see pp. 53–66; pp. 157–65.

— *Opgør med Kierkegaard*, Copenhagen: Gyldendal 1968.

— *Skabelse og tilintetgørelse—religionsfilosofiske betragtninger*, Copenhagen: Gyldendal 1978 (*Metafysik*, vol. 4), pp. 259–60.

Lønning, Per, *Samtidighedens situation*, Oslo: Land og Kirke 1954.

Magnussen, Rikard, *Søren Kierkegaard, set udefra*, Copenhagen: Ejnar Munksgaard 1942.

— *Det særlige Kors. Efterskrift til Bogen: Søren Kierkegaard, set udefra*, Copenhagen: Ejnar Munksgaard 1942.

Malantschuk, Gregor, *Dialektik og Eksistens hos Søren Kierkegaard*, Copenhagen: Hans Reitzel 1968.

— *Frihedens Problem i Kierkegaards Begrebet Angest*, Copenhagen: Rosenkilde & Bagger 1971.

— "Løgstrups Opgør med Kierkegaard," *Kierkegaardiana*, vol. 8, 1971, pp. 163–81.

— *Den kontroversielle Kierkegaard*, Copenhagen: Vinten 1976.

— *Fra Individ til den Enkelte. Problemer omkring Friheden og det etiske hos Søren Kierkegaard*, Copenhagen: C.A. Reitzel 1978.

— *Frihed og eksistens. Studier i Søren Kierkegaards tænkning*, ed. by Niels Jørgen Cappelørn and Paul Müller, Copenhagen: C.A. Reitzel 1980.

— *Nøglebegreber i Søren Kierkegaards tænkning*, ed. by Grethe Kjær and Paul Müller, Copenhagen: C.A. Reitzel 1993.

Malantschuk, Gregor and N.H. Søe, *Søren Kierkegaards Kamp mod Kirken*, Copenhagen: Munksgaard 1956 (*Søren Kierkegaard Selskabets Populære Skrifter*, vol. 6).

Martensen, Hans Lassen, *Om Tro og Viden, et Lejlighedsskrift*, Copenhagen: C.A. Reitzel 1867.

— *Den christelige Ethik. Den almindelige Del*, Copenhagen: Gyldendal 1871, see pp. 275–300.

Mikkelsen, Hans Vium, "Martin A. Hansen som dialektisk teolog. Eller: Martin A. Hansen mellem Kierkegaard og Løgstrup," in *PS. Om Martin A. Hansens korrespondance med kredsen omkring Heretica*, ed. by Anders Thyrring Andersen, Copenhagen: Gyldendal 2005, pp. 178–98.

Mylius, Johan de, "Af en endnu Levendes Papirer," in *Den udødelige. Kierkegaard læst værk for værk*, ed. by Tonny Aagaard Olesen and Pia Søltoft, Copenhagen: C.A. Reitzel 2005, pp. 11–34.

Müller, Mogens, "Historikerens Jesus, den historiske Jesus og kirkens Kristus-forkyndelse," *Dansk Teologisk Tidsskrift*, vol. 38, 1975, pp. 81–104.

Müller, Paul, "Betingelser for meddelelsen af det kristelige hos Søren Kierkegaard," *Dansk Teologisk Tidsskrift*, vol. 36, 1973, pp. 25–43.

— "Tvivlens former og deres rolle i erkendelsen af det historiske. En studie i Søren Kierkegaards erkendelsesteori," *Dansk Teologisk Tidsskrift*, vol. 37, 1974, pp. 177–216.

— *Kristendom, etik og majeutik i Søren Kierkegaards "Kjerlighedens Gjerninger,"* Copenhagen: Institut for Religionshistorie 1976.

— "Grundprincipperne i Søren Kierkegaards meddelelsesdialektik og deres anvendelse i forfatterskabet," *Dansk Teologisk Tidsskrift*, 1978, pp. 123–33.

— *Meddelelsesdialektikken i Søren Kierkegaard's Philosophiske Smuler*, Copenhagen: Institut for Religionshistorie 1979.

— *Søren Kierkegaards kommunikationsteori. En studie. Med forelæsningudkastene til "Den ethiske og den ethisk-religieuse Meddelelses Dialektik" (1847) særskilt udgivet som dokumentation*, Copenhagen: C.A. Reitzel 1984.

Møllehave, Johannes, "Identitet og kærlighed. En Kierkegaard-læsning," in his *Læsehest med æselører. Oplevelser med danske bøger fra H.C. Andersen og Blicher til Benny Andersen og Lola Baidel*, Copenhagen: Lindhardt & Ringhof 1979, pp. 70–94.

— *Til trøst*, Copenhagen: Lindhardt & Ringhof 1983.

— "Job—kærlighed og dæmoni," in *Kunsten og kaldet. Festskrift til biskop Johannes Johansen 4. marts 1990*, Herning: Poul Kristensen 1990, pp. 99–112.

— *Kærlighed og dæmoni. Hvorfor fejludvikler kærligheden sig?*, Copenhagen: Lindhardt & Ringhof 1992, pp. 20–38.

Møller, Jes Fabricius, *Grundtvigianisme i det 20. århundrede*, Copenhagen: Vartov 2005.

[Nielsen, Flemming Chr.], *Regine Olsens dagbog*, ed. by Erik Søndergaard Hansen, Højberg: Hovedland 2001.

Nielsen, Rasmus, "Om S. Kierkegaards 'mentale Tilstand,'" *Nordisk Universitets-Tidsskrift*, Copenhagen 1858, pp. 1–29.

— *Paa Kierkegaardske 'Stadier'. Et Livsbillede*, Copenhagen: Den Gyldendalske Boghandling 1860.

— *Grundideernes Logik*, vols. 1–2, Copenhagen: Den Gyldendalske Boghandling 1864.

— *Om »Den gode Villie« som Magt i Videnskaben*, Copenhagen: Den Gyldendalske Boghandling 1867.

— *Hr. Prof. Brøchners filosofiske Kritik gjennemset*, Copenhagen: Den Gyldendalske Boghandling 1868.

— *Om Hindringer og Betingelser for det aandelige Liv i Nutiden*, Copenhagen: Den Gyldendalske Boghandling 1868.

— *Religionsphilosophie*, Copenhagen: Den Gyldendalske Boghandling 1869.

Nordentoft, Kresten, *Kierkegaards psykologi*, Copenhagen: Hans Reitzels Forlag 1972.

— *"Hvad siger Brand-Majoren?" Kierkegaards opgør med sin samtid*, Copenhagen: G.E.C. Gad 1973.

— *Søren Kierkegaard. Bidrag til kritikken af den borgerlige selvoptagethed*, Copenhagen: Dansk Universitets Presse 1977.

Næsgaard, Sigurd, *En Psykoanalyse af Søren Kierkegaard*, Odense: Psykoanalytisk Forlag 1950.

Olesen, Michael, "Christelige Taler," in *Den udødelige. Kierkegaard læst værk for værk*, ed. by Tonny Aagaard Olesen and Pia Søltoft, Copenhagen: C.A. Reitzel 2005, pp. 269–86.

Olesen, Tonny Aagaard, "Et halvt århundrede med tryk på," in *Studier i Stadier. Søren Kierkegaard Selskabets 50-års Jubilæum*, ed. by Joakim Garff, Tonny Aagaard Olesen and Pia Søltoft, Copenhagen: C.A. Reitzel 1998, pp. 256–99.

— "Kierkegaardiana 1–20. Index with a short historical survey," *Kierkegaardiana*, vol. 21, 2000, pp. 201–27.

— "Om Begrebet Ironi"/"Forord," in *Den udødelige. Kierkegaard læst værk for værk*, ed. by Tonny Aagaard Olesen and Pia Søltoft, Copenhagen: C.A. Reitzel 2005, pp. 35–52; pp. 137–52.

Olesen Larsen, K., *En Fremstilling og Vurdering af Søren Kierkegaards Lære om Paradokset og denne Læres etiske Konsekvenser under særlig Hensyntagen til Forholdet mellem Hegel og Kierkegaard*, Copenhagen 1923 (unpublished— located in the K. Olesen Larsen archive at The Royal Library, no. 4.1 in the catalogue). Evaluated in *Festskrift udgivet af Københavns Universitet November 1924*, pp. 125–7.

— "Den uendelige fordring og kærligheden til næsten," *Tidehverv*, no. 1, 1952, pp. 4–12; no. 2, 1952, pp. 13–20; nos. 3–4, 1952, pp. 29–39; no. 5, 1952, pp. 44–56.

— *Søren Kierkegaard læst af K. Olesen Larsen*, ed. by Vibeke Olesen Larsen and Tage Wilhjelm, Copenhagen: G.E.C. Gad 1966.

— "Temaet i Søren Kierkegaards forfatterskab. Fragment" / "Paradoxbegrebet hos Søren Kierkegaard," in *I Ansvar og i Tro. K. Olesen Larsen 1899–1999* (selected articles by A. Kingo and Sten Vedstesen), vols. 1–2, Copenhagen: C.A. Reitzel 1999, vol. 2, pp. 7–13; pp. 205–66.

Olrik, H.G., "Hvem er Papegøjen i 'Lykkens Kalosker'?" *Nationaltidende*, January 31, 1930.

Ostenfeld, Ib, *Om Angst-Begrebet i Søren Kierkegaard: Begrebet Angest. En psykologisk Detailstudie*, Copenhagen: G.E.C. Gad 1933.

— *Søren Kierkegaards Psykologi. Undersøgelse og Indlevelse*, Copenhagen: Rhodos 1972.

Posselt, Gert, "Kierkegaard som boggiver," in *Tekstspejle. Om Søren Kierkegaard som bogtilrettelægger, boggiver og bogsamler*, Esbjerg: Rosendahls Forlag 2002, pp. 65–104.

Poulsen, Birgitte Kvist, "Begrebet Angest" in *Den udødelige. Kierkegaard læst værk for værk*, ed. by Tonny Aagaard Olesen and Pia Søltoft, Copenhagen: C.A. Reitzel 2005, pp. 119–36.

Prenter, Regin, "Frihedsbegrebet hos Sartre paa baggrund af Kierkegaard," in *Ordet og aanden. Reformatorisk Kristendom. Afhandlinger og artikler*, Copenhagen: Gad 1952, pp. 177–89.

— "Luther and Lutheranism," in *Kierkegaard and Great Traditions*, ed. by Niels Thulstrup and Marie Mikulová Thulstrup, Copenhagen: C.A. Reitzel 1981 (*Bibliotheca Kierkegaardiana*, vol. 6), pp. 121–72.

Quist, Wenche Marit, *Den enkelte og det mellemmenneskelige. Den etiske betydning af det mellemmenneskelige forhold hos Søren Kierkegaard*, Copenhagen: C.A. Reitzel 2000.

— "Sygdommen til Døden," in *Den udødelige. Kierkegaard læst værk for værk*, ed. by Tonny Aagaard Olesen and Pia Søltoft, Copenhagen: C.A. Reitzel 2005, pp. 311–28.

Rasmussen, Anders Moe, "Kierkegaards eksistenstænkning som idealismekritik. En analyse af Johannes Sløks Kierkegaard-tolkning," *Philosophia*, vol. 17, nos. 3–4, 1988, pp. 129–47.

Reinhard, Hedvig, "Søren Kierkegaard," *Tidehverv*, vol. 12, 1938, pp. 63–7, pp. 81–5, pp. 108–12; vol. 13, 1939, pp. 30–4, pp. 55–60, pp. 117–19; vol. 14, 1940, pp. 8–11, 67–73, pp. 106–9.

Reventlow, Christian, *Breve fra Skærsilden*, Copenhagen: Aschehoug 1924.

Roed, Susan, "Vejen fra kaos til kosmos—tre eks.: Grundtvig, Kierkegaard og Blixen," in *Pamves træ. Om krise, kunst og religiøsitet*, Århus: Forlaget Philosophia 1988, pp. 53–74.

Rohde, H.P., "Om Søren Kierkegaard som bogsamler. Studier i hans efterladte papirer og bøger paa Det kongelige Bibliotek," in *Fund og Forskning i Det kongelige Biblioteks Samlinger*, vol. 8, 1961, pp. 79–127.

— (ed.), *Auktionsprotokol over Søren Kierkegaards bogsamling / The Auctioneer's Sales Record of the Library of Søren Kierkegaard*, Copenhagen: Det Kongelige Bibliotek 1967.

Rohde, Peter P., *Et geni i en Købstad. Et essay om Søren Kierkegaard*, Oslo 1956 (Copenhagen: Gyldendal 1962).

Roos, H., *Søren Kierkegaard og Katolicismen*, Copenhagen: Ejnar Munksgaard 1952 (*Søren Kierkegaard Selskabets Populære Skrifter*, vol. 3).

Rosenberg, P.A., *Søren Kierkegaard, hans Liv, hans Personlighed og hans Forfatterskab. En Vejledning til Studiet af hans Værker*, Copenhagen: Karl Schønbergs Forlag 1898.

Ross, Alf, *Hvorfor Demokrati?*, Copenhagen: Munksgaard 1946

Rubow, Paul V., "Søren Kierkegaard," in *Georg Brandes' Briller. Ny forøget Udgave af "Georg Brandes og den kritiske Tradition i det nittende Aarhundrede,"* Copenhagen: Levin & Munksgaard 1932, pp. 101–65.

Scharling, Henrik, "Grundtvig, Søren Kierkegaard, H. Martensen," in his *Menneskehed og Christendom i deres historiske Udvikling. En Fremstilling af Historiens Filosofi*, vols. 1–2, Copenhagen: Gads 1872–74, vol. 2, pp. 274–308.

Schiødte, A.F., *Om de dialektiske Grundbegreber hos Søren Kierkegaard,* Copenhagen: Axel Schiødte 1874.

Schmidt, Robert, "Kierkegaard og H.C. Andersen," *Nationaltidende,* January 30, 1930.

— "Kierkegaard—Professor Brix," *Nationaltidende,* February 2, 1930.

Schousboe, Julius, *Om Begrebet Humor hos Søren Kierkegaard. En Filosofisk Afhandling,* Copenhagen: Arnold Busck 1925.

Skjoldager, Emanuel, *Søren Kierkegaards syn på samvittigheden. Med indledning af Gregor Malantschuk,* Copenhagen: Munksgaard 1967 (*Søren Kierkegaard Selskabets Populære Skrifter,* vol. 12).

— *At vælge sig selv i ansvar. Kierkegaard-essays,* Copenhagen: Munksgaard 1969 (*Søren Kierkegaard Selskabets Populære Skrifter,* vol. 14).

— *Hvorfor blev Søren Kierkegaard ikke Grundtvigianer,* Copenhagen: C.A. Reitzel 1977 (*Søren Kierkegaard Selskabets Populære Skrifter,* vol. 16).

— *At trænge til Gud. Indførelse i Søren Kierkegaards opbyggelige taler 1843–44,* Copenhagen: C.A. Reitzel 1980.

— *Den egentlige Kierkegaard. Søren Kierkegaards syn på kirken og de kirkelige handlinger,* Copenhagen: C.A. Reitzel 1982.

— *Søren Kierkegaard og mindesmærkerne,* Copenhagen: C.A. Reitzel 1983.

Sløk, Johannes, "Kierkegaards Bestemmelse af Incommensurabilitetens tvetydige Perspektiv," in *Forsynstanken. Et Forsøg paa en dogmatisk Begrebsbestemmelse,* Hjørring: Expres-Trykkeriets Forlag 1947, pp. 92–135.

— *Die Anthropologie Kierkegaards,* Copenhagen: Rosenkilde og Bagger 1954.

— "Tre Kierkegaard-tolkninger," *Kierkegaardiana,* vol. 1, 1955, pp. 89–101.

— *Søren Kierkegaard,* Copenhagen: G.E.C. Gad 1960.

— "Afmytologisering af Kierkegaard," *Dansk Teologisk Tidsskrift,* vol. 40, 1977, pp. 120–27.

— *Humanismens tænker,* Copenhagen: Hans Reitzel 1978.

— *Da Kierkegaard tav. Fra forfatterskab til kirkestorm,* Copenhagen: Hans Reitzel 1980.

— *Kierkegaards univers. En ny guide til geniet,* Copenhagen: Centrum 1983.

— *Mig og Godot,* Viby J.: Forlaget Centrum 1986.

— *Det her samfund!,* Viby J.: Forlaget Centrum 1989.

Stangerup, Henrik, "Kierkegaard hed han. Parodisk bidrag til halvfjerdsernes ideologikritik" and "Roger Poole: Kierkegaard er vor tids filosof," in his *Fangelejrens frie halvdel,* Copenhagen: Berlingske Forlag 1979, pp. 51–59; 61–73.

— "Søren Kierkegaard" in *Forfatternes forfatterhistorie,* ed. by Per Stig Møller, Copenhagen: Gyldendal 1980, pp. 89–97.

Stangerup, Henrik and Roger Poole, *Dansemesteren. Sider af Søren Kierkegaard,* Copenhagen: Gyldendal 1985, see especially pp. 225–30.

Svendsen, Werner, "Forord," to Frithiof Brandt and Else Rammel, *Søren Kierkegaard og pengene,* Copenhagen: Spektrum 1993, pp. 7–12.

Søe, N.H., *Subjektiviteten er Sandheden,* Copenhagen: Munksgaard 1949 (*Søren Kierkegaard Selskabets Populære Skrifter,* vols. 1–2).

— "Søren Kierkegaards Lære om Paradokset," in *Nordisk teologi. Idéer och män. Till Ragnar Bring*, Lund: C.W.K. Gleerup 1955, pp. 102–21.

— "Karl Barth og Søren Kierkegaard," *Kierkegaardiana*, vol. 1, 1955, pp. 55–64.

— "Gregor Malantschuk: Dialektik og Eksistens hos Søren Kierkegaard," *Kierkegaardiana*, vol. 7, 1968, pp. 196–200.

Søltoft, Pia, "The Unhappy Lover of Subjectivity: Is the Pseudonym Johannes Climacus an Unequivocal Figure?" *Kierkegaard Studies. Yearbook*, 1996, pp. 255–76.

— "Den enkelte og den anden" in *Studier i Stadier. Søren Kierkegaard Selskabets 50-års Jubilæum*, ed. by Joakim Garff, Tonny Aagaard Olesen and Pia Søltoft, Copenhagen: C.A. Reitzel 1998, pp. 117–35.

— *Svimmelhedens Etik. Om forholdet mellem den enkelte og den anden hos Buber, Lévinas og især Kierkegaard*, Copenhagen: Gads Forlag 2000.

— "Enten - Eller"/"Lilien paa Marken og Fuglen under Himlen" in Tonny Aagaard Olesen and Pia Søltoft (red.) *Den udødelige. Kierkegaard læst værk for værk*, Copenhagen: C.A. Reitzel 2005, pp. 53–70; pp. 287–302.

Sørensen, Villy, *Digtere og dæmoner. Fortolkninger og vurderinger*, Copenhagen: Gyldendal 1959, pp. 10–36.

— "Om det komiske. Med stadigt hensyn til Søren Kierkegaard," in his *Hverken-Eller. Kritiske betragtninger*, Copenhagen: Gyldendal 1961, pp. 196–210.

— "Søren Kierkegaard og Tryllefløjten," in his *Hverken-Eller. Kritiske betragtninger*, Copenhagen: Gyldendal 1961, pp. 191–5.

— *Kafkas Digtning*, Copenhagen: Gyldendal 1968, see pp. 179–89.

— *Mellem Fortid og Fremtid. Kronikker og kommentarer*, Copenhagen: Gyldendal 1969, see pp. 98–102; pp. 103–8; pp. 117–26.

— *Jesus og Kristus*, 2nd ed., Copenhagen: Gyldendal 1993 [1992], see p. 256.

— *Med Villy i midten—28 vidnesbyrd om Villy Sørensen*, ed. by Suzanne Brøgger, Erling Groth et al., Copenhagen: Gyldendal 2004, see pp. 314–15.

Teisen, Niels, *Kort Indlæg i Sagen mellem S. Kierkegaard og H. L. Martensen. Et Lejlighedsskrift*, Copenhagen: Karl Schønbergs Forlag 1884.

— *Til Overvejelse i Anledning af Prof. Høffdings Bog om S. Kierkegaard*, Odense: Milo'ske Boghand Forlag 1893.

— *Om Søren Kierkegaard's Betydning som kristelig Tænker*, Copenhagen: J. Frimodt 1903.

Thaning, Kaj, *Menneske først: Grundtvigs opgør med sig selv*, vols. 1–3, Copenhagen: Gyldendal 1963.

Thielst, Peter, *Søren og Regine. Kierkegaard, kærlighed og kønspolitik*, Copenhagen: Gyldendal 1980.

— *Latterens lyst. Det frigørende og distancerende grin*, Copenhagen: Tiderne Skifter 1988, pp. 38–51.

— *Livet forstås baglæns, men må leves forlæns. Historien om Søren Kierkegaard*, Copenhagen: Gyldendal 1994.

Thulstrup, Marie Mikulová, *Kierkegaard og pietismen*, Copenhagen: Munksgaard 1967 (*Søren Kierkegaard Selskabets Populære Skrifter*, vol. 13).

— *Kierkegaard, Platons skuen og kristendommen*, Copenhagen: Munksgaard 1970 (*Søren Kierkegaard Selskabets Populære Skrifter*, vol. 15).

— *Kierkegaard i kristenlivets historie*, Copenhagen: C.A. Reitzel 1991.

Thulstrup, Niels, "Die historische Methode in der Kierkegaard-Forschung—durch ein Beispiel beleuchtet," in *Symposion Kierkegaardianum, Orbis Litterarum*, tome X, fasc. 1–2, Copenhagen: Munksgaard 1955, pp. 280–96.

— *Katalog over Søren Kierkegaards Bibliotek*, Copenhagen: Munksgaard 1957.

— *Kierkegaards Forhold til Hegel og til den spekulative Idealisme indtil 1846*, Copenhagen: Gyldendal 1967.

— *Akcept og Protest. Artikler i udvalg*, vols. 1–2, Copenhagen: C.A. Reitzel 1981.

Toftdahl, Hellmut, *Kierkegaard først—og Grundtvig så. Sammenligning og vurdering*, Copenhagen: Nyt Nordisk Forlag/Arnold Busck 1969.

— "Debatten om Grundtvig og Kierkegaard. En kritisk gennemgang," *Grundtvig-Studier* (Copenhagen: Grundtvig-Selskabet) 1969, pp. 47–86 and the "Summary" on pp. 103–5.

— "Grundtvig og Søren Kierkegaard," in *Grundtvig-Studier* (Copenhagen: Grundtvig-Selskabet) 1973, pp. 30–49.

Troels-Lund, Troels Frederik, *Bakkehus og Solbjerg. Træk af et nyt Livssyns Udvikling i Norden*, Copenhagen: Gyldendal 1922.

— *Et Liv. Barndom og Ungdom*, Copenhagen: Hagerup 1924, pp. 207–47.

Tudvad, Peter, *Kierkegaards København*, Copenhagen: Politiken 2004.

— "SAK—en uvidenskabelig biografi om Søren A. Kierkegaard," *Information*, July 24–5, 2004.

Tøjner, Poul Erik, "Stilens tænker," in Poul Erik Tøjner, Joakim Garff and Jørgen Dehs, *Kierkegaards æstetik*, Copenhagen: Gyldendal 1995, pp. 9–68.

Vind, Ole, *Grundtvigs historiefilosofi*, Copenhagen: Gyldendal 1999, pp. 484–92.

Vodskov, Hans Sophus, "En Krise i Søren Kierkegaards Liv. S. Kierkegaards Efterladte Papirer, Bind V–VIII, 1849–53," in *Spredte Studier*, Copenhagen: Gyldendal 1884, pp. 1–30 (originally in *Illustereret Tidende*, 1881).

Walther, Bo Kampmann, *Øjeblik og tavshed: Læsninger i Søren Kierkegaards forfatterskab*, Odense 2002.

— "Stadier paa Livets Vei," in *Den udødelige. Kierkegaard læst værk for værk*, ed. by Tonny Aagaard Olesen and Pia Søltoft, Copenhagen: C.A. Reitzel 2005, pp. 183–94.

Weltzer, Carl, *Peter og Søren Kierkegaard*, Copenhagen: Gad 1936.

— *Grundtvig og Søren Kierkegaard*, Copenhagen: Gyldendal 1952.

Wigh-Poulsen, Henrik et al. (ed.), *Grundtvig—Kierkegaard: en samtale på høje tid*, Copenhagen: Vartov 2002.

Wind, H.C., *Religion og kommunikation. Teologisk hermeneutik*, Århus: Aarhus Universitetsforlag 1987, pp. 59–112.

— "Kierkegaard og det historiske," in *Kierkegaard og...hovedtemaer i forfatterskabet*, ed. by Christian T. Lystbæk og Lars Aagaard, Århus: Philosophia 2001, pp. 25–39.

Wivel, Klaus, *Næsten Intet. En jødisk kritik af Søren Kierkegaard*, Copenhagen: C.A. Reitzel 1999.

III. *Secondary Literature on Kierkegaard's Reception in Denmark*

Bøggild, Jacob, "Coming to Terms with the Tricky Twins. On the Scandinavian Reception of *Repetition* and *Fear and Trembling*," *Kierkegaard Studies. Yearbook*, 2002, pp. 290–309.

Bukdahl, Jørgen K., "Kierkegaard brugt i en marxistisk tid," in *Om Søren Kierkegaard—artikler i udvalg ved Jan Lindhardt*, Copenhagen: C.A. Reitzel 1981, pp. 147–65.

Diderichsen, Adam Thomas, "A Note on the Danish Reception of *The Concept of Anxiety*," *Kierkegaard Studies. Yearbook*, 2001, pp. 351–63.

Götke, Povl, "Recent Scandinavian Literature on *Works of Love*," *Kierkegaard Studies. Yearbook*, 1998, pp. 232–44.

Henriksen, Aage, *Methods and Results of Kierkegaard Studies in Scandinavia. A Historical and Critical Survey*, Copenhagen: Munksgaard 1951 (*Publications of the Kierkegaard Society*, vol. 1).

Himmelstrup, Jens, *Søren Kierkegaard. International Bibliografi*. Udgivet under medvirken af Kjeld Birket-Smith, Copenhagen: Nyt Nordisk Forlag/Arnold Busck 1962, pp. 53–101.

Holm, J. Eilschou, M. Müller and M. Oldenburg "Søren Kierkegaard-litteratur 1956–1960," *Kierkegaardiana*, vol. 7, 1968, pp. 252–67.

Jørgensen, Aage, *Kierkegaard-litteratur 1961–70*, Aarhus 1971.

— *Søren Kierkegaard litteratur 1971–1980*, Aarhus 1982.

— "Søren Kierkegaard Literature 1981–1991—A Bibliography," *Kierkegaardiana*, vol. 16, 1993, pp. 166–232.

— "Søren Kierkegaard Literaure 1992–1993—A Bibliography," *Kierkegaardiana*, vol. 17, 1994, pp. 221–36.

— "Søren Kierkegaard Literaure 1993–1994—A Bibliography," *Kierkegaardiana*, vol. 18, 1996, pp. 267–84.

— "Søren Kierkegaard Literaure 1994–1997—A Bibliography," *Kierkegaardiana*, vol. 19, 1998, pp. 207–41.

— "Søren Kierkegaard Literaure 1997–1998—A Biliography," *Kierkegaardiana*, vol. 20, 1999, pp. 353–69.

— "Søren Kierkegaard Literaure 1998–2001—A Bibliography," *Kierkegaardiana*, vol. 22, 2002, pp. 271–306.

— "Søren Kierkegaard Literaure 2002–2004—A Bibliography," *Kierkegaardiana*, vol. 23, 2004, pp. 241–66.

Kabell, Aage, *Søren Kierkegaard–Studiet i Norden*, Copenhagen: H. Hagerup 1948.

Malik, Habib C., *Receiving Søren Kierkegaard. The Early Impact and Transmission of His Thought*, Washington, D.C.: The Catholic University of America Press 1997.

Morsing, Ole, *Sprækker til det uendelige? Søren Kierkegaard i 1990'erne—en bog om bøgerne*, Århus: Slagmark 1996.

Mortensen, Finn Hauberg, "Kierkegaard in Scandinavia—A History of Radical Reception," in *Kierkegaard Revisited*, Berlin and New York; Walter de Gruyter 1997 (*Kierkegaard Studies Monograph Series*, vol. 1), pp. 410–41.

Nielsen, Edith Ortmann and Niels Thulstrup, *Søren Kierkegaard. Bidrag til en Bibliografi. Contributions towards a bibliography*, Copenhagen: Ejnar Munksgaard 1951.

Olesen, Tonny Aagaard, "The Painless Contradiction: A Note on the Reception of the Theory of the Comic in *Postscript*," *Kierkegaard Studies. Yearbook*, 2005, pp. 339–50.

Schjørring, Jens Holger, "Kierkegaard und die dänische Theologie der zwanziger und dreißiger Jahre," in *Die Rezeption Søren Kierkegaards in der deutschen und dänischen Philosophie und Theologie. Vorträge des Kolloquiums am 22. und 23. März 1982*, ed. by Heinrich Anz, Munich et al: Fink 1983 (*Text & Kontext*, Sonderreihe, vol. 15) (*Kopenhagener Kolloquien zur deutschen Literatur*, vol. 7), pp. 171–85.

Schulz, Heiko, "Rezeptionsgeschichtliche Brocken oder die *Brocken* in der deutschen Rezeption," *Kierkegaard Studies. Yearbook*, 2004, pp. 375–451.

Søltoft, Pia, "Recent Danish Literature on the *Upbuilding Discourses 1843 and 1844* and *Three Discourses on Imagined Occasions*," *Kierkegaard Studies. Yearbook*, 2000, pp. 251–60.

Thulstrup, Niels, "Studiet af Kierkegaard udenfor Skandinavien 1945–52. En kritisk skitse," *Dansk teologisk Tidsskrift*, vol. 16, no. 2, 1953, pp. 65–80.

— "Kierkegaard-Studiet i Skandinavien 1945–52—en kritisk oversigt," *Edda* (Oslo) 1954, pp. 79–122.

— *Kierkegaards Verhältnis zu Hegel: Forschungsgeschichte*, Stuttgart: Verlag W. Kohlhammer 1969.

— "Scandinavia," in *Kierkegaard Research*, ed. by Niels Thulstrup and Marie Mikulová Thulstrup, Copenhagen: C.A. Reitzel 1987 (*Bibliotheca Kierkegaardiana*, vol. 15), pp. 173–98.

Tullberg, Steen, "*Søren Kierkegaards Papirer* (1909–48 and 1968–78)—between Recension and Reception," *Kierkegaard Studies. Yearbook*, 2003, pp. 234–76 (published also in *Danske Studier*, Copenhagen: C.A. Reitzel 2003, pp. 132–72).

— "Die Rezeption der *Philosophischen Brocken* in Skandinavien," *Kierkegaard Studies. Yearbook*, 2004, pp. 306–27.

Wind, H.C., "Die Rezeption Kierkegaards in der neueren dänischen Theologie," in *Die Rezeption Søren Kierkegaards in der deutschen und dänischen Philosophie und Theologie. Vorträge des Kolloquiums am 22. und 23. März 1982*, ed. by Heinrich Anz, Munich et al: Fink 1983 (*Text & Kontext*, Sonderreihe, vol. 15), (*Kopenhagener Kolloquien zur deutschen Literatur*, vol. 7), pp. 187–209.

Norway:

"You Have No Truth Onboard!"
Kierkegaard's Influences on Norway

Thor Arvid Dyrerud

> Why should we respect those,
> who go about in "long" dress?
> *Sandkorn*[1]

In an account of student life in Kristiania in the 1860s, a high-spirited pastiche went "Read Kierkegaard, and you'll regret it; don't read him, and you'll also regret it."[2] The quotation reflects a duality experienced in the encounter with Kierkegaard's authorship. One could easily elevate this ambivalence to a general level, letting it stand for Kierkegaard's effect on Norway. On the one hand, he was celebrated and feted in mimetic passages like the one above; drinking bouts were arranged with toasting and speeches in woman's honor, following the pattern of the "Symposium" in *Stages on Life's Way*—altogether, there was pure joy at the universal spiritual power that had manifested itself in the Nordic countries. But in Norway, Kierkegaard also had a religious fate, primarily as a consequence of *The Moment* and the Church controversy of 1854–55, a battle that branded many of the young generation for the rest of their lives and that directly affected the social and cultural debate, partly with (soul-shaking) consequences. If there is any central focus in this article, it will precisely be the unpredictable and deeply disturbing figure Kierkegaard represents for Norway.

Writing about Søren Kierkegaard and Norway involves, to begin with, making clear that one will inevitably cross the boundaries between contemporary history, *Wirkungsgeschichte* (i.e., "effective history"), and reception history. Other countries stand at both linguistic and temporal removes from Kierkegaard's authorship, something that is not the case with Norway. Kierkegaard's writings were immediately accessible in Norway; there was no language barrier since Norwegian and Danish were then orthographically identical. Denmark and Norway had been in a union for just over four hundred years, and even if the political upheavals in 1814 resulted in the Danish throne losing Norway to Sweden, the cultural ties between the first two

---

[1]   Caspar Køhler Sandberg, *Den tveæggede Granstaur*, Fredrikshald: K. Sandberg 1856, p. 6.

[2]   Kristian Gløersen, *Sigurd*, Copenhagen: C.A. Reitzel 1887, p. 181.

countries remained strong. References to a Dano-Norwegian "common literature" died out only well into the nineteenth century.

In 1922 the Norwegian literary historian Gerhard Gran (1856–1925) wrote that "Kierkegaard has stamped his impression, either temporarily or permanently, on our theologians, our poets and writers, our pedagogues—yes, one even finds traces of him amongst our journalists."[3] This statement indicates how broadly Kierkegaard's polemics had affected the Norway of that time. Gran further claimed that Kierkegaard was one of the "most important fermenting agents" of Norwegian intellectual life ever. In a certain sense there can hardly be found a Norwegian author or intellectual who has not received impulses from Kierkegaard to a greater or lesser degree. It will not be possible to give a picture of the full spectrum of this here, but it is my modest ambition to demonstrate the richness of Kierkegaard's influence upon Norway. My point of entry to the material is from the history of ideas, a perspective that implies that a forgotten novel of the 1870s, an accountant from Halden, as well as a drama by Ibsen or one of Munch's pictures, all stand on equal footing with philosophical or theological dissertations, which is to say, the more academic and "official" interpretations of Kierkegaard's authorship.

A real reception history in Norway was first broached in the late 1870s. Following in the wake of George Brandes' book of 1877, *Søren Kierkegaard. A Critical Exposition*,[4] that marks the starting point for Kierkegaard studies, the Norwegian theologian Fredrik Petersen's great work, *Dr. Søren Kierkegaard's Preaching of Christianity*, was published.[5] It was from then that it is first possible to refer to a systematic interpretation of Kierkegaard's authorship, not only in Denmark or Norway, but anywhere. Parallel with this there was a shift of Norwegian opinion about Kierkegaard that is of great significance. During the first decades of the twentieth century an international disciplinary subject grew, wherein Kierkegaard eventually reached a sort of global supremacy in existential philosophy. In line with this, it becomes more and more problematic to speak about a genuine Norwegian comprehension or reception. Kierkegaard is now discussed to an increasing degree across borders, in a global network where Norwegian researchers also participate, but—paradoxically enough—to a lesser degree than one would expect. But before we come that far, we must enter into the then contemporary events.

I. Eroticism, Poetry, or Philosophy?

Kierkegaard's books were published in editions of 500 copies in the first half of the 1840s, all printed at Bianco Luno's Press in Copenhagen. Of these, a certain number were sold on commission by Norwegian book dealers. *Morgenbladet*, the

[3]   Gerhard Gran, *Alexander L. Kielland og hans samtid*, Stavanger: Dreyers Forlag 1922, p. 110.
[4]   George Brandes, *Søren Kierkegaard. En kritisk Fremstilling i Grundrids*, Copenhagen: Gyldendalske Boghandels Forlag (F. Hegel & Søn) 1877.
[5]   Fredrik Petersen, *Dr. Søren Kierkegaards Christendomsforkyndelse*, Christiania: P.T. Mallings Boghandel 1877.

country's first daily newspaper (from 1819), could thus announce on Wednesday, March 29, 1843, that the Tottrupske Book and Music Store had *Either/Or* by Victor Eremita for sale for 2 rix-dollars and 73 schillings. It can be concluded that it was with the publication of *Either/Or* that Kierkegaard attained a Norwegian readership. However, it is difficult to state precisely the number of readers at this point in time since many more individuals than today used the library to keep up with the latest literature. In the catalogue of the Christiania Cathedral School's library one finds *The Concept of Irony* (1841) and *Fear and Trembling* (1843). These were obtained a short time after publication and were accessible to both the school's teachers and students.[6]

Today, we cannot say much about reader traffic in the libraries of that day, but now and then we get a glimpse of it, as for example through the young Henrik Ibsen (1828–1906), who during the 1840s was an apothecary's apprentice at Grimstad on the Norwegian south coast. His friend of the time, Christopher Due (1827–1923), describes the great activity in the town's library: "In addition to the mutual personal sympathy and common literary interests—that year we eagerly studied Søren Kierkegaard's *Either/Or* and *Works of Love* amongst others."[7] I will leave Ibsen alone for the time being, only to bring him back at a later stage in his life, when he once and for all put the bottles of medicines aside in favor of the inkwell.

One does not find contemporary reviews of Kierkegaard's writings in Norwegian newspapers or journals. However, on March 17, 1846, *Morgenbladet* had a discussion in connection with the publication of the *Postscript* twenty days before. The newspaper cites Kierkegaard's first and last explanation, published at the end of the book, where he admits to his authorship of the pseudonymous works. *Morgenbladet* concludes: "And thus it is now that the common opinion is publicly confirmed, by ascribing to one author all those remarkable writings published over the space of 8 years, arousing surprise concerning authorial fertility, the likes of which has until now never been seen." The discussion reveals no knowledge of the remarkable publications *per se* but witnesses instead a curiosity and fascination with the *phenomenon* Kierkegaard, that provocative and interesting literary comet from Copenhagen.

This jibes well with other contemporary sources, all of which are mainly anecdotal in character. In Edvard Mørch's (1828–1908) book, *Kristiania-Memories*, we get a brief impression of how the students of the capital regarded Kierkegaard. Mørch describes this period as a philosophical and aesthetic time, when the young men of the coming generation smoked pipes and conversed with one another in a lofty manner. Some went so far in their admiration of Kierkegaard, Mørch writes, that they "...began in small ways to use, what they meant was a Kierkegaardian mode of expression—one didn't say 'that one's eyes hurt,' but rather 'that one had a sickly malady of the eyes.' "[8] At student flats, works like *Either/Or* or *Stages on Life's Way* were debated, but without anyone actually being well-versed in the content of these writings. It was nonetheless important that "an ideally equipped student should be infatuated by Hostrup and know his Kierkegaard."[9]

On certain formal occasions, such as when a comrade was traveling away, a party would be arranged in a larger student flat. All paid "12 schillings per head," which then went to the purchase of cognac and "powdered sugar," with the attendant boiling of water, and punch being made in the wash basin. Initially, things would go respectably: the young students—who were often from the countryside—chatted about the city's ladies they had seen and with whom, on rare occasions, they had talked, "comparing them to Cordelia in 'Johannes the Seducer's Diary or Alma' in 'Adam Homo' etc."[10] Later, the party would drift over to group singing, before people eventually moved out into town where they sang and danced around the Palace in Karl Johan's Street, to the great despair of the watch.

The most concrete traces of Kierkegaard from that time can be found in Henning Junghans Thue's (1815–51) *Reader in the Mother Tongue for Norwegians and Danes* from 1846.[11] This is a collection of model texts for use in the school at the advanced levels, and here Kierkegaard is represented by three small pieces: "Kvinden" from *Either/Or*, "Den Huslige Censur" from *Prefaces*, and finally "Den Lykkeligste Existens" from *Stages on Life's Way*, the latter of which was only seven months old when Thue's book went to press. Even though these do not represent any great body of text, it is still worth noting that the book was also used for teaching of the mother tongue in Norway. A later professor of history, Yngvar Nielsen (1843–1916), wrote in his memoirs of his student days at the Latin School in Christiania, "Our literary and aesthetic norm was to be taken from H.J. Thue's *Læsebog*, big and thick as it was."[12] Nielsen was a student from about the mid-1850s, and so Thue's reader had been in use for at least ten years by that time.

Thue, who was Head Teacher and Headmaster of Arendal's *Middel- og Realskole*,[13] was well qualified as a broker of Kierkegaard since he had, during a period of study in Copenhagen, been an *ex auditorio* opponent at the public defense of Kierkegaard's thesis on irony in 1841. In Thue's introduction to his selection of texts, he added a short biography of Kierkegaard, where he, on the basis of common opinion, dared to claim that Kierkegaard was in fact "the Great Unknown." One should here remember that Kierkegaard's name was at that point in time only found on a handful of edifying discourses. Additionally, Thue praises Kierkegaard for his productivity, his psychological powers of observation, and for his exemplary use of his native tongue even in the most difficult mental exercises. But it is, Thue writes, "especially on the erotic themes that he directs his intense investigations into the

---

[9]   Ibid, p. 20.

[10]   Ibid.

[11]   Henning Junghans Thue, *Læsebog i Modersmaalet for Norske og Danske*, Kristiania: A.D. Wulfsberg & Co. 1846.

[12]   Yngvar Nielsen, *En Christianesers Erindringer fra 1850- og 60-Aarene*, Kristiania and Copenhagen: Gyldendalske Boghandel / Nordisk Forlag 1910, p. 77.

[13]   At the time, a type of school beyond primary levels teaching the "practical" subjects of mathematics, modern languages, etc., as opposed to the classically-oriented traditional middle school.

deepest corners of the human heart."[14] It is, in other words, as a sublime eroticist that Kierkegaard is first presented to the Norwegian public.

In the table of contents at the beginning of his reader, Thue has categorized Kierkegaard's texts according to their genres, something that provides yet another indication of how he was read at the time. Thue classified Kierkegaard's text from *Either/Or* with "Epic Poetry," in the subcategory "Poetic Narrative," while the other two pieces fall under "Didactic Prose."

It does not take a very long look at Thue's attempt to place Kierkegaard into his own literary categories, before it becomes apparent that he must have been in a quandary about what type of texts these were since in them one finds a mixture of high and low styles, philosophical concepts in neat union with a literary presentation, teasing, irony, and the like. Thue chose the obvious solution: to place the texts partly under poetry, partly under narrative, under philosophy, and science. However, it is no easy task to determine how the three texts can thus be separated. What they have in common is that they are a sort of training in the higher eroticism, where woman, with her immediate genius in the direction of the sensual, her innocent delightfulness, makes the reflective man think twice about worldly existence.

That Kierkegaard is primarily identified by Thue as a sharp psychologist and expert eroticist, is interesting with regard to the reception that would later come to dominate the entire field of study: Kierkegaard as the passionate advocate of the individual, with the weight on the personal dedication to Christianity's totally overshadowing claim on human life. At this early point, however, there was no real theological reception—it is the poet Kierkegaard whom Thue finds interesting. Something that also agreed well with the young students already mentioned, who in a philosophical-aesthetic intoxication celebrated, apparently untroubled and without qualms, the fate that had so kindly placed a literature of Greco-Dionysian-Byronic format within their own linguistic sphere.

II. Can One Be a Priest in the Norwegian Church?

The matter takes another tone when we move on to the 1850s. Given that Kierkegaard was a literary and aesthetic source of inspiration in the 1840s, it was *The Moment* and the controversy of conscience of 1854–55 that really brought Kierkegaard to public attention, in fact, to such a degree that it was claimed that the so-called "Conscience Controversy" had greater significance in Norway than in Denmark. In 1901, theology professor Christopher Bruun concluded that Kierkegaard had "exercised a strong influence...upon all of Norwegian revivalism of the previous half-century."[15] However, twenty years later, Harald Beyer (1891–1960) wrote "But not least of all, the *freethinkers*...were able to make Kierkegaard their own."[16]

---

[14]   Thue, *Læsebog i Modersmaalet for Norske og Danske*, p. 487.
[15]   Christopher Bruun, "Lidt om Søren Kierkegaard," *For Kirke og Kultur*, 1901, p. 579.
[16]   Harald Beyer, *Søren Kierkegaard og Norge*, Kristiania: H. Aschehoug & Co. (W. Nygaard) 1924, p. 295.

The following pages will attempt to illuminate the somewhat dizzying chasm that yawns between these two citations: the circumstance that Kierkegaard has given significant nourishment to the Norwegian revivalist movement, only to have later imparted important impulses to cultural radicalism. To make this easier to grasp, I will concentrate on three important meetings in the Norwegian Students' Society.

In its own supplement to *Christiania-Posten*, on February 19, 1855, under the title "Was the Deceased Bishop Mynster a 'Witness for Truth,' " the Norwegian public could read in its entirety Kierkegaard's first article from *Fædrelandet* of December 18, of the previous year, where he frontally attacked Hans Lassen Martensen's (1808–84) eulogy for Bishop Mynster (1775–1854). The debate had attracted attention in Norway before, but now the editors opined that Norwegian readers must get a more detailed insight into the controversy since it "concerns every Christian and not least of all our Church." The newspaper's editorial was accompanied by a wish that "every reader will exclude all external influence, when he decides for himself, which of the parties in this instance is witness to the Truth."[17] Three days later, on February 22, the riposte came from the other side, also given in its entirety: "On the Occasion of Dr. S. Kierkegaard's Article in *Fædrelandet*," written by Bishop Martensen. Three days after that, Kierkegaard's reply to Martensen "There the Matter Rests"[18] was published—and so it continued, with several more Norwegian contributions to the controversy, in addition to reprintings of some of the most central Danish articles, as for example those by Jens Paludan-Müller (1813–99) and Rasmus Nielsen (1809–84).

A glance at the selections above shows that the "witness to truth" controversy not only—as previously thought—was referred to in Norwegian newspapers, but it was also to a large degree *carried out* in those papers under the eye of the Norwegian public. All of the articles referred to above were reprinted on the front page of the newspaper, and in many instances, they even filled all four columns and thus dominated the news.

Bjørnstjerne Bjørnson (1832–1910) later dramatically described the impression the controversy had made upon the collective consciousness: "It was in the days when *The Moment* struck like lightning; peals of thunder still rolling, Søren Kierkegaard was the master of our conceptions."[19] Bjørnson acts here like a reporter of a pure catastrophe of nature, but it would be—as we shall see below—only twenty years later that Bjørnson would become seriously involved in the consequences of these same reported peals of thunder.

Someone who found himself in the thick of it was Nils Hertzberg (1827–1911), later a government minister. At the time, he was a young student of theology, who wrote in his memoirs: "Kierkegaard's 'Øjeblikke' awoke in the first half of the 1850s a strong ferment among us younger theologians in Christiania." Disturbances began in the theologians' own student organization but quickly spread to wider circles and

17	"Var afdøde Biskop Mynster et 'Sandhedsvidne,' " *Christiania-Posten*, Supplement to *Christiania-Posten*, no. 2318, February 19, 1855.
18	See *SV1* XIV 15–21 / *M*, 9–15.
19	Citation from Beyer, *Søren Kierkegaard og Norge*, p. 191.

packed meetings of the main Student Society. Hertzberg relates that at one of these meetings, he led off with the following words:

> "Is it defensible to be a priest in the state Church?" Starting out from Kierkegaardian premises, I found that irresponsible. I still well remember how old Wexels, in a friendly, yet serious and worthy way, went against the proposition. Jørgen Moe, at the time priest at Krødsherred, laid down the law more sharply: amongst other things, he directed the following words at us: "How can you youths find it indefensible to become a priest in the State Church, where old Wexels has preached the Word of Christ before you could even button your trousers!"[20]

These authoritarian slaps were perhaps self-defeating. More decisively, Gisle Johnson (1822–94) was present on this occasion. He was a man of the new times, strongly touched by Kierkegaard, and even if he could not support the young people in everything, he had strong sympathy for their leanings. However, he thought the Church was in possession of the "pure Word and pure Sacraments," but is also said to have exclaimed that he "thanked God that he never became a priest."[21] These were noteworthy words from a man who used his life to train priests throughout the entire country; in its paradoxical way, this is very telling.

Gisle Johnson was Lecturer (later Professor) of Theology at the university, and also a teacher at the Practical Theological Seminary, giving his name to the most far-reaching and profoundly gripping revival movement that ever occurred in Norway: the "Johnsonian Revival." Ever since the overthrow of the *Konventikkelplakaten* of 1741[22] and the founding of the Norwegian Mission Society in 1842, the country had been characterized by a strongly Pietistically-toned revival. Johnson had not initiated it, but he became its undisputed leader and most marked proponent. In addition, he was also an important factor in stabilizing the split in the Church that came as a threat in the wake of the revival. The emphasis on a personal and sincere Christian ideal at the same time led to a dissatisfaction with the national Church and all the "freeloaders" who had, by virtue of baptism, obtained a free pass to church pews. The Revival's ideal congregation was the small born-again core—the sect—and not a group of fancily-dressed upper class citizens out for a Sunday walk. If Johnson was the revival movement's torch-bearer, he also, together with the Johnsonian priests, ensured to a large degree that the formation of the smaller church groups—the Inner Mission societies—took place within the national Church and not in opposition to it.

Johnson was aware of Kierkegaard from early on and was influenced by him; Johnson worked him—almost as if in a precautionary fashion—into his revivalist theology and his dogmatics. His *pistikk* (the name he gave to studies regarding the origin of and essence of belief) therefore contained several central congruencies with Kierkegaard's categories of existence. In Johnson, man is described in his natural state as being characterized by egoism, disharmony, pain, and angst. This

---

[20]   Nils Hertzberg, *Fra min Barndoms og Ungdoms Tid*, Kristiania: Aschehoug & Co. (W. Nygaard) 1909, p. 138.
[21]   Ibid, p. 137.
[22]   A decree that forbade those without higher education from preaching at prayer meetings.

points towards the next state, reached by a leap, and which corresponds to human existence under law. However, abiding in piety gives birth to a doubt that leads to the highest state, Christian belief, described by Johnson as "a strange form of humanity's personal existence."[23] It is this subjective component of Johnson's otherwise strong Lutheran orthodoxy that Hertzberg has in mind when he writes about Johnson being influenced by Kierkegaard—"both define the individual's task as reaching a personal relationship with God and the Gospel's inwardness."[24] In other words, Johnson was a Kierkegaardian, albeit of a pronouncedly confessional and Pietistic sort.

Hertzberg further writes that Johnson was also aware of the dangers of the official state Christianity, but in contradistinction to Kierkegaard, who was permeated by "a bitter, often ruthless satire," Johnson's warnings functioned "more positively, but did not on account of that carry lesser weight."[25] Kierkegaard had also given an important impetus to the revival movement of which Johnson was the foremost proponent, and with that, had also in a certain way prepared the ground for the dissatisfaction with the State Church that was now breaking out. Yet through the same Johnson, Kierkegaard was also watchfully assimilated into the Church's own bulwarks. Johnson had to a great degree prepared a systematic defense that now functioned as an effective shield in the fight that had arisen, whereby he could meet the young people halfway, and by doing so, ensure that they ended up on the right side. When Johnson, in the Student Society, thanked God that he had not become a priest, we see a latent irony in the statement that would have been worthy of Kierkegaard.

It is true enough that not everybody accepted Johnson's outstretched hand. Hertzberg absolutely lacked any leanings towards the priesthood, and many of his fellow students never took Holy Orders, or only followed that vocation late in life. The aforementioned Christopher Bruun became a theological candidate in 1856 but did not become a priest until 1893. He wrote, in 1878: "I couldn't be a priest. Certainly, for me clearly, what was greatest and most glorious was to preach Christianity....But I had read Søren Kierkegaard. And he had taught me to be a bit careful in the matter of becoming a priest."[26] Bruun had been Johnson's pupil but chose, as he later formulated it, to wrestle with Kierkegaard's paradoxes "instead of swallowing that Johnsonian hard tack porridge."

Even if Johnson's presence, at least in the capital, had put a lid on tempers, in some other places things did not go as smoothly. In Skien, Henrik Ibsen's birthplace, the priest Gustav Adolph Lammers (1802–78), after taking office as pastor, stimulated a revival that would attain great significance. In 1850, he built the country's first *bedehus*, a prayer meeting house, for the "awakened" elect, and in 1853 he founded *Skien's Inner Mission Society*, Norway's first inner mission organization. Lammers preached a strict Pietism with emphasis on individual salvation and witness. He had read many of Kierkegaard's writings, and it is claimed that he recommended to his

---

23   Citation from Einar Molland, *Fra Hans Nielsen Hauge til Eivind Berggrav*, Oslo: Gyldendal Norsk Forlag 1968, p. 36.
24   Hertzberg, *Fra min Barndoms og Ungdoms Tid*, p. 138.
25   Ibid.
26   Citation from Molland, *Fra Hans Nielsen Hauge til Eivind Berggrav*, p. 38.

friends the reading of *The Moment* especially since that "will clarify your view of the State Church."[27]

During the 1850s, Lammers steadily became more and more at odds with the State Church and its unholy blend of the worldly and the believers. On March 19, 1856, he wrote to the King and applied for resignation from the priesthood. On June 22 of the same year, Lammers preached his final sermon at Skien Church, and here, it is apparent that Kierkegaard played a significant role. Of the things that made it impossible for him to continue in his vocation, baptism and confirmation were central, and Lammers found these rituals to be one of the main causes of the Church's decay:

> Rather unbaptized and unconfirmed Children! Rather honest heathens, than to allow oneself to be driven by the bourgeois conditions and use the State Church's directions to keep on bringing up a family of liars and hypocrites! Rather the destruction of all that is good and dear in the world, than to play along any longer at this horrible game![28]

Not only was the content here inspired by Kierkegaard; the entire dramaturgy of the speech, from the concrete choice of words, to the rhetorical and polemic build-up and tone are, so to speak, directly taken from *The Moment.* "And now judge yourself," comes some lines further on, as if to underline from where the day's text is taken. It is *The Moment* no. 7 that lies at the basis of the above formulations regarding baptism and confirmation, and Lammers uses almost literally the same ameliorating words to the congregation, as those that are found in *The Moment* no. 7: "But I do not attack the congregation in what I write; it is led astray"—by the priests.[29]

A few weeks later Lammers and twenty-three others formally left the Norwegian Church and instituted a free congregation. The Scriptures would be the sole authority now, and infant baptism was eliminated. Two-hundred-and-eighteen people attached themselves to the congregation during the four years Lammers was the leader. He had greater expectations than that and surely believed that more priests would follow his example, but this did not happen. However, Lammers also was active in other parts of the country.

In 1857 he traveled north to Tromsø, where a strong religious revival had established itself. In *Norsk Kirketidende* from October 1856 we can read that already "one year ago, Kierkegaard's *The Moment* no. 7 was sent around from Tromsø to the inhabitants of the areas situated a few miles[30] south of Tromsø around Balsfjorddal."[31] For anyone familiar with Norwegian topography, this is dizzying information: the journey from Skien to Tromsø is almost equivalent to the distance from Skien to

---

[27]   H.G. Heggtveit, *Den norske Kirke i det nittende Aarhundrede: Et Bidrag til dens Historie,* vols. 1–2, Christiania: Cammermeyer 1905–20, vol. 2, p. 932.
[28]   G.A. Lammers, *Agskedsandragende og Afskedsord ved Nedlæggelsen af Embedet som Sognepræst til Skien,* Skien: Paa J. Melgaards Forlag 1856, p. 22.
[29]   *SV1* XIII, p. 259 / *M,* 245.
[30]   I.e., Norwegian miles, an old measure of distance of between 10 and 11.295 km, depending on the system used.
[31]   "Den religiøse Bevægelse paa Tromsø," *Norsk Kirketidende,* no. 42, October 19, 1856, pp. 461–7, see pp. 463–4.

Rome. If one takes into consideration the limited means of transportation of those times (the first railway came to Norway in 1855, a short line in the south) in that area—a long extended valley where the forces of nature, not people, set the agenda (with bitterly cold winter temperatures)—then one has a rough idea of what the traveler was up against.

In any case, the farmer Johan Bomstad was so moved, that he set out on a trip in the immediate area and "preached for withdrawal from the State Church."[32] At Eastertide, the resignations began, and already by June, 50 individuals had formally withdrawn themselves from the national Church. The latest twist was that a free congregation had been formed, with one Johan Hansen as leader. Once more, baptism was central to the criticism of official worship. The problem was, as *Norsk Kirketidende* lightly tut-tutted, that those in Tromsø had misunderstood Kierkegaard and "viewed him as a prophet." Kierkegaard's writings had been taken literally, something that was blamed on readers not being familiar enough with them to know that "he himself was laughing in the background at those, who were so weak in their convictions, that they took his word for the gospel truth."[33] This arrogance from a theological writer in the capital did nothing to dampen the urge for confrontation.

It is important here to point out that the revival that swept over the country was tied closely to, and was a continuation of the *lekmannsbevegelse* ("Layman's Movement") which had originated fifty years before with Hans Nielsen Hauge (1771–1824) and the first clash with the state Church. Hauge travelled around the country as a lay preacher between 1797 and 1804, and was arrested a number of times on the basis of the *Konventikkelplakaten* of 1741, the last time being in 1804, with the result that he was imprisoned for ten years. (*Konventikkelplakaten* was rescinded in 1842, and Norway enacted a liberal dissent law in 1853.) Hauge writes that his arrests at the time "aroused the ordinary people to the opinion that authority would obstruct the Good and allow the Evil to go unpunished."[34] At the start of the nineteenth century, 80% of the population supported itself through subsistence farming and fishing; Hauge's words can stand as markers for the first social upheaval in Norway. Here, for the first time it became apparent that there is a difference between those above and those below; between ordinary people's religious unfolding and an alienated state power, a rule of bureaucrats contra the common masses.

The Pietistic movement in Norway came in two waves, finding many outlets for expression: it contains within it an emerging class consciousness that would later take form as a farmers' revolt, where the Haugians played a considerable role. It is found in the national independence movement and represents an early reaction against industrialization, progress, and secularization; put briefly, Pietism is a modern phenomenon. It is against this background that the powerful effect that Kierkegaard's agitation against the "silk vestment priesthood" had in Norway must be seen.

It was to the newly-formed free congregation in Tromsø that Lammers was invited in 1857. The only catch was that Gisle Johnson had also been in Tromsø; the same

---

32   Ibid. p. 465.
33   Ibid.
34   Citation from Molland, *Fra Hans Nielsen Hauge til Eivind Berggrav*, p. 129.

year saw the publication of Johnson's book *Some Words on Child Baptism*,[35] later often referred to as "words at the right time." By 1859, it was all over: Lammers left the free congregation, saying now that everything was a "error" and an "escapade," reconciling himself entirely and fully to the Augsburg Confession, and rejoining the Norwegian Church—in other words, he had totally changed his view on infant baptism.

As was mentioned earlier, not everyone went along with joining the fold. For many, Kierkegaard had lit an inner flame that could not be controlled. In what follows, I shall portray a person who has until now been totally forgotten in Norway—a story and a fate that lie under the banner of *The Moment*, with the most dramatic outcome imaginable.

III. Kierkegaard's Norwegian Bannerman

East of Oslo, in the direction of Sweden, lies Halden, earlier called Fredrikshald. We can read in the local newspaper *Smaalenenes Amtstidende*'s issue from May 8, 1870 the following legal notice: "Agent Caspar Køhler Sandberg, 50 years old, widower with 6 children, is charged after the District's order...with having, during the holy service held at Fredrikshald's Church on the second day of Easter, taunted and insulted the serving priest, together with having disrupted and disturbed the proceedings in the Church." The accused, according to the charge, stood up, clapped his hands and addressed the priest with these ignominious words: "Priest, you lie. You besmirch the truth." According to one Adjunct Knudsen, who sat in the near vicinity, Sandberg (1819–96) had acted calmly and with an apparently considered stance to the scandalousness of his action. He ended his short speech by saying, "For whatever I with calm demeanor have said, I stand for judgment at the courts, should anyone have any complaint." And there was indeed a reckoning. Sandberg was sentenced to 32 days' imprisonment on bread and water, together with fines for his uncontrolled behavior in the church. The sentence was served between January 9 and February 10 of the following year.

If the courts thought that this would have a preventive effect, they had a second thought coming. Shrove Sunday, February 19, nine days after the sentence was served, Sandberg again went into the church, this time with his three oldest children in tow. The sermon was about baptism, and once more, Sandberg did not allow the priest's words to go unchallenged. With everybody aghast, he stood up again and stopped the sacred service. When the sexton was summoned, rushing to the pews to usher him out, Sandberg once again took his hat and staff and walked out in a dignified manner. Out in the entrance, he met the mayor, who astonished, asked him "Sandberg, what have you done!" The guilty party did not give much by way of an answer, instead asking politely if he had permission to go home. That he received, and with that, Sandberg left the church.[36]

---

[35]   Gisle Johnson, *Nogle Ord om Barnedaaben*, Kristiania: J. Dybwad 1857.
[36]   All the above citations from *Smaalenenes Amtstidende*, court notice of May 8, 1870.

The same day, he was visited by the police, who told him that he was forbidden to visit the church on Sundays. The following Sunday he was nonetheless put under full arrest in the church at 9 a.m. and placed in custody until the church service was over. During interrogation by the police, Sandberg explained that he had taken the stricture to mean that he may not "go into the Church on Sunday, but he had not done that since he had entered it on Saturday." The fact was that Sandberg had entered the church at 6 p.m. on Saturday, and had slept over in the gallery until the following day.

Sandberg could have avoided prosecution if he had promised to stay peaceful when inside the church, something he could not allow himself by reason of his convictions. With that, the way was open for a new round in the courts. Sandberg was accused and judged by the Lower Court [*Underretsdom*] to "15 days imprisonment on bread and water" and afterwards by a Higher Court [*Overretsdom*] to "10 days imprisonment after the Criminal Law's Chapter 10 paragraphs 4 and 5" for having interrupted the church service and harassing an official in the execution of an official duty. Sandberg, however, immediately appealed to the Superior Court [*Høyesterett*], and the final judgment in the case fell on November 29, 1871. The lower court verdict was confirmed, and, additionally, the accused was sentenced to pay a fee of 25 specie dollars.

The interesting thing about Sandberg in this connection, however, lies many years back in time before the described events. In his declaration in court, Sandberg claimed that he, "following the New Testament, regarded it as his right and duty, to have acted as stated." He also explained that he had, for sixteen years thought about taking a step in this direction, but he had not "until now found the right moment."[37] If we go back sixteen years, we find ourselves in 1855. Caspar Køhler Sandberg was living at the time to all appearances a blameless life in Fredrikshald, as a tradesman and as an agent for out-of-town trade, working additionally for insurance companies. He had moved there in 1842, and at 22 years of age, worked as a trade agent with Ludvig Breder, receiving official permission to trade in the town in 1845.

But even if that life, seen externally, appeared to be nothing other than a life which, from a middle-class viewpoint, was respectable in every way, there was nonetheless clearly much going on inside the tradesman's mind. He used a large part of his time to cultivate what was an entire authorial output. From about 1854–55, Sandberg regularly turned out small publications from his own press, written and financed by himself. In form and content these closely resemble Kierkegaard's *The Moment*, so much so that there is reason to believe that Sandberg saw himself as Kierkegaard's faithful follower in the battle against priests and official Christianity.

This becomes especially apparent when we read his little piece *Look out, You There in the Ship of the Church! You're Capsizing! You Have No Truth Onboard!* This little pamphlet was published in 1855 and consists of 23 pages. On page 2 we can read the following little explanation: "Written the 20th of July 1855. Sent to S. Kjerkegaard, whence remitted August 1st. Some few additions October the 5th."[38]

---

37   All citations from *Norsk Retstidende* (Kristiania), 1872, pp. 137–40.
38   Caspar Køhler Sandberg, *Varsko der i Kirkeskibene! I kuldseile! I have ikke Sandhed ombord!*, Fredrikshald: K. Sandberg 1855, p. 2.

Thus, there was a correspondence between Sandberg and Kierkegaard, without our knowing anything of its content, and one can only guess at what led to Sandberg's changes of October. It is of course tempting to think that Kierkegaard's answer contained suggestions for improving the text; the most probable explanation is, however, that news of Kierkegaard's collapse on the street and his admission to hospital on October 2, had reached Fredrikshald.

In all likelihood, Kierkegaard had kept his Norwegian disciple at some distance. In the piece he received from Sandberg, he could have read amongst other things the following: "Now, when it is crawling with 'Witnesses to Truth' on this Earth, nobody could possibly take offence if I also witness for the truth? I will then in all innocence testify: that God alone is the Witness to Truth, and that all Witnesses to Truth of these days, are dead pots of clay!"[39] This is not too far removed from something Kierkegaard could have written, but in other places, the philosopher met with a twisted caricature of himself and his polemics. "I must, with S. Kjerkegaard admit," Sandberg states a bit too intimately somewhat later, "that I also am a bit polemically inclined and have therefore had to curb myself, so that no polemic in the fashion of these times had edged itself into any of the above 7 sentences." The seven sentences, with the heading *To the Planet's Common Church Pastors!*[40] are, however, soon passed by, and now he can no longer contain himself. With great dudgeon, he fires the following opening salvo: "Hey there, you Witnesses of Truth! Why do you walk around in long dress? Do you think that God's truth lies within the black cassock?" He continues in the same vein, and ends his harangue of the priests in a breakneck crescendo: "You go about like monkeys, bearing the symbol of your effeminacy! 'Black' is the symbol of Satan: the Lie! Your ruffs are certainly the symbols of the Millstone!"[41]

It is easy to recognize the starting point for this polemic. Some months before, Kierkegaard had polemicized in *Fædrelandet* about the same theme, with reference to the gospels of both Mark and Luke in the New Testament, where it is stated that one should beware of those who go about in long dress. Variations on the same subject are found in several places in *The Moment*. Yet even though the origin for the polemics is from a single source, there is a great difference between the stylistic execution of the Dane and the Norwegian. Sandberg is well-read and broadly oriented with the intellectual landscape, but in contrast to Kierkegaard, he cannot contain himself: Kierkegaard's brilliantly tinged rhetoric constantly threatens to become bloated and vulgar in Sandberg's hands. The finely tuned and honed polemic from *The Moment* is like a razor with which Sandberg accidentally cuts himself just as often as he manages to dissect his opponents.

A glance at some of his other writings further confirms this tendency. In a periodical called *The Two-Edged Spruce-Stake!* from 1856, he threatens the tribe of priests with Norwegian law and imagines what would happen when he makes the claim that the priests must be removed because they are an insult, not only against God's word, but because they must also be judged as villains by the laws

---

[39]   Ibid. p. 20.
[40]   *Til klodens almindelige kirkepræster!*, see ibid., p. 21.
[41]   Ibid. p. 21.

of the nation. He ends with this declaration of war: "Form up and come out into the light, you Children of Darkness, because 'the Fire Chief and the Chief of Police' are coming soon to give you a thrashing, because you will get many stripes, because you say that you speak the truth and act accordingly!"[42]

In a later number of the same journal the rants reach greater heights. In an important paragraph of the publication, with the headline "Watch out below—in the Hold," he has identified the problem with these "Cicero-Plato-Grundtvig-Wexelsian numskulls," whereupon he thereafter takes up the investigation of priestly morality. In barely four pages, he manages to call the priests "Pigs," "Offspring of Lizards," "Vipers," "Foxes," "Spawn of Hell," "Satan's Envoys," "Godforsaken Scabby-necks," and many other pleasant things.[43] After he has given vent to himself, however, there follows what might be called the "positive" part of his message to the priests. Entirely after the Kierkegaardian pattern, he enjoins the priests to quit themselves of all worldly goods, give to the poor, be dead to this world, give up the struggles and obstinacies of existence, and let Christ and mercy enter into them for real, in order to work quietly and in everyday life—but now in truth and humility.

We are now in 1856, and the aforementioned Fire Chief's voice has stilled. Kierkegaard died only one month after Sandberg had put the final touches to the work that he had received back from Copenhagen. In *Den tveæggede Granstaur*, number 5, he eulogizes his Danish brother-in-arms in a separate section at the end, under the heading *Søren Kjerkegaard*. He writes here that the deceased "has been an essential reason for clarifying concepts both high and low relating to true Christendom and contemporary Christianity, something every thinker must admit!"[44] Possibly significant of his then-current mood, is the following text: first, without any transitional form, he lets loose at the one point where he is reportedly at odds with Kierkegaard. The Dane was mistaken on one point, namely, his view of marriage as being incompatible with true Christianity. Sandberg claims that Kierkegaard confused his own long struggle on that theme, whereby he had chosen to live in a single state, with the teaching of Christ and the apostles in the New Testament. He who would be a disciple of Christ is often acting cleverly by living unmarried, Sandberg claimed, since persecution's power loses its sting when one is not a father of a family, but one is on no account any better in the sight of God because of that. This shows, first of all, that Sandberg has in all likelihood become well-versed in Kierkegaard's later writings, and even here it is difficult to make a case for Kierkegaard having meant what Sandberg thought, as presented above. The abrupt and somewhat clumsy manner with which Sandberg leaps into the controversy also bears witness to something personal and precarious being latent in that question.

Sandberg uses, however, by far the greater portion of the text to defend Kierkegaard from the attacks upon him from various quarters. Sandberg strikes out left and right: Did, for example, Kierkegaard resist public acknowledgement of Christ's Name? "You're a bunch of bold liars!" He—Kierkegaard—who more than anyone else in

---

42   *Den tveæggede Granstaur*, no. 5, 1856, p. 8.
43   *Den tveæggede Granstaur*, no. 10, 1856, p. 10.
44   *Den tveæggede Granstaur*, no. 5, 1856, p. 6.

the nineteenth century, has proclaimed Christ's teachings publicly! Sandberg's view of what Kierkegaard thought is worth citing in its entirety:

> He was not against those, who "publicly" preached the teaching of Christ, but he was a hater of the "official," mainly State Church blather, that had got the name of Christianity, with the State bribing some sworn-in, decked-out monkeys to carry out, at a given time, "official" corvée services, like the pawnbroking or execution businesses! He was a hater of this "official" state-run corvée nuisance, where someone at a fixed, pre-determined hour would come reciting a historical concoction to convince us that *that* was Christianity! He was a hater of those, who are "official," clever, talented speakers of the Word; but who did not want to be doers of the Word![45]

The temperature and glowing heat of the above show with all clarity how strongly Sandberg identified himself with Kierkegaard. At the end of the article, the following angry outburst appears: "You toads! You children of midnight! Do you want to sully Kierkegaard's memory? You did not come forth into the light whilst he lived, but now that he is dead, you want to insult him!" That is something Sandberg will not quietly acquiesce to, and in his later writings he uses much space to defend his deceased fellow conspirator. He continues the fight against official Christianity on his own. In *Fragment of the Church Wreck*, published somewhat later in 1856,[46] he takes on the philosopher Monrad, Pastor Block, the astronomer Viggo Hansteen, Welhaven, and Wilhelm Birkedal, to name a few. Wexels comes out worst, accused of perjury since "he like Judas with the thirty pieces of silver, carries on commerce using Christ."[47] This is a repetitive note running throughout his writing, and in the same fashion infant baptism and confirmation also get a sound drubbing. All these themes have obvious roots in Kierkegaard, who in *The Moment* repeatedly ridicules the young priests who look out for their daily bread before they look for the Kingdom of God.

Right up until the end of the 1850s, Sandberg kept on writing. However, he paid a high price for it and not just monetarily. He sent broadsheets to everyone and often got them sent back with angry replies and advice to send them to a *certain place*. In the number he sent to Kierkegaard, he signed off as "The Smallest of the Small," with an explanatory note regarding his own person. Here he lists some of the labels his contemporaries have pasted on him, such as "Face of Outrageousness," "Pharisee," "The Bewildered Heart," "Dreamer," "The Half-Mad," and the like.[48] All of this convinced Sandberg that he found himself on the true, but narrow path. Nonetheless, some events had proved unpleasant. In one 1857 number of *Grannaalen*, literally *The Spruce Needle*, he calls on the Chief of Police to keep an eye on his house, given that a stranger has been up to his room and "placed rotten straw under my sleeping mattress!"[49]

---

[45]   Ibid. p. 7.
[46]   Caspar Køhler Sandberg, *Vragstumperne af Kirke-Skroget*, Frederikshald: K. Sandberg 1856.
[47]   Ibid., p. 9.
[48]   Sandberg, *Varsko der i Kirkeskibene*, p. 21.
[49]   *Grannaalen*, no. 17, 1857, p. 8.

In January of 1859, Sandberg formally resigned from the State Church, and two months later married Maren Henriksen. In the 1860s, his pen was still; he and Maren had, one after the other, eight children, something that surely made its demands on top of the daily work. In 1869, Maren died after having given birth to twins, and after a few months, the twins themselves died. It is not unlikely that this could have been a contributing factor to Sandberg, on the following Easter day, taking that step which led to bread and water.

Things worsened over the 1870s. Sandberg went back on his word to the Chief of Police to stay quiet in church, and he took up writing again—even writing to the king—with everything reaching a climax in 1879, when he printed a notice claiming that 40 men had banded together to discuss the foundation of a new faith and the creation of a new Church. This proved to have no basis in reality, but rumors about possible members began to fly about, something that necessitated the Fredrikshald layman and church critic Olaus Nielsen (1810–88) (among others) to come out to deny that he was to be one of the potential founders of the new church. Sandberg's printed words were now reported to the police.

In mid-January's *Smaalenens Amtstidende* of the following year, we can read the following disturbing lines: "Køhler Sandberg made a spectacle again on Sunday in Immanuel Church." The case had become so sensitive that it was forwarded to the Department of Justice. The debate raged in the Fredrikshald press, a public exchange of words in which Sandberg also participated, something that only made things worse. In October, Sandberg was interned in Ebenezer Hospital, and at the beginning of November the verdict fell: Sandberg was forcibly placed into Gaustad Mental Asylum for an indeterminate period. The newspapers were beside themselves, congratulating Fredrikshald now that the city was free of this pest, and added: "...one could only wish that a couple of other agitators in our society, whose megalomania is tangible enough, could follow along soon after."[50] Now, if nothing else, one bothersome voice was silenced.

Sandberg sat in Gaustad for seven years, doing the hospital's book-keeping. Even if the man was too mad to be let loose, he was a trustworthy businessman and accountant. In 1887, he managed to smuggle out an article to a publication called *Rodhuggeren*, something that led to his case being taken up anew. He was released the same year, but had no one to whom he could return. His children had been taken in hand by poor relief authorities, and were farmed out; some disappeared to America with new families. He settled in Kristiania, wrote now and then for the magazine *Rodhuggeren*, and in 1888 published once more: two small works that both have the same title "The Human Being in The Moment, so called in the Memory of Henr. Wergeland and S. Kierkegaard." Caspar Køhler Sandberg died in Khristiania Hospital on April 16, 1896.

When things in Fredrikshald were raging at their worst in 1880, Sandberg's editor at the book press of *Østlandske Tidende* ran into hard times. He too, had been threatened with being reported to the police for having printed Sandberg's articles. In March, editor R.J. Sørensen answered the criticism and pointed out that Søren Kierkegaard had notoriously written things just as bad or worse than those for which

---

[50]   *Smaalenenes Amtstidende*, Wednesday, November 3, 1880.

Sandberg was now to be imprisoned. Sørensen then cited a number of Kierkegaard's statements in *The Moment*, before concluding: "Had Køhler Sandberg been a candidate in theology like Søren Kierkegaard and had he been a rich man, he would have been called a character, for whom one had to show pity. But now?—You're giving him the suffering he has been looking for!"[51]

The difference between Denmark and Norway was that Copenhagen had a functioning literary public who, acting as a set of lightning rods, could neutralize the type of small uproar that Sandberg's pamphlets had stirred up. This was lacking in Norway, where instead, there was an especially charged and politicized field, something editor Sørensen touched upon when he gave the Johnsonian revival the blame for Sandberg's failure. Even though Sandberg's polemical style was exaggerated, the content of his message was not very different from what the revival also had preached throughout the entire country—even from the official lectern of the university.

But again, it was Caspar Køhler Sandberg and not Søren Kierkegaard, who was to suffer that modern martyrdom that the Dane had viewed as the necessary consequence of his own fight against the Establishment. In spite of Kierkegaard's gloomy predictions (themselves being just a few of the "wrongdoings" for which he expected his contemporaries would attack him), he was to a much greater degree in control of his own fate. Sandberg fought his battle without a safety net, without the nimbus of genius that surrounded his Danish model. Thus it was that the Norwegian participant in the "witness to truth" controversy would feel the full brunt of his own actions, be juridically persecuted, imprisoned, declared insane, and parked in the insane asylum.

IV. Kierkegaard Haunts Kristiania

The Sandberg affair is like an evil harbinger of the unpredictable guise Kierkegaard would assume in Norway in the years that followed. The same year that Sandberg was sentenced to bread and water for disturbing the peace in church, Georg Brandes held his famous Copenhagen lectures, in which most of what had earlier been seen as true and sacrosanct was sent packing. *Emigrantlitteraturen*, as Brandes' lectures are often called, heralds the modern breakthrough in the Nordic countries—cultural radicalism and free thinking—and as such, is one of the notable intellectual movements of the nineteenth century. That Kierkegaard had something to do with Brandes' settling of accounts with the established order, first became clear with all its shock effect five years later, when Brandes set out on a lecture tour in Sweden and Norway with the manuscript of his Kierkegaard book that came out a year later in 1877. Brandes' lecture in Kristiania in the autumn of 1876 would have far-ranging consequences for how Kierkegaard was to be regarded in Norway; beyond this, it left in its wake a schism in Norwegian ecclesiastical and cultural life.

Brandes' lectures on Kierkegaard took place in the festival hall of the student organization since he had been denied an official platform at the Karl Johan University

---

[51]   R. Sørensen, article in *Østlandske Tidende*, no. 27, Wednesday, March 3, 1880.

by the Academic Collegium, the University's highest governing body. Even before Brandes' arrival, there was a conflict, something that can be put down to the fact that word of his appearance in Sweden had reached the collegium's ears. The official reason for the Norwegian cancellation was that while in Sweden, Brandes had given a "very shocking treatment of one of the most important and most beautiful Biblical narratives,"[52] namely, that of Abraham and Isaac. In connection with an analysis of *Fear and Trembling*, Brandes had related a religious phenomenological explanation of the story, and called it a *legend*, noting that its function was to mark the transition from human to animal sacrifice. What was notable was that a doctor of literature and aesthetics from the University of Copenhagen had been denied admission to the university auditorium, and a debate in the newspapers came soon after. The Norwegian author Arne Garborg (1851–1924) supported the Collegium with the argument that Brandes came as an "agitator" not as a scholar.

In the student organization, however, Brandes was welcomed with an energetic and arranged applause, if we are to believe *Morgenbladet*'s reporter. As herald of the free word, he was applauded by the young. From the article, we can further read that the lecture had the title "Søren Kierkegaard's Significance for Literature and the Life of the Mind"[53] and based on *Morgenbladet*'s short summary, it is easy to recognize the theme that, in a reworked form, appeared the following year in a book with the title *Søren Kierkegaard. A Critical Exposition.*[54]

At this point, a short summary of the main lines of Brandes' thought is necessary. Brandes' aim was to demonstrate that Kierkegaard's inner life was warped from early on, that the strict and pietist Christianity under which he was raised had made him a misfit, otherworldly, and lacking any feel for history or science. Brandes did not doubt his genius—quite the opposite—but the larger part of Kierkegaard's writing, no matter how brilliant it was, had no connection with reality. It was a self-centered mirror universe that suffered from the pressure of a tortured and sickly pietism, giving only shadow-like, anaemic pictures of reality. "His fantasy was and remained a hothouse flower," Brandes wrote.[55]

Kierkegaard's authorship first attains reality with *The Moment* controversy. Brandes' belief is that the incongruity between Kierkegaard's critical-psychological genius, and his servile belief in authority created an inner conflict that in the end could no longer be contained. The dam burst first in 1854–55, according to Brandes. Then, the original pure source latent in Kierkegaard's being pours forth unfettered, and the *real* Kierkegaard (in whom Brandes has already invested his support)—in a titanic eruption of anger and with his entire rhetorical genius unleashed—strikes official Christianity a blow of a sort and violence that none had seen the like of until then.

[52] Quoted from Einar Molland, *Norges kirkehistorie i det 19. århundre*, vols. 1–2, Oslo: Gyldendal 1979, vol. 1, p. 320.
[53] "Søren Kierkegaard's Betydning for Literaturen og Aandslivet," see "Dr. Brandes Forelæsninger," *Morgenbladet*, Friday, December 15, 1876.
[54] Brandes, *Søren Kierkegaard. En kritisk Fremstilling i Grundrids.*
[55] Ibid., p. 11.

Kierkegaard's great madness, according to Brandes, was that he believed he had discovered the India of belief, but in reality, he had arrived at the America of *true personality*, the *individual*, and *freedom*. With Brandes as a guide, both the map and the landscape in an instant became completely unrecognizable. Brandes gave Kierkegaard a clean bill of health precisely at the point where theologians and Christianity saw him as going mad and a good part of the way down the corridors of full insanity. This revision of Kierkegaard's authorship, its aims, and goals, makes it possible for Brandes to easily utilize Kierkegaard's agitation against authority, but now with more wide-ranging consequences.

Brandes' involvement with Kierkegaard goes much deeper than many have been willing to admit; he himself had been greatly influenced by Kierkegaard, and had as a young man nearly overreached himself mentally by attempting Kierkegaard's Christian ideals of inwardness. Perhaps, more than any other contemporary, Brandes perceived Kierkegaard's literary greatness. But he also identified the paradoxical aspect in Kierkegaard's writing, its two-edged taking of a position *against*, and at the same time, *acting in* the modern. During his fight against official Christianity, Kierkegaard was asked what he really wanted, whereupon he answered:

> I want honesty. If this, then, is what the generation or the contemporaries want, if they want straightforwardly, honestly, candidly, openly, directly to rebel against Christianity and say to God "We cannot, we will not submit to this power"—but, please note, this is to be done straightforwardly, honestly, candidly, openly, directly—well, then strange as it might seem, I go along with it, because I want honesty.[56]

It is this uncompromising intellectual ethos that Brandes takes with him from Kierkegaard, in addition to a dearly purchased knowledge of how explosive a power the Kierkegaardian corpus possessed. It was Brandes who a few years later discovered Nietzsche, and the formulation "God is dead, and we are the ones who killed Him" can well be said to be an updated variation of the modern psycho-religious diagnosis Kierkegaard had pronounced thirty years before.

In the Norway of 1876, the times were not ripe for any of this. The Kierkegaard who had up to then spoken so vivaciously to hearts, who had set so many souls on fire just a bit more than twenty years before, and who had agitatedly encouraged the core of belief and seriousness of choice—now stood forth as freethinker and cultural radical Georg Brandes' foremost witness to truth. The shocked reactions were not long in coming. Theologian Fredrik Petersen (1839–1903) began his counter-lectures at the university only a few weeks later, and the Kierkegaardian Jens Christian Heuch (1838–1904), teacher at the pastoral seminary, and later bishop, charged right out immediately with a series of articles in *Luthersk Ugeskrift*. These are interesting on several accounts but especially because they bear the message about the precarious confusion that occurred.

These articles had the title "On Occasion of Dr. Brandes' Appearance in Kristiania," and one of Heuch's main aims was to erase any traces of "the heretical Jew" and "anti-Christian agitator" in young people's minds. What was disturbing about Brandes, according to Heuch, was that he seduced young and impressionable

---

[56]   "Hvad jeg vil?" *Fædrelandet*, no. 77, March 31, 1855 / *M*, 48.

individuals "to become something else from the ground up." He did that by being in possession of "heresy's passion...a strongly subjective truth [and] fanaticism's inwardness." Regarding the danger of Georg Brandes as an agitator, Heuch emphasized his extraordinary style, "glittering like fireworks...smoothly going down...resourcefulness, pertness, rashness, unabashedness, and fearlessness... elevated and sympathetically gripping"—in short, his "coloration of language and method of expression to a high degree determine the effect he has."[57]

Brandes' rhetoric had rightly enough just been forged in the Kierkegaardian armory, and after Heuch's little tirade, one can ask who was it who actually came to Kristiania in 1876. Paul V. Rubow wrote in his Brandes study of 1932 that the "most deeply seated matrix of *Emigrantliteraturen* is Kierkegaard's agitational writing from 1854–55."[58] Rubow argues here that the point of departure for modernism's breakthrough is rooted in Kierkegaard's fight against the Church. The *sloughing* I intimated above, in other words, can be said to be of fundamental character. That bodily metaphor is nothing I am making up. In connection with Brandes' lecture of 1876, the newspaper *Nær og Fjærn* stated: "Now, well—so it is Søren Kierkegaard's skin that he has stuffed with 'freethinking.' Why? 'Because the man, if he were still alive, would invariably have been a freethinker.' "[59] Yet if the meeting with the freethinker Brandes was haunting enough, in a short while it would become much worse.

V. Between Pietism and Cultural Radicalism

The seriousness of Brandes' appearance was not clear until Bjørnstjerne Bjørnson (1832–1910), Norway's chief poet and national figurehead, himself spoke at the student organization barely a year later. Bjørnson had throughout his entire life kept Kierkegaard at arm's length, and viewed that "damned consistent hair-splitting" as he called it, with a good deal of ambivalence. Yet when he received Brandes' book on Kierkegaard in the spring of 1877, the reading of it obviously caused a change in his comprehension of what the whole affair was about. In a letter to history professor Johan Ernst Sars (1835–1917) in June of the same year, we can read the following heartfelt report:

> Brandes' *Søren Kierkegaard* is the best he has written. A capable, often masterfully capable book, and in Kierkegaard's person, I think Pietism is killed; he himself has made sure of it by cruelly and honestly driving its conditions for existence to the limit, and with Brandes' pointing this out, there lies a deed, that almost matches Kierkegaard's own, in terms of contemporary significance.[60]

---

[57]   J.C. Heuch, "I Anledning af Dr. Brandes's Optræden i Kristiania," *Luthersk Ugeskrift*, 1877, pp. 31ff.

[58]   Paul V. Rubow, *Georg Brandes' Briller*, Copenhagen: Levin & Munksgaard 1932, p. 128.

[59]   Quoted from Jørgen Knudsen, *Georg Brandes: frigørelsens vej, 1842–77*, Copenhagen: Gyldendal 1985, p. 419.

[60]   Bjørnstjerne Bjørnson, *Brytnings-år. Med innledning og opplysninger*, Copenhagen and Kristiania: Gyldendalske Boghandel, Nordisk Forlag 1921, p.180. Letter dated June 16, 1877.

The contemporary significance became clear for everyone when, on October 31 of the same year, Bjørnson held a speech entitled "On Being in Truth" before a full house in the building of the Student organization.[61] The great intellectual and moral leader at the time was in the middle of a period of religious conflict, a spiritual turbulence that—since it was of national consequence—was followed with argus eyes from the Christian side. Bjørnson was already in controversy with several central Johnsonian priests, and it got worse when he and Pastor Heuch went toe-to-toe in an irreconcilable debate in the *Luthersk Ugeskrift*, something that would become the opening round in the fight between conservative and liberal theology. Bjørnson never had much sympathy for the Pietist revival in the country, but gave his support to Grundvig and the idea of an independent "Folk Church." After Grundtvig's death in 1872, the Norwegian and Danish Grundtvigians saw Bjørnson as a possible new leader, something that fell to pieces when Bjørnson broke entirely with Christianity in 1880, to the advantage of the new and modern household gods Comte, Mill, Spencer, Darwin, Renan, and Taine.

In introducing his speech at the student organization, Bjørnson emphasized that there "are new sources flowing into my being," and continued by saying that he experienced a strong compulsion, "such a need among us, that it must be expressed." What was on Bjørnson's mind was the dichotomy between Pietism's demand for obedience and submission against the Enlightenment's demand for truth and intellectual integrity. Everywhere in society, Bjørnson sees that progress and truth must give way to the principle of authority, which stands higher than truth in the order of things. To live in truth means to say what one thinks because when something is held back, young people are fundamentally spoiled in their wish for openness and truth. Society is, in other words, unhealthy because something is being suppressed: "These things are left unspoken; it is officially correct to keep quiet. That disturbs piety, they say. But this is what should be spoken about."[62] The echo from *The Moment*, "That should be said, so that it has been said" is tangible here, and Bjørnson was also the man to say what was on his mind.

His speech has, however, in style and rhetorical construction, more the form of a sermon than of a literary or academic lecture. Symptomatically, it states "What I, even though no priest, will say unto all of you...."[63] From the shelter of this position, Bjørnson does not hold back from polemicizing against King Oscar II, who himself in a September speech had issued the following challenge to the young students of Uppsala: "Honor thy father and thy mother: that thy days may be long upon the land." This old commandment is the one the young hear most often, Bjørnson claimed, and the words were true enough, but it is a type of truth of the same sort as "to tell the warrior, setting out, the words 'Thou shalt not kill!'" These are also true and right, but untimely and directly meaningless words in the given situation. And

---

[61] Bjørnson, "Om at være i Sandhed." Speech in the Student Organization on October 31, 1877, see *Virkelighetens forvaltere*, ed. by Egil Børre Johnsen, Oslo: Universitetsforlaget 1995, pp. 167–172.

[62] Bjørnson, "Om at være i Sandhed," p. 168.

[63] Ibid.

the situation in the year 1877, on October 31, was to overcome that blind piety for the established order: "We must especially have piety for *the Truth*."[64]

After this eye-opening dethronement of society's highest authority, Bjørnson let fly against the religious preaching in the country, which he found un-Christian and loathsome. "If I had been a priest in these days," it runs programmatically, "I would begin and end everything by saying "Truth is the highest, in it is also the highest wisdom."[65] So far, so good. These words could have been spoken from any pulpit in any church of the country. But in the next sentence, comes a refinement that makes the whole more complex: "But for every *Individual*, the most important thing is to be in truth."[66] Brandes' interpretation of Kierkegaard of a few months before has fallen between these two sentences, and with dramatic consequences.

One must remember here that Bjørnson still had not broken with his Christian faith—he had only reformulated it into a Kierkegaardian-Brandesian personal creed, where the demand for *personal truth* and intellectual integrity is placed above all—as a (temporary) pledge for truth. What Bjørnson does in his speech is to set aside society's political and religious authorities, and in their place substitute an unswerving demand for personal gravity and the enlightened truth, at the cost of the current order. He does this by "colonizing authority's genre," by posing like a priest delivering a radical agitation that pretends to be an edifying homily. He got the recipe from Brandes, who in like fashion colonized Kierkegaard's rhetoric in *The Moment* for use in the service of cultural radicalism. In connection with this, I will here make the claim that the combination of Kierkegaard and Brandes are the *sine qua non* of Bjørnson's speech of 1877.

Francis Bull (1887–1974), Norway's most famous literary historian, later spoke of this speech as "one of the main events of Norwegian cultural life of the 1870s."[67] And if one were to put forward a single event in effective history, where Kierkegaard's complex influence in Norway manifests itself at a particularly charged moment, it must be this. Many of the young students who were there would, with time, become the main actors in culture and society, including amongst others Gerhard Gran (1856–1925) and Christen Collin (1857–1926), who told Bull that "it became their goal to live up as closely as possible to the ideals that Bjørnson had awakened on that day in their minds and thought."[68] Together with Brandes' performance of the year before, these occasions changed the view of Kierkegaard in Norway. If the Danish philosopher had been a hard nut to crack during the Church controversy, with this, he had gone a long way toward being totally impossible. That he could be used in such strongly diverging projects as fervent revivalism, cultural radicalism, and freethinking, moreover, demanded systematic counter-measures. Kierkegaard was also put into a theological structure that year, something that further marks 1877 as a watershed in Norwegian effective history.

---

64   Ibid. p. 169.
65   Ibid. p. 170.
66   Ibid. p. 172.
67   Ibid.
68   Ibid.

VI. The Theological Settling of Accounts

Immediately after Georg Brandes' appearance in Kristiania in 1876, the theologian Fredrik Petersen (1839–1903) began his oppositional lectures at the University in Kristiania. Petersen had read Kierkegaard since the age of 17 or 18 and had worked systematically with the Dane's writings since the middle of the 1860s. Petersen had also reviewed Barfod's edition of Kierkegaard's *Efterladte Papirer* in *Morgenbladet* around the beginning of New Year 1870, in six long installments spread out over an equal number of Sundays. Petersen was also the one who was to take on the thankless job of bringing theological order to Kierkegaard's relationship with Christianity. It was a task which, seen afterwards, was only the first in a career of apologetics while he was Professor of Systematic Theology at the Kristiania university. In 1874, he took over the position from Gisle Johnson and in 1880 emerged as the spokesman for a new apologetics with the lecture "How Should the Church Respond to the Lack of Faith of the Present?," that introduced modern theology to Norway. But first, he had to lay the foundation of the Church's reply to the unmanageable Kierkegaard.

The book *Dr. Søren Kierkegaard's Preaching of Christianity* (1877) is almost 900 pages long, and represents the first systematic reading of Kierkegaard's authorship, not only in Norway, but in the entire world. The book places itself somewhere in the intersection of contemporary and reception histories, and, in spite of its enormous scope, the text is a rather precise locus for finding those special aspects of Kierkegaard's authorship that captured attention and—not least—those characteristics or properties one *did not* bother with—in any case from a theological point of view.

The book's gestation stretched out over nearly ten years, being developed mainly as a series of articles in *Theologiske Tidskrift* from spring 1868 onwards. In late 1877, however, in light of the then recent Brandes appearance, it was precarious to take the step of a full and authoritative publication, a point made in the afterword, where it is stated that Kierkegaard was so obscure that not only "Christ's friends but also his enemies" might be able to use the Dane for their own purposes. Petersen wrote that the philosopher's enemies "had inherited Kierkegaard's costume, inherited his clothes. Kierkegaard cannot be recognized through their spirit, even though some of them might outwardly appear Kierkegaardian enough."[69] These words are tacked onto the end of the book, and the choice of words, such as "clothes" and "costumes" reveals with all possible clarity how tightly the promotion of the book is tied to the incidents around Brandes' phantom-like appearance in Kristiania.

Petersen's study contains three parts: the book's first part locates Kierkegaard's authorship within the cultural and political contexts of his times, while part two presents Kierkegaard's production work by work, through extensive use of long and thorough analyses of Kierkegaard's text, as given by him, but also by Petersen. The third and final part weighs the value and significance of each work for culture generally and for theology in particular. Petersen supports Kierkegaard's critique of Biedermeier culture's banality and spiritual decline but at the same time rejects the medicine Kierkegaard has prescribed as the cure. Kierkegaard's absolutism and

---

[69]   Fredrik Petersen, *Dr. Søren Kierkegaards Christendomsforkyndelse*, Christiania: P.T. Mallings Boghandel 1877, p. 897.

heaven-storming subjectivity represent a superhuman position to Petersen: it is too eccentric and perhaps even a bit too elitist. Christianity stresses reconciliation and is a gift for those ordinary people who struggle, and to that degree, is not a special tournament ground for heralds and *knights of faith* with clever paradoxes and cunning dialectic. Here, Petersen is in agreement with his theological contemporaries in their general evaluation of Kierkegaard.[70]

In spite of this understandable stance of Petersen—in his role as the responsible theologian—his study also at times leaves the reader somewhat confused. This is primarily because his study seems surprisingly insensitive towards Kierkegaard's textual characteristics. Petersen points out by way of example Hegel and speculative philosophy as Kierkegaard's main enemies, but at the same time rejects the critique of Hans Lassen Martensen's dogmatics on the following ground: "Martensen's speculation is not heathen, but Christian speculation."[71] The apologetic *tour de force* now and then threatens to totally eradicate its own object of study.

VII. Two Readings of Either/Or in the Year 1877

Fredrik Petersen regarded *Either/Or* as Kierkegaard's main work, and his basis for thinking so was that he found a harmony and balance in the presentation that he had otherwise missed in the pseudonymous works. "We perceive this work in every aspect as Kierkegaard's *magnum opus*."[72] According to Petersen, Kierkegaard had, with this work, stated more clearly than anywhere else a *principle of freedom*, a spiritual fulcrum that has "obliterated philosophy's and aesthetics' power over life."[73] More strongly than anywhere else in Kierkegaard's work, *Either/Or* bears witness to a personal conversion, from pursuit of pleasure and philosophy, over to life's ethical and practical demands upon humanity.

It is not surprising that Fredrik Petersen chose Kierkegaard's Assessor Wilhelm as his witness to truth. But interestingly, it was precisely *Either/Or* that was Kierkegaard's most widely read book in Norway. This popularity was also the case for Petersen's generation, who were students during the 1850s and 1860s. During the same year that Petersen's dissertation was published (1877), a novel came out, which in spite of its obvious differences from Petersen, nonetheless indicates how Kierkegaard was read in those times. The novel was titled *Sigurd*, written by the philosopher's contemporary, Kristian Gløersen (1838–1916). We find here a description of the effect Kierkegaard had on a young man shaped by the strong Pietistic revival visited upon the country, the "Johnsonian movement" outlined above.

The main character Sigurd is a priest's son from Norway's Vestland district, who came to age in a little hamlet which in his childhood was visited by the revival. The parish priest, his father, suffers acute religious scruples, and the family home is

---

[70]   Cf. Svein Aage Christophersen, "—som en Fugl i angstfull flukt foran det kommende Uvir. Det pietistiske hos Søren Kierkegaard og Gisle Johnson," *Kirke og kultur*, no. 107, 2002, pp. 191–206.

[71]   Petersen, *Dr. Søren Kierkegaards Christendomsforkyndelse*, p. 519.

[72]   Ibid. p. 881.

[73]   Ibid.

gradually turned into a joyless Christian educational institute. Play is for the most part forbidden—in any case, on Sundays—and Sigurd uses most of his time on "edification" in the church, on morning and evening prayer services at home, not to mention Bible and psalm reading.

Sigurd is a pious and believing lad, but hatred and inward conflict build up within him, between an ascetic denial of the worldly, and a need for life and beauty. He breaks with his home and journeys to Kristiania to study, developing thereafter into an erudite dandy and hairsplitter, after the pattern of Kierkegaard's aesthete—and with an open wound at the heart of his being. "Read Kierkegaard, and you'll regret it; don't read him, and you'll also regret it," to repeat the dramatic pastiche.[74] From this point on, the novel's narrative structure changes from a straightforward relation into Sigurd's diary. A little way into the section "From *Sigurd's Diary* I" we meet Kierkegaard for the first time. Sigurd has borrowed *Either/Or* from the university library, and at four o'clock in the afternoon, he sits down to read. He does not put the book down until four o'clock the next morning. In the diary, we read how he has been cast out into a sea of feeling and thought so strong that he nearly has to hold onto his chair. His almost step-by-step reaction is given here:

> there was a powerful feeling of envy, or actually jealousy. After all, it was what had moved within my own soul, what I have felt, what I have thought, dark, unclear perhaps, but even so, my thoughts. Why has he taken the words from me? The third and permanent impression was joy, expectant joy: Here you will find the solution to the great mystery, the answer to the great question, the apothegm, that opens the door to life's, to beauty's, to the spirit's, innermost sanctum.[75]

Sigurd has found the doors to heaven, a philosophy, given voice by a Christian thinker, and one of an intellectual caliber and power shining light-years beyond any of those domestic sons of darkness who killed the joy of life in young people. What is more, he also becomes more comfortable meeting the contemptuous representatives of evolutionary teaching and progress since it was Kierkegaard's ethicist Wilhelm who had sketched the most precise picture of the time's leveling powers, and with that, the deep despair of which the aesthete A was a symptom. Most important of all is that Sigurd found in *Either/Or* the necessary intermediary between Christianity and life's mundane pleasures, something that he had painfully missed. The ethicist's simple style of living, his rich inner life, his aesthetic and—not least of all—his ethically "legitimate" desire for his wife, whilst living at the same time in eternity— this makes life complete for Sigurd. This point is marked by the author when he has Sigurd propose to his great love at the very end of the novel.

For both the real theologian Petersen and the fictional character Sigurd, it is *freedom* that is at stake. Petersen finds a concept of freedom in Kierkegaard, whereby the individual takes over the responsibility for his own life and own deeds, becoming master in his own house—choosing one's own self in one's own eternal validity, to paraphrase Kierkegaard. This concept of freedom was useful in the theologian's polemics against the deterministic scientific view of his time, Darwinism, that

---

[74]   Gløersen, *Sigurd*, p. 181.
[75]   Ibid. p. 182.

regarded the human being as an animal. Sigurd saw the problem in an entirely different fashion. Sigurd had plenty of feelings of dutifulness; the most important thing for him was that delight and the beauty of life were also subsumed into the ethicist's recovery of himself and his own eternal self-validation. Duty and delight can thus open onto a higher state and solve Sigurd's existential dilemma.

VIII. Henrik Ibsen—Philosophy as mis–en–scène

The literary and artistic aspects of Kierkegaard's authorship clearly did not rate highly in the established interpretation of his writing. Petersen's almost bureaucratic treatment of the Kierkegaardian corpus seems rigid and strange today, but it reflects the contemporary religious and ideological climate. These conflicts appear to have dimmed the dimensional depth and richness of perspective in Kierkegaard's literary art. This side of Kierkegaard's work did, however, resonate amongst authors and artists from the last half of the 1800s, and it is here that one must look to obtain a fuller picture of the ways Kierkegaard permeates the generations who followed him. In connection with this, it is natural to examine more closely the two Norwegian artists strongly imbued with impulses from Kierkegaard's writing, namely Henrik Ibsen and Edvard Munch (1863–1944).

Henrik Ibsen was 25 years old when Kierkegaard died in 1855, while the younger Edvard Munch came first into this world eight years later, in 1863. In other words, they represent the experience of two generations, and in addition, two widely differing forms of expression. In what follows, I shall outline some main currents in what I perceive as the salient points of contact between Kierkegaard and these later well-known Norwegians, without, I hope, doing either of them any injustice.

One point Kierkegaard and Ibsen undoubtedly have in common is (once again) Georg Brandes. As mentioned, Kierkegaard studies have their beginning with him in 1877. In 1867—ten years before—Brandes also wrote the first word-portrait of Henrik Ibsen, where he more than hints at a connection with Kierkegaard. Ibsen's *Love's Comedy* and *Brand*, which had attracted attention on account of their polemic weight, "presented no new thinking, but convert that already existing into verse and rhyme." Regarding *Brand* especially, Brandes wrote "Nearly every decisive thought in that work can be found in Kierkegaard, and the hero's life has its model in his. It actually seems that Ibsen had aspired to the honor of being called Kierkegaard's *Bard*."[76]

Brandes' undisguised suggestions of plagiarism sealed Ibsen's mouth forever regarding his relationship with the older Danish fellow writer. Monotonously he repeated that "I have simply read very little of S.K. and have understood even less."[77] As usual, Ibsen is just as reserved, as are his works—sealed and closed against such attempts at linkage like that alluded to above. Bjørnson accused Ibsen of taking his cues in writing from within *literature* and not *reality*, something at which Ibsen took great umbrage, as one who had stated that an author's greatest task was to *see*.

---

[76]   Georg Brandes, *Henrik Ibsen*, Copenhagen: Gyldendal 1898, p. 29.
[77]   Letter to the Danish publisher Frederik Hegel, March 8, 1867. Quoted from *Ibsenårbok*, Oslo: Universitetsforlaget 1985–86, p. 138.

These contemporary rivalries can be put aside here. Much has been written and said about Ibsen's influences from Kierkegaard, including many ill-considered statements, such as that of Brandes above. I believe that it is important to understand this in the right way, and perhaps one should take Ibsen at his own word. Namely, I think it is correct when Ibsen says he has not understood Kierkegaard, nor has the more systematic part of the Dane's philosophy awakened his interest to any degree worth mentioning. Ibsen's understanding and use of Kierkegaard move along totally different tracks, I submit, and in what follows I shall attempt to say something about this, together with giving an example of how Kierkegaard's writings might be a source of inspiration for Ibsen.

In her dissertation of 1923, Valborg Erichsen writes, regarding *Either/Or*, and also the later and thematically closely related "Silhouettes," that she has found something which "could also be the prologue to a greater part of modern psychological writing."[78] A few years later the Swede Erik Kihlman claimed in his study of the history of ideas that Kierkegaard had, with these writings, "presented a basis for a new drama...pointed the way to mental life's most secret land."[79] These observations point towards a fundamental characteristic in Kierkegaard's production, which is precisely, I will claim, that to which Ibsen's literary instincts have been receptive.

To begin with, that characteristic lies in how Kierkegaard transfers speculative philosophy's inventory of concepts onto a literary *mis en scène*. But that literary scene and its playing with philosophical concepts in new contexts, has also converged with the theater's stage. In Kierkegaard's conceptual world, Mozart, Shakespeare, Holberg, and the Royal Danish Theater's *stage* were just as important as the *writings* of Hegel and Schelling. Thoughts literally received legs to walk on, with a text that swarms with theatrical metaphors and pictures—that actively use both the stage, its figures and gestalts to think with.

The secret behind Kierkegaard's genius as a diagnostician of the modern hides itself in his talent for the metaphorical view. Hans Blumenberg criticizes in his metaphorology Descartes' demand for a language that is plain and clear, and argues that metaphors and pictures are not residual phenomena on the road of language from mythos to logos, but are constitutive for thought and philosophy in general.[80] This means that our possibilities for experiencing the new are neatly tied together with the ability to shape metaphors, an ability to see the similar in the dissimilar. Kierkegaard loads his text with so many figurative mental motifs, that someone working in a visual medium can read him like a psychological picture book, which, as we shall see, is in fact how Ibsen has read Kierkegaard.

Thematically, the first part of *Either/Or* is about the theater. We get penetrating portraits of female dramatic characters, from Sophocles' Antigone to Goethe's figures, Marie Beaumarchais and Elvira (from *Clavigo* and *Faust*, respectively). The Don Juan character is examined in detail, as is his victim Donna Elvira. Further on,

---

[78]   Valborg Erichsen, "Søren Kierkegaards betydning for norsk aandsliv," *Edda*, 1923, p. 260.
[79]   Erik Kihlman, *Ur Ibsen–Dramatikens idéhistoria*, Helsingfors: Søderstrøm 1921, p. 197.
[80]   Hans Blumenberg, *Paradigmen zu einer Metaphorologie*, Bonn: Bouvier 1960 (originally in *Archiv für Begriffsgeschichte*, vol. 6, 1960, pp. 7–142).

we can read a long review of Eugène Scribe's 1825 play, *The First Love*. All these
figures are part of the existential drama that plays out in *Either/Or*—a drama of
existence's possibilities which is also reflected in Kierkegaard's method of rewriting
available genres and creating new ones into his own text. Belief in philosophical
truths and the presentation of them *in* a text, has given way to a feeling and a need
for that which can be demonstrated *by* it.[81] The literary game, the playing with
pseudonyms as personas and representatives for different views of life, overlaps
with the theme, so to speak, and is thus constitutive for *Either/Or* as the first modern
existential theater. It is very unlikely that the young Ibsen was not aware of this.[82]

The point of intersection is with the *Symparanekromenoi* (i.e., fellow-dead), a
company of aesthetes who meet at night, whose activity and holy customs consist
of "the aphoristic coincidental devotions," and who not only speak and think
aphoristically, but also live aphoristically, as "aphorisms in life," outside society and
humanity's trivial routine:

> we who are not consonants in the clamor of life but are solitary birds in the stillness of
> night, assembled together on only one occasion to be edified by representations of the
> wretchedness of life, on the length of the day, and of the endless duration of time...we
> who believe in nothing but unhappiness.[83]

The aesthete's form of expression thus has discontinuity as precondition: aphorisms,
fragments, snippets from diaries, and "Literary Remains"—complete and finished
work would indicate the unity of being, something that is an illusion. A committed
and lasting relationship with the world is not to be found within the aesthetic—this
form of *repetition* belongs to the *ethical*. His private life of memoirs can only find
its expression in individual and genuine moods. Typically, *Either/Or* is in its entirety
comprised of private papers found in a desk or a "*Secretaire*" [cf. Latin, *secretum*],
and were never meant for the public. The aesthete, when we meet him throughout
the first part of *Either/Or* is, as existential figure, a representative of a set of modern
experiences. These are important, because they have generated a view of life, a
decided attitude towards the world.

---

[81] This is a paraphrase taken from Poul Erik Tøjner's essay on *Kierkegaards æstetik,
Stilens tænker* (Copenhagen: Gyldendal 1995, p. 43) where the point is precisely that
Kierkegaard's *style* represents the most serious attack on the general conception of what
philosophy and the truth are.

[82] He admitted to his first Norwegian biographer, Henrik Jæger, that he had read bits of
Either/Or and *The Moment*, but that it was not more than "about 4–5 sheets of paper." (Cited
from *Ibsenårbok*, 1985–86, p. 139.) The youthful Ibsen's friend from apothecary times in
Grimstad, Christopher Due, tells us the following: "Other than the mutual personal sympathy
and common literary interests—those years we eagerly studied Søren Kierkegaard's *Either/
Or*, *Works of Love*, among others" (quoted from *Aftenposten*, October 16, 1904). Jens Th.
Crawfurd has told H. Eitrem that "I myself many times brought books from old auntie for
Ibsen." He further remembers that she was thought to have had *Either/Or* in her collection.
(Citation after Michael Meyer, *Henrik Ibsen: en biografi*, Oslo: Gyldendal 1995 [1971],
p. 33).

[83] *SKS* 2, 214 / *EO1*, 220.

If we now move forward in time, taking a little detour to the young apothecary's apprentice in Grimstad, we find the poem "Balminder" with the subtitle "A Life Fragment in Poetry and Prose."[84] The titles here draw forth clear associations, as for example "A Life Fragment" and "A Diary's Last Pages." The young Ibsen writes about falling in love at a ball, an affair that outwardly is not very successful, but nonetheless has its value:

> ...don't let that moment to be ruined by drawing it out—I have found her—what more could I want?...I want to go home; I want to complete the last leaf in my journal with memories from the ball.—You are my life's rosy dawn![85]

This is no young man with marriage plans in mind described here—love is to be realized in art.

In the first edition of *Lady Inger*,[86] Nils Lykke tells how with his relationship with the deceased Lucia he has whiled away many an idle moment: "the best part of love is the memory, and I—have many memories." Falk[87] in *Love's Comedy* has evidently crash-landed in Fru Halm's garden with an idea of beauty and pleasure that jibes rather badly with the bourgeois *setting* he finds himself in. He makes a half-hearted attempt at mundane love, but quickly reveals the emptiness: "I enjoy the flower; that says a little, about who gets the dead remnant." He draws himself back with these calming words: "Forgive for everything, the big as well as the small. I want to remember nothing, but recall everything."[88]

With this little glimpse from Ibsen's early production, we shall now move forward to the more mature playwright. Traditionally, Kierkegaard's influence was tied to the reception of *Brand* as Ibsen's "leap" from the aesthetic to the ethical and religious state: the strong character of the priest with his *all or nothing* puts all earthly considerations aside for martyrdom and the self-imposed demand for the Absolute. Ibsen's dramaturgy hardly forms itself as schematically and reliably as that, and I shall here also call attention to an aspect of his next play, *Peer Gynt*, that has not been given consideration until now.

In 1867 Clemens Petersen (1834–1918, Denmark's great literary critic between Johan Ludvig Heiberg and Brandes) reviewed Peer Gynt in *Fædrelandet*. Petersen wrote there that the strange *passenger* who turns up in the fifth act, and who swims by Peer Gynt's side, "is namely angst, and the conversation between them clarifies his relation to the new factor, to angst."[89] In a letter to Bjørnson a few days later

---

[84]   "Balminder. Et Livsfragment i Poesi og Prosa." Quoted from Erichsen, "Søren Kierkegaards betydning for norsk aandsliv," p. 74.

[85]   Ibid.

[86]   Henrik Ibsen, *Fru Inger til Østråt: skuespil i fem handlinger*, Copenhagen 1857.

[87]   Cf. the aphorism from "Diapsalmata," where the aesthete compares himself with an "Eagle" who sporadically dives down from the mountain into reality, hunting after pictures he can weave into a tapestry in his eyrie.

[88]   Henrik Ibsen, *Love's Comedy*, London: Oxford University Press 1962, p. 201. ["*Tilgiv mig Alt, det Større som det Mindre. / Jeg Intet huske vil; (sagte) men Alt erindre.*"]

[89]   Quoted from Otto Hageberg's anthology, *Omkring "Peer Gynt." Vårt nasjonaldrama i den litterære debatt og kritikk gjennom 100 år*, Oslo: Gyldendal 1967, p. 46.

Ibsen complains about about the statement, and uses the following words: "He says that the strange passenger is the concept angst!"[90] Petersen never said that, and it is in many ways interesting that Ibsen almost by reflex connects the word directly with Kierkegaard—because that is what he does here when he talks about the concept of angst, which was not just any common contemporary concept, living its own life apart from Kierkegaard's little study of 1844.

Thanks to Brandes' insinuations about plagiarism mentioned above, Ibsen from then on denied any connection between Kierkegaard and his own production, just as he likewise denied having read anyone other than Holberg. Monotonously, Ibsen repeated that answer about the relationship between himself and the great Danish literary philosopher: "I have simply read very little of S.K. and have understood even less."[91] Nonetheless, there are several interesting parallels in Kierkegaard's presentation of angst in the scene from Peer Gynt that Petersen points out.

The strange passenger appears from nowhere out on the stormy sea, corpse-pale and frightening. Peer is on his way home after many years in exile, and all of a sudden the being is standing beside him out on deck. He is so pale that Peer asks him if he is sick, but he definitely is not—on the contrary, he sees the stormy weather as a blessing. Just as unobtrusively as he came, he disappears, only to show up again at precisely the moment the boat goes under during the storm. Peer has managed to haul himself up on the pitiful wreckage of the boat, when the foreign passenger comes swimming towards him and asks if he can hang on with the tip of his finger. Out on the open sea—on the 70,000 fathoms—he begins to examine Peer on angst's deep-rooted gravity:

Passenger: Friend,—have you *once* in each Half-year felt the earnestness of angst?

Peer Gynt: Sure, anyone's afraid when Danger threatens;— but your Words all have double-meanings.

Passenger: Yes, have you ever *one* time in Life had the Victory, that is given in angst?[92]

Right off, it is clear here that the passenger is talking about something totally different from what Peer understands; the pair find themselves in two different worlds. Peer is naturally enough, afraid out on the open waters of the sea, and also says so, i.e., that he is *afraid*. The passenger, on the other hand, consistently uses the word *angst*, a form of misunderstanding between the two that the text deliberately plays on. And which must be attributed to Ibsen's having had a conscious relation towards the

---

90   Ibid. p. 48.
91   Letter to Frederik Hegel, March 8, 1867. Quoted from *Ibsenårbok*, 1985–86, p. 138.
92   Henrik Ibsen, *Peer Gynt*, Minneapolis: University of Minnesota Press 1980, p. 164. ["Passageren: *Ven,—har De en gang blot hvert Halvaar / tilbunds fornummet Angstens Alvor?* Peer Gynt: *Rædd blir man jo, naar Faren truer;—/ med Deres Ord er satt på Skruer.—/* Passageren: *Ja, har De blot blot en gang i Livet / havt Sejren, som i Angst er givet?*"]

distinction between fear and angst, a distinction not common at the time, one that was first made explicit in *The Concept of Anxiety*.

The passenger's words about "angst's conquest" confuse Peer even more. To his question about whether the thought about victory, out on the rolling masses of waves, might not be a bit inappropriate, the passenger answers, "Was then, victory perhaps more likely, by your hearth, snug and quiet?"[93] A more Kierkegaardian and radical emphasis of existential seriousness can hardly be imagined. The victory of angst being spoken about here has little to do with conquering fear and dangerous situations, or survival at all. The thought rather could have been clipped right out of Chapter V of *The Concept of Anxiety*, i.e., "Anxiety as Saving through Faith," where it is stated that the person shall "learn to be anxious in order that he may not perish either by never having been in anxiety or by succumbing in anxiety. Whoever has learned to be anxious in the right way has learned the ultimate."[94]

The foreign passenger's function in the fifth and final act is to accentuate that which is the entire drama's thought and idea: the Gyntian I-relationship, which through the plot's many turns, never manages to coalesce around its own self. As when Peer in the Hall of the King of Dovre Trolls strikes out blindly around himself to escape a voice in the darkness. "Answer! Who are you?" asks Peer, and the voice replies "Myself. Can you say that?" "*What* are you?" and the voice answers: "The great Boyg."[95] The voice urges Peer to go around, but Peer wants to charge straight on through, and with that begins a hopeless struggle, where Peer wildly slashes at a fiend he cannot touch with a sword, before he sinks from exhaustion:

Peer Gynt: Strike!

Voice: The Boyg strikes not.

Peer Gynt: Fight! You must!

Voice: The great Boyg conquers without fighting.

Peer Gynt: If only it was some kind of spook, that could prick me!
          If only as much as a year-old troll!
          Only something to fight with. But here there is nothing.—[96]

If it makes sense to link the scene with the strange passenger with *The Concept of Anxiety*, one could, by extending this thought, very well read the entire *Peer Gynt* as a translation to the stage of one of the main forms of despair in *The Sickness unto Death*, namely, that which Kierkegaard describes as the despair of being unable to endure being one's own self. It is written or said somewhere, Peer Gynt remembers in the third act, without recalling where, "that if you gained the whole world, but

93   Ibid., p. 165.
94   *SKS* 4, 454 / *CA*, 155.
95   Ibsen, *Peer Gynt*, p. 64.
96   Ibid., p. 66.

lost yourself doing it, your prize was only a wreath around a cloven brow."[97] Peer gives no sources for this existential pathos, but one need not be more than passably musical to hear the notes of the Danish scribbler in these lines.

IX. Edvard Munch—The Picture in Mind

"When I write down all these notes with drawings, it is not to relate my own life. For me it means studying certain inheritable events that decide a person's life and fate, phenomena of madness in general. It is a study of the soul I have since I can of course study myself like an anatomical soul specimen."[98] These lines sound undeniably Kierkegaardian, apart from the reference to pictures. The text is written by none other than Edvard Munch, but Søren Kierkegaard is involved to the highest degree in this piece of writing. Immediately following the above passage, one reads, "Therefore I divide—as does Søren Kierkegaard—the work in two—The painter and his overly nervous friend the writer."[99] This passage is from Munch's notes for a novel in the form of a diary that he had thought of publishing under the title *A Mad Author's Diary*. The literary allusion to Kierkegaard's "The Seducer's Diary" in *Either/Or* is striking, as is the divide between the text's authorial *I* and the man behind the text, the painter.

But Kierkegaard has provided more than just a stylistic handle to Munch the author, something that Munch's own statements about these literary works also attest. In one of the notes to the diary he relates the experience of his encounter with Kierkegaard's texts: "When, one and a half years ago now, I sometimes read Kierkegaard—where in a strange way everything is as if I experienced it earlier—in another life."[100] So involved has he been with the Kierkegaardian universe, that—when he is going to write about his own life—he has to remind himself: "When I now collect notes—I must be careful not to let my choices be led by Kierkegaard."[101]

That Edvard Munch wrote, will surely surprise many. But he did, and he indicated that almost all of his paintings began as manuscripts, something that means he, to a large degree, wrote himself into his motifs. To what degree Kierkegaard's picturesque language also has influenced the *painter* Munch, is more difficult to determine. But there are also striking parallels here, once again directly relating to the themes in *The Concept of Anxiety*. In the work that Munch himself regarded as his crowning achievement, *Frieze of Life* (1892), there is a picture cycle he called *Angst of Living*. This consists of a series of angst motifs which, together, comprise the third of the frieze's four sequences. The first is *The Seed of Love*, the second *Love which Flowers and Dies*, then *Angst of Living*, and the last, *Death*. Some of Munch's

---

[97]   Ibid., p. 101.
[98]   Edvard Munch, *Geniets notater. Essays af Edvard Munch*, introduced by Thorvald Steen, Lysaker: Geelmuyden. Kiese 2000 (*Scandinavian Words*, vol. 18), p. 14.
[99]   Ibid., p. 15.
[100]   Quoted from Poul Erik Tøjner, *Munch—med egne ord*, Oslo: Forlaget Press 2000, p. 182.
[101]   Quoted from ibid..

best-known paintings are found in *The Frieze of Life*, such as *Madonna*, *Vampire*, and *The Scream*.

What is interesting is that the pictures that lead up to *The Scream* all revolve around angst as a theme. The first of these paintings is named *Evening at Karl Johan* (1892). The painting shows a crowd of people walking down the side of Karl Johan, the main street of present-day Oslo, pale as corpses and expressionless. Alone, out in the street itself, we see the contours of a solitary character who almost tries to steady his dizziness by focusing his gaze on a lighted second-floor window. This painting radiates angst; Munch then moves the entire theme over to the picture that received the title *Angst* (1894). But now the physical framework has been moved to Ekebergåsen (a high hill, directly above Oslo Hospital, where at the time both a mental asylum and a slaughterhouse were located). Under a blood-red sky, the same people now wander in groups up the footpath up to Valhallveien, just as pale and expressionless, but with this difference: the wanderers now have a railing with which to support themselves.

But the solitary individual who previously was visible on the margin of the Karl Johan picture is gone, missing, as if from having gone out of focus, only to reappear in another picture called *Despair* (1892). The picture's setting is the same as that of *Angst*. We are still on the pedestrian street above the city on Ekebergåsen, but the motif is in a particular way a mirror image: the crowds are on their way out of the field of view, leaving behind a lonesome person with a mask-like face, staring out at nothing. On the margin of a preliminary sketch for this picture, Munch wrote in pencil: "My friends went away—and I stood alone shaking with angst—and I felt that a great endless scream went through nature."[102] The year after, this expressionless and inwardly withdrawn mask cracks apart in the *The Scream*, that would go on to become one of the most familiar images in the history of art. The point is that leading up to this picture—the thematic center around which all else revolves—are Munch's studies on angst and despair.

What is central in this connection is not only that Munch uses angst as a theme here. That by itself is remarkable, considering how precisely he renders the *nothingness* of angst and its silent feeling of vertigo, just like Kierkegaard has so graphically described it. What is striking is that he additionally links angst and despair. The work by Kierkegaard that most explicitly follows up the theme of *The Concept of Anxiety* is *The Sickness unto Death*. The whole central concept in this book is precisely *despair*, a concept that stands in a precise relationship with angst. Whereas angst in Kierkegaard states the basic condition of divided human nature, despair is more the condition in which people find themselves when they became conscious of not being able to catch up with their authentic self. From *Either/Or* onward, despair had been a turning-point in the writings. It is this which is itself the keynote in the aesthete's life, as when we meet him in various guises from *Either/Or* to *Stages on Life's Way*. It is the aesthete, with whom Kierkegaard draws his psychological studies: the figure for the modern fragmented world, who tries to avoid loss of meaning by placing all his bets on living in and through *remembrance*.

---

[102]   Munch, *Geniets notater*, p. 96.

Perhaps it is precisely first with Munch that this modern figure, who in Kierkegaard is consistently denied any outer form of self-expression, is released from his sickness of reflection and demonic imprisonment and becomes clearly visible. In *The Concept of Anxiety* it is also stated "...for anxiety can just as well express itself by muteness as by a scream."[103]

X. The Twentieth Century—Positivism and Psychology

As was the case with Petersen and the theologians, Kierkegaard was also viewed from the disciplinary heights of philosophy with ambivalence and to some extent, rejection. The leading Norwegian philosopher of the last half of the 1800s was the Hegelian Marcus Jacob Monrad (1816–97). In his main work *Thought Directions in Recent Times* (1874) he states: "Kierkegaard's significance for the development of everyday thinking must not be looked down upon, notwithstanding the fact that he only seemed to be a lonely, inward-focused brooder."[104] Monrad was quite clear at an early stage about Kierkegaard's importance, but kept him at arm's length, primarily because the Dane, according to Monrad, lacked a sociological dimension in his thinking. Monrad is considered to have been the leading social philosopher for the Norwegian bureaucratically-administered state of the second half of the nineteenth century, and thus it is no small irony that the memorial ceremony marking Kierkegaard's death was led by the Hegelian Monrad at the Students' Society in Kristiania, in the new year, 1856.[105]

However, with modernism's breakthrough, Kant and Hegel were exchanged for Darwin, Mill, and Taine, and at the turn of the century, naturalism and positivism dominated philosophical studies at the university. A central player in getting modern empirical philosophy recognized at the university was Professor of Philosophy Arne Løchen (1850–1930). In 1902 he wrote an article in the journal *Samtiden* on the occasion of the publication of the first edition of Kierkegaard's *Samlede Værker* (1901–06), and this was well-suited for elucidating how Kierkegaard could be used and through which lenses he now was viewed.

Løchen had, as a young man and under the strong influence of Brandes, traveled to Paris in 1877 to attend Taine's lectures in literary history. Hippolyte-Adolphe Taine (1828–93) is perhaps the foremost French proponent of the revolt against Romanticism and idealism. Taine claimed that every text is directly connected to the author's personality and what he calls the *faculté maîtresse*—the "predominating faculty." The methodological ideal, borrowed from the natural sciences, that lies at the basis of Taine's literary studies treated in principle every text along the same lines as the study of rocks and plants. Texts could be broken down into their constituent parts and taxonomically classified by regularities such as *race, milieu, et*

[103]   *SKS* 4, 421 / *CA*, 119.

[104]   M.J. Monrad, *Tankeretninger i den nyere tid. Et kritisk rundskue*, Oslo: Tanum-Norli 1981 [1874], p. 84.

[105]   M.J. Monrad, "Mindebægeret over Søren Kierkegaard" (Studentersamfundet, January 14, 1856), *Illustreret Nyhedsblad*, no. 4, January 26, 1856.

moment (i.e., nation, environment, and time). Traditional humanities fields were thus transformed into a sort of botany of the mind.

With that in mind, it is interesting to look at some formulations in Løchen's article, where he describes Kierkegaard's personality. The health of our entire being, Løchen claims, "rests upon the harmony among our spiritual abilities, and an *Überkultur* or an inborn preponderance of a single trait [that] can therefore be viewed as both wealth and poverty, as health and sickness."[106] This is closely related to Taine's formulation of the predominating faculty, and, according to Løchen, it consists in Kierkegaard's case of a strong feeling of loneliness combined with an all-too-developed self-reflectivity and life of memory. Løchen gets this naturalistic formula from Brandes, who had identified Kierkegaard's spiritual wasteland with the soil and barren flatlands of Jutland, where his father had grown up.

With this as a point of departure. Løchen seeks to elucidate the connection between the *logical* and the *psychological* in Kierkegaard. According to Løchen, this rests in the schism between a self-sufficient life of recollection and a Christian revelation mentality. The necessity of a confrontation, both psychological and logical, between these occurs in Kierkegaard's *Philosophical Fragments*. Here the basic conflict is formulated for the first time: remembrance philosophy is directly challenged by bringing in a teacher who *is himself truth*, and who also brings along with him the necessary condition for grasping that truth—in a word, *faith*. From this time onwards, a logical break in the authorship was set into productive motion, as thought's offense, the paradox, and faith's subjective passion.

Thus Kierkegaard was mediated in Norway in the guise of French naturalistic psychology, first indirectly via Brandes during the late 1870s, and now from the rostrum of a Norwegian professor of philosophy. It is hardly surprising that the younger representatives of a new and "modern" century found much in Kierkegaard that grated. Løchen felt that much of Kierkegaard's polemics was dated, while a colleague, philosophy professor Anathon Aall (1867–1943), in harsher words consigned much of the Kierkegaardian mental world to a medieval Dark Age.[107] What, however, is interesting, is what empirical philosophers viewed as the positive aspects of Kierkegaard.

Løchen writes in his introduction that he, now an older man, must admit that "[the] dream of a science that can construct a philosophy of life to completion, is vanishing."[108] What remains is Kierkegaard, standing as the one who most strongly claimed that a philosophy of life is no science, that it is a "possession of the personality." In the light of the above statements, these words can at first seem somewhat paradoxical, but they are consistent enough. Kierkegaard functioned here as the spearhead of a struggle in Norway against rationalism and Hegelianism, and their ambitions to be the *objective* science *per se*. Philosophy of life is no science, and vice versa. This

---

[106]   Arne Løchen, "Søren Kierkegaard," in *Digtning og Vitenskap*, Kristiania: H. Aschehoug & Co. (W. Nygaard) 1913 [1902], p. 66.
[107]   Cf. Anathon Aall, *Filosofien i Norden. Til oplysning om den nyere tænknings og videnskabs historie i Sverige og Finland, Danmark og Norge*, Kristiania: H.A. Benneches Fond 1919 (*Videnskapsselskapets Skrifter*), see pp. 124ff.
[108]   Løchen, "Søren Kierkegaard," p. 64.

was an important principle for a methodological ideal that sought universal validity on equal terms with natural science. In keeping with this, Kierkegaard could be used as an ally in the fight against the blending together of science and religion. As with Brandes and the cultural radicals of the 1870s, Kierkegaard's teachings of true individuality had to be made common currency in the meaning of "every philosophy of life," so that Kierkegaard's specifically Christian premises would not stand as a decisive criterion.

The handful of articles by Løchen and Aall stood alone: they were not representative of any cohesive program of research or mediation of Kierkegaard in Norway. Were one to point out a general phenomenon at the beginning of the previous century, it would be that what is found by way of rudiments of Kierkegaardian studies tends towards a fragmentation of the philosopher into theology, philosophy, and psychology. This was also a trait that would become further pronounced in the years to come.

XI. From the Theological Confrontation to the World War

Fredrik Petersen's great trial of strength with Kierkegaard in 1877 should in retrospect be seen in the light of a large task he had set for himself, that—as was intimated above—of mediating between modern, secular thought, on the one hand, and a conservative and dogmatic theology, on the other. This project was kept active for as long as Petersen held his professorship, but it began to fall apart already upon his stepping down in 1903. The controversy regarding the appointment of liberal and "culturally friendly" theologians versus conservative ones at the University steadily intensified the discord, which reached a climax in 1906. An alternative "seminary" was established outside the University's control, the *Menighetsfakultetet*.[109] This rupture was formally accepted in 1913 (with an almost symbolic resonance, on the centenary of Kierkegaard's birth).

A growing awareness regarding Kierkegaard was also visible in the theological periodicals of the time. A growing number of articles about Kierkegaard were published in the magazine *For Kirke og Kultur*. One of these was by the previously mentioned Christopher Bruun, who defines Kierkegaard as "The master of Christian thought," praising him for having stressed the paradoxical aspect in Christianity which surpasses all reason: "He does it in his own excitable fashion, to be sure; but even so with a refreshing emphasis above all flat insipidity and all modern arrogance toward Divine Revelation."[110]

Six years later, Jens Tandberg (1852–1922), afterwards bishop and Primate of the Norwegian Church, gave a lecture for the Norwegian Students' Christian Association, wherein the earlier theological reservations regarding Kierkegaard were almost totally cleared away. Granted, Tandberg pointed out that Kierkegaard to certain degree was characterized by the eccentric exaggerations of genius, besides

---

[109]   The current English designation for this is The Norwegian Lutheran School of Theology.
[110]   Christopher Bruun, "Lidt om Søren Kierkegaard," *For Kirke og Kultur*, vol. 8, 1901, p. 590.

having a somewhat deficient view of the meaning of the congregation. But beyond this, the philosopher was a welcome irritant; he "acted like a salt for *Christian* life and *Christian* preaching."[111] Tandberg rounded off his speech with an unequivocal appeal: "Therefore I say to you young people: Read him! Study him! Work yourselves into his brilliant world of thought—You will gain from it throughout your entire Christian lives."[112] This was a new tune being played by responsible theological circles in Norway.

In 1913, one hundred years after Kierkegaard's birth, a number of articles were published in religious periodicals and newspapers over all of Scandinavia. Never since Brandes' Kierkegaardian road-show of 1876, had Kierkegaard been so topical. The difference was that now, so to speak, one had rescued the formerly captive Kierkegaard from the freethinker Brandes. Kierkegaard was once again legal tender in the theological grapplings then going on.

Nevertheless, it was in the 1920s and 1930s that Kierkegaard's spindly presence made itself felt in a serious way, in all its existential philosophical might. It is impossible to understand the enormous significance Kierkegaard would gain in philosophy and theology without considering the background of Europe's decline. The warnings against systemic thinking, herd mentality, the clash with the anonymizing and leveling power of the press, the irresponsibility of crowds, the individual as guarantor for morality and choice—all of this sounded rather different to those living through the First World War and after, than it did during Kierkegaard's lifetime. The Kierkegaard who had previously seemed both disturbed and overexcited, now gained a relevance that made him seem almost prophetic.

One example of this shift is the Dane Johannes Hohlenberg (1881–1960), who together with the Norwegian anthroposophist Alf Larsen (1885–1967), published the magazine *Janus* in Norway during 1933–41. In 1939, Kierkegaard was given his own number, and reading between the lines of what is written, one senses that evil forces were now ever tightening their grip around Europe. In the last article of that issue, titled "Søren Kierkegaard and the World," Hohlenberg reviews the entire history of reception, whereupon he concludes that Kierkegaard's own times lacked the necessary conditions to comprehend him. "But we who have darkening clouds above us," the article concludes "we know what he meant." "There remains a great hope and promise for the future in that more and more of the unconcerned passengers now are starting to listen to him, who first and by himself, sensed what was in store and pointed out the course to be steered, if we want our ship to be saved from the storm."[113]

In 1940, Hohlenberg's great biography *Søren Kierkegaard* was published,[114] later coming out in German, Dutch, English, French, and Japanese editions. This biography is the most widely read book about Kierkegaard ever written. With the 1920s, what can be called a systematic field of Kierkegaard studies appeared in Norway for the

---

[111]   Jens Tandberg, "Søren Kierkegaard. Foredrag i 'Norske studenters kristelige forbund,'" *For Kirke og Kultur*, vol. 14, 1907, pp. 166–77; pp. 198–210.

[112]   Ibid. p. 210.

[113]   Johannes Hohlenberg, "Søren Kierkegaard og Verden," *Janus*, no. 3, 1939, p. 320.

[114]   Hohlenberg, *Søren Kierkegaard*, Copenhagen: Hagerup 1940.

first time. On this occasion, instead of theologians and philosophers, it was literary historians and scholars of Nordic studies who took up the banner. In little more than a year, two significant works were published regarding Kierkegaard's influence on Norwegian intellectual life: Valborg Erichsen's "Søren Kierkegaard's Significance for Norwegian Intellectual Life"[115] and Harold Beyer's *Søren Kierkegaard and Norway*.[116] Both of these contains almost three hundred pages each, and it is in a certain way startling to have such ponderous essays in reception history appear, given that there had been only one academic work on Kierkegaard up until then. On the other hand, it was natural for a country with such a close relation to Kierkegaard that this initial research was reception and "effective history," i.e., *Wirkungsgeschichte*.

The studies were the result of advertized prizes, something that points in the direction of their being a thrust in a cultural-political consciousness-raising act, a statement of the importance of the intellect in a world suddenly reverting to barbarism. Another interesting characteristic is that these two studies can be said to represent a new view of Kierkegaard since the work was now being viewed as literature, as a coherent literary and intellectual feat. Previously, particular theological or philosophical areas of contention had always dominated the entire arena of Kierkegaardian debate.

Both Beyer and Erichsen concentrated themselves in the main on the literary impact Kierkegaard had on Norwegian literature. Both of them examine the greatest Norwegian authors such as Welhaven, Vinje, Ibsen, Bjørnson, and Garborg. They differ in that Erichsen is somewhat more thorough, more textually close and analytic, thus narrowing her material to a greater degree than Beyer, who for his part is stronger in the area of delineating the grand picture and wide connections.

In a way, these two works end and sum up an epoch in the understanding of Kierkegaard in Norway. On this side of the two World Wars, everything looks different, including Kierkegaard, who now is no longer by any means an exclusively Dano–Norwegian phenomenon, having become the godfather of central philosophical and theological mainstreams in Europe.

XII. 1855–1955—One Hundred Years of Simultaneity

Modern Norwegian academic studies of Kierkegaard find their real beginning in Per Lønning's (b. 1928) dissertation for his theological doctorate of 1954, *Simultaneity's Situation. A Study of Søren Kierkegaard's Understanding of Christianity*.[117] This dissertation brought the study of Kierkegaard in Norway up to the level of international research in the same field. Lønning was conversant with the work of all of the central theologians and philosophers from Germany, France, and the United States, individuals with whom he was also in personal contact. Furthermore, he had a familiarity with the steadily growing Nordic literature on Kierkegaard. The aim of

---

[115]   Valborg Erichsen, "Søren Kierkegaards betydning for norsk aandsliv," *Edda*, vol. 23, 1923, pp. 369–429.
[116]   Harald Beyer, *Søren Kierkegaard og Norge*, Kristiania: Aschehoug 1924.
[117]   Per Lønning, *Samtidighetens Situation. En studie i Søren Kierkegaards kristendoms forståelse*, Oslo: Forlaget Land og Kirke 1954.

the dissertation was to "try to bring clarity to what actually was an understanding of Kierkegaard and to what was a misunderstanding of Kierkegaard."[118] That was no mean task in 1955, given the enormous range of existing international Kierkegaard-inspired literature in fields such as dialectical theology, existential philosophy, and existential psychology.

In the great array of materials that already by that time had threatened to make Kierkegaard studies impossible for a single individual to master, choice and precise definition of method and lines of approach had become essential. Lønning's choice of *simultaneity* as a theme underlines his criticism of the use of Kierkegaard taken out of context that he found, for example, in parts of French existentialism in slogans such as "*existence précéde l'essence*," which according to Lønning, had nothing to do with Kierkegaard. Lønning goes in for a "historical" understanding of Kierkegaard (in opposition to a biographical or psychologisitic one), one that at the same time obliges itself to take seriously the reflections about humanity's conditions of existence presented in the writings. The task is thus the question of "the themes' own and timeless consistency and coherence."[119]

Kierkegaard's concept of simultaneity is, according to Lønning, not just one subject among many others of equal import but "the actual basic motif of Kierkegaard's comprehension of Christianity."[120] The idea here was to run a direct thread through the writings with this theme as the guideline.

Lønning's dissertation is divided into three lettered parts. Part *A* gives an analysis of the simultaneity concept with its point of departure in Frater Taciturnus' *Stages on Life's Way* (1845) and the thought that all authentic existence necessarily must express itself as "simultaneity." The simultaneity concept is developed further through its connection with existence's "formal dynamic." Part *B* is the longest section and examines "Simultaneity's Situation" in the encounter with Christ. Here above all, Johannes Climacus' thought experiment in *Philosophical Fragments* is thematized as the staged confrontation between the Socratic idea of truth and a truth that in a radical sense comes from the outside. The concluding part *C* deals with "Simultaneity's Situation" and the Church, and discusses to what degree Kierkegaard's comprehension of Christianity is in agreement with the idea of a church at all.

Lønning held the defense of his dissertation on the hundredth anniversary of Kierkegaard's death, on May 5, 1955, and the claim is that he met little resistance from his assigned opponents (Professors Paulus Svendsen and Johan B. Hygen). On the other hand, he got tit for tat in the newspaper *Morgenbladet* five days later, when Doctor of Theology Thorleif Boman raked Lønning over the coals under the title "Søren Kierkegaard Made Harmless." Boman's objections were not directed against formalities or thematic complaints as such; rather, they were aimed at the fact that Kierkegaard's simultaneity concept had been made into an object for academic consideration at all. "It managed on its own for a hundred years, but now the concept has been annexed by

---

[118]   Ibid., p. 8.
[119]   Ibid.
[120]   Ibid., p. 27.

academia and thereby made harmless as a revivalist call and penitential sermon. The rat poison no longer works. Søren Kierkegaard really is dead."[121]

So it was that even a hundred years after his demise, Kierkegaard could still incite controversy in Norway, and it is interesting to note the heat and seriousness that Boman's reaction represents. As we have seen earlier, the Norwegian understanding of Kierkegaard was permeated by an idiosyncratic Pietistic sincerity. That attitude was clearly still in force: the writings should be read for their vehemence and edification. The fear of Kierkegaard's ironic rants about "The Docents" who make a living by explaining life in *existence* in voluminous tomes, had thus affected Norwegian theologians far more deeply than their Danish brothers and sisters. In Denmark, such a reaction would have been almost unthinkable. It would take another fifty years before a theological dissertation on Kierkegaard saw the light of day in Norway. In the interim, Kierkegaard cast his direct and indirect influence on totally different fields in Norwegian academia.

XIII. Settling Accounts with Positivism

A direct, if somewhat surprising, influence of Kierkegaard can be traced in Norwegian social thought from the end of the 1950s, namely, in the showdown with positivism in the humanities and social sciences faculties at the University of Oslo. The controversy of the 1950s and 1960s between Hans Skjervheim (1926–99) and the philosopher Arne Næss (1912–2009) easily comes to mind here. Næss had been employed as professor of philosophy at the University of Oslo since 1939, and thus was the heir of the positivists Løchen and Aall. Næss had studied in Vienna in the mid-1930s and was influenced by the Vienna Circle's antimetaphysical program, its fight against traditional epistemology—subjectivism—to the advantage of an objective-psychological description. This can be most clearly seen in his doctoral dissertation of 1936, *Erkenntnis und wissenschaftliches Verhalten*. Regarded from a scientific-theoretical point of view, Næss claimed, there was in principle little difference between the study of men or rats, except that rats were "simpler" and that it was "permitted to experiment on them."[122] Later on, Næss turned more strongly towards logical and semantic themes, towards his *logical empiricism*. Næss was the leading philosophical presence at the University of Oslo right up to the beginning of the 1970s.[123]

Skjervheim registered his opposition for the first time in 1957, through his master's thesis in philosophy, *Objectivism and the Study of Man*. There he brings up a fundamental divide between the positivist and existentialist views of humanity and uses Kierkegaard directly in his argument. In the reckoning with objectivism's

---

[121]   Thorleif Boman, "Søren Kierkegaard er blitt ufarlig," *Morgenbladet*, May 10, 1955.
[122]   Quoted from Rune Slagstad, *De nasjonale strateger*, Oslo: Pax Forlag 1998, p. 406.
[123]   Arne Næss does not easily fit into fixed categories. Since the 1960s and 1970s, he has distinguished himself as an experienced mountaineer, Spinozist, environmental activist—and Kierkegaardian. In 1968, he published a shortened version of *Efterskriften*, with his own long foreword. On the back cover, an editor has taken the opportunity to feature a little epistle, signed Kierkegaard: "While the Grass grows, the Observer dies, calmly, for he was Objective."

different forms, such as "psychologism" and "sociologism," he uses Kierkegaard's analysis of "forms of despair" to show that these *-isms* lead to a fatalist view of humanity. Kierkegaard's view of humankind defined as a synthesis of *possibility* and *necessity* is sliced in half, so that one is left sitting with only necessity.

In an article from 1963, "Psychology and Human Self-Interpretation" Skjervheim's use of Kierkegaard is broadened.[124] The subject–object relationship in the natural sciences, as opposed to the humanities and social sciences, is central to the article. A totally different approach is necessary in the humanities and social sciences, Skjervheim says, citing thus Kierkegaard's definition of spirit from the introduction of *The Sickness unto Death*: "Man is spirit. And what is spirit? Spirit is self. But what is self? The self is a relationship, that relates itself to itself, or it is the relationship, where the relationship relates to itself."[125] Mankind is not viewed as being like any other thing in the world, having as its defining characteristic that it is a self-aware and acting *self*. Skjervheim therefore concludes saying that "the interpretation of self is constitutive for what mankind actually *is*; mankind *is* in a certain way its own self-interpretation."[126] Thus, the concepts and methods one uses in studies of individuals in the social sciences must have consequences.[127]

For Skjervheim, the confrontation with positivism was not just an academic game but also a question of the individual's freedom in modern society. Skjervheim is regarded as one of the most influential post–1945 social theorists in Norway, and thus has great significance as a critic of the Social Democratic state with its faith optimistically placed in scientific and technocratic solutions—a state that saw the light of day and grew after the Second World War.

In 1913, the philosopher and positivist Løchen used Kierkegaard in his argument for holding philosophies of life and values apart from science. The two World Wars separating Løchen and Skjervheim had a sharpening effect on views and the need for another methodological approach in the humanities.

The new Kierkegaard that emerged after the Second World War, *the humanist and existentialist*, was perhaps most clearly promoted from the relatively newly established Institute for the History of Ideas at the University of Oslo (now subsumed into the Department of Philosophy, Classics, History of Art and Ideas), first and foremost through the publication of Finn Jor's (b. 1929) master's thesis of 1954, *Søren Kierkegaard. The Existing Thinker* and Grete Børsand's (b. 1939) *Model and Challenge: A Kierkegaard*

---

[124]   Hans Skjervheim, "Psykologien og mennesket si sjølfortolkning," in *Mennesket*, ed. by Jon Hellesnes and Gunnar Skirbekk, Oslo: Universitetsforlaget 2002, pp. 90–103.
[125]   Ibid. p. 95.
[126]   Ibid. One might also mention here Tollak B. Sirnes as critic of the system who used Kierkegaard to support his arguments. Sirnes was a psychiatrist and pharmacologist, who published a string of scientific popularizations in the 1960s and 1970s in the tradition of Rollo May and Victor Frankl. Sirnes had a large readership at the time, and he cited and used Kierkegaard extensively, making Kierkegaard into the main theme of the book *Sann personlighet. Personlig sannhet. Kan Kierkegaard hjelpe oss?* Stavanger: Dreyer Bok 1979.
[127]   For a more detailed treatment of Skjervheim's relationship to Kierkegaard, see Ragnvald Kalleberg, "Kierkegaard som samfunnstenker," *Nytt Norsk Tidskrift*, no. 20, 2003, pp. 196–209.

Study.[128] Jor's work is a wide-scoped presentation of Kierkegaard, his biography and his authorship, holding up the importance of "*hin Enkelte*" as his main intellectual achievement. Børsand, on the other hand, is more detailed study of Kierkegaard's thoughts on role models. In both books there is a clear notion that Kierkegaard is the founding father of existentialism. These two scholars/authors have probably been the most widely read interpreters of Kierkegaard throughout this period, in the sense that they have reached a public also outside the academic arena.

XIV. Into the Twenty-First Century

During the 1970s, Kierkegaard was not held in high esteem in Norway. The leftist materialist trend at Norwegian universities did not leave much room for a Danish Golden Age thinker, oriented towards individualism. At decade's end there was nevertheless published, almost as if in defiance, a little collection of essays titled *Idea-Historical Fragments*, by the above mentioned Grete Børsand (now Heyerdahl). The subjects range from comparisons of Kierkegaard with his contemporary Hans Christian Andersen, to discussions with Adorno regarding *Works of Love*, to the young Hegel, Hermann Hesse, and Freud's views on women, with Kierkegaard as a sort of anchor point throughout. This is in many ways the most intellectually liberating and stimulating work written about Kierkegaard in Norwegian.[129]

One can also view Karstein Hopland's 1981 doctoral dissertation on Kierkegaard, *Actuality and Consciousness. A Study of Søren Kierkegaard's Anthropology*, as going against the grain. It was written at what was then the Institute for History of Religions at the University of Bergen. Hopland sees Kierkegaard's writing as a crisis, a crisis in the form of a break with the systematic and general thinking of idealism, but a break that at critical points also represents an exciting continuation of certain parts of German idealism. Kierkegaard restates and reduces idealism's *absolute self* to a *human self*—that is, his new "idea system," according to Hopland. "The characterization of Kierkegaard's thought as 'anthropology' is a way of expressing this idea."[130] Unfortunately, Hopland's dissertation was never published and made known to a larger readership.

The 1980s marks the beginning of a new and lasting interest in Kierkegaard's work. The first Norwegian philosophical dissertation about Kierkegaard appeared then, in 1985: Kjell Eyvind Johansen's (b. 1945) *The Concept of Repetition in Søren Kierkegaard*.[131] If one looks at international research, this is undeniably a somewhat ironic situation, but the reason for this is that the Institute of Philosophy in Oslo was

---

[128]   Finn Jor, *Søren Kierkegaard: den eksisterende tenker*, Oslo: Land og kirke 1954; Grete Børsand, *Forbilde og utfordring: en Kierkegaard-studie*, Oslo: Tanum 1966.
[129]   Grete Børsand Heyerdahl, *Idéhistoriske smuler. Essays om litteratur og filosofi, kjærlighet og undertrykkelse- om Hegel, Kierkegaard, H.C. Andersen, Freud, Hermann Hesse, Adorno*, Oslo: Gyldendahl Norsk Forlag 1979.
[130]   Karstein Hopland, *Virkelighet og Bevissthet. En studie i Søren Kierkegaards antropologi*, Bergen: Religionsvitenskapelig Institutt, University of Bergen 1981, p. II.
[131]   Kjell Eyvind Johansen, *Begrepet gjentagelse hos Søren Kierkegaard*, Oslo: Solum Forlag 1988.

dominated by analytical philosophy from the 1950s until into the 1970s, with little emphasis given to continental philosophy. Two exceptions to the picture are Egil A.Wyller (a Christian Platonist and *henologist*) and the internationally renowned Kierkegaard researcher Alastair Hannay (b. 1932), who has been in Norway since 1961. Perhaps best known for his translations into English for the Penguin Classics series, Hannay has given Kierkegaard a wider readership; however, through his teaching at the University of Oslo, he has also made a considerable contribution to recent Norwegian philosophical interest in Kierkegaard.

Johansen's dissertation addresses itself to investigating the status and content of the concept *Repetition* throughout its career in Kierkegaard's writing. Kierkegaard himself perceived it as a genuinely new philosophical concept, his *terminus*. The concept appears in Kierkegaard partly as an epistemological and ontological challenge, and partly as an imperative for action in an ethical and religious sense, Johansen claims, and it is this "parallelism" in *Repetition* that his dissertation attempts to encompass.[132] Johansen mainly does this through readings of works such as *Fear and Trembling*, *The Concept of Anxiety*, *Philosophical Fragments*, and *Concluding Unscientific Postscript*, in addition to *Repetition*. Johansen, however, is also the first philosopher in Norway to include the "edifying discourses" in his study, something that attests to a fresh look at Kierkegaard's authorship.

This new look at Kierkegaard's writing is also part of what characterizes the growing interest of the 1980s and 1990s.[133] The literary aspects of Kierkegaard's work were then coming into focus. It was now claimed that when the theologians and the philosophers tried to impose a consistent and thematic stringency upon the work (where the rather uncooperative Kierkegaard never himself decided if he was poet, philosopher or theologian), they at the same time missed many of the most essential insights of that writing. The polyphonic and intertextual playing with pseudonyms and different genres challenges—and thematizes—the problematical relationship

---

[132]   Ibid., p. 9.

[133]   The Norwegian Søren Kierkegaard Society (*Det Norske Søren Kierkegaard Selskap*) was founded in 1996. Finn Jor took the initative for the establishment of a Norwegian society at a spring 1996 seminar in Copenhagen, where an interim board was elected. The Society was formally instituted later that same year, in the premises of the Philosophical Project Centre in Oslo. The intention behind starting the Society was to have it act as a prism for Kierkegaard interest in Norway at all levels. The Society has operated under the aegis of the Norwegian Academy of Science (Det Norske Videnskabs-Akademi) in central Oslo, where 2 to 3 lectures are held each semester. These have reflected a broad public interest in Kierkegaard in Norway, and at their best, have functioned as a forum for young Kierkegaard researchers. The Society has arranged large seminars and conferences: *Kierkegaard og det sceniske* (1996, Det Norske Videnskabs-Akademi); *Filosofi og Samfunn* (1997, Kristiansand); *Søren Kierkegaard og Norsk Kulturliv* (2000, Det Norske Studentersamfund, Chateau Neuf); *Øieblikket—sannheten gitt utenfra?* (2005, Det Norske Videnskabs-Akademi, in conjunction with the 150th commemoration of Kierkegaard's death); *Søren Kierkegaard og Henrik Ibsen—fuldt og helt, ikke stykkevis og delt* (2006, Vartov, Copenhagen). The Society has also published one number of *Småskrifter* (1997) together with *Filosofi og Samfunn* (Finn Jor, ed., Høyskoleforlaget 1998). See also www.kierkegaard.no

between *production* and *interpretation* of text, and thus offers a much more refined criticism of philosophy's claims to truth than was earlier realized.

Two significant works are conspicuous as different answers to the postmodern interest in Kierkegaard, and both are strongly colored by a cross-disciplinary approach to the material. The first is Eivind Tjønneland's (b. 1956) doctoral dissertation of 1999, *Ironi som Symptom. En kritisk studie av Søren Kierkegaards Om Begrepet Ironi*.[134] Tjønneland's fields are the history of ideas and literary criticism, and he stands in the line of the literary and critical tradition originating with Brandes. His dissertation rejects the New Rhetoric's readings by Jacques Derrida and Paul de Man, and instead takes up the cause for a symptomatic reading inspired by Freud. The aim is not to psychoanalyze Kierkegaard, but to reach a concept of intertextuality that has room for "the text's intention."

The starting point is Kierkegaard's own thesis on irony, and put succinctly, one can say that Tjønneland's dissertation attempts to show how, and for what purposes, Kierkegaard incorporated other texts into his own. The manner of the forming of the irony concept would have drastic consequences, Tjønneland claims since it imposes strong governance on how religious matters are presented in Kierkegaard's later writing. Tjønneland's dissertation represents a thorough and perhaps unique comparative reading of central authors such as K.W.F. Solger, Henrich Steffens, Gotthilf H. Schubert, and H. Theodor Rötscher—contemporaries of Kierkegaard, all of whom we know were read by him.

In 2005, Marius G. Mjaaland (b. 1971) defended his dissertation on Kierkegaard, *Autopsy. Death and the View of Self [among KIERKEGAARD's Aporias]*, written for a doctorate in theology.[135] Mjaaland is a philosopher and theologian, and his dissertation, like Tjønneland's, is characterized by an interdisciplinary approach. However, in contrast to Tjønneland, Mjaaland uses Derrida and deconstructionism positively, as a springboard for a reading of Kierkegaard's texts. The dissertation represents additionally one of the most comprehensive analyses of Derrida in Norwegian.

Mjaaland's study of death as a theological and philosophical problem takes its starting point in two of Kierkegaard's works, the discourse "At a Graveside" and the great *The Sickness unto Death*. Throughout the seven sections of his dissertation, Mjaaland tries to zero in on death as Kierkegaard and Derrida tried to portray it, as something that neither admits to understanding nor explanation, wedging itself between the Self and the Other, challenging the barrier between reason and madness. Mjaaland's text has a meditative character, and is, in accordance with deconstructionist practice, more concerned with process than with conclusions.

Coming from theological quarters, this is a totally new tack since there is no longer any talk about what Kierkegaard *really* meant, or what he should have meant—as had often been the case in those same religious circles earlier. Kierkegaard's

---

[134]   Eivind Tjønneland, *Ironi som Symptom. En kritisk studie av Søren Kierkegaard's Om Begrebet Ironi*, doctoral dissertation, University of Bergen 1999.

[135]   Marius G. Mjaaland, *Autopsi. Døden og Synet på Selvet [blant KIERKEGAARDS aporier]*, Oslo: UniPub, Universitetet i Oslo 2005. (English translation: *Autopsia. Self, Death and God after Kierkegaard and Derrida*, Berlin and New York: Walter de Gruyter 2008 (*Kierkegaard Studies. Monograph Series*, vol. 17).)

authorship is for both Tjønneland and Mjaaland—in spite of all other differences between them—a point of departure for critical reflection, and their dissertations, with a cross-disciplinary approach and openness to various modern theories thus represent, it is hoped, a new trend in Norwegian Kierkegaard research. This new openness is made even more apparent by the notable circumstance that both of these dissertations are being made available through translation to an international public. Tjønneland's dissertation is already available in German,[136] while Mjaaland's study has now appeared in English.

XV. Concluding Effective-Historical Postscript

Kierkegaard's production was read by a contemporary public in Norway, and his showdown with the Church in 1854–55 in many ways had a stronger effect here than in Denmark. The controversy about *The Moment* actualized and sharpened an already existing Pietist revival in Norway. The ambiguity in Kierkegaard's radicalism, however, became clear with Georg Brandes' enlistment of him in the service of freethinking and cultural radicalism at the end of the nineteenth century. A special characteristic in Norwegian cultural debate since then has been the irreconcilable frontlines between *Pietism* and *cultural radicalism*. It is precisely in the particularly Norwegian absolutist formulations of these "modern" projects, that we recognize Kierkegaard's hidden hand.

"I always namely write, so to speak, under Kierkegaard's eyes," went the words of Alexander Lange Kielland (1849–1906) in 1888. Kierkegaard's close intellectual proximity has given a creative push to Norwegian authors and artists, while at times appearing to have had a paralyzing effect on philosophers and theologians. For a long while, Kierkegaard was refused academic consideration, and those few who did write about him often appeared to be somewhat conscience-stricken. A new interdisciplinary approach to Kierkegaard around the start of the new millennium has produced more research in a few decades than did the entire preceding 150 years. To put it bluntly, one can therefore state that it was necessary to remove the ideological spectacles and read Kierkegaard anew, in order to establish a genuine research tradition in Norway.

---

[136]   Tjønneland, *Ironie als Symptom. Eine kritische Auseinandersetzung mit Søren Kierkegaards "Über den Begriff der Ironie,"* Frankfurt am Main: Peter Lang 2004 (*Texte und Untersuchungen zur Germanistik und Skandinavistik*, vol. 54).

Bibliography

I. Norwegian Translations and Editions of Kierkegaard's Works

Læsebog i Modersmaalet for Norsk og Danske, tilligemed en Exempelsamling af den svenske Literatur og med Æsthetiske og literaturhistoriske Oplysninger, ed. by Henning Junghans Thue, Kristiania: A.D. Wulfsberg & Co. 1846.

"Derved bliver det," *Christiania-Posten*, no. 2323, February 25, 1855.

"Var afdøde Biskop Mynster et 'Sandhedsvidne,' " *Christiania-Posten*, Supplement to *Christiania-Posten*, no. 2318, February 19, 1855.

Søren Kierkegaard. I utvalg, ed. by Anna Klaussen, Oslo: Olaf Norlis Forlag 1929 (several later editions).

"Søren Kierkegaard. Et Udvalg af hans direkte opbyggelge Skrifter," in *Fra dansk kirke- og kristenliv. Fra J.P. Mynster til Vilhelm Beck*, ed. by Olaf Moe, Oslo: Lutherstiftelsen 1930 (*Hovedverker av den kristne litteratur fra kirkefedrene til nutiden*, vol. 12), pp. 127–97.

Søren Kierkegaard, trans. and ed. by Harald Beyer, Oslo: Gyldendal 1942 (several later editions).

Søren Kierkegaards budskap. Skrifter i utvalg, ed. by Anna Klaussen, Oslo: Arne Gimnes Forlag 1943.

Enten-Eller. Et Livsframent 2, Oslo: Hagerup 1950.

Øjeblikket (a selection), ed. by Erling Nielsen, Oslo: Cappelen Norsk Forlag 1955.

Søren Kierkegaard. Utdrag af verker, trans. by Finn Jor, ed. by Per Lønning, Oslo: Forlaget Land og Kirke 1955.

Søren Kierkegaard (a selection), ed. by Arne Næss, Oslo: Pax Forlag 1966.

Begrebet Angest, ed. by Finn Jor, Oslo: Gyldendal Norsk Forlag 1969 (2nd ed., 1981).

Frygt og Bæven, ed. by Finn Jor, Oslo: Gyldendal Norsk Forlag 1969.

Avsluttende uvitenskaplig etterskrift til "De philosophiske smuler" (a selection), trans. and ed. by Arne Næss, Oslo: Pax 1994.

Forførerens dagbok, trans. by Knut Johansen, ed. by Eivind Tjønneland, Oslo: Bokvennen 1995 (2nd ed., 1999) (*Romantikerserien Den Blå blomst*, vol. 17).

"Barmhjertighed, en Kjerlighedens Gjerning, selv om den intet kan give og intet formaaer at gjøre," *ARR—idéhistorisk tidsskrift*, ed. by Thor Arvid Dyrerud, no. 1, 1998, pp. 24–33.

Kjærlighetens gjerninger, 2. serie, ed. by Egil A. Wyller, Oslo: Spartacus Forlag AS / Andresen & Butenschøn AS 1998.

Begrepet angst, trans. by Knut Johansen, ed. by Thor Arvid Dyrerud, Oslo: Oktober 2001 (2nd ed., 2005).

Filosofiske smuler, eller En smule filosofi, trans. and ed. by Knut Johansen, Oslo: Damm Forlag 2004.

Filosofiske smuler, ed. by Arild Waaler and Christian Fink Tolstrup, Oslo: Damm Forlag 2004.

II. Secondary Literature on Kierkegaard in Norway

Aall, Anathon, "Søren Kierkegaard," in his *Filosofien i Norden. Til oplysning om den nyere tænknings og videnskabs historie i Sverige og Finland, Danmark og Norge*, Kristiania: H.A. Benneches Fond 1919 (*Videnskapsselskapets Skrifter*), see pp. 121–64.

Ågotnes, Knut, "'Jeg sidder rolig som Klintekongen,' Refleksjon og pasjon hos Adam Smith, Friedrich Schlegel og Søren Kierkegaard," *Norsk Filosofisk Tidsskrift*, vol. 36, 2001, pp. 242–55.

Andersen, Kristen, "Den religiøse motsetning mellem Søren Kierkegaard og Henrik Ibsen. Foredrag på Universitetet i Oslo, April 16, 1928," *For Kirke og Kultur*, vol. 35, no. 4, 1928, pp. 213–33.

Anonymous, "Kierkegaard har atter i en Opsats...," *Bergensposten*, no. 100, February 11, 1855.

Anonymous, "Dr. Brandes' Forelæsninger," *Morgenbladet*, no. 346 A, December 15, 1876.

Aubert, Axel H., *Maieutikk: en studie av den maieutiske kunst ut i fra forfatterskapet til Platon og Kierkegaard*, M.A. Thesis, Trondheim: Norges teknisk-natur vitenskapelige universitet, Filosofisk institutt 2000 (*Filosofisk institutts-publikasjonsserie*, vol. 36).

Beyer, Harald, *Søren Kierkegaard*, Oslo: Olaf Norlis Forlag 1925.

— "Søren Kierkegaard i nutidens Tyskland," *For Kirke og Kultur*, vol. 41, 1934, pp. 424–9.

— "Søren Kierkegaard og svensk litteratur," *For Kirke og Kultur*, vol. 56, no. 8, 1951, pp. 500–4.

— "Nietzsche og Kierkegaard," *Edda. Nordisk tidsskrift for litteraturforskning*, vol. 6, 1955, pp. 161–72.

Boman, Thorleif, "Søren Kierkegaard som den kristne Kirkes reformator," *For Kirke og Kultur*, vol. 60, 1955, pp. 449–55.

Børsand, Grete, *Forbilde og utfordring: En Kierkegaard studie*, Oslo: Tanum 1966 (*Idé og tanke*, vol. 14).

Bruun, Christopher, "Lidt om Søren Kierkegaard," *For Kirke og Kultur*, vol. 8, no. 10, 1901, pp. 579–91.

Christensen, Tor Bjarne, "Det irrasjonelles filosof," *Prosopopeia*, no. 2, 1999, pp. 44–52.

Christoffersen, Svein Aage, "—som en Fugl i angstfull flukt foran det kommende Uveir. Det pietistiske hos Søren Kierkegaard og Gisle Johnson," *Kirke og Kultur*, no. 57, 2002, pp. 191–206.

Dingstad, Ståle, "Om å lese—Hegel i lys av Kierkegaard," *AGORA. Journal for Metafysisk Spekulasjon*, nos. 3–4, 1994, pp. 261–71.

— "Om Kierkegaards 'In vino veritas'—en gjentagelse," in *Hilsen. En bok til Arne Melberg i anledning 60-årsdagen*, ed. by Trond Haugen et al., Oslo: Gyldendal Norsk Forlag 2002, pp. 49–63.

Dyrerud, Thor Arvid, "Det kierkegaardske regnskap: et (uautorisert) efterskrift," *ARR–idéhistorisk tidsskrift*, ed. by Thor Arvid Dyrerud, no. 1, 1998, pp. 33–5.

— "*...ikke et eneste Ord af mig selv*. Søren Kierkegaard og hans biografer," *AGORA. Journal for Metafysisk Spekulasjon*, no. 3, 2004, p. 12–45.

Elster, Kristian, "Søren Kierkegaard: Efterladte Papirer," *Dagsposten*, October 27–8, 1880 (republished in *Fra det moderne gjennombrudds tid. Litteraturkritikk og artikler 1868–1880 i utvalg*, ed. by Willy Dahl, Bergen: J.W. Eide Forlag 1981, pp. 201–4).

— "Et Par Ord om Dr. S. Kierkegaards Angreb paa Biskop Mynsters Eftermæle," *Christiania–Posten*, no. 2335, March 9, 1855.

Engebretsen, Rune A., *Kierkegaard and Poet–Existence with Special Reference to Germany and Rilke*, Ph.D. Thesis, Stanford University 1980.

Grelland, Hans Herlof, *Tausheten og øyeblikket: Kierkegaard, Ibsen, Munch*, Kristiansand: Høyskoleforlaget 2007.

Hale, Frederick, "The Impact of Kierkegaard's Anticlericalism in Norway," *Studia Theologica*, vol. 34, 1980, pp. 153–71.

Harket, Håkon, Eivind Tjønneland, Poul Erik Tøjner and Joakim Garff, *Innøvelse i Kierkegaard: fire essays*, Oslo: Cappelen Norsk Forlag 1996.

Haslund, Irene, *Tid og væren: en sammenligning mellom Kierkegaards og Heideggers tidsfilosofi*, Trondheim: Norges teknisk-naturvitenskapelige universitet 1997 (*Filosofisk institutts publikasjonsserie*, vol. 25).

Heyerdahl, Grete Børsand, *Forbilde og utfordring: en Kierkegaard-studie*, Oslo: Johan Grundt Tanum Forlag 1966.

—*Idéhistoriske smuler. Essays om litteratur og filosofi, kjærlighet og undertrykkelse— om Hegel, Kierkegaard, H.C. Andersen, Freud, Hermann Hesse, Adorno*, Oslo: Gyldendal Norsk Forlag 1979.

Henriksen, Jan-Olav, *The Reconstruction of Religion. Lessing, Kierkegaard and Nietzsche*, Grand Rapids, Michigan: Eerdmans 2001, pp. 75–129.

Hohlenberg, Johannes, "Søren Kierkegaard og den Enkelte," *Janus*, no. 3, 1939, pp. 244–62.

Holgernes, Bjørn, *Angst i eksistensfilosofisk belysning: en studie i Irvin D. Yalom og Søren Kierkegaard*, Kristiansand: Høyskoleforlag 2004.

Hopland, Karstein, *Virkelighet og bevissthet. En studie i Søren Kierkegaards antropologi*, Bergen: Religionsvitenskapelig Institutt, Universitetet i Bergen 1981.

— "Rasjonalistiske smuler hos Søren Kierkegaard," *Kierkegaardiana*, vol. 14, 1988, pp. 38–48.

— *Introduksjon til Søren Kierkegaards Begrebet angest*, Bergen: Universitetet i Bergen, Institutt for religionsvitenskap 1990 (*Stensilserie. Religionsvitenskapelige institutt*, vol. 47).

— "Kristendom og lidelse—introduksjon til Søren Kierkegaards kristendomsfilosofi," *For Kirke og Kultur*, no. 102, 1997, pp. 251–71.

Johansen, Kjell Eyvind, *"Begrebet Gjentagelse" hos Søren Kierkegaard*, Oslo: Solum Forlag 1988.

— "The Problem of Knowledge in the Ethics of Kierkegaard's *Works of Love*," *Kierkegaardiana*, vol. 17, 1994, pp. 52–65.

— "Kierkegaard on Religious Belief and Risk," *Kierkegaardiana*, vol. 19, 1998, pp. 43–57.

— " 'Fear and Trembling'—the Problem of Justification," *British Journal for the History of Philosophy*, vol. 10, 2002, pp. 261–76.

Jor, Finn, *Søren Kierkegaard. Den eksisterende tenker*, Oslo: Forlaget Land og Kirke 1954.

— (ed.), *Den levende Kierkegaard*, trans. by Lars Roar Langslet et al., Oslo: Gyldendal Norsk Forlag 1969 (originally as *Kierkegaard vivant. Colloque organisé par l'Unesco à Paris du 21 au 23 avril 1964*, ed. by René Maheu, Paris: Gallimard 1966).

— *"Til hiin Enkelte": Søren Kierkegaards liv og verk*, Oslo Oktober 1995.

— *Kjærlighetens gjerninger. En roman om Søren og Regine*, Oslo: Pantagruel Forlag 1997.

— (ed.), *Filosofi & samfunn: Søren Kierkegaard: en vandring i filosofi, teologi, psykologi, litteratur. Bearbeidede foredrag fra første "Filosofi & samfunn"—konferanse, holdt i Kristiansand, september 1997*, Kristiansand: Høyskoleforlaget 1998.

Jostad, Morten, "Øyeblikkets kunst," *For Kirke og Kultur*, no. 102, 1997, pp. 243–50.

Kalleberg, Ragnvald, "Kierkegaard som samfunnstenker," *Nytt Norsk Tidsskrift*, no. 20, 2003, pp. 196–209.

Koppang, Ole, "Quelques pensées kierkegardiennes dans la philosophie de Jean Wahl," *Symposion Kierkegaardianum*, Copenhagen: Munksgaard 1955 (*Orbis literarum*, Tome 10, fasc. 1–2), pp. 112–17.

Løchen, Arne, "Søren Kierkegaard," in his *Digtning og Videnskap*, Kristiania: Aschehoug 1913, pp. 63–79 (originally published in *Samtiden*, vol. 13, no. 1, 1902, pp. 77–88).

Lønning, Per, *Samtidighetens Situation*, Oslo: Forlaget Land og Kirke 1954.

— "Kierkegaard's 'Paradox,' " *Symposion Kierkegaardianum*, Copenhagen: Munksgaard 1955 (*Orbis literarum*, Tome 10, fasc. 1–2), pp. 156–65.

Mjaaland, Marius G., *Om fri vilje*, M.A. Thesis, Philosophy Department, University of Oslo 1999.

— "En sann tviler. Søren Kierkegaard og negativ teologi," *Ung Teologi*, vol. 1, 2000, pp. 21–35.

— "Et åpent sår i selvet," *Kirke og Kultur*, vol. 106, 2001, pp. 85–96.

— "På de 70.000 favne. Ole Hallesby møter Søren Kierkegaard," *Kirke og Kultur*, vol. 107, 2002, pp. 207–21.

— "Death and Aporia," *Kierkegaard Studies. Yearbook*, 2003, pp. 395–418.

— "Den kunst at blive taus. Søren Kierkegaard om bønn, lidelse og glede," *Over Alt*, vol. 3, 2003, pp. 11–17.

— "Døden—denne mægtige Tænker. Apori, skrift og kjærlighetens gjerninger, *Kirke og Kultur*, vol. 108, 2003, pp. 149–62.

— "X. Alterität und Textur in Kierkegaards *Krankheit zum Tode*," *Neue Zeitschrift für systematische Theologie und Religionsphilosophie*, 2005, pp. 58–80.

— *Autopsi. Døden og Synet på Selvet [blant KIERKEGAARDS aporier]*, Oslo: UniPub, Universitetet i Oslo 2005 (*Acta theologica*, vol. 12). (English translation: *Autopsia. Self, Death and God after Kierkegaard and Derrida*, Berlin and New York: Walter de Gruyter 2008 (*Kierkegaard Studies Monograph Series*, vol. 17).)

Moe, Steinar, "Den 'heftige Opblusen i Fosvik.' Om forholdet mellom presten Gustav A. Lammers i Skien og tenkeren Søren Kierkegaard," in his (ed.) *Radikale profiler i dansk og norsk kirkeliv fra ca. 1850 til ca. 1900. Artikkelsamling*, Tønsberg: Høgskolen i Vestfold 1996.

Monrad, M.J., "Søren Kierkegaard" (Eulogy), *Illustreret Nyhedsblad*, no. 47, November 24, 1855.

— "Mindebægeret over Søren Kierkegaard" (Lecture at the Student Society, January 14, 1856), *Illustreret Nyhedsblad*, no. 4, January 26, 1856.

Paludan-Müller, Jens, "Dr. Kierkegaards Angreb paa Mynsters Eftermæle," *Christiania-Posten*, no. 2325, February 27, 1855.

Petersen, Fredrik, "Dr. Søren Kierkegaards Efterladte Papirer," *Morgenbladet*, no. 22 A, January 23, 1870 (and the following five Sundays).

— *Dr. Søren Kierkegaards Christendomsforkyndelse*, Christiania: P.T. Mallings Boghandel 1877.

Rothholz, Walter, "Einflüsse Grundtvigs und Kierkegaards," in *Die politische Kultur Norwegens. Zur Entwicklung einer wohlfahrtsstaatlichen Demokratie*, Baden-Baden: Nomos Verlag 1986, pp. 94–100.

Sandberg, Caspar Køhler, *Varsko der i Kirkeskibene! I kuldseile! I have ikke Sandhed ombord!* Fredrikstad: K. Sandberg 1855.

— *Den tveæggede Granstaur*, Fredrikshald: K. Sandberg 1856.

— *Den tveæggede Granstaur*, no. 5, Fredrikshald: K. Sandberg 1856.

— *Den tveæggede Granstaur*, no. 10, Fredrikshald: K. Sandberg 1856.

— *Den tveæggede Granstaur*, no. 12, Fredrikshald: K. Sandberg 1856.

— *Vragstumperne af Kirke-Skib-Skroget*, Fredrikshald: K. Sandberg 1856.

— *Solens Øie. Tilegnet Den, som skal komme*, Fredrikshald: K. Sandberg 1856.

— *Solens Øie. (Tilegnet Den, som skal komme.) Kjerlighed. † Sandhed*, Fredrikshald: K. Sandberg 1856.

— *Grannaalen*, no. 18, Fredrikshald: K. Sandberg 1857.

Sirnes, Tollak B., *Sann personlighet. Personlig sannhet. Kan Kierkegaard hjelpe oss?* Stavanger: Dreyer Bok 1979.

Sødal, Helje Kringlebotn, "Henrik Ibsens 'Brand'—illustrasjon på en teleologisk suspensjon av det etiske?" *Edda. Nordisk tidsskrift for litteraturforskning*, vol. 99, 1999, pp. 63–70.

Sommerfelt, Wilhelm, *Søren Kierkegaard. Utgit efter forfatterens død af nogle venner*, Kristiania: Cammermeyers Boghandel 1922.

Svendsen, Paulus, "Søren Kierkegaard—5. mai 1963" (Lecture at the University of Copenhagen), *Kierkegaardiana*, vol. 5, 1964, pp. 7–22.

Tandberg, Jens, "Søren Kierkegaard. Foredrag i 'Norske studenters kristelige forbund,'" *For Kirke og Kultur*, vol. 14, 1907, pp. 166–77; pp. 198–210.

Tjønneland, Eivind, *Ironie als Symptom. Eine kritische Auseinandersetzung mit Søren Kierkegaards Über den Begriff der Ironie*, Frankfurt am Main: Peter Lang Verlag 2004 (*Texte und Untersuchungen zur Gemanistik und Skandinavistik*, vol. 54).

Wyller, Egil A., "Ibsen og Kierkegaard. Tre tekst-henvisninger," *AGORA. Journal for Metafysisk Spekulasjon*, nos. 2–3, 1993, pp. 302–10.

Waaler, Arild, "Søren Kierkegaard—en fremmed i verden," *For Kirke og Kultur*, no. 102, 1997, pp. 229–41.

III. Secondary Literature on Kierkegaard's Reception in Norway

Anz, Heinrich, " 'Seinerzeit eine Art makabre Modefigur.' Aspekte der Wirkungs-geschichte Søren Kierkegaards in der skandinavischen Literatur," in *Kierkegaard Studies. Yearbook*, 1999, pp. 204–20.

Beyer, Harald, "Søren Kierkegaards Betydning for norsk Aandsliv," *Edda. Nordisk tidsskrift for litteraturforskning*, vol. 19, no. 1, 1923, pp. 1–143.

— *Søren Kierkegaard og Norge*, Kristiania: H. Aschehoug 1924.

Boer, Richard, "Kierkegaard in Noorwegen," *Onze eeuw*, vol. 24, no. 1, 1924, pp. 152–69.

Bøggild, Jacob, "Coming to Terms with the Tricky Twins. On the Scandinavian Reception of *Repetition* and *Fear and Trembling*," *Kierkegaard Studies. Yearbook*, 2002, pp. 290–309.

Delgaauw, Bernhard, "De Kierkegaardstudie in Scandinavië," *Tijdschrift voor Filosofie*, vol. 33, 1971, pp. 737–78; vol. 38, 1976, pp. 136–58; vol. 43, 1981, pp. 117–62.

Dyrerud, Thor Arvid, " 'Nordic Angest': Søren Kierkegaard and *The Concept of Anxiety* in Norway," *Kierkegaard Studies. Yearbook*, 2001, pp. 364–78.

Erichsen, Valborg, "Søren Kierkegaards betydning for norsk aandsliv," *Edda. Nordisk tidsskrift for litteraturforskning*, vol. 19, 1923, pp. 369–429.

Flottorp, Haakon, *Kierkegaard and Norway: A Study of "Inwardness" in History with Illustrative Examples from Religion, Literature, and Philosophy*, Ph.D. Thesis, Colombia University, New York 1955.

Götke, Povl, "Recent Scandinavian Literature on *Works of Love*," *Kierkegaard Studies. Yearbook*, 1998, pp. 232–44.

Kabell, Aage, *Kierkegaardstudiet i Norden*, Copenhagen: H. Hagerup 1948.

Kihlmann, Erik, "Kierkegaard i Norge," *Nya Argus*, vol. 17, no. 14, 1924, pp. 170–2.

Landmark, Johan Daniel, *Fortolkninger til Søren Kierkegaards ungdomshistorie*, Trondhjem: Det kgl. Norske videnskabers selskab 1926 (*Det kgl. Norske videnskabers selskabs skrifter*, vol. 4).

— "Til drøftelsen av Kierkegaards notat II A 805," *Det Kgl. norske videnskabers selskabs forhandlinger*, vol. 6, no. 50, 1933, pp. 189–91.

— "Om Søren Kierkegaard: Biskop Kierkegaards brev til professor Fr. Petersen," *Det kgl. Norske videnskabers selskabs forhandlinger*, vol. 9, no. 17, 1936, pp. 62–4.

Mortensen, Finn Hauberg, "Kierkegaard in Scandinavia. A History of Radical Reception," in *Kierkegaard Revisited. Proceedings from the Conference "Kierkegaard and the Meaning of Meaning It," Copenhagen, May 5–9, 1996*, ed. by Niels Jørgen Cappelørn and Jon Stewart, Berlin and New York: Walter de Gruyter 1997 (*Kierkegaard Studies Monograph Series*, vol. 1), pp. 410–41.

Norris, John A., "The Validity of A's View of Tragedy with Particular Reference to Ibsen's 'Brand,' " in *International Kierkegaard Commentary, Either/Or, Part I*, ed. by Robert L. Perkins, Macon, Georgia: Mercer 1995, pp. 143–57.

Svendsen, Paulus, "Norwegian Literature," in *The Legacy and Interpretation of Kierkegaard*, ed. by Niels Thulstrup and Marie Mikulová Thulstrup, Copenhagen: C.A. Reitzel 1981 (*Bibliotheca Kierkegaardiana*, vol. 8), pp. 9–39.

Thulstrup, Niels, "Scandinavia," in *Kierkegaard Research*, ed. by Niels Thulstrup and Marie Mikulová Thulstrup, Copenhagen: C.A. Reitzel 1987 (*Bibliotheca Kierkegaardiana*, vol. 15), pp. 173–99.

Tullberg, Steen, "Die Rezeption der *Philosophischen Brocken* in Skandinavien," *Kierkegaard Studies. Yearbook*, 2004, pp. 306–27.

Sweden:

Kierkegaard's Reception in Swedish Philosophy, Theology, and Contemporary Literary Theory

Jonna Hjertström Lappalainen and Lars-Erik Hjertström Lappalainen

I. A Reception by Single Individuals Seeking the Truth

One thing that makes the Swedish reception interesting is that it started very early, already in Kierkegaard's own lifetime. There are two well-known Swedish interpreters, Torsten Bohlin (1889–1950) and Lars Bejerholm (b. 1930), and there are a few more interesting interpreters worth mentioning. But their achievements have had no effect on the Swedish reception, and it looks indeed as if this history of reception lacks all sense of continuity. With the Swedish debate concerning Kierkegaard's attack on the Danish Church as the only exception, every new interpreter seems to rise up out of a vacuum, feeling himself called upon to introduce Kierkegaard anew. It follows that most of what has been published in Sweden on Kierkegaard are introductions, and their form is always the same: an introductory part about his engagement to Regine Olsen and his painful relationship to his father, after which follows a biographically oriented description of the authorship, work by work. Our article will mainly focus on the books which attempt to move beyond merely introducing Kierkegaard. When one gets deeper into texts that are better informed, a certain tendency in the Swedish reception appears, i.e., an interest in Kierkegaard's view on religious and subjective truth.

II. Translations

All the early translations into Swedish come from Kierkegaard's religious production, and they were done by men with an interest in religion, often with some personal connection to the revivalist movement. The very first volume, *Eighteen Edifying Discourses* (1852), was published when Kierkegaard was still alive,[1] and he had

---

Thanks to Stefan Borg, Björn Kumm, and Clara Cederberg for their help with this article.

[1] *Aderton Uppbyggeliga Tal* [*Eighteen Upbuilding Discourses* (the first fourteen of the *Upbuilding Discourses* from 1843–44)], trans. by Th. Wensjoe, vol. 1 in *Walda Skrifter af S. Kierkegaard* [Selected Writings of S. Kierkegaard], Mariestad: Hos P.W. Karström 1852 (reprinted in 1853 in five different off-prints).

a copy of it on his bookshelf. Other translations during Kierkegaard's lifetime are *For Self-Examination*,[2] some of the *Edifying Discourses*,[3] and parts of *Practice in Christianity*.[4] In 1855 several translations appeared in relation to Kierkegaard's attack on the Church. There are two works that were published and translated anonymously by the religiously interested J.G. Wahlström (1814–85), a member of the board of the socialist newspaper *Aftonbladet*.[5] Another anonymous translation, which very likely was done by Oskar Patrick Stürzen-Becker (1811–69), is a selection of Kierkegaard's articles attacking the Church.[6] In the following decades, there appeared several translations, all from the explicitly religious parts of his works, e.g., *Works of Love*,[7] *Practice in Christianity*,[8] and *The Sickness unto Death*.[9]

Kierkegaard was not introduced outside the theological or ecclesiastical sphere until 1902, when the first Swedish translation of "The Seducer's Diary" appeared.[10] But not until the translation of a selection from *Either/Or* and the translation of *Fear and Trembling* by Richard Hejll (1889–1963)[11] is it possible to discern an interest in Kierkegaard beyond the theology. After this, "The Seducer's Diary" appeared

---

[2]   *Selfpröfning för vår tid*, trans. by P.M. Elmblad, Stockholm: N. Markus, Nylander & Co. 1852.

[3]   *Hvad vi läre af Liljorna på marken och foglarna under himmelen* [*What We Learn from the Lilies in the Field and from the Birds of the Air*], trans. by P.M. Elmblad, Norrköping: Östlund & Bergling 1852; *Liljorna på marken och foglarna under himlen. Tre andeliga tal* [*The Lilies in the Field and the Birds of the Air*], trans. by P.M. Elmblad, Stockholm: N Marcus Nylander & Co. 1853.

[4]   *Kommen! Kommen!* [Come! Come! (selections from *Practice in Christianity*)] (no translator given), published anonymously by Hans Jakob Lundborg, Uppsala: Wahlström 1853; "Den stora underbara inbjudningen" [The Great Wonderful Invitation (selections from *Practice in Christianity*)], trans. by P.M. Elmblad under the pseudonym Kd in *Frids-budbäraren. Tidning för den inre missionen*, 1854–55.

[5]   *Hvad Kristus dömmer om officiell kristendom* [*What Christ Judges about Official Christianity*], trans. by J.G. Wahlström, Uppsala: Wahlström & Co. 1855; *Ögonblicket* [*The Moment*], nos. 1–9, trans. by J.G., Uppsala: Wahlström & Co. 1855.

[6]   *Den officiella kristendomen är icke det nya Testamentets kristendom. Framställning av dr Sören Kierkegaards polemik mot statskyrkan i Danmark* [The Official Christianity is not the Christianity of The New Testament. Description by Dr. Sören Kierkegaard's polemic against the State Church in Denmark (selections from Kierkegaard's articles in *Fædrelandet*)], trans. and ed. by Oscar Patrick Sturzen-Becker, Copenhagen: S. Triers tryck 1855.

[7]   *Kärlekens gerningar. Några christliga betraktelser i form af tal*, trans. by Gustaf Tomée, Stockholm: Bonniers förlag 1862.

[8]   *Inöfning i kristendom af Anti-Climacus*, trans. by O.A. Stridsberg, Stockholm: Z. Haeggström 1879.

[9]   *Sjukdomen til Döds*, trans. by Zacharias Göransson, introduction. Waldemar Rudin, Stockholm: A.V. Carlsons förlag 1881.

[10]   *Förförarens dagbok*, trans. and ed. by David Sprengel, Stockholm: 1902 (*Mästerverk ur världslitteraturen*, vol. 2).

[11]   *Valda stycken ur Sören Kierkegaards tankevärld* [Selected Parts from Sören Kierkegaards World of Thought (Selections from *Either/Or, Edifying Discourses* and Kierkegaard's journals)], Stockholm: Albert Bonniers förlag 1916; *Fruktan och bävan* [*Fear and Trembling*], Stockholm: Björck & Börjessons 1920.

in several editions by different translators (1919, 1969, and 1995).[12] There is also a translation of selections from Kierkegaard's diaries, allegedly by Anna Bohlin.[13] Furthermore, Lars Göransson's (1919–94) and Stig Ahlgren's (1910–96) selected translations were published, both of which pick out parts of Kierkegaard's early authorship leading up to the *Concluding Unscientific Postscript*.[14] These have been reprinted several times. In the 1990s, Stefan Borg (b. 1954) initiated his ongoing project to make all the famous works of Kierkegaard available in Swedish.

III. The Very First Swedish Kierkegaard Texts

The very first opportunity to read about Kierkegaard in Swedish arose in the Swedish newspapers from 1844, when Stürzen-Becker, using the pseudonym Orvar Odd, wrote articles in *Aftonbladet* about daily life in the Danish capital. These articles were later revised and published in *Beyond the Sound* in 1846.[15] Stürzen-Becker concludes that Kierkegaard seems to be more talked about than actually read. Three years later, in 1849, Fredrika Bremer (1801–65) had a different opinion in her portrayal of prominent personalities in Copenhagen, *Life in the Nordic Countries*. She describes Kierkegaard as a modern Simon Stylites, who "has a considerable audience, in particular among the ladies."[16] At the time of Kierkegaard's attack on the Church in 1855, there were new reports from Stürzen-Becker, this time in *Öresundsposten*.[17] Other reports were to be found in *Wäktaren* and in *Aftonbladet*.[18]

---

[12]   *Förförarens dagbok* (no translator is given), Stockholm: Bonnier 1919; *Förförarens dagbok*, trans. by Per Sörbom, Stockholm: Wahlström & Widstrand 1969; *Förförarens dagbok*, trans. by Nils Tengdahl, Gothenburg: Vinga Press 1995.

[13]   *Sören Kierkegaards Dagbok*, ed. by Torsten Bohlin, Stockholm: Svenska Kyrkans Diakonistyrelsens Bokförlag 1928.

[14]   *Skrifter i urval. Med inledningar och textförklaringar av Billeskov Jansen* [Selected Works, Introductions and Comments by Billeskov Jansen], vols. 1–2, trans. and selected by Stig Ahlgren, Stockholm: Wahlström & Widstrand 1954–57 (selections from *Either/Or* and *Stages on Life's Way*) (reprinted in 1977); *Kierkegaard*, trans. and ed. by Lars Göransson, Stockholm: Forum 1956 (selections from *Either/Or*, *Stages on Life's Way*, *Repetition*, and *Concluding Unscientific Postscript*) (reprinted in 1969 and 1979); *Begreppet ångest* [*The Concept of Anxiety*], trans. by Stig Ahlgren and Nils Kjellström, ed. with commentaries by F.J. Billeskov Jansen, Stockholm: Wahlström & Widstrand 1963 (reprinted in 1977 and 1986); *Antingen-eller. Ett livsfragment* [*Either/Or*], trans. by Stig Ahlgren and Nils Kjellström, selected and commented by F.J. Billeskov Jansen, Stockholm: Wahlström & Widstrand 1963 (reprinted in 1967, 1977, and 1986).

[15]   [Sturzen-Becker, Oscar Patrick], Orvar Odd, *Hinsidan Sundet. Danska epistlar av Orvar Odd* [Beyond the Sound. Danish Epistles by Orvar Odd], vols. 1–2, Stockholm: Bonnier 1846.

[16]   *Lif i Norden. Skizz*, Stockholm: Bagge 1849, p. 54.

[17]   *Öresundsposten*, March 26, August 6, October 19, October 22, November 9, November 12, November 14, and November 19, 1855.

[18]   *Aftonbladet*, January 13, February 10, October 29, October 30, October 31, November 3, and November 7, 1855.

Beside the news reports there is one theoretical Swedish article about Kierkegaard in his lifetime, "Sören Kierkegaard. A Literary and Historical Picture" in *Tidsskrift för Litteratur* in 1851, written by Albert Theodor Lysander (1822–90).[19] The article, which is a deep and comprehensive study, tries to capture the line of development in Kierkegaard's authorship. It seems that Kierkegaard himself read and appreciated Lysander's article.[20]

Even if the present article does not specifically deal with Kierkegaard's influence on Swedish literature, the great importance he has had for several Swedish authors must be mentioned. This influence is of course due to the fact that Denmark and Sweden are both geographically and linguistically very close. The two Scandinavian languages are so similar that a Swede might read Danish almost as he would his mother tongue. Therefore, it is hardly surprising that Kierkegaard was, and still is, being read by Swedish authors. August Strindberg (1849–1912), probably the most famous Swedish writer internationally acknowledged in his diaries that he was influenced by Kierkegaard.[21]

IV. The Effects of Kierkegaard's Attack on the Danish Church in Sweden[22]

Apart from the news reports covering the Danish Church battle, there was a certain amount of Swedish theological interest in Kierkegaard's radical standpoint. But no

[19]   Albert Theodor Lysander, "Sören Kierkegaard. Litterär-historisk teckning," *Tidsskrift för Litteratur*, vol. 1, no. 10, 1851, pp. 227–53.
[20]   This is mentioned by Nils Åke Sjöstedt in *Sören Kierkegaard och svensk litteratur. Från Fredrika Bremer till Hjalmar Söderberg* [Sören Kierkegaard and Swedish Literature. From Fredrika Bremer to Hjalmar Söderberg], Gothenburg: Wettergren & Kerbers förlag 1950, p. 25.
[21]   August Strindberg, *Samlade skrifter* [Collected Works], vols. 1–55, Stockholm: Bonnier 1912–20, see vol. 18, pp. 383–430. Selma Lagerlöf (1858–1940) also read Kierkegaard, for example while writing *Gösta Berling's Saga*. Georg Brandes' Swedish lover Victoria Benedictsson (1850–88), who wrote under the pseudonym Ernst Ahlgren, is another author known to have been influenced by Kierkegaard. There is an extended description of this in the book *Sören Kierkegaard och svensk litteratur* by Nils Åke Sjöstedt. Two other authors who clearly show a Kierkegaard influence are Ola Hansson (1860–1925) and Gustaf Otto Adelborg (1883–1965). Section five in Ola Hansson's book *Sensitiva Amorosa* (Stockholm: Almqvist & Wiksell 1957), is thought to deal with the suffering inflicted by Regine Olsen on Kierkegaard. Chapter 2 in Adelborg's book *Om det personligt andliga* [About the Personally Spiritual] (Stockholm: Wahlströms & Widstrand 1907), contains an essay about Kierkegaard: "Till minnet af S. Kierkegaard" [In Memory of S. Kierkegaard]. Among other authors under Kierkegaard's influence are Pär Lagerqvist (1891–1974), Hjalmar Söderberg (1869–1941), and Lars Gyllensten (1921–2006). The latter has published several texts explicitly dealing with Kierkegaard: "Synpunkt Sören Kierkegaard" [Viewpoint on Sören Kierkegaard], *Prisma*, vol. 3, no. 2, 1950, pp. 72–3; "Intervju med pseudonymen 'SK'" [Interview with the pseudonym "SK"], in his *Nihilistiskt credo*, Stockholm: Bonnier 1964, pp. 83–92; "Magister Kierkegaard om ironi" [Magister Kierkegaard on Irony], *Res Publica*, vol. 22, 1992, pp. 7–19.
[22]   For a more detailed account of different aspects of early Swedish reactions to Kierkegaard's attack on the Church, see Nils Åke Sjöstedt, *Sören Kierkegaard och svensk litteratur. Från Fredrika Bremer till Hjalmar Söderberg* (Gothenburg: Wettergren & Kerber

articles defending the Swedish Church can be found, and, most significantly, initially no effort was made to make Kierkegaard's ideas compatible with the teaching of the Swedish Church. On the contrary, Kierkegaard's position is presented to the Swedish audience in its most extreme aspects. Until Valter Lindström's effort to mediate between Kierkegaard and the Church, the accepted view in Sweden is that Kierkegaard's ideas contradict those of the ecclesiastical community.

This is a view that appeared already in 1855 in Wilhelm Flensburg's (1819–97) remarkable article "Dr. Kierkegaard's Struggle against official Christianity."[23] According to Flensburg, the polemic is justified. Kierkegaard is precisely the "police officer" needed by the Church: the ecclesiastical community has lost its vitality and purpose. But Flensburg is also critical; he doubts that Kierkegaard's notion of "the spiritual man's Christianity" would be a viable alternative to the religiosity of the mass that he condemns. Flensburg agrees that Christian faith is a question of isolation, and the more isolation a man can stand, the more spiritual he gets. The highest degree of isolation is achieved when man loves God in hatred towards man. But according to Flensburg, Kierkegaard's mistake is that he turns this hatred into a goal in itself, instead of treating it as a means. Kierkegaard's Christianity thus becomes the "dark cult of hatred" instead of the religion of love, which by no means excludes a community between believers, once they have found salvation.[24] Flensburg also claims that Kierkegaard's attack undermines itself: on the one hand, the image of Christ as a model is emphasized and his role as redeemer is denied, which implies that spiritual man is becoming self-sufficient.[25] On the other hand, Kierkegaard forces us to accept that man no longer is born as spiritual man; that modern man is too weak to be receptive to the religious.[26] This means that "the spiritual man's Christianity" is no longer available to modern man. Flensburg thus, somewhat surprisingly, reaches the conclusion that the best thing for modern, spiritless man is to content himself with the religiosity of the mass, i.e., accept official religiosity and stick to the official Church!

The basis of Flensburg's literal interpretation, i.e., that Kierkegaard's view is incompatible with that of the ecclesiastical community, provides the foundation for later Swedish interpreters. Lysander, who elsewhere expressed his admiration for Kierkegaard, by no means disregards Kierkegaard's attack on the Church. Instead, Lysander himself clearly rejected this side of Kierkegaard, which he demonstrates in a poem he wrote for an official festive occasion in Lund in 1856.[27]

Nils Åke Sjöstedt (b. 1916) points out that both Waldemar Rudin (1833–1921) and Zacharias Göransson (1823–81) were fascinated by Kierkegaard's radical standpoint. But they agreed that the best option was to refrain from presenting

---

1950), pp. 28–37. Our account does not contradict Sjöstedt's description, but it also includes contributions to the debate that have been published since 1950.

[23]   Wilhelm Flensburg, "Dr. Kierkegaards kamp mot den officiella Christendomen," *Svensk Kyrkotidning,* vols. 15–16, 1855, pp. 225–34; pp. 241–56.

[24]   Sjöstedt, *Sören Kierkegaard och svensk litteratur,* p. 242.

[25]   Ibid., pp. 243ff.

[26]   Ibid., p. 252.

[27]   Ibid., p. 22.

it to the Swedish public, since they did not think that Kierkegaard's ideas were well enough understood to open the Swedish mind to this strong critique.[28] It is noteworthy, though, that, despite his fascination, Rudin did not leave the Swedish Church. In fact, he became both a pastor and a professor of theology. But some of Rudin's contemporary colleagues did leave the official Church, preferring other Christian activities.[29]

Torsten Bohlin, the best-known Swedish Kierkegaard scholar, emphasized the incompatibility of Kierkegaard's ideas with life within the ecclesiastical community. Bohlin is also the first Swede to recognize that Kierkegaard's critique of the Church is a challenge to the single individual to take a stand. Bohlin makes clear that the single individual who embraces Kierkegaard's existential philosophy cannot also naively embrace the ecclesiastical community. At the same time, Bohlin, exactly as Rudin, spent his entire life within the Church (he became a bishop and wrote several texts in defence of the ecclesiastical community). The difference is that Bohlin was explicitly critical, not only of Kierkegaard's attack on the Danish Church, but also of several fundamental aspects of his philosophy. While Rudin's relationship to Kierkegaard deeply affected him, Bohlin keeps his distance, regarding Kierkegaard as a tool in his own intellectual development. This also explains how Bohlin manages to keep up the tradition from Flensburg: to present Kierkegaard as a radical critique of the ecclesiastical community.

Not until Valter Lindström's (1907–91) critique of Bohlin was there a Swedish attempt to suggest that Kierkegaard might be compatible with life within the ecclesiastical community. Lindström can be seen as the first Swede to present a softer Kierkegaard, a Kierkegaard who does not demand that one fundamentally change one's life.

The crucial point of disagreement between Bohlin and Lindström is whether the attack on the Church is a consequence of Kierkegaard's philosophy right from the start or not. Bohlin held that Kierkegaard's refutation of the community could be traced back to his early works. Bohlin further claimed that this is due to the fact that Kierkegaard focuses too much on the paradox rather than on personal religious experience.[30] Bohlin holds that Kierkegaard's focus is to intellectualize the personal religious *experience* into a *thought* of the paradox. Bohlin even regarded the paradox as a Hegelian idea that Kierkegaard did not manage to supersede; thus he insists that Kierkegaard did not, despite his intentions, liberate himself from his intellectualist philosophy.[31]

---

[28]   Sjöstedt refers to a correspondence between Göransson and Rudin, see ibid., p. 29.

[29]   Sjöstedt mentions a few clergymen and laymen, influenced by Kierkegaard, who actively dissociated themselves from the Swedish church, see ibid., pp. 31ff.

[30]   Here one can see the influence of Flensburg. Flensburg claims that the conflict concerns whether Christ is regarded only as an ideal or if he is also regarded as a redeemer. This is the crucial question, as both Bohlin and Lindström are concerned. According to Bohlin, Christ is treated as an ideal only in Kierkegaard's early writings, while Lindström's view is that Kierkegaard starts out with a dual image of Christ, and it is not until later in his writings that Kierkegaard sees the image of Christ as an ideal and as the sole correct one.

[31]   Torsten Bohlin, *Kierkegaards dogmatiska åskådning i dess historiska sammanhang* [Kierkegaard's Dogmatic View in its Historical Context], Uppsala: Svenska Kyrkans Diakonistyrelses Bokförlag 1925, see pp. 432–6.

Lindström, on the other hand, held that Kierkegaard's refutation of the community was due to a crucial breach in his view of faith. This breach is shown by the late Kierkegaard's emphasis on suffering.[32] Per Wagndal (1907–2000) made this debate, which lasted several decades, the key point of his dissertation *Kierkegaard's Problem of Community* (1954).[33] Wagndal distinguishes between two aspects of loneliness in Kierkegaard's work. The first aspect he understands as inner loneliness, and the second as geographical loneliness in time and space. Wagndal then claims that only the former aspect is crucial for the Christian single individual, which is why Kierkegaard's work ought to be reinterpreted in order to show that Kierkegaard's striving for loneliness is possible within a Christian community.[34] Later on, Thure Stenström (b. 1927) takes part in this discussion in an *excursus* to his dissertation from 1961. He makes short shrift of Wagndal's distinctions, arguing that Wagndal, by confusing the distinction between the ethical and the aesthetic, presents the very kind of quantitative dialectics that Kierkegaard opposed.[35]

In 1962 there was one last noteworthy contribution to this debate by Berndt Gustafsson (1920–75). In his book *That very Night...A Study in Kierkegaard's Theory of Decline*[36] he shows how the very development of Kierkegaard's thought, that ends in the attack on the official Church, starts with *The Concept of Irony* from 1841; with Kierkegaard's description of Socrates there the rise of the single individual is presented as a movement away from the established order. Most of all, he gives a well-informed description of Kierkegaard's studies in ecclesiastical history and shows that Kierkegaard regarded the ecclesiastical history as an ongoing decline.[37]

---

[32]   Valter Lindström, *Efterföljelsens teologi* [The Theology of Imitation], Stockholm: Diakonistyrelsens förlag 1956, see p. 227.

[33]   There are also two Danish descriptions of the Swedish reaction to Kierkegaard's attack on the Danish Church: Aage Henriksen and Aage Kabell conclude their descriptions of the Swedish Kierkegaard reception in two quite different ways. Henriksen describes Lindström's critique of Bohlin as correct insofar as the contradictions found by the latter are caused by the problematic way in which he isolates certain parts of Kierkegaard's writings. At the same time, Henriksen claims there is a need for a deeper understanding than Lindström's of Kierkegaard's writings as a whole. (Cf. Aage Henriksen, *Methods and Results of Kierkegaard Studies in Scandinavia*, Copenhagen: Munksgaard 1951.) Kabell, for his part, claims that Bohlin's response to his critics was accepted by Danish experts, who saw this as a way of demolishing the view of those Swedish theologians who tried to interpret Kierkegaard as compatible with a ecclesiastical community. Even though all the main participants in the Swedish debate were active in the Swedish Church, this debate did not in any deeper sense affect the institution as such; the discussion took place within an academic sphere. (Cf. Aage Kabell, *Kierkegaardstudiet i Norden* [Kierkegaard Studies in the Nordic Countries], Copenhagen: H. Hagerup 1948, p. 181.)

[34]   Per Wagndal, *Gemenskapsproblemet hos Sören Kierkegaard* [Kierkegaard's Problem of Community], Lund: Gleerup 1954, pp. 113–17.

[35]   Thure Stenström, *Den ensamme. En motivstudie i det moderna genombrottets litteratur* [The Lonesome One. A Study of Motives in the Rise of the Modern in Literature], Stockholm: Natur & Kultur 1961, see chapter 3 ("Kierkegaard and Brandes"), p. 339.

[36]   Berndt Gustafsson, *I den natt...Studier i Kierkegaards förfallsteori*, Stockholm: Diakonistyrelsens bokförlag 1962.

[37]   Ibid., pp. 73ff.

Further he claims that, according to Kierkegaard, the crucial mistake happened during the Middle Ages, when self-denial came to be regarded as something exceptional that was to be rewarded. Interestingly enough, Gustafsson's point is that the late Kierkegaard's emphasizing of suffering is due to the fact that man, in order to become Christian, has to free himself from the medieval mistake that self-denial is a suffering to be rewarded. Instead, suffering is the very mode of preparation for an existence in faith. This is not to make suffering an aim in itself; it is still but a means, a means to make sure that man stands alone instead of being safely embedded in an established order. The late Kierkegaard's emphasis on suffering is thus not, as Lindström among others claimed, a breach in Kierkegaard's view of faith. The difference is that the intention is now to show that the aim, an existence in faith, has become harder than ever before to attain.[38] To this Gustafsson adds that it is important to notice the difference between the *Upbuilding Discourses* and the late articles. While the *Discourses* speak of grace to the single individual, the late articles recite the law to the *publicum*.[39] Gustafsson's book also contains several analyses of Kierkegaard's view on ecclesiastical practical matters, e.g., baptism and the holy communion.[40]

V. Swedish Kierkegaard Reception in Theology and Philosophy

In the description above, it became clear that the early Swedish interest in Kierkegaard was prevalent mainly among theologians. It is within theology that Kierkegaard's emphasis on the individual person started to become a topic in Sweden, mainly thanks to Rudin. Rudin is often regarded as the very first Kierkegaardian in Sweden, but he was not the first Swede to write about Kierkegaard. The first more substantial text was Lysander's article, mentioned above. But there is also another interesting text that appeared before Rudin's *Sören Kierkegaard's Personality and Authorship. An Essay.*[41] This other early text is *About the Possibility of a Christian Philosophy—*

---

38   Ibid., p. 81.
39   Ibid., pp. 25–6.
40   Gustafsson also has in a remarkable article from 1958 ("Kierkegaard och kyrkoåret" [Kierkegaard and the Ecclesiastical Year], *Svensk teologisk kvartalstidskrift*, vol. 2, 1958, pp. 96–110), compared Kierkegaard's and Bishop Mynster's understanding of the ecclesiastical year. He claims that a Christian in Kierkegaard's sense presupposes a different attitude to the ecclesiastical year than does a Christian in Mynster's sense: if everyday life has to be guided by the thought that eternity is present in the moment, i.e., if holy history is present here and now in the single individual's life, this must affect the relation to the ecclesiastical year. The ecclesiastical festivities therefore are not supposed to be popular festivities celebrated in confidence as an aspect of bourgeois life. Instead, they are supposed to be in accordance with the idea of the possibility of eternity in time. One of Gustafsson's examples is that Advent can no longer be celebrated as an expectation of Christmas; rather, it should be an expectation of suffering.
41   Rudin Waldemar, *Sören Kierkegaards person och författarskap. Ett försök*, Uppsala: A. Nilsson 1880.

Aphorisms by Zacharias Göransson.[42] Göransson's book is a stringent and elegant statement showing how Kierkegaardian philosophy demonstrates the impossibility of proving a religious truth. Göransson's text is interesting, since it indicates that there was an early discussion about Kierkegaardian theoretical thought. Also Oswald Kuylenstierna's (1865–1932) text, *Sören Kierkegaard. The Thinker and the Truth Seeker*, is worth mentioning, since Kuylenstierna, already in 1898, manages to present Kierkegaard as an existentialist.[43] Between Rudin and Bohlin, Torgny Segerstedt (1876–1945) is regarded as the great Swedish authority on Kierkegaard. Segerstedt praises Kierkegaard's efficient dismissal of every effort to use intellectual conclusions to confirm truth in faith. In his book, *The Problem of Religious Truth* (1912),[44] he asks why the question of truth in faith arises at all in Western religions. With his historical point of departure and his comparison with other religions, Segerstedt is the first Swede to introduce Kierkegaard's idea of subjectivity into a more academic discourse.

In the shadow of Bohlin and Lindström another Swede struggled to introduce Kierkegaard to Swedish readers. Richard Hejll has been disregarded, partly because of his political opinions, partly because of his fanatical side. Nevertheless, he is of interest, since he was the first Swede to translate some of Kierkegaard's early pseudonymous works (*Fear and Trembling* and selections from *Either/Or*). He is also interesting because of his deep and serious struggle to apply existential philosophy to his own life, not least at a political level, where he criticizes democracy as the very embodiment of the domination of the mass and the many.

In 1916 Hejll wrote *True and False Religiosity*, where he among other things criticizes Segerstedt's interpretation of Kierkegaard as too academic and too didactic.[45] In 1944 Hejll started publishing his own periodical, *The Single Individual*.[46] In this publication he presents his Kierkegaardian critique of what he sees as contemporary stupidity and the institutionalization of this stupidity in the shape of democratic government. Since Hejll presented his criticism at a time, near the end of the Second World War, when Europe was a congeries of shaky states, devastated by war, and since at the same time he expressed his sympathy with Germany, it is hardly surprising that he was met with complete silence. His periodical was banned from many public libraries. Hejll's isolation forced him further into resentment and fanaticism, which explains why his aspiration to challenge democracy from a Kierkegaardian point of departure—the single individual—never was and still is not treated seriously.

With the increasing interest in Marxism during the 1960s, there were some lame efforts in Sweden to emphasize the philosophical importance of Kierkegaard. The most interesting name in this respect is Arnold Ljungdahl (1901–68). In polemic with

---

[42]   Zacharias Göransson, *Om möjligheten av en Christlig Philosophi—aforismer*, Uppsala: F.C. Askerberg 1859.
[43]   Kuylenstierna, Oswald, *Sören Kierkegaard. Tänkaren och sanningssökaren*, Stockholm: Bonnier 1898.
[44]   Torgny Segerstedt, *Det religiösa sanningsproblemet*, Stockholm: Bonnier 1912.
[45]   Richard Hejll, *Sann och falsk religiositet. En kritisk studie över det moderna tänkandet*, Stockholm: Minerva 1916.
[46]   *Den enskilde: Tidskrift för de ensamma*, ed. by Richard Hejll, Ramlösabrunn 1944–62.

the positivist tendency of Swedish analytical philosophy, he presented Kierkegaard's philosophy as a complex description of the burden of modern man's life situation. Ljungdahl argues that even if Kierkegaard's philosophy cannot in any concrete manner guide man in his wish to become a good citizen, it can still be helpful by deepening man's understanding of responsibility and freedom.[47] Ljungdahl in 1964 also published a well-informed, philosophically relevant, and accessible introduction to Kierkegaard, *The Problem Kierkegaard*.[48] In Sweden, this decade was, as mentioned above, dominated by analytic philosophy, and Kierkegaard's Christian, existential, and unsystematic thought was not approved of. The leading Swedish philosopher at the time, Ingemar Hedenius (1908–82), wrote several articles on Kierkegaard, showing a never-ending interest in those aspects of Kierkegaard's thought that Hedenius labels "unphilosophical." These aspects are presented by Hedenius in an interesting manner. At the same time, his view is that Kierkegaard's philosophical and theological production is impossible to enjoy.[49]

While the existential Marxists and the analytic decision-theorists kept introducing Kierkegaard over and over again to the Swedes, another Swede, Lars Bejerholm, made an international name for himself with his historically related dissertation on Kierkegaard, *The Dialectics of Communication*, in 1962.[50] One, among several, of Bejerholm's merits, is that the method of indirect communication is presented as separate from the aims of the method, and as an efficient method. Thus Bejerholm displays a distinction between an ineffable aspect of faith and an unsayable aspect of ethics.[51] Bejerholm's dissertation also provides an initiated and pragmatic interpretation of Kierkegaard's use of pseudonyms and further a well-informed description of the influence of the academic and cultural environment on Kierkegaard's thought.

During the 1970s and 1980s there were some sporadic publications on Kierkegaard in Sweden, for example, an article by Mats Furberg (b. 1933),[52] and two dissertations in theology: *Time and Eternity in Kierkegaard* by Lennart Koskinen (b. 1944)[53] and *Man's Ontological Predicament: a Detailed Analysis of Sören Kierkegaard's Concept of Sin with Special Reference to The Concept of Dread* (1984) by Edward

[47]   Arnold Ljungdal, "Existentialisten Kierkegaard" [The Existentialist Kierkegaard], *Zenit*, nos. 4–5, 1962, pp. 11–13; p. 16.
[48]   Arnold Ljungdal, *Problemet Kierkegaard*, Stockholm: Nordstedts 1964.
[49]   See Ingemar Hedenius, "Om Sören Kierkegaard" [About Sören Kierkegaard], *Tiden*, vol. 36, no. 7, 1944, pp. 423–37 and Ingemar Hedenius, "Kierkegaard och kärleken" [Kierkegaard and Love], in his *Om stora män och små* [About Great Men and Small Men], Stockholm: Rabén & Sjögren 1980, pp. 103–16.
[50]   Lars Bejerholm, *Meddelelsens dialektik. Studier i Sören Kierkegaards teorier om språk, kommunikation och pseudonymitet*, Lund: Publications of the Kierkegaard Society 1962.
[51]   Ibid., pp. 87–8.
[52]   Mats Furberg, "Möjliga teser hos Johannes Climacus" [Possible Theses of Johannes Climacus], *En filosofibok tillägnad Anders Wedberg* [A Philosophy Book Dedicated to Anders Wedberg], Stockholm: Bonnier 1978, pp. 35–50.
[53]   Lennart Koskinen, *Tid och evighet hos Kierkegaard*, Lund: Nya Doxa 1980.

A. Harris (b. 1952).[54] Harris' dissertation is an effort to present five definitions of sin, according to Kierkegaard. Since his dissertation, Harris has published several books on Kierkegaard.[55] Even if his presentation is influenced by analytic philosophy and thus mainly conceptually oriented, he is an example of a clergyman who tries to practice Kierkegaard's existentialism in a highly pragmatic manner. He interprets Kierkegaard's work as a spiritual instruction, written for the purpose of helping others.[56]

VI. Kierkegaard Reception in Sweden Today

During the 1990s, when Kierkegaard's importance to modernity and post-modernity became more accepted and studied around the world, a Swedish interest in Kierkegaard was also awakened, especially in relation to a modern theory of literature. It should be emphasized that while Kierkegaard definitely has influenced Swedish writers, he has also been a regular subject of Swedish literary studies ever since Georg Brandes' (1842–1927) book *Sören Kierkegaard* was published in Sweden in 1877.[57] Some examples are *The Rich Estate* (1946) by Klara Johansson (1875–1948),[58] *Sören Kierkegaard and Swedish Literature* (1950) by Nils Åke Sjöstedt,[59] and *The Lonesome One* (1961) by Thure Stenström.[60] In the 1990s there was an increase in the number of articles published, and now it is not just a question of introducing Kierkegaard but rather of understanding our time by using his philosophy. Arne Melberg (b. 1942) has published two articles dealing with the importance of repetition. He claims that repetition has to be understood, not only as an existential category but as a textual one as well.[61] In *Readings of Nothingness*

---

[54]   Edward A. Harris, *Man's Ontological Predicament, A Detailed Analysis of Sören Kierkegaard's Concept of Sin with Special Reference to The Concept of Dread*, Uppsala: Acta Univeritatis Upsaliensis 1984.

[55]   Edward A. Harris, *Friends of God: In Search of Self, Ultimate Reality and Love*, Stockholm: Sprirtual Future 2003; *Gör ditt val: en introduktion till Kierkegaards subjektivitetsteori* [Make your Choice: An Introduction to Kierkegaard's Theory of Subjectivity], Stockholm: Spiritual Future 2003, in Swedish as *Kristen andlighet: sökandet efter jaget, den slutgiltiga verkligheten och villkorslös kärlek* Stockholm: Spiritual Future 2004.

[56]   Harris, *Kristen andlighet*, pp. 94–112.

[57]   Georg Brandes, *Sören Kierkegaard*, trans. under supervision of the author by Olof Arvid Stridsberg, Stockholm: Seligman 1877 (Swedish original edition) (originally in Danish as *Søren Kierkegaard: en kritisk Fremstilling i Grundrids*, Copenhagen: Gyldendal 1877).

[58]   Klara Johansson, "Noter till Sören Kierkegaards liv" [Notes on Søren Kierkegaard's Life], in her *Det rika stärbhuset*, Stockholm: Wahlström & Widstrand 1946, pp. 149–87 (2nd ed., 1947).

[59]   Sjöstedt, *Sören Kierkegaard och svensk litteratur*.

[60]   Stenström, *Den ensamme. En motivstudie i det moderna genombrottets litteratur*.

[61]   Arne Melberg, "*Repetition* (in the Kierkegaardian sense of the Term)," *Diacritics*, vol. 20, no. 3, 1990, pp. 71–87, see p. 75; Melberg, "Kierkegaard's Gjentagelse: The Moment of Repetition," in *Kunst og mening* [Art and Meaning] ed. by Karin Gundersen and Ståle Wikshåland, Oslo: Norges allmenvitenskapelige forskningråd 1992.

(2000), Anders Olsson (b. 1949) presents Kierkegaard's negative theology as a kind of nihilism, destroying the domination of the Platonic–Christian tradition, since it begins by liberating faith from the traditional manner of legitimization, which has safeguarded it for ages.[62] One issue of the literary magazine *Aiolos* had Kierkegaard as its main topic in 1998.[63] During these last decades two new introductions were also published: Allan Green's (1910–93) *Kierkegaard among his Contemporaries*,[64] and Ingmar Simonsson's (b. 1951) *Kierkegaard in our Time*.[65] Also Peter Thielst's *Life is Understood Backwards—But One Has to Live it Forward*,[66] and Joakim Garff's *SAK* have been translated into Swedish.[67] The most interesting name in this context is Jan Holmgaard (b. 1960). One third of his dissertation from 1998, *The Self in the Text*, deals with Kierkegaard.[68] Holmgaard takes his point of departure in "The Seducer's Diary," going on to show how the intrigues of the seducer might be read as a *production*, as self-producing imaginary poetic moments. The reflecting seducer is described as searching for female immediacy, originality and substantiality, all of which is lacking in Kierkegaard's reflecting male. The seducer's productivity does not get hold of her substantiality (of course), but, according to Holmgaard, he gains, if still fragmentary, a fundament for his own poetic substantiality. In Holmgaard's next book, *An Ironical History*,[69] this theme is pursued further when he asks for the aesthetic subject's relationship to the given actuality and history.

From the amount of texts and translations published, one can conclude that Kierkegaard, at least for the time being, has settled into Swedish academic and cultural life. To this one can add two recent publications which have collected works from several Kierkegaard scholars who are currently active at Swedish universities: the literary magazine *Lyrikvännen* in 2004 published an issue with Kierkegaard as its theme. In 2005, the anthology *The Thinker's Manifold* was published; this book contains the papers presented at a Nordic Kierkegaard conference arranged by the Department of Nordic Languages at the University of Lund.[70] The main part of the papers are written by scholars active in Sweden. Yet even if it is possible to claim that a group of Swedish Kierkegaard scholars is emerging, there is still an absence of discussion among them.

---

[62]   Anders Olsson, *Läsningar av Intet*, Stockholm: Bonnier 2000.
[63]   *Aiolos*, nos. 6–7, 1997–98.
[64]   Allan Green, *Kierkegaard bland samtida. Personhistoriska skisser*, Eslöv: Gondolin 1995.
[65]   Ingmar Simonsson, *Kierkegaard i vår tid*, Stockholm: Themis förlag 2002.
[66]   Peter Thielst, *Man förstår livet baklänges—men måste leva det framlänges*, trans. by Carla Wiberg, Stockholm: Raben & Sjögren 1995.
[67]   Joakim Garff, *SAK*, trans. by Hans Dalén, Nora: Nya Doxa 2002.
[68]   Jan Holmgaard, *Jaget i texten*, Stockholm: Aiolos förlag 1998, see chapter 3 ("Självdiktandet").
[69]   Jan Holmgaard, *En ironisk historia*, Stockholm: Aiolos förlag 2003.
[70]   *Tänkarens mångfald. Nutida perspektiv på Sören Kierkegaard*, ed. by Lone Koldtoft, Jon Stewart and Jan Holmgaard, Gothenburg & Stockholm: Makadam förlag 2005.

Bibliography

I. Swedish Translations of Kierkegaard's Works

Aderton Uppbyggeliga Tal [*Eighteen Upbuilding Discourses* (the first fourteen of the *Upbuilding Discourses* from 1843–44)], trans. by Th. Wensjoe, vol. 1 in *Walda Skrifter af S. Kierkegaard* [Selected Writings of S. Kierkegaard], Mariestad: Hos P.W. Karström 1852 (reprinted in 1853 in five different off-prints).

Hwad vi läre af liljorne på marken och foglarna under himmelen. Trenne tal af S Kierkegaard [*What We Learn from the Lilies in the Field and from the Birds of the Air*], trans. by P.M. Elmblad, Norrköping: Östlund & Bergling 1852.

Selfpröfning för vår tid [*For Self-Examination*], trans. by P.M. Elmblad, Stockholm: Rylander 1852.

Walda Skrifter af S. Kierkegaard [Selected Writings of S. Kierkegaard (the four last discourses of the *Eighteen Upbuilding Discourses*) (cf. above)], vol. 2, trans. by Thure Wensjoe, Mariestad: P.W. Karström 1852.

Kommen! Kommen! [Come! Come! (selections from *Practice in Christianity*)] (no translator given), published anonymously by Hans Jakob Lundborg, Uppsala: Wahlström 1853.

Liljorna på marken och foglarna under himlen. Tre andeliga tal af S Kierkegaard [*The Lilies in the Field and the Birds of the Air*], trans by P.M. Elmblad, Stockholm: Rylander 1853.

"Den stora underbara inbjudningen" [The Great Wonderful Invitation (selections from *Practice in Christianity*)], trans. by P.M. Elmblad under the pseudonym Kd, in *Frids-budbäraren. Tidning för den inre missionen*, 1854–55.

Den officiella kristendomen är icke det nya Testamentets kristendom. Framställning av dr Sören Kierkegaards polemik mot statskyrkan i Danmark [The Official Christianity is not the Christianity of The New Testament. Description of Dr. Sören Kierkegaard's Polemic against the State Church in Denmark (selections from Kierkegaard's articles in *Fædrelandet*)], trans. and ed. by O.P. Sturzenbecker, Copenhagen 1855.

Detta skall sägas så vare det sagdt [This Must Be Said; So Let it Be Said], Uppsala 1855.

Hvad Kristus dömmer om officiell kristendom [What Christ Judges about Official Christianity], trans. by J.G. Wahlström, Uppsala: Wahlström & Co. 1855 (reprinted, 1858).

Ögonblicket [*The Moment*], nos. 1–9, trans. by J.G. Wahlström. Uppsala: Wahlström & Co. 1855 (reprinted, 1858).

Guds oföränderlighet. Ett tal [*The Changelessness of God. A Discourse*] (no translator given), Wisby 1858.

Kärlekens gerningar. Några christliga betraktelser i form af tal [*Works of Love*], trans. by Gustaf Tomée, Stockholm: Bonniers förlag 1862.

"Öfwerstepresten"—"Publikanen"—"Synderskan" ["The High Priest," "The Tax Collector" and "The Woman who was a Sinner"], trans. by Waldemar Rudin, Stockholm 1867.

Till sjelfpröfning, samtiden anbefaldt [*For Self-Examination*] (no translator given), Stockholm: Hæggström 1876.

Inöfning i kristendom. Af Anti–Climacus [*Practice in Christianity*], trans. by O.A. Stridsberg, Stockholm: Z Haeggström 1879.

Sjukdomen til Døds. En kristlig psykologisk utveckling till uppbyggelse och uppväckelse. Af Anti-Climacus [*The Sickness unto Death*], trans. by Zacharias Göransson, introduction by W. Rudin, Stockholm: Carlson 1881.

Två skriftetal af S. Kierkegaard [*Two Discourses at the Communion on Fridays*], trans. by Theodor Mazér, Stockholm: A.V. Carlsons förlag 1883 (reprinted, Stockholm: Svenska Kyrkans Diakonistyrelsens Bokförlag 1919).

Kristliga tal af S. Kierkegaard [*Christian Discourses*], trans. by Zacharias Göransson, introduction by Waldemar Rudin, Uppsala: W. Schulz 1892.

Förförarens dagbok ["The Seducer's Diary"], trans. and ed. by David Sprengel, Stockholm: Bonnier 1902 (*Mästerverk ur världslitteraturen*, vol. 2).

"En 'allmän kyrkobön' af Sören Kierkegaard" [A General Intercession by Sören Kierkegaard] (extracts from *Practice in Christianity*)], *Vår lösen*, vol. 4, 1913, pp. 182–3.

Valda stycken ur Sören Kierkegaards tankevärld [Selected Parts from Sören Kierkegaard's World of Thought (selections from *Either/Or*; non-specified fragmentary selections from the *Edifying Discourses* and Kierkegaard's journals)], trans. by Richard Hejll, Stockholm: Albert Bonniers förlag 1916.

Förförarens dagbok ["The Seducer's Diary"] (no translator is given), Stockholm: Bonnier 1919.

Fruktan och bäven. Dialektisk lyrik av Johannes de silentio [*Fear and Trembling*], trans. by Richard Hejll, Stockholm: Björck & Börjesen 1920 (*Berömde filosofer*, vol. 16) (revised ed. by Stefan Borg, Nora: Nimrod 1995).

Kierkegaard (translation of the second part of *Judge for Yourself!*), trans. and ed. by Richard Hejll, Stockholm: Albert Bonniers förlag 1926.

Till självprövning, samtiden anbefalld [*For Self-Examination*], trans. by Anna Bohlin, Stockholm: Svenska Kyrkans Diakonistyrelsens Bokförlag 1926 (*Religiösa klassiker*, vol. 3).

Sören Kierkegaards dagbok [Sören Kierkegaard's Diary], trans. by Anna Bohlin, ed. by Torsten Bohlin, Stockholm: Svenska Kyrkans Diakonistyrelsens Bokförlag 1928.

Axplockning ur Sören Kierkegaards skrifter. Försök av Karolina Lindström [A Small Selection from Sören Kierkegaard's Works. An Essay by Karolina Lindström (selections from *Either/Or, Fear and Trembling* and some of *The Upbuilding Discourses*)], Stockholm: Seelig & Co. 1934–37.

Övning i kristendom [*Practice in Christianity*], trans. by Henrik Hägglund, Stockholm: Svenska Kyrkans Diakonistyrelse Bokförlag 1939.

Skrifter i urval. Med inledningar och textförklaringar av Billeskov Jansen [Selected Works, Introductions and Comments by Billeskov Jansen (selections from *Either/Or* and *Stages on Life's Way*)], vols. 1–2, trans. and ed. by Stig Ahlgren, Stockholm: Wahlström & Widstrand 1954–57 (reprinted, 1977).

Kierkegaard (selections from *Either/Or, Stages on Life's Way, Repetition* and *Concluding Unscientific Postscript*), trans. and ed. by Lars Göransson, Stockholm: Forum 1956 (reprinted, 1969, 1979).

Forførerens dagbog ["The Seducer's Diary"] (Danish edition), postscript by Niels Kofoed, Stockholm: Bonnier 1959 (*Levande litteratur*).

Begreppet ångest [*The Concept of Anxiety*], trans. by Stig Ahlgren and Nils Kjellström, selected and ed. by F.J. Billeskov Jansen, Stockholm: Wahlstöm & Widstrand 1963 (reprinted, 1977, 1986; revised translation by Stefan Borg, Nimrod: Nora 1996).

Antingen-eller [*Either/Or*], trans. by Stig Ahlgren and Nils Kjellström, selected and ed. by F.J. Billeskov Jansen, Stockholm: Wahlstöm & Widstrand 1964 (reprinted, 1967, 1977, 1986).

Förförarens dagbok ["The Seducer's Diary"], trans. by Per Sörbom, Stockholm: Wahlström & Widstrand 1969.

Sören Kierkegaard (fragmentary selections), trans. and ed. by David Olsson, Västerhaninge: David Olsson 1970.

"Om begreppet ironi" [*On The Concept of Irony* (a small selection)] (no translator given), *Res Publica*, vol. 22, 1992.

Förförarens dagbok ["The Seducer's Diary"], trans. by Nils Tengdahl, Gothenburg: Vinga Press 1995.

Upprepningen [*Repetition*], trans. by Stefan Borg, Nora: Nimrod 1995.

Sjukdomen till döds [*The Sickness unto Death*], trans. by Stefan Borg, Nora: Nimrod 1996.

Filosofiska smulor [*Philosophical Fragments*], trans. by Stefan Borg and Thomas Andersson, Nora: Nimrod 1997.

Om min författarverksamhet [*On My Work as an Author*], trans. by Jan Holmgaard, *Aiolos*, vols. 6–7, 1997–98.

Avslutande ovetenskaplig efterskrift [*Concluding Unscientific Postscript*], trans. by Stefan Borg, Nora: Nimrod 1999.

Antingen-eller [*Either/Or*], trans. by Stefan Borg, Önneköp: Nimrod 2002.

"En möjlighet" [A Possibility (excerpts from *Stages on Life's Way*)], trans. by Stefan Borg, *Lyrikvännen*, vol. 5, 2004.

II. Selected Secondary Literature on Kierkegaard in Sweden

Adelborg, Gustaf Otto, *Om det personligt andliga. Till minnet af S. Kierkegaard* [About the Personal Spiritual. In Memory of S. Kierkegaard], Stockholm: Wahlströms & Widstrand 1907.

Ahlberg, Alf, "Sören Kierkegaard," *Studiekamraten*, vol. 8, 1955, pp. 187–9.

— "Den religiösa existentialismen" [The Religious Existentialism], *Årsbok för Sveriges kristliga studentrörelse*, 1963, pp. 38–50.

Arb, Siv, "Harriet Löwenhjelm and Sören Kierkegaard" [Harriet Löwenhjelm och Sören Kierkegaard], *Ord och bild*, vol. 69, 1960, pp. 491–503.

Atterling, Henry, "Sören Kierkegaard. Inför ett 150-årsminne" [Sören Kierkegaard. Before his 150th birthday], *Tro och liv*, vol. 2, 1963, pp. 56–64.

Bejerholm, Lars, *Meddelelsens dialektik. Studier i Sören Kierkegaards teorier om språk, kommunikation och pseudonymitet* [The Dialectics of Communication. Studies in Sören Kierkegaard's Theories about Language, Communication and Pseudonymity], Lund: Publications of the Kierkegaard Society 1962.

— "Sören Aabye Kierkegaard," *Vandringar med böcker*, vol. 4, no. 12, 1963, pp. 1–4.

Benedikt, Ernst, "Sören Kierkegaard och judendomen" [Sören Kierkegaard and Judaism], *Judisk tidskrift*, vol. 30, 1957.

Benzow, Kristofer, "Strindberg och S. Kierkegaard" [Strindberg and S. Kierkegaard], in his *Idealitet och religiösitet*, Lund: Gleerup 1921, pp. 48–66.

— "Vid skiljevägen" [By the Cross-road] (on Kierkegaard and Ibsen), *Vår lösen*, vol. 20, 1929, pp. 110–11.

— "Sören Kierkegaard och existentialismen" [Sören Kierkegaard and Existentialism], *Svensk tidskrift*, vol. 38, no. 4, 1951, pp. 223–8.

— "Sören Kierkegaard. Ett hundraårsminne" [Sören Kierkegaard. A Centenary], *Svensk tidskrift*, vol. 42, 1955, pp. 449–62.

Berglund, Emil, "Søren Kierkegaard. En kritisk studie" [Søren Kierkegaard. A Critical Study], *Kyrklig tidskrift*, vol. 19, 1913, pp. 438–68.

Björkhem, John, *Sören Kierkegaard i psykologisk belysning* [Sören Kierkegaard Seen from a Psychological Perspective], Uppsala: Nybom 1942.

Bohlin, Torsten, *Sören Kierkegaard,* Uppsala: Svenska Kyrkans Diakonistyrelses Bokförlag 1918.

— *Sören Kierkegaards etiska åskådning med särskild hensyn till begreppet "Den enskilde"* [Sören Kierkegaard's Ethical View with Special Reference to the Concept of the Single Individual], Uppsala: Almqvist & Wiksell 1918.

— *Pontus Wikner och Sören Kierkegaard. Några jämforande synpunkter* [Pontus Wikner and Sören Kierkegaard. Some Comparisons], Uppsala: Svensk Kristlig Studentrörelses Förlag 1919.

— *Sören Kierkegaard och nutida religiöst tänkande* [Kierkegaard and Contemporary Religious Thought], Stockholm: Svenska Kyrkans Diakonistyrelses Bokförlag 1919.

— *Kierkegaards dogmatiska åskådning i dess historiska sammanhang* [Kierkegaard's Dogmatic View in its Historical Context], Uppsala: Svenska Kyrkans Diakonistyrelses Bokförlag 1925.

— "Aktuella Kierkegaardsproblem" [Contemporary Kierkegaard Problems], *Svensk teologisk kvartalstidskrift*, vol. 2, no. 2, 1926, pp. 125–43.

— "Krisens teologi. Luther och Kierkegaard" [Theology of Crisis. Luther and Kierkegaard], in his *Tro och uppenbarelse. En studie till teologiens kris och "krisens teologi"* [Faith and Revelation. A Study on the Crisis of Theology and the Theology of Crisis], Stockholm: Svenska Kyrkans Diakonistyrelses Bokförlag 1926, pp. 100–54. (In German as *Glaube und Offenbarung. Eine kritische Studie zur dialektischen Theologie*, trans. by Ilse Meyer-Lüne, Berlin: Furche Verlag 1928.)

— "Kierkegaards teologiska aktualitet" [The Theological Actuality of Kierkegaard], *Teologinen aikakauskirja*, 1930, pp. 120–7 (Tampere).

— *Sören Kierkegaard. Mannen och verket* [Sören Kierkegaard. The Man and his Work], Uppsala: Svenska Kyrkans Diakonistyrelses Bokförlag 1939.

— "Sören Kierkegaard och Regine Olsen" [Sören Kierkegaard and Regine Olsen], *Svenska dagblad*, November 17, 1940, pp. 11–12.

— "Enten-Eller. Ett 100-årsminne" [Either/Or. A Century], *Svenska dagbladet*, March 21, 1943, p. 13.

— *Kierkegaards tro och andra Kierkegaardstudier* [Kierkegaard's Faith and Other Kierkegaard Studies], Stockholm: Svenska Kyrkans Diakonistyrelses Bokförlag 1944.

— "Kring Wikner och Kierkegaard" [Kring Wikner and Kierkegaard], *Årsbok för kristen humanism*, vol. 6, 1944, pp. 92–102.

— "Var Kierkegaard individualist?" [Was Kierkegaard an Individualist?], *Vår lösen*, vol. 35, 1944, pp. 94–102.

— "En upplysning" [An Enlightenment], *Svensk teologisk kvartalstidskrift*, vol. 21, 1945, pp. 74–81.

— "Kierkegaard och Nietzsche" [Kierkegaard and Nietzsche], *Meddelelser af Søren Kierkegaard Selskabet*, vol. 2, 1950, pp. 28–31 (Copenhagen).

Bolander, Nils, "Kierkegaard - redivivus," *Vår lösen*, vol. 46, 1955, pp. 292–300.

Bolin, Asta, "Vårt heliga tvivel" [Our Holy Doubt], *Västerås stiftsbok 1964*, Falun: Västerås stiftsråd 1963, pp. 72–81.

Born, Eric von, "Tanke och Handling hos Kierkegaard" [Thought and Action in Kierkegaard], *Vår lösen*, vol. 47, 1956, pp. 283–5.

Brandell, Georg, "Människouppfattningen hos Sören Kierkegaard och i Goethes *Faust* [The Views of Man in Sören Kierkegaard and in Goethe's *Faust*], *Religion och kultur*, vol. 25, 1954, pp. 100–3.

Bremer, Fredrika, *Lif i Norden. Skizz* [Life in the Nordic Countries. An Outline], Stockholm: Bagge 1849, see pp. 53–5.

Brudin Borg, Camilla, "Lust och lärdom. Gyllenstens Sju vise mästare om kärlek och erotiska motiv hos Kierkegaard Inclinations and Learning" [Gyllensten's Seven Wise Masters about Love and Erotic Motives in Kierkegaard], *Tidskrift för litteraturvetenskap*, vol. 1, 1999, pp. 86–104.

— "Genren och undantaget betraktat med hjälp av Sören Kierkegaards *Gjentagelsen*" [Genre and the Exception Seen through Søren Kierkegaard's *Repetition*], *Genrer och genreproblem: teoretiska och historiska perspektiv / Genres and Problems of Genre: Theoretical and Historical Perspectives*, Göteborg: Daidalos 2003, pp. 406–13.

— "Det dubbla tilltalet i brevet till den verkliga läsaren i Søren Kierkegaards *Gjentagelsen*," [The Double Address to the Real Reader in Søren Kierkegaard's *Repetition*], in *Den litterära textens förändringar: studier tillägnade Stina Hansson*, ed. by Stefan Ekman, Mats Malm and Lisbeth Stenberg, Stockholm and Stehag: Symposion 2007, pp. 190–9.

Demker, Marie, "Självmordets dialektik. En studie av Kierkegaards *Sjukdomen till döds*" [The Dialectics of Suicide. A Study of Kierkegaard's *The Sickness unto Death*], *Filosofisk tidskrift*, vol. 1, 2005, pp. 3–19.

Eklund, R.R., "Kierkegaard-reflexioner" [Kierkegaard Reflexions], *Nye Argus*, vol. 13, nos. 16–17, pp. 137–8.

Englund, Claes, "Kring Kierkegaards 'Krisen og en Krise i en Skuespillerindes Liv'" [About Kierkegaard's *The Crisis and a Crisis in the Life of an Actress*], *Ord och bild*, vol. 1, 1961, pp. 54–60.

Flensburg, Wilhelm, "Dr. Kierkegaards kamp mot den officiella Christendomen" [Dr. Kierkegaard's Struggle against the Official Christianity], *Svensk Kyrkotidning*, vols. 15–16, 1855, pp. 225–34; pp. 241–56.

Foconi, Stefan, "Konsten att skriva komplext. Om Kierkegaards ironi" [*The Art of Complex Writing. About Kierkegaard's irony*], *Artes*, vol. 30, no. 4, 2004, pp. 104–12.

Furberg, Mats, "Möjliga teser hos Johannes Climacus" [Possible Theses of Johannes Climacus], *En filosofibok tillägnad Anders Wedberg* [A Philosophy Book Dedicated to Anders Wedberg], Stockholm: Bonnier 1978, pp. 35–50.

Göransson, Zacharias, *Om möjligheten av en Christlig Philosophi—aforismer* [About the Possibility of a Christian Philosophy—Aphorisms], Uppsala: F.C. Askerberg 1859.

Green, Allan, *Kierkegaard bland samtida. Personhistoriska skisser* [Kierkegaard among his Contemporaries. Outlines of Personal Histories], Eslöv: Gondolin 1995.

Gustafsson, Berndt, "Kierkegaard och kyrkoåret" [Kierkegaard and the Ecclesiastical Year], *Svensk teologisk kvartalstidskrift*, vol. 2, 1958, pp. 96–110.

— *I den natt...Studier i Kierkegaards förfallsteori* [That Very Night...A Study in Kierkegaard's Theory of Decline], Stockholm: Diakonistyrelsens bokförlag 1962.

Gustafsson, Madeleine, "Kierkegaard," in *Författarnas litteraturhistoria* [Literature History of Authors], vols. 1–3, ed. by Björn Håkanson, Stockholm: Författarförlaget 1980–82, vol. 2, pp. 141–50.

— "Die Schattenphilosophie des 19. Jahrhunderts" [The Shadow-Philosophy of the Nineteenth Century]," *Deutsche Zeitschrift für europäisches Denken*, vol. 37, 1983, pp. 73–81.

Gyllensten, Lars, "Sören Kierkegaard," *Utsikt*, vol. 2, no. 3, 1949, pp. 14–15.

— "Synpunkt på Sören Kierkegaard" [Viewpoint on Sören Kierkegaard], *Prisma*, vol. 3, no. 2, 1950, pp. 72–3.

— "Intervju med pseudonymen 'SK' " [Interview with the Pseudonym "SK"], in his *Nihilistiskt credo*, Stockholm: Bonnier 1964, pp. 83–92.

— "Magister Kierkegaard om ironi" [Magister Kierkegaard on Irony], *Res Publica*, vol. 22, 1992, pp. 7–19.

Häggqvist, Björn, "Ur tråkighetens historia. Tre stadier" [From the History of Boredom. Three Stages], *Tidskrift*, vol. 4, 1977, pp. 3–6.

Hansson, Ola, *Sensitiva amorosa*, Stockholm: Almqvist & Wiksell 1957.

Harris, Edward A., *Man's Ontological Predicament, A Detailed Analysis of Sören Kierkegaard's Concept of Sin with Special Reference to The Concept of Dread*, Uppsala: Acta Univeritatis Upsaliensis 1984.

— *Gör ditt val: en introduktion till Kierkegaards subjektivitetsteori* [Make your Choice: An Introduction to Kierkegaard's Theory of Subjectivity], Stockholm: Spiritual Future 2003.

— *Friends of God: In Search of Self, Ultimate reality and Love*, Stockholm: Spiritual Future 2003. (In Swedish as *Kristen andlighet: sökandet efter jaget, den slutgiltiga verkligheten och villkorslös kärlek*, Stockholm: Spiritual Future 2004.)

Hedenius, Ingemar, "Om Sören Kierkegaard" [About Søren Kierkegaard], *Tiden*, vol. 36, no. 7, 1944, pp. 423–37.

— "Om Sören Kierkegaard" [About Søren Kierkegaard], in his *Tro och vetande* [Faith and Knowledge], Stockholm: Bonnier 1949, pp. 331–56.

— "Kierkegaard och kärleken" [Kierkegaard and Love], in his *Om stora män och små* [About Great Men and Small Men], Stockholm: Rabén & Sjögren 1980, pp. 103–16.

Hejll, Richard, *Den enskilde: Tidskrift för de ensamma* [The Single Individual. Periodical for the Lonesome], Ramlösabrunn 1944–62.

— *Sann och falsk religiositet. En kritisk studie öfver det moderna fritänkeriet* [True and False Religiosity. A Critical Study of Modern Free Thinking], Stockholm: Minerva 1916, see pp. 151–87.

— "Sören Kierkegaard. Till förståelse" [For an Understanding of Søren Kierkegaard], *Edda*, vol. 25, no. 38, 1938, pp. 350–93.

— "Mystikern Sören Kierkegaard" [The Mystic Søren Kierkegaard], *Janus*, vol. 7, no. 3, 1939, pp. 263–81.

— "Sören Kierkegaard and David Friedrich Strauss" [Sören Kierkegaard and David Friedrich Strauss], *Edda*, vol. 27, no. 40, 1940, pp. 43–51.

— "Sören Kierkegaard och den europeiske kulturens undergång" [Sören Kierkegaard and the Destruction of European Culture], *Den enskilde: Tidskrift för de ensamma*, vol. 4, nos. 3–4, 1948, pp. 69–116.

— "Sören Kierkegaard och den 'enskildes' förkunnare" [Sören Kierkegaard and the Proclaimer of the Single Individual], *Den enskilde: Tidskrift för de ensamma*, vol. 11, no. 2, 1955, pp. 28–30.

— "Sören Kierkegaards angrepp på den kristna kyrkan" [Sören Kierkegaard's Attack on the Christian Church], *Den enskilde: Tidskrift för de ensamma*, vol. 11, no. 4, 1955, pp. 45–52.

Herbert, G., *Kierkegaard och Herbart. En jämförelse mellan deras framställning av själens historia* [Kierkegaard and Herbart. A Comparison between their Descriptions of the Soul's History], Uppsala: Almqvist & Wiksell 1934.

Hjertström Lappalainen, Jonna, "Den rädda människans skuld" [The Guilt of the Frightened Man], *Lyrikvännen*, vol. 5, 2004, pp. 107–13.

— "Den osägbare. Den enskildes betydelse i *Fruktan och bävan*" [The Unsayable One. The Importance of the Single Individual in *Fear and Trembling*], in *Tänkarens mångfald. Nutida perspektiv på Sören Kierkegaard* [The Thinker's Manifold. Contemporary Perspectives on Sören Kierkegaard], ed. by Lone Koldtoft, Jon

Stewart and Jan Holmgaard, Gothenburg & Stockholm: Makadam förlag 2005, pp. 12–25.

Holmgaard, Jan, "*Spegelns öga. En läsning av* Förförarens dagbok" [The Eye of the Mirror. A Reading of the Diary of the Seducer], *Aiolos*, nos. 6–7, 1997–98, pp. 103–29.

— *Jaget i texten* [The Self in the Text], Stockholm: Aiolos förlag 1998, see chapter 3 ("Självdiktandet").

— "Att bedra in i det sanna" [To Deceive into Truth], *Glänta*, vol. 4, 1999, pp. 44–56.

— *En ironisk historia* [An Ironical History], Stockholm: Aiolos förlag 2003.

— "Skillnadens estetik. Några anteckningar med utgångspunkt i Sören Kierkegaard" [The Aesthetic of Difference], *Artes*, vol. 29, no. 2, 2003, pp. 21–5.

— "Ett stigande och fallande likt lärkans. Om det poetiska i en passage hos Kierkegaard" [A Climbing and Falling like the Lark. About the Poetic in a Kierkegaardian Passage], *Lyrikvännen*, vol. 5, 2004, pp. 114–21.

— "Förförelse och kropp hos Kierkegaard. Några synpunkter på estetisk teori—en skiss" [Seduction and Body in Kierkegaard. Some Aspects in Aesthetic Theory— An Outline], *Tänkarens mångfald. Nutida perspektiv på Sören Kierkegaard* [The Thinker's Manifold. Contemporary Perspectives on Sören Kierkegaard], ed. by Lone Koldtoft, Jon Stewart and Jan Holmgaard, Gothenburg and Stockholm: Makadam förlag 2005, pp. 67–77.

Holmquist, Hjalmar, "Till Sören Kierkegaards minnefest" [To Celebration of Sören Kierkegaard's Memory], *Svensk tidskrift*, vol. 3, 1913, pp. 277–83.

Horgby, Ingvar, "Misshandlad Kierkegaard" [Maltreated Kierkegaard], *Kristet forum*, vol. 1, 1965, pp. 20–1.

— "Kierkegaards svar på den gnostiska utmaningen" [Kierkegaard's Answer to the Gnostic Challenge], *Exil*, No. 1, August, 1968, pp. 1–10.

Hultgren, Gunnar, "Mysteriet Kierkegaard" [The Mysterium Kierkegaard], *Vår lösen*, vol. 31, 1940, pp. 317–26.

Isakson, Karl-Gustav, "Sören Kierkegaard och den paradoxale kristendomen" [Sören Kierkegaard and Paradoxical Christianity], *Frikyrklig ungdom*, no. 4, 1940, pp. 58–60.

Johannesson, Hans-Erik, "Kierkegaard—dialektisk diktare" [Kierkegaard— Dialectic Poet], *Artes*, vol. 2, 1978, pp. 122–5.

Johansson, Klara, "Noter till Sören Kierkegaards liv" [Notes on Søren Kierkegaard's Life], in her *Det rika stärbhuset* [The Rich Estate], Stockholm: Wahlström & Widstrand 1946, pp. 149–87 (2nd ed., 1947).

Jørgensen, Poul Henning, "Från Kierkegaard till Sartre" [From Kierkegaard to Sartre], *Kyrkornas värld*, vol. 8, 1962, pp. 250–6.

Kihlmann, Erik, "Ibsen och Kierkegaard" [Ibsen and Kierkegaard], in his *Ur Ibsen–dramatikens idéhistoria. En studie i dansk–norsk litteratur*, Ph.D. Thesis, Helsingfors: Söderström 1921, see pp. 197–239.

— "Kierkegaard som verklighetsskildrare" [Kierkegaard as a Describer of Reality], *Nya Argus*, vol. 23, no. 17, 1930, pp. 222–5.

Koskinen, Lennart, *Tid och evighet hos Kierkegaard* [Time and Eternity in Kierkegaard], Lund: Nya Doxa 1980.

— *Sören Kierkegaard och existentialismen—om tiden, varat och evigheten* [Sören Kierkegaard and Existentialism—About Time, Being and Eternity], Nora: Nya Doxa 1994.

Kuylenstierna, Oswald, *Sören Kierkegaard. Tänkaren och sanningssökaren* [Sören Kierkegaard. The Thinker and the Truth Seeker], Stockholm: Bonnier 1898.

Larson, Kate, "Det heliga mörkret—att falla uppåt. En studie kring Jobs lidande och dess mening" [The Holy Darkness—To Fall Upwards. A Study on Job's Suffering], *Vår lösen*, vol. 86, 1995, pp. 375–85.

Larsson, Hans, "Två Kierkegaardsmotiv i litteraturen" [Two Kierkegaard Motifs in Literature], in his *Litteraturintryck* [Impressions of Literature], Stockholm: Bonnier 1926, pp. 105–16.

Lehmann, Edvard, "Sören Kierkegaard," in his *Män och deras tro. Luther, Pascal, Rousseau, Carlyle, Kierkegaard* [Men and their Faith. Luther, Pascal, Rousseau, Carlyle, Kierkegaard], Lund: Gleerup 1920, pp. 217–79.

Linderholm, Emanuel, "Sören Kierkegaards barndom och ungdom. Några kritiska synpunkter" [Sören Kierkegaard's Childhood and Youth. Some Critical Remarks], *Bibelforskaren*, vol. 32, 1915, pp. 225–42.

Lindström, Valter, "Kierkegaards Individualism" [Kierkegaard's Individualism], *Svensk Teologisk Kvartalstidskrift*, vol. 19, no. 1, 1943, pp. 18–32.

— *Stadiernas teologi. En Kierkegaardstudie* [Theology of Stages. A Kierkegaard Study], Lund: Gleerup 1943 (2nd ed., 1947).

— "Kierkegaards tolkning av självförnekelsen såsom kristendomens livsform" [Kierkegaard's Interpretation of Self-Denial as the Life-form of Christianity], *Svensk teologisk kvartalstidskrift*, vol. 26, nos. 3–4, 1950, pp. 326–34.

— *Efterföljelsens teologi* [The Theology of Imitation], Stockholm: Diakonistyrelsens förlag 1956.

— "Den första trosartikeln i Kierkegaards författarskap" [The First Doctrine of Faith in Kierkegaard's Authorship], *Svensk teologisk kvartalstidskrift*, vol. 56, 1980, pp. 97–104.

— "Diskussionen kring den siste Kierkegaard" [*The Discussion about the Last Kierkegaard*], *Svensk teologisk kvartalstidskrift*, vol. 63, 1987, pp. 24–31.

Linnel, Karin, "Det absoluta och ovissheten hos 'Hiin Enkelte' " [The Absolute and the Uncertainty in "Hiin Enkelte"], *Tänkarens mångfald. Nutida perspektiv på Sören Kierkegaard* [The Thinker's Manifold. Contemporary Perspectives on Sören Kierkegaard], ed. by Lone Koldtoft, Jon Stewart and Jan Holmgaard, Stockholm and Gothenburg: Makadam förlag 2005, pp. 78–119.

Ljungdal, Arnold, "Existentialisten Kierkegaard" [The Existentialist Kierkegaard], *Zenit*, nos. 4–5, 1962, pp. 11–13; p. 16.

— *Problemet Kierkegaard* [The Problem Kierkegaard], Stockholm: Nordstedts 1964.

Löfgren, Åke and Ofstad Harald, "Morality, Choice and Inwardness. Judge William's Distinction between the Aesthetic and the Ethical Way of Life," *Inquiry*, vol. 8, 1965, pp. 33–73.

Ludvig, Nils, "Kierkegaard eller Grundtvig? Sommarminnen från Fana i Norge 1951" [Kierkegaard or Grundtvig? Memories from the Summer in Fana in Norway 1951], *Lunds stifts årsbok*, vol. 51, 1959, pp. 43–8.

— *Mål i sikte* [Aim in View], Lund: Gleerups 1963.

Lundstedt, Göran, "Regine och Frida. Två tablåer—om Kierkegaard och Birger Sjöberg" [Regine and Frida. Two Schedules—About Kierkegaard and Birger Sjöberg], *Studiekamraten*, vol. 55, no. 8, 1973, pp. 148–9.

Lysander, Albert Theodor, "Sören Kierkegaard. Litterär-historisk teckning" [Sören Kierkegaard. Literary-Historical Picture], *Tidskrift för litteratur*, vol. 1, no. 10, 1851, pp. 227–52.

Melberg, Arne, "*Repetition* (in the Kierkegaardian sense of the Term)," *Diacritics*, vol. 20, no. 3, 1990, pp. 71–87.

— *Mimesis: en repetition*, Stockholm/Stehag: Symposion 1992, see pp. 147–76.

Norrby, Tore, *Sören Kierkegaard*, Stockholm: Wahlström & Widstrand 1951.

Nymann, Alf, "Kierkegaard och hans släkt. Ett stycke arvstragik i dansk bildningshistoria" [Kierkegaard and his Family. A Tragic Heritage in Danish Education History], *Samtid och framtid*, vol. 9, 1955, pp. 369–96.

— "Sören Kierkegaard och en köpenhamnsk nyckelroman från 1830-talet" [Sören Kierkegaard and a Roman-a-Clef in Copenhagen in the 1830s], *Nordisk tidskrift*, vol. 31, Nr 6, 1955, pp. 294–9.

Olsson, Anders, *Läsningar av Intet* [Readings of Nothingness], Stockholm: Bonnier 2000.

Ottesen, Christian, "Förföraren" [The Seducer], *Pequod*, vol. 26, December, 1999.

Rudin, Waldemar, "Har Sören Kierkegaard förnekat försoningsläran" [Did Sören Kierkegaard Deny the Doctrine of Atonement?], *Wäktaren*, no. 46, 1864.

— *Sören Kierkegaards person och författarskap. Ett försök* [Sören Kierkegaard's Personality and Authorship. An Essay], Uppsala: A. Nilsson 1880.

Segerstedt, Torgny, "Antiintellektualismen" (on Pascal and Kierkegaard), in his *Det religiösa sanningsproblemet* [The Problem of Religious Truth], Stockholm: Bonnier 1912, pp. 149–61.

— *Det religiösa sanningsproblemet* [The Problem of Religious Truth], Stockholm: Bonnier 1912.

— "Sören Kierkegaard," in his *Gammal och ny religiositet* [Old and New Religiosity], Stockholm: Bonnier 1915, pp. 73–9.

Simonsson, Ingmar, *Kierkegaard i vår tid* [Kierkegaard in our Time], Stockholm: Themis förlag 2002.

— "Kierkegaards heteronyma författarskap" [Kierkegaard's Heteronymous Authorship], *Lyrikvännen* 5, 2004, pp. 94–106.

Sjöstedt, Nils Åke, *Søren Kierkegaard och svensk litteratur. Från Fredrika Bremer till Hjalmar Söderberg* [Søren Kierkegaard and Swedish Literature. From Fredrika Bremer to Hjalmar Söderberg], Gothenburg: Wettergren & Kerber 1950.

Stenström, Thure, *Den ensamme. En motivstudie i det moderna genombrottets litteratur* [The Lonesome. A Studie of Motives in the Rise of the Modern in Literature], Stockholm: Natur & Kultur 1961, see chapter 3 ("Kierkegaard and Brandes").

— *Existentialismen, Studier i dess idétradition och litterära yttringar*, Stockholm: Natur & Kultur 1966.

— "Kierkegaard, Geijer och universitetet" [Kierkegaard, Geijer and the University], *Samlaren. Tidskrift för svensk litteraturvetenskaplig forskning*, vol. 114, 1993, pp. 5–14.

— "Sören Kierkegaard och liljorna på marken" [Sören Kierkegaard and the Lilies in the Field], *Svensk teologisk kvartalskrift*, vol. 77, no. 3, 2001, pp. 98–106.

— "Joakim Garff, *SAK Sören Aabye Kierkegaard. En biografi*" [Joakim Garff, *SAK Sören Aabye Kierkegaard. A Biography*], *Samlaren. Tidskrift för svensk litteraturvetenskaplig forskning*, vol. 123, 2003, pp. 362–9.

Strindberg, August, *Samlade skrifter* [Collected Works], vols. 1–55, Stockholm: Bonnier 1912–20, see vol. 18, pp. 383–430.

[Sturzen-Becker, Oscar Patrick], *Hinsidan Sundet. Danska epistlar av Orvar Odd* [Beyond the Sound. Dansih Epistles by Orvar Odd], vols. 1–2, Stockholm: Bonnier 1846.

Vinge, Louise, "Kierkegaards kvinnosyn och ett dockhem" [Kierkegaard's View of Women and a Doll's House], *Res Publica*, vol. 18, 1991, pp. 161–4.

Wagndal, Per, "Sören Kierkegaard och samhället" [Sören Kierkegaard and the Society], *Vår lösen*, vol. 44, 1953, pp. 189–97.

— *Gemenskapsproblemet hos Sören Kierkegaard* [Kierkegaard's Community Problem], Lund: Gleerup 1954.

Wiklander, Roy, "Kierkegaard och den indirekta meddelelsen" [Kierkegaard and the Indirect Communication], *Tänkarens mångfald. Nutida perspektiv på Sören Kierkegaard* [The Thinker's Manifold. Contemporary Perspectives on Sören Kierkegaard], ed. by Lone Koldtoft, Jon Stewart and Jan Holmgaard, Gothenburg and Stockholm: Makadam förlag 2005, pp. 130–212.

Wiklander, Roy and Christina Runquist, "Att förverkliga sig själv" [*To Realize One's Self*], *Svensk teologisk kvartalstidskrift*, no. 1, 1997, pp. 11–22.

Wirtanen, Atos, "Den ultrakristne och Antikrist" [The Ultra Christian and Anti-Christ], *Samtid och framtid*, vol. 4, 1960, pp. 230–2.

Wohlstein, Herman, "Till den moderna humanismens kris. Sören Kierkegaard och Martin Buber" [To the Crisis of Modern Humanism. Sören Kierkegaard and Martin Buber], *Religion och kultur*, June, 1964, pp. 38–41.

III. Secondary Literature on Kierkegaard's Reception in Sweden

Anz, Heinrich, " 'Seinerzeit eine Art macabre Modefigur.' Aspekte der Wirkungs-geschichte Søren Kierkegaards in der Skandinavischen Literatur," *Kierkegaard Studies. Yearbook*, 1999, pp. 204–19.

Bejerholm, Lars, "Bohlin," in *The Legacy and Interpretation of Kierkegaard*, ed. by Niels Thulstrup and Marie Mikulová Thulstrup, Copenhagen: C.A. Reitzel 1981 (*Bibliothecha Kierkegaardiana*, vol. 8), pp. 222–3.

Benedikt, Ernst, "Nyare Kierkegaardlitteratur" [Newer Kierkegaard Literature], *Svenska dagbladet*, January 6, 1951.

Benzow, Kristofer, "S. Kierkegaard och nordisk diktning" [S. Kierkegaard and Nordic Poetry], *Årsbok för kristen Humanism*, 1949, pp. 24–43.

Beyer, Harald, "Søren Kierkegaard og svensk litteratur" [Sören Kierkegaard and Swedish Literature]," *Kirke og Kultur*, vol. 56, 1951, pp. 500–4.

Bøggild, Jacob, "Coming to Terms with the Tricky Twins. On the Scandinavian Reception of *Repetition* and *Fear and Trembling*," *Kierkegaard Studies. Yearbook*, 2002, pp. 290–309.

Delgaauw, Bernhard, "De Kierkegaardstudie in Scandinavië," *Tijdschrift voor Filosofie*, vol. 33, 1971, pp. 737–78; vol. 38, 1976, pp. 136–58; vol. 43, 1981, pp. 117–62.

Dymling, Carl, "Sören Kierkegaard i nyaste forskningars ljus" [Sören Kierkegaard in the Light of the Newest Research], *Religion och kultur*, vol. 15, no. 3, 1944, pp. 142–7.

Götke, Povl, "Recent Scandinavian Literature on *Works of Love*," *Kierkegaard Studies. Yearbook*, 1998, pp. 232–44.

Hansen, Holger, "Søren Kierkegaard och Sverige" [Søren Kierkegaard and Sweden], *Nordisk Tidskrift*, vol. 22, 1946, pp. 52–9.

Hejll, Richard, "Sören Kierkegaard och Sverige" [Sören Kierkegaard and Sweden], *Den enskilde: Tidskrift för de ensamma*, vol. 4, nos. 3–4, pp. 104–5.

Henriksen, Aage, *Methods and Results of Kierkgaard Studies in Scandinavia*, Copenhagen: Munksgaard 1951.

Horgby, Ingvar, "Kierkegaardinflytandets historia" [History of Kierkegaard's Influence], *Kristet forum*, vol. 3, 1964, pp. 82–4.

Kabell, Aage, *Kierkegaardstudiet i Norden* [Kierkegaard Studies in the Nordic Countries], Copenhagen: H. Hagerup 1948.

Liedgren, Emil, "Kierkegaard i Sverige. Några anteckningar till hudraårsminnet af hans födelse" [Kierkegaard in Sweden. Some Notes to the Centenary of his Birth], *Vår lösen*, vol. 4, 1913, pp. 177–82.

Mortensen, Finn Hauberg, "Kierkegaard in Scandinavia. A History of Radical Reception," in *Kierkegaard Revisited. Proceedings from the Conference "Kierkegaard and the Menaing of Meaning It," Copenhagen, May 5–9, 1996*, ed. by Niels Jørgen Cappelørn and Jon Stewart, Berlin and New York: Walter de Gruyter 1997 (*Kierkegaard Studies Monograph Series*, vol. 1), pp. 410–41.

Sjöstedt, Nils Åke, *Kierkegaard och svensk litteratur. Från Fredrika Bremer till Hjalmar Söderberg* [Kierkegaard and Swedish Literature. From Fredrika Bremer to Hjalmar Söderberg], Gothenburg: Wettergren & Kerbers förlag 1950.

— "Swedish Literature," in *The Legacy and Interpretation of Kierkegaard*, ed. by Niels Thulstrup and Marie Mikulová Thulstrup, Copenhagen: C.A. Reitzel 1981 (*Bibliotheca Kierkegaardiana*, vol. 8), pp. 40–53.

Thulstrup, Niels, "Scandinavia," in *Kierkegaard Research*, ed. by Niels Thulstrup and Marie Mikulová Thulstrup, Copenhagen: C.A. Reitzel 1987 (*Bibliotheca Kierkegaardiana*, vol. 15), pp. 173–99.

Tullberg, Steen, "Die Rezeption der *Philosophischen Brocken* in Skandinavien," *Kierkegaard Studies. Yearbook*, 2004, pp. 306–27.

Finland:

The Reception of Kierkegaard in Finland

Janne Kylliäinen

I. 1849–1915

Finns received their first impressions of Kierkegaard from rumors and secondary literature. Kierkegaard became known through intermediaries such as Fredrika Bremer (1801–65), Hans Lassen Martensen (1808–84), Georg Brandes (1842–1927), and Waldemar Rudin (1833–1921).

Kierkegaard appeared in Finland for the first time in 1849 in pages of the magazine *Litteraturblad för allmän medborgerlig bildning*.[1] The purpose of this literary magazine was, through its surveys of the newest literature, to civilize society and to build a proper civil society. It was founded and edited by the Hegelian philosopher Johan Vilhelm Snellman (1806–81).[2] In an overview of Swedish literature, Snellman presents the new book by Fredrika Bremer, *Lif i Norden*.[3] Snellman quotes *in extenso* the long passage that describes cultural life in Copenhagen and presents to the reader, among others, the solitary and unapproachable Kierkegaard.[4]

Two years later, in 1851, there was a review of the Swedish translations of Hans Lassen Martensen's works *Den christelige Dogmatik* and *Dogmatiske Oplysninger* in the same magazine.[5] In his review the new editor of *Litteraturblad*, the historian Sven Gabriel Elmgren (1817–97), mentions among Martensen's decided opponents "a certain man of letters, Sören Kierkegaard, who is unknown everywhere else,

---

[1] Johan Vilhelm Snellman, "Svensk Litteratur," *Litteraturblad för allmän medborgerlig bildning*, no. 10, 1849, pp. 281–96.

[2] At the time Finland was a part of Russian empire with only a very limited autonomy and without a strong national culture. J.V. Snellman was the head of the moderate Finnish nationalists who through legal and cultural measures tried to liberate the Finnish society from Russian control. Part of Snellman's strategy to build up Finnish culture and society was to keep windows open for international ideas through his *Litteraturblad*.

[3] Fredrika Bremer, *Lif i Norden*, Stockholm: Bagge 1849.

[4] Johan Vilhelm Snellman, "Svensk Litteratur," *Litteraturblad för allmän medborgerlig bildning*, no. 10, 1849, p. 292.

[5] Sven Gabriel Elmgren, "Litteraturöfversigt," *Litteraturblad för allmän medborgerlig bildning*, no. 7, 1851, pp. 193–207. The translations Elmgren refers to in the title of his review read as follows: "*Den christeliga dogmatiken, framställd af H. Martensen*. Öfversättning af. Th. Wensjoe. Mariestad 1849. *Dogmatiska upplysningar, en tillfäldighetsskrift af H. Martensen*. Öfversättning. Mariestad 1850" (Ibid., pp. 198–9.).

but in Denmark has managed to gain a certain reputation through his writings that are wordy and apparently of poor quality." According to Elmgren's informants, this Kierkegaard acts as a kind of prophet for selfishness, a prophet with "unclear thoughts, dull irony and a mass of banalities which his admirers rank high as humorous witticisms. He teaches that men should become themselves, think their personal existence and throw all the unnecessary knowledge, all big and general thoughts overboard."[6] It seems likely that Elmgren received his information straight from Martensen's writings.[7]

While the moderate *Litteraturblad* was not very receptive to Kierkegaard's ideas, the more radical students were. Already in 1852 Kierkegaard was referred to by the students who were critical towards the State Church, and in the 1850s and 1860s the name of Kierkegaard came up now and then in student meetings and discussions.[8] How deep this interest in Kierkegaard was is hard to evaluate for lack of documentation.

In the late 1870s, the lectures of Georg Brandes published in Sweden under the title *Sören Kierkegaard* stimulated interest in the man behind the ideas also in Finland.[9] This book by Brandes remained influential for a long time.[10] Another Swedish book that influenced Finnish reception of Kierkegaard for decades was the treatise *Sören Kierkegaards person och författarskap* by the professor Waldemar Rudin.[11] For the clergy, Rudin seems to have served as the guarantor of Kierkegaard's deep religious character.[12]

---

[6]   Ibid., pp. 200–1.

[7]   See Kalle Sorainen, "Kierkegaard och Finland," *Kierkegaardiana*, vol. 2, 1957, p. 65.

[8]   See Mikko Juva, *Suomen sivistyneistö uskonnollisen vapaamielisyyden murroksessa 1848–1869*, Helsinki: Suomen kirkkohistoriallinen seura 1950, p. 85; p. 207; pp. 302–3.

[9]   Georg Brandes, *Sören Kierkegaard*, Stockholm: Jos. Seligmann 1877.

[10]   Brandes' book was reviewed with praise by Martin Wegelius, the composer, conductor and the founder of the Institute for Music in Helsinki ("Georg Brandes: *Sören Kierkegaard*," *Finsk Tidskrift*, no. 2, 1878, pp. 64–7). It was criticized by Herman Råbergh, the deacon of The theological faculty of the University of Helsinki in his review of Waldemar Rudin's treatise on Kierkegaard ("Sören Kierkegaards Person och författerskap, ett försök af W. Rudin, första afdelningen. Uppsala 1880," *Tidskrift för teologi och kyrka*, vol. 4, 1880, pp. 231–4). Brandes' book remained influential for a long time. Two examples: The novelist Volter Kilpi reports that Brandes by his "completely ignorant and, at crucial issues, negative critique" made him study Kierkegaard's works in 1896 (Volter Kilpi, *Vieras, vieras minä olen kaikille*, ed. by Pirjo Lyytikäinen, Helsinki: Suomalaisen Kirjallisuuden Seura 1993, p. 170; p. 177). On the other hand, Erik Ahlman, the philosopher, refers to Brandes in 1924 with approval in his review of the Finnish translation of *The Sickness unto Death* [*Kuolemansairaus*], in *Valvoja-Aika*, vol. 2, 1924, pp. 220–1.).

[11]   Waldemar Rudin, *Sören Kierkegaards person och författarskap*, Uppsala: A. Nilsson 1880. Still in 1908, in his article on Kierkegaard, Heikki Linnove refers to the works of Brandes and Rudin that he assumes many of his readers to be acquainted with (Heikki Linnove, "Piirteitä Sören Kierkegaardin elämänkatsomuksesta," *Aika*, vol. 2, 1908, p. 862).

[12]   In the review quoted above, Herman Råbergh presents the book by Rudin as a corrective to Brandes. In the preface for his translation of *For Self-Examination* Gustaf Adolf Heman, the priest and novelist, refers to Rudin in same spirit. (See *Itsensä koettelemiseksi*

The first Finnish translations of Kierkegaard came out in 1898. The choice and the place of publication are somewhat surprising: the first texts to appear were two of the *Three Discourses at the Communion on Fridays*, "The Tax Collector" and "The Woman Who Was a Sinner," and they came out in Savonlinna, a small town in eastern Finland. The texts were published also as an offprint, but originally they appeared in a small Christian newspaper *Friend of the People*.[13] The chief editor of this weekly newspaper was the bishop of Savonlinna, Gustaf Johansson (1844–1930), the former professor of Dogmatics and Ethics at the University of Helsinki and the future archbishop in Turku. Johansson's diaries show that he had been studying the works of Kierkegaard earlier in the 1890s, and so it is quite possible that the first translations were made by the bishop himself.[14]

One of Johansson's former disciples during his university time and his associate in later missions, Gustaf Adolf Heman (1855–1917), a parson and writer, translated *For Self-Examination*. It was published in 1907 as volume one in a planned series of *Søren Kierkegaard's Works* by the publishing house Werner Söderström Ltd. (WSOY). Together with it was published volume number two, a translation of "The Seducer's Diary." Unfortunately, that was to be the last in the series![15]

The translator of "The Seducer's Diary" was the young poet Veikko Antero Koskenniemi (1885–1962). As a poet, critic and later professor at the University of Turku, Koskenniemi was to become one of the most prominent figures in Finnish literature of the first half of the twentieth century. But in 1907 Koskenniemi had only just published his first collection and started as a critic in the conservative newspaper *Uusi Suometar*, and the conservative literary magazine *Aika*. Koskenniemi himself wrote how he at this time lived spellbound by Kierkegaard and read all the secondary literature available on him. Kierkegaard's personality interested Koskenniemi, and he admired Kierkegaard as a poet and refined psychologist, but the rigorous religious thinker and moral philosopher was never close to his heart.[16] Kierkegaard's influence might be visible in some of his poems, both in their language and themes. The language of Koskenniemi is lofty and often filled with pathos. He was one of the first to introduce urban themes into Finnish poetry, and he was occupied with the

---

[*For Self-Examination*], trans. by Gustaf Adolf Heman, *Sören Kierkegaardin teoksia* [Søren Kierkegaard's Works], vols. 1–2, Porvoo: WSOY 1907, vol. 1, p. X.)

[13]   *Kansan ystävä*, nos. 15–18, April 14–May 5, 1898, pp. 57–8; pp. 61–62; pp. 65–6; pp. 69–71.

[14]   See Yrjö J.E. Alanen, *Gustaf Johansson*, Porvoo: WSOY 1947, p. 190. Johansson, who was a charismatic university teacher and leader of the Church, had a pietistic background and he had great respect for the religious inwardness of the pietistic movement. In the late 1860s, as a young theologian he had studied in Tübingen under Johann Tobias Beck who is said to have been one of the first theologians in Germany to pay attention to Kierkegaard. Ibid., p. 37.

[15]   *Sören Kierkegaardin teoksia*, 1907. What happened to this project of WSOY is unknown.

[16]   See Veikko Antero Koskenniemi, *Vuosisadanalun ylioppilas*, Porvoo: WSOY 1947, pp. 237–9.

fragility of human existence, describing the solitude of man often in a melancholic mood, but also urging for a heroic overcoming of destiny.[17]

The publisher was cautious enough to ask Waldemar Rudin to write a preface to *Søren Kierkegaard's Works* in order to make ensure a correct understanding of "The Seducer's Diary." In one way or other the diary must have fascinated people at the time since, in the very same year 1907, another less well-known translation of it was published in Tampere.[18] The theme of seduction could have become popular partly due to the best-selling seducer novel, *The Song of the Blood-Red Flower* by Johannes Linnankoski.[19] But Linnankoski himself had included *Either/Or* among the works to be read while preparing himself for his own authorship, and so it is hard to judge who was the first to seduce.[20]

Another important author who had studied *Either/Or* already by 1896 was Volter Kilpi (1874–1939). Kilpi has himself stated the central importance of Kierkegaard for his work,[21] and it has been claimed that among Finns one can hardly find a more Kierkegaardian spirit than the essayist and novelist Kilpi.[22] In his works Kilpi focuses on the inwardness of man and, like Kierkegaard, he tests philosophical ideas psychologically in fictive characters that represent them. In his *Batsheba* and *Parsifal* he analyzes the stages of desire in the manner of Kierkegaard.[23] In the essay collection *On Man and Life* he makes a sharp distinction between the inner and outer, and connects the inner with the eternal.[24] As the moral ideal for man he sets the task to live in truth, and among the few great thinkers that have been able to represent the truth in an authentic way Kilpi names Kierkegaard as the only Nordic example.[25] In the characters of his later masterpiece *In Alastalo Hall* there are reminiscences of

---

[17]   Later Koskenniemi became convinced that only Mussolini and Hitler could save the West from the red barbarians, and he was one of the central promoters of German culture in Finland in the 1930s and 1940s.

[18]   *Viettelijän päiväkirja* ["The Seducer's Diary"], trans. by Siimes Kanervio, Tampere: Sulo Toivonen 1907. Siimes Kanervio appears to have translated many kinds of books from a variety of different languages.

[19]   Johannes Linnankoski, *Laulu tulipunaisesta kukasta*, Porvoo: WSOY 1905.

[20]   Aarne Anttila, *Vihtori Peltonen—Johannes Linnankoski*, Part II, Porvoo: WSOY 1927, p. 22. Pirjo Lyytikäinen claims that at the turn of the century *Either/Or* had become a "textbook" in seduction and aestheticism all over Nordic countries and that particularly Kierkegaard's analysis of Don Juan had contributed to the popularity of the figure of the seducer. See Pirjo Lyytikäinen, *Narkissos ja sfinksi*, Helsinki: Suomalaisen Kirjallisuuden Seura 1997, p. 114; p. 178.

[21]   Kilpi states this in a letter to Alvar Renqvist on January 30, 1936 (quoted in Pirjo Lyytikäinen, *Mielen meri, elämän pidot*, Helsinki: Suomalaisen Kirjallisuuden Seura 1992, p. 200), and in a letter to Vilho Suomi on March 21, 1938 (*Vieras, vieras minä olen kaikille*, ed. by Pirjo Lyytikäinen, Helsinki: Suomalaisen Kirjallisuuden Seura 1993, pp. 118–19). Besides Kierkegaard, Kilpi names Plato and Schopenhauer as the most important sources of his ideas (ibid., p. 170).

[22]   Helge Ukkola, "Kierkegaard ja jälkimaailma," *Teologinen aikakauskirja*, vol. 66, 1961, p. 163.

[23]   Volter Kilpi, *Batsheba*, Helsinki: Otava 1900; Kilpi, *Parsifal*, Helsinki: Otava 1902.

[24]   Kilpi, *Ihmisestä ja elämästä*, Helsinki: Otava 1902, p. 93; p. 102.

[25]   Ibid., p. 119.

the theory of stages and of Kierkegaard's conception of faith and humor.[26] Religious despair and anxiety, and indirectly perhaps paradoxical faith, are the themes of the last published work by Kilpi, *At Sealed Gates*.[27]

Of the classics of Finnish literature, one may mention also Juhani Siljo (1888–1918) as an author possibly influenced by Kierkegaard. Siljo was a poet and a critic with a strong ethical pathos. The universe of his texts is occupied by the contradictions of life, ascetic ideals, the will that aims at the eternal, and the need to make a choice between an authentic ethical existence and a cozy but impersonal life among the masses. Siljo had a pietistic background, and in school he had a charismatic teacher of religion Mauno Rosenthal, who was an enthusiastic admirer of Kierkegaard.[28] It is not known whether he studied Kierkegaard extensively, but among his notes there are quotations from Kierkegaard's works.[29]

Siljo and especially Koskenniemi were active contributors to *Aika* [Time], a literary magazine published by moderate Finnish nationalists. For *Aika* Koskenniemi translated some of the "Diapsalmata" from *Either/Or* in 1909.[30] The year before *Aika* had published an article by Heikki Linnove that gave an overview of Kierkegaard's thoughts and works.[31] The tone of the article is idealizing and romantic; the themes of individuality, inwardness and absoluteness are highlighted. In 1911 and 1913 similar articles were published in the theological journal *Vartija* [Guardian] by Antti J. Pulkkinen and Aukusti Oravala.[32] In 1915 Linnove published his translation of *The Lily in the Field and the Bird of the Air*.[33]

One may conclude that by the First World War, Kierkegaard had settled down also in Finland, at the time the northwestern corner of the Russian empire. He had received readers and admirers both among the Swedish- and the Finnish-speaking population of the country, and both within aesthetic and religious circles.

---

[26]   Kilpi, *Alastalon salissa*, Helsinki: Otava 1933.

[27]   Kilpi, *Suljetuille porteille*, Helsinki: Otava 1938. Kilpi feels close to Kierkegaard for whom faith goes hand in hand with doubt (See Volter Kilpi, *Vieras, vieras minä olen kaikille*, Helsinki: Suomalaisen Kirjallisuuden Seura 1993, p. 106; pp. 118–19). Kilpi, however, does not commit himself to Christianity in the manner of Kierkegaard, and he differs from Kierkegaard also in regarding art as the carrier of the Truth and in attaching ethical value to it.

[28]   See Kalle Sorainen, *Juhani Siljo oman minuutensa rakentajana*, Helsinki: Otava 1936, pp. 21–5. Wounded in the Finnish civil war against the socialists, Siljo died as a young man and became a pattern for the following generation of rightist poets.

[29]   See Kalle Sorainen, "Kierkegaard och Finland," *Kierkegaardiana*, vol. 2, 1957, p. 68.

[30]   "Søren Kierkegaardin lauselmia" [Lines from "Diapsalmata"], trans. by Veikko Antero Koskenniemi, in *Aika*, vol. 3, 1909, pp. 644–6.

[31]   Heikki Linnove, "Piirteitä Sören Kierkegaardin elämänkatsomuksesta," *Aika*, vol. 2, 1908, pp. 862–8; pp. 917–22. Linnove was a theologian who earned his living as a teacher.

[32]   The article by Antti J. Pulkkinen, "Sören Kierkegaard," *Vartija*, vol. 24, 1911, pp. 231–46, concentrates on Kierkegaard's conflict with the church and shows understanding for Kierkegaard's position. The article by Aukusti Oravala, "Sören Aabye Kierkegaard," *Vartija*, vol. 26, 1913, pp. 150–7, presents Kierkegaard on the occasion of his centennial.

[33]   *Kedon kukka ja taivaan lintu* [*The Lily in the Field and the Bird of the Air*], trans. by Heikki Linnove, Porvoo: WSOY 1915 (2nd revised ed., 1939; 3rd ed., 1990.)

II. 1916–62

Next follows the beginning of academic Kierkegaard research. As with translations, we have again an unexpected forerunner, the radical philosopher Rolf Lagerborg (1874–1959), an advocate of behaviorist and physiologic psychology and an active member of the Prometheus Society, the purpose of which was to liberate minds from the hegemony of the Christian Church. In 1916 Lagerborg published an article on the question "To what extent is Søren Kierkegaard fit for defending emotional tendencies within the sphere of religion?"[34] Lagerborg answers, polemically against the Swedish theologians Gillis Petersson Wetter (1887–1926) and Torgny Segerstedt (1876–1945): only to certain extent since in the end Christian truth is not only a subjective matter to Kierkegaard, not just a matter of emotions, passions. Later, in 1922 and 1923, Lagerborg published another article where he examines Kierkegaard's personality as a representative of psycho-pathological religious phenomena.[35] As a second forerunner, one could mention Erik Kihlman (1895–1933), who discusses Kierkegaard extensively in his dissertation *On the History of Ideas of Ibsen's Dramatic Art*.[36]

However, one must consider Kalle Sandelin (1893–1983) who later used the name Kalle Sorainen, as the first genuine Finnish Kierkegaard specialist. At the Department of Theoretical Philosophy of the University of Helsinki he defended the first academic dissertation on Kierkegaard in Finland, entitled *The Development of Søren Kierkegaard's Idea of Personality in Connection with the Danish Philosophical Currents of the Early Nineteenth Century*.[37] With the "idea of personality" Sandelin refers to the clear consciousness of the value of individual experience and the attempt to do justice to such a consciousness in oneself and in others. As such, the idea of personality counterbalances the idea of authority. According to Sandelin, the idea of personality has had many notable representatives in the Nordic Countries, among others Johan Ludvig Runeberg, JohanVilhelm Snellman, Erik Gustaf Geijer, Søren Kierkegaard, and Harald Høffding.[38]

In his dissertation Sandelin takes a diachronic approach to Kierkegaard's thought. Sandelin traces first the appearances of the idea of personality in Danish philosophical

---

[34]   Rolf Lagerborg, "I vad mån är Sören Kierkegaard egnad att stöda känslosamma riktningar på det religiösa området?" in *Festskrift tillägnad Vitalis Norström*, Gothenburg: Wettergren & Gerber 1916.

[35]   Rolf Lagerborg, "Synpunkter på Sören Kierkegaard," *Arkiv för psykologi och pedagogik*, vol. 1, 1922, pp. 185–202; vol. 2, 1923, pp. 174–87.

[36]   Erik Kihlman, *Ur Ibsen-dramatikens idéhistoria*, Helsinki: Söderström 1921.

[37]   Kalle Sandelin, *Søren Kierkegaardin persoonallisuusaatteen kehittyminen Tanskan filosofisten virtausten yhteydessä viime vuosisadan alkupuolella*, Pori: Satakunnan kirjateollisuus 1927.

[38]   Sandelin might have been influenced by Harald Høffding in the choice of the subject of his study. Already in 1911 Høffding had given a series of lectures at the University of Helsinki on the idea of personality in philosophy, and these lectures had been also translated and published in Finnish (see Harald Høffding, *Persoonallisuusperiaate filosofiassa* [The Principle of Personality in Philosophy], trans. by Zacharias Castren, Helsinki: Otava 1911). Sandelin came to know Høffding personally in the 1920s.

discourses of the early 1800s. Then he describes how the idea starts to take shape in Kierkegaard's journals and notebooks, and further, how it gets formulated and developed in his published works.

Sandelin investigates first Danish discourses on the relationship between faith and knowledge. At the beginning of the nineteenth century, Henrik Steffens (1773–1845) attached cosmic significance to the free individual personality as carrier of truth and fulfiller of the purpose of nature. In order to grasp the deepest religious truths, a human being is to turn to his own divine nature. Steffens' lectures pointed the way for a whole generation but created also a tension among its members. The tension makes itself known in a series of debates in which Grundtvig championed the supremacy of Christian faith against the defenders of human knowledge and reason—Hans Christian Ørsted (1777–1851), Jens Baggesen (1764–1826), Henrik Nikolaj Clausen (1793–1877), and Jakob Peter Mynster (1775–1854). Later the members of the next generation—Frederik Christian Sibbern (1785–1872), Johan Ludvig Heiberg (1791–1860), Poul Martin Møller (1794–1838), and Hans Lassen Martensen—each in his own way tried to bring philosophical activity into harmony with Christianity. But the tension between faith and reason came alive again with the debate on the principle of contradiction and with bishop Mynster's writings against naturalism and the left-Hegelians in the late 1830s and early 1840s. Aware of the earlier debates and witness to the later ones, the young Kierkegaard begins to develop his own view about the relationship between faith and reason. Unable to find spiritual satisfaction in either rationalist theology or Hegelian philosophy, he comes to see scientific research and Christian faith as, in the final analysis, mutually exclusive ways to the truth. In his texts the problematic relationship between faith and reason is aggravated into a dilemma that only a personal decision can solve: either reason or faith. Only such a decision opens the way for personal development towards the truth. In this way Kierkegaard most emphatically brings the idea of personality to the center of the quest for truth.

Sandelin investigates next the idea of personality in Danish discussion on ethics. As an ethical idea, the idea of personality already had a long history in Danish discussions. The idea of a free and autonomous ethical personality is already present in the dramas of Ludvig Holberg (1684–1754). In his comical characters the idea is present indirectly. Later, the idea was nurtured by Anders Sandøe Ørsted (1778–1860), Henrik Steffens, and Niels Treschow (1751–1833) and challenged by the deterministic views of Frantz Gotthard Howitz (1789–1826). In the works of Kierkegaard's teachers, then, the idea is harmonized with the idea of the natural development of a concrete individual. Sibbern writes about sporadic development that has many separate starting points and goes through many contradictions, but aims at harmonious unity; if the development is healthy, its end result will be a sound individual, who is in harmony with his or her nature. In a similar spirit Poul Martin Møller advocates "personal truth" [*personlig Sandhed*] and diagnoses different forms of affectation that distort it. This is the background for Kierkegaard's idea of personality that connects the quest for truth with the development of the individual ethical-religious character. Against this background, however, Kierkegaard's account of true personality stands out due to its emphasis on negativity. Sandelin goes through Kierkegaard's authorship and points out how, step-by-step, the negative aspects in Kierkegaard's idea of personality overcome the positive ones. First there is the development towards positive personality—towards personality that is in harmony with its own nature, its fellow human beings, and with the totality it belongs to: in Judge William there is a clear consciousness of the value of individual experience and a striving to do justice to such a consciousness in oneself and others. However, in the writings that follow, with the turn towards genuine religiousness, the idea of personality falls prey to conflicts and contradictions. In order to save the true relationship to God, a person has to deny his nature, renounce the world, and break immediate relationships with other human beings.

Sandelin concludes that with his strong emphasis on the subjectivity of truth and on the personal relationship to God, Kierkegaard indeed affirms and intensifies the idea of personality. However, at the same time he negates essentially all the other positive aspects that his compatriots had attached to the idea of personality. Against the ideal of a Christian with sound understanding and healthy ethical spirit, Kierkegaard posits anxiety and guilt and faith that goes against reason. In his authorship the absolute truth takes the place of personal life-views, and obedience to God supersedes the harmonious development of human faculties. Thus, despite the strong presence of personal inwardness in all that Kierkegaard has written, it is questionable whether one is to regard him among the representatives of the idea of personality after all. The evaluation of Sandelin's dissertation by professor Arvi Grotenfelt (1863–1941) was in the main positive. Grotenfelt praised Sandelin's expertise but would have wished more determination in the conclusions of the doctoral candidate.[39]

Later, Sandelin earned his living as a Swedish teacher in secondary schools, but he continued to study Kierkegaard and published numerous articles on the different aspects of his thought in a variety of scholarly and literary publications—after 1936 under the name Kalle Sorainen. A younger Kierkegaard scholar, Helge Ukkola (1921–93) gives witness to Sorainen's "most enthusiastic, at times even imitating interest in Kierkegaard."[40] Sorainen applied for a professorship several times and at several different universities.[41] For example, in 1953 he applied for the professorship of Practical Philosophy at the University of Helsinki but, like all the other applicants, Sorainen was evaluated as unqualified for the post by the analytical philosophers Eino Kaila (1890–1958) and Oiva Ketonen (1913–2000).[42] In his *Filosofien i Norden efter 1900*, Søren Holm mentions Sorainen among the philosophical lone wolves in Finland.[43]

There are reasons why an enthusiastic Kierkegaard scholar was bound to become a lone wolf in the Finnish philosophical atmosphere. After the charismatic logical empiricist Kaila had become the professor of Theoretical Philosophy of the University

---

[39]   Minutes of the Historico–Philological Faculty 1927, Archives of the University of Helsinki.

[40]   Helge Ukkola, *Romantiikan vanavedessä*, Tampere: Tampereen yliopistopaino 1973, pp. 148–9.

[41]   Oral information received from Raili Sorainen, the daughter of Kalle Sorainen.

[42]   Later, in 1959, the professorship was granted to young Jaakko Hintikka, the star disciple of G.H. von Wright. (See Mikko Salmela, *Suomalaisen kulttuurifilosofian vuosisata*, Helsinki: Otava 1998, pp. 384–7.)

[43]   Søren Holm, *Filosofien i Norden efter 1900*, Copenhagen: Munksgaard 1967, p. 167.

of Helsinki in 1930, the philosophical climate had turned clearly analytical.[44] Kaila and his followers did consider Kierkegaard and his followers as important thinkers, but hardly as representatives of the great tradition of *scientific* philosophy worthy of serious *scientific* study.[45] Among the philosophers with an academic position, only Erik Ahlman (1892–1952), who worked as a professor first in Jyväskylä (1935–48) and then in Helsinki (1948–52), took the ideas of Kierkegaard seriously in his scholarly works. Like Sorainen, Ahlman had been studying in Helsinki under the old professor Grotenfelt who had had his roots in the German idealistic tradition. Ahlman was interested in Nietzsche, phenomenology, existential philosophy, psychoanalysis, and the problem of authentic spiritual existence. He appreciated Kierkegaard's depth psychology and appears to have gained insights into the structure of the human spirit especially while reading *The Sickness unto Death*.[46]

The last-mentioned work had been published in a Finnish translation in 1924.[47] In 1926 followed the translation of *Works of Love*.[48] Both were translated by Juho Hollo (1885–1967) who later became a professor in pedagogy. In the end of his *Theory of Pedagogy*, which is still used as a university textbook, Hollo designates love as the basis of all pedagogy. Hollo refers to the chapter "Love Builds Up" and maintains that all the fine perceptions and advice to be found in this chapter and throughout the *Works of Love* should be considered as pure pedagogy. If one substitutes "upbringing" and "to bring up" for Kierkegaard's expressions "upbuilding" and "to build up," the result is an outstanding treatise on one of the most basic phenomena and events in pedagogy.[49] The influence of Kierkegaard is perceptible also in Hollo's treatment of aesthetic and ethical upbringing, humor, and irony.[50] Later, the educationalist and philosopher of education Urpo Harva (1910–94) admitted Kierkegaard among the fifteen greatest philosophers ever in his *Great Thinkers*, a textbook even more widely read than Hollo's.[51] This short introduction to the history of philosophy has served through fifteen editions as a basic textbook in many schools and colleges for four decades. The chapter on Kierkegaard is sympathetic and without serious mistakes.

---

[44]   Kaila himself counted "angst philosophers" such as Kierkegaard among the "pathological cases" (see Ilkka Niiniluoto, "Eino Kaila ja 1950-luku," in *Avoin ja suljettu*, ed. by Anna Makkonen, Helsinki: Suomalaisen Kirjallisuuden Seura 1992, p. 184).

[45]   Eino Kaila, *Inhimillinen tieto*, Helsinki: Otava 1939, pp. 219–20; Georg Henrik von Wright, *Logik, filosofi och språk*, Helsinki: Söderström 1957, pp. 16–19; Jaakko Hintikka, "Suomen filosofisen tutkimuksen tila ja tulevaisuus," in *Ajatus*, vol. 24, 1967, pp. 145–9.

[46]   Erik Ahlman, "Sören Kierkegaard: *Kuolemansairaus*," *Valvoja-Aika*, vol. 2, 1924, pp. 218–21; Erik Ahlman, *Totuudellisuuden probleemi*, Porvoo: WSOY 1929, especially pp. 50–7.

[47]   *Kuolemansairaus* [*The Sickness unto Death*], trans. by Juho Hollo, Porvoo: WSOY 1924.

[48]   *Rakkauden teot* [*Works of Love*], trans. by Juho Hollo, Porvoo: WSOY 1926.

[49]   Juho Hollo, *Kasvatuksen teoria*, Porvoo: WSOY 1927, p. 122.

[50]   Ibid., pp. 101–11.

[51]   Urpo Harva, *Suuria ajattelijoita*, Helsinki: Otava 1955.

In theology the thought of Kierkegaard was approached by Lennart Pinomaa (1901–96).[52] According to Pinomaa personal engagement, being personally interested, is common to the thinking of both Luther and Kierkegaard. In this respect one may well speak of the existential character of Luther's theology: Luther's total view of life and world is existentially determined by the torments of his conscience. Moreover, in both Luther and Kierkegaard despair that endangers the whole of existence occupies a central position, and from despair faith opens up as the only way out. However, Pinomaa points out that despair issues in a different way in the two thinkers. In Luther, despair issues from religious scruples, but in the philosophy of Kierkegaard it issues from epistemological and ethical considerations.[53] Pinomaa's interest in Kierkegaard continued in the 1950s. As professor of systematic theology he gave a course of lectures on Kierkegaard in 1950–51 and again in 1957–58.

Of other theologians, Eelis Gulin (1893–1975), the professor of exegetics, published his translation of the eulogy on Abraham from *Fear and Trembling* in the journal *Teologinen aikakauskirja* in 1942.[54] Jaakko Toivio (1915–2000) published two articles in the same journal, first on Kierkegaard's struggle against the Church, then on the carrying of the burden as a determinant of Kierkegaard's personality.[55] The occasion of the latter article was the publication of the Finnish translation of "The Gospel of Sufferings" from *Upbuilding Discourses in Various Spirits* by Niilo Syvänne (1900–86).[56]

The young theologian Helge Ukkola (1921–93) became thoroughly immersed in Kierkegaard. Ukkola's dissertation, *Existing Man. The Problem of Man as Presented in Søren Kierkegaard's Thought*, is an attempt to give an overview of Kierkegaard's thought by focusing on his conception of man.[57] According to Ukkola, Kierkegaard is, in all of his writings, occupied with the problem of man. For Kierkegaard man as such is not real [*virkelig*] and therefore Kierkegaard's thought is not concerned with being man as such, but with the process of becoming man. By "existing" Kierkegaard refers to the task of becoming a self. The process of existence is described in the light of the idea that man becomes self-conscious in front of God. While the content of Kierkegaard's concepts change and his concepts have even diametrically opposed meanings in different contexts; the inner structure of his thought is, according to

[52]   Lennart Pinomaa, *Der existenzielle Character der Theologie Luthers*, Helsinki: Suomalainen tiedeakatemia 1940.
[53]   Ibid., pp. 7–13. See also Lennart Pinomaa, "Eksistentiaalinen ja teologinen ajattelu," *Teologinen aikakauskirja*, vol. 47, 1941, pp. 236–56.
[54]   "Ylistyspuhe Aabrahamista" [Eulogy on Abraham], trans. by Eelis G. Gulin, *Teologinen aikakauskirja*, vol. 47, 1942, pp. 14–23.
[55]   Jaakko Toivio, "Kierkegaardin taistelu kirkkoa vastaan," *Teologinen aikakauskirja*, vol. 44, 1939, pp. 123–44; Jaakko Toivio, "Kierkegaardin persoonallisuus 'kuormankantamisen' valottamana," *Teologinen aikakauskirja*, vol. 53, 1948, pp. 180–9. Toivio's background was in Evangelical Pietism. He earned his living as a teacher and educationalist.
[56]   *Kärsimysten evankeliumi* ["The Gospel of Sufferings"], trans. by Niilo Syvänne, Porvoo: WSOY 1948. Syvänne was held in esteem both as a practitioner and as a teacher pastoral care in hospitals. His background was in Pietism.
[57]   Helge Ukkola, *Eksistoiva ihminen. Ihmisen ongelma Søren Kierkegaardin ajattelussa*, Helsinki: Suomalainen teologinen kirjallisuusseura 1961.

Ukkola, one entity. The uniformity of Kierkegaard's thought is the result of the basic problem behind all of Kierkegaard's writings, that of becoming a self, i.e., that of becoming a Christian. However, this uniformity cannot be brought out by a mere analysis of the content of Kierkegaard's concepts. The analysis of the concepts must be combined with giving them a certain task in elucidating the existence of man, the process of becoming self-conscious in front of God, the process of becoming a Christian.[58]

Man as described by Kierkegaard is not an autonomic being of philosophic anthropology but a theonomic *homo theologicus*, inevitably dependent on God. Ukkola qualifies Kierkegaard's anthropological conceptions as neither dogmatic-theological nor philosophic-ontological but existential-Christian. Man is meant to be relatively free with the responsibility of choice, but still existing in everything on the basis of the God-relationship. Relationship to God is a factor that inevitably shapes man's existence. God's infinite, eternal and absolute demand for the God-relationship and God-consciousness is hidden in man's existence and therefore the subject is always active, always moving and striving.

Ukkola underscores that Kierkegaard's thought concerns not only objective doctrine but also subjective attitude. The standard of existence is not Christianity as such, but the deepening of the attitude of a human being towards the content of his life and the "how" of becoming Christian which expresses the content of Christianity. Therefore Kierkegaard's thought must not be judged according to the normal principles of dogmatics. From the point of view of the care of souls, Kierkegaard's thinking is a treasure store. Supporting *ecclesia militans* and advocating the real adoption of Christianity, Kierkegaard walked in the footsteps of Martin Luther. According to Ukkola, Kierkegaard certainly cannot be understood if his polemical inferences are taken to be his doctrine of faith, as Torsten Bohlin (1889–1950) took them. Kierkegaard is a unique guide, when it comes to the dialectical understanding of Christianity and the problems of man's existing and striving. He who, even as a scholar, is satisfied with being a mere individual existing human being will learn from Kierkegaard to understand his problem and being.

Ukkola had some problems in getting his dissertation accepted. The first version of it was turned down, the final one received a low mark *(lubenter approbatur)*.[59]

---

[58]   Ukkola claims that as a basis of his analyses the researcher must have a synthetic-intuitive total-view. The validity of his results, however, is decided in part by his own inner evidence. Here Ukkola argues against G.H. von Wright, a representative of analytical philosophy, who had stamped the philosophy of Kierkegaard as "subjectivism that can only be lived through, not explained." Ukkola claims that a scholar must aim at a scientific explanation, but in evaluating its results he cannot give up his own inner evidence (ibid., p. 12, n1). Ukkola criticizes also the method of motive research practiced by Valter Lindström and other representatives of Lundian theology (ibid., pp. 18–19).

[59]   In his official statement, professor Lauri Haikola (1917–87), himself a follower of Lundian theology, criticizes Ukkola's unscientific, subjectivistic view of knowledge, his categorical judgments on the work of other scholars, his unclear and often entangled language, his lack of genuine discussion with other scholars and his lack of critical distance to the research object Kierkegaard (The Minutes of the Faculty of Theology, Archives of University

The reception of the dissertation reportedly embittered Ukkola's life.[60] He did not give up doing research, however, but published a number of monographs, in most of which the ideas of Kierkegaard are examined. Most notable of these is perhaps *Love for One's Neighbor in the Thought of Søren Kierkegaard.*[61] For his research, Ukkola received support from the Society for Theological Research in which he was himself the central figure.[62] He ended up being an instructor of philosophical anthropology at the University of Tampere. Since the studies of Ukkola, only Master's Theses have been written on Kierkegaard in academic theology.

During the Kierkegaard renaissance and existential vogue from the 1920s to 1950s numerous more popular theological writings on Kierkegaard were published in newspapers, essay collections, theological journals, and literary magazines. Among the contributors were professors (Arvi Grotenfelt, Olof Enckell, Rafael Gyllemberg, Valter Lindström, Lennart Pinomaa) priests (Jaakko Toivio, Lauri Pohjanpää), and bishops (Max von Bonsdorff, Eino Sormunen).

With regard to literary authors, interest in Kierkegaard was show by Ragnar Rudolf Eklund (1895–1946) who published his Kierkegaard reflections in the magazine *Nya Argus* in 1920.[63] Also the first prose works by Kerttu-Kaarina Suosalmi (1921–2001), *Sin* and *Virgin*, reflect strong Kierkegaard influence.[64] A strong enthusiasm about Kierkegaard is shown by Pentti Saarikoski (1937–83), one of the most celebrated figures of postwar Finnish literature.[65] In his posthumous diaries from the years 1953–57, Kierkegaard and Kierkegaardian ideas come up again and again. On May 3, 1956 the future poet writes: "At the moment Kierkegaard's thoughts are to me nourishment such as I couldn't do without....For three years I have conversed with him, and it seems to me that the more I draw from the sea, the more it expands. I lust for his words. I love his sentences. I desire to kiss the yellowed pages of his books."[66] With Kierkegaard the young Saarikoski tries to approach true Christianity as a single

---

of Helsinki). At least part of the critique is without doubt justified: the language of Ukkola is, indeed, unclear and entangled.

[60]   Oral information from Elias Muilu, who knew Ukkola and his wife personally. Ukkola had difficulties in human relationships and in working life as a priest and teacher. He tended to be violent.

[61]   Helge Ukkola, *Lähimmäisenrakkaus Søren Kierkegaardin ajattelussa*, Helsinki: Suomalainen teologinen kirjallisuusseura 1964.

[62]   In the preface of one of his books Ukkola calls this society the *Finnish Søren Kierkegaard Society* (see Helge Ukkola, *Ihmisestä on kysymys*, Tampere: Tampereen yliopisto 1983, p. 5).

[63]   Ragnar Rudolf Eklund, "Kierkegaard-reflexioner," *Nya Argus*, vol. 13, no. 16–17, 1920, pp. 137–8.

[64]   Kerttu-Kaarina Suosalmi, *Synti*, Helsinki: Otava 1957; Kerttu-Kaarina Suosalmi, *Neitsyt*, Helsinki: Otava 1964. Suosalmi has told of this influence in a lecture "How My Works Have Come Into Being," see *Miten kirjani ovat syntyneet*, vol. 2, ed. by Ritva Haavikko, Porvoo: WSOY 1980, pp. 179ff.

[65]   Saarikoski has apparently received as schoolboy a motivation to study Kierkegaard from his Swedish teacher Kalle Sorainen, see Pentti Saarikoski, *Asiaa tai ei*, Helsinki: Otava 1980, pp. 123–4.

[66]   Pentti Saarikoski, *Nuoruuden päiväkirjat*, Helsinki: Otava 1984, p. 399.

individual. He detests the hypocritical Church and the theologians who try to make Kierkegaard into a pious and conformist Lutheran, "a mixer of syrup."[67] Saarikoski rebels against the spiritless bourgeoisie and detests its collective illusions. He devotes himself to the dialectics of the paradoxical truth that prefers a prostitute to a philistine, assumes the mask of a clown and plunges into his own, private anxiety.[68] Later, in the beginning of the 1960s, dialectical materialism and its optimism took the place of mystic and desperate existentialism in the heart of Saarikoski. Now Saarikoski states that typical for the works of Kierkegaard is "terrible melancholy that is refracted into, at its worst, pathological irony, strained rigorism, romantic and cold individualism." Kierkegaard's attitude toward life now turns out to be "romantic and wrong"; Kierkegaard himself is "one of the most obvious masochists in world literature."[69] One could claim, however, that Saarikoski, as a personality, retained many similarities with Kierkegaard through his Marxist period, and in his last years he apparently again felt closer to Kierkegaard and Christianity.[70]

III. 1963–2005

In the collective and scientific spirit of the 1960s and 1970s there seems to have been precious little room for the advocate of personal inwardness and subjectivity. A translation of *The Concept of Anxiety* came out in 1964.[71] The work was done by psychologists Eila and Johan Weckroth, but there are no other traces of Kierkegaard interest within the subject of psychology. In theology, besides the works by Ukkola, there were studies on Kierkegaard only at the undergraduate level. In philosophy, professors worked strictly within the analytical tradition while a large and active part of the students was interested in Marxism.

In the first half of the 1980s analytical philosopher Ingmar Pörn (b. 1935) published two articles on Kierkegaard. In these articles Pörn, who had taken an interest in Kierkegaard as a student in the 1950s, adapts Kierkegaard's ideas to the analytical theory of action and the self.[72]

At the beginning of the 1980s the young analytical philosopher Esa Saarinen (b. 1953) became interested in the phenomenon of punk rock and wanted to bring some of its spirit into academic philosophy. The "punk doctor" Saarinen did not hesitate to appear polemically in the media, and he soon became a celebrity. Next he turned to existentialism and wrote a book on Sartre; then he wrote a series of

---

[67]   Ibid., p. 128; pp. 137–8; p. 248.
[68]   Ibid., pp. 78–9; p. 104; p. 157; p. 167; pp. 169–71; p. 269. See also Pauliina Arola, *Nuori Saarikoski etsii itseään*, Master's Thesis, University of Helsinki 2000.
[69]   Pentti Saarikoski, "Kierkegaardista," *Parnasso*, vol. 10, no. 6, 1960, p. 277.
[70]   See Torsti Lehtinen, *Hyvän ja pahan tällä puolen*, Helsinki: Kirjapaja 1991, pp. 85–91.
[71]   *Ahdistus* [*The Concept of Anxiety*], trans. by Eila and Johan Weckroth, Jyväskylä: Gummerus 1964.
[72]   Ingmar Pörn, "On the Dialectic of the Soul: An Essay on Kierkegaard," in *Essays in Philosophical Analysis*, ed. by Ingmar Pörn, Helsinki: Societas Philosophica Fennica 1981 (*Acta Philosophica Fennica*, vol. 32), pp. 198–210; Ingmar Pörn, "Kierkegaard and the Study of the Self," *Inquiry*, no. 27, 1984, pp. 199–205.

other books. In 1985 he published his *A History of Western Philosophy from Top to Top, from Socrates to Marx*.[73] One of the 16 star philosophers whom Saarinen presents with energy and enthusiasm in this bestseller is Kierkegaard,[74] the extreme subjectivist who takes his reader to the border of the irrational and beyond. Saarinen portraits Kierkegaard as a proto-existentialist for whom abstract, objective truth was not enough, for whom the only meaningful truth was "the truth for me." Kierkegaard fixed philosophy in the existing subject, and for Kierkegaard philosophy was action, not theory. According to Saarinen, he was the first to discover the difference between existence and authentic existence, and did not hesitate to choose the latter.

In 1990 the public came to know a discipline of Saarinen, Heidi Liehu (b. 1967) who defended her doctoral thesis, entitled *Kierkegaard's Theory of Stages and Its Relation to Hegel*.[75] After the event, the chairman of the public defense, professor Ilkka Niiniluoto wrote a report on the event to the Historico-Linguistic Faculty: "The public defense of the doctoral thesis of the 22-year-old Heidi Liehu was a media event rare of its kind in university. Because of the prior sensation, the event was scheduled to take place in Porthania Hall II [which is a very large lecture hall]. And indeed, there were up to 300 interested listeners, among them the deacons of Historico-Philological and of Theological Faculty, members of the Finnish Academy, emeritus professors, students, authors, artists and reporters. The buzz of TV- and video cameras accompanied the beginning of the event at 10.15; the photographers continued their ceaseless and at times irritating snapping until 11.10."[76]

In her dissertation, Liehu analyzes the theory of stages as the main theme of Kierkegaard's philosophy and shows how Kierkegaard's view of man provides the structural framework for this theory. Thirdly, she examines systematically the connections between the theory of stages and the philosophy of Hegel.

Liehu examines in detail Kierkegaard's theory of stages and shows point by point how it is in opposition with Hegel's philosophy—how Kierkegaard used the ideas he appropriated from Hegel against Hegel. Both Hegel's criticism of Romantic aesthetism and his description of ethics are transformed in Kierkegaard's hands into a criticism against Hegel himself. The critique Hegel had directed against Romanticism is directed against Hegel's system: just as a romantic daydreamer, a Hegelian speculator forgets his concrete existence and fails to focus on his personal life. On the other hand, Judge William, the adherent to the Hegelian conception of universal *Sittlichkeit* ethics, slides little by little in the direction of the aesthetic stage. Transforming desire into duty, he is a parody of a truly ethical man. At the stage of religion, Kierkegaard's critique of Hegel bursts forth in all its strength. For Hegel, religion as an objective institution transcends the role of irrational and subjective faith, whereas for Kierkegaard, it is precisely faith that transcends religion and is

---

[73]   Esa Saarinen, *Länsimaisen filosofian historia huipulta huipulle, Sokrateesta Marxiin*, Porvoo: WSOY 1985.

[74]   By 2004 the book had been reprinted eight times and it had sold over 21,000 copies, a huge amount for a philosophical work in a small country like Finland.

[75]   Heidi Liehu, *Kierkegaard's Theory of Stages and Its Relation to Hegel*, Helsinki: Societas Philosophica Fennica 1990 (*Acta Philosophica Fennica*, vol. 47).

[76]   Archives of the Department of Philosophy, University of Helsinki.

given the leading role. Moreover, Kierkegaardian dialectics is turned against the Hegelian: the dialectical transitions between the different spheres are not necessary and conceptual, but depend on man's will and choice.

According to Liehu, the views of Hegel and Kierkegaard on the relationship between God and man differ essentially from each other. For Hegel, spirit is the unity of polarities, their mediation; for example, finitude and infinitude are identical, for neither would exist without the other. Thus a finite man becomes authentically self-conscious when he becomes conscious of himself as a part of the infinite spirit, and at the same time as a vehicle for the self-consciousness of this world spirit. On the contrary, Kierkegaard emphasizes throughout his corpus the absolute difference between man and God. According to Kierkegaard finitude and infinitude are not mediated, but remain distinct. This difference reflects the Christian pathos of Kierkegaard's philosophy. Only faith realizes man as a "positive third" between the opposite components of the synthesis, and in this way man becomes infinite and eternal only by God's help. Christ, the object of faith, is not the rational mediation of temporality and eternity, and of humanity and divinity, he is the Absolute Paradox.

In his statement, the opponent *ex officio*, professor Mark C. Taylor praised the "extremely ambitious and uncommonly insightful study" by Ms. Liehu. Taylor extols "Ms. Liehu's sophisticated grasp of the secondary literature." According to Taylor, Ms. Liehu "has surveyed works of Hegel, Kierkegaard, and the relationship between Hegel and Kierkegaard with extreme care. Her readings of these studies are accurate and suggestive." "In sum," Taylor concludes, "Ms. Liehu's dissertation is an original and significant scholarly contribution. I am confident that it will be received by the international scholarly community. It should be widely reviewed and discussed. Moreover, future studies of Hegel and Kierkegaard will have to take into account the contribution that Ms. Liehu has made. This is a work of lasting significance."[77] After her dissertation, Heidi Liehu went to Paris where she studied under Jacques Derrida. She has published works of poetry, novels, and feminist philosophy. She maintains that Kierkegaard is there behind all that she does, but she has not continued academic research on Kierkegaard for the time being.

During the most recent years the most prominent Kierkegaard interpreter in Finland has been Torsti Lehtinen (b. 1942). Lehtinen is a versatile writer who has produced novels, poetry, drama, translations, and books on philosophy. As a young man, Lehtinen lived in Copenhagen and came to know Danish. While studying philosophy at the University of Helsinki, he became attracted to existentialism. Behind all the philosophers of existence there loomed the figure of Kierkegaard and so Lehtinen became absorbed in his works.

In 1988, Lehtinen published his translation of "Diapsalmata," which sold so well that it has appeared in a second edition.[78] In 1990, he published the first Finnish Kierkegaard biography *Søren Kierkegaard, the Philosopher of Passion, Anxiety and*

---

[77]   Archives of the Department of Philosophy, University of Helsinki.

[78]   *Välisoittoja* ["Diapsalmata"], trans. by Torsti Lehtinen, Helsinki: Kirjapaja 1988 (2nd ed., Helsinki: Kirjapaja 1997).

Humor.[79] This compact and vivid introduction into the philosopher of the stages of existence has been reprinted three times. In 1992 he published his translation of *Concluding Unscientific Postscript,* which by the year 2004 had gone through altogether four editions and sold almost 6,000 copies.[80] In 1996 came out a translation of "In vino veritas,"[81] and in 2001, a translation of *Fear and Trembling.*[82] Lehtinen has also translated the popular introduction into Kierkegaard by Peter Thielst, *Livet forstås baglæns, men må leves forlæns,* published in 1999. He has discussed Kierkegaard in his essays and articles, on many public occasions, in the media, and in his recent study *Existentialism, the Philosophy of Freedom.*[83] For Lehtinen philosophy is art, life itself is the best academy and Kierkegaard, the philosopher of passion and freedom who lived through his own philosophy, a matchless interpreter of life.

Of the other Kierkegaard scholars, the philosopher Jyrki Kivelä (b. 1962) has studied the connections between the philosophers of faith, Hume, Hamann, and Kierkegaard in his licentiate dissertation.[84] In the study of literature Leena Eilittä (b. 1959) has examined Kierkegaard's influence on Kafka in her *Approaches to Personal Identity in Kafka's Short Fiction: Freud, Darwin, Kierkegaard.*[85] Olli Mäkinen (b. 1953) has translated *Repetition* and the essay "The Immediate Erotic Stages" from *Either/Or.*[86] The translations also make up one chapter in Mäkinen's doctoral dissertation entitled *The Modern, Repetition and Irony. Søren Kierkegaard's Aesthetic Aspects and Joseph Heller's "Catch-22."*[87] In his dissertation, Mäkinen studies Kierkegaard as a modernist and interprets modernism in the light of Kierkegaard's philosophy. The themes of movement, repetition, leveling, fascinating illusions, simulation, pretence, and the ironic style are Kierkegaard's points of contact with literary modernism, maintains Mäkinen. Mäkinen wants to demonstrate that Kierkegaard can be interpreted as a pre-modernist and that a Kierkegaardian interpretation of Heller's *Catch-22* is valid and possible.

---

[79]   Torsti Lehtinen, *Søren Kierkegaard, intohimon, ahdistuksen ja huumorin filosofi,* Helsinki: Kirjapaja 1990.

[80]   *Päättävä epätieteellinen jälkikirjoitus* [*Concluding Unscientific Postscript*], trans. by Torsti Lehtinen, Porvoo: WSOY 1992 (several later editions).

[81]   *In vino veritas,* trans. by Torsti Lehtinen, Porvoo: WSOY 1996.

[82]   *Pelko ja vavistrus* [*Fear and Trembling*], trans. by Torsti Lehtinen, Porvoo: WSOY 2001.

[83]   Torsti Lehtinen, *Eksistentialismi, vapauden filosofia,* Helsinki: Kirjapaja 2002.

[84]   Jyrki Kivelä, *Uskon filosofit: Hume, Hamann, Kierkegaard,* Licentiate Thesis, University of Helsinki 1996.

[85]   Leena Eilittä, *Approaches to Personal Identity in Kafka's Short Fiction: Freud, Darwin, Kierkegaard,* Helsinki: Academica Scientiarum Fennica 1999 (*Suomalaisen tiedeakatemian toimituksia, Series Humaniora,* vol. 302).

[86]   *Toisto* [*Repetition*], trans. by Olli Mäkinen, Jyväskylä: Atena 2001; *Mozart-esseet* ["The Immediate Erotic Stages"], trans. by Olli Mäkinen, Helsinki: Like 2002.

[87]   Olli Mäkinen, *Moderni, toisto ja ironia. Søren Kierkegaardin estetiikan aspekteja ja Joseph Hellerin "Catch-22,"* Oulu: Oulun yliopisto 2004 (*Acta Universitatis Ouluensis, Series B,* vol. 55).

Of the younger scholars, the philosopher Janne Kylliäinen (b. 1969) has published a translation of the *Philosophical Fragments*[88] and the first article in Finnish to discuss Kierkegaard's political views.[89] The philosopher Annika Eronen (b. 1977) has published an article on Kierkegaard's and Wittgenstein's views on ethics and religious knowledge.[90] The theologian Olli-Pekka Vainio (b. 1976) has published an article on Kierkegaard's adherence to the Christian dogma[91] and a monograph on Kierkegaard as a theologian.[92]

Although there have been no public sensations comparable to the one raised by the dissertation of Heidi Liehu, one may claim that at the moment interest in Kierkegaard is on the rise in Finland.

---

[88]   *Filosofisia muruja* [*Philosophical Fragments*], trans. by Janne Kylliäinen, Helsinki: Summa 2003.

[89]   Janne Kylliäinen, "Kierkegaardin (anti)poliittinen ajattelu," *Tiede & edistys*, vol. 30, no. 3, 2005, pp. 140–57.

[90]   Annika Eronen, "Etiikan ja uskonnollisen tiedon luonne Wittgensteinin ja Kierkegaardin mukaan," in *Filosofinen tieto ja filosofin taito*, ed. by Petri Räsänen and Marika Tuohimaa, Tampere: Tampere University Press 2003 (*Acta Philosophica Tamperiensis*, vol. 2), pp. 148–60.

[91]   Olli-Pekka Vainio, *"Fides qua, fides quae?* Søren Kierkegaard ja uskon propositionaalinen sisältö," *Teologinen aikakauskirja*, vol. 108, no. 3, 2003, pp. 215–24.

[92]   Olli-Pekka Vainio, *Sören Kierkegaardin teologia*, Helsinki: Kirjapaja 2004.

Bibliography

I. Finnish Translations of Kierkegaard's Works

Publikaani ["The Tax Collector"], trans. n.n., Savonlinna: Etelä-Savon kirjapaino 1898.

Syntinen vaimo ["The Woman Who Was a Sinner"], trans. n.n., Savonlinna: Etelä-Savon kirjapaino 1898.

Itsensä koettelemiseksi [*For Self-Examination*], trans. by Gustaf Adolf Heman, *Sören Kierkegaardin teoksia*, vol. 1–2, Porvoo: WSOY 1907, vol. 1.

Viettelijän päiväkirja ["The Seducer's Diary"], trans. by Veikko Antero Koskenniemi, *Sören Kierkegaardin teoksia*, vol. 1–2, Porvoo: WSOY 1907 vol. 2 (2nd revised ed., 1960; 3rd ed., 1989).

Viettelijän päiväkirja ["The Seducer's Diary"], trans. by Siimes Kanervio, Tampere: Sulo Toivonen 1907.

"Søren Kierkegaardin lauselmia" [Lines from "Diapsalmata"], trans. by Veikko Antero Koskenniemi, *Aika*, vol. 3, 1909, pp. 644–6.

Kedon kukka ja taivaan lintu [*The Lily in the Field and the Bird of the Air*], trans. by Heikki Linnove, Porvoo: WSOY 1915 (2nd revised ed., 1939; 3rd ed., 1990).

Kuolemansairaus [*The Sickness unto Death*], trans. by Juho Hollo, Porvoo: WSOY 1924.

Rakkauden teot [*Works of Love*], trans. by Juho Hollo, Porvoo: WSOY 1926.

"Ylistyspuhe Aabrahamista" [Eulogy on Abraham], trans. by Eelis G. Gulin, in *Teologinen aikakauskirja*, vol. 47, 1942, pp. 14–23.

Kärsimysten evankeliumi ["The Gospel of Sufferings"], trans. by Niilo Syvänne, Porvoo: WSOY 1948.

Ahdistus [*The Concept of Anxiety*], trans. by Eila and Johan Weckroth, Jyväskylä: Gummerus: 1964.

Välisoittoja ["Diapsalmata"], trans. by Torsti Lehtinen, Helsinki: Kirjapaja 1988 (2nd ed., 1997).

Päättävä epätieteellinen jälkikirjoitus [*Concluding Unscientific Postscript*], trans. by Torsti Lehtinen, Porvoo: WSOY 1992 (several later editions).

In vino veritas, trans. by Torsti Lehtinen, Porvoo: WSOY 1996.

Pelko ja vavistus [*Fear and Trembling*], trans. by Torsti Lehtinen, Porvoo: WSOY 2001.

Toisto [*Repetition*], trans. by Olli Mäkinen, Jyväskylä: Atena 2001.

Mozart-esseet ["The Immediate Erotic Stages"], trans. by Olli Mäkinen, Helsinki: Like 2002.

Filosofisia muruja [*Philosophical Fragments*], trans. by Janne Kylliäinen, Helsinki: Summa 2003.

II. Secondary Literature on Søren Kierkegaard in Finland

Ahlman, Erik, "Sören Kierkegaard: *Kuolemansairaus*" [Sören Kierkegaard: *The Sickness unto Death*], *Valvoja-Aika*, vol. 2, 1924, pp. 218–21.

Eilittä, Leena, *Approaches to Personal Identity in Kafka's Short Fiction: Freud, Darwin, Kierkegaard*, Helsinki: Academica Scientiarum Fennica 1999 (*Suomalaisen tiedeakatemian toimituksia, Series Humaniora*, vol. 302).

Eronen, Annika, "Etiikan ja uskonnollisen tiedon luonne Wittgensteinin ja Kierkegaardin mukaan" [The Nature of Ethics and Religious Knowledge According to Wittgenstein and Kierkegaard], in *Filosofin tieto ja filosofinen taito*, ed. by Petri Räsänen and Marika Tuohimaa, Tampere: Tampere University Press 2003 (*Acta Philosophica Tamperiensis*, vol. 2), pp. 347–55.

Kihlman, Erik, *Ur Ibsen-dramatikens idéhistoria* [On the History of Ideas of Ibsen's Dramatic Art], Helsinki: Söderström 1921.

Kivelä, Jyrki, *Uskon filosofit: Hume, Hamann, Kierkegaard* [The Philosophers of Faith: Hume, Hamann, Kierkegaard], Licentiate Thesis, University of Helsinki 1996.

Kylliäinen, Janne, "Kierkegaardin (anti)poliittinen ajattelu" [Kierkegaard's (Anti)political Thought], *Tiede & edistys*, vol. 30, no. 3, 2005, pp. 140–57.

Lagerborg, Rolf, "I vad mån är Sören Kierkegaard egnad att stöda känslosamma riktningar på det religiösa området?" [To What Extent is Søren Kierkegaard Fit for Defending Emotional Tendencies within the Sphere of Religion?], in *Festskrift tillägnad Vitalis Norström*, Gothenburg: Wettergren & Gerber 1916, pp. 347–55.

— "Synpunkter på Sören Kierkegaard" [Points of View on Søren Kierkegaard], *Arkiv för psykologi och pedagogik*, vol. 1, 1922, pp. 185–202; vol. 2, 1923, pp. 174–87.

Lehtinen, Torsti, *Søren Kierkegaard, intohimon, ahdistuksen ja huumorin filosofi* [Søren Kierkegaard, a Philosopher of Passion, Anxiety and Humor], Helsinki: Kirjapaja 1990.

— "Paradoksin käsite Søren Kierkegaardin ajattelussa" [The Concept of Paradox in the Thought of Søren Kierkegaard], *Teologinen aikakauskirja*, vol. 102, no. 1, 1997, pp. 11–25.

Liehu, Heidi, *Søren Kierkegaardin teoria ihmisen eksistensitasoista* [Søren Kierkegaard's Theory of the Stages of Human Existence], Helsinki: Helsingin yliopisto 1989 (*Reports from the Department of Philosophy, University of Helsinki*, vol. 2).

— *Kierkegaard's Theory of Stages and Its Relation to Hegel*, Helsinki: Societas Philosophica Fennica 1990 (*Acta Philosophica Fennica*, vol. 47).

— "Kierkegaard ja kolmen tason tunteet" [Kierkegaard and the Passions in Three Stages], in *Tunteet*, ed. by Ilkka Niiniluoto and Juha Räikkä, Helsinki: Yliopistopaino 1996, pp. 65–76.

Linnove, Heikki, "Piirteitä Sören Kierkegaardin elämänkatsomuksesta" [Aspects of Søren Kierkegaard's Life-View], *Aika*, vol. 2, 1908, pp. 862–8; pp. 917–22.

Mäkinen, Olli, *Moderni, toisto ja ironia. Søren Kierkegaardin estetiikan aspekteja ja Joseph Hellerin "Catch-22"* [The Modern, Repetition and Irony. Søren Kierkegaard's Aesthetic Aspects and Joseph Heller's *Catch-22*], Oulu: Oulun yliopisto 2004 (*Acta Universitatis Ouluensis, Series B*, vol. 55).

Oravala, Aukusti, "Sören Aabye Kierkegaard," *Vartija*, vol. 26, 1913, pp. 150–7.

Pinomaa, Lennart, "Eksistentiaalinen ja teologinen ajattelu" [Existential and Theological Thinking], *Teologinen aikakauskirja*, vol. 46, 1941, pp. 236–56.

Pörn, Ingmar, "On the Dialectic of the Soul: An Essay on Kierkegaard," in *Essays in Philosophical Analysis*, ed. by Ingmar Pörn, Helsinki: Societas Philosophica Fennica 1981 (*Acta Philosophica Fennica*, vol. 32), pp. 198–210.

— "Kierkegaard and the Study of the Self," *Inquiry*, no. 27, 1984, pp. 199–205.

Pulkkinen, Antti J., "Sören Kierkegaard," *Vartija*, vol. 24, 1911, pp. 231–46.

Råbergh, Herman, "Sören Kierkegaards Person och författareskap; ett försök af W. Rudin" [The Personality and Authorship of Søren Kierkegaard; an Essay by W. Rudin], *Tidskrift för teologi och kyrka*, vol. 4, 1880, pp. 231–4.

Saarikoski, Pentti, "Kierkegaardista" [On Kierkegaard], *Parnasso*, vol. 10, no. 6, 1960, pp. 276–7.

Saastamoinen, Tyyne, "Elävä ja kuollut Kierkegaard" [The Living and the Dead Kierkegaard], *Parnasso*, vol. 6, no. 1, 1956, pp. 24–8.

Sandelin, (Sorainen), Kalle, "Geijerin ja Kierkegaardin persoonallisuusaate" [The Idea of Personality in Geijer and Kierkegaard], *Ajatus. Filosofisen yhdistyksen vuosikirja*, vol. 2, 1927, pp. 131–40.

— *Søren Kierkegaardin persoonallisuusaatteen kehittyminen Tanskan filosofisten virtausten yhteydessä viime vuosisadan alkupuolella* [The Development of Søren Kierkegaard's Idea of Personality in Connection with the Danish Philosophical Currents of the Early Nineteenth Century], Pori: Satakunnan kirjateollisuus 1927.

Sorainen, Kalle, "Kierkegaard kasvattajana" [Kierkegaard as a Pedagogue], *Kasvatus ja koulu*, vol. 23, 1943, pp. 173–9.

— "Kierkegaard och Høffding" [Kierkegaard and Høffding], in *Eros och Eris. Kulturessäer tillägnade professor Rolf Lagerborg*, ed. by The Westermarck Society, Helsinki: Söderström 1944, pp. 266–85.

— "Kierkegaard und Leibniz" [Kierkegaard and Leibniz], *Ajatus. Filosofisen yhdistyksen vuosikirja*, vol. 17, 1952, pp. 177–86.

— "Kierkegaard kirjallisuudentutkijana" [Kierkegaard as a Student of Literature], in *Sydänpäivä. Juhlakirja Aarne Anttilalle*, ed. by Rafael Koskimies and Sulo Haltsonen, Helsinki: Suomalaisen Kirjallisuuden Seura, 1952 (*Kirjallisuudentutkijain seuran vuosikirja*, vol. 12), pp. 225–37.

Toivio, Jaakko, "Kierkegaardin taistelu kirkkoa vastaan" [Kierkegaard's Struggle against the Church], *Teologinen aikakauskirja*, vol. 44, 1939, pp. 123–44.

— "Kierkegaardin persoonallisuus 'kuormankantamisen' valottamana" [Kierkegaard's Personality in the Light of the 'Carrying of the Burden'], *Teologinen aikakauskirja*, vol. 53, 1948, pp. 180–9.

Ukkola, Helge, *Eksistoiva ihminen. Ihmisen ongelma Søren Kierkegaardin ajattelussa* [Existing Man. The Problem of Man as Presented in Søren Kierkegaard's Thought], Helsinki: Suomalainen teologinen kirjallisuusseura 1961 (*Suomalaisen teologisen kirjallisuusseuran julkaisuja*, vol. 71).

— "Kierkegaard ja jälkimaailma" [Kierkegaard and Posterity], *Teologinen aikakauskirja*, vol. 66, 1961, pp. 159–66.

— *Lähimmäisenrakkaus Søren Kierkegaardin ajattelussa* [Love for One's Neighbor in the Thought of Søren Kierkegaard], Helsinki: Suomalainen teologinen kirjallisuusseura 1964 (*Suomalaisen teologisen kirjallisuusseuran julkaisuja*, vol. 75).

— "Eros ja agape Søren Kierkegaardin ajattelussa" [Eros and Agape in the Thought of Søren Kierkegaard], in *Rakkauden filosofia*, ed. by Esa Saarinen, Lilli Alanen and Ilkka Niiniluoto, Porvoo: WSOY 1984, pp. 182–97.

— "Søren Kierkegaardin eksistentiaalinen dialektiikka" [Søren Kierkegaard's Existential Dialectics], *Teologinen aikakauskirja*, vol. 93, 1988, pp. 392–6.

Vainio, Olli-Pekka, *"Fides qua, fides quae?* Søren Kierkegaard ja uskon propositionaalinen sisältö" [*Fides qua, fides quae?* Søren Kierkegaard and the Propositional Content of Faith], *Teologinen aikauskirja*, vol. 108, no. 3, 2003, pp. 215–24.

— *Sören Kierkegaardin teologia* [Søren Kierkegaard's Theology], Helsinki: Kirjapaja 2004.

Wegelius, Martin, "Georg Brandes: *Sören Kierkegaard,*" *Finsk Tidskrift*, no. 2, 1878, pp. 64–7.

III. Secondary Literature on Kierkegaard's Reception in Finland

Hamberg, Lars, "Søren Kierkegaard i Finland" [Søren Kierkegaard in Finland], *Meddelelser fra Søren Kierkegaard Selskabet*, no. 4, 1952, pp. 125–8.

Sorainen, Kalle, "Kierkegaard och Finland" [Kierkegaard and Finland], *Kierkegaardiana*, vol. 2, 1957, pp. 61–9.

— "Finland," in *Kierkegaard Research*, ed. by Niels Thulstrup and Maria Mikulová Thulstrup, Copenhagen: C.A. Reitzel 1985 (*Bibliotheca Kierkegaardiana*, vol. 15), pp. 125–33.

Ukkola, Helge, *Eksistoiva ihminen. Ihmisen ongelma Søren Kierkegaardin ajattelussa* [Existing Man. The Problem of Man as Presented in Søren Kierkegaard's Thought], Helsinki: Suomalainen teologinen kirjallisuusseura 1961 (*Suomalaisen teologisen kirjallisuusseuran julkaisuja*, vol. 71), pp. 20–2.

— *Romantiikan vanavedessä: eksistentialismi, ekspressonismi* [In the Wake of Romanticism: Existentialism, Expressionism], Tampere: Tampereen yliopisto 1973 (*Acta universitatis Tamperensis*, vol. 150), pp. 147–50.

Iceland:

"Neglect and Misunderstanding": The Reception of Kierkegaard in Iceland

Vilhjálmur Árnason

This article is divided into two main parts. In the first part, the reception of Kierkegaard by Icelanders living in Copenhagen is described. The critique of Kierkegaard by an Icelandic theologian, Magnús Eiríksson, and Kierkegaard's response, is briefly described. In the second part, the reception of Kierkegaard in Iceland is discussed mainly in the light of publications of Kierkegaard's works and writings about them, academic teaching about Kierkegaard and his influences upon theology, philosophy, and literature in Iceland in the nineteenth and twentieth century.

I. In Copenhagen

Iceland was part of the Danish kingdom in the nineteenth century, and Copenhagen was thus the capital of Iceland. There was no university in Iceland until 1911, and so before that most students sought their university education in Copenhagen. Many of these students knew of Kierkegaard and were even acquainted with him. Among these were the so-called "Fjölnismenn," a group of four students who published the journal *Fjölnir* about Icelandic language, culture, and politics. As most other Icelandic students in Copenhagen in the nineteenth century, the Fjölnismenn were preoccupied with matters related to Iceland's independence.[1] But they were also interested in theological matters and followed the theological debates in Denmark at the time. At the instigation of Þorgeir Guðmundsson (1794–1871), an Icelandic pastor in Lolland, they translated Jakob Peter Mynster's *Reflections on the Christian Doctrine of Faith* into Icelandic in 1839.[2] Mynster's book became very popular

 I thank Óttar Norðfjörð for research assistance, Kristján Árnason, Sigurbjörn Einarsson, Ástráður Eysteinsson, Aðalgeir Kristjánsson, Einar Sigurbjörnsson, and Jóhanna Þráinsdóttir for providing valuable information. Thanks are also due to the University of Iceland Research Fund for grant enabling this research.
[1]   See Aðalgeir Kristjánsson, *Nú heilsar þér á Hafnarslóð: ævir og örlög í höfuðborg Íslands 1800–1850* [Copenhagen Greets you Now: Lives and Destinies in the Capital of Iceland 1800–1850], Reykjavík: Nýja bókafélagið 1999.
[2]   Jakob Peter Mynster, *Hugleiðingar um höfuðatriði kristinnar trúar* [*Betragtninger over de christelige Troeslærdomme*, vols. 1–2, Copenhagen: Gyldendalske Boghandels Forlag

in Iceland. Although the Fjölnismenn sometimes mention Kierkegaard in private letters, there are no indications that they introduced Kierkegaard's ideas to Icelandic readers.

Later, one member of the "Fjölnismenn" group, the poet and natural scientist Jónas Hallgrímsson (1807–45) seems to have distanced himself from Mynster's theology. Incidentally, in his poem "The Pipit" ["Grátittlingurinn"], which was first presented in February 1843,[3] he draws upon the example of Abraham, the subject matter of Kierkegaard's *Fear and Trembling*, which was published that same year. "In this poem," the English translator, Dick Ringler, writes, "Jónas reacts sharply against the conception of God that informs the story of Abraham and Isaac in the Old Testament....Jónas insists that the behavior of human beings, at their best, is governed by spontaneous compassionate impulses toward their fellow creatures; also that God is a God of love and compassion." Hence:

> Out in Iceland, a little
> ardent boy could hardly
> aim at imitating
> Abraham's brave behavior.[4]

Although this poem cannot be regarded as a reaction to Kierkegaard's rendering of the Abraham's story in *Fear and Trembling*, the poet, as Páll Valsson points out, is clearly reacting to contemporary theological discussions arising from the difficulty of reconciling the demands of obedience in the Old Testament and the unquestioning love of the New.[5] There is no doubt that the poet Hallgrímsson knew of Kierkegaard; in the year 1843 he signs one of his letters "Victor Eremita," the author of *Either/Or*.[6]

The general attitude of Icelandic students towards Kierkegaard, however, seems to have been one of curiosity but indifference. A little story told by Jón Helgason (1866–1942), bishop in Iceland 1917–38, in an article in memory of his father's centennial is telling in this regard. Helgason writes about his father's student years in Copenhagen:

> He heard Søren Kierkegaard preach at least once, in the Castle Church, but without being impressed by this spiritual giant [*andlega stórmenni*] at the pulpit. In general, his reaction was similar to that of most students in those days, not understanding Kierkegaard; in addition, his attacks upon the church and teachings of the times must have made it difficult

---

1837] (the translators are not mentioned), ed. by Þorgeir Guðmundsson (priest in Gloslunde and Græshave), Copenhagen: Brunnich 1839. On this see Páll Valsson, *Jónas Hallgrímsson. Ævisaga* [Jónas Hallgrímsson. A Biography], Reykjavík: Mál og menning 1997, pp. 204–5.

[3]   Jónas read the poem to the Fjölnir Society in Copenhagen on February 11, 1843.

[4]   Dick Ringler, *Bard of Iceland: Jónas Hallgrímsson, Poet and Scientist*, Madison: University of Wisconsin Press 2002, p. 230. The poem, as well as Ringler's commentary, can be read at www.library.wisc.edu/etext/Jonas/Gratittling/Gratittling.html.

[5]   Páll Valsson, "Dýrðardæmi Abrahams" [Abraham's Glorious Example], in *Tímarit Máls og menningar* [Journal of the Society for Language and Culture], vol. 57, no. 3, 1996, pp. 50–63.

[6]   Valsson, *Jónas Hallgrímsson. Ævisaga*, p. 398.

for young students preparing for the priesthood to sympathize with this otherwise wise man, one of the greatest that the Danes have had.[7]

A. Magnús Eiríksson and Grímur Thomsen

There is one clear exception from the seeming indifference towards Kierkegaard in Icelandic circles in nineteenth-century Copenhagen. An Icelandic theologian, Magnús Eiríksson (1806–81), took an active part in the theological debate in Denmark at the time. He was, like Kierkegaard, a harsh critic of Hans Lassen Martensen (1808–84) who had replaced Mynster as bishop of Zealand. But although Magnús shared Kierkegaard's opposition to the Hegelian philosophy of religion,[8] he also criticized Kierkegaard's theology. Magnús was mainly critical of two of Kierkegaard's positions: the idea that faith is a paradox and what he took to be the ascetism of Kierkegaard's view of the Christian life. In a book he wrote against Kierkegaard, *Is Faith a Paradox and "on the strength of the Absurd"?*[9] by Theophilus Nicolaus, a pseudonym in the spirit of Kierkegaard, Eiríksson argues that Kierkegaard's "radical wrongheadedness" (*radicale Vildfarelser*) resides in the position of regarding faith in the divine incarnation, which surely never took place, as the true Christian belief. Eiríksson based his theology upon historical criticism and rationalism and rejected as paradoxical many articles of the Christian faith, such as the Incarnation, because they fly in the face of human understanding. Nevertheless, Magnús argued that the very core of the evangelical faith is quite compatible with human reason.[10]

Kierkegaard did not publicly respond to this criticism but in his journals, there are letters addressed to Theophilus Nicolaus,[11] where he says that Eiríksson's rationalism has done away with Christianity and replaced it with faith according to the Old Testament.[12] Kierkegaard shows, for example, how Eiríksson's confusion resides in neglecting the distinction between the person of faith and the observing third party (*Trediemand*), like Johannes de silentio who is trying to understand the person of faith and thus, negatively, trying to throw light upon it.[13] Kierkegaard argues that

[7]   Jón Helgason, "Helgi lektor Hálfdánarson. Æfiminning í tilefni af aldarafmæli hans" [Lecturer Helgi Hálfdánarson. In Memory of his Centennial], in *Prestafélagsritið. Tímarit fyrir kristindóms- og kirkjumál* [The Journal of the Pastors Society], vol. 8, 1926, p. 9.
[8]   As Joakim Garff points out, Kierkegaard did not appreciate Eiríkson's company in this matter, see Joakim Garff, *Søren Kierkegaard. A Biography*, trans. by Bruce H. Kirmmse, Princeton and Oxford: Princeton University Press 2005, pp. 425–7.
[9]   Theophilus Nicolaus [Magnús Eiríksson], *Er Troen et Paradox og "i Kraft af det Absurde"? et Spørgsmaal foranledigt ved "Frygt og Bæven, af Johannes de silentio," besvaret ved Hjelp af en Troes-Ridders fortrolige Meddelelser, til fælles Opbyggelse for Jøder, Christne og Muhamedanere af bemeldte Troes-Ridders Broder Theophilus Nicolaus*, Copenhagen: Chr. Steen & Søn 1850.
[10]   Eiríkur Albertsson, *Magnús Eiríksson. Guðfræði hans og trúarlíf* [Magnús Eiríksson. His Theology and Religious Life], Reykjavík: Ísafoldarprentsmiðja 1938 pp. 84–5.
[11]   He also mentions "Tro, overtro og vantro" [Faith, too much Faith and Lack of Faith] by Magnús Eiríksson.
[12]   *Pap.* X–6 B 72.
[13]   *Pap.* X–6 B 79 / *JP* 1, 10.

in Eiríksson's discussion of his position "the misunderstanding is so enormous that there is hardly a hope of an understanding."[14]

Magnús Eiríksson wrote his criticism of Kierkegaard only in Danish, and he did not publish anything on the subject in Icelandic. In 1938, however, Eiríkur Albertsson defended a doctoral dissertation on Magnús Eiríksson at the Department of Theology at the University of Iceland, where he devotes a subchapter to Eiríksson's criticism of Kierkegaard.[15] He also wrote a chapter on the theology and dogmatic divisions in Denmark in the earlier part of the nineteenth century where he summarizes Kierkegaard's teachings.[16]

Magnús Eiríksson was not the only Icelander who was mentioned in Kierkegaard's journals. In 1845 Kierkegaard criticizes Grímur Thomsen (1820–96), a public official, poet and philosopher, for making use of his works, such as *Fear and Trembling* and *Either/Or*, in his dissertation on *Om Lord Byron*[17] without referring to them.[18] Later, Thomsen wrote a philosophical article on "Space and Time" in *Skírnir* where he criticizes Hegelian attempts to synthesize philosophy and Christianity. The article is in the spirit of Kierkegaard although he is not mentioned. In a M.A. Thesis about Thomsen, Kristján Jóhann Jónsson (b. 1949) argues that his thought developed from strong Hegelian influences towards themes in the spirit of Kierkegaard.[19]

"Hegel, Rasmus Nielsen and Sören Kierkegaard were his men," writes the poet Benedikt Gröndal (1826–1907) about Thomsen.[20] In a private letter (dated in Iceland August 7, 1847) to the "Fjölnismenn"-fellow Brynjólfur Pétursson, Thomsen asks about news of "Kirkjugarður" [Churchyard] and Pétursson responds in a letter, dated August 20, 1847: "Sören Churchyard is now altogether ignored, so the only thing I can tell you about him is that I saw him once, as I was walking with Olsen, the brother of his former fiancée."[21]

---

[14]		*Pap.* X–6 B 82 / *JP* 6, 6601.

[15]		Eiríkur Albertsson, *Magnús Eiríksson. Guðfræði hans og trúarlíf*, Reykjavík: Ísafoldarprentsmiðja 1938, pp. 81–7.

[16]		Ibid., pp. 34–6.

[17]		Grímur Thorgrímsson Thomsen, *Om Lord Byron*, Copenhagen: Andreas Frederik Høst 1845.

[18]		*SKS* 18, 273, JJ:400 / *JP* 5, 5844. *Either/Or* is in fact mentioned in the thesis. Joakim Garff argues with reference to this case that to be a disciple of Kierkegaard could be regarded as theft in his eyes, see Garff, *Søren Kierkegaard. A Biography*, p. 646.

[19]		Kristján Jóhann Jónsson, *Kall tímans. Um ritgerðir Gríms Thomsen 1841–1845* [The Call of Time. On the Writings of Grímur Thomsen 1841–1845] (M.A. Thesis in Icelandic Literature, Reykjavik: University of Iceland 2002), published as *Kall tímans: um rannsóknir Gríms Thomsen á frönskum og enskum bókmenntum* [The Call of Time. Grímur Thomsen's Research of French and English Literature], ed. by Ásdís Egilsdóttir, Reykjavík: Bókmenntafræðistofnun Háskóla Íslands 2004, p. 18; pp. 43–4; p. 133; pp. 206–7; pp. 236–7.

[20]		Benedikt Gröndal, *Dægradvöl*, [Passtime], Reykjavík: Skuggsjá 1983, p. 101. See also Hannes Pétursson, "Lítið eitt um Grím" [A Few Things about Grímur], in *Lesbók Morgunblaðsins* [The Newspaper's Literary Supplement], vol. 71, no. 45, 1996, p. 4.

[21]		Brynjólfur Pétursson, *Bréf* [Letters], ed. by Aðalgeir Kristjánsson, Copenhagen: Hið íslenska fræðafélag / The Icelandic Theoretical Society 1964, p. 131. Kristjánsson tells me that this is the only place where Kierkegaard is mentioned in Pétursson's letters (conversation November 17, 2004).

II. In Iceland

Søren Kierkegaard's works are not mentioned in the records of the Icelandic Prestaskóli, Lutheran Seminary, although this does not preclude that his ideas were "indirectly" introduced to students. The seminary was founded in 1847, and its first director was Pétur Pétursson (1808–91), who studied theology in Copenhagen from 1829 to 1834. Jón Helgason, the aforementioned bishop, states that Pétursson was one of the first to introduce Martensen's theology into the Icelandic Church, an interpretation which dominated it for the next 50 years.[22] Student lecture notes from the period, as well as the manuscripts of Pétursson's own lectures, show that Pétursson lectured on Martensen's *Christian Dogmatics*.[23] In the records of the seminary in 1856, newly published works by Kierkegaard are mentioned: *This Must Be Said; So Let It Be Said*,[24] and *What Christ Judges of Official Christianity*,[25] both from 1855. The pamphlets *The Moment* from 1855 are also mentioned.

The only other indications that Kierkegaard was at all known in Iceland are that his publications are always mentioned in *Skírnir*, the newsletter of the Icelandic Literary Society, which was published in Copenhagen for most of the nineteenth century. Twelve original editions of Kierkegaard's works are in the Icelandic National Library, but it is not known when they were bought for the library.[26] The oldest recorded reception of a book by Kierkegaard is from 1868, *What Christ Judges of Official Christianity* (1855). The library inherited many books by professor and minister Andreas Frederik Krieger (1817–93) and three of the original editions are marked F. Krieger.[27] A newsbrief about Kierkegaard's death also appeared in *Skírnir* 1856, written by Arnljótur Ólafsson (1823–1904) a theologian, economist, and logician. He writes: "His works have awakened many from a spiritual slumber, and they will in the future awaken still more."[28]

But there certainly was no awakening in the spirit of Kierkegaard in nineteenth-century Iceland. Although it is likely that he was known in academic circles, he was not publicly discussed, although he is sometimes discussed in private letters which, of course, were a major form of intellectual communication at the time.[29]

---

[22]   Jóhanna Þráinsdóttir, "Kierkegaard gegn Martensen" [Kierkegaard against Martensen], unpublished B.A. thesis at the Department of Theology, Reykjavik: University of Iceland 2000, p. 10; Jón Helgason, *Kirkjusaga* [The History of the Church], Reykjavík 1922, p. 185.

[23]   Hans Lassen Martensen, *Den christelige Dogmatik*, Copenhagen: C.A. Reitzel 1849 [In English as *Christian Dogmatics*, Edinburgh: T. & T. Clark 1898]. See Þráinsdóttir, "Kierkegaard gegn Martensen," pp. 10–11.

[24]   *SV1* XIV, 83–92 / *M*, 71–7.

[25]   *SV1* XIV, 139–49 / *M*, 127–37.

[26]   Þráinsdóttir, "Kierkegaard gegn Martensen," p. 8.

[27]   Ibid, p. 9.

[28]   Arnljótur Ólafsson, "Fréttir" [News], in *Skírnir* [Journal of The Icelandic Literary Society], 1856, vol. 30, pp. 30–1.

[29]   An example is Matthías Jochumsson, a prominent nineteenth-century poet, translator and priest (1835–1920), who mentions Kierkegaard at least twice in his letters, see *Bréf Matthíasar Jochumssonar* [The Letters of Matthías Jochumsson], ed. by Steingrímur Matthíasson, Akureyri: Bókadeild Menningarsjóðs 1935, p. 359; p. 608.

A telling example of this public neglect is a book on the nineteenth century by Ágúst H. Bjarnason,[30] who became a professor of philosophy (or philosophicum) at the University of Iceland when it was founded in 1911. This book discusses the main thinkers of the newly ended century and has interesting chapters about Hegel, Schleiermacher, Schopenhauer, Nietzsche, Spencer, Marx, and Comte, to mention a few important thinkers. But Kierkegaard is not even mentioned! In an article about Magnús Eiríksson in 1924, Professor Bjarnason mentions Kierkegaard briefly, quoting Schwanenflügel's words that Kierkegaard was "one of the greatest philosophers and theologians of the Nordic countries."[31]

A. Twentieth Century

It is worth noting that in 1923 a short book (of 86 pages) by Kort K. Kortsen (1882–1939), entitled *Sören Kierkegaard*, was published in Icelandic translation a year before it appeared in Danish.[32] This text is largely biographical but it also discusses some of Kierkegaard's main ideas and debates. This publication was the second in the series of the The Danish–Icelandic Society in Iceland on themes from Danish cultural history. Kortsen was at the time a lecturer in Danish language and literature at the University of Iceland.

B. Teaching

As said already, the University of Iceland was founded in 1911 but works by Kierkegaard or by authors who discuss his ideas do not appear on the reading lists of Icelandic students at the new national University. This changed only in 1944 when Sigurbjörn Einarsson (b. 1911) started teaching a course on the philosophy of religion, using the text *From the Renaissance to our Age* by N.H. Søe.[33] This book, which is a general overview, has about a fifteen-page long discussion about Kierkegaard.[34] According to Sigurbjörn, he did not discuss Kierkegaard in any detail in this course, but this was probably the first time that his ideas were explicitly

---

[30]   Ágúst H. Bjarnason, *Nítjánda öldin* [The Nineteenth Century], Reykjavík: Bókaverzlun Guðmundar Gamalíelssonar 1904.

[31]   Ágúst H. Bjarnason, "Um Magnús Eiríksson" [On Magnús Eiríksson], in *Skírnir* [Journal of The Icelandic Literary Society], vol. 98, 1924, p. 39. The context of the reference to Schwanenflügel is that he had likened Magnús Eiríksson to Kierkegaard claiming that the former was a great character while the latter was a great philosopher. The poet Matthías Jochumsson also refers to Schwanenflügel's words in his autobiography, see Matthías Jochumsson, *Sögukaflar af sjálfum mér* [Stories about Myself], Reykjavík: Ísafoldarprentsmiðja 1959, p. 177.

[32]   Kort Kristian Kortsen, *Sören Kierkegaard/Gefið út að tilhlutun Íslandsdeildar Dansk-íslenska félagsins*, Reykjavík: Prentsmiðjan Acta 1923. See Svend Ranulf, "Kort Kristian Kortsen," in *Aarsberetning 1938–1939*, Copenhagen: Universitetsforlaget i Aarhus 1939, p. 10.

[33]   N.H. Søe, *Fra Renæssancen til vore Dage: Filosofisk Tænkning med særligt Henblik paa de moralske og religiöse Problemer*, Copenhagen: Gads Forlag 1945.

[34]   Ibid., pp. 184–200.

taught in the Department of Theology at the University of Iceland.[35] Sigurbjörn, who had become acquainted with Kierkegaard's ideas during his studies in Uppsala, was himself very interested in Kierkegaard although he has unfortunately never written about him.

When Sigurbjörn Einarsson became bishop of Iceland in 1959, he was succeeded by Jóhann Hannesson at the Department of Theology, and he continued using Söe's book. In 1962, Hannesson started a new course called "The History of Western Philosophy after Kant" and used for it a book by Harald Schjelderup, *The History of Philosophy from the Renaissance to the Present Age*, which also has a short discussion about Kierkegaard.[36] Hannesson was more of an explicitly existentialist theologian than Einarsson, who was mostly influenced by the theology of Karl Barth. In 1969, Hannesson published an essay on "Heidegger and the Basic Tenets of Existential Philosophy" which shows clearly his knowledge of Kierkegaard, although he is very much in the background of the essay. Þórir Kr. Þórðarson, professor of the Old Testament, briefly mentions Kierkegaard's account of Abraham's temptation in an article from 1988.[37]

It is indicative of Kierkegaard's standing in the consciousness of Icelandic theologians that in a debate about existential theology in the journal of the Icelandic Church, *Kirkjuritið*, from 1974–75, Kierkegaard is only mentioned as the originator of existentialism, while Heidegger, Sartre, Nietzsche, and Bultmann play a larger role in the discussion. A more recent example is a book on Christian ethics by an Icelandic theologian where Kierkegaard's ideas are ignored, although many existential-theological themes are extensively discussed.[38]

In the mid-1980s, Vilhjálmur Árnason (b. 1953), philosopher and part-time lecturer, taught an elective course on existential philosophy at the Department of Theology where themes from Kierkegaard's writings were prominent. Árnason also regularly taught a course for students of humanities at the University of Iceland on nineteenth-and twentieth-century history of ideas where Kierkegaard was introduced. Árnason's doctoral dissertation was largely a critical assessment existential ethics and dealt partly with Kierkegaard.[39] In 1990, Árnason along with pastor Karl Sigurbjörnsson, who later became the bishop of Iceland, taught a seminar on *Fear and Trembling* and *Repetition* for students of theology. In 1995, Árnason taught a

---

[35]   Interview October 26, 2004.

[36]   Harald K. Schjelderup, *Filosofiens historie fra renaissancen til nutiden*, Kristiania: Gyldendalske Boghandel 1924.

[37]   Þórir Kr. Þórðarson, "Akedah: Freisting Abrahams" [Akedah: The Temptation of Abraham], in *Trú og þjóðfélag. Afmælisrit dr. Þóris Kr. Þórðarsonar* [Faith and Society. A Festschrift for Þórir Kr. Þórðarson], Reykjavik: Institution of Theology and Skálholt Press 1994, pp. 129–40.

[38]   Sigurjón Árni Eyjólfsson, *Kristin siðfræði í sögu og samtíð* [Christian Ethics, Historical and Contemporary], Reykjavík: Hið íslenska bókmenntafélag/The Icelandic Literary Society 2004.

[39]   Vilhjálmur Árnason, *The Context of Morality and the Question of Ethics: From Naive Existentialism to Suspicious Hermeneutics*, Ph.D. Thesis in philosophy, Department of Philosophy, Purdue University, December 1982, Ann Arbor UMI Dissertation Services 1982.

joint seminar for students of philosophy and theology on *Fear and Trembling* and *The Sickness unto Death*. These were probably the first courses explicitly offered on Kierkegaard writings for students at the University of Iceland. Since then, Sigríður Þorgeirsdóttir (b. 1958), associate professor of philosophy, has taught seminars on Kierkegaard for students of both philosophy and theology. In the last ten years, four B.A. theses have been written on Kierkegaard at the Department of Philosophy at the University of Iceland, and one at the Department of Theology.

In April 1998 two seminars on Kierkegaard's philosophy were held in the Nordic house in Reykjavík under the title: "To Choose or not to Choose: That is the Question." Þorgeirsdóttir gave a paper on "Kierkegaard in Iceland" and Jon Høyer, lecturer in Danish at the University of Iceland, spoke about Kierkegaard's authorship. Specially invited lecturers were Joakim Garff, who talked about his biography on Kierkegaard, and Finn Hauberg Mortensen, whose lecture was on "The Seducer's Diary" from *Either/Or*. In relation to this seminar, the published works from the new Kierkegaard edition were on display in the Nordic house, and the media covered this event.[40] To my knowledge, this is the first meeting which was publicly held in Iceland explicitly to discuss Kierkegaard's works.

Nowadays, there is a good chance that most students who study philosophy in the secondary school or at college, or general readers interested in philosophy, will become acquainted with Kierkegaard through reading some of the overview works in philosophy that are available in Icelandic translations, such as *Sophie's World* by Jostein Gaarder, *History of Philosophy* by Gunnar Skirbekk and Nils Gilje, and *Philosophy* by Martin Levander, all of which discuss Kierkegaard in an introductory way. There is also a very short discussion of Kierkegaard in the only Icelandic *History of Ideas* by Ólafur Jens Pétursson.

C. Translations and Writings

The first Icelandic translations of texts by Kierkegaard were published in the journal *Eimreiðin*; these were fragments from the "Diapsalmata" and *The Moment*.[41] The next Icelandic translation did not appear until 1956, when the pastor Gunnar Árnason rendered *Lilies of the Fields and the Birds of the Air*, which was published in the journal of the Icelandic church, *Kirkjuritið*.[42] In 1963 pastor Árnason appeared again in *Kirkjuritið* with a translation of "Solomon's Dreams" from *Stages on Life's Way* and a fragment from the "Diapsalmata."[43] In a short introduction to these translations,

---

40   *Lesbók Morgunblaðsins* [The Newspaper's Literary Supplement], April 16, 1998.

41   "Brotabrot úr ritum Sörens Kierkegaards" [Fragments from the Works of Sören Kierkegaard], containing "Úr Diapsalmata" [From "Diapsalmata"] and "Þetta kalla menn að vera kristinn" úr *Öjeblikket* [This is regarded as Being a Christian from *The Moment*], trans. by Guðjón Baldvinsson, in *Eimreiðin*, vol. 17, no. 1. 1911, pp. 49–51; pp. 51–2.

42   "Liljur vallarins og fuglar himinsins" ["Lilies of the Fields and the Birds of the Air"], trans. by Gunnar Árnason, in *Kirkjuritið* [Journal of the Church], vol. 22, no. 10, 1956, pp. 482–4.

43   "Draumur Salómons" ["Solomon's Dream" (from "Guilty?"/"Not Guilty" in *Stages on Lifes Way*)] and "Úr Diapsalmata" [From "Diapsalmata"], trans. by Gunnar Árnason, in *Kirkjuritið* [Journal of the Church], vol. 29, no. 5, 1963, pp. 222–4; p. 224.

Árnason writes that this publication is in celebration of Kierkegaard's 150th birthday: "It is remarkable that selections of the best from the works of this most influential man, has not long appeared in Icelandic. That should be remedied."[44]

The remedies have been few and far between. In 1966, the first full book by Kierkegaard, *Repetition*, was translated by a young philosopher, Þorsteinn Gylfason (1942–2005).[45] Gylfason wrote an introduction to the book, where he told about Kierkegaard's life and discussed the ideas of *Repetition*. In a book review of this publication, Kristján Árnason (b. 1935), who had studied philosophy and literature in Germany, wrote that the Icelanders had for a long time neglected this "greatest intellectual of the Nordic countries" and those who had given him their attention had been accused of plagiarism and misunderstanding, referring to the experience of Magnús Eiríksson and Grímur Thomsen. "But better late than never, and now it seems that Icelanders are keen to make up for this neglect and misunderstanding of Kierkegaard...."[46] Árnason was at the time working on a manuscript in Danish on Kierkegaard and the Greeks which has never been published.[47] A synopsis of this thesis, entitled "Recollection and Repetition—Kierkegaard and the Greeks" has been published in Danish.[48] Árnason also read a paper, "Kierkegaard and Philosophy," on this topic to the Icelandic Philosophical Society in 1977. In the late 1990s, Dr. Gígja Gísladóttir (b. 1937) gave lectures in the Icelandic Philosophical Society and in the Society for Eigthteenth Century Studies on the subject of her doctoral thesis about Hegel and Kierkegaard.[49]

It is not until the very end of the twentieth century that something resembling a Kierkegaard wave of interest passed over Iceland. In the year 2000, two books by Kierkegaard were published in the Theroretical Classics Series [*Lærdómsrit*] of the Icelandic Literary Society, under the editorship of Vilhjálmur Árnason. These were the "sister" books *Fear and Trembling* and *Repetition*.[50] The former was translated by

---

[44]   G[unnar] Á[rnason], Introductory words to "Draumur Salómons" [Solomon's Dream], in *Kirkjuritið* [Journal of the Church], vol. 5, 1963, p. 222.

[45]   *Endurtekningin* [*Repetition*], trans. by Þorsteinn Gylfason, Reykjavik: Helgafell 1966.

[46]   Kristján Árnason, *"Endurtekningin"* [*"Repetition"*], in *Tímarit Máls og menningar* [Journal of the Society for Language and Culture], vol. 28, 1967, p. 190.

[47]   It is available, however, in the Icelandic National library.

[48]   Kristján Árnason, "Erindring og gentagelse. Kierkegaard og Grækerne" [Recollection and Repetition—Kierkegaard and the Greeks], in *Filosofi og samfunn—Søren Kierkegaard* [Philosophy and Society—Søren Kierkegaard], ed. by Finn Jor, Kristiansand: Høyskoleforlaget Norwegian Academic Press 1998, pp. 197–203. Also in Kristján Árnason, *Hið fagra er satt* [The Beautiful Is True], Reykjavik: The Institute for Literature and the University of Iceland Press 2004, pp. 115–21.

[49]   Gígja Gísladóttir, *Kierkegaard contra Hegel: Either/Or, A Caricatured Facsimile of The Philosophy of Mind*, Ph.D. Thesis in philosophy, Department of Philosophy University of Texas at Austin 1991, Ann Arbor: UMI Dissertation Services 1995.

[50]   *Uggur og ótti* [*Fear and Trembling*], trans. by Jóhanna Þráinsdóttir, introduced by Kristján Árnason, Reykjavik: Hið íslenzka bókmenntafélag/The Icelandic Literary Society 2000 (Theoretical Classics Series, ed. by Vilhjálmur Árnason); *Endurtekningin* [*Repetition*], trans. by Þorsteinn Gylfason, Reykjavik: Hið íslenzka bókmenntafélag/The Icelandic Literary Society 2000 (Theoretical Classics Series, ed. by Vilhjálmur Árnason).

Jóhanna Þráinsdóttir, who also wrote on the historical background of the text, placing it in the context of the theological debates in early nineteenth-century Denmark, especially Kierkegaard's relationship to the bishops Mynster and Martensen. Þráinsdóttir, who was already an established translator, was studying theology at the time and this translation kindled her interest in Kierkegaard and the context of ideas which he grew out of and responded to. She wrote her B.A. Thesis on Kierkegaard and his relation to Martensen. Kristján Árnason, Associate Professor of Comparative Literature, wrote a rather extensive introduction to this edition of *Fear and Trembling*. The translation of *Repetition* was a renewed edition of Gylfason's translation from 1966 with an extended introduction and renewed notes by the translator, taking new Kierkegaard scholarship into account. In the wake of these publications, one of the cultural journals in Iceland, *Tímarit Máls og menningar*, devoted a thematic issue to Kierkegaard, with articles by Kristján Árnason, Vilhjálmur Árnason, Jóhanna Þráinsdóttir, and Birna Bjarnadóttir.[51] In January 2001, The Icelandic Philosophical Society held a meeting where the new edition of *Fear and Trembling* and *Repetition* was discussed. There were also discussions and introductions about Kierkegaard in cultural programs on radio and television following this publication.

D. Literature

In his book on the history of Icelandic literature, Stefán Einarsson writes that the poet Stefán Hörður Grímsson once said about himself that he was "the only one among Icelandic poets reading Kierkegaard."[52] Many have seen existential themes in the poetry of Steinn Steinar (1908–58), and he has been interpreted in the light of Kierkegaard.[53] One interpreter writes, however, that Steinar probably never read Kierkegaard but that he appropriated ideas that were "in the air" around the middle of the last century. That time was characterized by socialist ideas in literary circles which did not square well with prevailing ideas about Kierkegaard. Steinar was disillusioned by socialism, and existential themes are prevalent in his poetry.

When Birna Bjarnadóttir (b. 1960) wrote her article in the thematic issue on Kierkegaard, she was a student of comparative literature at the University of Iceland, working on a doctoral thesis about the Icelandic writer Guðbergur Bergsson.[54] In a chapter, entitled "The Aesthetics of the Paradox," Bjarnadóttir analyses Bergsson's literary aesthetics in light of Kierkegaardian themes from the *Repetition* and *Fear*

---

[51]   *Tímarit Máls og menningar* [Journal of the Society for Language and Culture], vol. 61, no. 4, 2000.

[52]   Stefán Einarsson, *Íslensk bókmenntasaga 874–1960* [Icelandic Literary History 874–1960], Reykjavik: Snæbjörn Jónsson & Co 1961. I have not been able to find the reference to Grímsson's own words.

[53]   Silja Aðalsteinsdóttir, "Þú og ég sem aldrei urðum til: existensíalismi í verkum Steins Steinarr" [You and I Who Never Existed: Existentialism in The Works of Steinn Steinarr], in *Skírnir* [Journal of The Icelandic Literary Society], ed. by Ólafur Jónsson, vol. 155, 1981, pp. 309–36.

[54]   Birna Bjarnadóttir, *Holdið hemur andann. Um fagurfræði í skáldskap Guðbergs Bergssonar* [The Flesh Tames The Spirit. On Aesthetics in The Fiction of Guðbergur Bergsson], Reykjavik: The University of Iceland Press 2003.

and Trembling, drawing partly on Derrida's reading of the latter.[55] It is interesting that in this first doctoral thesis written in comparative literature at the University of Iceland, Kierkegaard plays a prominent role. Bjarnadóttir shows that Bergsson's writings are, in his own unique way, characterized by existential thinking, where the aesthetic takes the place of the religious in the individuals' struggle to live and give meaning to their lives:[56] "While Kierkegaard wrote with passion about the dilemma of love and responsibility, highlighting thereby the issue of belief, Bergson's treatment of these themes runs deep, portraying a passionate relation of life and art."[57] Bjarnadóttir has also interpreted the poetry of the Icelandic poet Ísak Harðarson in light of Kierkegaard's ideas.[58]

The edition of *Repetition* and *Fear and Trembling* seems to have inspired the literary theorist Eiríkur Guðmundsson who has published 39 reflections on Icelandic reality of today.[59] One of Bjarnadóttir's and Guðmundsson's former teachers, Matthías Viðar Sæmundsson (1954–2004), wrote his Master's thesis about existential themes in the literary works of three Icelandic novelists: Gunnar Gunnarsson, Thor Vilhjálmsson, and Geir Kristjánsson.[60] Sæmundsson argues that while the others are mostly influenced by Sartre and Camus, Kierkegaardian themes are more apparent in the works of Gunnar Gunnarsson (1889–1975). Gunnarsson lived for a long time in Denmark and was most likely familiar with Kierkegaard's works.[61]

Going farther back in time, Sigurður Nordal (1886–1974), the renowned professor of Icelandic literature, gave public lectures in Reykjavík in the winter of 1918–19 where he put forth a theory about two major themes in the story of human development or in the art of life. These two themes are in many aspects akin to Kierkegaard's aesthetic and ethical ways of life and, Nordal discusses Kierkegaard a few times in these lectures, especially "The Diary of a Seducer" from *Either/Or*. In his

---

[55]   Jacques Derrida, "Whom to Give to (Knowing Not to Know)," in *The Gift of Death*, trans. by David Wills, Chicago: University of Chicago Press 1995, pp. 53–81.

[56]   Incidentally, one of Bergsson's stories, entitled "An Image of Man from the Bible" is an interpretation of the story of Abraham and Isaac, see Guðbergur Bergsson, "Mannsmynd úr Biblíunni," in *Maðurinn er myndavél* [Man is a Camera], Reykjavík: Forlagið 1988, pp. 7–21.

[57]   Birna Bjarnadóttir, "Summary," in *Holdið hemur andann* [The Flesh Tames the Spirit], Reykjavik: The University of Iceland Press 2003, p. 252.

[58]   Birna Bjarnadóttir, "Í mótsögn tilfinninga. Um játningar Ísaks Harðarssonar" [In a Paradox of Emotions. On Ísaks Harðarson's Confessions] in *Skírnir* [Journal of The Icelandic Literary Society], vol. 172, pp. 219–37.

[59]   Eiríkur Guðmundsson, *39 þrep á leið til glötunar* [39 Steps to Ruination], Reykjavík: Bjartur 2004, nos. 7 and 14.

[60]   The revised published version is only about Gunnarsson: Matthías Viðar Sæmundsson, *Mynd nútímamannsins. Um tilvistarleg viðhorf í sögum Gunnars Gunnarssonar* [The Image of Modern Man. On Existential Themes in the Novels of Gunnar Gunnarsson], Reykjavík: Menningarsjóður 1982. No references are made to books by Kierkegaard in this thesis, only to secondary sources.

[61]   In a short biography, Prof. Sveinn Skorri Höskuldsson writes that the young Gunnarsson read philosophical authors, like Nietzsche and Schopenhauer, but Kierkegaard is not explicitly mentioned, see Sveinn Skorri Höskuldsson, *Skáldið á Skriðuklaustri* [The Writer at Skriðuklaustur], Reykjavík: AB 1989 (without page numbers).

first lecture, Nordal writes: "Behind the debate about beneficial and harmful books, I now saw a conflict between two views on life, often called ethical and artistic, and which are mainly known from the works of Søren Kierkegaard."[62] In his introduction to Nordal's lectures, which were first published in 1986, Þorsteinn Gylfason draws attention to this kinship with Kierkegaard and argues that some of Kierkegaard's works, in particular *Either/Or* and *Stages on Life's Way* had considerable direct and indirect impact on Sigurður Nordal. Páll Skúlason, Professor of Philosophy at the University of Iceland, also argues that Nordal's existential themes are influenced by Kierkegaard.[63]

F. Conclusion

In this article, the Icelandic reception of Kierkegaard, both among Icelanders in nineteenth-century Copenhagen and in Iceland, has been discussed. It has become clear that Kierkegaard has received relatively little attention by Icelanders with the clearest exceptions of Grímur Thomsen and Magnús Eiríksson. Icelandic theology has not been significantly influenced by Kierkegaard's ideas, although a few leading figures of the Church read and admired him. Sigurbjörn Einarsson, the former bishop of Iceland, said that to his knowledge Kierkegaard never gained any popularity in this country.[64] Again, with the exception of Magnús Eiríksson, Icelandic theologians in the nineteenth century followed the theology of Mynster and Martensen which Kierkegaard furiously attacked. Moreover, in contrast to Mynster's theology, Kierkegaard's writings were somehow alien to the Icelanders and did not appeal to their spiritual situation.[65] Therefore, they did not feel they needed to respond to his ideas or make up their mind with respect to them.[66]

Icelandic interest in, and influence from, Kierkegaard has been more relevant in the areas of philosophy and literature, especially in the last decades of the twentieth century.[67] This interest brought its main fruit in 2000 when scholarly editions of *Repetition* and *Fear and Trembling* appeared in Icelandic translations. These editions have plowed the ground for Kierkegaard scholarship which is still only in

---

[62]   Sigurður Nordal, *Einlyndi og marglyndi* [To Will One Thing or Many], ed. by Þorsteinn Gylfason and Gunnar Harðarson, Reykjavík: Hið íslenzka bókmenntafélag/The Icelandic Literary Society 1986.

[63]   Páll Skúlason, "Tilvistarstefnan og Sigurður Nordal" [Existentialism and Sigurður Nordal], in *Skírnir* [Journal of The Icelandic Literary Society], ed. by Vilhjálmur Árnason, vol. 161, 1987, pp. 309–36.

[64]   My conversation with him, October 22, 2004.

[65]   The same in fact applies to Grundtvig who never had any followers in Iceland.

[66]   Conversation with Sigurbjörn Einarsson, October 22, 2004.

[67]   The Icelandic philosopher Logi Gunnarsson (b. 1964) published a paper entitled "Climbing Up the Ladder: Nonsense and Textual Strategy in Wittgenstein's *Tractatus*," in *Journal of Philosophical Research*, no. 26, 2001, pp. 229–86. This is a paper by two fictional authors—Gunnarsson, just like Kierkegaard, is not the author—Johannes philologus and Johannes commentarius. The pseudonymous authorship of the book and its formal structure is supposed to reflect Kierkegaard's influence on Wittgenstein. (In Icelandic as *Stigi Wittgensteins*, trans. by Elmar Geir Unnsteinsson and Vidar Thorsteinsson, Reykjavík: University of Iceland Press and Institute of Philosophy 2005.)

the beginning phase in Iceland. Perhaps the social conditions for the reception of Kierkegaard's existential thought are more favorable generally now in an affluent consumer culture than in the traditional mostly rural society that Iceland was until around the middle of the last century.

Bibliography

I. Icelandic Translations of Kierkegaard's Works

"Brotabrot úr ritum Sörens Kierkegaards" [Fragments from the Works of Sören Kierkegaard], containing "Úr Diapsalmata" [From "Diapsalmata"] and "Þetta kalla menn að vera kristinn" úr *Öjeblikket* ["The Sort of Person Who Is Called a Christian" from *The Moment*], trans. by Guðjón Baldvinsson, in *Eimreiðin*, vol. 17, no. 1. 1911, pp. 49–51; pp. 51–52.

"Liljur vallarins og fuglar himinsins" ["Lilies of the Fields and the Birds of the Air"], trans. by Gunnar Árnason, *Kirkjuritið*, vol. 22, no. 10, 1956, pp. 482–4.

"Draumur Salómons" [Solomon's Dream (from "Guilty?"/"Not Guilty," in *Stages on Lifes Way*)] and "Úr Diapsalmata" [From "Diapsalmata"], trans. by Gunnar Árnason, *Kirkjuritið*, vol. 29, no. 5, 1963, pp. 222–4; p. 224.

Endurtekningin [*Repetition*], trans. by Þorsteinn Gylfason, Reykjavik: Helgafell 1966.

"Úr *Synspunktet for min Forfatter-Virksomhed*" [Fragment from *The Point of View of My Work as an Author*], trans. by Vilhjálmur Árnason and used as a motto of his book *Siðfræði lífs og dauða. Erfiðar ákvarðanir í heilbrigðisþjónustu* [Ethics of Life and Death. Difficult Decisions in Health Care], Reykjavik: The Centre for Ethics and the University of Iceland Press 1993 and 2003, p. 5.

"Ómar úr strengleikum: úrval úr 'Diapsalmata. Ad se Ipsum' í *Enten-eller*" [Selections from the "Diapsalmata. Ad se Ipsum" in *Either/Or*], trans. by Þorsteinn Gylfason, *Jón á Bægisá*, vol. 1, 1994, pp. 74–7.

Endurtekningin [*Repetition*], trans. by Þorsteinn Gylfason, Reykjavik: Hið íslenzka bókmenntafélag/The Icelandic Literary Society 2000 (*Theoretical Classics Series*, ed. by Vilhjálmur Árnason).

Uggur og ótti [*Fear and Trembling*], trans. by Jóhanna Þráinsdóttir, introduced by Kristján Árnason, Reykjavik: Hið íslenzka bókmenntafélag/The Icelandic Literary Society, 2000 (*Theoretical Classics Series*, ed. by Vilhjálmur Árnason).

"Úr *Andránni (Øieblikket)*" [From *The Moment*], trans. by Kristján Árnason, *Tímarit Máls og menningar*, vol. 61, no. 4, 2000, pp. 15–16; pp. 33–4; p. 46.

II. Secondary Literature on Kierkegaard in Iceland

Ágústsdóttir, María, "Hyggið að liljum vallarins..." [Consider the lilies of the field...], in *Náttúrusýn* [Visions of Nature], ed. by Róbert H. Haraldsson and Þorvarður Árnason, Reykjavik: The Centre for Ethics and the University of Iceland Press 1994, pp. 159–68.

Albertsson, Eiríkur, *Magnús Eiríksson. Guðfræði hans og trúarlíf* [Magnús Eiríksson. His Theology and Religious Life], Reykjavík: Ísafoldarprentsmidja 1938.

Árnason, Kristján, "Endurtekningin" [Review of the Icelandic first Edition of *Repetition*], in *Tímarit Máls og menningar*, vol. 28, no. 2, 1967, pp. 190–2.

— "Arfur Hegels" [Hegel's Heritage], in *Skírnir*, vol. 161, 1987, pp. 302–6.

— "Sjálfsþekking og sjálfsval" [Knowing Oneself and Choosing Oneself], in *Tímarit Máls og menningar*, vol. 61, no. 4, 2000, pp. 6–14.

— *Hið fagra er satt* [The Beautiful is True] (A collection of essays, a few of which discuss Kierkegaard), Reykjavik: The Institute for Literature and the University of Iceland Press 2004.

Árnason, Vilhjálmur, *Broddflugur* [Gadflies] (A collection of essays, a few of which discuss Kierkegaard), Reykjavik: The Centre for Ethics and the University of Iceland Press 1997.

— "Að velja sjálfan sig. Tilraunir Kierkegaards um mannlífið" [Choosing Oneself. Kierkegaard's Experiments with Being Human], *Tímarit Máls og menningar*, vol. 61, no. 4, 2000, pp. 17–32.

Bjarnadóttir, Birna, "Hvers vegna er dauðinn besta gjöfin, Kierkegaard?" [Why is Death the Best Gift, Kierkegaard?], *Tímarit Máls og menningar*, vol. 61, no. 4, 2000, pp. 47–62.

— *Holdið hemur andann. Um fagurfræði í skáldskap Guðbergs Bergssonar* [The Flesh Tames the Spirit. On Aesthetics in the Fiction of Guðbergur Bergsson], Reykjavik: The University of Iceland Press 2003.

Björnsson, Sigurjón, "Endurminning og endurtekning" [Recollection and Repetition], "Í skugga óttans" [In the Shadow of Fear] (Review of the Icelandic edition of *Repetition* and *Fear and Trembling*), *Morgunblaðið*, November 23, 2000.

Dal, Gunnar "Kierkegaard," in *Existentialismi* [Existentialism], Reykjavik: Vikurútgáfan 1978, pp. 17–20.

— "Danir eru gáfuð þjóð—Sören Kierkegaard frægastur norrænna heimspekinga" [The Danes are a Gifted Nation—Sören Kierkegaard the Most Famous of Nordic Philosophers"], in *Að elska er að lifa* [To Live is to Love] (Gunnar Dal in conversation with Hans Kristján Árnason), Reykjavík: HKÁ 1994, pp. 99–101.

Gísladóttir, Gígja, *Kierkegaard contra Hegel: Either/Or, A Caricatured Facsimile of The Philosophy of Mind*, Ph.D. Thesis in philosophy, Department of Philosophy University of Texas at Austin 1991, Ann Arbor: UMI Dissertation Services 1995.

Magnússon, Ketill B., "Tilvera og tilbrigði við hana—vangaveltur um kenningar Sörens Kierkegaards" [Reflections on Existential Themes in the Teachings of Sören Kierkegaard], unpublished BA Thesis in philosophy, Reykjavik: University of Iceland 1993.

Nordal, Sigurður, *Einlyndi og marglyndi* [To Will One Thing or Many], Reykjavik: Hið íslenzka bókmenntafélag/The Icelandic Literary Society 1986, esp. pp. 166–76.

Ólafsson, Arnljótur, "Fréttir" [News], *Skírnir*, vol. 30, 1856, pp. 30–1.

Pétursson, Ólafur Jens, *Hugmyndasaga* [History of Ideas], Reykjavik: Mál og menning 1989, pp. 240–1.

Ragnarsdóttir, Margrét, "Ógn og skelfing" [Fear and Trembling], unpublished BA Thesis in philosophy, Reykjavik: University of Iceland 1996.

Skúlason, Páll, "Tilvistarstefnan og Sigurður Nordal" [Existentialism and Sigurður Nordal], in *Skírnir* (Journal of The Icelandic Literary Society), vol. 161, 1987, pp. 309–36.

Þráinsdóttir, Jóhanna, "Að verða einstaklingur" [Becoming an Individual], unpublished BA Thesis in philosophy, Reykjavik: University of Iceland 2001.

— "Kierkegaard gegn Martensen" [Kierkegaard against Martensen], unpublished BA thesis in theology, Reykjavik: University of Iceland 2000.

— "Sögulegt baksvið *Uggs og ótta*" [Historical background of *Fear and Trembling*], in *Uggur og ótti* [*Fear and Trembling*], Reykjavík: Hið íslenzka bókmenntafélag/ The Icelandic Literary Society 2000.

— "Er trúin þverstæða? Gagnrýni Magnúsar Eiríkssonar á trúarskoðunum Kierkegaards í *Ugg og Ótta*" [Is Faith a Paradox? Magnús Eiríksson's Critique of Kierkegaard's Theological Position in *Fear and Trembling*], *Tímarit Máls og menningar*, vol. 61, no. 4, 2000, pp. 35–45.

Viðarsdóttir, Kolbrún H., "Um Sören Aabye Kierkegaard, heimspeki hans og umfjöllun um kvíðann" [On Sören Aabye Kierkegaard, his Philosophy and Reflections on Dread], unpublished BA Thesis in philosophy, Reykjavik: University of Iceland 1997.

III. Secondary Literature on Kierkegaard's Reception in Iceland

None.

PART II

Western Europe

Great Britain:

From "Prophet of the Now" to Postmodern Ironist (and after)

George Pattison

In 1852 the antiquarian Andrew Hamilton published a two-volume account of the *Sixteen Months in the Danish Isles* that he had passed in the years 1849 and 1850. As well as containing many delightful descriptions of Danish mores and of the repercussions of the historic events of the time, Hamilton seems to have rapidly acquired a competence in Danish and records conversations with many of the leading figures of Danish society, including Bishop Mynster, to whom the book is dedicated. In a chapter on the history and life of the Church in Denmark, after discussing Mynster, Grundtvig and, briefly, Martensen, Hamilton concludes with a couple of pages on Kierkegaard. "There is," he wrote

> a man whom it is impossible to omit in any account of Denmark, but whose place it might be more difficult to fix; I mean Sören Kierkegaard. But as his works have, at all events for the most part, a religious tendency, he may find a place among the theologians. He is a philosophical Christian writer, evermore dwelling, one might almost say harping, on the theme of the human heart. There is no Danish writer more earnest than he, yet there is no one in whose way stand more things to prevent his becoming popular. He writes at times with an unearthly beauty, but too often with an exaggerated display of logic that disgusts the public. All very well, if he were not a popular writer, but it is for this he intends himself.[1]

Hamilton goes on to single out *Works of Love* and *The Sickness unto Death* for special praise, adding some often quoted lines about Kierkegaard's "invisible dwelling," peripatetic habits, and his own dread of introducing himself, for fear that he would be "mercilessly pumped and sifted."[2]

This was almost certainly Kierkegaard's first appearance in print in the English language. It was followed, fairly shortly afterwards, by an episode in the English translation of Fredrika Bremer's novel *Hertha*, an episode that the author had in fact instructed the translator to leave out. In the course of a river-journey, the eponymous heroine is accosted by an earnest young man who presses upon her a copy of

---

[1]   Andrew Hamilton, *Sixteen Months in the Danish Isles*, London: Bentley 1862, p. 269.
[2]   Ibid., p. 270.

Kierkegaard's "This Must be Said, so Let it Now be Said," one of the tracts from the "Attack on Christendom" of his last years. The English text reprints a couple of pages of Kierkegaard's text, and we are told that, on reading it, Hertha "felt that a combating and suffering heart throbbed here in unison with her own, embittered, bleeding, loving, and still, though as in the midst of the flames, seeking to lay hold upon God; and she felt less solitary in the world."[3] Shortly afterwards, however, she tosses the pamphlet into the waves, finding the words "too much absorbed by the combat" and not giving her a sufficient view of the victory to which it should lead. It is perhaps of further interest that, in a subsequent episode, she is led by distant singing to a communion service in a woodland church—a scene which offers a very different kind of religiosity.

However, these early, unconnected, appearances did not mark any sustained recognition of Kierkegaard, either in the English-speaking world in general, or in Britain in particular (*Hertha* was in fact translated and published in the United States). Such a sustained reception would be a long time coming, and it is really only in the inter-war years that we can begin to speak of a real presence of Kierkegaard's life and thought in Britain. In the following sketch of the reception of Kierkegaard in these islands, I shall divide the story into three phases. The first runs up to the First World War. Even though this period sees a number of reviews, articles, and a monograph dealing with Kierkegaard appear in English, his reception is fragmentary and scattered. The second period, from after the First World War through to the 1970s sees the emergence of a Kierkegaard who is, generally speaking, associated by most commentators with such then current theological and philosophical movements as the theology of crisis (i.e., Karl Barth and his followers) and existentialism. If the years immediately after the Second World War probably marked the high-point of this period, the 1970s saw a significant decline in interest, and it was widely assumed that, as existentialism became eclipsed, Kierkegaard would disappear along with it. The third period begins in the 1980s, but really gathers momentum around 1990. Here Kierkegaard re-emerges as a significant figure worthy of solid historical and textual study and also as a newly contemporary voice, especially in contexts stimulated by or reacting to the "postmodernity" of the last quarter of the twentieth century, such that he can even be hailed "the first postmodern ironist."[4] In this presentation I shall comment on the salient works and issues that came to the fore in each of these periods, and I realize that what I offer falls significantly short of a total accounting. I shall not venture beyond this retrospective view into the domain of prognostication, but will close with a few comments on the situation as it is at the time of writing. Before proceeding to survey the material, however, several further preliminary remarks are in place.

Firstly, it is important to be aware of the distinctiveness of philosophical, theological, and what one might call cultural contexts of reception. The Kierkegaard

---

[3]   Quoted from Habib C. Malik, *Receiving Søren Kierkegaard: The Early Impact and Transmission of his Thought*, Washington, D.C.: Catholic University of America Press 1997, p. 65.

[4]   Julian Evans, "The First Postmodern Ironist," *The New Statesman*, October 30, 2000, pp. 30–1.

who proved attractive to those interested in the modernist breakthrough in art and literature was, often, a different Kierkegaard from the one who spoke to those enthused by dialectical theology. Sometimes these areas of reception often operated more or less in isolation from each other, at other times, perhaps especially in more recent Kierkegaard literature, they have interacted quite closely.

Secondly, whilst these last comments could probably be said of the reception of Kierkegaard across Europe and North America in the twentieth century, there is a further factor to be aware of in the case of the British reception. This has to do with the peculiar intellectual and religious constitution of modern Britain. For, albeit in ways that are sometimes hard to pin down, it is clear that there have been significant variations in the reception of Kierkegaard between the component parts of Britain. Especially in theology, the Presbyterianism of Scotland has meant that there was always an openness to European currents of Protestant theology that was often lacking in England. Similarly, the strong Free Church tradition in Wales possibly provided a certain "point of contact" for some aspects of Kierkegaard's thought. Perhaps there is also something about the national identity of small nations that plays a part here. Conversely, a thinker sometimes known by the motto "Either/Or" would always be likely to encounter resistance in a religious climate that has traditionally prided itself on its *via media* or both-and approach! At the same time, the dominance of analytic philosophy, especially in England, meant that Kierkegaard was tarred with the prevailing suspicion towards most continental philosophy that characterized the analytical school. Although in recent years Kierkegaard has come to be engaged with by philosophers coming from this background, especially in moral philosophy, it has generally only been where continental philosophy was acknowledged as a legitimate philosophical discourse that interest in Kierkegaard was able to flourish in British philosophy—which makes his reception by philosophers perhaps even more irregular and episodic than is the case with theologians.

Finally, it should be pointed out that insular as it so often is, Britain is by no means cut off from the rest of the world. At many points, and especially in contemporary academic circles, it is not always easy to draw a line between Britain and the wider English-speaking world. North American and British scholars attend each others' conferences, read and comment on each others' books, and generally share many important horizons, even if distinctive traits remain. At the same time, throughout the period under review there were many educated Britons who were fluent in modern European languages and who were therefore not solely dependent on English-language translations of or literature about Kierkegaard. Such thinkers and writers as Heidegger, Sartre, and Camus, all of whom made significant comments on Kierkegaard, were relatively widely read in their original languages before translations became available and, once translated, were often assimilated into the native discourse.

I. The First Period of Reception: The Beginnings to the First World War

After the isolated references by Hamilton and Bremer, perhaps the first coherent account of Kierkegaard's thought to appear in English was, curiously enough, in the English translation of the General Part of Hans Lassen Martensen's *Christian Ethics*, which appeared in T. & T. Clark's distinguished Foreign Theological Library in 1873.[5] Kierkegaard is discussed in a chapter entitled "Socialism and Individualism," and the section dealing with him runs to nineteen pages. Martensen commences with the declaration that Kierkegaard "with great talent and powerful one-sidedness, has been with us the advocate of individualism."[6] He goes on to portray Kierkegaard as part of a nominalistic reaction to a "speculative and aesthetic intoxication about ideas."[7] Kierkegaard's distinctiveness is in his emphasis on the individual. Martensen recognizes in this "the category of Christianity and of Theism."[8] Kierkegaard, he says, therefore "ought to make common cause with those philosophic and theological writers who specially desire to promote the principle of Personality as opposed to Pantheism" (perhaps including himself)—but "This is very far from being the case."[9] Instead, Kierkegaard insists on what Martensen calls the "doubtful proposition" that "subjectivity is truth" and engages in a "reckless polemic against speculation."[10] Martensen then goes on to discuss Kierkegaard's attack on the delusion of Christendom, and strongly emphasizes his subject's Socratic inspiration. Indeed, Martensen even concedes that it must be granted to Kierkegaard "That Christianity is a vast delusion or misapplication of a name"—but on condition that it is also acknowledged that this is only as regards "those who lack the mind of the Spirit to discriminate between the apparent and the unseen."[11] But if, against Kierkegaard, we once allow that there are also those who have this mind, then we also allow for what Kierkegaard consistently refused: the Church. A similar formula applies to Kierkegaard's views of society. Martensen concedes that there has been much "dissolution" in the age, but, he says, it is also an age of "remodellings." Kierkegaard's "pessimism," however, does not allow him to see this. Christianity, Martensen insists, requires the existence of the Church. Kierkegaard's "ascetic-practical" individualism is that of an individual who is "cut off from the Church" and who is, therefore, also "deprived of 'the Church's God,' deprived of the fullness of the revelation of God."[12]

It is not to the present purpose to debate the merits of Martensen's (perhaps predictable) characterization. It is, however, not insignificant that this will have been the first substantial account of Kierkegaard's thought that many English-language readers will have encountered. In many ways it can be said to have set the tone for

---

[5]   In the light of comments in the previous paragraph it is worth noting that T. & T. Clark were an Edinburgh-based publisher, strongly associated with publishing Reformed theology. Martensen's *Christian Dogmatics* also appeared in this series. Martensen is described in the publisher's blurb as "The greatest Scandinavian, perhaps the greatest Lutheran, divine of our century."

[6]   Hans Lassen Martensen, *Christian Ethics (General)*, Edinburgh: T. & T. Clark 1873, p. 217.

[7]   Ibid., p. 218.

[8]   Ibid., p. 220.

[9]   Ibid., p. 222.

[10]   Ibid., pp. 222–3.

[11]   Ibid., p. 228.

[12]   Ibid., p. 235.

much subsequent Kierkegaard literature in English, even where this is not dependent on Martensen.

In the last part of the nineteenth century and the beginnings of the twentieth, theological journals saw a trickle of reviews of Kierkegaard books appearing in German. Some of these were reviewed in British journals.[13] It is not unreasonable to suspect a certain recognition of the name becoming current amongst the better-read and European-oriented theologians, but probably little more than that.

The next significant step came from a rather different direction, from the circles of modernist culture. Mabel Stobart published two articles dedicated to Kierkegaard in the literary journal *The Fortnightly Review*, "New Light on Ibsen's Brand" and "The 'Either-Or' of Sören Kierkegaard."[14]

George Bernard Shaw had published his book *The Quintessence of Ibsenism* in 1891, and Ibsen was, at the time of Stobart's first article, still regarded as a quintessentially radical and "modern" author. The core of the article is, unsurprisingly, the suggestion that in his *Brand* Ibsen had "clothed in dramatic drapery some of the tenets propounded in the neglected works of Kierkegaard."[15] In pursuing this argument, Stobart presents a Kierkegaard who is almost Nietzschean: "In a word, we are told that Christianity is rotten to the core, and nothing but the Augean cleansing, by the *Will* of man, of its seductive doctrines, its lip-service, its prostitution of prayer, its corrupting ritual, can destroy the human and restore the original purity of the Divine element in man."[16] Yet, this appeal to a "Divine element" in man is immediately qualified by the remark that "whether, even at its best, the human Will contains a latent power of conquest is, apparently, in Kierkegaard's mind, open to question."[17] Stobart's conclusion it that, on Kierkegaard's view, "Man—the higher nature of man—may and can escape annihilation and attain salvation, but, on conditions which appear too hard for the multitude , who still, in this present state of their evolution, carry too much of the gregarious and of the animal in their nature."[18] Whether Stobart's categories ("the Divine element in man," "the higher nature of man," etc.) really reflect Kierkegaardian thought is clearly open to question, yet it is also significant that that was how Kierkegaard could be seen by one not yet schooled in the discipline of a structured reception history.

---

[13]   For example, the references to "the able and vivacious Dane's discussions of two questions of considerable interest to the theologian, *viz.*, whether a man should become a martyr for the truth, and what the difference is between a genius and an apostle" in the anonymous "Notices" of *The Critical Review of Theological and Philosophical Literature*, vol. 13, Part 2, 1913, p. 182 (this *Review* too was published by T. & T. Clark). At greater length is the review by Richard Bell of the German versions of O.P. Monrad's monograph and a number of volumes of Kierkegaard's own *Gesammelte Werke* in *Review of Theology and Philosophy*, vol. 6, 1910, pp. 304–8.

[14]   Mabel A. Stobart, "New Light on Ibsen's 'Brand,' " in *The Fortnightly Review*, vol. 66, 1899, pp. 227–39; Mabel A. Stobart, "The 'Either-Or' of Sören Kierkegaard," in *The Fortnightly Review*, vol. 71, 1902, pp. 53–60.

[15]   Stobart, "New Light on Ibsen's 'Brand,' " p. 227.

[16]   Ibid., p. 229.

[17]   Ibid.

[18]   Ibid., p. 239.

If, in her first article devoted to him, Miss Stobart had hailed Kierkegaard as the "Copenhagen apostle," he appears in the second as "the Tycho Brache, as he has been called, of Danish philosophy."[19] Much of this article is given over to praising Kierkegaard in a variety of ways: his writings have "an intellectual brilliancy and an almost magical power of fascination," an "effulgent, yet clear and restful radiance"; the "Diary of the Seducer" is a "web woven with a delicacy worthy of a high priest anxious for the reputation of the cult he represents" and "it is with a breathless interest that we follow the psychological manipulations of Kierkegaard's representative pastmaster in the science of Aesthetic emotion"—though it is written with a "charming simplicity of style."[20] Yet, though Stobart is duly charmed by the literary values of the first part of *Either/Or*, despite "the greater intrinsic value" of the second, her conclusion is that there is more to Kierkegaard than a mere man of letters. Although she refers to Brandes in her 1899 article, her conclusion now gives a quite different ordering of the Nietzsche/ Kierkegaard relationship than his. Addressing the question as to why Kierkegaard is not better known, she suggests that

> had this talented thinker been solely either philosopher or lyrical writer, he must long ago have received his desserts, but that he is at once too didactic for the poetic reader, and too lyrical for the philosophic taste of the period, philosophy having been till within recent years regarded as a dry and abstruse science ill-mated with the more fanciful muses. But now the Zeit-Geist of the Age demands a bridge over the gulf which has hitherto divided the few abstract and purely scientific philosophic thinkers on the one side, from mankind with its ritualistic and dogmatic religion upon the other, and the time has perhaps come when, disappointed with the illusionary nature of thinkers who, like Nietzsche, put away realities to find consolation in pretty coloured clouds, the large and increasing number of spiritually ambitious who have cast off the swaddling clothes of superstition can appreciate the helpful works of an earnest and vigorous thinker such as Sören Kierkegaard.[21]

Most readers today will probably find this an odd characterization of Nietzsche, and Stobart's view of Kierkegaard may be more enthusiastic than careful, but it is clear that by 1902 Kierkegaard had found at least one well-informed and appreciative reader on British shores.

In an article appearing in the avant-garde weekly journal *The New Age* on September 19 (Part 1) and 26 (Part 2), 1908, entitled "Ibsen, Nietzsche and Kierkegaard," Dr. Angelo Rappaport seems to offer a judgement on the respective merits of Kierkegaard and Nietzsche opposite to that of Stobart. These men, Rappaport believes, are amongst a rare company of "serious, deep natures"[22] that includes "Flaubert and Renan, Carlyle and Emerson...Dosotieffsky [and] Wagner."[23] Of the three mentioned in his title Rappaport says that "The unrest of their souls drove them out from the

---

[19]   Stobart, "The 'Either-Or' of Sören Kierkegaard," p. 53.
[20]   Ibid., p. 53; p. 53; p. 57; p. 58; p. 58.
[21]   Ibid., p. 60.
[22]   Angelo S. Rappaport, "Ibsen, Nietzsche and Kierkegaard," *The New Age*, vol. 3, no. 21, 1908, pp. 408–9; vol. 3, no. 22, 1908, pp. 428–9; see vol. 3, no. 21, 1908, p. 408.
[23]   Rappaport, "Ibsen, Nietzsche and Kierkegaard," *The New Age*, vol. 3, no. 21, 1908, p. 409.

safe haven of traditionalism and faith upon the surging waves of enquiry in search of new lands, of new worlds, of new gods, and of new ideals."[24] However, Ibsen and Kierkegaard proved themselves in the last resort to be "democratic," their view of the ideal was that it should be for "everyone," since everyone can, in principle, become "the exception." Rappaport's conclusion is that, as a result, they "were never morally free, and, therefore, although they began as Titans, they finished as petty reformers....They had gone out in their respective vessels in search of new lands, but Ibsen's and Kierkegaard's voyage was a circular tour. They returned—sadder, perhaps wiser, men—to their native homes."[25] Nietzsche, however, "an Italian by thought and culture" did not return, he alone lived the truly aristocratic spirit, only "his land is not the land of Everyman"[26]—and it is this Nietzschean aristocratism that is, in Rappaport's view, the better outcome.

It is perhaps worth adding that Rappaport's method of using a roll-call of supposedly kindred spirits by which to locate his subject is a device that recurs at many points in the reception of Kierkegaard in Great Britain, as, doubtless, elsewhere. Kierkegaard himself was familiar with the saying that to know a man's friends was to know the man,[27] and I shall at a number of points draw attention to commentators' use of such listings and, sometimes, rankings, as indicative of where exactly they were placing Kierkegaard in the cultural and intellectual horizon of their time. Although Nietzsche and Dostoevsky would prove fairly constant companions, there could be considerable variations in the lists of Kierkegaard's supposed associates, as we shall see.

By 1910, then, Kierkegard would have been a name known to some, however few, in literary circles as a representative of the same cultural movement that was better known through such representatives as Ibsen and Nietzsche. That his importance was such as to merit the efforts of translation and comment that followed their work (and, we might add, that of Dostoevsky, at this time being translated by Constance Garnet), was not a judgement ventured by any at this time.

The religious reception of Kierkegaard's thought in this period is, perhaps, somewhat more substantial, and, where it occurs, somewhat more positive than the stirrings of literary interest. Works of Kierkegaard appearing in German were reviewed in theological journals, especially within the Reformed tradition. Theological readers would also have been able to read Martensen's remarks, although not all were put off by them.

An early sign that Kierkegaard had much to offer modern theology can be glimpsed in P.T. Forsyth, a Scottish Baptist theologian, who mostly lived and worked in England. Forsyth himself would come to be known in the history of modern theology as a precursor of Barth in his attack on theological liberalism. Interestingly, however (and unlike Barth in this respect), Forsyth had himself passed through a liberal and, more particularly, Hegelian phase. Of special interest for Forsyth's

---

[24]   Ibid., p. 408.

[25]   Rappaport, "Ibsen, Nietzsche and Kierkegaard," *The New Age*, vol. 3, no. 22, 1908, p. 429.

[26]   Ibid.

[27]   *SKS* 5, 250 / *EUD*, 253.

reading of Kierkegaard is that this phase was marked by a significant focus on art and aesthetics, on which he produced two substantial books, *Religion in Recent Art* and *Christ on Parnassus*.[28] In the introduction to the latter Forsyth says, "I am preaching Hegel."[29] However, by the end of this study he declares that it is ultimately Christian faith and not philosophy that provides the best guide to art: "Art is not life, and faith is. Art does not prescribe a morality, and faith does. Christ did not come as a subject for Art, but as an object of faith and giver of life."[30] And: "Fantasy is one thing, and faith is another, and it is Faith that guides life...."[31] If Forsyth found his own movement from the aesthetic, through the ethical to the religious prefigured in Kierkegaard, he does not say so, though his closing discussion in *Christ on Parnassus* has teasing Kierkegaardian resonances. In fact he seems to have made only one direct reference to Kierkegaard in his published work, in *The Work of Christ*, where he introduces an extended quotation from the Dane:

> There is a timely saying of that searching Christian genius Kierkegaard—the great and melancholy Dane in whom Hamlet was mastered by Christ: "For long the tactics have been: use every means to move as many as you can—to move everybody if possible to enter Christianity. Do not be too curious whether what they enter *is* Christianity. My tactics have been, with God's help, to use every means to make it clear what the demand of Christianity really is—if not one entered it." The statement is extreme; but that way lies the Church's salvation—in its ante-Nicene relation to the world; its pre-Constantinian, non-established relation to the world, and devotion to the Word. Society is hopeless except for the Church.[32]

This is, of course, a very different judgment on the Church from that which emerges from Kierkegaard's own "Attack"—however, it should be remembered that Forsyth was writing precisely from within a non-established ecclesiastical tradition and that the Church he sought to promote was precisely not a Church "by law established."

Baron Friedrich von Hügel came from a very different ecclesiastical wing again, from within the circle of Catholic theological modernizers that emerged, briefly, at the beginning of the twentieth century before being slapped down by the Anti-modernist oath imposed on all Catholic clergy. Von Hügel, living and writing in England, never took an oppositional stance to the Church, yet he engaged with contemporary Protestant theology and contemporary philosophy, particularly in its idealist and personalist forms, in an open and irenic way that was unique in Catholic theology at that time. In 1912 von Hügel published a very substantial study *Eternal Life: A Study of its Implications and Applications* (again published by T. & T. Clark), a work which was given its second edition a year later.

Von Hügel includes two-and-a-half pages on Kierkegaard in his "Contemporary Survey." In his inimitably ponderous style he describes his subject as "the deep,

---

[28]   Peter Taylor Forsyth, *Religion in Recent Art*, London: Hodder and Stoughton 1905; *Christ on Parnassus*, New York and Toronto: Hodder and Stoughton 1911.

[29]   Forsyth, *Christ on Parnassus*, p. viii.

[30]   Ibid., p. 293.

[31]   Ibid., p. 299.

[32]   P.T. Forsyth, *The Work of Christ*, London: Independent Press 1910, p. xxxii.

melancholy, strenuous, utterly uncompromising Danish religionist," going on to speak of him as "a spiritual brother of the great Frenchman, Blaise Pascal, and of the striking English Tractarian, Hurrell Froude...." "Kierkegaard is especially interesting," he adds, "in that he, a modern of the moderns, is as massively *ontological* in his religion as any ancient."[33] Much of the brief discussion is taken up with an extended quotation from what the Baron calls the *Final Unscientific Postscript* that illustrates this "ontological" commitment, both in terms of the emphasis on the reality of God and of God's difference from humanity. However, although such an emphasis would have been congenial to von Hügel, he concludes that Kierkegaard combines it with "an excessive because exclusive" treatment "of the eschatological, the other-worldly, movement in Our Lord's teaching."[34] The upshot is that "it is Kierkegaard's profound apprehension of the Ontology and the Difference which renders him religiously deep and powerful, beyond all the Subjectivists and Identity-thinkers put together; and it is his lack of insight as to the Likeness which leaves his life strained to the verge of insanity."[35]

Although they devote little enough space to Kierkegaard, Forsyth and von Hügel were each amongst the big hitters of their respective theological traditions and each, in their different ways, clearly saw in him a figure worthy of respect and attention. Much less well-known was the Anglican clergyman Francis W. Fulford. For most of his career, Fulford, born in Cambridge in 1876, was a parish priest of the Church of England, dying in office at Watlington in Norfolk.[36] Fulford was thus a perhaps unlikely candidate to be the author of the first book-length study of Kierkegaard in English, published in 1911, *Sören Aabye Kierkegaard: A Study*.[37] Probably Fulford's book was never widely read, yet it is a competent survey of the main texts and topics of the authorship, studied in the original Danish and not in German translation.

Fulford states that Kierkegaard was "by common consent the greatest thinker Denmark has produced." He sets about an exposition of Kierkegaard's thought with special emphasis on his religious message. He offers an outline of Kierkegaard's life and a summary of the major works, though not *Either/Or*. He divides Kierkegaard's thought into the "destructive teaching" and the "constructive teaching." Destructively, Kierkegaard opposes Luther, the established Church, the "religion of Thought" and human beings' feebleness and inability to suffer. However, constructively, "The main interest of Kierkegaard is to set forth the religious man and the Christian man in their ideal." Fulford summarizes the teaching of the three spheres, the religious sphere being defined as "that of completeness." Emphasizing the category of inwardness, Fulford uses Kierkegaard's division of religion into religiousness A and B, although whether his application of these terms closely reflects Kierkegaard's

---

[33] Friedrich von Hügel, *Eternal Life: A Study of its Implications and Applications*, 2nd ed., Edinburgh: T. & T. Clark 1913, p. 260.
[34] Ibid., p. 261.
[35] Ibid., p. 262.
[36] See the obituary in *The Times*, July 24, 1941. It is probably a pure coincidence, but Fulford, like several later British Kierkegaard scholars, including Roger Poole and the present author, was educated at the Perse School, Cambridge.
[37] Francis W. Fulford, *Sören Aabye Kierkegaard: A Study*, Cambridge: Wallis 1911.

own is questionable. "A" comprises a sense of the nothingness of man, an attitude of trust and contentment, the simplicity of love towards one's fellow human beings and "repetition," understood both as a virtue and as a blessing on this stage of religion. "B" includes Abraham, the conviction of sin (with reference to *The Concept of Anxiety*), and following the example of Jesus Christ.

Fulford accepts the Christian premises of Kierkegaard's work and, anticipating complaints from "the average man," "the liberal thinker," and "the conservative," he insists that the real question is: does Kierkegaard's thought "harmonize with the mind of Christ"? His own criticisms of Kierkegaard include a disagreement concerning the Reformation, which Fulford does not see as a revolt against "the Example." In connection with this he notes that there must be that in Christ which is beyond imitation. He also disagrees about the nature of sin, which, he believes, is not only to be understood in terms of disbelief in Christ, and he stresses that we must remember to keep faith with man as well as with God. And, he complains, Kierkegaard limits the divine help to those who desire it. Against Kierkegaard, he says, Christianity should not be withheld from children.

I have perhaps given more space to these first adumbrations of Kierkegaard reception prior to the First World War than their intrinsic stature may merit. Partly this is because this is a less well-known phase of the story; partly it is because the sources themselves are not readily accessible. Taken together, they scarcely constitute a coherent story of reception, and, even by the summer of 1914, that totemic "end of the nineteenth century," it is scarcely possible to talk about a substantial presence of Kierkegaard in British life. Nor is there any clear or direct line to the subsequent history of Kierkegaard reception in Britain, shaped by a very different and darker intellectual, cultural and religious situation.

II. From the First World War to the 1970s

In the interwar period the picture changes dramatically. There can be little doubt that this is, in the first instance, provoked by the role of Kierkegaard in the dialectical theology of Karl Barth and in the philosophy of existence, both of which burst onto the scene in the 1920s. Even where the primary texts, such as Barth's *Commentary on the Letter to the Romans* and Heidegger's *Being and Time* were not known first-hand, they exerted a rapid influence on the English-speaking world—and even where they were not favorably received. Of these, it is especially Barth and the theologians influenced by or reacting to him who serves as the main stimulus to studying Kierkegaard. In the preface to his 1950 book *Kierkegaard: The Melancholy Dane*, H.V. Martin wrote that, during his theological training,

> when I began to study Karl Barth, I found that he seemed to crystallize clearly much of what was already undefined in my mind. I became a "Barthian." Though I have moved on since then, I still feel greatly in debt to Barth, chiefly because it was through him I was introduced to the work of Sören Kierkegaard.[38]

---

[38]   Harold Victor Martin, *Kierkegaard: The Melancholy Dane*, London: Epworth Press 1950, p. 7. In the same year Martin published another short introduction, *The Wings of Faith:*

Back in 1935, in the Preface to his *Kierkegaard: His Life and Thought*, one of the two studies of Kierkegaard to be published in Britain in that year, E.L. Allen wrote that "When he [Kierkegaard] fainted in the streets of Copenhagen in 1855, he seemed meant only for the sensation of a day. But the World-war wrote in blood the commentary on his writings, and today he is acclaimed by philosophers like Heidegger and Jaspers, theologians like Barth and Hirsch...."[39]

Allen's own task, as he puts it, is "to fill a gap," since the man and the thought thus acclaimed "on the Continent with Marx and Nietzsche, is with us but a rumour of a name."[40] Allen's conclusion, however, is somewhat negative: "Of Kierkegaard himself we must say....that he was a valiant fighter in a cause he did not rightly understand. He was too concerned with sacrificing reason to the God-man to be able to follow the Master."[41] From Allen's point of view, faced with the choice of Christianity and culture, Kierkegaard chose Christianity: "His choice was a heroic one, but few are likely to follow him in it."[42] "The vain struggle of this lonely, sensitive genius to reconcile himself to Christianity is one of the unhappiest chapters in the history of the human spirit....[A]gainst the last enemy within himself, his native melancholy, he was powerless." Kierkegaard, finally, and in the last line of the book was thus "left alone with stark fact, despotic demand, and suffering upon suffering."[43] Kierkegaard chose a path of perpetual opposition, but Allen believes that the Christian is only required to oppose modern civilization when the latter "is so many money-bags plus so many bayonets," but "where it is social conscience and the fearless love of truth [the Christian] will count it an honour to be numbered amongst its children."[44]

As a gloss on Allen's judgement on Kierkegaard it should be noted that he also wrote a small book entitled *Bishop Grundtvig: A Prophet of the North*, which concludes by opposing Kierkegaard to Grundtvig and roundly endorsing the latter's embrace of "the new world of democracy and social endeavour, national solidarity and human rights" and affirming Grundtvig's "First a man, and then a Christian."[45]

John A. Bain, in *Sören Kierkegaard: His Life and Religious Teaching*, also acknowledges the lack of awareness of Kierkegaard in Britain, but he does not lay so much stress on the Barthian connection. "The extent to which Barth's theology has been affected is doubtful. In many points Barth's thinking is on similar lines to that of the Danish writer, to whom, however, I understand Barth does not attribute

---

A Consideration of the Nature and Meaning of the Christian Faith in the Light of the Work of Søren Kierkegaard, London: Lutterworth Press 1950.

[39]   Edgar Leonard Allen, *Kierkegaard: His Life and Thought*, London: Stanley Watt, 1935, p. vii.

[40]   Ibid.

[41]   Ibid., p. 205.

[42]   Ibid., p. 204.

[43]   Ibid., p. 206.

[44]   Ibid., p. 205.

[45]   E.L. Allen, *Bishop Grundtvig: A Prophet of the North*, London: James Clarke 1948, p. 94.

much influence to the formation of his thought."[46] Bain does, however, also note that "Kierkegaard has been much used by Husserl, Heidegger, and others in the newer philosophical school in Germany."[47] Bain too ends with a highly qualified assessment of Kierkegaard's merits: "He had serious defects that hindered him from being a power for good in the Church and community of his day," deficiencies which included his "die-hard political conservatism," and his "exaggerated individualism": "We are not taught to go into God's presence and say: 'My Father,' but 'Our Father,' and are thereby taught that in the most fundamental element of our religious life we are to link ourselves continually with our fellow men."[48] The "great mistakes" of Kierkegaard's life are thus not having married Regine Olsen and not having "an occupation or profession that would have kept him in daily contact with his fellow men."[49] If he had married and had a job, Bain says, "he would have learned that religious theories must be tested by their power to fit the facts of human experience."[50] Yet

> while making these reservations and recognising that his religion is not that of Christ, we can at any rate hear in his voice an echo of John the Baptist calling on men to repent of all unreality in their religion, all sham and pretence, and to search our hearts and lives to see if we are nearer to the God who revealed Himself in Christ than was he who made such burning appeals to his countrymen to repent and turn to God.[51]

Bain offers as an appendix thirty-five pages of short extracts from Kierkegaard's writings.

In 1937 Kierkegaard merits a chapter of the distinguished Scottish theologian H.R. Mackintosh's *Types of Modern Theology*, alongside Schleiermacher, Hegel, Ritschl, Troeltsch, and Barth.[52] Clearly, like other Scottish theologians, Mackintosh was deeply informed by the German theological tradition, but we may say that, with this book, by a theologian of stature, Kierkegaard definitively enters the British theological field as a thinker of the first rank. If Mackintosh's theology, bearing the stamp of Scottish Calvinism, was intrinsically more open to the kind of negativity we find in Kierkegaard than that of English thinkers molded by deep convictions as to the necessity of always looking for a *via media*, he nevertheless shares Allen's and Bain's view that, in the last resort, Kierkegaard was, simply, too one-sided. However, his chapter begins on a more positive note:

> No account of leading modern types of Theology would be complete, or even intelligent, which omitted the work of Sören Kierkegaard. He has been called "the greatest Christian thinker of the past century," "the greatest of all Christian psychologists." And such

---

[46]   John A. Bain, *Sören Kierkegaard: His Life and Religious Teaching*, London: SCM 1935, p. 11.
[47]   Ibid., p. 10.
[48]   Ibid., p. 117.
[49]   Ibid., p. 118.
[50]   Ibid., p. 119.
[51]   Ibid.
[52]   Hugh Ross Mackintosh, *Types of Modern Theology: Schleiermacher to Barth*, London: Collins/Fontana 1964 [London: Nisbet & Co. 1937].

an estimate, in spite of apparent extravagance, is a finger-post it would be unwise to ignore.[53]

Yet we are also given notice that there is a "Hamlet-like strain" in Kierkegaard and that his teaching "has in it the elements of a deeply shadowed life." The affinity with Barth is noted and accepted, and Kierkegaard is compared to Tertullian for having given to theology "a new set of terms—existence and existential, incognito (used of Jesus Christ), contemporaneous, moment, offence, perpendicular, tension, decision and the like."[54]

Though Kierkegaard is indeed "subjective," "[a] mind so gravely realistic could never have been tempted by the subjectivity of 'religion without an object.' "[55] Yet, after tracing the "stages on life's way" under the title "the successive levels of human life," Mackintosh finds the actual view of God held by Kierkegaard to be inadequate. The unknowability of God, coupled with the necessity of God for human life, engendered in Kierkegaard a situation of religious torture and an unrelenting imperative of sacrifice, including the sacrifice of all humanly comprehensible predicates for God. "It is," Mackintosh comments, "hard to believe that, as a general conception, this reproduces with fidelity the teaching of the New Testament."[56] "That God is unfathomable is a basal element in all true theology; that God is the 'absolutely Unknown' is a position separated from the other by the whole diameter of being. Scripture gives it no support."[57] The same applies to Kierkegaard's Christology. Noting that the emphasis on absurdity is not to be turned too glibly against Kierkegaard—"It is not to be thought that a man of Kierkegaard's supreme ability could revel in mere nonsense for its own sake"[58]—Mackintosh finds that Kierkegaard's insistence on "unmitigated paradox" "is curiously out of touch, in particular, with the picture of Jesus Christ in Gospel and Epistle."[59]

What we see in Kierkegaard are thus two irreconcileable conceptions of God: "God as Holy Love" and God as absolute transcendence, before whom man is sheer nothingness. "There is no way of bringing these two conceptions of God together in a mind which has submitted trustfully to the Christian revelation," writes Mackintosh.[60] Yet his conclusion mitigates the criticism of Kierkegaard in a manner different from that of Allen or Bain:

> In that brave, tragic life of faith and genius, impulses were moving for all of which we must not claim Biblical sanction. We repudiate his error, while yet we find no cause to doubt the truth of his impassioned affirmation that for him also the certainty of God's fatherly love in Christ was "the Archimedean point." Under his theology, so piercing

---

[53]   Ibid., p. 209.
[54]   Ibid., p. 210.
[55]   Ibid., p. 216.
[56]   Ibid., p. 230.
[57]   Ibid., pp. 230–1.
[58]   Ibid., p. 234.
[59]   Ibid., p. 237. Of course, it is not to the point of the present article to contest the misreading of Kierkegaard committed by Mackintosh on these key theological points.
[60]   Ibid., p. 250.

in insight, so mixed in quality, we may fitly inscribe the words of Pascal: "in great men everything is great—their faults as well as their merits."[61]

1937 also saw the publication by Oxford University Press (soon to be the English publishers of Swenson's and Lowrie's translations of Kierkegaard) of a pair of essays by Theodor Haecker, under the title *Søren Kierkegaard* (note, at last, the Danish ø!).[62] In church terms, Haecker, a Catholic layman, approached Kierkegaard with a very different set of presuppositions from those of Mackintosh. Haecker's greatest significance in terms of Kierkegaard reception undoubtedly lies in the German-speaking world, but in the essays published in Britain in 1937 he does offer a distinct, perhaps "Catholic," angle by drawing on Kierkegaard's religious meditations, not least those for the sacrament of the altar, to supplement his polemical and philosophical works. Thus it was not in an absurd faith but in love that Haecker found the key to Kierkegaard's thought:

> His motto was the Benedictine motto *Ora et labora*, so that he could say "my genius is my prayer." Nor was it merely a matter of holding out until one day all would be over, but of enduring and bearing it because it never ceases: because there is eternity: eternal blessedness or eternal despair. And as a result of his great struggles he received that precious acquisition, the belief that God is love. Even if he had never said so, although in fact he does, it is clear which was his favourite text, for it was the subject of nearly all his discourses and he was for ever paraphrasing it. Little wonder, then, that it was this verse from the epistle of S. James: "Every good gift and every perfect gift is from above, and cometh down from the Father of lights with whom is no variableness, neither shadow of turning."[63]

By this time, Kierkegaard himself was starting to appear in English translation. Lee M. Hollander had published a small anthology of texts in the United States in 1923, though this was probably not widely known in Britain. David Swenson's translation of *Philosophical Fragments* appeared in 1936;[64] in 1937 a section of *Upbuilding Discourses in Various Spirits*, under the title *Purify Your Hearts* was published in Britain in the translation by A.S. Aldworth and W.S. Ferrie, who would go on to translate the other two parts as well.[65] In 1938, Alexander Dru, translator of Haecker's book (and introduced to Kierkegaard's work by Haecker

---

[61]   Ibid., p. 251.
[62]   Theodor Haecker, *Søren Kierkegaard*, trans. by Alexander Dru, London: Oxford University Press 1937.
[63]   Ibid., p. 50.
[64]   *Philosophical Fragments*, trans. by David Swenson, Princeton, New Jersey: Princeton University Press 1936.
[65]   *Purify Your Hearts* (a section of *Upbuilding Discourses in Various Spirits*), trans. by A.S. Aldworth and W.S. Ferrie, London: C.W. Daniel, 1937 (Aldworth and Ferrie were, in fact, a married couple, as well as collaborators in translating Kierkegaard). Reviewed in the journal *Purpose, Purify your Hearts!* found itself between the same covers as essays by, e.g., T.S. Eliot and Henry Miller—new company for Kierkegaard to keep!

himself in the 1920s[66]) published a substantial selection from the journals with Oxford University Press, a text which would become many readers' first port of call in acquainting themselves with Kierkegaard. Walter Lowrie (1868–1959) also published his first translation of *The Point of View* and other associated writings with Oxford the following year.[67] Translations of other major works followed in quick succession, and by the mid-1940s a solid body of Kierkegaard's writing was available in English. Not only that, but Lowrie's massive biography, about forty per cent of which consists of quoted materials, was published in 1938, shaping many English-language readers' perceptions of its subject. Herbert Read, perhaps the most eminent British art critic of his generation, recalls in his autobiographical *Annals of Innocence and Experience* how he had begun looking for Kierkegaard's works in German and French translations as a result of references in German philosophy, but it is to Haecker's, Dru's, and Lowrie's works and translations that he refers when discussing the influence Kierkegaard had on him, and it is Lowrie's translation he rewrites as poetry in a rather beautiful rendering of a passage from the *Either/Or* essay on Mozart and which he likens to a poem of Rilke.[68]

The stage was now set for the rumors originating in France and Germany to become realities in Britain, and Kierkegaard was set to become a tangible cultural presence. As Charles Williams, the Oxford University Press editor responsible for the Kierkegaard translations wrote in his own survey of Christian history, *The Descent of the Dove*: "as Kierkegaard becomes fashionable, which is already beginning to happen...He will be explained...His imagination will be made to depend on his personal history, and his sayings will be so moderated in our minds that they will soon become not his sayings but ours."[69]

Williams' prediction of fashionableness was borne out, doubtless added to by the emergence in France of philosophers such as Sartre and writers like Camus, who, under the banner "existentialism", cited Kierkegaard as a decisive progenitor. In an article in the BBC journal *The Listener*, and based on a broadcast talk he had given, T.S. Gregory hailed Kierkegaard in 1946 as "The Prophet of the Now" and in similar vein Evelyn Waugh's novel *The Loved One*[70] contains a conversation between two expatriate Englishmen living in California, in the course of which Kierkegaard is cited in a list of fashionable names "being talked about in London," including Kafka,

---

[66]   On the relationship between Haecker and Dru, see John Heywood-Thomas and Hinrich Siefkin, "Theodeor Haecker and Alexander Dru: A Contribution to the Discovery of Kierkegaard in Britain," *Kierkegaardiana*, vol. 18, 1996, pp. 173–90.

[67]   *The Point of View for My Work as an Author: A Report to History and Related Writings*, trans. and ed. by Walter Lowrie, New York: Harper Torchbooks 1939.

[68]   Herbert Read, *Annals of Innocence and Experience*, London: Faber and Faber 1946, pp. 116–23.

[69]   Charles Williams, *The Descent of the Dove: A Short History of the Holy Spirit in the Church*, London: Collins/Fontana 1963 [London: Longmans & Co. 1939], pp. 193–4. Williams was, incidentally, a central member of the "Inklings," a literary and religious circle based in Oxford, also including C.S. Lewis and J.R.R. Tolkien, and he was a religious poet, novelist, and writer in his own—always somewhat quirky—right.

[70]   Evelyn Waugh, *The Loved One: An Anglo-American Tragedy*, London: Little, Brown & Co. 1948.

Connolly, Compton-Burnett, and Sartre. The influential London *World Review* included in its August 1949 number a prettily illustrated translation of Kierkegaard's journal for his 1840 journey to Jutland.[71] The same number had contributions by John Rothenstein (Director of the Tate Gallery), Harold Macmillan, William Saroyan, Karl Barth, Karl Jaspers, Stephen Spender, Mervyn Peake, and John Heath-Stubbs, as well as discussions of Henry Moore, W.H. Auden, and what Macmillan called "the Strasbourg Experiment." If we can judge a man by the company he keeps, then, we must say that Kierkegaard was now at the epicenter of cultural and intellectual life.

In the opening line of his charmingly conversational Introduction to a further substantial contribution to British Kierkegaard literature, *Kierkegaard Studies* (also from 1948), Thomas Henry Croxall (1893–1960) wrote that "Kierkegaard is in the air these days."[72] Indeed, Lord Lindsay of Birker, Master of Balliol College, Oxford, who offered a preface to Croxall's book had in that same year held a series of addresses on "St Paul and Kierkegaard" in his college chapel.[73] Croxall sets out his book in three main sections, "Man," "Christianity," and "God" and seeks to read his subject in the double-focus of the Bible and the present age. What he sees in Kierkegaard, then, is precisely a Christian thinker who can meet the challenge of modernity and answer it in intellectual terms as powerful as those in which the challenge is made. Concerning the Bible, Croxall insists that, as Kierkegaard himself frequently claimed, "we may be sure that there is a vital connexion between his philosophy and the Bible" and that this applies as much to what Croxall calls "the philosophical and psychological works" as to "the religious works," even if the "Biblical nexus" is less obvious in these cases.[74] Interestingly (if—as his own comments suggest—unusually), Croxall avoids dwelling on the biographical side of Kierkegaard. Approaching him in these terms is, he says, "becoming dangerous" and can lead to the impression that he was mad. "But Kierkegaard is *not* mad. He often tilts the boat of his dialectic till it lists terribly, especially in his attack on the Danish Church at the close of his life. That often makes him lopsided, but rarely... downright false; for he is...always at the helm of his listing boat."[75] However, he acknowledges that the life is important, and refers his readers to Lowrie's *Short Life* of Kierkegaard.[76] A music scholar and organist, Croxall's book interestingly offers a chapter on Music, in the section on "Man."

As well as his *Kierkegaard Studies* and the translation of the Jutland journal for *World Review*, Croxall would go on to make further contributions to Kierkegaard literature in England by translating a selection of meditations from the "devotional"

---

[71]   "A Pilgrimage to Jutland," trans. by Thomas Henry Croxall, in *World Review*, New Series, No. 6, August 1949.

[72]   Thomas Henry Croxall, *Kierkegaard Studies*, London and Redhill: Lutterworth 1948, p. 11.

[73]   Alexander Dunlop Lindsay, *Selected Addresses*, privately published, Cumberland 1957, pp. 65–97.

[74]   Croxall, *Kierkegaard Studies*, p. 12.

[75]   Ibid., pp. 18–19.

[76]   Walter Lowrie, *A Short Life of Kierkegaard*, Princeton, New Jersey: Princeton University Press 1942.

works, published in 1955,[77] and *Glimpses and Impressions of Kierkegaard*,[78] containing translations of contemporary memoirs and other biographical materials, including the recollections of Hans Brøchner, Henriette Lund, and a range of materials relating to the attack on the Church.

The wisdom of Croxall's reservations about the value of the biographical approach is borne out by the extent to which a kind of amateur psycho-analysis was often applied to the genesis of Kierkegaardian ideas in this period of reception, with mysterious paternal goings-on in 2 Nytorv usually being to blame. Lowrie's biography, as well as the introductory notes to his translations, gave a cue to such speculations, but they were widespread. In 1959 Rudolph Friedman offered an extreme example in his 60-page psycho-analytical study, *Kierkegaard: The Analysis of the Psychological Personality*. The usual myths are recycled, sometimes with embellishments, as when the oft-mooted one-off visit to a brothel seems to have become a regular occurrence: "In moods of drunken dissipation Kierkegaard visited prostitutes."[79] Again, Kierkegaard is compared with Nietzsche, and seems again to have fallen short of the latter's "Dionysian, life-giving Imago," a shortcoming that his death, however, appears to have finally made good:

> As the setting sun of death touched him, Kierkegaard shone forth with the power of the Primæval Father, a rock of bronze, a nineteenth-century *Hermanns Denkmal*, assaulting the heavens with his sword, amidst the endless pine trees of the Teutoburg mountains. For the last time the schizophrenic Imago came near to nature, and heard the sap running down the trees. Not only with the harsh and terrible radiance of the Father-God, but in part touched with the soft contours of youth, the monumental figure rose aloft. Kierkegaard gave historical reality to that special union of psychological Imago and youth which constitutes genius. The tendrils of his spirit, reaching upwards, became wrapt in the skyleaf of the clouds. In the infinite pathos of death, the pure and sublime spirit experienced the full potency of his never-realized manhood.[80]

Such overripe speculation was, happily, to prove a *non plus ultra* in this line of interpretation!

At the same time as the Christian (and the psycho-analyzed) Kierkegaard, the existentialist Kierkegaard was also at the centre of contemporary action in the late 1940s and early to mid-1950s. Even before the war, Werner Brock's *Contemporary German Philosophy* had firmly identified the Dane as pivotal to the development of modern German philosophy which, for Brock, meant primarily Heidegger.[81]

---

[77]   *Meditations from Kierkegaard*, trans. and ed. by T.H. Croxall, London: James Nisbet 1955—interestingly this was published just one year before Perry LeFevre published *The Prayers of Kierkegaard* in the United States, a pointer to one way in which Kierkegaard was being read at this time.
[78]   Thomas Henry Croxall, *Glimpses and Impressions of Kierkegaard*, Welwyn: James Nisbet 1959.
[79]   Rudolph Friedman, *Kierkegaard: The Analysis of the Psychological Personality*, London: Peter Nevill 1959.
[80]   Ibid., p. 55.
[81]   See Werner Brock, *An Introduction to Contemporary German Philosophy*, Cambridge: Cambridge University Press 1935, especially pp. 72–86.

Guido Ruggieros' introductory book on *Existentialism*, translated into English in 1945, opened "One hundred years ago in Copenhagen...."[82] H.J. Blackham's *Six Existentialist Thinkers* described its subjects as "marvellously gifted, highly trained, masters of Western culture, with exceptional seriousness of purpose and a profound personal experience,"[83] and the book began with what, in such studies, would become an obligatory first chapter on Kierkegaard. (The other five existentialist thinkers dealt with were Nietzsche, Jaspers, Marcel, Heidegger, and Sartre.) Colin Wilson's *The Outsider* was undoubtedly negligent with scholarly accuracy, but this didn't prevent the book being a massive success in its time and influential on a generation of readers in the way that cult classics are. This was the era of the "angry young men," and Kierkegaard was enlisted as one of the decisive historical progenitors of the contemporary outsider—this time in such mixed company as George Fox, Blake, Tolstoy, Dostoevsky, Nietzsche, Nijinsky, Hemingway, Hesse, and Gurdjieff![84]

Of course, not everyone was persuaded that all this excitement about the "melancholy Dane" was a good thing. Writing polemically from a "Humanist" standpoint, one Hector Hawton reaffirmed faith in progress and declared that "In the present fevered condition of the divided world it is disastrous to preach that tensions must be maintained and not resolved, because of some supposed metaphysical necessity. It is cowardly and false to say that humanity is doomed and that we must therefore choose Despair."[85] It is, of course, the existentialists he sees as primarily culpable with regard to such disastrous preaching, with Kierkegaard at their head, epitomizing "the spiritual pride of an egoist incapable of real feeling."[86] As regards Kierkegaard's conviction that faith cannot be rationally justified, "You can, of course, stubbornly stick to an assertion against your rational judgement, and make a virtue of the perpetual discomfort that this involves, but it is odd to recommend this schizophrenic procedure as a means of unifying the personality....I do not think that the plight of Pascal and Kierkegaard represents the universal human condition, although they may be right in insisting that it is the outcome of carrying Christianity through to its logical conclusion."[87] Nevertheless, we do owe to Hawton the delicious description of Kierkegaard as "a dandiacal saint, a Savonarola of the boulevards."[88]

For such reasons as Hawton's humanist faith in the need to base one's life on rationally justifiable propositions (and, of course, the perception that Kierkegaard allowed no scope for the rational procedures involved in such justification), the

---

[82]   Guido de Ruggiero, *Existentialism*, London: Secker and Warburg 1946, p. 5.
[83]   Harold John Blackham, *Six Existentialist Thinkers*, London, Routledge and Kegan Paul 1961 [1952], p. 164.
[84]   See Colin Wilson, *The Outsider*, London: Victor Gollancz 1956. Kierkegaard was also given a chapter in Wilson's sequel, *Religion and the Rebel*, London: Gollancz 1957, where he now finds himself in a family tree running from Jacob Boehme, through Nicholas Ferrar, Blaise Pascal, Emanuel [*sic*] Swedenborg, William Law, John Henry Newman, Kierkegaard himself, and on to George Bernard Shaw, Wittgenstein, and Whitehead!
[85]   Hector Hawton, *The Feast of Unreason*, London: Watts and Co. 1952, p. 224.
[86]   Ibid., p. 67.
[87]   Ibid., p. 80.
[88]   Ibid., p. 58.

religious and cultural interest in Kierkegaard in these years was scarcely matched by any corresponding philosophical reception. For as Blackham had remarked:

> Even in these days, academic groves are cool and sequestered, and it is understandable that in such quarters a pulpit philosophy should be resented and deplored, for the new friars, more frothily corruptive of youth than the ancient sophists, let loose an immense untidiness and with uncouth shouts set up their morality show and parade the hectic of disease against a backcloth of the vast and vague.[89]

This is, of course, a view which many Anglo-Saxon philosophers would still be naturally disposed to accept (despite the continuing rumors of Kierkegaard's influence on or, at least, appeal to Wittgenstein). To the extent that a philosophical reception happened at all in Britain in this period, it was most likely to be within the relatively limited field of philosophy of religion—and, in any case, practiced by theologians. The American James Collins' *The Mind of Kierkegaard*[90] was widely read, but perhaps the first significant British philosophical study was John Heywood-Thomas's *Subjectivity and Paradox* (1957).[91]

Although setting Kierkegaard's work in its historical background, and attentive to the mediation of Hegel via J.L. Heiberg and H.L. Martensen, Heywood-Thomas' main aim is to show Kierkegaard's potential contribution to contemporary philosophy of religion. Kierkegaard was no mere irrationalist, but his emphasis on subjectivity and paradox can and should be read in terms of explicating the peculiar logic of faith. This logic is pointed to by Kierkegaard's distinction between faith and proof. By this he means that faith is not the sort of thing that can be dealt with by the kind of proofs that are valid in law, in science or in mathematics. However, at the same time as challenging the view that rational argument and philosophical justification offer appropriate aims and methods with regard to religion, and thus defending the religious person's instinctive independence of philosophy's "dangerous help,"[92] Kierkegaard was also critical of the identification of religion with experience, as exemplified in Schleiermacher. In this respect, religious faith can, after all, be said to have a certain kind of objectivity, albeit of a very different kind from that of the "speculative philosopher" who "seems to tell us what goes on in the mind of God."[93]

By way of a critical discussion of J.L. Stevenson's sophisticated re-presentation of the view that ethical statements have no other foundation than that they articulate proposals for action of which we happen to approve, Heywood-Thomas argues that ethical statements do, after all, have a certain kind of objectivity and that this is what Kierkegaard too is attempting to say. "We see, then, that questions of ethics, like questions of logic, are concerned, not with subjective relations—that is, with

---

[89]   Blackham, *Six Existentialist Thinkers*, p. 164.

[90]   James Collins, *The Mind of Kierkegaard*, London: Secker and Warburg 1954.

[91]   John Heywood-Thomas, *Subjectivity and Paradox*, Lampeter: Edwin Mellen Press 1994 (this is a reprint of the 1957 Blackwell edition).

[92]   Ibid., p. 156.

[93]   Ibid., p. 162.

256 George Pattison

what is 'attractive' (to-me or to-you) or with what 'seems right'...but with objective concepts."[94]

Something analogous holds also in the case of religious statements, Heywood-Thomas argues. There is a real difference between the man whom the glorious sunset reminds of the sunsets at home and the man whom it moves to sing praises to God, "The former is entirely a matter of attitude, whereas the second is not."[95] That the religious statement has a certain, if peculiar, kind of objectivity—and that just this is the point of Kierkegaard's invocation of paradox—is teased out with the use of Stephen Toulmin's notion of limiting questions. There is a point where there is no point continuing to ask the question "Why?" The logic of "God" is not that of a conclusion to an argument but of a marker that indicates the limit where argument must stop.

Yet Kierkegaard's service is not only to have clarified the logic of religious assertions, it is also, in Heywood-Thomas's terms, to have "brought the person of the thinker into philosophy"[96] and to have reminded the world that the "divorce of philosophy and life," far from being the normal state of affairs that it is assumed to be by modern philosophers, may equally well be seen as "a betrayal of the legacy Socrates had given to philosophy."[97] If we once accept this personal dimension, then we will see that it is quite legitimate to say of religion that "ontology and autobiography are related, so that to say that I believe God exists *means* that I worship Him."[98]

Debates about the nature and justification of religious language—the "logic" of "God-talk"—dominated British philosophy of religion for much of the period, and whilst Kierkegaard was largely absent from such discussions, the kind of view put forward by Heywood-Thomas on the basis of his interpretation of Kierkegaard did continue to be represented in such debates. To that extent, we may say that Kierkegaard at least contributed to persuading philosophers to accept—or at least to think twice before rejecting—the special claim of religious statements not to be outlawed on the grounds of failing the tests of verifiability and falsifiability.

As the writings of the time show, and folk memory also testifies, the popularity of Kierkegaard in the 1940s and 1950s doubtless had much to do with a heightened sense of crisis in culture, thought, and society, with what was experienced as a renewed sense of sin, of it being an "age of anxiety," as the title of W.H. Auden's 1947 poem had it (and, in this connection, one might point to a number of poets who received Kierkegaard as, in a sense, one of their own: Auden himself, of course, but also Ian Crichton-Smith and R.S. Thomas incorporated Kierkegaardian themes into their work and, indeed, wrote poems *about* Kierkegaard).[99] As the "age of anxiety"

---

[94]   Ibid., p. 164.
[95]   Ibid., p. 165.
[96]   Ibid., p. 173.
[97]   Ibid., p. 174.
[98]   Ibid., p. 182.
[99]   The Thomas poems are "Kierkegaard," in *Collected Poems 1945–90*, London: Dent 1993, p. 162; See Rowan Williams, "Suspending the Ethical. R.S. Thomas and Kierkegaard," in *Echoes to the Amen: Essays After R.S. Thomas*, ed. by Damian Walford Davies, Cardiff: University of Wales Press 2003.

passed away, however, and the more upbeat era of the 1960s replaced that of the angry young men, interest in Kierkegaard, as in the other existentialists began to wane. Kierkegaard was not included in the prestigious and influential "Modern Masters" series, though virtually every other major figure of his age was.

A small trickle of works did continue to be published. In 1966 Ronald Grimsley's *Kierkegaard and French Literature* offered a survey of Kierkegaard's relationship to French literature.[100] As a purely scholarly work, Grimsley's book perhaps looked towards a later phase of Kierkegaard reception in Britain, and was, in any case, already far from the febrile atmosphere in which Kierkegaard had become "the prophet of the Now." In 1973 Grimsley also published a "biographical introduction" to Kierkegaard in the "Leaders of Modern Thought" series. Here Grimsley depicts Kierkegaard as an intellectual ancestor of existentialism, but universalizes his significance into a characteristic emphasis on the "pervasive intimate connection" between a thinker's ideas and his "personal involvement in the subject-matter of his thought,"[101] thus provoking later generations to ask more deeply about what it means to be a human being. In 1968, the philosopher Patrick Gardiner gave the Dawes Hicks Lecture on Philosophy on *Kierkegaard's Two Ways*, followed in 1988 by an introductory work in the "Past Masters" series.[102] Yet, from the mid-1960s through to the early-1980s, it is broadly safe to say that, apart from an occasional scholarly article,[103] little significant new work on Kierkegaard appeared in Britain. Doubtless, a certain collective memory about him continued in university teaching, in the Church and amongst general readers, even if this was often only second-hand, but, circa 1980, many drew the conclusion that Kierkegaard, along with existentialism belonged safely to the past.

III. The 1980s to the Present

As we turn to the latest period of Kierkegaard reception in Britain, we are dealing for the most part with scholars who are still active. The story to be told is therefore one whose conclusion and, therefore, significance is still wide open. It is at the very least clear, however, that, whatever else has happened, Kierkegaard has once more become an acknowledged figure in debates about religion, ethics, and culture. Even if the literature relating to Kierkegaard is rarely "popular" (and, in any case, the nature of popular publishing and media culture has itself been transformed since the late 1940s), it is substantial, growing and, for the most part, accessing a higher level of scholarly resources than those used by or, mostly, available to the commentators of the 1940s and 1950s. At the same time, whilst it was always the

---

[100]   Ronald Grimsley, *Kierkegaard and French Literature*, Cardiff: University of Wales Press 1966.
[101]   Ronald Grimsley, *Leaders of Modern Thought: Kierkegaard; A Biographical Introduction*, London: Studio Vista 1973, p. 114.
[102]   Patrick Gardiner, *Kierkegaard's Two Ways*, London 1968 (*Proceedings of the British Academy*, vol. 54); Patrick Gardiner, *Kierkegaard*, Oxford: Oxford University Press 1988.
[103]   For example, W. Glyn Jones, "Sören Kierkegaard and Poul Martin Møller," *Modern Language Review*, vol. 60, 1965, pp. 73–82.

case that Britain was never completely isolated intellectually from either Europe or the United States, it is characteristic for the last quarter of a century of Kierkegaard studies in the British Isles that they have participated in a genuinely international community of scholarship, of which the research institutions of St. Olaf College in Minnesota and the Kierkegaard Research Centre at the University of Copenhagen have been particularly important foci. British scholars have regularly participated in international conferences, and the main British conferences in the period (Sunderland 1984, Durham 1991, Lancaster 1995, Cambridge 1998, Leeds 2001) all had a strong presence of North American and European scholars and, occasionally, from further afield. Similarly, British scholars are now generally well-represented in collected and serial volumes such as the *International Kierkegaard Commentary*, *Kierkegaardiana*, and the *Kierkegaard Studies Yearbook*, as witness contributions in recent years by Harvie Ferguson, David Law, John Lippitt, George Pattison, Roger Poole, Hugh Pyper, Steven Shakespeare, as well as by scholars who have studied in Britain, such as Niels Nymann Eriksen, Ulrich Knappe, Adrian Van Heerden, and Jolita Pons, all of whom have in some degree participated in the British Kierkegaard studies environment.[104] With regard to this "globalization," Kierkegaard studies thus represents in microcosm a tendency that can be observed across the humanities.

The first sign of a "new wave" of interest in Kierkegaard amongst philosophers was the appearance in 1982 of Alastair Hannay's contribution to the "Arguments of the Philosophers" series, entitled, simply, *Kierkegaard*.[105] In terms of placing Kierkegaard philosophically, Hannay's book had a breadth unequalled in any previous British contribution. Not only is Kierkegaard made a conversation partner for Hegel, but the relevance of his thought to issues in Kantian moral philosophy is also brought out, as well as a significant emphasis being placed on his critique of the age. Resident for many years in Norway, Hannay's command of the Danish language and sources for Kierkegaard's thought would continue to mark both his scholarly work and his celebrated translations of a sequence of key Kierkegaard texts for Penguin Classics, starting in 1985 with *Fear and Trembling*. As well as co-editing *The Cambridge Companion to Kierkegaard*, Hannay went on to produce what, he emphasized, as very much an *intellectual* biography of Kierkegaard, *Kierkegaard: A Biography*. As opposed to the virtually synchronous biography by Garff, Hannay's work eschews personal details, but instead focuses on putting Kierkegaard into his intellectual context. Many of his contributions to conferences and collected works have also been published together as *Kierkegaard and Philosophy: Selected Essays*.[106]

---

[104]   One might also mention here the work of Mark Dooley, who, as a citizen of the Irish Republic, is certainly not "British" yet who works in a certain proximity to Britain. See especially Mark Dooley, *The Politics of Exodus: Kierkegaard's Ethics of Responsibility*, New York: Fordham University Press 2001.

[105]   Alastair Hannay, *Kierkegaard*, London: Routledge and Kegan Paul 1982.

[106]   *The Cambridge Companion to Kierkegaard*, ed. by Alastair Hannay and Gordon Marino, Cambridge: Cambridge University Press 1998; Alastair Hannay, *Kierkegaard: A Biography*, Cambridge: Cambridge University Press 2001; Alastair Hannay, *Kierkegaard and Philosophy: Selected Essays*, London: Routledge 2003.

What we see in Hannay is very much a philosopher's approach to Kierkegaard and it has been a strong feature of the recent Kierkegaard reception in Britain that philosophers have been amongst its most significant contributors. This is in stark contrast to the 1950s, and is due partly to an opening up of the analytic tradition from within, particularly in connection with, on the one hand, the influence of Wittgenstein (witness Hannay himself and, e.g. D.Z. Phillips[107]) and, on the other, the enlivening of ethics as an area of philosophical enquiry (witness Anthony Rudd's *Kierkegaard and the Limits of the Ethical*[108]). At the same time there are now universities in Britain where the continental tradition post-Kant is an acceptable and even a normal part of the philosophical context. In this regard the reading of Kierkegaard in the context of Heideggerian and post-Heideggerian French philosophy has been a salient feature of the contemporary philosophical—and theological—reading of Kierkegaard. A prelude to this approach was the social and political philosopher Gillian Rose's *The Broken Middle: Out of our Ancient Society*, in the early chapters of which Kierkegaard becomes a partner-in-dialogue for critically articulating and reflecting on some of the crucial, and excruciating, pressures forcing law and ethics apart in our modern ("ancient!") society. This not only involves Rose in rereading Kierkegaard's relation to Hegel, but also brings him into a conversation in which Blanchot, Kafka, Freud, and Lacan are important fellow participants. Not the least important aspect of Rose's book is her alertness to the importantly different Jewish perspective on the issues of law and ethics that acquire Kierkegaardian shape in the interpretation of the Akedah and in such questions as whether or not to marry.[109] Rose taught in Warwick, one of the British universities best known for its openness to continental philosophy. Another such university is Essex, with which several contemporary British philosophers with interests in Kierkegaard have strong associations. Amongst these are Michael Weston, whose *Kierkegaard and Modern Continental Philosophy*[110] provided a usable and perceptive guide to the links between Kierkegaard and the world of post-Heideggerian continental thought. John Lippitt's *Humour and Irony in Kierkegaard's Thought* developed from a Ph. D. Thesis taken at Essex,[111] and another sometime Essex teacher was Stephen Mulhall,

---

[107]   On Phillips' abiding interest in Kierkegaard see, e.g., D.Z. Phillips, "Authorship and Authenticity: Kierkegaard and Wittgenstein," in *Wittgenstein and Religion*, Basingstoke: Macmillan 1993, pp. 200–19; D.Z. Phillips, "Self-Deception and Freedom in Kierkegaard's *Purity of Heart*," in *Kierkegaard and Freedom*, ed. by James Giles, Basingstoke: Palgrave 2000, pp. 156–71.

[108]   Anthony Rudd, *Kierkegaard and the Limits of the Ethical*, Oxford: Oxford University Press 1993.

[109]   Gillian Rose, *The Broken Middle: Out of our Ancient Society*, Oxford: Blackwell 1992.

[110]   Michael Weston, *Kierkegaard and Continental Philosophy*, London: Routledge 1994.

[111]   John Lippitt, *Humour and Irony in Kierkegaard's Thought*, Basingstoke: Macmillan 2000; see also John Lippitt, *Routledge Philosophy Guidebook to Kierkegaard and Fear and Trembling*, London: Routledge 2003.

whose *Inheritance and Originality* brings Kierkegaard into dialogue with Stanley Cavell, Wittgenstein (again!), and Martin Heidegger.[112]

Just as recent continental philosophy has itself allowed or encouraged the line between philosophy and literature to become blurred or, at the very least, contestable, so, in the case of Kierkegaard, an awareness of the tendency associated with Derrida opened up possibilities that were especially vigorously exploited in the controversial *Kierkegaard: The Indirect Communication* by Roger Poole. Insisting on rejecting what he regarded as the dominant "blunt reading" that equated "Kierkegaard" with his pseudonyms, Poole's work brought into sharp focus the language and literary complexity of Kierkegaard's texts, a focus that necessarily displaced the evaluation of Kierkegaard in terms purely of his "ideas" or "arguments." Kierkegaard's own works do not need to be deconstructed since they deconstruct themselves and, in doing so, effect a deconstruction of their Hegelian subject-matter. Kierkegaardian Christianity is, in turn, relocated by Kierkegaard into the impossible language of the "sign of contradiction," a contradiction in which the human body itself becomes the locus of the terrifying tensions and gyrations that such a sign is compelled to undergo in an era dominated by the monolingual signs of mass media culture.[113]

This sense for the literary dimension of Kierkegaard's text as being integral to its philosophical and, indeed, religious significance has been echoed in much recent British work on Kierkegaard. Mulhall's *Inheritance and Originality*, already mentioned, is engrossed by issues around the difficulty of writing philosophy. George Pattison's work, often situated on the frontier between philosophy and theology, has similarly emphasized that the way in which Kierkegaard writes is indissociable from the religious strategy underpinning much of the authorship, and vice versa.[114] In this perspective the theory of indirect communication expounded by Kierkegaard himself as an explanation for why he wrote pseudonymously can be shown to have many levels of complexity and, to use Bakhtin's term, many polyphonic voices to which Kierkegaard's own theory scarcely does sufficient justice. The dialogical space of Kierkegaard's semiosphere thus opens up both to encompass his supposedly "direct" religious works[115] and to incorporate the horizon of his contemporary literary, popular, and urban culture.[116]

Independently of, and perhaps to some extent prior to the new wave of British philosophical approaches, Kierkegaard was from early on a key figure in the etiology of the "non-realist" interpretation propounded by the Cambridge theologian Don Cupitt in such books as *Taking Leave of God* (1980) and popularized in his BBC television

---

[112]   Stephen Mulhall, *Inheritance and Originality: Wittgenstein, Heidegger, Kierkegaard*, Oxford: Oxford University Press 2001.

[113]   Roger Poole, *Kierkegaard: The Indirect Communication*, Charlottesville: University of Virginia Press 1993.

[114]   George Pattison, *Kierkegaard: The Aesthetic and the Religious*, London: SCM Press 1998 [1992].

[115]   Pattison, *Kierkegaard's Upbuilding Discourses: Philosophy, Literature, Theology*, London: Routledge 2002.

[116]   Pattison, *"Poor Paris!" Kierkegaard's Critique of the Spectacular City*, New York and Berlin: Walter de Gruyter 1999; Pattison, *Kierkegaard, Religion, and the Nineteenth Century Crisis of Culture*, Cambridge: Cambridge University Press 2002.

series *The Sea of Faith* (1984), which made available to a wide public the issues at the center of contemporary radical theology.[117] According to Cupitt, Kierkegaardian subjectivity is an early statement of the true state of religion in the modern, and soon to be post-modern, world: that religion is not a response to a reality "out there" but is the free and imaginative creation by the individual of a synthesis of his or her central values and aspirations. Cupitt's influence did much to put Kierkegard back on the agenda of theologians, even though many typically responded by challenging the particular interpretation he offered. Like the philosophers, Cupitt too was open to the influences coming from Derrida, Foucault, and others, although, in some respects, this influence tended to lead him away from Kierkegaard, who remained caught—in Cupitt's view—in a perhaps too-metaphysical version of subjective transcendence.

A recent theological approach that is characterized by close attention to the linguistic and literary dimensions of Kierkegaard's work have been Hugh Pyper's many contributions to widely referenced Kierkegaard collections and resources, which not only bring to bear a great literary sensitivity but also the knowledge and experience of a scholar of the Hebrew Bible. Pyper's readings are always fiercely original and, often, pointedly humorous. Characteristic is the article "The Apostle, the Genius and the Monkey," which Pyper rounds off with a comic but entirely apt illustration from the Scottish author Neil Munro to illustrate Kierkegaard's use of Lichtenberg's aphorism that there are works like mirrors which, if an ape looks in them, no apostle can look out.[118] Yet there are always serious issues at play in Pyper's work, as testified by the article "Forgiving the Unforgivable: Kierkegaard, Derrida and the Scandal of Forgiveness," which examines the question of whether there are certain crimes, especially war crimes, that it is right to forgive.[119]

Another theological reader of Kierkegaard who both engages with Derrida and is attentive to the specifically textual characteristics of Kierkegaard's writing is Steven Shakespeare, whose *Kierkegaard, Language and the Reality of God* offers a subtle response to Cupitt that resists an easy opposition between (conservatively)

---

[117]   Don Cupitt, *Taking Leave of God*, London: SCM Press 1980; Don Cupitt, *The Sea of Faith* (new ed.), London: SCM Press 2003, pp. 148–61.

[118]   Hugh Pyper, "The Apostle, the Genius and the Monkey: Reflections on the Mirror of the Word," in *Kierkegaard on Art and Communication*, ed. by George Pattison, Basingstoke: Macmillan 1992, pp. 125–36.

[119]   Pyper, "Forgiving the Unforgivable: Kierkegaard, Derrida and the Scandal of Forgiveness," *Kierkegaardiana*, vol. 22, 2002, pp. 7–23. Pyper's other Kierkegaardian publications to date are: "Adam's Angest: The Myth of Language and the Language of Mythology," *Kierkegaard Studies. Yearbook*, 2001, pp. 78–95; "Beyond a Joke: Kierkegaard's *Concluding Unscientific Postscript* as a Comic Boo," in *Concluding Unscientific Postscript to Philosophical Fragments*, ed. by Robert L. Perkins, Macon, Georgia: Mercer University Press 1997 (*International Kierkegaard Commentary*, vol. 12), pp. 149–68; "Cities of the Dead: The Relation of Person and Polis in Kierkegaard's *Works of Love*," in *Kierkegaard: The Self in Society*, ed. by George Pattison and Steven Shakespeare, Basingstoke: Macmillan 1998, pp. 125–38; "The Lesson of Eternity: Christ as Teacher in Hegel and Kierkegaard," *Philosophical Fragments* and *Johannes Climacus*, ed. by Robert L. Perkins, Macon, Georgia: Mercer University Press 1994 (*International Kierkegaard Commentary*, vol. 7), pp. 129–46.

realist and (radically) non-realist.[120] Shakespeare's work is marked by a keen sense that Kierkegaard's whole manner of communication requires handling with care, not least when one or other theological school wishes to enlist him in their cause. This can, for example, be seen in his response to John Milbank's article "The Sublime in Kierkegaard."[121] Appreciative of Milbank's sense for the ambiguity and ultimate weaknesses of a purely secular, rational approach to religion, Shakespeare nevertheless—and contra Milbank—draws attention to that in Kierkegaard which resists being used to legitimate any direct theological meta-narrative and, especially, any unambiguous celebration of the Church as a privileged site of God's presence in the world.[122]

Jolita Pons' *Stealing a Gift: Kierkegaard's Pseudonyms and the Bible* might also be counted amongst approaches that bring together a religious interpretation of Kierkegaard with a concern for the literary dynamics of his work.[123] Although the author is Lithuanian and the book was published in the United States, it is developed from work done in Cambridge in the 1990s—and, as previously emphasized, it is in some ways artificial to isolate the contemporary scholarly reception of Kierkegaard in purely geographical terms. Clare Carlisle's *Kierkegaard and Movement* similarly brings together a philosophical examination of Kierkegaard's category of movement with attention to the way in which the text itself moves and sets the reader in motion.[124]

These by no means exhaust the theological interest in Kierkegaard in the last decade and a half, which covers a wide spectrum of approaches. David Law documented Kierkegaard's relation to the long history of Christian negative theology,[125] whilst both neo-Barthian and radically orthodox theologians have made serious and appreciative approaches to the Dane.[126] Far from being the first postmodern ironist, Murray Rae's Kierkegaard becomes the first critic of such ironic postmodern theologies as that of William Hamilton. Where Hamilton reduces the "truth" of Christianity to the fictions that we construct about Christ, and thus to the personal existence of the contemporary Christian communicator, Kierkegaard "in

---

[120]   Steven Shakespeare, *Kierkegaard, Language and the Reality of God*, Aldershot: Ashgate 2001. See also Steven Shakespeare, "Stirring the Waters of Language," in *The Heythrop Journal*, vol. 37, no. 4, October 1996, pp. 421–36.

[121]   John Milbank, "The Sublime in Kierkegaard," in *Post-Secular Philosophy: Between Philosophy and Theology*, ed. by Philipp Blond, London: Routledge 1998, pp. 131–56.

[122]   See Steven Shakespeare, "Better Well-Hanged than Ill-Wed: Kierkegaard and Radical Orthodoxy," in *Deconstructing Radical Orthodoxy*, ed. by Douglas Hedley and Wayne J. Hankey, Aldershot: Ashgate 2005, pp. 133–48.

[123]   Jolita Pons, *Stealing a Gift: Kierkegaard's Pseudonyms and the Bible*, New York: Fordham University Press 2004.

[124]   Clare Carlisle, *Kierkegaard's Philosophy of Becoming: Movements and Positions*, Albany: State University of New York Press 2005.

[125]   David Law, *Kierkegaard as Negative Theologian*, Oxford: Clarendon Press 1993. See also contributions to the *International Kierkegaard Commentary*.

[126]   For the former see Murray Rae, *Kierkegaard's Vision of the Incarnation: By Faith Transformed*, Oxford: Clarendon Press 1997; for the latter see Milbank, "The Sublime in Kierkegaard."

contrast to the post-modern myopia" "refuses to make the situation and authority of the subject the whole of what is communicated. We also *bear witness* and this implies a reality and a truth which is not of our making."[127] Other theological readers of Kierkegaard include Julia Watkin, whose personal assistance and encouragement to so many Kierkegaard scholars over many years is scarcely deducible from her relatively few writings, and something similar could be said of Peter Vardy, who over many years has led innumerable students to Kierkegaard, and who established the annual Kierkegaard "birthday dinner" in London.[128] At the same time a perhaps surprisingly sympathetic account of Kierkegaard (given some of his stated views on women), and of his importance in the history of the human understanding of the self, has been offered by the feminist thinker Daphne Hampson. In her *After Christianity*, Hampson largely focuses on Kierkegaard as offering the clearest statement from within Christianity concerning the impossibility of reconciling the yield of modern, post-Enlightenment knowledge with Christian doctrine.[129] In *Christian Contradictions*, however, he is given a far more constructive role. The book focuses on the differing structures of Lutheran and Catholic thought, with a special emphasis on their respective modellings of human selfhood. In Kierkegaard she sees someone who, to a considerable extent, brings together the strong points of each tradition in an entirely novel idea of the self. Hampson writes: "Kierkegaard's model for what it means to be a self in relationship to God is the most sophisticated of which I am aware in the Western Christian tradition."[130] Why is this? It is because, as against the dominant Lutheran tradition, Kierkegaard allows for a genuine element of self-affirmation in his depiction of the human God-relationship—yet this moment of self-affirmation is not grounded in the kind of metaphysical schema that, Hampson assumes, has been rendered incredible by the Enlightenment and that, nevertheless, remains a key element in Catholic anthropology. The Kierkegaardian self is a self that cannot be except by being-in-relationship, dynamically self-developing and open to grow through its interactions with human others and with God.

A further study that deserves mention is Harvie Ferguson's *Melancholy and the Critique of Modernity*. Hard to categorize in neat disciplinary terms, Ferguson's work operates in the triangle of social science, philosophy, and psychology. Seeing in the famed Kierkegaardian melancholy more than a private foible, Ferguson shows it to be revelatory of fundamental aspects of modern life, but also to be conquerable by the way of Kierkegaardian edification.[131]

It is time to sum up. And the first thing to be said is that whether we look to philosophy or theology (or, to a lesser extent, to literary studies) Kierkegaard has, in the last twenty years, re-emerged as an important figure in the contemporary

---

127   Rae, *Kierkegaard's Vision of the Incarnation: By Faith Transformed*, p. 232.
128   See, however, Julia Watkin, *Kierkegaard*, London: Geoffrey Chapman 1997; Peter Vardy, *Kierkegaard*, London: Fount 1996.
129   See Daphne Hampson, *After Christianity*, London: SCM Press 1993, pp. 21–5.
130   Daphne Hampson, *Christian Contradictions: The Structures of Lutheran and Catholic Thought*, Cambridge: Cambridge University Press 2001, p. 282.
131   Harvie Ferguson, *Melancholy and the Critique of Modernity: Kierkegaard's Religious Psychology*, London: Routledge 1995.

intellectual field—but how important? Clearly the kind of epochal claims being made on his behalf in the 1940s are rarely heard today, nor can we expect that he will ever acquire the canonical status of a Kant or a Hegel in philosophy, or a Schleiermacher or a Barth in theology (though such claims are still occasionally heard). Yet his unique challenge to both disciplines to reflect on their own assumptions and agendas, and his exemplification of how both philosophy and theology can be done "in a new key," to borrow Suzanne Langer's phrase, are likely to remain an acknowledged presence and, even if, in some sense, marginal, then marginal in a distinctive and not negligible way.

Does this mean that Kierkegaard has become a figure of purely academic interest, whether as a contributor to theory or the matter of historical enquiry? Or, if no longer a prophet of "the Now," is he still, in some pressing sense, our contemporary? It is always hard to quantify such things, but at some level it is clear that Kierkegaard remains part of the general horizon of culture, being occasionally entangled in contemporary works of British literature[132] as well being the subject of newspaper articles,[133] radio broadcasts, and even cartoons[134]—not to mention being cited on a *Frankie Goes to Hollywood* album cover. Perhaps *Frankie Goes to Hollywood* is hardly contemporary by now, and ephemera are, by definition, ephemeral. Although such testimony is more scattered and, by definition, intellectually weaker than a strong academic discourse, it supports the view that the strength and depth of the contemporary academic reception of Kierkegaard in Britain reflects a perception that he remains, in some non-trivial sense, a contemporary figure, whose work can inspire, provoke, annoy, intrigue, and, for some, bring to faith.

---

[132]   Especially David Lodge, *Therapy*, Harmondsworth: Penguin 1996.
[133]   Julian Evans, "Leader of the Awkward Squad," *The Guardian*, November 20, 1998, p. 31.
[134]   See "Biff," *The Guardian Weekend*, February 1, 1997, p. 8, and November 11, 2000 (the last featuring an imaginary meeting between Kierkegaard and Comte!).

Bibliography

I. Selected British Translations of Kierkegaard's Works

Purify Your Hearts! A "Discourse for a Special Occasion", the First of Three "Edifying Discourses in a Different Vein" Published in 1847 at Copenhagen, by S. Kierkegaard, trans. by A.S. Aldworth and W.S. Ferrie, London: The C.W. Daniel Company 1937.

The Journals of Søren Kierkegaard, ed. by Alexander Dru, London et al.: Oxford University Press 1938 (new ed. entitled *The Soul of Kierkegaard: Selections from His Journal*, Mineola, New York: Dover Publications 2003).

The Present Age and Two Minor Ethico-Religious Treatises, trans. by Alexander Dru and Walter Lowrie, London and New York: Oxford University Press 1940.

Meditations from Kierkegaard, trans. and ed. by T.H. Croxall, London: James Nisbet 1955.

The Present Age, and On the Difference between a Genius and an Apostle, trans. by Alexander Dru, introduced by Walter Kaufmann, New York: Harper & Row 1962.

Fear and Trembling, trans. and ed. by Alastair Hannay, Harmondsworth: Penguin 1985.

The Sickness unto Death, trans. and ed. by Alastair Hannay, Harmondsworth: Penguin 1989.

Either/Or. A Fragment of Life, trans. and ed. by Alastair Hannay, Harmondsworth: Penguin 1992.

Papers and Journals: A Selection, trans. and ed. by Alastair Hannay, Harmondsworth: Penguin 1996.

A Literary Review, trans. and ed. by Alastair Hannay, Harmondsworth: Penguin 2001.

Johannes Climacus. Or: A Life of Doubt (a translation of *De omnibus dubitandum est*), trans. by T.H. Croxhall, ed. and revised by Jane Chamberlain, London: Serpent's Tail 2001.

The Kierkegaard Reader, ed. by Jane Chambarlain and Jonathan Rée, Malden, Massachusetts: Blackwell 2001.

Kierkegaard's Journals and Notebooks, vols. 1–11, ed. by Niels Jørgen Cappelørn, Alastair Hannay, David Kangas, Bruce H. Kirmmse, George Pattison, Vanessa Rumble, and K. Brian Söderquist, Princeton and Oxford: Princeton University Press 2007ff.

II. Selected Secondary Literature on Kierkegaard in Great Britain

Allen, E.L., *Kierkegaard: His Life and Thought*, London: Stanley Watt 1935.
— *Bishop Grundtvig: A Prophet of the North*, London: James Clarke 1948.
Bain, John A., *Sören Kierkegaard: His Life and Religious Teaching*, London: SCM 1935.
Blackham, H.J., *Six Existentialist Thinkers*, London: Routledge and Kegan Paul 1961 [1952].
Carlisle, Clare, *Kierkegaard's Philosophy of Becoming: Movements and Positions*, Albany: State University of New York Press 2005.
Croxall, T.H., *Kierkegaard Studies*, London and Redhill: Lutterworth 1948.
Dooley, Mark, *The Politics of Exodus: Kierkegaard's Ethics of Responsibility*, New York: Fordham University Press 2001.
Ferguson, Harvie, *Melancholy and the Critique of Modernity: Kierkegaard's Religious Psychology*, London: Routledge 1995.
Forsyth, Peter Taylor, *Religion in Recent Art: Being Expository Lectures on Rossetti, Burne–Jones, Watts, Holman Hunt, and Wagner*, Manchester: s.n. 1889.
— *The Work of Christ*, London: Independent Press 1910.
— *Christ on Parnassus*, New York and Toronto: Hodder and Stoughton 1911.
Fulford, Francis Woodbury, *Sören Aabye Kierkegaard: A Study*, Cambridge: H.W. Wallis 1911.
Gardiner, Patrick, *Kierkegaard's Two Ways*, London: British Academy 1968 (*Proceedings of the British Academy*, vol. 54).
Grimsley, Ronald, *Kierkegaard and French Literature*, Cardiff: University of Wales Press 1966.
— *Leaders of Modern Thought: Kierkegaard: A Biographical Introduction*, London: Studio Vista 1973.
Haecker, Theodor, *Søren Kierkegaard*, trans. by Alexander Dru, London: Oxford University Press 1937.
Hannay, Alastair, *Kierkegaard*, London: Routledge and Kegan Paul 1982.
— (ed., together with Gordon Marino), *The Cambridge Companion to Kierkegaard*, Cambridge: Cambridge University Press 1998.
— *Kierkegaard: A Biography*, Cambridge: Cambridge University Press 2001.
— *Kierkegaard and Philosophy: Selected Essays*, London: Routledge 2003.
Hawton, Hector, *The Feast of Unreason*, London: Watts and Co. 1952.
Heywood-Thomas, John, *Subjectivity and Paradox*, Lampeter: Edwin Mellen Press 1994 [1957].
Hügel, Friedrich von, *Eternal Life: A Study of its Implications and Applications*, Edinburgh: T. & T. Clark 1912.
Jones, W. Glyn, "Sören Kierkegaard and Poul Martin Møller," *Modern Language Review*, vol. 60, 1965, pp. 73–82.
— *Kierkegaard*, Oxford: Oxford University Press 1988.
Law, David, *Kierkegaard as Negative Theologian*, Oxford: Clarendon Press 1993.
Lindsay, A.D., *Selected Addresses*, privately published, Cumberland 1957.
Lippitt, John, *Humour and Irony in Kierkegaard's Thought*, Basingstoke: Macmillan 2000.

— *Routledge Philosophy Guidebook to Kierkegaard and Fear and Trembling*, London: Routledge 2003.

Martin, H.V., *Kierkegaard: The Melancholy Dane*, London: The Epworth Press 1950.

— *The Wings of Faith: A Consideration of the Nature and Meaning of the Christian Faith in the Light of the Work of Søren Kierkegaard*, London: Lutterworth Press 1950.

Milbank, John, "The Sublime in Kierkegaard," in *Post-Secular Philosophy: Between Philosophy and Theology*, ed. by P. Blond, London: Routledge 1998, pp. 131–56.

Mulhall, Stephen, *Inheritance and Originality: Wittgenstein, Heidegger, Kierkegaard*, Oxford: Oxford University Press 2001.

Pattison, George, *Kierkegaard: The Aesthetic and the Religious*, London: SCM Press 1998 [1992].

— *"Poor Paris!" Kierkegaard's Critique of the Spectacular City*, New York and Berlin: Walter de Gruyter 1999.

— *Kierkegaard, Religion, and the Nineteenth Century Crisis of Culture*, Cambridge: Cambridge University Press 2002.

— *Kierkegaard's Upbuilding Discourses: Philosophy, Literature, Theology*, London: Routledge 2002.

Phillips, D.Z., "Authorship and Authenticity: Kierkegaard and Wittgenstein," in *Wittgenstein and Religion*, Basingstoke: Macmillan 1993, pp. 200–19.

— "Self-Deception and Freedom in Kierkegaard's *Purity of Heart*," in *Kierkegaard and Freedom*, ed. by James Giles, Basingstoke: Palgrave Macmillan 2001, pp. 156–71.

Poole, Roger, *Kierkegaard: The Indirect Communication*, Charlottesville: University of Virginia Press 1993.

Pyper, Hugh, "The Apostle, the Genius and the Monkey: Reflections on the Mirror of the Word," in *Kierkegaard on Art and Communication*, ed. by George Pattison, Basingstoke: Macmillan 1992, pp. 125–36.

— "The Lesson of Eternity: Christ as Teacher in Hegel and Kierkegaard," *Philosophical Fragments* and *Johannes Climacus*, ed. by Robert L. Perkins, Macon, Georgia: Mercer University Press 1994 (*International Kierkegaard Commentary*, vol. 7), pp. 129–46.

— "Beyond a Joke: Kierkegaard's *Concluding Unscientific Postscript* as a Comic Boo," in *Concluding Unscientific Postscript to Philosophical Fragments*, ed. by Robert L. Perkins, Macon, Georgia: Mercer University Press 1997 (*International Kierkegaard Commentary*, vol. 12), pp. 149–68.

— "Cities of the Dead: The Relation of Person and Polis in Kierkegaard's *Works of Love*," in *Kierkegaard: The Self in Society*, ed. by George Pattison and Steven Shakespeare, Basingstoke: Macmillan 1998, pp. 125–38.

— "Adam's Angest: The Myth of Language and the Language of Mythology," *Kierkegaard Studies. Yearbook*, 2001, pp. 78–95.

— "Forgiving the Unforgivable: Kierkegaard, Derrida and the Scandal of Forgiveness," *Kierkegaardiana*, vol. 22, 2002, pp. 7–23.

Read, Herbert, *Annals of Innocence and Experience*, London: Faber and Faber 1946.

Rappaport, Angelo S., "Ibsen, Nietzsche and Kierkegaard," in *The New Age*, vol. 3, no. 21, 1908, pp. 408–9; vol. 3, no. 22, 1908, pp. 428–9.

Rudd, Anthony, *Kierkegaard and the Limits of the Ethical*, Oxford: Oxford University Press 1993.

Ruggiero, Guido de, *Existentialism*, London: Secker and Warburg 1946.

Shakespeare, Steven, "Stirring the Waters of Language," *The Heythrop Journal*, vol. 37, no. 4, October 1996, pp. 421–36.

— *Kierkegaard, Language and the Reality of God*, Aldershot: Ashgate 2001.

— "Better Well-Hanged than Ill-Wed: Kierkegaard and Radical Orthodoxy," in *Deconstructing Radical Orthodoxy*, ed. by Douglas Hedley and W. Hankey, Aldershot: Ashgate 2005, pp. 133–48.

Stobart, Mabel A., "New Light on Ibsen's 'Brand,' " *The Fortnightly Review*, vol. 66, 1899, pp. 227–39.

— "The 'Either-Or' of Sören Kierkegaard," *The Fortnightly Review*, vol. 71, 1902, pp. 53–60.

Vardy, Peter, *Kierkegaard*, London: Fount 1996.

Weston, Michael, *Kierkegaard and Continental Philosophy*, London: Routledge 1994.

Williams, Charles, *The Descent of the Dove: A Short History of the Holy Spirit in the Church*, London: Collins/Fontana 1963 [London: Longmans & Co. 1939].

Wilson, Colin, *The Outsider*, London: Victor Gollancz 1956.

— *Religion and the Rebel*, London: Gollancz 1957.

III. Selected Secondary Literature on Kierkegaard's Reception in Great Britain

Anderson, James Maitland, "Sören Kierkegaard and the English-speaking World," *Hovedstaden*, no. 4, 1913, pp. 7–8.

Barrett, Lee C., "A History of the Reception of *Philosophical Fragments* in the English Language," *Kierkegaard Studies. Yearbook*, 2004, pp. 328–50.

Grimsley, Ronald, "England," in *Kierkegaard Research*, ed. by Niels Thulstrup and Marie Mikulová Thulstrup, Copenhagen: C.A. Reitzel 1987 (*Bibliotheca Kierkegaardiana*, vol. 15), pp. 109–24.

Hannay, Alastair, "A Kind of Philosopher: Comments in Connection with Some Recent Books on Kierkegaard," *Inquiry*, no. 18, 1975, pp. 354–65.

Heywood-Thomas, John, "The Influence of Kierkegaard's Thought on Contemporary English-Speaking Theology," *Liber Academicae Kierkegaardiensis Annuarius*, vol. 1, 1977–78, ed. by Alessandro Cortese, Copenhagen: C.A. Reitzel 1980, pp. 41–62.

— "Influence on English Thought," in *The Legacy and Interpretation of Kierkegaard*, ed. by Niels Thulstrup and Marie Mikulová Thulstrup, Copenhagen: C.A. Reitzel 1981 (*Bibliotheca Kierkegaardiana*, vol. 8), pp. 160–77.

Heywood-Thomas, John and Hinrich Siefken, "Theodor Haecker and Alexander Dru: A Contribution to the Discovery of Kierkegaard in Britain," *Kierkegaardiana*, vol. 18, 1996, pp. 173–90.

Jones, W. Glyn, "Søren Kierkegaard in English Translation," *Yearbook of Comparative and General Literature*, vol. 35, 1986, pp. 105–11.

Kraushaar, Otto Frederick, "Kierkegaard in English," *Journal of Philosophy*, no. 39, 1942, pp. 561–83; pp. 589–607.

Malik, Habib C., *Receiving Søren Kierkegaard: The Early Impact and Transmission of his Thought*, Washington, D.C.: Catholic University of America Press 1997.

Maude, Mother Mary, "A Kierkegaard Bibliography," *Theology*, no. 41, 1941, pp. 297–300.

Moore, W.G., "Recent Studies of Kierkegaard," *The Journal of Theological Studies*, vol. 40, 1939, pp. 225–31.

Schilling, Peter Andrew, *Sören Kierkegaard and Anglo-American Literary Culture of the Thirties and Forties*. Ph.D. Thesis, Columbia University, New York 1994.

Sechi, Vanina, "Perspectives in Contemporary Kierkegaard Research," *Meddelelser fra Sören Kierkegaard Selskabet*, no. 4, 1953, pp. 10–12.

Steere, Douglas V., "Kierkegaard in English," *Journal of Religion*, no. 24, 1944, pp. 271–8.

Stewart, Jon, "The Reception of Kierkegaard's *Nachlaß* in the English-Speaking World," *Kierkegaard Studies. Yearbook*, 2003, pp. 277–315.

Summers, Richard and John Heywood-Thomas, "British Kierkegaard Research. A Historical Survey," *Kierkegaardiana*, vol. 15, 1991, pp. 117–35.

Taylor, Mark Lloyd, "Recent English Language Scholarship on Kierkegaard's Upbuilding Discourses," *Kierkegaard Studies. Yearbook*, 2000, pp. 273–99.

Ward, Rodney A., "The Reception of Soren Kierkegaard into English," *The Expository Times*, 107, 1995, pp. 43–7.

Woodbridge, Hensley Charles, "A Bibliography of Dissertations Concerning Kierkegaard Written in the U.S., Canada and Great Britain," *American Book Collector*, 12, 1961, pp. 21–2.

— "Søren Kierkegaard: A Bibliography of His Works in English Translation," *American Book Collector*, 12, 1961, pp. 17–20.

The Netherlands and Flanders

Kierkegaard's Reception in the Dutch-Speaking World

Karl Verstrynge

Writing an article on the reception of Søren Kierkegaard in the Dutch-speaking world is difficult for two main reasons. The *first* kind of difficulty will be shared by every author who sets himself the task of mapping and measuring the reception of Kierkegaard's thought in any area or age. More than that, the problem seems to be rooted in the core of Kierkegaard's philosophy. For how should one interpret the term "reception" when one knows that Kierkegaard meticulously paid attention to the way he communicated his thoughts and when one is aware that, more than anyone before him, he tried to steer the effects his writings caused among their reading public. The Dane distanced himself on several occasions from the writings he produced and meticulously judged his readers' relevance according to the way they existentially appropriated the underlying message of his "*pia fraus*."[1] If one of Kierkegaard's main purposes is to reveal the reader to himself, thereby establishing an inwardness in him that "does not interest the world,"[2] then the intended outcome of this enterprise is *eo ipso* hidden from anyone who looks upon it from a merely historical point of view.

A *second* difficulty is more specifically related to this article's sphere of interest. In dealing with the "Dutch-speaking world," one is not only going beyond the national borders dividing the Netherlands and Belgium. With the latter country at stake, one has in addition to take into account the language boundary between the Dutch-speaking part, "Flanders" (Vlaanderen), and the French-speaking "Walloon provinces" (Wallonie). And although the Netherlands and Flanders share the same language, one is to some extent also confronted with cultural and religious-ideological differences. Casting a quick glance at the genesis of both nations explains these divergences. Between the fourteenth and the sixteenth centuries Belgium and the Netherlands formed one and the same territory placed under a foreign government. But from 1648 on the Reformed Northern Netherlands withdrew from Spanish domination and became independent, whereas the Southern Netherlands—present-day Belgium—remained under a Spanish, repressive, and Catholic regime. After Napoleon's defeat at Waterloo in 1815 both regions were reunited a last time as the

---

[1]   *SKS* 21, 19–20, NB6:21 / *JP* 6, 6205.
[2]   *SV1* XIII, 607 / *PV*, 121.

United Kingdom of the Netherlands. But linguistic (Dutch vs. French) and religious (Protestantism vs. Catholicism) divergences culminated in the independence of the kingdom of Belgium in 1830. From 1970 on and after a long-lasting linguistic conflict within the borders of Belgium, Flanders gained relative autonomy as a Dutch-speaking community with the Walloon provinces as its French-speaking counterpart. As we will explain, these undeniable divergences between Flanders and the Netherlands also made a difference in the reception of Kierkegaard's authorship and thought.

In dealing with the *first* difficulty, one cannot but admit that writing the history of a Kierkegaard reception runs counter to the intentions Kierkegaard had in mind with his authorship, especially with the writings under his own name. His explicit "break with the public" and his preference of "that single individual whom I with joy and gratitude call *my* reader"[3] is in line with his aversion to those authors who explicitly strive for recognition. Those "premise-authors," as he called them in *The Book on Adler*, mirror their productions to the premises and the demands of the times. They merely "want to produce an effect...[and] want their writings to win an extraordinary distribution and to be read, if possible, by all humankind."[4] An "essential author," on the other hand, remains unaffected by the success he or she gains in publishing. If a true author "should never need [public money, gracious applause, forbearing indulgence...]," then it does not matter what his or her reception is to be like—if there is to be any reception at all.[5]

Be that as it may, finding and classifying those readers that were able to accept with their right hand the writings that were "offered with the right hand"[6] is a hopeless task. Moreover, one is well aware that Kierkegaard never judged scholars, professors, or assistant professors as the ones most likely to account for that type of reader. Does this mean then that a vast majority of books and articles on Kierkegaard are not important or even that all secondary literature is in fact quite useless? Well, we certainly don't have to rush to conclusions. Kierkegaard's reluctant attitude towards being widely read does of course not exclude his wish to be read at all. In aiming to arrive at "that single individual," the aesthetic production is especially accomplished "to try to establish a rapport with people."[7] This maieutical intention gave rise to a wide variety of—adequate or inadequate—interpretations, and inevitably provoked confusion and misunderstanding. The latter not only goes for his contemporaries, but also for later readers and especially for those who were additionally struggling with linguistic difficulties. It is precisely the purpose of the present study to take into account the considerable amount of heterogeneous ways in which Kierkegaard's writings have been received, translated, and interpreted within the countries of my interest.

With regard to the *second* difficulty, I will have to give an account of some cultural differences between Flanders and the Netherlands. Because of the close affiliation

---

3   *SV1* XIII, 528 / *PV*, 37.
4   *Pap.* VII–2 B 235, p. 9 / *BA*, 10.
5   *Pap.* VII–2 B 235, p. 13 / *BA*, 14.
6   *SV1* XIII, 527 / *PV*, 36.
7   *SV1* XIII, 533 / *PV*, 44.

between Flemish and French culture, on the one hand, and the strong influence of German thinking on the Dutch intellectual world in the nineteenth century, on the other hand, Kierkegaard's thought entered Flanders through different channels than was the case for the Dutch introduction to his works. So it is not surprising that in Catholic Flanders Kierkegaard did not enter the stage until the 1940s and has for most part been of philosophical concern, whereas (northern) Reformed Dutch readers and scholars chiefly became interested in him for theological reasons. Since until the late 1960s, Catholic authorities marked the existing books on Kierkegaard as "forbidden literature" or allowed them to be read only with "strict reservation," any popular dissemination of his thoughts in Flanders was not likely to be expected.[8] The very reason why he used to be abused in Flanders turned the Dane into an object of interest in the Reformed Netherlands.

In unfolding Kierkegaard's reception in the Dutch-speaking countries, I will first deal with the reception of his thought in the Netherlands before bringing in the subsequent introduction of his authorship in Flanders. In doing so, I will fall back on earlier studies that focused upon Kierkegaard reception in Dutch-language literature. The very first person who tried to give a survey of Kierkegaard reception in the Netherlands was Maarten van Rhijn (1888–1966). In 1929 he published his article "Kierkegaard in the Netherlands" in the periodical *Algemeen weekblad voor christendom en cultuur*.[9] For the next article on Kierkegaard's influence and reception in the Netherlands, one had to wait until 1987 when Bernard Delfgaauw and Geert van den Bos wrote their article for the "Kierkegaard Research" volume of the *Bibliotheca Kierkegaardiana*.[10] Although the authors entitled the article "Holland (The Netherlands)" and largely dealt with their fatherland, they also gave a short account of the situation in Flanders. Part of that article resulted from Geert van den Bos' doctoral research, published two years later as *Traces of Kierkegaard. The Dutch Kierkegaard Literature between 1880 and 1930*.[11] As the

---

[8]   Cf. *Lectuur repertorium*, tome 2, Antwerp and Amsterdam: Vlaamsche Boekcentrale/ De R.K. Boek-Centrale 1934, p. 747. This compendium of books, published in both the Netherlands and Flanders, includes the moral qualifications for all works as assessed by the Catholic Church, in accordance with the index and the church laws that it maintained until then. The severest moral qualification, "forbidden," prohibited believers from reading certain books "under penalty of mortal sin," unless "for valid reasons one possesses a reading permission" (ibid., tome 2, pp. XIII–XIV). Almost all translations of Kierkegaard, with exception of *The Concept of Anxiety* which was strictly reserved for specialists, were classed as "forbidden literature." Not before the edition of the *Lectuur repertorium* from 1969 were the moral qualifications of Kierkegaard's books moderated. Cf. Diederik Grit, "Het begin van de Kierkegaardreceptie in Nederland en Vlaanderen," *Geschiedenis van de wijsbegeerte in Nederland*, vol. 4, 1993, pp. 52–4.

[9]   Maarten van Rhijn, "Kierkegaard in Nederland," *Algemeen weekblad voor christendom en cultuur*, vol. 5, no. 26, 1929, pp. 1–2.

[10]   Gerard van den Bos and Bernard Delfgaauw, "Holland (The Netherlands)," in *Kierkegaard Research*, ed. by Niels Thulstrup and Marie Mikulová Thulstrup, Copenhagen: C.A. Reitzel 1987 (*Bibliotheca Kierkegaardiana*, vol. 15), pp. 160–72.

[11]   Gerard van den Bos, *Sporen van Kierkegaard; De Nederlandse Kierkegaard-literatuur tussen 1880-1930*, Ph.D. Thesis, University of Nijmegen 1989.

subtitle makes clear, his study is restricted to the period 1880–1930, and due to this Flemish Kierkegaard reception is left out of consideration. Nevertheless, the book gives a very detailed account of the "pre-scientific stage" of Kierkegaard reception and proves to be very fruitful for the present article. The last contribution came from Diederik Grit. His article "The Beginning of the Kierkegaard Reception in the Netherlands and Flanders" was published in the journal *Geschiedenis van de wijsbegeerte in Nederland en Vlaanderen* in 1993,[12] and functions as a supplement both to the study of van den Bos and the article in *Bibliotheca Kierkegaardiana*. On the bibliographical side I could bring Karel Eisses' *One Hundred and Fifty Years of Traces of Søren Kierkegaard. Dutch Bibliography from 1846–2000. Translations, Studies and References* to the task.[13] His bibliography provides the Kierkegaard scholar with a detailed survey of Kierkegaard literature and broader traces of his work in the Dutch-speaking countries.

I. Early Kierkegaard Entries and the Edifying Reception

Generally speaking, Kierkegaard entered the Dutch field of language through German studies and translations, especially those from the theologian Albert Bärthold who introduced Kierkegaard to (North) Germany,[14] and the German translation of Georg Brandes' book on Kierkegaard.[15] Although there existed cultural relations between the Netherlands and Denmark at the time, none of them was such that it imported Kierkegaard's reputation or thought to the Netherlands or Flanders.[16] Hence, it is of no surprise that the very first mention of Kierkegaard in the Netherlands does not emanate from a Dane but from a German Romantic and specialist in literary history, Eduard Boas (1815–53). In 1846 the literary journal *De tijd* published a translated

---

[12]   Diederik Grit, "Het begin van de Kierkegaard receptie in Nederland en Vlaanderen," *Geschiedenis van de wijsbegeerte in Nederland en Vlaanderen*, vol. 4, 1993, pp. 49–54.

[13]   Karel Eisses, *Honderdvijftig jaar (in de voet) sporen van Søren Kierkegaard. Nederlandstalige bibliografie van 1846–2000. Vertalingen, studies en verwijzingen*, North-field: Kei-produkties 2000. A condensed version of this bibliography was published by Paul Cruysberghs and Karel Eisses as "Søren Kierkegaard, een bibliografie," in *Tijdschrift voor filosofie*, vol. 63, 2001, pp. 107–6.

[14]   See, for example, Albert Bärthold, *Noten zu Søren Kierkegaards Lebensgeschichte*, Halle: Julius Fricke 1876; Albert Bärthold, *Die Bedeutung der ästhetischen Schriften Søren Kierkegaards mit Bezug auf Georg Brandes: "Søren Kierkegaard, ein literarisches Charakterbild,"* Halle: Julius Fricke 1879, and Albert Bärthold, *Zur theologischen Bedeutung Søren Kierkegaards*, Halle: Julius Fricke 1880.

[15]   Georg Brandes, *Søren Kierkegaard. Ein literarisches Charakterbild*, Leipzig: Barth 1879.

[16]   Cf. Bernard Delfgaauw's article "Jacob Nieuwenhuis en het Deense denken ten tijde van Kierkegaard," in *Algemeen Nederlands tijdschrift voor wijsbegeerte*, vol. 68, no. 3, 1976, pp. 190–7. See also van den Bos, *Sporen van Kierkegaard*, p. 9: "There was no Dutchman who came back from his travels through Scandinavia with reports from a certain Kierkegaard, and neither was Kierkegaard brought here by globetrotting or immigrated Danes" (my translation).

article of his, entitled "The Danish Literature of the Present Age."[17] The article dated originally from 1843 and in spite of its predominantly negative appreciation of Kierkegaard, his original and literary qualities are praised. But since Kierkegaard at the time was not at all available in Dutch translation, the reference did not bring forth further Kierkegaard-interest.

It took another thirty years until a second Kierkegaard reference turned up, but this time it was an original Dutch one. In Johannes van Vloten's (1818–83) *Brief History of New Literature* of 1876, Kierkegaard is situated within the tradition of religiously inspired Danish prose writers.[18] Here as well the appreciation concerns his brightness and literary style, but between the few lines dedicated to the Dane one reads disapproval. Along with Grit we can argue that as a typical representative of modern thinkers, Van Vloten sticks to a pure rational approach of religion, and explicitly relies on Spinoza whose collected works he edited.[19] Therefore, it is not surprising that this reference gained as little influence as Boas', because now Kierkegaard was disregarded on ideological grounds.[20]

The first to bring up Kierkegaard with real empathy was Allard Pierson (1831–96). This former priest and professor at Heidelberg wrote in 1880 a review of Georg Brandes' *Søren Kierkegaard Ein literarisches Charakterbild*, published in *De tijdspiegel*.[21] Although none of the later commentators on Kierkegaard explicitly mentions Pierson, his introduction had greater importance than the ones preceding it. Apart from some biographical remarks and its focus on Bärthold's translation of *Practice in Christianity*,[22] his review already draws the contemporaries' attention to opposite Kierkegaard interpretations, since it brings up Bärthold's edifying understanding over against Brandes' aesthetic reading of Kierkegaard. More than his predecessors, Pierson seems to have given the starting shot for the regular appearance of heterogeneous notes on Kierkegaard, ranging from mere mentions of his name, columns or orienting articles to book reviews or short translations from German editions of his work.

---

[17]   Eduard Boas, "De Deensche Letterkunde van dezen tijd," *De Tijd*, vol. 2, no. 1, 1846, pp. 225–78. See also "Het begin van de Kierkegaardreceptie in Nederland en Vlaanderen," *Geschiedenis van de wijsbegeerte in Nederland*, pp. 50–1.

[18]   Cf. Johannes van Vloten, *Beknopte geschiedenis der nieuwe letteren*, Amsterdam: P.N. Van Kampen & Zn. 1876, p. 517. There van Vloten depicts Kierkegaard "...both as writer and human being [as an] odd character, and in 1856 [*sic*] abused and indigently descended in the grave" (my translation).

[19]   Cf. Boas, "Het begin van de Kierkegaardreceptie in Nederland en Vlaanderen," *Geschiedenis van de wijsbegeerte in Nederland*, pp. 51–2.

[20]   So the famous Dutch novelist Frederik van Eeden, who also sympathized with the modern trend of "De tachtigers" [The Eighties Movement], writes in his diary: "Kierkegaard is tough. I have no patience to follow his abstractions. These speculations in our poor language are so unscientific that I shrink back from it." Quoted from Diderik Grit, *Driewerf zalig Noorden*, Maastricht: Universitaire pers Maastricht 1994, p. 87 (my translation).

[21]   Allard Pierson, "Georg Brandes, *Søren Kierkegaard. Ein literarisches Charakterbild*. Leipzig, 1879," *De tijdspiegel*, vol. 37, 1880, pp. 117–22.

[22]   *Einübung im Christentum von Søren Kierkegaard*, trans. by A. Bärthold, Halle: Julius Fricke 1878.

In the first two decades of Dutch reception most, if not all, Kierkegaard acknowledgements stem from authors with a mere practical-theological approach to his writings. What is striking hereby is that especially one group or trend within the religious circles set the tone, i.e., the "ethical theologians." Ethical theology, being the most progressive persuasion within the Dutch Reformed Church, basically held that the revealed truth is not so much intended for man's understanding of it, as it is destined for the heart and the will (ethos) of the human being. The word "ethical" refers to the inner, spiritual life of man and aims to accentuate the personal relation to the God-man. From the beginning on, and especially in their evangelic review *Stemmen voor waarheid en vrede* [Voices for Truth and Peace], several articles appeared which introduced Kierkegaard to the Netherlands. So shortly after Pierson's introduction of Kierkegaard in the more humanistic and political review *De tijdspiegel*, one finds several articles that try to situate the Dane within the ethical-theological context or provide the reader with partial translations of edifying pieces that are invariably based on German editions. In particular, the brothers Aart and Gerrit Jonker were leading voices, the former being the first to publish in 1886 a Dutch translation of Kierkegaard in a separate volume *For Self-Examination. Recommended to the Present Age*[23] translated from the first German Kierkegaard edition by Christian Hansen.[24] Some years later, in 1893, a second full translation appeared, entitled *What We Learn from the Lilies in the Field and from the Birds of the Air*.[25] The book was translated by Hendrikus Barger and also based on a German edition, this time Alfred Puls' translation from 1891.[26] It is worth mentioning that already at that time Barger wrote in his preface that introducing Kierkegaard to the Dutch public was no longer necessary, because "it has been done by a more competent hand than mine, since Aart Jan Theodorus Jonker called attention to him [Kierkegaard] already more than once."[27]

The mere edifying way in which the ethical theologians presented Kierkegaard set the tone for the years to come. Bernard Delfgaauw is right to argue that Kierkegaard for "twenty years remained almost exclusively the 'possession' of ethical theology,"[28] and in *Traces of Kierkegaard* van den Bos correctly concludes that the "biographical-theological-edifying approach" to be found in *Stemmen voor waarheid en vrede* "will appear to be of overriding importance for the coming decades: one translates translations and follows for the most part the interpretations of foreign interpreters."[29]

---

[23]   *Wees gewaarschuwd! door S. Kierkegaard*, from German trans. by Aart Jonker, Rotterdam: J.M. Bredée 1886.
[24]   *Zür Selbstprüfung der Gegenwart empfohlen*, trans. by Christian Hansen, Erlangen: Deichert 1862.
[25]   *Aanmerkt de leliën des velds en de vogelen des hemels*, from German trans. by Hendrikus Barger, Rotterdam: J.M. Bredée 1893.
[26]   *Was wir lernen von den Lilien auf dem Felde und den Vögeln unter dem Himmel. Drei Reden van Søren Kierkegaard*, trans. by Alfred Puls, Gotha: E.F. Thienemann 1891.
[27]   *Aanmerkt de leliën des velds en de vogelen des hemels*, 1893, p. 5 (my translation).
[28]   Delfgaauw, "Jacob Nieuwenhuis en het Deense denken ten tijde van Kierkegaard," p. 197 (my translation).
[29]   van den Bos, *Sporen van Kierkegaard*, p. 60 (my translation).

With the publication of *Selection from the Works of Søren Kierkegaard* in 1905,[30] a new wind started to blow for Kierkegaard's thought in the Netherlands. Although its translator, Regina Chantepie de la Saussaye, also has to be classed among the ethical theologians,[31] the publication not only contributed to Kierkegaard's growing name, but also sowed the seeds for a new perspective on his thoughts. This was due to the fact that the selected texts—chosen by the Copenhagen professor Edvard Lehmann (1862–1930)—were supposed to give the most complete picture possible of Kierkegaard's work. So among edifying texts and strictly religious passages, one finds fragments from Kierkegaard's aesthetic and pseudonymous productions, now for the first time translated directly from the Danish source. But in spite of the wide interest in the book—the second edition already appeared in 1906—a lot of confusion arose from it. The seeds sown did not bring the expected fruits, since what passed for the book's innovation turned out to be its defect. Nowhere is it mentioned from which books the excerpts are taken, nor is their correlation explained or is their pseudonymous status accounted for. Also the person introducing the book, Isaac van Dijk (1847–1922), who equally belonged to the ethical-theological circles, passed over that crucial information. After having known Kierkegaard as a sheer edifying author, the ignorant Dutch reader all of a sudden is confronted with pagan texts apparently originating from one and the same brain.

A successor to Chantepie's anthology appeared in 1911, but this *New Selection from the Works of Søren Kierkegaard* brought no improvement.[32] Book reviewers, even the ones that were well-disposed towards Kierkegaard's thought, were unanimous in their opinion that these rather random collections of texts mainly gave raise to greater misunderstanding, intellectual resistance, and confusion of minds. The advantage that a direct perusal of Kierkegaard and his Scandinavian interpreters now became possible in the Dutch reader's own tongue did not outweigh the uncertainties that came along with both anthologies. The fact that little cracks in the traditional edifying conception of Kierkegaard became noticeable, made van den Bos qualify the influence of both anthologies as a "shuffling of the cards"[33] rather than a full rediscovery of the Dane. The lack of an adequate introduction may have aroused confusion and misunderstandings, but at least different texts were brought into the picture providing the conditions for a renewed interpretation of the Dane's proper intentions.

---

[30]   *Keur uit de werken van Søren Kierkegaard*, trans. by Regina Chantepie de la Saussaye, introduced by Isaac van Dijk, Haarlem: De erven F. Bohn 1905 (2nd ed., 1906; 3rd revised ed., 1919).

[31]   She was married to Pierre Chantepie de la Saussaye, who was a prominent professor at the University of Groningen and leading member of the ethical theologians.

[32]   *Nieuwe keur uit de werken van Søren Kierkegaard*, trans. by Regina Chantepie de la Saussaye, introduced by Isaac van Dijk, Haarlem: De erven F. Bohn 1911 (2nd ed., 1920).

[33]   van den Bos, *Sporen van Kierkegaard*, p. 191 (my translation).

II. Scholarly Interest in Kierkegaard

From the turn of the nineteenth century on, people who did not belong to ethical theology concerned themselves with commenting upon Kierkegaard. Entries from (modern) theologians like Johan Appeldoorn (1861–1945) and Tjeerd Cannegieter (1846–1929) show that a new interest arose or at least indicate that the dominance of a purely edifying Kierkegaard approach no longer prevailed. Especially with Willem Leendertz (1883–1970), also a Protestant theologian, the Dutch Kierkegaard reception slowly entered a new phase. Leendertz was the first in the Netherlands to take Kierkegaard as a subject for a scholarly thesis and is generally considered to be the "Nestor" of the Dutch Kierkegaard study. In the jubileum year 1913 he defended his dissertation entitled *Sören Kierkegaard* at the University of Groningen, with Isaac van Dijk as his advisor.[34] But prior to that Leendertz already showed an intense interest in Kierkegaard and a great familiarity with his works in a pamphlet entitled *How Does One Get Closer to Kierkegaard?*[35] In coming up with an answer to the question which he set himself with the title of the essay, he outlined some conditions to meet the requirement of a "serious Kierkegaard study": "Knowledge of European Romanticism, Danish culture, the Danish language and of the entire work of Kierkegaard," "congeniality with his entire thought" (not only with parts of the authorship), "averting from rationalism" and "being a Christian" appeared to him to be the main requirements for such an undertaking. In his dissertation, Leendertz aimed to fulfill those demands. Based on the first edition of the *Samlede Værker*, he determines the goal of his research as an effort to "give an exposition of Kierkegaard's religious-philosophical basic principles."[36] In doing so, he presents in a first part a chronological, well-documented overview of Kierkegaard's authorship and of the stages therein contained. In a second part he tries to situate Kierkegaard within the broader sphere of Romanticism, Hegelianism, and Socratic thought. His labor yielded rich rewards. Critics showed unanimous approval for Leendertz' study, although not all of them were yet convinced of Kierkegaard's decisive importance for the world of thought.

However revealing Leendertz' efforts were at the time, they did not bring about a crucial breakthrough for Kierkegaard research in the Netherlands. Leendertz' work may be mentioned in several later publications, yet it took another twenty-three years until a second dissertation was published.[37] A sudden flourishing of scientific research did not occur, but two new translations came out. Regina Chantepie, no doubt encouraged by the commercial success of her *Selection from the Works of Søren Kierkegaard* and *New Selection from the Works of Søren Kierkegaard*,

---

[34]   Willem Leendertz, *Sören Kierkegaard*, Amsterdam: A.H. Kruyt 1913.
[35]   Willem Leendertz, *Hoe komt men dichter bij Kierkegaard?* Groningen: privately published 1908.
[36]   Ibid., p. 2 (my translation).
[37]   Taeke Dokter, *De structuur van Kierkegaards oeuvre* [The Structure of Kierkegaard's Authorship], Ph.D. Thesis, Assen: Van Gorcum 1936. The thesis was defended at the state University of Groningen as well. This only contributes to the remarkableness that Dokter himself does not refer a single time to Leendertz's dissertation.

published *Edifying Discourses* in 1918, a modified translation of twelve discourses.[38] One year later Jacqueline Maris-Fransen delivered with *Works of Love* the first integral translation of a Kierkegaard manuscript from Danish.[39] From the works chosen for translation it is clear that even if the foundations for a broader scope on Kierkegaard's work were laid, the approach to Kierkegaard remained mainly of an edifying nature and rested for the most part on personal and religious sympathies with the Dane. Leaving Leendertz aside, one can claim that from a philosophical, literary, or psychological point of view, Kierkegaard still was hardly investigated. Although his name was included in an encyclopedia surprisingly early—already in 1886 Kierkegaard was mentioned in the *Illustrated Encyclopedia*[40]—he did not appear in a compendium of the history of philosophy before 1949.[41]

From the 1930s on the tide was about to turn. The rise and influence of dialectical theology with the Swiss school of Karl Barth and Emil Brunner, and the importance of existential philosophy with such authors as Martin Heidegger and Karl Jaspers, gave the Kierkegaard interest a new zest. The Dutch dialectical theologians criticized ethical theology because of its intellectualism and its incapacity to deal adequately with the problem of the paradox. Worth mentioning here is Theodorus Haitjema (1888–1972) who introduced Karl Barth to the Netherlands. He sympathized with Kierkegaard's insights but opposed them to ethical theology.[42] Also Maarten van Rhijn (1888–1966) explains very briefly the relation of the Swiss theologians to Kierkegaard's thought in his article "Kierkegaard in the Netherlands."[43] But his piece is more of relevance because it is the very first attempt to look back upon the reception of Kierkegaard in the Netherlands. Willem Aalders' (1870–1945) contributions, on the other hand, were of greater importance for Kierkegaard's role in the new theological and philosophical movements. In particular, his article "The Word 'Existence' in Modern Scholarly Language,"[44] where he explicitly linked dialectical theology with Kierkegaardian thought, was quite influential in intellectual circles.

---

[38]   *Stichtelijke redenen, bijeengebracht uit de werken van Sören Kierkegaard*, trans. by Regina Chantepie de la Saussaye, Haarlem: De erven F. Bohn 1918 (2nd revised ed., 1922).
[39]   *Liefdedaden*, trans. by Jacqueline Maris-Fransen, foreword by Isaac van Dijk, Zeist: J. Ploegsma 1919.
[40]   *Geïllustreerde encyclopaedie, woordenboek voor wetenschap en kunst, beschaving en nijverheid*, 2nd ed., tome 9, ed. by A. Winkler Prins, Rotterdam: Elsevier, 1886, p.384. The author of the piece is not mentioned.
[41]   Willem Leendertz, "Kierkegaard, Schopenhauer, Nietzsche & de existentie-philosophie", in *Philosophia; beknopt handboek tot de geschiedenis van het wijsgerig denken*, vols. 1–2, ed. by Hendrik Van Oyen, Utrecht: De Haan 1949, vol. 2, pp. 337–78.
[42]   See Theodorus Haitjema, "Paradoxaal, maar niet anti-intellectualistisch," in *Nieuwe theologische studiën*, vol. 7, 1924, pp. 129–43.
[43]   van Rhijn, "Kierkegaard in Nederland," in *Algemeen weekblad voor christendom en cultuur*, p. 1.
[44]   Willem Aalders, "Het woord 'existentie' in het moderne wetenschappelijke spraakgebruik," in *Mededeelingen der koninklijke akademie van wetenschappen*, Amsterdam: Noord-Hollandsche Uitgevers-maatschappij 1933 (*Afdeling letterkunde, serie A*, no. 75), pp. 23–68.

These new points of departure detached Dutch Kierkegaard reception from
the embrace of ethical theology or at least gradually effaced its explicit mark.
In general, one could say that ideological matters became less important for
the Dane's reception, that the tone started to be more sober and terse, and that a
scientific approach to his thoughts won ground. A good example of this tendency
is Klaas Schilder (1890–1952), a Dutch Reformed minister who frequently relied
on Kierkegaard for the focus and explanation of his topic. He obtained his doctoral
degree in 1933 at the University of Erlangen with a German-language dissertation
on the history of the concept of "paradox"[45] and mentions Kierkegaard on several
occasions with a critical and scholarly tone. The prominent phenomenologist of
religion and later minister of art, education and science, Gerardus van der Leeuw
(1890–1950) was the first to publish on Kierkegaard in a Dutch philosophical
review.[46] I have already touched upon Taeke Dokter's dissertation *The Structure
of Kierkegaard's Authorship* (1936), which was probably the ultimate sign for the
fact that knowledge of Kierkegaard in the Netherlands got rid of its edifying roots
and was more and more involved in contemporary philosophical debates. In these
years also, psychological interest in Kierkegaard's thought arose. The psychiatrist
Pieter Hendrik Esser was one of the first to introduce Kierkegaard to the world of
psychology and psychiatry. Between 1936 and 1940 he published some articles
on Kierkegaard in *Nederlandsch tijdschrift voor psychologie*, and his anthology
Hours with Kierkegaard from 1941 contained several fragments from Kierkegaard's
collected works and journals, albeit all translated from German.[47]

It is not surprising that in this period new and complete translations of
Kierkegaard's texts appeared. In 1931 the first non-edifying translation appeared. The
Dutch novelist Siegfried van Praag (1899–2002) translated *The Concept of Anxiety*[48]
and delivered the following year a good translation of *Fear and Trembling*,[49] both
based on the Danish text. But also religious texts kept on being translated. "What
We Learn from the Lilies in the Field and from the Birds of the Air" appeared a
second time in 1937, now directly translated from Danish by A. Alma.[50] The Dutch
poet Roel Houwink (1899–1987) delivered some—albeit freely and from German
translated—selected texts of Kierkegaard's religious work and extracts from his

[45]   Klaas Schilder, *Zur Begriffsgeschichte des "Paradoxon" mit besonderer
Berücksichtigung Calvins und das nach-Kierkegaardschen "Paradoxon,"* Kampen: Kok
1933.
[46]   Gerardus van der Leeuw, "De psychologie van Kierkegaard," *Algemeen Nederlands
tijdschrift voor wijsbegeerte en psychologie*, vol. 27, no. 5, 1934, pp. 21–5.
[47]   *Uren met Kierkegaard*, from German and English trans. by Pieter Esser, Baarn:
Drukkerij Hollandia 1941.
[48]   *Angst*, trans. by Siegfried van Praag, Amsterdam: De Gulden Ster 1931 (2nd ed.,
1936).
[49]   *Vrees en beven*, trans. by Siegfried van Praag, annotated by A.B. Drachmann,
Amsterdam: De Gulden Ster 1932 (2nd ed., Putten: C.J. Terwee 1937).
[50]   *De lelie des velds en de vogel des hemels*, trans. by A. Alma, foreword by Willem
Aalders, Rotterdam: A. Voorhoeve v/h J.M. Bredée 1937.

journals.[51] His nice booklets were rather meant for broad popular reading and were not averse to using poetic license.

III. Introduction of Kierkegaard in Flanders and the Post-War Period

As I sketched above, Dutch interest in Kierkegaard after 1930 extended from the ethical theologians to the whole Protestant world. Not only was the reading public increasing, but also scientific and philosophical interest in Kierkegaard's thought was growing. The 1940s brought yet another turn for Kierkegaard reception, in that also Flanders and the Catholic intellectual world started to take an interest in his writings.

In my introduction I have already touched upon the fact that it was not by accident that Kierkegaard was introduced much later in a region that was predominantly Catholic. Indeed, partly on linguistic grounds but especially because of religious reasons, Catholic Flanders awakened sixty years later than the Protestant part of the Netherlands when it came to its reception of Kierkegaard. The Dutch philosopher Cornelis Struyker Boudier is also of the opinion that Flanders' initial dislike for Kierkegaard's thought was based on religious motives. In his historical overview of Catholic philosophical life in the Netherlands and Belgium, he rightly remarks that "so little as the Dutch and Belgian Catholic philosophers—and theologians—have shown interest in the greatest religious genius of the last century, Søren Kierkegaard, so much have they paid attention to the one whom E. Przywara ever named 'the Catholic Kierkegaard,' cardinal John Henry Newman."[52] As mentioned before, the fact that the reading of Kierkegaard's books was prohibited by the Catholic authorities certainly did not help Kierkegaard's reception in the Catholic sphere of influence.[53]

The first Flemish mention goes back to 1923, when a certain G.G. van Bergen reviewed *For Self-Examination* in *Vlaamsche arbeid*, a literary journal for Flemish and Catholic young people.[54] Van Bergen says that it is not surprising that in Flanders Kierkegaard has been unknown for a long time, and goes on by giving an account of the main themes in his thinking. Although he is fairly positive in

---

[51]   *Uit de dagboeken van Søren Kierkegaard*, trans. by Roel Houwink, Baarn: Bosch en Keuning 1935 (*Libellenserie*, no. 87); *De leerschool van het lijden*, trans. by Roel Houwink, Gravenhage: J.N. Voorhoeve 1936 (*Brandende kaarsen*, no. 6) (3rd ed., 1942, 6th ed., 1946); *Over de naastenliefde*, trans. by Roel Houwink, Amsterdam: uitg. Mij. Holland 1937; *Weest daders van het woord. Een woord voor den tegenwoordige tijd ter overdenking aangeboden*, trans. by Roel Houwink, Gravenhage: J.N. Voorhoeve 1938 (*Brandende kaarsen*, nos. 20–21³ (3rd ed., 1945); *Enkeling en menigte; een woord voor alle tijden*, trans. by Roel Houwink, Amsterdam: uitg. Mij. Holland 1939.
[52]   Cornelis Struyker Boudier, *Wijsgerig leven in Nederland en België 1880–1890*, vols. 1–6, Nijmegen and Baarn: Ambo 1985–91, vol. 2, pp. 245–6 (my translation).
[53]   Cf. footnote 8.
[54]   G. van Bergen, "Zelfonderzoek. S. Kierkegaard, *Zur Selbstprüfung der Gegenwart anbefohlen* (vert. A. Dorner en Chr. Schrempf; Diederichs Verlag, Jena, 1922)," in *Vlaamsche arbeid*, vol. 18, 1923, pp. 24–6.

his review, his introduction was not at all influential. Between 1931 and 1938, another twelve Kierkegaard reviews appeared in several Catholic—both Dutch and Flemish—reader's guides. But unlike van Bergen, their tenor was overall negative, and it appeared that all the reviewers combined "admiration for style with fear of content."[55]

From 1939 on, the tide was about to turn. In December of that year, the Louvain philosopher Alphonse De Waelhens (1911–81) wrote in *Tijdschrift voor filosofie* his article "Kierkegaard and the Existentialists. Some Notes."[56] With De Waelhens' article, published in the year of foundation of the journal, things definitely took a different direction for Kierkegaard's thought in Flanders. What is striking is that he was introduced to Kierkegaard by the works and translations of the French philosopher Jean Wahl (1888–1974), whom he knew personally and frequently refers to in footnotes. From his criticism of Kierkegaard, one can very well feel that he did not study the author from first-hand information. But the way he relates the Dane to later existential philosophers, in particular Martin Heidegger and Karl Jaspers, definitely gave the reader at the time a good account of Kierkegaard's position in the latest philosophical movements. Especially in combination with phenomenology, De Waelhens saw a crucial and original significance reserved for Kierkegaard in the history of philosophy. In his opinion Kierkegaard's view on subjectivity was fruitful since it emphasized the need for a radical transcendence, whereas phenomenology could deliver the philosophical method he thought was lacking in Kierkegaard's thought.

From De Waelhens' article onward, Flemish (and Walloon) Catholic philosophers and theologians occupied themselves with Kierkegaard. Also, Catholic interest in him in the Netherlands kept on growing, and a dialogue between both countries on Kierkegaard's thoughts became possible. Partly the beginning of a gradual secularization within Catholicism, but especially the rise and expansion of the philosophy of existence after the Second World War guaranteed Kierkegaard's success. In compendia of the history of philosophy and in introductions to existentialism (for example, those of Cornelis van Peursen, Hans Redeker, and Bernard Delfgaauw), the Dane is explicitly mentioned as the founder of the existential trend in philosophy. His work now found its way to both academic circles and average readers as is witnessed by the increasing number of doctoral researchers, on the one hand, and translations of Kierkegaard's works on the other. Jan Sperna Weiland (b. 1925) was the third scholar after Leendertz and Dokter to deliver a doctoral thesis mainly or entirely based on Kierkegaard's thoughts. In 1951, at the University of Groningen where his predecessors also earned their degrees, he defended and published his English manuscript *Humanitas Christianitas: A Critical Survey of Kierkegaard's and Jaspers' Thoughts in Connection with Christianity.*[57] Sperna Weiland's translations

[55]   Grit, "Het begin van de Kierkegaardreceptie in Nederland en Vlaanderen," *Geschiedenis van de wijsbegeerte in Nederland*, p. 54 (my translation).
[56]   Alphonse De Waelhens, "Kierkegaard en de existentialisten. Enkele nota's," *Tijdschrift voor philosophie*, vol. 1, no. 1, 1939, pp. 827–51.
[57]   Jan Sperna Weiland, *Philosophy of Existence and Christianity. Kierkegaard's and Jaspers' Thoughts on Christianity*, Assen: Van Gorcum 1951.

and many articles were of importance and provided a broad basis for further Kierkegaard propagation. In 1955 his translation of the *Philosophical Fragments*[58] appeared and three years later *The Concept of Anxiety*.[59] Both books gained extra value for their clear introduction and illuminating annotations, which was a good reason for their re-edition in one volume in 1995.[60]

Also in 1955, and following the earlier success of Chantepie's anthologies, Willem Leendertz came up with a new selection of journal entries and fragments from Kierkegaard's works.[61] In overcoming the deficiencies of his predecessor, he introduced and ordered the fragments chronologically, which gave the book a biographical character. It the same year Bernard Delfgaauw published his first of seven studies in *Tijdschrift voor filosofie*, entitled "Kierkegaard Studies in Scandinavia."[62] With his informative, well-documented, and clearly written surveys of Scandinavian and especially Danish studies on Kierkegaard, he enabled Dutch and Flemish scholars to be kept informed about international Kierkegaard literature for a period of more than twenty-five years.

The controversial Catholic sociologist and philosopher Victor Leemans (1901–71) was the first in Flanders to publish a monograph devoted to Kierkegaard. His book *Sören Kierkegaard* has an introduction by De Waelhens and offers a specialized and yet clearly written initiation to Kierkegaard's thought.[63] Not only De Waelhens enriched Leemans' insights, but the Dominican theologian Joannes Walgrave also proved to be influential. Walgrave, was a specialist in Thomas Aquinas, Cardinal Newman, and fundamental theology, and in the 1950s he devoted several articles and thoughts to Kierkegaard's work in the periodical *Kultuurleven* and the aforementioned *Tijdschrift voor filosofie*. Another Flemish and Catholic philosopher, Louis Dupré, who specialized in Marx and Hegel, published in 1958 his high-quality study *Kierkegaard's Theology or the Dialectic of Becoming a Christian*.[64] Also later, during his professorship at Yale University, he frequently paid attention to Kierkegaard, religion, and Christianity in various publications.

In the same year of the appearance of Dupré's book, another Dutch publication came out that had considerable importance for Kierkegaard study in the Dutch-

---

[58]   *Wijsgerige kruimels of Een kruimeltje filosofie*, trans. by Jan Sperna Weiland, Utrecht: Bijleveld 1955.
[59]   *Het begrip angst*, trans. by Jan Sperna Weiland, Utrecht: Erven J. Bijleveld 1958 (2nd ed., 1966).
[60]   *Wijsgerige kruimels & Het begrip Angst*, trans. by Jan Sperna Weiland, Baarn: Ambo 1995.
[61]   *Fragmenten*, trans. by Willem Leendertz and Nanne Boelen-Ranneft, Haarlem: De erven F. Bohn 1955.
[62]   Bernard Delfgaauw, "Kierkegaard Studies in Scandinavië, I–VII," *Tijdschrift voor filosofie*, I, in no. 17, 1955, pp. 523–30 (II, in no. 17, 1955, pp. 699–710; III, in no. 18, 1956, pp. 121–9; IV, in no. 17, 1959, pp. 317–43; V, in no. 33, 1971, pp. 737–78; VI, in no. 38, 1976, pp. 136–58; VII, in no. 43, 1981, pp. 117–62.)
[63]   Victor Leemans, *Sören Kierkegaard*, introduced by Alphonse De Waelhens, Antwerp: Standaard boekhandel 1956 (2nd ed., 1956).
[64]   Louis Dupré, *Kierkegaards theologie of dialektiek van het christen-worden*, Utrecht: Het spectrum, Antwerp: Standaard boekhandel 1958.

speaking world. Hans van Munster (b. 1925), a Dutch Friar Minor who in 1956 obtained his doctorate at the Catholic University of Leuven, published his study *The Philosophical Thoughts of the Young Kierkegaard 1831–1841.*[65] The book was an adaptation of his doctoral work that focused on the early developments of and influences on Kierkegaard's thought. It enjoyed an excellent reception in philosophical reviews, and from then on its author became a central figure in the propagation and popularization of Kierkegaard's thoughts. In 1957 Van Munster translated, introduced, and published a selection of diary entries, followed two years later by *Kierkegaard's Discourses.*[66] Six years later, his introduction for the common reader *Søren Aabye Kierkegaard* came about,[67] and in that same year 1963 a very good translation of *The Sickness unto Death* saw the light.[68]

In general one can observe an intense period of Kierkegaard translations from 1955 on. I have already mentioned the translations of Sperna Weiland, but also other scholars started to translate Kierkegaard's work directly from Danish. In 1957, Johan Grooten introduced and translated *De omnibus dubitandum est,*[69] in 1958 Johan Vanderveken published the translation of *Repetition,*[70] and in 1959 Simon van Lienden published the text "The Difference between a Genius and an Apostle" as a separate volume.[71] After the publication of Johannes Hohlenberg's book on Kierkegaard, which had already been translated in 1949,[72] translations of foreign studies began to appear. In 1959 Walter Lowrie's introduction came out, and other Kierkegaard studies such as those of Gregor Malantschuk, Johannes Sløk, and Marguérite Grimault soon followed.[73]

---

[65]   Hans van Munster, *De filosofische gedachten van de jonge Kierkegaard, 1831–1841,* Arnhem: Van Loghum Slaterus 1958.
[66]   *Kierkegaards redevoeringen,* trans. by Hans van Munster, Utrecht and Antwerp: Het spectrum 1959.
[67]   Hans van Munster, *Søren Aabye Kierkegaard,* Tielt: Lannoo 1963.
[68]   *Over de vertwijfeling: de ziekte tot de dood,* trans. by Hans van Munster and Alle Klaver, Utrecht and Antwerp: Het spectrum 1963.
[69]   *Johannes Climacus. De omnibus dubitandum est,* trans. by Johan Grooten, Antwerp: De Nederlandsche boekhandel 1957.
[70]   *De herhaling,* trans. and annotated by Johan Vanderveken, introduced by L. Flam, Amsterdam and Antwerp: Wereldbibliotheek 1958 (2nd ed., 1960).
[71]   *Over het verschil tussen een genie en een apostel,* trans. by Simon van Lienden, foreword by K.A. Deurloo, Zeist: N.C.S.V. 1959 (*Eltheto brochure,* no.1).
[72]   Johannes Hohlenberg, *Søren Kierkegaard,* trans. by Saskia Ferwerda, Utrecht: Erven J. Bijleveld 1949.
[73]   Walter Lowrie, *Het leven van Kierkegaard,* trans. by H.C. de Wolf, Utrecht and Antwerp: Het spectrum 1959 (originally as *A Short Life of Kierkegaard,* Princeton: Princeton University Press 1942); Gregor Malantschuk, *In het voetspoor van Kierkegaard. Een inleiding tot zijn oeuvre,* trans. by Wim Scholtens, introduced by Bernard Delfgaauw, Den Haag: H.P. Leopolds uitg. Mij. 1960 (originally as *Indførelse i Søren Kierkegaards Forfatterskab,* Copenhagen: C.A. Reitzel 1953); Johannes Sløk, *Søren Kierkegaard,* trans. by G.J. Drooglever Fortuyn, introduced by Jan Sperna Weiland, Amsterdam: W. ten Have 1967 (originally as *Søren Kierkegaard,* Copenhagen: G.E.C. Gad 1960); Marguérite Grimault, *Kierkegaard. Leven en werk,* trans. by Frans Bakker, Utrecht and Antwerp: Het spectrum 1967 (originally as *Kierkegaard par lui-même,* Paris: Éditions du Seuil 1962).

During the 1960s Kierkegaard caught the eye of liberal thinkers. Leopold Flam (1912–95), professor at the Free University of Brussels, dedicated several articles to the Dane between 1961 and 1966, among others, in his journal *Dialoog*, and wrote an introduction to the aforementioned translation of *Repetition*. His book *Thinking and Existing* contains several references to Kierkegaard and deals concretely with Kierkegaardian themes.[74] In May 1963, the State University of Ghent organized a Kierkegaard meeting in commemoration of Kierkegaard's 150th birthday. The publication that followed contained some valuable articles, evaluating Kierkegaard's influence on European literature, unfolding his theory of the stages, and situating him in modern philosophy.[75]

Another famous name that rose in Dutch Kierkegaard literature at the time was Wim Scholtens. From 1970 on, the Carmelite father dedicated several articles to the religious works of Kierkegaard in the Carmelite journal *Speling* and the Dominican journal *Tijdschrift voor geestelijk leven*. He translated integral works of Kierkegaard, such as *For Self-Examination, Fear and Trembling, Johannes Climacus or De omnibus dubitandum est*, and *Judge for Yourself*.[76] But Scholtens especially made a name for himself by translating and compiling diary entries, aphorisms, and excerpts of Kierkegaard's writings, thereby unlocking the Dane for a broad public. To name a few: *The Unknown Kierkegaard. His Works—His Prayers*,[77] *Prayers*,[78] *Wild Geese. Journal Entries 1846–1855*,[79] *Pamphlets against the Established Church*[80] and *Aphorisms*.[81] But Scholtens' insights and clear expositions also proved to be very useful for Kierkegaard scholars. In *All Foolishness Aside. Kierkegaard as a Psychologist*[82] he puts Kierkegaard's thought in the perspective of psychology and

---

[74]   Leopold Flam, *Denken en existeren*, Amsterdam and Antwerp: Wereldbibliotheek 1964.

[75]   *Kierkegaard herdenking*, ed. by Alex Bolckmans and Robert Raes, et. al., Gent: Rectoraat Rijksuniversiteit Gent 1964.

[76]   *Tot zelfonderzoek, mijn tijdgenoten aanbevolen*, ["For Self-Examination Recommended to the Present Age"], trans. by Wim Scholtens, Baarn: Ten Have 1974; *Vrees en beven [Fear and Trembling]*, trans. by Wim Scholtens, Baarn: Ten Have 1983; *Johannes Climacus ofwel Men moet aan alles twijfelen*, trans. by Wim Scholtens, Kampen: Kok Agora 1986; *Oordeel zelf! Tot zelfonderzoek, mijn tijdgenoten aanbevolen* ["Judge for Yourself! For Self-Examination Recommended to the Present Age"], trans. by Wim Scholtens, Baarn: Ten Have 1990.

[77]   *De onbekende Kierkegaard. Zijn Werken—Zijn Gebeden*, trans. by Wim Scholtens, Baarn: Ten Have 1972.

[78]   *Gebeden*, trans. by Wim Scholtens, Baarn: Ten Have 1976.

[79]   *Wilde ganzen. Dagboeknotities 1846–1855*, trans. by Wim Scholtens, Baarn: Ten Have 1978.

[80]   *Schotschriften tegen de gevestigde kerkelijkheid*, trans. by Wim Scholtens, Baarn: Ten Have 1980.

[81]   *Aforismen*, trans. by Wim Scholtens, Baarn: Ten Have 1983.

[82]   Wim Scholtens, *Alle gekheid op een stokje. Kierkegaard als psycholoog*, Baarn: Ten Have 1979.

in *"Look, here Language is Bursting..." Mysticism in Kierkegaard*,[83] Kierkegaard's
work is related to mysticism.

All in all one could say that by the end of the 1970s and under the influence
of devoted Kierkegaard scholars such as the aforementioned van Munster and
Scholtens, Kierkegaard was fully given his rightful place in the history of thought.
His works and thought had come to stay both for a common reading public and for
the scholarly world, in the Netherlands as well as in Flanders.

IV. Recent Years

To date, no full Dutch translation of Kierkegaard's collected works is available.
Although almost all the pseudonymous works have been translated separately—some
of them in several editions—and although a great deal of the edifying authorship is
available in translation, a complete edition of Kierkegaard's authorship has not been
realized so far. Overall, one could say that from the 1950s on each decade had its
fair share of Kierkegaard translations. In 1981 two valuable translations were added
to the list. Pieter van Reenen translated *Practice in Christianity*,[84] and Jan Marquart
Scholz published a separate translation of "The Seducer's Diary."[85] The latter in
particular had some special importance because it confronted the reading public for
the first time with a full translation of a purely aesthetic Kierkegaard text. To this
day, Marquart Scholz is regarded as a very good Kierkegaard translator. In 1987 he
made a splendid translation of *Stages on Life's Way*,[86] and in 2000 he succeeded very
well in translating *Either/Or* in its entirety.[87]

From the end of the 1980s on, a curious increase of Kierkegaard interest
is noticeable. Apart from the appearance of some new translations such as "The
Immediate Erotic Stages or the Musical-Erotic,"[88] *Journals*,[89] *Works of Love*,[90] and
Sperna Weiland's re-translation of *Philosophical Fragments* and *The Concept of
Anxiety*,[91] quite a large amount of Dutch secondary literature has been published.
Kierkegaard research especially has flourished, given the number of Ph.D.s that

---

[83]   Wim Scholtens, *"Kijk, hier barst de taal": Mystiek bij Kierkegaard*, Averbode: Kok,
Kampen-Altiora 1991.
[84]   *Oefening in christendom*, trans. by Pieter van Reenen, Utrecht: Bijleveld 1981.
[85]   *Het dagboek van de verleider*, trans. by Jan Marquart Scholtz, epilogue by Egil
Törnqvist, Amsterdam: De arbeiderspers 1981.
[86]   *Stadia op de levensweg*, vols. 1–2, trans. and annotated by Jan Marquart Scholtz,
introduced by Wim Scholtens, Amsterdam: Meulenhoff 1987.
[87]   *Of/of*, trans. by Jan Marquart Scholtz, Amsterdam: Boom 2000.
[88]   *De onmiddellijke erotische stadia of het muzikaal-erotische. Over Mozarts Don
Giovanni*, trans. and annotated by Renée Vink, introduced by Etty Mulder, Leiden: Plantage
and G&S 1991.
[89]   *Dagboeken*, trans. by Cora Polet, introduced and annotated by Sybren Polet,
Amsterdam: De arbeiderspers 1991.
[90]   *Daden van liefde*, trans. and annotated by Maria Veltman, introduced by Michael
Abbott, Leuven and Apeldoorn: Garant 1993.
[91]   *Wijsgerige kruimels & Het begrip angst*, trans. by Jan Sperna Weiland, Baarn: Ambo
1995.

were written about Kierkegaard both at philosophical and theological faculties. Quite some studies are also available in a published form. One discovers a general trend to religious subjects, but one also finds special attention paid to the ethical perspectives in Kierkegaard. A good number of separate articles deal with aesthetical themes but very often in the light of Kierkegaard's theory of the stages. In answering the question what the reason might have been for this considerable growth, one no doubt will have to refer to an increasing interest in the relation between philosophy and religion during the last decade of the former century, on the one hand, and a more general revival of existentialism and existentialist topics, on the other. The monograph *Søren Kierkegaard as a Philosopher. The Way back to the Subject* by Johan Taels initiated a fair amount of Dutch and Flemish scholars into Kierkegaard, but also helped average readers to get introduced in his thought.[92] Sister Maria Veltman's efforts to familiarize a broader public with the Dane were also meritorious. In 1987 she published two introductory books, thereby unlocking Kierkegaard's thought mainly with translations of his letters, diaries, and fragments of the works. Her translation and annotation of *Works of Love*[93] in 1993 provided a necessary and well-selling successor to Maris-Fransen's translation of 1919. Three compilations of essays: *Kierkegaard and the Twentieth Century*[94] and *The Living Kierkegaard*,[95] edited by Etienne Kuypers, and Bernard Delfgaauw's *Kierkegaard: Truth and Humanity?*[96] equally expressed and contributed to Kierkegaard's growing popularity. Other introductory translations appeared such as a fine translation of Patrick Gardiner's well-known introduction *Kierkegaard*[97] and Frits Florin's *Against Despair. Closer to Kierkegaard in 52 Texts.*[98] In 2005 Udo Doedens published *In the Light of Contradiction—Convincing Thoughts of Søren Kierkegaard*, a collection of notes to some upbuilding thoughts of Kierkegaard that will certainly encourage people of the present age.[99]

---

[92]   Johan Taels, *Søren Kierkegaard als filosoof. De weg terug naar het subject*, introduced by Wim Scholtens, Leuven: Universitaire pers Leuven 1991.

[93]   *Daden van liefde* [*Works of Love*], trans. by Maria Veltman, Leuven and Apeldoorn: Garant 1993.

[94]   *Kierkegaard en de twintigste eeuw* (with contributions by Bernard Delfgaauw, Etienne Kuypers, Wim Scholtens, and Maria Veltman), ed. by Etienne Kuypers, Kampen: Kok Agora 1989.

[95]   *De levende Kierkegaard* (with contributions by Paul Cruysberghs, Etienne Kuypers, Wim Scholtens, Jan Sperna Weiland, Johan Taels and Julia Watkins), ed. by Etienne Kuypers, Leuven and Apeldoorn: Garant 1994.

[96]   Bernard Delfgaauw, *Kierkegaard—Waarheid en menselijkheid?* Kampen, Pelckmans and Kapellen: Kok Agora 1995.

[97]   Partick Gardiner, *Kierkegaard*, Rotterdam: Lemniscaat 2001.

[98]   *Tegen de vertwijfeling. Dichter bij Kierkegaard in 52 teksten*, trans. by Frits Florin, Kampen: Agora 2003. In 2006 Florin also published *A Passionless Age. The Actuality of Kierkegaard's Social Criticism* (*Een passieloze tijd. De actualiteit van Kierkegaards maatschappijkritiek*, Kampen: Ten Have 2006), a retranslation of Kierkegaard's *Two Ages* with an introductory essay.

[99]   Udo Doedens, *In het teken van tegenspraak – steekhoudende gedachten van Søren Kierkegaard*, Zoetermeer: Meinema 2005.

The intense Kierkegaard activity of the last decade induced some members of the universities of Antwerp and Leuven—Paul Cruysberghs, Johan Taels, and Karl Verstrynge—to set up an interuniversity research group on Kierkegaard. In an attempt to unite for the first time people from both the Netherlands and Flanders with an interest in Kierkegaard, a Kierkegaard workshop was organized in November 1999. Its theme was "How to Speak? The Problem of Communication in Søren Kierkegaard." In 2001 the presented papers were published in a special issue of *Tijdschrift voor filosofie* entitled *Søren Kierkegaard. Speaking and Being Silent.*[100] Two years later the research group held a first international Kierkegaard conference in Flanders at the universities of Leuven and Antwerp, with the theme "Immediacy and Reflection in Kierkegaard's Thought." Here as well proceedings were published, this time in a separate volume.[101] From 2003 a project for a Kierkegaard chronicle has been set up, intending to deal with primary and secondary literature on Kierkegaard published after 2000. A first edition of this chronicle, which is basically an attempt to carry on and catch up with Delfgaauw's above-mentioned "Kierkegaard Studies in Scandinavia," appeared in December 2005.[102]

Also on a broader and more popular basis, some noticeable initiatives have been taken. In 1990 a "Werkgroep Kierkegaard" ("Study Group Kierkegaard") has been founded in Antwerp, led by Inigo Bocken. Its main objective is to make the person and the works of Kierkegaard more widely known by organizing meetings on a regular basis. On the occasion of the commemoration of the fiftieth anniversary of the liberation of Antwerp, some of its members published a collection of papers entitled, *Kierkegaard and the Modern Thinking in a Liberated City.*[103] In the Netherlands a "Leerkring" (Learning Circle) around Kierkegaard has been established, where texts of Kierkegaard are read, translated, and discussed under the direction of Lineke Buijs and Andries Visser. Karel Eisses, for his part, has been running a Dutch website on Kierkegaard since 2002, providing extensive bibliographical material and informing the Dutch-speaking world about the latest Kierkegaard news.[104] Last but not least, some Kierkegaard scholars,[105] both from Holland and Flanders, joined forces and established in October 2006 a scientific board that will guide a new series of translations of Kierkegaard's works. In doing so, some titles that were no longer available and no longer matched present-day standards will be obtainable again, and above all the lack of a substantial series of Kierkegaard translations in the Dutch-speaking countries will finally be overcome.

---

[100]   *Søren Kierkegaard. Spreken en zwijgen* (*Tijdschrift voor filosofie*, vol. 63, no. 1), 2001.

[101]   *Immediacy and Reflection in Kierkegaard's Thought*, ed. by Paul Cruysberghs, Johan Taels and Karl Verstrynge, Leuven: Leuven University Press 2003.

[102]   "Descriptive Bibliography. Recent Kierkegaard Literature: 2000–2004," *Tijdschrift voor filosofie*, vol. 67, no. 4, 2005, pp. 767–814.

[103]   *Kierkegaard en het moderne denken in een bevrijde stad*, ed. by J. Van Otten, B. Van Parijs and C. Vonck, Antwerp: Werkgroep Kierkegaard Antwerp 1994.

[104]   See http://www.kierkegaard.nl/.

[105]   Paul Cruysberghs, Udo Doedens, Frits Florin, Johan Taels, Karl Verstrynge, Andries Visser, Pieter Vos, Onno Zijlstra.

In conclusion, one can claim that the history of Kierkegaard reception in the Dutch-speaking countries shows nowhere in its development significant gaps when it comes to the attention paid to the Dane's thought. Even if it took some decades until his thought via Germany crossed the Dutch borders, and even if periods of high and low intensity succeeded one another, the claim is still valid that overall there has always been a fair and steady interest in Kierkegaard's thought. After ethical theology dominated the first two decades of the Dane's reception and left the reading public with a one-sided edifying picture of his thought, modern theologians embarked on a study of Kierkegaardian themes and gradually opened up the authorship to its full dimensions. After the Second World War they were followed by the philosophical interest of Flemish Catholic and liberal thinkers. The subsequent publication of some good introductions and the regular appearance of Dutch translations also gave many non-specialists the occasion to get involved with Kierkegaard's thought. But by definition it is an impossible task to measure the effect of the Dane's maieutical aims on the individuals—scholars as well as average readers—who concerned themselves with his authorship. To deal with Kierkegaard's reception implies, more than is the case for any other authorship, to abstract from the author's intentions. Thus understood, the increase of Kierkegaard interest in the Dutch language area of the last decade does not reveal a single thing about the success of the Dane's fundamental aspirations of upbuilding and awakening. If "only the knowing whose relation to existence is essential is essential knowing,"[106] then any external knowledge about the way Kierkegaard has been received must be accidental to the true meaning of the influence Kierkegaard was willing to exert. Involuntarily, it leaves one with the feeling of writing with one's "left hand" when it comes to disclosing something about those who accepted the authorship with their right.

---

[106]   *SKS* 7, 181 / *CUP1*, 197.

Bibliography[107]

I. Dutch Translations of Kierkegaard's Works

"Leerrede van Sören Kierkegaard" [A Sermon of Søren Kierkegaard], from German trans. by Aart Jonker, *Stemmen voor waarheid en vrede*, vol. 17, no. 2, 1880, pp. 406–26.

"Søren Kierkegaard," trans. by V.D. [*sic*], *Stemmen voor waarheid en vrede*, vol. 17, no. 1, 1880, pp. 177–208.

"Het vreugdevolle van een eeuwig gewin door een tijdelijk verlies" ["The Joy of It That the Happinness of Eternity Still Outweighs Even the Heaviest Temporal Suffering" from *Upbuilding Discourses in Various Spirits*], from German trans. by Aart Jonker, *Stemmen voor waarheid en vrede*, vol. 19, no. 2, 1882, pp. 281–300.

Wees gewaarschuwd! door S. Kierkegaard [Be Warned! by S. Kierkegaard (translation of *For Self-Examination. Recommended to the Present Age*)], from German trans. and ed. by Aart Jonker, Rotterdam: J.M. Bredée 1886.

"Onze roeping om de mensen die wij zien lief te hebben" ["Our Duty to Love the People We See"], from German trans. by Aart Jonker, *Stemmen voor waarheid en vrede*, vol. 28, 1891, pp. 125–54.

Aanmerkt de leliën des velds en de vogelen des hemels ["What We Learn from the Lilies in the Field and the Birds of the Air" from *Upbuilding Discourses in Various Spirits*], from German trans. by Hendrikus Barger, Rotterdam: J.M. Bredée 1893.

Keur uit de werken van Søren Kierkegaard [Selection from the Works of Søren Kierkegaard], trans. by Regina Chantepie de la Saussaye, introduced by Isaac van Dijk, Haarlem: De erven F. Bohn 1905 (2nd ed., 1906, 3rd revised ed., 1919).

Nieuwe keur uit de werken van Søren Kierkegaard [New Selection from the Works of Søren Kierkegaard], trans. by Regina Chantepie de la Saussaye, introduced by Isaac van Dijk, Haarlem: De erven F. Bohn 1911 (2nd ed., 1920).

Stichtelijke redenen, bijeengebracht uit de werken van Sören Kierkegaard [Upbuilding Discourses, Collected from the Works of Sören Kierkegaard], trans. by Regina Chantepie de la Saussaye, Haarlem: De erven F. Bohn 1918 (2nd revised ed., 1922).

---

[107]   This bibliography is partly based on Karel Eisses' *Honderdvijftig jaar (in de voet) sporen van Søren Kierkegaard. Nederlandstalige bibliografie van 1846–2000. Vertalingen, studies en verwijzingen.* In the first section, titles are arranged by date of publication. When several titles are published in a same year, they are ordered alphabetically. All translations referred to in section I of this bibliography are from Danish, except when otherwise indicated.

Liefdedaden [*Works of Love*], trans. by Jacqueline Maris-Fransen, foreword by Isaac van Dijk, Zeist: J. Ploegsma 1919.

"Avondmaalsrede over Lucas 7:47" ["III: The Woman Who Was a Sinner. Luke 7:47" from *Three Discourses at the Communion on Fridays*], trans. by Ph.L. van Rhijn, *Stemmen voor waarheid en vrede*, vol. 62, 1925, pp. 675–88.

Angst [*The Concept of Anxiety*], trans. by Siegfried van Praag, Amsterdam: De Gulden Ster 1931 (2nd ed., 1936).

Vrees en beven [*Fear and Trembling*], trans. by Siegfried van Praag, annotated by A.B. Drachmann, Amsterdam: De Gulden Ster 1932 (2nd ed., Putten: C.J. Terwee 1937).

Uit de dagboeken van Søren Kierkegaard [From the Diaries of Søren Kierkegaard], trans. by Roel Houwink, Baarn: Bosch en Keuning 1935 (*Libellenserie*, vol. 87).

De leerschool van het lijden ["The Joy of It That the School of Sufferings Educates for Eternity" from *Upbuilding Discourses in Various Spirits*], trans. by Roel Houwink's Gravenhage: J.N. Voorhoeve 1936 (*Brandende kaarsen*, no. 6) (3rd ed., 1942, 6th ed., 1946).

De lelie des velds en de vogel des hemels ["What We Learn from the Lilies in the Field and the Birds of the Air" from *Upbuilding Discourses in Various Spirits*], trans. by A. Alma, foreword by Willem Aalders, Rotterdam: A. Voorhoeve v/h J.M. Bredée 1937.

Over de naastenliefde [Selections from *Works of Love*], trans. by Roel Houwink, Amsterdam: uitg. Mij. Holland 1937.

Weest daders van het woord. Een woord voor den tegenwoordige tijd ter overdenking aangeboden [Be Doers of the Word. A Word for the Present Age Presented for Consideration], trans. by Roel Houwink, Gravenhage: J.N. Voorhoeve's 1938 (*Brandende kaarsen*, nos. 20–21³) (3rd ed., 1945).

Enkeling en menigte; een woord voor alle tijden [The Single Individual and Crowd], trans. by Roel Houwink, Amsterdam: uitg. Mij. Holland 1939.

Uren met Kierkegaard [Hours with Kierkegaard], from German and English trans. by Pieter Esser, Baarn: Drukkerij Hollandia 1941.

Fragmenten [Fragments], trans. by Willem Leendertz and Nanne Boelen-Ranneft, Haarlem: De erven F. Bohn 1955.

Wijsgerige kruimels of Een kruimeltje filosofie [*Philosophical Fragments*], trans. by Jan Sperna Weiland, Utrecht: Bijleveld 1955.

Een keuze uit zijn dagboeken [A Selection from his Diaries], trans. by Hans van Munster, Utrecht and Antwerp: Het spectrum 1957 (2nd ed., 1958).

Johannes Climacus. De omnibus dubitandum est, trans. by Johan Grooten, Antwerp: De Nederlandsche boekhandel 1957.

De herhaling [*Repetition*], trans. by Johan Vanderveken, introduced by L. Flam, Amsterdam and Antwerp: Wereldbibliotheek 1958, 2nd ed., 1960.

Het begrip angst [*The Concept of Anxiety*], trans. by Jan Sperna Weiland, Utrecht: Erven J. Bijleveld 1958 (2nd ed., 1966).

Kierkegaards redevoeringen [Kierkegaard's Sermons], trans. by Hans van Munster, Utrecht and Antwerp: Het spectrum 1959.

Over het verschil tussen een genie en een apostel [*On the Difference between a Genius and an Apostle*], trans. by Simon van Lienden, foreword by K.A. Deurloo, Zeist: N.C.S.V. 1959 (*Eltheto brochure*, no.1).

"De sterking in de innerlijke mens" ["Strengthening in the Inner Being" from *Three Upbuilding Discourses*], trans. by Frits Florin, *Kultuurleven*, vol. 30, 1963, pp. 751–67.

Over de vertwijfeling: de ziekte tot de dood [*The Sickness unto Death*], trans. by Hans van Munster and Alle Klaver, Utrecht and Antwerp: Het spectrum 1963.

"Komt allen tot mij..." ["Come Here, All You Who Labor and Are Burdened, and I Will Give You Rest" from *Practice in Christianity*], trans. by Frits Florin, *Tijdschrift voor geestelijk leven*, vol. 23, no. 2, 1967, pp. 586–94.

Dagboeknotities; een keuze [Diary Notes: A Selection], trans. by Wim Scholtens, foreword by Bernard Delfgaauw, Baarn: Ten Have 1971 (2nd ed., 1971).

"Gebeden van Kierkegaard" [Prayers of Kierkegaard], trans. by Wim Scholtens, *Tijdschrift voor geestelijk leven*, vol. 27, 1971, pp. 409–20.

"S. Aabye Kierkegaard: teksten over doel en methode van gebed" [S. Aabye Kierkegaard: Texts about Goal and Method of Prayer], trans. by Wim Scholtens, *Tijdschrift voor geestelijk leven*, vol. 27, 1971, pp. 259–66.

De onbekende Kierkegaard [The Unknown Kierkegaard], trans. by Wim Scholtens, Baarn: Ten Have 1972.

De naakte waarheid. Aforismen en andere korte notities [The Naked Truth. Aphorisms and other Short Notes], trans. by Wim Scholtens, Baarn: Ten Have 1974.

Tot zelfonderzoek, mijn tijdgenoten aanbevolen [*For Self-Examination. Recommended to the Present Age*], trans. by Wim Scholtens, Baarn: Ten Have 1974.

Gebeden [Prayers], trans. by Wim Scholtens, Baarn: Ten Have 1976.

Wilde ganzen. Dagboeknotities 1846–1855 [Wild Geese. Diary Notes 1846–1855], trans. by Wim Scholtens, Baarn: Ten Have 1978.

Schotschriften tegen de gevestigde kerkelijkheid [Pamphlets against the Established Church], trans. by Wim Scholtens, Baarn: Ten Have 1980.

Het dagboek van de verleider ["The Seducer's Diary"], trans. by Jan Marquart Scholtz, epilogue by Egil Törnqvist, Amsterdam: De arbeiderspers 1981.

Jezus, de dwarsligger; dagboeknotities [Jesus, the Obstructionist; Diary Notes], trans. by Wim Scholtens, Baarn: Ten Have 1981.

Oefening in christendom [*Practice in Christianity*], trans. by Pieter van Reenen, Utrecht: Bijleveld 1981.

Denken en zijn: Afsluitend onwetenschappelijk naschrift (Ch.II); Een literaire bespreking (Ch.III) [*Concluding Unscientific Postscript*: Chapter II; *Two Ages*. Chapter III], trans. by Gerard Rasch, introduced and annotated by Teddy Petersen, Meppel and Amsterdam: Boom 1982 (2nd ed., 1988).

Aforismen [Aphorisms], trans. by Wim Scholtens, Baarn: Ten Have 1983.

Vrees en beven [*Fear and Trembling*], trans. by W.R. Scholtens, Baarn: Ten Have 1983.

Johannes Climacus ofwel Men moet aan alles twijfelen [*Johannes Climacus or De Omnibus Dubitandum est*], trans. by Wim R. Scholtens, Kampen: Kok Agora 1986.

Søren Kierkegaard: een biografische schets aan de hand van zijn geschreven nalatenschap [Søren Kierkegaard: a Biographical Sketch by Way of his Written Legacy], trans. by Maria Veltman, Assen and Maastricht: Van Gorcum 1987.

Søren Kierkegaard. Een kennismaking door een keuze uit dagboeken, brieven en werken [Søren Kierkegaard. An Introduction by Way of a Selection from his Diaries, Letters and Works], trans. by Maria Veltman, Kampen: Kok 1987.

Stadia op de levensweg [*Stages on Life's Way*], vols. 1–2, trans. and annotated by Jan Marquart Scholtz, introduced by Wim Scholtens, Amsterdam: Meulenhoff 1987.

Kierkegaards werken. Een inleiding [Kierkegaard's Works. An Introduction], trans. by Wim Scholtens, Baarn: Ten Have 1988.

Oordeel zelf! Tot zelfonderzoek, mijn tijdgenoten aanbevolen [*Judge for Yourself! For Self-Examination. Recommended to the Present Age*], trans. by Wim Scholtens, Baarn: Ten Have 1990.

Dagboeken [Diaries], trans. by Cora Polet, introduced and annotated by Sybren Polet, Amsterdam: De arbeiderspers 1991.

De onmiddellijke erotische stadia of Het muzikaal-erotische. Over Mozarts Don Giovanni ["The Immediate Erotic Stages or the Musical-Erotic"], trans. and annotated by Renée Vink, introduced by Etty Mulder, Leiden: Plantage/G&S 1991.

"De drang tot afwisseling" ["Rotation of Crops" (from *Either/Or*)], trans. by Annelies van Hees, *De tweede ronde, tijdschrift voor literatuur*, vol. 13, no. 3, 1992, pp. 72–5.

Plankenkoorts en drankzucht: De crisis en een crisis in het leven van een actrice; De heer Phister als kapitein Scipio [*The Crisis in a Crisis in the Life of an Actress and Phister as Captain Scipio*], trans. by Wim Scholtens, Baarn: Ten Have 1992.

Daden van liefde [*Works of Love*], trans. and annotated by Maria Veltman, introduced by Michael Abbott, Leuven and Apeldoorn: Garant 1993.

Over het begrip ironie [*The Concept of Irony*], trans. and annotated by Willem Breeuwer, introduced by Wim R. Scholtens, Amsterdam and Meppel: Boom 1995.

Wijsgerige kruimels & Het begrip angst [*Philosophical Fragments* and *The Concept of Anxiety*], trans. by Jan Sperna Weiland, Baarn: Ambo 1995.

Of/of [*Either/Or*], trans. by Jan Marquart Scholtz, Amsterdam: Boom 2000.

Tegen de vertwijfeling. Dichter bij Kierkegaard in 52 teksten [Against Despair. Closer to Kierkegaard in 52 Texts], trans. by Frits Florin, Kampen: Agora 2003.

Een passieloze tijd. De actualiteit van Kierkegaards maatschappijkritiek [A Passionate Time (translation of *Two Ages*)], trans. by Frits Florin, Kampen: Ten Have 2006.

Vrees en beven [*Fear and Trembling*], trans. by Andries Visser, ed. by Frits Florin and Karl Verstrynge, Budel: Damon 2006.

II. Secondary Literature on Søren Kierkegaard in the Netherlands and Flanders

Aalders, Willem, "Het woord 'existentie' in het moderne wetenschappelijke spraakgebruik" [The Word "Existence" in Modern Scholarly Language], in

Mededeelingen van de koninklijke akademie van wetenschappen, Amsterdam: Noord-Hollandsche UM 1933 (*Afd. letterkunde, serie A*, no.75), pp. 23–68.

Appeldoorn, Johan, "Søren Kierkegaard. Harald Höffding, *Sören Kierkegaard als Philosoph*. Frommann: Stuttgart 1896," *Theologisch tijdschrift*, vol. 34, 1900, pp. 227–60.

— "Boekbeoordeling van Søren Kierkegaard, *Zwei ethisch-religiöse Abhandlungen*" [Book review of Søren Kierkegaard, *Two Ethical-Religious Discourses*], *Theologisch tijdschrift*, vol. 37, 1903, pp. 61–5.

Bakker, Reinout, "Kierkegaard, de denker vanuit de existentie" [Kierkegaard, the Thinker from Existence], *Ad fontes*, vol. 2, 1962, pp. 117–24.

Barger, Hendrikus, "Sören Kierkegaard, *Keur uit de werken van Søren Kierkegaard*. Vertaald door R.C.S." [Sören Kierkegaard, *Selection from the Works of Søren Kierkegaard*. Translated by R.C.S.], *Stemmen voor waarheid en vrede*, vol. 42, 1905, pp. 725–63.

van den Beld, A., "Over Kierkegaards notie van de suspensie van het ethische" [On Kierkegaard's Notion of the Suspension of the Ethical], *Bijdragen*, vol. 39, 1978, pp. 424–39.

Bense, Max, "Pascal en Kierkegaard," *Nederlandsch tijdschrift voor psychologie*, vol. 11, 1943–1944, pp. 58–66.

Berendsen, Desiree, "Kiezen voor Kierkegaard" [Chosing for Kierkegaard], *Gereformeerd theologisch tijdschrift*, vol. 100, 2000, pp. 136–42.

van Bergen, G., "Zelfonderzoek. S. Kierkegaard, *Zur Selbstprüfung der Gegenwart anbefohlen* (vert. A. Dorner en Chr. Schrempf; Diederichs Verlag, Jena, 1922)" [Self-Examination. S. Kierkegaard, *Zur Selbstprüfung der Gegenwart anbefohlen* (vert. A. Dorner en Chr. Schrempf; Diederichs Verlag, Jena, 1922)], *Vlaamsche arbeid*, vol. 18, 1923, pp. 24–6.

Boer, Richard "Kierkegaard in Noorwegen" [Kierkegaard in Norway], *Onze eeuw*, vol. 24, no. 1, 1924, pp. 152–69.

van den Borre, Roger, "Sören Kierkegaard en Elias Canetti. Een kort en een lang schrijversleven" [Sören Kierkegaard and Elias Canetti. A Short and a Long Writer's Life], *Yang*, vol. 25, 1989, pp. 124–31.

van Brederode, Désanne, "Een sprong in het duister. Enkele gedachten bij Kierkegaards *Vrees en Beven*" [A Leap in the Dark. Some Reflections on Kierkegaard's *Fear and Trembling*], *De revisor*, vol. 26, nos. 3–4, 1999, pp. 127–35.

Casparie, Paul, "Schuld. Waarom heeft hij de verloving verbroken?" [Guilt. Why Did He Break Off the Engagement?], *Filosofie magazine*, vol. 2, no. 7, 1993, pp. 13–15.

Cornelis, Geert, "Vrijheid van geloof en van rationeel denken bij Søren Kierkegaard" [Freedom of Faith and of Rational Thinking in Søren Kierkegaard], *Tijdschrift voor de studie van de verlichting en van het vrije denken*, vol. 18, nos. 1–2, 1990, pp. 73–106.

Cruysberghs, Paul, "Behoud de begeerte" [Maintain the Desire], *Onze alma mater*, vol. 46, no. 2, 1992, pp. 197–219.

— "Kierkegaard en Mozart, een verhaal over zinnelijkheid, begeerte en verleiding" [Kierkegaard and Mozart, a Story of Sensuousness, Desire and Seduction], *Onze alma mater*, vol. 47, no. 1, 1993, pp. 56–83.

— "De grote alliantie van esthetiek, ethiek en religie bij Kierkegaard. Naar aanleiding van de Nederlandse vertaling van *Of/of*" [The Big Alliance of Aesthetics, Ethics and Religion in Kierkegaard. On the Occasion of the Dutch Translation of *Either/ Or*], *Acta comparanda*, vol. 12, 2001, pp. 22–50.

— "Esthetische en demonische geslotenheid bij Kierkegaard. Naar aanleiding van het verhaal over de meerman in *Vrees en beven*" [Aesthetical and Demonic Enclosing Reserve in Kierkegaard. On the Occasion of the Merman in *Fear and Trembling*], *Tijdschrift voor filosofie*, vol. 63, 2001, pp. 55–85.

Cruysberghs, Paul, Johan Taels and Karl Verstrynge (eds.), "Descriptive Bibliography. Recent Kierkegaard Literature: 2000–2004," *Tijdschrift voor filosofie*, vol. 67, no.4, 2005, pp. 767–814.

Delfgaauw, Bernard, "De existentie-filosofie sinds de oorlog" [The Philosophy of Existence Since the War], *Katholiek archief*, vol. 9, 1954, pp. 741–76.

— "Kierkegaard studies in Scandinavië I," *Tijdschrift voor philosophie*, no. 17, 1955, pp. 523–30.

— "Kierkegaard studies in Scandinavië II," *Tijdschrift voor philosophie*, no. 17, 1955, pp. 699–710.

— "Kierkegaard-congres te Kopenhagen, 10–16 Aug. 1955," *Algemeen tijdschrift voor wijsbegeerte en psychologie*, vol. 48, 1955–56, pp. 98–106.

— "Kierkegaard studies in Scandinavië III," *Tijdschrift voor philosophie*, no. 18, 1956, pp. 121–9.

— "Kierkegaard studies in Scandinavië IV," *Tijdschrift voor philosophie*, no. 21, 1959, pp. 317–43.

— "Existentialisme," *Dietsche warande en belfort*, vol. 62, 1962, pp. 120–30.

— "Kierkegaard studies in Scandinavië V," *Tijdschrift voor filosofie*, no. 33, 1971, pp. 737–78.

— "Kierkegaard studies in Scandinavië VI," *Tijdschrift voor filosofie*, no. 38, 1976, pp. 136–58.

— "Jacob Nieuwenhuis en het Deense denken ten tijde van Kierkegaard" [Jacob Nieuwenhuis and Danish Thought at the Time of Kierkegaard], *Algemeen tijdschrift voor wijsbegeerte*, vol. 68, 1976, pp. 190–7.

— "Kierkegaard en Marx over democratie" [Kierkegaard and Marx on Democracy], *De gids*, vol. 141, no. 7, 1978, pp. 466–80.

— "Kierkegaard studies in Scandinavië VII," *Tijdschrift voor filosofie*, no. 43, 1981, pp. 117–162.

— "Oriëntatie: Kierkegaard in Denemarken" [Orientation: Kierkegaard in Denmark], *Wijsgerig perspectief*, vol. 24, 1983–84, pp. 57–60.

— *Kierkegaard—Waarheid en menselijkheid?* [Kierkegaard—Truth and Humanity?], Kampen and Pelckmans, Kapellen: Kok Agora 1995.

van Dijk, August, *Perspectieven bij Kierkegaard* [Perspectives in Kierkegaard], introduced by Willem Aalders, Amsterdam: H.J. Paris 1940.

Dijkstra, R., "Søren Kierkegaard 1813–1855," *Bloesem en vrucht: Maandschrift uitgegeven door het Christelijk Letterkundig Verbond*, vol. 4, 1915, pp. 726–41.

Doedens, Udo, *Het eenvoudige leven—volgens Søren Kierkegaard* [The Simple Life—According to Søren Kierkegaard], Baarn: Ten Have 1999.

— "Het gewicht van de eeuwigheid" [The Weight of Eternity], *Wijsgerig perspectief,* vol. 42, no. 4, 2002, pp. 5–15.

— *In het teken van tegenspraak—steekhoudende gedachten van Søren Kierkegaard* [In the Light of Contradiction—Convincing Thoughts of Søren Kierkegaard], Zoetermeer: Meinema 2005.

Dokter, Taeke, *De structuur van Kierkegaard's oeuvre* [The Structure of Kierkegaard's Oeuvre], Assen: Van Gorcum 1936.

— "Sören Kierkegaard," *Onder eigen vaandel,* vol. 14, 1939, pp. 37–56.

— "De stem van Sören Kierkegaard" [The Voice of Sören Kierkegaard], *Wending,* vol. 1, 1946–47, pp. 41–7.

Doornenbal, Robert, "Søren Kierkegaard als voorloper van postmodern denken" [Søren Kierkegaard as Precursor of Postmodern Thought], *Beweging,* vol. 58, no. 6, 1994, pp. 113–15.

Doude van Troostwijk, Chris, "De tragiek van het innerlijk leven: Kierkegaards moderne Antigone" [The Tragedy of the Inner Life: Kierkegaard's Modern Antigone], *Wijsgerig perspectief,* vol. 42, no. 4, 2002, pp. 16–26.

Dupré, Louis, "S. Kierkegaard. Schets van zijn innerlijke ontwikkeling" [S. Kierkegaard. Sketch of His Inner Development], *Streven,* vol. 9, no. 1, 1955–56, pp. 217–25.

— *Kierkegaards theologie of dialektiek van het christen-worden* [Kierkegaard's Theology or Dialectics of Being a Christian], Utrecht: Het spectrum, Antwerp: Standaard boekhandel 1958.

Van Eekert, Geert, "Sören Aabye Kierkegaard," *Streven,* vol. 59, no. 1, 1992, pp. 648–51.

Esser, Pieter, "Kierkegaards ontwikkeling en uitgroei als psychologisch probleem" [Kierkegaard's Growth and Development as a Psychological Problem], *Nederlandsch tijdschrift voor psychologie,* vol. 4, 1936–37, pp. 150–66.

— "Kierkegaard en de 'existentieele' psychologie" [Kierkegaard and the "Existential" Psychology], *Nederlandsch tijdschrift voor psychologie,* vol. 5, 1937–38, pp. 355–63.

Fetter, Johan, *Inleiding tot het denken van Kierkegaard* [Introduction to Kierkegaard's Thought], Assen: Uitg. Born 1953 (3rd ed., 1960).

Flam, Leopold, "S. Kierkegaard, de ketter" [S. Kierkegaard, the Heretic], *Nieuw Vlaams tijdschrift,* vol. 11, 1957, pp. 408–21.

— "Waarom me Kierkegaard interesseert?" [Why is Kierkegaard interesting to me?], *Dialoog,* vol. 2, 1961–62, pp. 68–70.

— "Kierkegaard (1813–1963)," *Dialoog,* vol. 3, 1962–63, pp. 241–61.

— "Kierkegaard (geboren op 5 mei 1813)," *Tijdschrift Vrije Universiteit Brussel,* vol. 5, 1962–63, pp. 204–16.

— "Kierkegaard (1813–1963), II," *Dialoog,* vol. 4, 1963–64, pp. 1–12.

— "De onmogelijke liefde van Sören Kierkegaard" [Sören Kierkegaard's Impossible Love], *Dialoog,* vol. 6, 1965–66, pp. 232–49.

Florin, Frits, "Søren Kierkegaard," *Kultuurleven,* vol. 30, 1963, pp. 725–8.

— *Geloven als noodweer. Het begrip "het religieuze" bij S. Kierkegaard* [To Believe as Heavy Weather. The Concept of 'the Religious' in S. Kierkegaard], Kampen: Agora 2002.

van Gennep, Frederik, "Sören Kierkegaard: De absolute ongelijkheid" [Sören Kierkegaard: the Absolute Inequality], *In de waagschaal*, vol. 16, 1987–88, pp. 69–77.

Glas, Gerrit, "Pas op de plaats voor Kierkegaard" [To Mark Time for Kierkegaard], *De Reformatie*, vol. 77, vol. 23, no. 2, 2000, pp. 432–34.

Grauls, W., "De romantische levenshouding en haar kritiek door S. Kierkegaard" [The Romantic Attitude to Life and Its Critique by S. Kierkegaard], *Kultuurleven*, vol. 20, 1953, pp. 14–20.

Grit, Diederik, "Gerard Dick van den Bos, *Sporen van Kierkegaard* (1989)" [Gerard Dick van den Bos, *Traces of Kierkegaard* (1989)], *Tijdschrift voor skandinavistiek*, vol. 13, no. 1, 1992, pp. 137–43.

Grooten, Johan, "Het probleem der 'onrechtstreekse mededeling' bij Kierkegaard" [The Problem of "Indirect Communication" in Kierkegaard], *Handelingen van het twintigste Vlaamse Filologencongres, Antwerp 7–9 april, 1953*, pp. 260–3.

— "Søren Kierkegaard," *Tijdschrift voor opvoedkunde*, vol. 1, no. 2, 1955–56, pp. 109–22.

Haitjema, Theodorus, "Paradoxaal, maar niet anti-intellectualistisch" [Paradoxical, but not Anti-Intellectual], *Nieuwe theologische studiën*, vol. 7, 1924, pp. 129–43.

Hameete, Gepke, *Kierkegaard: van exemplaar naar de enkeling* [Kierkegaard: from Specimen to Single Individual], Delft: Eburon 1990.

Hart, Maarten, "De dagboeken van Søren Aabye Kierkegaard" [The Diaries of Søren Aabye Kierkegaard], *Maatstaf*, vol. 30, nos. 11–12, 1982, pp. 28–42.

Haspels, George, "Kierkegaard vertaald" [Kierkegaard Translated], *Onze eeuw*, vol. 5, no. 2, 1905, pp. 475–85.

Havelaar, Just, "Kierkegaard (N.a.v. *Kierkegaard im Kampf mit sich selbst* (Chr. Schrempf), Fromanns Verlag, Stuttgart)" [Kierkegaard (in Response to *Kierkegaard im Kampf mit sich selbst* (Chr. Schrempf), Fromanns Verlag, Stuttgart)], *De stem*, vol. 3, 1923, pp. 177–81.

van der Hoeven, Johan, "Kierkegaard en Marx als dialectische critici van Hegel" [Kierkegaard and Marx as Dialectical Critics of Hegel], *Philosophia reformata*, vol. 34, 1969, pp. 85–100.

— "Kierkegaard en Marx als dialectische critici van Hegel II" [Kierkegaard and Marx as Dialectical Critics of Hegel II], *Philosophia reformata*, vol. 35, 1970, pp. 100–18.

— "Kierkegaard en Marx: twee revolutionaire baanbrekers van een nieuwe periode" [Kierkegaard and Marx: Two Revolutionary Pioneers of a New Period], *Mededelingen van de vereniging voor Calvinistische wijsbegeerte*, 1970, pp. 4–10.

— "Kierkegaard en Marx als dialectische critici van Hegel III" [Kierkegaard and Marx as Dialectical Critics of Hegel III], *Philosophia reformata*, vol. 36, 1971, pp. 125–54.

— "Kierkegaard en Nietzsche als stormvogels I & II" [Kierkegaard and Nietzsche as Petrels I & II], *Beweging*, vol. 49, 1985, pp. 8–11; pp. 41–3.

Hubbeling, Hubertus, " 'Als het ogenblik in de tijd eens beslissende betekenis had...' Een kritisch-logische analyse van Søren Kierkegaards argumentatie in het eerste hoofdstuk van de *Wijsgerige kruimels*" ["If the Moment is to Acquire Decisive Significance..." A Critical-Logical Analysis of Søren Kierkegaard's Argumentation in the First Chapter of *Philosophical Fragments*], *Bijdragen*, vol. 34, 1973, pp. 383–96.

Huizing, G., "Vaarwel Kierkegaard" [Farewell Kierkegaard], *In de waagschaal*, vol. 25, 1969–70, pp. 436–8.

—"Over de vertwijfeling bij S.A. Kierkegaard (I & II)" [On Despair in S.A. Kierkgaard (I & II)], *In de waagschaal*, vol. 26, 1997, pp. 366–70; pp. 401–5.

Jonker, Gerrit, "Sören Kierkegaard. Eene voorlezing" [Sören Kierkegaard. A Lecture], *Stemmen voor waarheid en vrede*, vol. 28, 1891, pp. 737–74.

— "Sören Kierkegaard. De enkele" [Sören Kierkegaard. The Single Individual], *Stemmen voor waarheid en vrede*, vol. 35, 1898, pp. 1099–1129.

Kierkegaard herdenking [Kierkegaard Commemoration], ed. by Alex Bolckmans, Robert Raes et. al., Gent: Rectoraat Rijksuniversiteit Gent 1964.

Kuypers, Etienne, *Met de hoed in de hand: Kierkegaard als pedagoog* [Cap in Hand: Kierkegaard as Educator], Maastricht: Climacus 1985.

— *Spelen met beelden; een theoretisch kritische studie over de zin of onzin van een christelijk-religieus-georiënteerde-pedagogie(k) onder auspiciën van S.A. Kierkegaard* [To Play with Images; a Theoretical Critical Study of the Meaning and Meaninglessness of a Christian-Religious-Orientated-Theory of Education Under the Auspices of S.A. Kierkegaard], Assen and Maastricht: Van Gorcum 1987.

—(ed.), *Kierkegaard en de twintigste eeuw* [Kierkegaard and the Twentieth Century], (with contributions by Bernard Delfgaauw, Etienne Kuypers, Wim Scholtens and Maria Veltman), Kampen: Kok Agora 1989.

— "Kierkegaards opmerkingen over de noodzaak van een socratisch nihilisme" [Kierkegaard's Comments on the Necessity of a Socratic Nihilism], *Filosofie*, vol. 3, no. 4, 1993, pp. 22–7.

— (ed.), *De levende Kierkegaard* [The Living Kierkegaard], (with contributions by Paul Cruysberghs, Etienne Kuypers, Wim Scholtens, Jan Sperna Weiland, Johan Taels and Julia Watkin), Leuven and Apeldoorn: Garant 1994.

— "Muzikale levenskunst. De esthetische voltooiing van Kierkegaards dialectische pedagogiek der existentiesferen" [Musical *Savoir-Vivre*. The Aesthetic Perfection of Kierkegaard's Dialectial Educational Theory of the Spheres of Existence], *Acta comparanda*, vol. 10, 1999, pp. 46–75.

Lansink, Cyril, "Het geheim van de ironie" [The Secret of Irony], *Wijsgerig perspectief*, vol. 35, no. 6, 1994–95, pp. 173–9.

— "Tussen woord en daad. Over het menselijk pathos volgens Kierkegaard" [Between Word and Deed. On the Human Pathos according to Kierkegaard], *Bijdragen*, vol. 57, 1996, pp. 189–210.

— "De vrijheid tussen beeld en werkelijkheid. Kierkegaards ethiek in de roman *Stiller* van Max Frisch" [Freedom between Image and Reality. Kierkegaard's Ethics in the novel *Stiller* of Max Frisch], *Filosofie*, vol. 6, no. 6, 1996–97, pp. 23–6.

— *Vrijheid en ironie. Kierkegaards ethiek van de zelfwording* [Freedom and Irony. Kierkegaard's Ethics of Becoming a Self], Leuven: Peeters 1997.
— "Vertwijfeling, weemoed en vertrouwen. Kierkegaard over ervaringen van tijdelijkheid" [Despair, Melancholy and Faith. Kierkegaard on Experiences of Temporality], *Speling*, vol. 51, no. 4, 1999, pp. 93–8.
— "Ironie als deugd. Tussen absolutisme en relativisme" [Irony as Virtue. Between Absolutism and Relativism], *De Uil van Minerva*, vol. 16, no. 1, 1999–2000, pp. 21–9.
— "Søren Kierkegaard over keuzevrijheid en morele vrijheid. (N.a.v. Søren Kierkegaard, *Of-Of*, 2000)" [Søren Kierkegaard on Freedom of Choice and Moral Freedom. (On the Occasion of Søren Kierkegaard, *Either/Or*, 2000)], *Filosofie magazine*, vol. 9, no. 3, 2000, pp. 40–4.
— "De ironicus op de beklaagdenbank. Kierkegaards kritiek op de romantiek" [The Ironist in the Dock. Kierkegaard's Critique of Romanticism], *Streven*, vol. 68, no. 2, 2001, pp. 771–9.
— "Zelfontkenning en zelfaanvaarding. De betekenis van de onthechting in het denken van Schopenhauer en Kierkegaard" [Self-Denial and Self-Acceptance. The Meaning of Detachment in the Thought of Schopenhauer and Kierkegaard], *Tijdschrift voor filosofie*, no. 63, 2001, pp. 87–106.
Leemans, Victor, "Kierkegaardiana," in *Kultuurleven*, vol. 21, 1954, pp. 376–8.
— "De wordingsjaren van Sören Kierkegaard" [The Years of Genesis of Sören Kierkegaard], *Tijdschrift voor philosophie*, vol. 17, 1955, pp. 623–62.
— "Kierkegaard en onze tijd" [Kierkegaard and Our Age], *Dietsche warande en belfort*, vol. 56, 1956, pp. 386–91.
— *Sören Kierkegaard*, introduced by Alphonse De Waelhens, Antwerp: Standaard boekhandel 1956 (2nd ed., 1956).
Leendertz, Willem, *Hoe komt men dichter bij Kierkegaard?* [How Does One Get Closer to Kierkegaard?], Groningen: privately published 1908.
— "Naar aanleiding van een nieuwe preekenbundel: *Stichtelijke redenen, bijeengebracht uit de werken van Søren Kierkegaard*" [On the Occasion of a New Volume of Sermons: *Upbuilding Discourses, Collected from the Works of Sören Kierkegaard*], *Stemmen des tijds*, vol. 8, no. 3, 1919, pp. 25–43.
— "De 'nulpuntexistentie' (n.a.v. Friedrich Carl Fischer, *Die Nullpunkt-Existenz. Dargestellt an der Lebensform Sören Kierkegaards*, München: C.H. Beck Verlagsbuchhandlung 1933)" [The "Zero-Existence" (on the Occaion of Friedrich Carl Fischer, *Die Nullpunkt-Existenz. Dargestellt an der Lebensform Sören Kierkegaards*, München: C.H. Beck Verlagsbuchhandlung 1933)], *Predikant en dokter*, vol. 4, no. 2, 1934, pp. 31–8.
— "Kierkegaard, Schopenhauer, Nietzsche & de existentie-philosophie" [Kierkegaard, Schopenhauer, Nietzsche & the Philosophy of Existence], *Philosophia; beknopt handboek tot de geschiedenis van het wijsgerig denken*, vols. 1–2, ed. by Hendrik Van Oyen, Utrecht: De Haan 1949, vol. 2, pp. 337–78.
— "Sören Kierkegaard," *Nederlands theologisch tijdschrift*, vol. 10, 1955–56, pp. 65–75.

van der Leeuw, Gerardus, "De psychologie van Kierkegaard" [The Psychology of Kierkegaard], *Algemeen tijdschrift voor wijsbegeerte en psychologie*, vol. 27, no. 5, 1934, pp. 21–5.

Lehmann, Edvard, "Søren Kierkegaard. 5 mei 1813–5 mei 1913," *Onze eeuw*, vol. 13, no. 3, 1913, pp. 54–66.

Leijen, Arie, "Essentieel auteurschap, existentiële mededeling en 'intrusie van buitenaf.' Beschouwing bij het artikel van Karl Verstrynge" [Essential Authorship, Existential Communication and 'Intrusion from Outside.' Opinion on the Article of Karl Verstrynge], *Tijdschrift voor filosofie*, no. 63, 2001, pp. 50–53.

de Marees van Swinderen, J., "Søren Kierkegaard," *Leven en werken, onafhankelijk Tijdschrift voor religie en cultuur*, vol. 2, 1917, pp. 408–34.

Meininger, J., "Sören Kierkegaard en zijn *Joannes Climacus*" [Sören Kierkegaard and his Joannes Climacus], *De idee*, vol. 35, 1957, pp. 1–16.

Merks, Rob, *De begrippen ironie en humor in het denken van Søren Kierkegaard* [The Concepts of Irony and Humor in the Thought of Søren Kierkegaard], Oosterbeek: De bosbespers 1980.

Molenaar, P., "Pascal en Kierkegaard" [Pascal and Kierkegaard], *Stemmen des tijds*, vol. 20, no. 1, 1931, pp. 580–94.

Montagne, Nicole, "De verleider" [The Seducer], *Dietsche warande en belfort*, vol. 145, no. 3, 2000, pp. 307–12.

van Munster, Hans, "Een analyse van Kierkegaards proefschrift" [An Analysis of Kierkegaard's Dissertation], *Tijdschrift voor philosophie*, no. 18, 1956, pp. 347–80.

— "Kierkegaards kritiek op Andersen. De verhouding tussen persoon en situatie" [Kierkegaard's Critique of Andersen. The Relation between Person and Situation], *Algemeen tijdschrift voor wijsbegeerte en psychologie*, vol. 50, 1957–58, pp. 82–9.

—*De filosofische gedachten van de jonge Kierkegaard, 1831–1841* [The Philosophical Thoughts of the Young Kierkegaard, 1831–1841], Arnhem: Van Loghum Slaterus 1958.

— "Kierkegaard als christen" [Kierkegaard as a Christian], *Kultuurleven*, vol. 30, 1963, pp. 739–50.

— *Søren Aabye Kierkegaard*, Tielt: Lannoo 1963.

— "Creativiteit en traditie. De betekenis van Kierkegaard" [Creativity and Tradition. The Significance of Kierkegaard], *De nieuwe mens*, vol. 18, 1966–67, pp. 66–79.

— *Wijsheid van Kierkegaard* [Wisdom of Kierkegaard], Tielt: Lannoo 2006.

Nauta, Lolle, "Incognito onderweg; portret van Sören Kierkegaard" [Incognito on the Way: Portrait of Sören Kierkegaard], *Wending*, vol. 18, 1963, pp. 246–51.

van den Nieuwenhuizen, Martien, *Dialectiek van de vrijheid. Zonde en zondevergeving bij Søren Kierkegaard* [Dialectics of Freedom. Sin and Forgiveness of Sins in Søren Kierkegaard], Assen: Van Gorcum 1968.

Noordmans, Oepke, "Het begrip 'angst' bij Kierkegaard" [The Concept of "Anxiety" in Kierkegaard], *Kerk en theologie*, vol. 30, 1979, pp. 178–82.

Oosterbaan, J., "De enkeling en het algemene in het denken van Sören Kierkegaard" [The Single Individual and the Universal in the Thought of Sören Kierkegaard],

Algemeen tijdschrift voor wijsbegeerte en psychologie, vol. 55, 1962–63, pp. 123–36.

Van Otten, Josephine, B. Van Parijs and Chris Vonck (eds.), *Kierkegaard en het moderne denken in een bevrijde stad* [Kierkegaard and Modern Thinking in a Liberated City] (with contributions by Elsebeth Bank, Magda Beek, Safet Bektovic, Inigo Bocken, Jacques Caron, Jan Gysen, Levi Matuszczak, Aad J. van der Perk, Josephine Van Otten, Nicolas Van Vosselen and Leslie Versweyveld), Antwerp: Werkgroep Kierkegaard 1994.

Overboom, A., "De enkeling van Kierkegaard, meer dan een zoeker naar zichzelf" [Kierkegaard's Single Individual, More than a Seeker after Himself], *Tijdschrift voor filosofie*, no. 48, 1986, pp. 416–48.

van Peursen, Cornelis, "Existentieel getij. S. Kierkegaard, *Wijsgerige kruimels* (vert./ aant. J. Sperna Weiland, 1955)" [Existential Tide. S. Kierkegaard, *Philosophical Fragments* (trans./ann. J. Sperna Weiland 1955)], *Wending*, vol. 11, 1956–57, pp. 561–72.

Pierson, Allard, "Georg Brandes, *Søren Kierkegaard. Ein literarisches Charakterbild.* Leipzig 1879," *De tijdspiegel*, vol. 37, 1880, pp. 117–22.

Polet, Sybren, "De filosoof met het percuteerhamertje" [The Philosopher with the Percussion Hammer], *Maatstaf*, vol. 39, no. 4, 1991, pp. 52–9.

Pont, Johannes, "Søren Kierkegaard," *Stemmen uit de Lutherse kerk in Nederland*, vol. 2, 1896, pp. 97–125.

Van Raemdonck, Ivon, "Kierkegaard en Nietzsche" [Kierkegaard and Nietzsche], *Dialoog*, vol. 6, 1965–66, pp. 214–31.

Ramaker, Wim, "De subjectiviteit is de waarheid. Over Sören Kierkegaard" [Subjectivity is the Truth. On Sören Kierkegaard], *Literama*, vol. 20, no. 3, 1985–86, pp. 103–17.

van Rhijn, Maarten, *Søren Kierkegaard; een indruk van zijn leven en denken* [Søren Kierkegaard: An Impression of his Life and Thinking], Baarn: Bosch en Keuning 1941.

Rispens, Jan, "De enkele" [The Single Individual], *Ontmoeting*, vol. 5, 1950–51, pp. 467–72.

Van Roey, Marc, "Kierkegaard en Hegel. Paradox en bemiddeling" [Kierkegaard and Hegel. Paradox and Mediation], *Acta comparanda*, vol. 9, 1998, pp. 51–60.

van Ruler, Arnold, "De beteekenis van Kierkegaard voor de theologie" [The Significance of Kierkegaard for Theology], *Vox theologica*, vol. 11, 1939–40, pp. 79–85.

Schilder, Klaas, *Zur Begriffsgeschichte des "Paradoxon"—Mit besonderer Berücksichtigung Calvins und des Nach-Kierkegaardschen "Paradoxon"* [On the Conceptual History of the "Paradoxon"—With Special Consideration of Calvin and of the Post-Kierkegaardian "Paradoxon"], Kampen: J.H. Kok 1933.

Scholtens, Wim, "Je kunt het niet leren (Gebed bij Kierkegaard)" [You Cannot Learn It (Prayer in Kierkegaard)], *Speling*, vol. 22, 1970, pp. 181–91.

—— "Het tragi-komische bij Sören Kierkegaard" [The Tragicomic in Sören Kierkegaard], *Speling*, vol. 23, 1971, pp. 57–71.

— "Sören Aabye Kierkegaard: over bidden en danken" [Sören Aabye Kierkegaard: On Praying and Thanking], *Tijdschrift voor geestelijk leven*, vol. 28, 1972, pp. 485–94.

— "Kierkegaard en de gewone man" [Kierkegaard and the Common Man], *Jeugd en cultuur*, vol. 18, 1972–73, pp. 11–15.

— "Kierkegaard en Sokrates, de plaats van de ironie in het geestelijk leven" [Kierkegaard and Socrates, the Place of Irony in Spiritual Life], *Tijdschrift voor geestelijk leven*, vol. 30, 1974, pp. 203–7.

— "Oekumene en mede-menselijkheid bij Søren Kierkegaard" [Oecumenism and Humanity in Søren Kierkegaard], *Kosmos en oecumene*, vol. 9, 1975, pp. 139–45.

— "Schriftmeditatie bij Sören Kierkegaard" [Scriptural Meditation in Sören Kierkegaard], *Tijdschrift voor geestelijk leven*, vol. 31, 1975, pp. 233–41.

— "Gods voorzienigheid bij Kierkegaard" [God's Providence in Kierkegaard], *Tijdschrift voor geestelijk leven*, vol. 32, 1976, pp. 486–93.

— "Politiek en evangelische raden bij Søren Kierkegaard" [Political and Evangelical Councils in Søren Kierkegaard], *Tijdschrift voor geestelijk leven*, vol. 33, 1977, pp. 298–309.

— *Alle gekheid op een stokje. Kierkegaard als psycholoog* [All Foolishness Aside. Kierkegaard as a Psychologist], Baarn: Ten Have 1979.

— "Søren Kierkegaard, angst en emancipatie" [Søren Kierkegaard, Anxiety and Emancipation], *Kultuurleven*, vol. 47, no. 2, 1980, pp. 721–36.

— "De mystieke geëngageerdheid van Søren Kierkegaard (1813–1855)" [The Mystical Commitment of Søren Kierkegaard (1813–1855)], *Speling*, vol. 33, 1981, pp. 37–41.

— "Kierkegaard, Jezus en de brave burgerij" [Kierkegaard, Jesus and the Good Bourgeoisie], *Tijdschrift voor geestelijk leven*, vol. 37, 1981, pp. 5–17.

— "Kierkegaard: 'enkeling' als protest tegen nivellering" [Kierkegaard: "The Single Individual" as Protest Against Leveling], *Speling*, vol. 34, 1982, pp. 52–7.

— "Kierkegaards utopia: gemeenschap in caritas" [Kierkegaard's Utopia: Community in Caritas], *Speling*, vol. 34, 1982, pp. 77–81.

— "Humor raakt het wezen van de mens (Humor bij Kierkegaard)" [Humor Touches upon the Core of Human Being (Humor in Kierkegaard)], *Speling*, vol. 40, 1988, pp. 6–13.

— "Flierefluiter, vrouwenhater, feminist. Kierkegaards opvattingen over de vrouw" [Loafer, Woman-Hater, Feminist. Kierkegaard's Views on Woman], *Mara*, vol. 3, no. 2, 1989–90, pp. 33–8.

— *"Kijk, hier barst de taal": mystiek bij Kierkegaard* [Look, here Language is Bursting...": Mysticism in Kierkegaard], Kampen-Altiora, Averbode: Kok 1991.

— "Kierkegaard en het Hebreeuws" [Kierkegaard and Hebrew], *Interpretatie*, vol. 3, no. 1, 1995, pp. 28–30.

— "Kierkegaard en de riooljournalistiek" [Kierkegaarde and Gutter Journalism], *Filosofie*, vol. 5, no. 2, 1995–96, pp. 26–9.

Sperna Weiland, Jan, "Het begrip transcendentie in de filosofie van Kierkegaard" [The Concept of Transcendance in the Philosophy of Kierkegaard], *Vox theologica*, vol. 20, 1949–50, pp. 9–18.

— *Philosophy of Existence and Christianity. Kierkegaard's and Jaspers' Thoughts on Christianity*, Assen: Van Gorcum 1951.

— "Kierkegaard en de nieuwbouw der ethiek" [Kierkegaard and the New Estate of Ethics], *Vox theologica*, vol. 26, 1955–56, pp. 41–51.

— "Sören Aabye Kierkegaard (1855–1955)," *Wending*, vol. 10, 1955–56, pp. 509–16.

Spier, Johannes, "Aan de hand van Regine Olsen door de wereldgeschiedenis" [With Regine Olsen through World History], *Bezinning*, vol. 10, 1955, pp. 281–9.

Taels, Johan, *Søren Kierkegaard als filosoof. De weg terug naar het subject* [Søren Kierkegaard as a Philosopher. The Way Back to the Subject], introduced by Wim Scholtens, Leuven: Universitaire pers Leuven 1991.

— "Søren Kierkegaard over de liefde" [Søren Kierkegaard on Love], *Ethische perspectieven*, vol. 3, no. 4, 1993, pp. 226–8.

— "Waarom is de werkelijkheid zo onwerkelijk? Søren Kierkegaards grondintuïtie" [Why is Reality so Unreal? Søren Kierkegaard's Basic Intuition], *Parodos*, vol. 41, 1995, pp. 5–15.

— "Ethische nabijheid. Kierkegaard over de verhouding tussen denken en doen" [Ethical Nearness. Kierkegaard on the Relation between Thinking and Doing], *Filosofie*, vol. 6, no. 6, 1996–97, pp. 19–22.

— "Spreken in eigen naam. Primitiviteit, woord en taaldaad bij Søren Kierkegaard" [To Speak in One's Own Name. Primitivity, Word and Speech Act in Søren Kierkegaard], *Tijdschrift voor filosofie*, no. 63, 2001, pp. 7–31.

— "Wat het betekent een mens te zijn" [What it Means to Be a Human Being], *Wijsgerig perspectief*, vol. 42, no. 4, 2002, pp. 27–39.

Veltman, Maria, "Verwondering—Is Kierkegaards visie nog geldig voor onze tijd?" [Amazement—Is Kierkegaard's View Still Valid for Our Age?], *Communio, internationaal katholiek tijdschrift*, vol. 12, no. 4, 1987, pp. 292–9.

— *Het ontwaken van de menselijke geest. Zelfbewustwording in de werken van Kierkegaard* [The Awakening of the Human Spirit. Self-Awakening in the Works of Kierkegaard], Leuven and Apeldoorn: Garant 1993.

Verhofstadt, Edward, "Een gestalte in het werk van Kierkegaard. Mozarts Don Juan" [A Figure in the Works of Kierkegaard: Mozart's Don Juan], *Nieuw Vlaams tijdschrift*, vol. 11, 1957, pp. 1061–75.

Verhoof, Koos, "Het Godsvertrouwen van Abraham. Enkele kanttekeningen bij een analyse van Sören Kierkegaard" [Abraham's Faith in God. Some Comments on an Analysis of Sören Kierkegaard], *De Uil van Minerva*, vol. 12, no. 2, 1995–96, pp. 83–102.

Verstrynge, Karl, "Kierkegaards begrip van de vertwijfeling als intensivering van het bewustzijn. Over *De ziekte tot de dood*" [Kierkegaard's Concept of Despair as Intensification of Consciousness. On *The Sickness unto Death*], *Tijdschrift voor filosofie*, no. 59, 1997, pp. 434–59.

— "De autonomie van de esthetiek in Kierkegaards *Enten/Eller*. Over ledigheid en verveling" [The Autonomy of Aesthetics in Kierkegaard's *Either/Or*. On Idleness and Boredom], *Algemeen tijdschrift voor wijsbegeerte*, vol. 92, 2000, pp. 293–305.

— "Met Kierkegaard tegen Kierkegaard. Essentieel auteurschap en existentiële mededeling" [With Kierkegaard against Kierkegaard. Essential Authorship and Existential Communication], *Tijdschrift voor filosofie*, no. 63, 2001, pp. 33–49.

— "Tegen de keer. Kierkegaard en de secularisatie" [Against the Tide. Kierkegaard and Secularization], *Wijsgerig perspectief*, vol. 42, no. 4, 2002, pp. 40–54.

— *De hysterie van de geest. Melancholie en zwaarmoedigheid in het pseudonieme œuvre van Kierkegaard* [Hysteria of the Spirit. Melancholy and Heavy-Mindedness in the Pseudonymous Oeuvre of Kierkegaard], Leuven: Peeters 2003.

— " 'Over de brug der zuchten de eeuwigheid in.' Søren Kierkegaard en de melancholie" ["Over the Bridge of Sighs into Eternity." Søren Kierkegaard and Melancholy], *Streven*, vol. 71, 2004, pp. 499–509.

De Visscher, Jacques, "Kultuurleven beknopt. Over de gevestigde kerkelijkheid. (N.a.v. Kierkegaards *Schotschriften tegen de gevestigde kerkelijheid*, 1980)" [Cultural Life in Brief. On the Established Church. (On the Occasion of Kierkegaard's *Pamphlets against the Established Church*, 1980)], *Kultuurleven*, vol. 48, no. 2, 1981, pp. 663–7.

— "Rigorisme en scepticisme—Over Pascal en Kierkegaard (Kritische bibliografie)" [Rigorism and Scepticism—On Pascal and Kierkegaard (Critical Bibliography)], *De Uil van Minerva*, vol. 14, 1997–98, pp. 109–27.

Vogelsang, Peter, *Oprecht veinzen. Over Kierkegaards* Over het begrip ironie, vooral met betrekking tot Socrates *(1841)*, [Feigning Sincerely. On Kierkegaard's *The Concept of Irony with Continual Reference to Socrates* (1841)], Groningen: Peter F. Vogelsang 1999.

Vos, Pieter, "Om het naakte bestaan: Kierkegaard over het christelijk geloof" [About the Naked Existence: Kierkegaard on Christian Faith], *Beweging*, vol. 63, no. 2, 1999, pp. 34–7.

— *De troost van het ogenblik: Kierkegaard over God en het lijden* [The Comfort of the Moment: Kierkegaard on God and Suffering] Baarn and Kampen: Ten Have 2002.

van der Waals, Jacqueline, "Bespreking naar aanleiding van *Liefdedaden—Eenige christelijke overwegingen in den vorm van redevoeringen door Sören Kierkegaard*" [Review on the Occasion of *Works of Love—Some Christian Deliberations in the Form of Discourses*], *Leven en werken, maandschrift voor meisjes en jonge vrouwen*, vol. 6, no. 4, 1920, pp. 240–55.

— "Kierkegaard," *Onze eeuw*, vol. 21, no. 3, 1921, pp. 171–89; pp. 274–95.

De Waelhens, Alphonse, "Kierkegaard en de hedendaagse existentialisten. Enkele nota's" [Kierkegaard and the Existentialists. Some Notes], *Tijdschrift voor philosophie*, vol. 1, 1939, pp. 827–51.

— "Geschiedenis van de hedendaagsche wijsbegeerte: S. Kierkegaard, *Purify your Hearts* (trans. from the Danish by A.S. Aldworth and W.S. Ferrie, London: C.W. Daniel Company 1937); Walter Lowry, *Kierkegaard* (Oxford: Oxford University Press 1938)" [History of Contemporary Philosophy. S. Kierkegaard, *Purify your Hearts* (trans. from the Danish by A.S. Aldworth and W.S. Ferrie, London: C.W. Daniel Company 1937); Walter Lowry, *Kierkegaard* (Oxford: Oxford University Press 1938)], *Tijdschrift voor philosophie*, vol. 2, 1940, pp. 669–71.

Walgrave, Joannes, "Philosophie en literatuur in het existentialisme" [Philosophy and Literature in Existentialism], *Kultuurleven*, vol. 18, 1951, pp. 671–87.

— "Bij het centenarium van Kierkegaard's dood" [At the Centenary of Kierkegaard's Death], *Kultuurleven*, vol. 22, 1955, pp. 667–76.

— "De ware Kierkegaard en de kerk" [The True Kierkegaard and the Church], *Kultuurleven*, vol. 23, 1956, pp. 411–20.

Walravens, Else, "Eenzaamheid en gemeenschap in de filosofie van S. Kierkegaard (I & II)" [Loneliness and Community in the Philosophy of S. Kierkegaard (I & II)], *Dialoog*, vol. 11, 1970–71, pp. 143–56; pp. 187–207.

— "Eenzaamheid en gemeenschap in de filosofie van S. Kierkegaard (III)" [Loneliness and Community in the Philosophy of S. Kierkegaard (III)], *Dialoog*, vol. 12, 1971–72, pp. 189–97.

Walravens, Jan, "De boodschappers van Kronos, I: Inleiding tot Kierkegaard" [The Messengers of Kronos, I: Introduction to Kierkegaard], *De Vlaamse gids*, vol. 33, 1949, pp. 145–51.

Westerlinck, Albert, "Een Vlaams boek over Kierkegaard" [A Flemish Book on Kierkegaard], *Dietsche warande en belfort*, vol. 57, 1957, pp. 55–60.

van der Wouden, Ries, "De zwaarte van licht. Kundera en de paradox van Kierkegaard" [The Weight of Light. Kundera and the Paradox of Kierkegaard], *Krisis*, vol. 9, no. 34, 1989, pp. 47–57.

Zijlstra, Onno, "De wandelaar en de ober. Wittgenstein en Kierkegaard over esthetiek en ethiek/religie" [The Walker and the Waiter. Wittgenstein and Kierkegaard on Aesthetics and Ethics/Religion], *Katern*, vol. 2, 1992, pp. 47–57.

— "Kierkegaard en het esthetische" [Kierkegaard and the Aesthetic], *Communiqué*, vol. 8, no. 3, 1992, pp. 35–45.

— "Muziek, tijd en taal: Kierkegaard en Schopenhauer" [Music, Time and Language: Kierkegaard and Schopenhauer], *Communiqué*, vol. 11, no. 1, 1994, pp. 59–74.

Zuidema, Sietse, "Het existentialisme bij Kierkegaard I & II" [Existentialism in Kierkegaard I & II], *Philosophia reformata*, vol. 15, 1950, pp. 40–6; pp. 49–65.

van der Zwaag, Klaas, "Bekering, levenskeus en de dialectiek van het geloof bij Søren Kierkegaard" [Conversion, Existential Choice and Dialectics of Faith in Søren Kierkegaard], *Theologia reformata*, vol. 43, 2000, pp. 226–51.

Zwanepol, Klaas, "Kierkegaard, Hegel en de theologie" [Kierkegaard, Hegel and Theology], *Communiqué*, vol. 8, no. 3, 1992, pp. 23–34.

III. Secondary Literature on Kierkegaard's Reception in the Netherlands and Flanders

van den Bos, Gerard, *Sporen van Kierkegaard; De Nederlandse Kierkegaard-literatuur tussen 1880–1930* [Traces of Kierkegaard. The Dutch Kierkegaard Literature between 1880 and 1930], Ph.D. Thesis, Katholieke Universiteit te Nijmegen, Nijmegen 1989.

van den Bos, Gerard and Bernard Delfgaauw, "Holland (The Netherlands)," in *Kierkegaard Research*, ed. by Niels Thulstrup and Marie Mikulová Thulstrup,

Copenhagen: C.A. Reitzel 1987 (*Bibliotheca Kierkegaardiana*, vol. 15), pp. 160–72.

Cruysberghs, Paul and Karel Eisses, "Søren Kierkegaard, een bibliografie" [Søren Kierkegaard, a Bibliography], *Tijdschrift voor filosofie*, no. 63, 2001, pp. 107–26.

Eisses, Karel, *Honderdvijftig jaar (in de voet) sporen van Søren Kierkegaard. Nederlandstalige bibliografie van 1846–2000. Vertalingen, studies en verwijzingen* [One Hundred and Fifty Years of Traces of Søren Kierkegaard. Dutch Bibliography from 1846 to 2000. Translations, Studies and References], Northfield, MN: Keiprodukties 2000 (3rd ed.).

Grit, Diederik, "Het begin van de Kierkegaardreceptie in Nederland en Vlaanderen" [The Beginning of Kierkegaard Reception in the Netherlands and Flanders], *Geschiedenis van de wijsbegeerte in Nederland*, vol. 4, 1993, pp. 49–54.

van Rhijn, Maarten, "Kierkegaard in Nederland" [Kierkegaard in the Netherlands], *Algemeen weekblad voor christendom en cultuur*, vol. 5, no. 26, 1929, pp. 1–2.

Germany and Austria:

A Modest Head Start: The German Reception of Kierkegaard

Heiko Schulz

Before delving into the historical survey of Kierkegaard reception a few preliminary remarks seem advisable in order to clarify what can and what cannot be expected from the following essay:

(1) As the title suggests, I will exlusively treat the reception of Kierkegaard in the "German-Speaking World." That is to say, I will (with very few exceptions) restrict my overview to a number of authors, whose mother-tongue is German *and* who write or have written in this language.[1] I will concentrate on the German and Austrian sources.

(2) Although translation is a form of reception (and also indicates some kind and cultural context),[2] I will not give any detailed analysis or make any comparison of existing Kierkegaard translations in German. Although this would indeed be an important and fascinating project in its own right, it is beyond the scope of the present article. There simply exist too many translations to be able to fully account for their specific profiles, their similarities and differences, their merits and shortcomings etc. within the framework of a history of reception like the one I am supposed to tell.[3]

---

[1]   Therefore Johannes Sløk's excellent book, *Die Anthropologie Kierkegaards*, Copenhagen: Rosenkilde and Bagger 1954, will only be mentioned in passing (namely here and now), but not discussed in detail. Likewise German translations of books or articles dealing with or reflecting the influence of Kierkegaard, will (a few exceptions notwithstanding) at best and for the sake of completeness be mentioned in the bibliography since strictly speaking they belong to and are part of the reception history of the country and language in which they were originally published.

[2]   See Heiko Schulz, "Rezeptionsgeschichtliche Brocken oder die *Brocken* in der deutschen Rezeption," *Kierkegaard Studies. Yearbook*, 2004, pp. 375–451; p. 378.

[3]   I have tried elsewhere to outline some problems of translating Kierkegaard into German, if only with reference to the *title* of (two of) his books; see Schulz, "Rezeptionsgeschichtliche Brocken," pp. 380–4 (see especially p. 380, note 14, where further sources tackling the problem of translating Kierkegaard into German are quoted); see also Heiko Schulz, "Rezeptionsgeschichtliche Nachschrift oder die *Nachschrift* in der deutschen Rezeption. Eine forschungsgeschichtliche Skizze," *Kierkegaard Studies. Yearbook*, 2005, pp. 351–99; pp. 354–7.

(3) I will focus on explicit and direct reflections of Kierkegaard in some German authors, thus deliberately downplaying the importance of implicit and/or indirect ones.[4] *Indirect* references seem to me to be simply irrelevant since in the present context we do not want to know anything in particular about B's (implicit and/ or explicit) reception of Kierkegaard, as it is deliberately or inadvertently made manifest in the writings of A, but rather about A's *own* (implicit and/or explicit) references to the former. By contrast, the relevance of *direct and implicit* references can hardly be overestimated (especially with regard to what I consider "productive reception," see below). However, quite often the respective passages will not only be difficult to identify, but, furthermore, their content and significance as purportedly Kierkegaardian reflections can often be reconstructed only in a more or less speculative manner. Although I do not feel myself entitled to completely ignore this type of reception, I will, in the following, nevertheless gravitate towards the direct and explicit type—a decision which should prove all the more plausible since the mass of relevant sources that I am left with even under these restricted conditions is still immense.

(4) A further distinction (that I only mention in passing, without constantly referring to it in the following) has to be made between *material* and *intentional* reflections. Some, but not all material reflections are intentional, and vice versa. Author B may believe and intend to do justice to what author A (here, Kierkegaard) has written, as he writes about or at least explicitly refers to him, but he may in fact be wrong in believing *that* he does. On the other hand, there might occur purely material reflections of A's views in B's writings without the latter having intended and/or known about them—maybe even without being *able* to intend or know about them (for example, for mere historical reasons). Furthermore, this distinction is not to be confused with the previous one between implicit and explicit references: every explicit reference is, as such, intentional, but not vice versa, for it may as well be implicit. By contrast, both implicit and explicit references are sometimes also material; however, they need not be.

(5) In the following I will draw on these two distinctions in order for mere heuristical reasons to characterize and make use of six basic types and/or attitudes of reception: reception without production; production without reception; unproductive reception; productive reception; receptive production; mixed types or borderline-cases. Let me briefly describe these types: A *reception without production* is a reception that leaves no literary traces—even *if* the recipient is a writer and even if Kierkegaard has left some impression on him or her. In this latter case, B may have read A's (here, Kierkegaard's) works, and she may in fact have incorporated what B takes to be their "message" into his or her own conduct and behavior in

---

[4]   I define *explicit* references as material and/or nominal ones: author A *writes about and/or mentions* Kierkegaard. *Implicit* references are purely material: certain passages in author A's text can be read as a (deliberate or involuntary, critical or affirmative) *reflection* of Kierkegaardian ideas and/or writings. By *direct* references (which, as such, can be both explicit and implicit) I mean passages in author A's *own* writings that refer to Kierkegaard. By contrast, an *indirect* reference is mediated through a *third party* mentioned or referred to in author A's text; as such, it can also be either explicit or implicit.

some way or other; however, A's writings themselves have left no verifiable traces—either of an explicit or of a purely material kind—in B's own literary production. By contrast, *production without reception* not only *presupposes* a literary output on B's part but this output must also contain and make manifest certain—*nota bene*, purely *material*—reflections of A's work in B's own production, although B has in fact never taken notice (or has not even been able to take notice, for example, for mere historical reasons) of the former. A reception is *unproductive*, if and only if, although author A *has* evidently been taken note of by author B (be it ever so sporadically or briefly), this reception has left at best marginal (explicit or implicit) traces in B's writings (of course, such traces can be of the affirmative or of the critical sort). A genuinely *productive reception* is characterized by the central role that author A's work takes on in author B's work vis-à-vis type, content, and genesis—even if explicit or implicit traces of the former are only recognizable in isolated passages of the latter. The term *receptive production* has been coined to designate the most frequent and prominent type of reception: author B's referring to author A by means of explicitly and directly addressing the latter's work, if only to a limited extent (for example, in form of an article or a passage in a book). Finally, there may also be *mixed types or borderline-cases*, in particular between productive reception and receptive production: for instance, if, on the one hand, author B's work reflects the impact of Kierkegaard (be it affirmatively or critically)—if only implicitly; and if, on the other hand, substantial portions of B's work are explicitly and directly devoted to Kierkegaard's thought, then we may speak of a *unity between productive reception and receptive production.*[5]

(6) Completeness is a noble aim in matters of reception; however, it would hardly be possible to achieve, even if I were to deal with a much more restricted number of authors, texts, and traditions than I do.[6] Thus a (hopefully representative) *selection* of what appear to be major forces in the history of German Kierkegaard reception will be indispensable. And this decision goes hand in hand with yet another: articles and papers on Kierkegaard in periodicals or anthologies will largely (that is, with few exceptions) be ignored due to the fact that it is virtually impossible to get a complete picture of these resources even in purely bibliographical terms, much less in terms of the history of reception.

(7) Except for the previous typological remarks the reader should not expect from the following survey any reflections on a hermeneutics of reception as such. In other words, nothing will be said about the concept, the history, the implications and problems, the function(s), forms, preconditions, and limits of what we usually

---

[5]   Among German philosophers Karl Jaspers or Theodor W. Adorno would be a case in point; Emanuel Hirsch might be mentioned as a theological example (see below).

[6]   Needless to add that even *if* we were to attain a complete picture of all relevant sources and traditions within the history of Kierkegaard's reception in Germany this would not at the same time yield any, much less any perfect self-transparency of the very same history in philosophical terms: "*Daß Wirkungsgeschichte je vollendet gewußt werde, ist eine ebenso hybride Behauptung wie Hegels Anspruch auf absolutes Wissen, in dem die Geschichte zur vollendeten Selbstdurchsichtigkeit gekommen und daher auf den Standpunkt des Begriffs erhoben sei*" (Hans-Georg Gadamer, *Wahrheit und Methode. Grundzüge einer philosophischen Hermeneutik*, Tübingen: J.C.B. Mohr 1975 [1960], p. 285).

call and maybe all too easily take to be self-evident as "reception."[7] Instead, all
I am offering is a piece of straightforward "descriptive intellectual history" that
finds itself content to uncover a number of more or less obvious biographical and
intertextual connections between Kierkegaard and his successors. Nothing less—yet
also nothing more.

I. Pre-Reception: The Unproductive Years, 1840–99

(1) There were only very few—*nota bene*, direct and explicit—German references
to Kierkegaard during his lifetime. Most of them can be traced back to "the German-
educated Danish theologian Andreas Frederik Beck (1816–61)."[8] Beck, who had
studied theology in Copenhagen and Kiel came under the influence of D.F. Strauss
and subsequently published several mostly anti-theological pamphlets and articles
(against Grundtvig, among others). He attended the oral defense of Kierkegaard's
dissertation and later on accompanied the latter's literary career with a handful
of surprisingly diligent and overall sympathetic, if at times also critical reviews
and articles, some of which were written and published in German.[9] Despite his
criticisms—especially addressed to certain formative ideas in *The Concept of
Irony*[10]—Beck obviously felt great respect for Kierkegaard (contrary to, for instance,
Grundtvig, Martensen, Rasmus Nielsen and others who fared a lot worse in his
judgment); in particular, he enthusiastically welcomed the former's attack on the
Danish Church, for, in his opinion, this attack played "into atheist and sectarian
hands and suited their purposes."[11]

---

[7]   As to this, see, for example, Heinz-Robert Jauss, "Rezeption, Rezeptionsästhetik," in
Historisches Wörterbuch der Philosophie, vol. 8, ed. by Joachim Ritter et al., Basel: Schwabe
1992, pp. 996–1004.

[8]   My source here is Habib C. Malik, *Receiving Søren Kierkegaard. The Early Impact
and Transmission of His Thought*, Washington, D.C.: Catholic University of America Press
1997, p. 17; my emphasis. Malik's book is indispensable reading for anyone seriously
interested in studying the early international history of Kierkegaard reception up to the mid-
1920s. For further information about A.F. Beck and his relation to Kierkegaard, see Malik,
Receiving Kierkegaard, pp. 17ff.; pp. 47–50; p. 71; p. 127.

[9]   See, in particular, *Deutsche Jahrbücher für Wissenschaft und Kunst*, no. 222, 1842,
pp. 885–8, continued in *Deutsche Jahrbücher für Wissenschaft und Kunst*, no. 223, 1842,
pp. 889ff.: This German review of Kierkegaard's *Concept of Irony*—to which Kierkegaard
himself ironically responded in *Fædrelandet*, no. 904, 1842—"represents the earliest existing
piece on Kierkegaard, and indeed the first printed mention of his name, in the German
language" (Malik, *Receiving Kierkegaard*, p. 18). Kierkegaard is also briefly mentioned in
Beck's article "Übersichtliche Darstellung des jetzigen Zustandes der Theologie in Dänemark,"
Theologische Jahrbücher, vol. 3, 1844, p. 501. A couple of years later Beck wrote a German
piece on "Martensen und Kierkegaard," *Nordischer Telegraph*, no. 89, 1850, pp. 1095–6,
discussing (Kierkegaard's criticism of) Martensen's dogmatics. Finally, he published two
German articles in the *Darmstädter Allgemeine Kirchenzeitung* (September 22, 1855, and
January 31, 1856), reporting about Kierkegaard's *Kirkekampen*.

[10]   See Malik's summary of Beck's key arguments, in *Receiving Kierkegaard*, p. 19.

[11]   Ibid., p. 127.

In 1845 a comparatively elaborate German review of Kierkegaard's *Philosophical Fragments* appeared—in fact, the only contemporary German review of a pseudonymous work at all. Unfortunately, the author preferred to remain anonymous.[12] Interestingly enough, though, he started his review by praising Kierkegaard—without mentioning his name—as "*eine[n] der produktivsten Schriftsteller Dänemarks.*"[13] Thus, he was obviously aware both of Kierkegaard's earlier work and of Kierkegaard himself as its actual author (in particular, namely, as the author of the pseudonymous writings). This could have been a hint for Kierkegaard himself that it was A.F. Beck—as indeed it was[14]—who had raised his voice again. For as early as 1845 no more than a handful contemporaries would have known about these facts, at least not in the German-speaking world. Beck then goes on to give a fairly detailed paraphrase of the text, focusing on its major concepts and ideas (moment, God in time, paradox, offense, faith, contemporaneity, etc.). Deliberately withholding any criticism, he moderately praises the book for its methodical originality. The method itself is said to lead to a strict mutual implication of—or as he puts it an "absolute relation"—between the objective (here, the paradox) and the subjective (here, faith) dimensions of the religious consciousness:

> *Das Verfahren des Verf. besteht darin, durch Aufstellung der christlichen Grund-voraussetzung als allgemeiner Hypothese die Bestimmung im menschlichen Leben zu finden, die derselben entspricht, die im Grunde selbst in jener Voraussetzung enthalten ist. Das Resultat ist, daß das Verhältnis zwischen dem* Objektiven *und Subjektiven als* absolutes *gedacht werden müsse, anders ausgedrückt, daß das erstere ein* Paradox *wird, das nur mittels des* Glaubens *angeeignet wird.*[15]

Beck's review was obviously brought to Kierkegaard's attention and, surprisingly enough (given his usual abstinence from any such practice), he explictly refers to it in a long footnote in the *Postscript*.[16] The reference is noteworthy in at least three respects. First, it provides us "with a rare example of Kierkegaard commenting on his own reception."[17] Secondly, the text does not give us any hint as to whether Kierkegard was aware of the fact that Beck was the author of the review or not. Finally, its overall critical tendency notwithstanding,[18] the comment finds unexpectedly appreciative

---

[12] See *Neues Repertorium für die theologische Literatur und kirchliche Statistik*, vol. 2, 1845, pp. 44–8. The text is reprinted as Anonymous, "Philosophische Brocken oder ein Bißchen Philosophie," in *Materialien zur Philosophie Søren Kierkegaards*, ed. by Michael Theunissen and Wilfried Greve, Frankfurt am Main: Suhrkamp 1979, pp. 127–131.
[13] Anonymous, "Philosophische Brocken oder ein Bißchen Philosophie," in *Materialien*, p. 127.
[14] In 1847 Beck publicly declared in a Danish theological journal that he himself was the author of the anonymous review from 1845: see *SKS* K7, 249.
[15] Ibid.
[16] See *SKS* 7, 249–53n / *CUP1*, 274–7n.
[17] Malik, *Receiving Kierkegaard*, p. 52.
[18] Here the main objection is that the author of the review is lacking any adequate sense for the overall indirect strategy of the book: "The report is didactic [*docerende*], purely and simply didactic; consequently the reader will receive the impression that the pamphlet is also didactic. As I see it, this is the most mistaken impression one can have of it." (*SKS* 7, 250 /

words for the reviewer: he "is brief and refrains almost entirely from what is usually found in reviews, the introductory and concluding examination-ceremony of lauding the author, of citing him for special distinction or perhaps even for special distinction and congratulations."[19]

Except for very few proven instances of a reception without production there is,[20] to the best of my knowledge, only one further direct and explicit reference to Kierkegaard to be found within the German-speaking world during the former's lifetime: Johann Georg Theodor Grässe (1814–85), a literary historian and librarian from Leipzig, refers to the "*Hegelianer Kierkegaard*"[21] (!) in a short passage of his massive survey of European literature which came out in 1848. Here a brief (and partly inaccurate) paraphrase of *Either/Or* leads to the overall judgment that the book as a whole "*ist mit solcher objectiven Originalität abgefaßt, daß man das leider in Deutschland noch nicht gekannte Buch zu den besten Produkten der modernen Dänischen Literatur zählen darf.*"[22]

(2) It is all but surprising that shortly after Kierkegaard's death (not only) German references to the deceased are almost exclusively restricted to his attack on the Danish Lutheran Church. Thus, for instance, the bi-weekly *Copenhagener Zeitung*, a paper addressed to the German-speaking community in Copenhagen, published thirteen longer articles in 1856, in which a thorough report (and critique) of Kierkegaard's standpoint and strategy in the *Kirkekamp* was given, accompanied by several excerpts from *The Moment* in German translation.[23] Even prior to these excerpts some selections of the (then available nine) *The Moment* issues had been translated into German by the Royal Prussian consul general to the Danish monarchy, Ryno Quehl (1821–64). Quehl had been present at Kierkegaard's funeral, and in a book he later wrote about Denmark he devoted about twenty pages to an account and

CUP1, 275; see also *SKS* 18, 259, JJ:362 / *JP* 5, 5827) In my opinion this critique does not do full justice to the review, however, which "*stell[t] es dem Ermessen eines jeden anheim, ob er in dieser apologetischen Dialektik Ernst oder etwa Ironie suchen will*" (Anonymous, "Philosophische Brocken," p. 131).

[19]   *SKS* 7, 249n / *CUP1*, 274n. Theunissen and Greve rightly assume that this "*ganz und gar ungewöhnliche Behandlung...auf Kierkegaards Genugtuung über die Tatsache [deutet], über die Grenzen Dänemarks hinaus nun auch im Ursprungsland der zeitgenössischen Philosophie Beachtung gefunden zu haben*" (*Materialien*, ed. by Theunissen and Greve, p. 132).

[20]   For instance, Malik points to a certain Dr. Edmund Zoller who obviously read Danish and was interested in Danish culture since his friend, the famous historian and philologist Christian Molbech (1783–1857), had asked Kierkegaard for a copy of the first edition of *Either/Or* in order to send it to Zoller—a request with which Kierkegaard willingly complied. See Malik, *Receiving Kierkegaard*, pp. 54–5.

[21]   Johann Georg Th. Grässe, *Geschichte der Poesie Europas und der bedeutendsten außereuropäischen Länder vom Anfang des 16. Jahrhunderts bis auf die neueste Zeit*, Leipzig: Arnoldische Buchhandlung 1848, p. 979.

[22]   Ibid. See also Malik, *Receiving Kierkegaard*, p. 55.

[23]   A summary of the articles can be found in Malik, *Receiving Kierkegaard*, pp. 126–7.

translation of Kierkegaard's controversial views, to which he added a biographical sketch and a detailed description of the incidents at the funeral.[24]

Almost simultaneously the first Catholic raised his voice—and about the same topic: Joseph Edmund Jörg (1819–1901), the German historian and conservative politician, published an article in 1856 about the religious movements in Scandinavia—an article that dealt almost exclusively with Kierkegaard's attack on the Danish Church and which made abundant use of the resources provided by Beck, Quehl, and the *Copenhagener Zeitung*.[25] It does not come as a surprise that Jörg praises Kierkegaard for his polemic against the Lutheran Church, while simultaneously criticizing him for having failed to draw the appropriate conclusion: *"[S]chon unmittelbar von der logischen Entwicklung seiner Grundanschauung aus wäre...der katholische Kirchenbegriff auf Hrn. Kierkegaard's Weg gelegen."*[26]

(3) With respect to the history of reception, the 1860s still proved unable to break the spell of the *Kirkekamp*. Meanwhile the first two complete German translations of Kierkegaardian texts had been published, and this already at the beginning of the decade.[27] However, both of them were taken from the *corpus* of Kierkegaard's post-1850 writings. This programmatic restriction may not only be read as a significant *cause* for the further direction and tendency of the process of reception in Germany (as characterized above), but also as a *manifestation* or expression of that tendency. Slowly but steadily things began to change, however. For one thing, Moritz Lüttke (dates unknown), a German theology student who apparently knew Danish quite well, travelled to Scandinavia in 1863 and one year later published a book describing his impressions of the trip with special reference to the present state of the Northern church.[28] One paragraph of his account is exclusively devoted to Kierkegaard, and here for the first time the focus is on one of the pseudonymous works: Kierkegaard's overall intention, says Lüttke, is to call attention to "the truth," that is: to Christianity. However, according to Kierkegaard, the truth is only accessible from, in fact

---

[24]   See Ryno Quehl, *Aus Dänemark*, Berlin: Verlag der Deckerschen Geheimen Ober-Hofbuchdruckerei 1856, pp. 277–97. More on Quehl in Malik, *Receiving Kierkegaard*, pp. 124–5.

[25]   See Joseph Edmund Jörg, "Streiflichter auf die neueste Geschichte des Protestantismus: Die religiösen Bewegungen in den scandinavischen Ländern," *Historisch-politische Blätter für das Katholische Deutschland*, no. 38, 1856, pp. 1–30. The article reappeared, in revised and expanded form, in Joseph Edmund Jörg, *Geschichte des Protestantismus in seiner neuesten Entwicklung*, vols. 1–2, Freiburg: Herder 1858, vol. 2, pp. 336–50.

[26]   Jörg, "Streiflichter," p. 28.

[27]   In 1861 the first complete, though clumsy translation of the nine issues of *The Moment* was published under the title *Christentum und Kirche. "Die Gegenwart." Ein ernstes Wort an unsere Zeit, insbesondere an die evangelische Geistlichkeit*, Hamburg: Hestermann 1861 (translator unknown). One year later the theology student Christian Hansen published *Zur Selbstprüfung der Gegenwart empfohlen*, Erlangen: Deichert 1862.

[28]   See Moritz Lüttke, *Kirchliche Zustände in den skandinavischen Ländern Dänemark, Norwegen, Schweden. Mittheilungen aus der Gegenwart*, Elberfeld: H.L. Friderichs 1864 (as to Kierkegaard see pp. 45–58). For a brief summary of Lüttke's Kierkegaard reading see Schulz, "Rezeptionsgeschichtliche Nachschrift," pp. 358–9.

tantamount to the standpoint of subjectivity: " *'Die Subjectivität ist die Wahrheit,' das würde in seinem Sinne gesprochen sein.*"[29]

At roughly the same time another step forward was taken by Johann Tobias Beck (1804–78), a protestant theology professor at the University of Tübingen, who through his teaching and (though to a lesser degree) his writings influenced many generations of students. Apparently he also made some of them (Albert Bärthold, Christoph Schrempf, and Hermann Gottsched, in particular) read Kierkegaard.[30] To a great extent, however, his own writings reveal only implicit traces of the latter's thought, thus making their author a borderline case between reception without production and productive reception.[31] Beck's enthusiasm for Kierkegaard was apparently stimulated and mediated through reading the two books that were already accessible in German at that time (see above); by contrast, *Fear and Trembling* (which under the title *Furcht und Beben* was obviously sent to him in manuscript, translated by an unknown Scandinavian student of his) did not find his approval.[32] In his opinion de silentio's account of Abraham "*ist allzu sehr überwachsen von üppigen Reden..., wo der Text der Schrift in seinem objektiven Schweigen unübertrefflich ist.*"[33]

(4) In all probability it was Beck, "*der zuerst die deutsche protestantische Theologie auf den großen Dänen hinwies...zu einer Zeit, da Kierkegaard selber in Deutschland noch völlig unbekannt war.*"[34] However, a rather dramatic change occurred when two of Beck's former students started spreading the word. Both of them profoundly influenced the subsequent reception of Kierkegaard in Germany— although in quite different directions. The first was Albert Bärthold (dates unknown) who after studying in Tübingen worked as a pastor in Halberstadt (Eastern Germany). From 1872 onwards Bärthold not only published a growing number of excerpts from Kierkegaard's pseudonymous and non-pseudonymous writings but soon also complete works in German translation.[35] His pertinent writings make

---

[29]   Lüttke, *Kirchliche Zustände*, p. 48.

[30]   A lively introduction to Beck's theology can be found in Karl Barth, *Die protestantische Theologie im 19. Jahrhundert. Ihre Vorgeschichte und ihre Geschichte*, 4th ed., Zürich: Theologischer Verlag 1981, pp. 562–9 (as to Beck's enthusiasm for Kierkegaard see ibid., pp. 563–4.). Kierkegaard himself possessed Beck's early work *Die christliche Lehr-Wissenschaft nach den biblischen Urkunden. Ein Versuch. Erster Theil. Die Logik der christlichen Lehre*, Stuttgart: Verlag der Chr. Belser'schen Buchhandlung 1841 (*ASKB* 425).

[31]   Brief surveys of Beck's Kierkegaard reception are accessible in Malik, *Receiving Kierkegaard*, pp. 220–1; pp. 271–2; p. 311; Schulz, "Rezeptionsgeschichtliche Brocken," pp. 386–7. A more detailed account is given by Walter Ruttenbeck, *Sören Kierkegaard. Der christliche Denker und sein Werk*, Berlin: Trowitzsch & Sohn 1929, pp. 282–6. Ruttenbeck points to several common themes in Kierkegaard and Beck (the philosophy of personality, the concept of existence, the critique of Hegel, one-sided individualism, etc.); note also that Beck called his own sermons "Christliche Reden" (see ibid., p. 282)!

[32]   See Ruttenbeck, *Kierkegaard*, p. 282.

[33]   Thus Beck in his so-called "Zwischenreden," Ruttenbeck, *Kierkegaard*, p. 282.

[34]   Ibid., pp. 283–4.

[35]   The excerpts that Bärthold translated and published were often (and most confusingly) interrupted by commenting passages from his own pen; they include *Einladung und Ärgernis. Biblische Darstellung und christliche Begriffsbestimmung von Søren Kierkegaard*, trans. and ed. by Albert Bärthold, manuscript, Halberstadt 1872; *Sören Kierkegaard. Eine Verfasser-*

him an excellent example of what I take to be borderline cases between receptive production and productive reception; for not only his secondary works,[36] but also and in particular his other writings bear witness to the fact that his whole religious and theological outlook, circling around the concept of "personality," was permeated with Kierkegaardian ideas.[37] Bärthold read the authorship as essentially religious, thus believing in Kierkegaard's self-interpretation as a religiously (not theologically![38]) motivated author. According to Bärthold, Kierkegaard's whole authorship was dominated right from the start by two functionally corresponding intentions: first, the introduction of Christianity into Christendom, by inculcating the former "als neue *Existenzmitteilung;*"[39] secondly, and as a functionally subordinate means to realize that goal, "*die Ausarbeitung der Persönlichkeit durch alle Lebenssphären,*"[40] a project which culminated in the attempt to confront the reader with the ideality of what it means to be or become a Christian.

Bärthold's impact was primarily mediated through his translations. With some qualification this can also be said of yet another significant early Kierkegaard catalyst

---

Existenz eigner Art. Aus seinen Mittheilungen zusammengestellt, trans. and ed. by Albert Bärthold, Halberstadt: Frantz 1873; *Aus und über Søren Kierkegaard. Früchte und Blätter,* trans. and ed. by Albert Bärthold, Halberstadt: Frantz'sche Buchhandlung 1874; *Zwölf Reden,* trans. and ed. by Albert Bärthold, Halle: J. Fricke 1875; *Von den Lilien auf dem Felde und den Vögeln unter dem Himmel. Drei Reden Søren Kierkegaards,* trans. and ed. by Albert Bärthold, Halberstadt: H. Meyer 1876; *Lessing und die objective Wahrheit. Aus Søren Kierkegaards Schriften,* trans. and ed. by Albert Bärthold, Halle: J. Fricke 1877 (also containing *Rasmus Nielsen über Glauben und Wissen gegen Martensen*); *Die Lilien auf dem Felde und die Vögel unter dem Himmel. Drei fromme Reden.—Hoherpriester—Zöllner—Sünderin. Drei Beichtreden von Søren Kierkegaard,* trans. and ed. by Albert Bärthold, Halle: J. Fricke 1877; *Søren Kierkegaard. Ausgewählt und bevorwortet,* trans. and ed. by Albert Bärthold, Hamburg: Agentur des rauhen Hauses 1906. In addition Bärthold translated three complete pseudonymous works: *Einübung im Christentum,* trans. and ed. by Albert Bärthold, Halle: J. Fricke 1878; *Die Krankheit zum Tode. Eine christliche psychologische Entwicklung zur Erbauung und Erweckung,* trans. and ed. by Albert Bärthold, Halle: J. Fricke 1881; *Stadien auf dem Lebenswege. Studien von Verschiedenen. Zusammengebracht, zum Druck befördert und hrsg. von Hilarius Buchbinder;* trans. and ed. by Albert Bärthold, Leipzig: J. Lehmann 1886.

[36]   Bärthold's Kierkegaard studies include *Noten zu Søren Kierkegaards Lebensgeschichte,* Halle: Fricke 1876; *Die Bedeutung der ästhetischen Schriften Sören Kierkegaards mit Bezug auf G. Brandes: "Søren Kierkegaard, ein literarisches Charakterbild,"* Halle: Fricke 1879; *Zur theologischen Bedeutung Sören Kierkegaards,* Halle: Fricke 1880; *S. Kierkegaards Persönlichkeit in ihrer Verwirklichung der Ideale,* Gütersloh: Bertelsmann 1886; *Geleitbrief für Søren Kierkegaard: "Ein Bisschen Philosophie,"* Leipzig: Richter 1890.

[37]   See, for instance, Albert Bärthold, *Was Christentum ist. Zur Verständigung über diese Frage,* Gütersloh: Bertelsmann 1884; also *Die Wendung zur Wahrheit in der modernen Kulturentwicklung,* Gütersloh: Bertelsmann 1885.

[38]   See Albert Bärthold, *Zur theologischen Bedeutung Sören Kierkegaards,* Halle: Fricke 1880, p. 47; p. 75.

[39]   Albert Bärthold, *Die Bedeutung der ästhetischen Schriften Sören Kierkegaards,* Halle: Julius Fricke 1879, p. 18.

[40]   Ibid.

in Germany—the soon to be infamous Christoph Schrempf (1860–1944), who just like the former began as a student of J.T. Beck in Tübingen. And like his immediate predecessor, Schrempf, too, may be regarded as a paradigmatic borderline-case between productive reception and receptive production.[41] However, "whereas Bärthold maintains a consistently sympathetic disposition toward Kierkegaard, Schrempf soon overcomes his initial enthusiasm as he allows himself to be sucked into the swirl of *fin de siècle* scepticism and malaise."[42] After occasionally referring to Kierkegaard in an early book from 1884 called *Die Grundlagen der Ethik*, Schrempf started to publish numerous shorter and longer papers, articles, and reviews exclusively devoted to the Danish thinker, the earliest of which dates from 1886.[43] In the subsequent years Schrempf gained some notoriety even outside the rather small early Kierkegaard circles, and this for three reasons, all of which had to do with Kierkegaard. First, after studying Danish in order to attain first-hand knowledge of his philosophical hero, Schrempf produced in 1890 his first translation, consisting of the *The Concept of Anxiety* and the *Philosophical Fragments*.[44] Many more were to follow later on, until finally in 1922 the first complete edition of Kierkegaard's published works was available in German.[45] Schrempf's repeatedly revised, highly idiosyncratic, and at times breathtakingly free renditions of the Kierkegaardian texts soon became *the* authoritative voice at least for many German Kierkegaard scholars—scholars who did not possess the language skills to draw on the original in order not to have to rely on Schrempf.[46] The somewhat dubious quality of his translations not withstanding, it can hardly be denied that (in addition to Bärthold) Schrempf promoted German

---

[41]   A comprehensive survey of Schrempf's Kierkegaard reception is given by Malik, *Receiving Kierkegaard*, pp. 311–15; pp. 332–8; see also Schulz, "Rezeptionsgeschichtliche Brocken," pp. 389ff.

[42]   Malik, *Receiving Kierkegaard*, p. 311.

[43]   All pertinent texts are conveniently gathered in volume 12 of Christoph Schrempf, *Gesammelte Werke*, vols. 1–16, Stuttgart: Frommanns 1935. As mentioned above, the earliest of these texts dates from 1886, the latest one from 1935. By far the largest part of volume 12 consists of Schrempf's numerous forewords and afterwords to the various German translations of Kierkegaard's works that he edited and published. In addition, vols. 10 and 11 of the same edition contain Schrempf's infamous Kierkegaard biography, originally published in two volumes: *Sören Kierkegaard. Eine Biographie*, Jena: Diederichs 1927–28.

[44]   The book was given the somewhat misleading title *Zur Psychologie der Sünde, der Bekehrung und des Glaubens. Zwei Schriften Sören Kierkegaards*, Leipzig: F. Richter 1890. The translations served as a basis for the respective volumes of Schrempf's later edition of Kierkegaard's collected works (see the following note).

[45]   Sören Kierkegaard, *Gesammelte Werke*, vols. 1–12, Jena: Diederichs 1909–22. Schrempf had planned to add four volumes of edifying discourses. Only two of them were actually published, however: Sören Kierkegaard, *Leben und Walten der Liebe*, Jena: Diederichs 1924 (*Erbauliche Reden*, vol. 3); *Christliche Reden*, Jena: Diederichs 1929 (*Erbauliche Reden*, vol. 4).

[46]   As to a discussion of Schrempf's translations, see, for instance, Malik, *Receiving Kierkegaard*, pp. 312–15. Principal problems of translating Kierkegaard into German have more recently been discussed by Eberhard Harbsmeier, "Von der 'geheimen Freudigkeit des verborgnen Wohlstandes.' Zum Problem deutscher Kierkegaard Übersetzungen," *Kierkegaardiana*, vol. 17, 1994, pp. 130–41.

Kierkegaard scholarship tremendously through his translations and, though to a lesser degree, his secondary writings. The second reason for his becoming increasingly well-known at least within the academic public is his (equally often revised) prefaces and postscripts to the various volumes of Kierkegaard's *Gesammelte Werke* plus his two-volume biography of the latter. These publications served as a platform for Schrempf to spread and elaborately defend his own, highly eclectic, and often polemical message about the Danish writer. In a nutshell the message goes like this: Kierkegaard's writings (in particular, his pseudonymous ones) inadvertently promote and justify religious unbelief and/or scepticism—the very same unbelief or scepticism that Schrempf enthusiastically subscribes to and practices himself. Schrempf arrives at this highly idiosyncratic conclusion by deliberately radicalizing a principle that he has found in Kierkegaard himself (or more exactly, in Climacus): the principle of subjectivity as truth.[47] This principle is, according to Schrempf, in Kierkegaard's authorship always and mistakenly restricted to the sheer act of subjectively (that is volitionally and/or passionately) *appropriating* something as already objectively given—a proposition, in other words, the objective truth of which is and shall never be called into question. Thus, for instance, the whole problem of the *Fragments* boils down to the question, "*welche Folgen für die Selbsterkenntnis und die Stellung zu Christus [der] Glaube nach sich zieht.*"[48] However, the purely dogmatical *premise* or presuppositon of answering this question is, according to Schrempf, completely left out of the picture—the premise, namely, that Jesus was indeed the Son of God, so that in any case no historical scrutiny is required in order to be able to become contemporary with him via faith. Schrempf does not share this view, of course: "*Wer mit Jesus wirklich gleichzeitig werden will muß auch den historischen Jesus wirklich vor Augen haben wollen; er muß sich also mit den Nachrichten über ihn historisch beschäftigen und wird von ihnen selbst zur Kritik an ihnen genötigt.*"[49] Schrempf concludes that Kierkegaard's own principle of subjectivity (here understood as the will to unconditional sincerity) both compels us to the attempt to draw a reliable picture of the historical Jesus *and* to the acknowledgment of his non-divine character as the actual outcome of this attempt. Accordingly, the very same Kierkegaard, "*der durch Climacus das Christentum wieder in sein Recht einsetzen will,*" inadvertently justifies "*den theoretischen und praktischen Unglauben.*"[50] Schrempf himself was courageous and honest enough to draw the consequences of adopting such a stance by personally appropriating it and acting accordingly. In 1891 he renunciated his clerical vows and departed from service in the Lutheran Church in Württemberg—which is a third reason for his becoming widely known at that time. In fact, the so-

---

[47] As to Schremph's quite sophisticated account of the various meanings of this principle in Kierkegaard, see Schrempf, *Werke*, vol. 12, pp. 225ff.; also Schulz, "Rezeptionsgeschichtliche Nachschrift," pp. 365–8.

[48] Schrempf, *Werke*, vol. 12, p. 58; see ibid., p. 206; p. 424.

[49] Ibid., p. 59; see ibid., pp. 429–50.

[50] Ibid., p. 217.

called "Schrempf-affair" caused a sensation throughout the land, well beyond the borders of the Church.[51]

(5) It is plain to see that Schrempf not only knew but was probably also influenced by the account of Kierkegaard given by Georg Brandes. This account was made accessible and popular even prior to Brandes' own infamous Kierkegaard biography from 1877[52] through his friend and translator Adolf von Strodtmann (1829–79).[53] As a literary scholar Strodtmann published an extensive survey of Danish culture that among other things contains a longer paragraph on Kierkegaard, in which the author explicitly refers to Brandes' critical views—and this about four years prior to the latter's publication of his own book.[54] Strodtman views Kierkegaard as a genius poet and psychologist who in his attempt to live and defend Christianity in its pure ideality turned out to be "*der letzte, ehrlichste und geistig bedeutendste Nachzügler der Romantik in unserer Zeit.*"[55] However, as such he was, according to Strodtmann, also a tragic figure:

> *[D]as Tragische ist vor Allem, daß..., gerade indem er...aus voller Überzeugung das von Grund aus paradoxe und übernatürliche Wesen des Christentums schilderte, bewiesen hat, daß es theoretisch undenkbar, praktisch unmöglich ist....In diesem Sinne ist Kierkegaard's ganze Literatur nur eine beweisende Note zu Feuerbach's "Wesen des Christentums." Er hat seinen Nachfolgern die schneidigsten Waffen geschmiedet, aber sie wenden sich wider sein eigenes Werk.*[56]

---

[51]   Malik's view of Schrempf is less sympathetic at this point; it is summed up as follows: "The picture one inevitably tends to form of Schrempf during the 1890s, particularly in relation to Kierkegaard, is a contradictory one: nonconformist, calculating opportunist, and sincere soul-searcher wrapped together. It is a picture of a spiritually confused and intellectually unstable man." (Malik, *Receiving Kierkegaard*, p. 337.)

[52]   It was anonymously translated and published in Germany as early as 1879 under the title *Søren Kierkegaard. Eine kritische Darstellung*, Leipzig: Reclam 1992 (reprint of the edition of 1879). As to Brandes' own Kierkegaard reception, inasmuch as it is presented in his book from 1877, plus some contemporary reactions to it, see, for instance, Malik, *Receiving Kierkegaard*, pp. 245–60.

[53]   Adolf Strodtmann himself translated and edited Brandes' book as *Søren Kierkegaard. Ein literarisches Charakterbild*, Hildesheim and New York: Olms 1975 (reprint of the Leipzig ed. 1879). I am inclined to believe that (in addition to the one mentioned in the previous footnote) this is in fact a second German translation of Brandes' *Søren Kierkegaard. En kritisk Fremstilling i Grundrids* from 1877. I cannot prove this, however, since Strodtmann's book has not been accessible to me. In any case, it is wrong to identify the *anonymous* translation from 1879 with the one *Strodtmann* provided in the very same year—which I erroneously did in "Rezeptionsgeschichtliche Brocken," p. 392 (note 48).

[54]   See Adolf Strodtmann, *Das geistige Leben in Dänemark. Streifzüge auf den Gebieten der Kunst, Literatur, Politik und Journalistik des skandinavischen Nordens*, Berlin: Paetel 1873. As to the passage on Kierkegaard, see ibid., pp. 95–125 (it also contains translations from *Either–Or*); the reference to Brandes, whom Strodtmann later calls "*[den] echte[n] geistige[n] Erbe[n] Sören Kierkegaard's*" (ibid., p. 125), is found ibid., p. 101. Strodtmann's role in German Kierkegaard reception is briefly touched upon in Malik, *Receiving Kierkegaard*, pp. 228–32.

[55]   Strodtmann, *Das geistige Leben*, p. 123.

[56]   Ibid., p. 124.

Georg Brandes may be one of those successors that Strodtmann had in mind.[57] It must be admitted, though, that his diagnosis does not capture the general tendency of the secondary output up to the end of the century—not in Germany, at any rate. For one thing, the number of pertinent books to be mentioned here is pretty small.[58] For another, even the monographs exclusively devoted to Kierkegaard are mostly theologically oriented, and this in a more or less academic fashion, thus without normally showing traces of any freethinking spirit whatsoever. Moreover, when it comes to giving a comprehensive account of Kierkegaard's then still untranslated (pseudonymous) writings in particular and his overall intentions in general, most of these works not only rely on the very few translated Danish secondary sources available at that time,[59] but quite often also heavily draw on Bärthold's views and expertise. E.A.F. Jessen's (dates unknown) book from 1895 is a case in point.[60] Summarizing recent religious developments and conflicts in Denmark, it also contains a paragraph on Kierkegaard. Here Jessen, implicitly following Bärthold, arrives at the conclusion that the former's main intention "*ist..., seinen Mitmenschen dazu zu verhelfen, durch Buße und Glauben zu selbständigen christlichen Persönlichkeiten sich auszugestalten.*"[61] Jessen himself subcribes to such an ideal, yet feels himself compelled to criticize Kierkegaard for having interpreted it in a one-sidedly individualistic fashion. Invoking yet another, this time Danish first-hand authority, his account culminates in a confrontation of Kierkegaard and Martensen, in which he takes sides with the latter:

Martensen vertritt...die Verbindung des Christlichen mit dem Humanen. S. Kierkegaard bekämpft sie leidenschaftlich. Martensen huldigt der Totalitätsbetrachtung und dem Socialismus auf kirchlichem Gebiet. S. Kierkegaard huldigt dagegen einem ausgeprägten

[57] See Schulz, "Rezeptionsgeschichtliche Brocken," pp. 392–3.

[58] Ernst Esmach, *An Sören Kierkegaard*, Leipzig: Richter 1885; Gleiss, Otto, *Aus dem evangelischen Norden. Zeugnisse vom Christo in Predigten aus der skandinavischen Kirche unserer Zeit*, Gütersloh: Bertelsmann 1882; E.A.F. Jessen, *Die Hauptströmungen des religiösen Lebens der Jetztzeit in Dänemark*, Gütersloh: Bertelsmann 1895; E. Lorentz, *Über die sogenannten ästhetischen Schriften Sören Kierkegaards*. Leipzig: Richter 1892; Monachus [pseudonym], *Relative Absoluta? Oder der Weg zur Geistesfreiheit und freien Liebe. Traumphantasien*, Leipzig: Dieter 1899; K. Walz, *Sören Kierkegaard, der Klassiker unter den Erbauungsschriftstellern des 19. Jahrhunderts. Ein Vortrag*, Gießen: Ricker 1898; Frederik Winkel Horn, *Geschichte der Literatur des skandinavischen Nordens von den älteren Zeiten bis auf die Gegenwart*, Leipzig: Schlicke 1880.

[59] Harald Høffding, *Sören Kierkegaard als Philosoph*, trans. and ed. by Albert Dorner and Christoph Schrempf, 3rd ed., Stuttgart: Frommann 1922 (1st German ed., 1896); Hans L. Martensen, *Aus meinem Leben*, vol. 3, trans. and ed. by A. Michelsen, Karlsruhe and Leipzig: Reuther 1884; Marcus J. Monrad, *Denkrichtungen der neueren Zeit. Eine kritische Rundschau*, trans. and ed. by the author, Bonn: Weber 1897; Henrik Scharling, *Humanität und Christenthum in ihrer geschichtlichen Entwicklung, oder: Philosophie der Geschichte aus christlichem Gesichtspunkte*, trans. and ed. by A. Michelsen, Gütersloh: Bertelsmann 1874–75.

[60] See the previous footnote.

[61] Jessen, *Hauptströmungen*, p. 87.

Individualismus. Martensens Wahlspruch heißt: Reich Gottes und der Einzelne. S. Kierkegaards: Nur der Einzelne.[62]

These rather sporadic, if explicit accounts of and references to Kierkegaard within the second half of the nineteenth century should not make us overlook the possibility of a simultaneous Kierkegaard reception without production, production without reception, and unproductive reception, respectively. Although moving onto rather speculative ground here (especially regarding the first type that, for this very reason, will have to be ignored in the following) some names and ideas may at least be mentioned that could be of some importance in this respect. For instance, both Albrecht Ritschl (1822–89) and Wilhelm Herrmann (1846–1922) claim that it is anthropology, more specifically, the believer's first-person perspective which functions as the sole ground, starting-point and necessary condition of theology (instead of metaphysics as onto-theology); such a view demonstrates at least some, if purely material, traces of Kierkegaard's thought. If so, both authors may be classified as borderline cases between production without reception and unproductive reception—it would probably seem rather far-fetched to suggest that they deserve to be called productive recipients instead. Something similar holds in the case of Hermann Cremer (1834–1903) and his (plea for the necessity of a) "paradox-theology,"[63] yet also for a number of prominent authors outside of theology. Thus, Wilhelm Dilthey (1833–1911) "enjoys the distinction of being the earliest philosopher of world renown to have known about and studied Kierkegaard's thought."[64] Apparently an article from 1889, written by Harald Høffding (1843–1931) and published in Dilthey's *Archiv für Geschichte der Philosophie*, awakened the latter's interest in Kierkegaard. In the following years he seems to have read most of the German translations available at that time, until in 1899 he wrote a quite sophisticated review of Høffding's *Kierkegaard als Philosoph*, published in 1896 in Schrempf's translation[65]—a review which bears witness to an astounding expertise in and sympathy for the Danish thinker.[66] Finally, as some have suggested, even the sociologist Ferdinand Tönnies (1855–1936), who personally knew Schrempf and Høffding (if also the latter's book, is uncertain),

---

[62]   Ibid., p. 81; as to Jessen's preference for Martensen at this point, see ibid., p. 93.

[63]   As to Ritschl and Herrmann, see Bärthold's comments, in *Zur theologischen Bedeutung*, pp. 21ff., pp. 53ff.; p. 56; pp. 58–9; in addition, Ruttenbeck, *Kierkegaard*, pp. 278–81. It must be admitted, though, that the references given by the two authors are not very specific. Cremer's relation to Kierkegaard is also treated by Ruttenbeck, see *Kierkegaard*, pp. 286–9; in addition, see Schulz, "Rezeptionsgeschichtliche Brocken," p. 401.

[64]   Malik, *Receiving Kierkegaard*, p. 326.

[65]   Harald Höffding, *Sören Kierkegaard als Philosoph*, trans. and ed. by Albert Dorner and Christoph Schrempf, Stuttgart: Frommann 1896.

[66]   The review is to be found in *Archiv für Geschichte der Philosophie*, vol. 12, 1899, pp. 358–60. See also Malik's paraphrase in *Receiving Kierkegaard*, pp. 326–7. The young Ernst Troeltsch (to whom I will return later) wrote an additional review of Høffding's book; it was published in *Theologischer Jahresbericht*, vol. 16, 1896–97, pp. 539–40. As far as Dilthey is concerned Malik points to the notion of "life possibilities" (*Lebensmöglichkeiten*) that Dilthey found and appreciated in Kierkegaard's theory of the stages. Apart from Dilthey some authors have also suggested a certain idea-historical connection between Kierkegaard and Emil Lask (1875–1925); see Ruttenbeck, *Kierkegaard*, p. 376.

may have pondered Kierkegaard's purported 'individualism' while working on his *magnum opus, Gemeinschaft und Gesellschaft*, which came out in 1887.[67]

II. Reception: The Productive Years, 1900–45

(1) In light of the previous survey Paul Tillich's claim that Kierkegaard remained "*völlig unbekannt*"[68] in Germany up until the late nineteenth century calls for correction. However, it is not completely beside the point. If some interested student, eager to make himself familiar with the "teachings" of the great Danish thinker, tried, at the beginning of the twentieth century, to lay his hands on and read all available first- and second-hand sources, he would have had to be content with no more than a rather restricted selection—a selection that was far from representative, much less from being complete, in any case.[69] Thus, Günther Dehn's (a later professor of Practical Theology in Bonn) account does not seem to be overly idiosyncratic, when he, recalling in his autobiography the year 1902, which saw him living and studying in Berlin, characterizes the situation as follows:

> *Kierkegaard...[war] damals in Deutschland noch ziemlich unbekannt. Ich war an ihn gekommen durch das umfangreiche Werk "Sören Kierkegaards agitatorische Schriften und Aufsätze" 1896, herausgegeben von Dorner und Schrempf. Wenn man damals noch mehr von Kierkegaard erfahren wollte, mußte man mühsam suchen. Der erste Band der großen Ausgabe seiner Werke erschien erst 1905 [sic] bei Diederichs. Es gab fast nur die Einzelausgaben von Bärthold, die schon in den siebziger Jahren erschienen und im allgemeinen nicht mehr zu haben waren.*[70]

For all its historical inaccuracies, Dehn's statement at least indicates that there must have been an increasing awareness of and interest in Kierkegaard by the turn of the century, in any case within German academic circles and in particular theological ones. Following Albert Bärthold and Christoph Schrempf, the Austrian philosopher,

---

[67]   See Malik, *Receiving Kierkegaard*, p. 335. It is interesting to note that Bärthold discussed Kierkegaard's "sociology" in terms of the "Unterschied zwischen *Gemeinschaft* und *Gesellschaft*" (Bärthold, *Zur theologischen Bedeutung*, p. 60; original emphasis; as to the context, see ibid., pp. 60ff.) as early as 1880, that is, seven years prior to the publication of Tönnies' famous book.

[68]   Paul Tillich, *Philosophie und Schicksal. Schriften zur Erkenntnislehre und Existenzphilosophie*, vol. 4 (1961) in Tillich, *Gesammelte Werke*, vols. 1–14, ed. by Renate Albrecht, Berlin: Walter de Gruyter and Stuttgart: Evangelisches Verlagswerk 1959–75, p. 147.

[69]   I have given a rough survey of the German Kierkegaard monographs available at that time, which may add up to about a dozen. Also by 1900 sixteen titles containing writings from Kierkegaard's own pen were available, eight of which being more or less complete pseudonymous works (*Training in Christianity, The Sickness unto Death, Fear and Trembling, Either/Or, Stages on Life's Way, The Concept of Anxiety, Philosophical Fragments*). The rest consisted mostly of (Bärthold's) excerpts plus a number of edifying discourses and some late writings.

[70]   Günther Dehn, *Die alte Zeit, die vorigen Jahre. Lebenserinnerungen*, Munich: Chr. Kaiser 1962, p. 78.

essayist, cultural critic, and physiognomist Rudolf Kassner (1873–1959) seems to have walked on stage precisely at this time as a third prominent witness—and simultaneously, promotor—of such a growing awareness and interest. Kassner was the first Catholic to "spread the word," although more were to follow in due course. He had discovered Kierkegaard in 1899, thanks to the intermediary of a German Protestant pastor who had given him Schrempf's 1896 translation of the former's polemical writings.[71] Kassner got hooked immediately—even more so, as he suffered from polio, which made him prone to identify with Kierkegaard's ominous "thorn in the flesh." In 1902 Kassner started to conduct a regular reading circle in Vienna, where writings from Kierkegaard, Tolstoy, Stefan George, and others were read and discussed among several first-rate intellectuals. However, the main feat of the Austrian author for the reception was a long introductory article that he published four years later in the then very well known and widely distributed literary journal, *Die neue Rundschau*, under the title "Sören Kierkegaard—Aphorismen."[72]

The crucial claim defended by Kassner in this article appears in its last section bearing the title "the form." It comprises three elements: Kierkegaard was one of the greatest artists who ever lived; he was also one of the greatest humorists; his most important accomplishment is the discovery of the form or the idea of the single individual ("*der Einzelne*").[73] How do these three elements hang together? Part of the answer concerns Kassner's Platonic, expressivistic anthropology: being human is tantamount to being expressive, by virtue of bestowing form on everything experienced, including the experiencing subject itself. For instance, we express something—or ourselves—as beautiful by using (or painting or presenting) a picture; we express something as just or legitimate by using (or issuing or appealing to) a law; we express something as true by using (or formulating or arguing for) a judgment, and so forth. Sure enough, we do so also for epistemological, at least hermeneutical reasons: "*Die Menschen* verstehen sich *untereinander, indem sie sich Form und Ausdruck geben.*"[74] But we do so for sheer ontological reasons also, that is, because to do so is simply part and parcel of our nature as human beings: "*Alles menschliche Leben* ist *Ausdruck und Form.*"[75] Unfortunately, the realization of our expressive nature goes hand in hand with a fatal tendency to multiply and at the same time unify form and expression: "*Je mehr Formen und Ausdrücke,...umso besser scheint für das Leben der einzelnen Dinge gesorgt zu sein, und die menschliche Weisheit steht am höchsten im Preise dort, wo sie für alle einzelnen Dinge, für*

---

[71]   I am drawing here and in the following on Malik's instructive account: *Receiving Kierkegaard*, pp. 357–61; as to Kassner's Kierkegaard reception in general see also Steffen Steffensen, "Kassner und Kierkegaard. Ein Vortrag," *Orbis Litterarum*, no. 18, 1963, pp. 80–90; Schulz, "Rezeptionsgeschichtliche Brocken," pp. 418ff.

[72]   See Rudolf Kassner, "Sören Kierkegaard—Aphorismen," *Die neue Rundschau*, vol. 17, pp. 513–43. Owing to its importance, the article was later reprinted several times and in modified form, respectively. It is also included in Rudolf Kassner, *Sämtliche Werke*, ed. by Ernst Zinn and Klaus E. Bohnenkamp, vols. 1–10, Pfullingen: Neske 1969–91; vol. 2, 1974, pp. 39–97; as to the different versions of the essay see the editors' note, ibid., p. 519.

[73]   See Kassner, *Sämtliche Werke,* vol. 2, pp. 95; p. 97; p. 91.

[74]   Ibid., p. 89; my emphasis.

[75]   Ibid.; my emphasis.

*alle Formen und Ausdrücke...*eine *Form,* einen *Ausdruck,* ein *Gesetz hat."*[76] Thus, something experienced as great also seems to call for being labelled or expressed as "great." And the more experiences to the same effect can be subsumed under the same category, the better. In light of this perspective it would seem odd, indeed grotesque, to experience something as "great" and nevertheless call or express it as "wretched," or to experience something "unhappy" and yet call or express it as "happy," etc. However, "making distinctions" in this sense is precisely what Kierkegaard does and asks for—while at the same time living and articulating the one and only form that seemed appropriate to him, namely the (idea of the) single individual. In doing so, he proved to belong to the rare species of genius. For, according to Kassner, it is the capacity and privilege of the genius to creatively reduce the variety of forms to just one: for Pascal it was the (idea of the) cloister, for Nietzsche the superman, for Plato the idea as such; Kierkegaard, however, *"fand die Form im—Einzelnen."*[77] Now, the single individual cannot simply be reduced to an individual entity in the Platonic sense, as such existing in time and space as part of the phenomenal world, while at the same time participating (both ontologically and epistemically) in a corresponding idea as part of the *mundus intelligibilis.* Rather, the single individual is as such polemically, in fact even paradoxically, opposed to any such universal form that it should most easily be subsumed under. As a single individual, a human being has to be conceived of as an entity, which is, for instance, beautiful or just, precisely by expressing itself in such a way as to actually appear ugly and unjust—and by accepting, in fact even intending itself to appear so. Furthermore, on Kassner's reading "single individual" and *"Christian"* are closely related to or bound up with each other in this respect: wherever (and presumably also, *only* where) one finds the latter, there is also the former. *"Der Einzelne ist gleichsam die eingeborene Form des Christen, die Form aber, in der ihn die Anderen verstehen, ist der Widerspruch, das Paradox. Gleichwie der Grieche schön oder gut war, so erregt der Christ, der Einzelne, Widerspruch. Der Einzelne produziert das Paradox."*[78]

Finally, by stimulating refusal, provoking opposition, and witnessing the paradox, the Christian and as such *"der Einzelne [ist] die Überwindung der Tautologie."*[79] To call or express something as "great," thereby pretending that the usage of this term (or a corresponding expression of it) is congruent with a common, indeed, universal experience to that effect, is for Kassner an integral feature of logic; logic, however, boils down to pure tautology.[80] Humans think and understand each other, *"indem sie das Große groß, das Kleine klein, das Einsame einsam, das Glückliche glücklich sein lassen."*[81] Now, to turn this tautological logic upside down (in the sense described above) requires and is in fact an expression of humor; in this sense *"Humor ist umgekehrte Logik."*[82] And since existing and expressing oneself humorously is a form

---

[76]   Ibid., p. 90.
[77]   Ibid., p. 91; as to Pascal, Nietzsche, and Plato, see ibid., p. 92.
[78]   Ibid., p. 93.
[79]   Ibid., p. 94.
[80]   See ibid., pp. 89; pp. 94–5.
[81]   Ibid., p. 89.
[82]   Ibid., p. 97.

of art, and since, furthermore, Kierkegaard proves, especially in his pseudonymous writings, to be one of the greatest humorists, he can also be deemed a great artist— even more so, since being and expressing himself as an artist belonged to his very nature *as* the single individual that he actually was: "*Kierkegaard war Künstler, wie ein Anderer Mensch ist.*"[83]

(2) Kierkegaard's impact on Kassner was "so powerful and lasting that it permeated all his thoughts and writings throughout the successive phases of his development."[84] Therefore, following Bärthold, Schrempf, and a few others, the Austrian author is another excellent example of what I take to be a typological borderline case in the reception: here between receptive production and productive reception.[85] In both respects he functioned as an important catalyst for promoting the subsequent study and reception of Kierkegaard.[86] This promotion stretched mainly in two directions: On the one hand, Kassner's own enthusiasm for the Danish author infected a number of poets and belletristic writers whom he was personally acquainted with, most notably Rainer Maria Rilke (1875–1926). It must be admitted, though, that it was not Kassner himself who introduced Rilke to Kierkegaard. The two men did not meet until 1907, and Rilke knew Kierkegaard already since 1901, when he had borrowed a copy of a German selection of the latter's *Christian Discourses* (1848) that also contained an appendix of translated extracts about Kierkegaard as a person from the pen of his niece Henriette Lund (1829–1909).[87] The book and especially Lund's recollections apparently left a great impression on Rilke.[88] After also having studied

---

[83]   Ibid., p. 95.

[84]   Malik, *Receiving Kierkegaard*, p. 359.

[85]   I have tried elsewhere to account for the genuinely productive aspect of Kassner's Kierkegaard reception in greater detail, particularly with regard to his doctrine of paradox; see Schulz, "Rezeptionsgeschichtliche Brocken," pp. 418ff.

[86]   Some lesser names who may also be responsible for having drawn attention to Kierkegaard, at least within the literary world, are mentioned by Helen Mustard: "Sören Kierkegaard in German Literary Periodicals, 1860–1930," *The Germanic Review*, vol. 26, 1951, pp. 83–101; here pp. 93–4.

[87]   See Sören Kierkegaard, *Ausgewählte Christliche Reden. Mit einem Anhang: Kierkegaard's Familie und Privatleben nach den persönlichen Erinnerungen seiner Nichte H. Lund*, trans. and ed. by Julie von Reincke, 2nd ed., Gießen: Töpelmann 1909 [1901]. As to Rilke's Kierkegaard reception in context, see Malik, *Receiving Kierkegaard*, pp. 360–5; a more extensive treatment is provided by Rune Engebretsen, *Kierkegaard and Poet–Existence with Special Reference to Germany and Rilke*, unpublished Ph.D. Thesis, Stanford University 1980. Rilke may be one of the first German poets to be influenced by and explicitly to refer to Kierkegaard; however, purely material reflections can be found earlier, even in Kierkegaard's own times: compare, for instance, Edgar Eilers who in his *Probleme religiöser Existenz im "Geistlichen Jahr." Die Droste und Søren Kierkegaard*, Werl: Coelde 1953, points to Annette von Droste–Hülshoff (1797–1848). See also Erwin Kobel, who assumes that Theodor Fontane (1819–98) was perhaps "*der erste Dichter deutscher Sprache, in dessen Werk sich Einwirkungen Kierkegaards zeigen.*" (Erwin Kobel, "Theodor Fontane—ein Kierkegaard Leser?" *Jahrbuch der deutschen Schillergesellschaft*, vol. 36, 1992, pp. 255–87, here p. 287).

[88]   See Malik's report, in *Receiving Kierkegaard*, pp. 361–2.

Max Dauthendey's translation of "The Seducer's Diary," which came out in 1903,[89] he began reading Kierkegaard more seriously, until in 1904 he decided and actually started to learn Danish with the help of his publisher Axel Juncker (1870–1952), who was fluent in the language. Compared to these well-established facts, an assessment of Kassner's later influence on Rilke's reception of Kierkegaard (after 1907) is no easy task. For one thing Rilke himself has left no records of it; for another, his "early attraction to Kierkegaard seems to have resulted more from an interest in his life than in his philosophy or his Christian faith"[90]—and this interest could have easily been awakened and kept alive by just being drawn to the sources mentioned above plus further reading. Finally and typologically speaking, Rilke's receptive attitude towards Kierkegaard is more of a borderline case between reception without production and production without reception: not only has he left behind almost nothing of considerable length and substance *about* Kierkegaard (apart from and outside of the scattered reflections in his letters); it is also quite difficult to even find unambiguous traces of purely *implicit and/or material* reflections of the latter's thought throughout Rilke's authorship.[91] Moreover, one must not forget that a certain Scandinavian craze began to spread among German intellectuals at the turn of the century, triggered especially by Henrik Ibsen. Consequently, the "*Verbindung von Schwermut, Opfer und Einsamkeit*,"[92] which many perceived as a Scandinavian character trait, was adopted as an attitude by a considerable number of German authors, including Rilke; however, this trait could have easily been traced back and attributed by the latter not only to Kierkegaard, but also to other seminal figures of Scandinavian culture at that time, for instance to Jens Peter Jacobsen.[93]

(3) Most of the more or less prominent figures influenced by Kassner's crusade for Kierkegaard remained on the verge of unproductive reception and production without reception.[94] This notwithstanding, Kassner's initiatives were often also

---

[89]   Sören Kierkegaard, *Das Tagebuch des Verführers*, trans. and ed. by Max Dauthendey, Leipzig: Insel 1903.

[90]   Malik, *Receiving Kierkegaard*, p. 364.

[91]   For instance, the parallels between Rilke's *Aufzeichnungen des Malte Laurids Brigge* (1904–10) and Kierkegaard's *Repetition* that von Kloeden points to in order to justify his claim that Rilke's book deliberately (if implicitly) refers to the book, seem to me to be rather vague and unspecific (see Wolfdietrich von Kloeden, "Einfluß und Bedeutung im deutschsprachigen Denken," in *The Legacy and Interpretation of Kierkegaard*, ed. by Niels Thulstrup and Marie Mikulová Thulstrup, Copenhagen: Reitzel 1981 (*Bibliotheca Kierkegaardiana*, vol. 8), pp. 54–101, here p. 56). The impact of Jens Peter Jacobsen is probably much stronger here; see Borge Gedso Madsen, "Influences from J.P. Jacobsen and Sigbjörn Obstfelder on Rainer Maria Rilke's *Die Aufzeichnungen des Malte Laurids Brigge*," *Scandinavian Studies*, no. 3, 1954, pp. 105–14.

[92]   Kloeden, "Einfluß und Bedeutung," p. 55.

[93]   See Malik, *Receiving Kierkegaard*, p. 364.

[94]   Two prominent Austrian authors are a case in point: Arthur Schnitzler (1862–1931) and Hugo von Hofmannsthal (1874–1929). Both had read Brandes' book and at least Hofmannsthal also knew Kassner's pertinent writings. In addition he possessed several translations of Kierkegaard's own works and repeatedly referred to *Buch des Richters* in his *Aufzeichnungen und Tagebücher* covering the years 1904–21 (as to the references, see Malik, *Receiving Kierkegaard*, p. 365). If the presence of an author in a (review-)periodical may

instrumental in leading others to write *about* Kierkegaard, and it is interesting to note that sometimes the biographical interest was either dominant here, too, or at least functioned as a point of departure for further reflection. This was the case, for instance, with the early Georg Lukács (1885–1971).[95] At that time Lukács obviously admired Kassner and certainly also knew the latter's Kierkegaard article from 1906; for a couple of years later he came up with an essay of his own, which clearly reflected Kassner's account. The text which was originally published in Hungarian soon reappeared in a collection of German essays called *Die Seele und die Formen*.[96] Here Lukács' point of departure is Kierkegaard's relation to Regine, and the central idea of his essay recapitulates the overall message of the book in a nutshell: form founders upon ("*zerschellt an*") soul or life. Kierkegaard, according to Lukács, "built his whole life [= soul] upon a gesture [= form]": the gesture of "waving goodbye," as it were, to Regine, that is, of breaking the engagement, and in doing so determined the entire course of his further existence. This gesture symbolizes Kierkegaard's heroic attempt to *match* "form" to "life," and he deserves to be praised and admired for this heroism in Lukács' opinion. However, ultimately his (just like any corresponding) attempt was bound to fail, so that in looking back Kierkegaaard's life resembles a tragedy—the gesture has been a "vain effort," after all.[97] It is plain to see that Kierkegaard's "attempt," as conceived by Lukács, reflects Kassner's description of the Kierkegaardian "single individual" and thus corroborates the assumption of Kassner's repercussion in Lukács' (early) work.[98]

(4) Right from the beginning of his literary career Lukács was a prolific and highly original writer, so that a typological assessment of his Kierkegaard reception is no easy task. Again, I would tend to speak of a borderline case, this time between unproductive and productive reception. At roughly the same time, yet to a certain

---

serve as an index for his overall significance within the contemporary literary world, then Mustard's conclusion is indeed telling: "Up to 1913...German literary circles apparently either did not know Kierkegaard or were not interested in him....The indifference of the literary world is in sharp contrast to the keen interest of theological, philosophical, even pedagogical circles, as shown by the number of articles in professional journals in those fields." (Helen Mustard, "Sören Kierkegaard," p. 95.)

[95]   On Lukács' relation to Kassner, see Malik, *Receiving Kierkegaard*, pp. 357ff., on the former's Kierkegaard reception in general see ibid., pp. 354–7; also Michael Theunissen and Wilfried Greve, "Einleitung: Kierkegaards Werk und Wirkung," in *Materialien zur Philosophie Søren Kierkegaards*, ed. by Michael Theunissen and Wilfried Greve, Frankfurt am Main: Suhrkamp 1979, pp. 12–104, here pp. 76–7.

[96]   See Georg Lukács, *Die Seele und die Formen. Essays*, Berlin: Fleischel 1911. The Kierkegaard essay is found pp. 61–90: "Das Zerschellen der Form am Leben: Sören Kierkegaard und Regine Olsen."

[97]   Here Malik (*Receiving Kierkegaard*, p. 355) points to a biographical parallel in Lukács who also had a brief and unhappy relationship with a woman named Irma Seidler, who committed suicide in 1911.

[98]   In my "Rezeptionsgeschichtliche Brocken," pp. 394–5, I have dealt with the later, Marxist Lukács' and his attempt to incorporate Kierkegaard into the "geistige Vorgeschichte Hitlers" (Theunissen and Greve, "Einleitung," p. 76): see Georg Lukács, *Die Zerstörung der Vernunft*, vol. 1, *Irrationalismus zwischen den Revolutionen*, 2nd ed., Darmstadt and Neuwied: Luchterhand 1979, pp. 219–69.

degree apparently independent of both Lukács and Kassner, we find in Germany a slowly, but steadily growing number of more or less receptively productive Kierkegaard scholars. Though perhaps due, first and foremost, to the impact of (the German version of) Høffding's book, which, as mentioned above, had been published in 1896, it is nevertheless remarkable that most of the pertinent titles focus on Kierkegaard as a philosopher. Some of these accounts arrive at highly idiosyncratic conclusions, probably because essential sources were still (or at least seemed) missing,[99] and also because solid hermeneutical standards had not yet been established within German Kierkegaard scholarship. For instance, one author maintains (with regard to Kierkegaard's ethics) that it is "*unsere unbedingte Pflicht... den Weg durch den Engpass der autonomen Sittlichkeit zu nehmen, wenn wir uns nicht gegen das göttliche Gnadengeschenk der Vernunft versündigen wollen und gedankenlos zugreifen und tollkühn handeln sollen*"[100]—a claim which obviously misses the point in Kierkegaard's ethico-religious dialectic, as it is spelled out, among others, by the latter's *alter ego* Johannes de silentio in *Fear and Trembling*. Another author feels inclined to criticize what he takes to be Kierkegaard's lack of historical sense: "*Sein stetes Werden des Existierenden dachte er sich als ein abgerissenes Werden für sich existierender Einzelheiten, bei dem jede wesentliche Veränderung mit einem gewaltsamen Ruck vor sich geht. Kierkegaard hatte nicht den geringsten historischen Sinn.*"[101] Yet another cannot help but "pathologize" Kierkegaard, reducing his thought to a personal, idiosyncratic conflict, largely based on anxiety; this anxiety, in turn, allegedly prevented its victim from realizing that his doctrine of God, as in fact having grown out of such a pathological impulse, can be refuted by simply elucidating its genesis: "*Die Angst als Grundgefühl erzeugt als Kontrast die Vorstellung der Erlösung von derselben, Gott und ewige Seligkeit. Da aber die Angst das Gegenwärtige ist, so wird die Welt als Leiden und durch Leiden erst zur Seligkeit führend gedacht und Gott thronend in Trauer und grausam, schliesslich zum Heil.*"[102] Admittedly, Kierkegaard has occasionally hit upon some piece of insight; but this, according to the author, is true also of shamans and oracles. At any rate, in the end it will be "*die Wissenschaft..., welche solche Naturen versteht und deutet und darum nach und nach unschädlich, d.h. unwirksam, machen wird.*"[103]

(5) These few randomly chosen examples may give us a rough impression of the *status quo* of contemporary Kierkegaard scholarship in Germany at the beginning of the twentieth century. Things got a lot more focused—yet with respect to the

---

[99] See, for instance, Philipp Münch, *Die Haupt- und Grundgedanken der Philosophie Sören Kierkegaards in kritischer Beleuchtung*, Leipzig: Richter 1901; the author notes (p. 6) that "*alle Citate und Inhaltsangaben der* 'unwissenschaftlichen Nachschrift'" are taken from the German version of Høffding's book. Münch's approach is paradigmatic for German Kierkegaard reception at the beginning of the twentieth century.

[100] Münch, *Haupt- und Grundgedanken*, p. 78.

[101] Karl Hoffmann, *Zur Literatur und Ideengeschichte. Zwölf Studien*, Dresden: Carl Reissner 1909, p. 32.

[102] Julius Baumann, *Deutsche und außerdeutsche Philosophie der letzten Jahrzehnte dargestellt und beurteilt. Ein Buch zur Orientierung auch für Gebildete*, Gotha: Perthes 1903, p. 493.

[103] Ibid., p. 494.

history of reception also more complicated—after, roughly, 1910. Here the first keywords that come to mind are *Der Brenner* and Theodor Haecker (1879–1945). Habib C. Malik sums up the historical significance of their relationship nicely: "Through Theodor Haecker, Kierkegaard entered *Der Brenner* and found his way into the lives of those making up the 'Brenner Circle.' Through this periodical he shone with a new face on the German intellectual scene, a face that had hitherto been obscured by the Schrempf Kierkegaard."[104] *Der Brenner* (the title refers to the famous Alpine pass of the same name) was an Innsbruck-based fortnightly cultural periodical, founded by Ludwig von Ficker (1880–1967); its first issue came out in 1910, and from then on it quickly gained momentum as a focal point of cultural ferment—not only because of the high artistic and/or intellectual rank of its prominent or soon to be prominent authors (Georg Trakl, Hermann Broch, etc.), but also because of numerous illustrious recipients, including, among others, Martin Heidegger and the Mann brothers. One of the regular contributors was the Tyrolian author, poet, church-critic and Nietzsche-enthusiast Carl Dallago (1869–1949). Von Ficker had given Haecker's first publication, *Sören Kierkegaard und die Philosophie der Innerlichkeit*, and Dallago got hooked immediately.[105] He talked the editor into inviting Haecker to join the *Brenner* circle—an invitation which the latter gladly accepted. Now, in a sense Dallago's enthusiasm for Kierkegaard and/or Haecker is all but surprising: his world-view, influenced by Nietzsche, had made him an ardent admirer of some purported "heros" of human history; to these he sentimentally referred as *reine Menschen* (pure men): Socrates, Jesus, Lao Tzu, Walt Whitman, etc. Haecker's account of Kierkegaard as a world-historically significant "hero of inwardness" seemed to corroborate both this world-view in general and Kierkegaard's own place among these privileged exemplars of the human race in particular. Haecker's own reading of the Danish author is a bit more sophisticated, though. He writes: Kierkegaard

> *hatte von der Vorsehung die Aufgabe erhalten, auf das Christliche aufmerksam zu machen, aber ohne das Recht, es als Apostel zu verkündigen. Ehe er zum Christen gelangte, mußte er als Denker, der er war, alle Existenzformen, soweit sie vom Geist aus gesehen werden, durchlaufen, denn der Christ steht am Ende. So ist sein Werk die Darstellung (in Innerlichkeit) der humanen Existenzformen.*[106]

The fact that his works are *inward* accounts of the subsequent human forms and stages of human existence indicates that they indirectly express Kierkegaard's own spiritual development and existential progress in the course of writing them: "*Kierkegaard wuchs durch jedes Werk, das er schuf,*"[107] and through this process of "growing (in) inwardness" his own *understanding* of the true nature of inwardness and inward growth was simultaneously fostered and expressed itself more and more adequately.

---

[104]   Malik, *Receiving Kierkegaard*, p. 391; the following overview is heavily indebted to Malik's account, see pp. 367–92.
[105]   Theodor Haecker, *Sören Kierkegaard und die Philosophie der Innerlichkeit*, Munich: Schreiber 1913.
[106]   Ibid. p. 10.
[107]   Ibid.

In this sense his whole authorship is, according to Haecker, both a paradigmatic expression and an increasingly adequate account of inwardness as such, in fact, a philosophy of inwardness. Formally speaking, this philosophy culminates in the claim that to *fulfill* the task of existence and to *understand* what it actually amounts to are but two sides of the same coin: one cannot have one without the other. Materially speaking, it is Christianity—and Christianity alone—that provides and also perfectly expresses both: "*Selig zu* sein *in Furcht und Zittern*"[108] and simultaneously to *understand* that the task is precisely this, in other words that it is tantamount to existing in inwardness. In Haecker's essay this overall systematic claim functions as the background for assessing Kierkegaard's role within modern philosophy. In his opinion Bergson is the one who comes closest to what Kierkegaard was up to, because Bergson's philosophy is a "*Philosophie des Werdens und der Freiheit*" and for this reason might also serve as a valuable "*Anleitung zum Verständnis der Gedanken Kierkegaards.*"[109] Regrettably, though, Kierkegaard's writings have failed to realize their own central propadeutical purpose of determining and introducing into the true nature of Christianity, and this, in particular, with regard to Nietzsche's fatal influence on the common picture of Christianity: for the latter's apparently radical critique of Christianity had in fact just beaten a caricature to death.[110] In his attempt to sharply distinguish between the realms of ojectivity and subjectivity, Kierkegaard actually has but two peers in modern Western thought. One of them is Pascal who in his attempt to preserve the ideality of Christian faith has, just like Kierkegaard, "*vom Verstand alles erpreßt, was er hergeben kann, aber er kann eben nicht alles geben.*"[111] In this respect Kierkegaard's intentions also resemble Kant's, whom Haecker considers the second candidate for comparison. However,

[d]ie Philosophie Kants...ist die möglichst weite Entfernung des Denkens vom Leben, von der Existenz, vom Werden, vom einzelnen, konkreten Menschen und führte so zur Bestimmung des Transzendentalen als eines entinnerlichten Mediums, in dem sich Subjekt und Objekt zur Wissenschaft treffen. Die Philosophie Kierkegaards...ist die größtmögliche Annäherung des Denkens an das Leben, an die Existenz, an das Werden, an den einzelnen, konkreten Menschen.[112]

So much for Haecker's early account of Kierkegaard and its repercussions in the *Brenner*-circle, especially in Dallago. Where, when and under which circumstances Haecker himself got involved with Kierkegaard is hard to tell; with some probability, though, "it was his fellow Swabian Christoph Schremph who first introduced [him]...to Kierkegaard's works."[113] Soon Haecker started to learn Danish in order to read Kierkegaard in the original—if only to find out pretty quickly that Schrempf's translations were often unreliable. Thus, after having been invited to contribute to the *Brenner*, he set out to deliver his own renditions of Kierkegaard's texts, and this

108 Ibid., p. 68 (my emphasis).
109 Ibid., p. 13.
110 See ibid., pp. 56–7.
111 Ibid., p. 41.
112 Ibid., p. 19.
113 Malik, *Receiving Kierkegaard*, p. 376.

with a special focus on those parts of the authorship that had been overlooked or deliberately ignored by Schrempf, namely the edifying discourses, the journals, and the book on Adler.[114] However, in spite of the mutually fruitful cooperation between Haecker and the *Brenner* for several years, a greater distance between both parties made itself noticeable around 1921. This was the year when Haecker, after having discovered and struggled with the writings of John Henry Newman for a number of years, finally converted to Catholicism.[115] It was Dallago, in particular, whom he had gradually drifted away from, and this because of the apparently overly individualistic tendencies in the latter's Kierkegaard reading. Step by step Dallago had substituted Kierkegaard for Nietzsche, finding in the former's attack on Christendom and the Church "a new standard of values for men," thus "celebrating his own bohemian version of Kierkegaardian individualism."[116] By contrast, Haecker was moving closer to the Catholic Church, and by comparing Newman with Kierkegaard's pertinent writings from 1846 on, he finally arrived at the conclusion that Kierkegaard's attack on the ecclesiastical authorities "was done out of love for them and not as a sign of rebellion or rejection of religious authority."[117] Haecker's conclusion is far from singular or idiosyncratic; rather, it reflects a not so uncommon usurpation tendency in certain Catholic writers who sympathize with Kierkegaard. Precisely those parts of his authorship, which, according to these writers, can be approved of, must be deemed crypto-Catholic in nature; and the rest—at least so they tell us—cannot be approved of.[118]

(6) At first sight it may seem odd that[119] it was not Schrempf, but the *Brenner* circle (Haecker, in particular) which proved instrumental for spreading the Kierkegaardian gospel to a wider German-speaking audience. However, even though by 1914 ten of the twelve volumes comprised by the former's edition of Kierkegaard's *Gesammelte Werke* had already been published, it can barely be overlooked that the edition itself was still a more or less academic affair. Obviously, Schrempf's efforts would have hardly reached a wider audience without the *Brenner's* most effective intermediary

---

[114] For a complete list of Haecker's translations see the bibliography at the end of my article. As far as I can see the first two pieces were a rendition of *Der Pfahl im Fleische* (Innsbruck: Brenner-Verlag 1914) and *Kritik der Gegenwart*, a translation of the third part of *Two Ages* (as to Haecker's reasons for this selection, see Malik, *Receiving Kierkegaard*, pp. 378–9). Numerous edifying discourses plus selections from the journals were to follow during the subsequent years, most of which were published at first in *Der Brenner*. Haecker's rendition of *The Book on Adler* came out in 1917 under the title *Der Begriff des Auserwählten* (Hellerau: Hegner).

[115] It was the year also, when his translation of Newman's *Grammar of Assent* came out.

[116] Malik, *Receiving Kierkegaard*, p. 383. For a survey of Dallago's approach to Kierkegaard, see pp. 382–3. Dallago's own writings on Kierkegaard are listed in the bibliography at the end of my article.

[117] Malik, *Receiving Kierkegaard*, p. 385.

[118] Elsewhere I have dealt with this tendency in fuller detail—namely with reference to Haecker's infamous essay *Der Begriff der Wahrheit bei Sören Kierkegaard* (Innsbruck: Brenner 1932); see Schulz, "Rezeptionsgeschichtliche Nachschrift," pp. 371ff.

[119] As, for instance, Malik maintains, in *Receiving Kierkegaard*, p. 371.

role since the latter was bought, read, and appreciated by large parts of the culturally interested public in Germany and Austria—and yet also by many academics. Apparently more than a few of these have been initiated into the Kierkegaardian cosmos through Haecker's translations in the Austrian periodical.[120] Now, due, first of all, to the quite remarkable number of translated works already circulating and available in Germany around 1915 (Schrempf's volumes, numerous individual editions, the *Brenner* texts), and due, secondly, to the fact that the First World War and its devastating social, political, economical, moral, and spiritual circumstances had rendered large parts of European culture both attentive and susceptible to what was taken to be Kierkegaard's quest for a radical transformation and renewal from within, it is all but surprising that his popularity spread almost exponentially and quickly reached a climax during those years. As the German theologian Erich Schaeder put it in 1914: "*Kierkegaard erlebt einen neuen Tag.*"[121] Up until then, the situation had appeared rather simple and straightforward, with respect to the history of reception: a couple of catalysts or key figures, often known for and because of their translations (Bärthold, Schrempf, Kassner, Haecker); in addition, some more or less prominent appropriations on a purely personal level, without any considerable amount of implicit, much less of explicit output (Rilke, Lukács, et al.), plus, finally, a rather unimpressive number of secondary sources of highly uneven quality. Almost overnight things changed dramatically, an explosion took place, as it were, both in terms of productive reception, receptive production, and their respective literary output. In what follows I will give a rudimentary survey of both strands, starting with some exemplary instances of a genuinely productive reception.

For mere chronological reasons, I will begin by taking a very brief look at Franz Kafka (1883–1924) as a representative index of Kierkegaard's impact within the German literary world at that time.[122] Whereas Rilke, Schnitzler, Hofmannsthal, and

---

[120]   Just to mention one famous example in passing: Martin Heidegger began subscribing to *Der Brenner* in 1911 (see Malik, *Receiving Kierkegaard*, p. 391). In 1915 Haecker's translation of "At a Graveside" ("An einem Grabe") was published in *Brenner–Jahrbuch*, vol. 5. This was the first translation of the text, and it remained the only one available until 1922, when Haecker had it reprinted in his own edition of Sören Kierkegaard, *Religiöse Reden*, Munich: Wiechmann 1922 (here pp. 173–220). In fact, no other translation appeared between this one and the publication of Heidegger's *Sein und Zeit* (1927). Now, it has been rightly argued that the discourse in question contains "*die existentialontologische Todesphilosophie so vollständig, daß man sich unwillkürlich ihrer erinnert, wenn man in* Sein und Zeit *liest, von Kierkegaards 'erbaulichen' Schriften sei 'philosophisch mehr zu lernen als von den theoretischen'* " (Theunissen and Greve, "Einleitung," p. 70). Thus, it seems highly likely that Heidegger not only knew the discourse well, but, furthermore, that the source of his knowledge was Haecker's rendition of it in *Der Brenner*.

[121]   Erich Schaeder, *Theozentrische Theologie. Eine Untersuchung zur dogmatischen Prinzipienlehre*, vols. 1–2, Leipzig: Deichert 1909–14, vol. 2, 1914, p. 142.

[122]   Kafka's Kierkegaard reception is treated, for instance, in Malik, *Receiving Kierkegaard*, pp. 365ff.; Wolfgang Lange, "Über Kafkas Kierkegaard Lektüre und einige damit zusammenhängende Gegenstände," *Deutsche Vierteljahresschrift für Literaturwissenschaft und Geistesgeschichte*, vol. 60, pp. 286–308; Theunissen and Greve, "Einleitung," pp. 55–6; Peter Tschuggnall, *Das Abraham-Opfer als Glaubensparadox. Bibeltheologischer Befund, literarische Rezeption, Kierkegaards Deutung*, Frankfurt am Main: Peter Lang 1990,

others, whom I have either mentioned already or who could at least be mentioned in the present context,[123] seem to remain this side of a productive reception in any stricter sense, many passages in Kafka's writings are clearly reminiscent of Kierkegaard, even if they do not explicitly or not even deliberately refer to him. Occasionally, though, Kafka directly addresses the Danish genius. Thus, in 1913 he notes (in his journals) that he just received the *Buch des Richters*.[124] He then goes on, saying: "*Wie ich es ahnte, ist sein Fall trotz wesentlicher Unterschiede dem meinen sehr ähnlich zumindest liegt er auf der gleichen Seite der Welt. Er bestätigt mich wie ein Freund.*"[125] Kafka thought he had found a spiritual *alter ego* in Kierkegaard, and indeed, particularly in retrospect many parallels show up in their biography, their attitudes, and their inner conflicts: Kafka's father was of special importance for him; he broke off his engagement (in fact, three times!); he was in a permanent struggle to be or become a Christian; he died not long after his 40th birthday, etc. Around 1918, Kafka was, as is well documented in his letters and journals, deeply immersed in Kierkegaard's pseudonymous works, especially *Either/Or*, *Fear and Trembling*, and *Repetition*—all of which he read in the Schrempf translation.[126] Especially *Fear and Trembling* left a lasting impression, for Kafka repeatedly returned to the book, pondering varying versions of the Abraham story and trying to criticize Kierkegaard's interpretation from a Jewish standpoint. In a letter to Max Brod from 1918 he complained that Kierkegaard payed no attention to the (conflicts of the) ordinary man as possibly being reflected in the Abraham story; instead, the former painted "*den ungeheuren Abraham in die Wolken.*"[127] Three years later Kafka imagined "*an alternative Abraham,*" one who does not make the "leap of faith," for he finds the idea perfectly reasonable that the same God who had once given him everything he could wish for should eventually ask for a return and sacrifice of

---

pp. 65–6. See also Ralph P. Crimmann, *Franz Kafka. Versuch einer kulturphilosophischen Interpretation*, Hamburg: Kovac 2004; Wiebrecht Ries, *Transzendenz als Terror. Eine religionsphilosophische Studie über Franz Kafka*, Heidelberg: Schneider 1977.

[123]   Karl Kraus (1874–1936) belongs in this latter category. Kraus was an enormously important figure in the contemporary German and Austrian literary world before and during the First World War. The *Brenner* circle (especially Dallago and Haecker) obviously adored him. However, although (a) it is highly likely that Kraus knew Kierkegaard; (b) some of the former's famous essays (in his periodical *Die Fackel*) seem like "continuations of the writings of Constantin Constantius" (Malik, *Receiving Kierkegaard*, p. 374); (c) Kraus occasionally quotes from Kierkegaard's critique of the press, but it is unclear, whether and to what extent he actually read and was influenced by Kierkegaard (see also ibid., pp. 368–9; pp. 374–5). Thus, it seems safe to consider him another borderline case between production without reception and unproductive reception.

[124]   What is meant here is the selection of journal entries, translated and edited by Hermann Gottsched under the title *Buch des Richters* (Jena and Leipzig: Diederichs 1905). See Franz Kafka, *Gesammelte Werke in zwölf Bänden*, ed. by Hans-Gerd Koch, Frankfurt am Main: Fischer 1994; vol. 10, p. 191.

[125]   Ibid.

[126]   See, for instance, Kafka, *Werke*, vol. 11, p. 236; p. 299; other references in Malik, *Receiving Kierkegaard*, p. 366.

[127]   Letter to Max Brod, March 1918; quoted from Tschuggnall, *Das Abraham-Paradox*, p. 65.

what he had bestowed upon him in the first place. At the same time, however, such
an Abraham would be a comical figure, something like a Don Quixote, "*der die
Forderung des Opfers sofort, bereitwillig wie ein Kellner zu erfüllen bereit wäre, der
das Opfer aber doch nicht zustandebrächte, weil er von zu Hause nicht fort kann,
er ist unentbehrlich.*"[128] These few references already confirm the assumption that
Kafka's reception of Kierkegaard is of a highly productive and original, if somewhat
eclectic kind, even though it must be admitted that we may hardly speak of a receptive
production in the proper sense of the word, due to the relatively small number of
explicit and unambiguous references to the Danish author. This notwithstanding,
various other passages in Kafka's works bear witness to the fact that Kierkegaard's
writings (*Fear and Trembling*, in particular) functioned as a constant source of
inspiration, indeed of a lifelong passion for the German author.[129]

(7) Ernst Troeltsch (1865–1923) is an excellent example of what I take to be
unproductive reception: a form of reception, in other words, which is based on a
fair amount of knowledge, but leaves no or at best marginal traces in the respective
author's literary output. Before the turn of the century Troeltsch's interest in the
Danish writer had been awakened and had also been kept alive for some time,
probably due to the respect that Høffding and Dilthey had shown (see above).
My guess is that Troeltsch was initially drawn to Kierkegaard, because the latter
obviously called for being read as one of those intellectuals who had developed
a keen sense for the crisis that modern European Christianity underwent and who
had also provided a highly original solution for the crisis. Over the years, however,
Troeltsch showed a growing dissatisfaction with the solution itself, which as being
based on the idea of an historically and socially unmediated decision for the truth
of the Christian paradox by way of faith led to an unacceptable individualism *qua*
pietism in his opinion.[130] In the end, Kierkegaard, belongs, according to Troeltsch,
to the "*Gegend der Sektenreligion*" with its characteristic split between Christianity
and world.[131]

Karl Holl (1866–1926), the great German church historian, had already raised a
similar objection in 1911, claiming that a certain antisocial tendency in the history
of Lutheranism jeopardized the preservation of Luther's own true intentions, to the
effect that "*der Persönlichkeitsgedanke...sich gegen den Gemeinschaftsgedanken
wendete, ihn abschwächte, oder gar, wie dies bei den großen Individualisten, am*

---

[128] Letter to Robert Klopstock, June 1921; quoted after Tschuggnall, *Das Abraham-Opfer*, p. 66.

[129] Worth mentioning are, with respect to *Fear and Trembling*, the Sortini episode from *Das Schloß* (see Kafka, *Werke*, vol. 4, pp. 258–66), plus a number of pertinent parables (see, for instance, ibid., vol. 8, p. 11); some of the aphorisms are also highly illuminating as possible Kierkegaardian echoes; see, for example, Franz Kafka, "Betrachtungen über Sünde, Leid, Hoffnung und den wahren Weg," in *Gedanke und Gewissen. Essays aus 100 Jahren*, ed. by Günther Busch and J. Hellmut Freund, Frankfurt am Main: Fischer 1986, pp. 172–83.

[130] I have tackled Troeltsch's critique of Kierkegaard's purported "ahistoricism" elsewhere in greater detail: see Schulz, "Rezeptionsgeschichtliche Brocken," pp. 402ff.

[131] Ernst Troeltsch, "Ein Apfel vom Baume Kierkegaards [1921]," in *Anfänge der dialektischen Theologie*, ed. by J. Moltmann, vols. 1–2, 4th ed., Munich: Kaiser 1987, vol. 2, 1987, pp. 134–40, here p. 137).

entschiedensten bei Sören Kierkegaard, eingetreten ist, ihn völlig auflöste."[132] At that time the charge of abstract individualism was repeatedly raised against Kierkegaard, often combined with the critique of the latter's alleged ahistoricism,[133] and this (not only, but) especially within those liberal Protestant circles that theologians like Troeltsch and Holl paradigmatically represented.[134]

(8) Generally speaking, theology had always held a special place within the history of (German) Kierkegaard reception, and this from the very beginning.[135] However, the peak of its historical impact was reached in the early 1920s up to the 1930s, in other words, roughly after the First World War. This peak was reached thanks to the ever-growing influence of a German counter-movement to liberal theology: the (inappropriately) so-called dialectical theology and their protagonists Karl Barth, Emil Brunner, Friedrich Gogarten, Rudolf Bultmann, and Paul Tillich.[136] None of these (they all worked as academic theologians at German-speaking, and in Tillich's case at American universities) can be called Kierkegaard scholars in any academic sense of the word. Nor did they publish or write much *about* Kierkegaard.[137] However,

---

[132]   Karl Holl, *Gesammelte Aufsätze zur Kirchengeschichte*, vol. 1, 6th ed., Tübingen: J.C.B. Mohr 1932, p. 479; for a more friendly assessment, see ibid., pp. 24–5. It has only recently come to my attention that Holl not only knew, but also lectured on Kierkegaard, and this as early as 1908: See Matthias Wilke, *Die Kierkegaard Rezeption Emanuel Hirschs. Eine Studie über die Voraussetzungen der Kommunikation christlicher Wahrheit*, Tübingen: J.C.B. Mohr 2005, pp. 51–4.

[133]   I have given a more detailed account of this latter objection (and its main representatives from Georg Brandes to Karl Löwith) in "Rezeptionsgeschichtliche Brocken," pp. 393ff.

[134]   That such a liberal critique occasionally grew to a veritable polemic against Kierkegaard is shown, by among others, Albert Schweitzer. In a letter to Martin Buber (dating from 1936) Schweitzer writes: "*Warum setzen Sie sich des langen und breiten mit diesem armen Psychopathen Kierkegaard auseinander? Das ist doch kein Denker. Ich kann ihn nicht ohne Widerwillen lesen....Er ist erst durch alles, was man über ihn schrieb, zum Denker gemacht worden.*" Schweitzer's remark is reprinted in Martin Buber, *Briefwechsel aus sieben Jahrzehnten*, vols. 1–3, ed. by G. Schaeder, Heidelberg: L. Schneider 1972–75, vol. 2 (1973), pp. 625–6; see also vol. 3, 1975, p. 276.

[135]   For a comparatively early, but surprisingly knowledgeable survey of German theological Kierkegaard reception up to 1921, see Werner Elert, *Der Kampf um das Christentum. Geschichte der Beziehungen zwischen dem evangelischen Christentum in Deutschland und dem allgemeinen Denken seit Schleiermacher und Hegel*, Munich: Beck 1921, pp. 430–4.

[136]   Adorno even goes so far as to maintain "*Die gesamte dialektische Theologie war Kierkegaard Nachfolge in Karl Barth auch die seiner Unbeirrbarkeit.*" See Theodor W. Adorno, "Kierkegaard noch einmal," in *Materialien*, ed. by Theunissen and Greve, pp. 557–75, here p. 560.

[137]   In fact, many passages of their published works can be aptly characterized as an " 'Incognito'-Rezeption." See Martin Kiefhaber, *Christentum als Korrektiv. Untersuchungen zur Theologie Søren Kierkegaards*, Mainz: Grünewald 1997, p. 18; an excellent case in point is Dietrich Bonhoeffer, for instance, see ibid. As to the latter's Kierkegaard reception and/or relation to Kierkegaard's thought in general, see, for instance, Jeffrey B. Kelly, "The Influence of Kierkegaard on Bonhoeffer's Concept of Discipleship," *Irish Theological Quarterly*, vol. 41, 1974, pp. 148–54; David R. Law, "Christian Discipleship in Kierkegaard, Hirsch and Bonhoeffer," *Downside Review*, vol. 120, 2002, pp. 293–306; Heinrich T. Vogel, *Christus*

all or at least most of them exerted a profound influence on generations of students and extra-academic circles alike, and this also and in particular as multiplicators of (their particular reading of) Kierkegaard's thought. They have done so, in particular, through intensive teaching and lecturing, but also—and that is of crucial importance in the present context—through their own writings. These writings bear witness, each in their own way, to a highly productive, if at times also idiosyncratic, appropriation of the Kierkegaardian universe.

Having started pretty much as a theologian in the liberal vein, Karl Barth (1886–1968) later turned his back on his former teachers (Adolf von Harnack, Wilhelm Herrmann, Ernst Troeltsch, and others), when he discovered that most of them, in fact large parts of the German intellectual elite had been brainwashed, as it were, into wholly uncritical and chauvinistic supporters of the "German cause" in 1914. In Barth's view this had hardly happened by accident; on the contrary, the process of modern secularization as a whole seemed to be determined by a fatal mesalliance of politics and religion, or more exactly of Luthern conservatism, on the one hand, and of what Barth perceived as cultural-Protestant arrogance, on the other hand—an arrogance always susceptible to confusing the proper realms of the divine and the human. Not surprisingly, Barth saw in Kierkegaard a most welcome ally in his fight against such a confusion; and not surprisingly either that he favored Kierkegaard's later writings (after 1846) in his hope of finding support for his case.[138]

---

als Vorbild und Versöhner. Eine kritische Studie zum Problem des Verhältnisses von Gesetz und Evangelium im Werke Sören Kierkegaards, Th.D., Humboldt-University Berlin 1968, see especially pp. 297–303.

[138]   As to Barth's Kierkegaard reception see, for instance: Wilhelm Anz, "Die Wirkungsgeschichte Kierkegaards in der dialektischen Theologie und der gleichzeitigen deutschen Philosophie," in *Die Rezeption Søren Kierkegaards in der deutschen und dänischen Philosophie und Theologie*, ed. by H. Anz et al., Copenhagen and Munich: Fink 1983, pp. 11–29, here pp. 13–16; Egon Brinkschmidt, *Sören Kierkegaard und Karl Barth*, Neukirchen–Vluyn: Neukirchener 1971; Hermann Deuser, *Dialektische Theologie. Studien zu Adornos Metaphysik und zum Spätwerk Kierkegaards*, Munich and Mainz: Grünewald 1980, pp. 19–32; Anders Gemmer and August Messer, *Sören Kierkegaard und Karl Barth*, Stuttgart: Strecker & Schröder 1925; Wolfdietrich von Kloeden, "Das Kierkegaard Bild Karl Barths in seinen Briefen der 'Zwanziger Jahre.' Streiflichter aus der Karl Barth-Gesamtausgabe," *Kierkegaardiana*, vol. 12, 1982, pp. 93–102; Alastair McKinnon, "Barths Verhältnis zu Kierkegaard," *Evangelische Theologie*, vol. 30, 1970, pp. 57–69; Wolfhart Pannenberg, *Problemgeschichte der neueren evangelischen Theologie in Deutschland. Von Schleiermacher bis zu Barth und Tillich*, Göttingen: Vandenhoeck & Ruprecht 1997, pp. 180–7; Ruttenbeck, *Sören Kierkegaard*, pp. 303–9; Schulz, "Rezeptionsgeschichtliche Brocken," pp. 404ff.; Niels-Henning Søe, "Karl Barth," in *The Legacy and Interpretation*, pp. 224–37. Barth himself briefly (though not very informatively) commented on his own Kierkegaard reception in retrospect, see "Dank und Referenz," *Evangelische Theologie*, vol. 23, 1963, pp. 337–42. It is also interesting to note that in his famous *Die protestantische Theologie im 19. Jahrhundert. Ihre Vorgeschichte und ihre Geschichte* (4th ed., Zurich: Theologischer Verlag 1981), Kierkegaard is completely ignored. Maybe Barth had a sense for the inappropriateness of incorporating Kierkegaard in a historical survey that saw him in the company of purely academic theologians.

Barth had started to read Kierkegaard's *Augenblicksschriften* as early as 1909, but apparently remained unimpressed at first. While working on the second edition of his famous *Römerbrief*,[139] he returned to them. In addition, he read Kierkegaard's journals (in Gottsched's selected edition from 1905) plus the *Fragments*, accompanied by some later pseudonymous and non-pseudonymous writings. Apart from also being stimulated by Franz Overbeck,[140] his interest in the Danish writer was in all probability reawakened by his friend Eduard Thurneysen.[141] Now, instead of actually deserving the label "dialectic" (the use of the term was actually not based on any self-attribution on the part of the respective theological movement) as a characteristic of its epistemological and/or ontological preferences, the anti-liberal theology of the *Römerbrief* is more or less "diastatic" in nature. As such, it emphasizes, as Barth puts it in his famous preface, "*das, was Kierkegaard den 'unendlichen qualitativen Unterschied' von Zeit und Ewigkeit genannt hat.*"[142] As opposed to what many scholars assume, Barth does not refer to the *Postscript* here, however, but rather—as is often the case in the *Römerbrief*—to *Training in Christianity*, a text, which apart from *Works of Love* was his favorite source of reference at this point.[143] Barth's highly productive, if at times also eclectic use of Kierkegaardian sources and ideas throughout the central chapters of the book would deserve a separate treatment; suffice it to say that, in particular, his polemic against religion as a purely human and as such sinful enterprise and his critique of mundane ethics, independent of revelation, are subterraneously breathing, as it were, the spirit of (the late) Kierkegaard.[144] Gradually, however, Barth's overall affirmative attitude towards Kierkegaard, as it is found in his writings of the early 1920s, is counterbalanced by and substituted with a somewhat more critical attitude later. Here Barth raises objections against what he takes to be Kierkegaard's crypto-pietistical theology of faith, which in his opinion favors the idea of a "*legitimes Privatchristentum.*"[145] In addition, he criticizes Kierkegaard's "*negative Dialektik*"[146] of the stages, taken as a process of ever increasing inwardness. According to Barth, this idea includes and promotes a transfiguration of human existence and falls under the verdict of natural theology, which, as such, inadvertently tends to invoke the principle of *Werkgerechtigkeit*.

(9) Emil Brunner (1889–1966), professor of Systematic Theology at the University of Zurich, was Barth's part-time companion and ally in his fight for a new

---

[139]   See Karl Barth, *Der Römerbrief,* 12th reprint of the second ed. from 1922, Zurich: Theologischer Verlag 1978.
[140]   See Barth, *Der Römerbrief,* p. VII; also Pannenberg, *Problemgeschichte,* p. 180.
[141]   For pertinent references from Barth's correspondence with Thurneysen, see Kloeden, "Einfluß und Bedeutung," pp. 61–2.
[142]   Barth, *Der Römerbrief,* p. XIII.
[143]   See ibid., p. 73; p. 262; p. 424 (references to *Practice in Christianity*) and ibid., p. 428 and p. 481 (references to *Works of Love*; in both cases Barth is using the Schrempf edition); see also Schulz, "Rezeptionsgeschichtliche Nachschrift," p. 353.
[144]   See, Barth, *Der Römerbrief,* pp. 211–53; pp. 410–510.
[145]   Karl Barth, *Die Kirchliche Dogmatik,* vol. 4.1, Zollikon and Zurich: Evangelischer Verlag 1953, p. 769.
[146]   Anz, "Die Wirkungsgeschichte," p. 16.

way of doing theology. In 1934, however, the two drifted apart and into different theological directions, due to their then famous disputes about "nature and grace" and the viability and/or possibility of a natural theology.[147] In contrast to Barth, Brunner occasionally also wrote and published papers and essays directly devoted to Kierkegaard,[148] and in general his overall style of thinking was influenced by the latter to a much greater degree than is the case with his former "brother in arms."[149]

Regarding Kierkegaard's theological, philosophical, and historical significance, Brunner declares that he must be considered a neighbor and direct successor of Kant. Both thinkers are said to have the same starting-point and to deal with the same fundamental problem: *"[d]ie Qualität: Ernst, oder...[d]ie Gottesfurcht, der unbestechliche Sinn für das, was Kierkegaard die qualitative Differenz zwischen Gott und Mensch nennt."*[150] The will to face and to do justice (both in theory and in practice) to the insurmountable boundary or gap between God and man, is what Kant and Kierkegaard have in common: *"[A]n dieser Grenze zu wachen, das ist der eigentümliche Gehalt...der kritischen Philosophie,"*[151] and it is also the pivot of Kierkegaard's existential dialectics. The only, yet also decisive difference between the two thinkers lies, according to Brunner, in Kant's ultimate (and all but accidental) optimism as a philosopher and as a child of the Enlightenment. In contrast to Kierkegaard, he proved unable to subscribe to the radical and essentially paradoxical claim that *"das wesentliche Merkmal der menschlichen Existenz die Schuld sei,"*[152] and, furthermore, that under this presupposition the possibility of regaining full integrity as a human being does not rest within human autonomy, but can only come from outside—from God. Perhaps Kant, just like Kierkegaard, would have been able and willing to realize that in effect an act of God, thus conceived, amounts to nothing less but a *"Bruch mit der Immanenz, mit dem Denkmöglichen,"*[153] and that its actuality and/or possibility (namely, as a divine revelation) can neither be refuted nor asserted on purely philosophical grounds. In any case, in contrast to his Danish successor, Kant proved unable to admit of such a possibility.

This early statement already gathers, in a nutshell, the chief ingredients of Brunner's later Kierkegaard reading. Moreover, it points to certain facets of his theological project as a whole. This project aims at a so-called "eristic" theology, which, as such,

---

[147] The dispute is nicely documented and analyzed in Christof Gestrich, *Neuzeitliches Denken und die Spaltung der dialektischen Theologie*, Tübingen: J.C.B. Mohr 1977, pp. 172–206.

[148] See, for instance, Emil Brunner, "Das Grundproblem der Philosophie bei Kant und Kierkegaard," in *Sören Kierkegaard*, ed. by Heinz-Horst Schrey, Darmstadt: Wissenschaftliche Buchgesellschaft 1971, pp. 1–18 [1924]; "Die Botschaft Sören Kierkegaards," in *Ein offenes Wort. Vorträge und Aufsätze 1917–1962*, ed. by Emil Brunner-Stiftung, Zurich: Theologischer Verlag 1981, pp. 209–26 [1930].

[149] Brunner's Kierkegaard reception is treated in Kloeden, "Einfluß und Bedeutung," pp. 68–75; Ruttenbeck, *Sören Kierkegaard*, pp. 314–18; Schulz, "Rezeptionsgeschichtliche Brocken," pp. 406–7; Theunissen and Greve, "Einleitung," pp. 58ff.

[150] Brunner, "Das Grundproblem," pp. 3–4.

[151] Ibid., p. 4.

[152] Ibid., p. 15.

[153] Ibid., p. 17.

consists of both anthropological or philosophical and strictly theological or dogmatical elements. Its major "point of contact" (*Anknüpfungspunkt*) is an anthropologically significant phenomenon (here, despair), the analysis of which proceeds maieutically. As such, it tries to impose upon its addressee—the "natural consciousness," *ex hypothesi* inflicted by despair—an awareness of the inevitability of assessing the truth or untruth of the theological diagnosis, going along with the analysis, about the true cause and cure of the despair in question: namely, sin and redemption. This being said, it does not come as a surprise that Brunner, contrary to Barth, tended to favor Kierkegaard's "middle works," especially the pseudonymous ones up to 1849, over against the late writings from the *Kirkekamp* period. Nor does his complaint come unexpected that in Barth the "*Problem der Aneignung, das bei Kierkegaard zugestandenermaßen im Mittelpunkt steht...kaum vorkommt.*"[154] After his dispute with Barth, Brunner successively unfolded his theological program in the larger works from the 1930s and 1940s: first, in his voluminous anthropology, a book which in Brunner's own words is deeply indebted to and rooted in the "*anthropologischen Arbeit Kierkegaards*";[155] secondly, and from a more epistemological perspective, in *Offenbarung und Vernunft* (1941). Kierkegaard's impact and formative role with regard to program, method, and content on Brunner's theology notwithstanding, it is worth noting also that he occasionally found it necessary to criticize the Danish thinker.[156]

(10) It is obvious that Rudolf Bultmann (1884–1976) was, and remained, much more steeped in the liberal tradition that he grew up with (especially the theology of his former teacher Wilhelm Herrmann) than, say, Barth. To a certain extent this is true also of his original and highly productive appropriation of Kierkegaard—an appropriation, which Barth, for this very reason, could approve of just as little as of Bultmann's theology in general. However, even though it must be admitted that Bultmann's way of invoking Kierkegaardian ideas and resources clearly belonged to the "incognito" type,[157] it can hardly be denied that, compared to the rest of his fellow

---

[154]   Emil Brunner, *Dogmatik*, 3rd ed., vols. 1–3, Zürich and Stuttgart: Zwingli-Verlag 1960, vol. 3, p. 246.

[155]   Emil Brunner, *Der Mensch im Widerspruch, Die christliche Lehre vom wahren und vom wirklichen Menschen*, Zurich: Zwingli-Verlag 1937, p. 18.

[156]   Compare, for instance, Brunner's critique of Kierkegaard's "reductionist" approach to the problem of the so-called historical Jesus in the *Fragments* (see *SKS* 4, 300 / *PF*, 104), in *Offenbarung und Vernunft. Die Lehre von der christlichen Glaubenserkenntnis*, Zurich: Zwingli-Verlag 1941, p. 131; see also his *Dogmatik*, vol. 1, Zurich and Stuttgart: Zwingli-Verlag 1960, p. 45.

[157]   Kierkegaard and his writings are explicitly referred to in very few places; his writings are referred to almost without exception by quoting the respective volume of the Schrempf edition; see, in particular, Rudolf Bultmann, *Das Evangelium des Johannes*, 10th ed., Göttingen: Vandenhoeck & Ruprecht 1962, p. 46; p. 148; p. 431 (references to *Fragments*); p. 94; p. 161; p. 275; p. 331; p. 469 (*Training in Christianity*); pp. 449–50 (*Christian Discourses*); p. 405 (*Works of Love*). In *Geschichte und Eschatologie* (3rd ed., Tübingen: J.C.B. Mohr 1979), Kierkegaard is mentioned only once (p. 87); in *Theologie des Neuen Testaments* (Tübingen: J.C.B. Mohr 1948) and *Geschichte der synoptischen Tradition* (Göttingen: Vandenhoeck & Ruprecht 1921) Kierkegaard is completely absent.

"dialectical theologians," he integrated these resources into his own exegetical and sytematical thinking in a much more substantial and overall consistent way.[158]

We do not know for sure when exactly Bultmann stumbled upon Kierkegaard for the first time; the fact is that as early as 1923 he started cooperating with Martin Heidegger who had just accepted a professorate at the University of Marburg, where Bultmann also taught, and who was deeply influenced by Kierkegaard at that time. It is also a fact that in a letter to Karl Barth dating from December 10, 1926, Bultmann explained to the latter the guiding principles and intentions of his own recently published Jesus book,[159] and this by explicitly drawing on the "Incognito" Christology of the *Fragments*.[160] Finally, in 1927 Bultmann published an extensive review of a book written by Emanuel Hirsch,[161] in which he stated as his (and also Hirsch's) primary intention, "*die Theologie aus den Irrwegen des Idealismus... und der Mystik...heraus[zu]führen und dabei die theologische Arbeit Kierkegaards fruchtbar [zu] machen.*"[162] There can be no doubt that Bultmann realized this intention throughout his writings in the years to come and did so by making use of resources provided by the *Fragments* and *Works of Love*, in particular.[163]

Space does not allow me to adequately account for the wealth of aspects and nuances in Bultmann's highly productive Kierkegaard appropriation. However, I would like to provide at least a couple of keywords covering and recapitulating some of Bultmann's main intentions, inasmuch as they reflect a Kierkegaardian impact. Among those, worth mentioning are the quest to appropriate the Christian faith under the conditions of modernity; the restructuring of biblical exegesis and hermeneutics in terms of focusing on the opposition of Greek ontology and Christian "existentialism"; the transformation of the Socratic search for the good into the Christian quest for human authenticity and self-transparency; the analysis of the particular temporality of the believer's "eschatological existence" in his or her

---

[158] Bultmann's Kierkegaard reception is discussed by, among others, Anz, "Zur Wirkungsgeschichte Kierkegaards," pp. 17–20; Cora Bartels, *Kierkegaard receptus. Die theologiegeschichtliche Bedeutung der Kierkegaard Rezeption Rudolf Bultmanns*, Göttingen: Vandenhoeck & Ruprecht 2008; Jørgen K. Bukdahl, "Bultmann," in *The Legacy and Interpretation*, pp. 238–42; Hermann Fischer, *Die Christologie des Paradoxes. Zur Herkunft und Bedeutung des Christusverständnisses Sören Kierkegaards*, Göttingen: Vandenhoeck & Ruprecht 1970, pp. 96–111; Enno Rudolph, "Glauben und Wissen. Kierkegaard zwischen Kant und Bultmann," in *Die Rezeption Sören Kierkegaards*, pp. 152–70; Schulz, "Rezeptionsgeschichtliche Brocken," pp. 407–11; H.C. Wolf, *Kierkegaard and Bultmann: The Quest of the Historical Jesus*, Minneapolis: Augsburg 1965.
[159] Rudolf Bultmann, *Jesus*, 15th ed., Tübingen: J.C.B. Mohr 1951 [1926].
[160] The letter is reprinted in *Karl Barth—Rudolf Bultmann. Briefwechsel 1922–1966*, ed. by Bernd Jaspert, Zurich: Evangelischer Verlag 1971, pp. 63ff.
[161] Emanuel Hirsch, *Jesus Christus der Herr. Theologische Vorlesungen*, Göttingen: Vandenhoeck & Ruprecht 1926.
[162] Rudolf Bultmann, *Glauben und Verstehen*, vols. 1–4, 7th ed., Tübingen: J.C.B. Mohr 1972, vol. 1 p. 85.
[163] As to the function and significance of the *Fragments* for Bultmann's theology in general and his Kierkegaard reception in particular, see, for instance, Anz, "Zur Wirkungsgeschichte Kierkegaards," pp. 17–20; Schulz, "Rezeptionsgeschichtliche Brocken," pp. 408–11.

instantaneous transgression to a new self-understanding before God; the insistence on the paradoxical nature of such transgression as a result of a divine revelation; the critique of the mythical (in Climacus' terms, metaphysical) self-understanding of existence as indicating a state of offense in relation to Christianity.

Most of these keywords, plus the corresponding themes, ideas, and theories crop up in almost any given place throughout Bultmann's published work. In terms of their significance for the history of reception none of them is surpassed, however, by Bultmann's major accomplishment: a productive appropriation and modification of Kierkegaard's infamous doctrine of the Incarnation as a "world-historical *nota bene*," confessed and preached by the apostles and, as such, deemed as sufficient for the possibility of faith in the succeeding generations of followers.[164] To begin with, Bultmann's primary—and one is tempted to add, his one and only—question is, "*[wie] aus dem Verkündiger Jesus der Verkündigte Jesus Christus wird.*"[165] This is, first of all, a historical question and thus it belongs to the domain of biblical exegesis. However, Bultmann's proper interest is epistemic in nature. He wants to know, "*wie ein geschichtliches Ereignis das eschatologische sein und als solches heute begegnen kann.*"[166] More specifically, he not only and primarily tries to understand how it was possible, historically and/or psychologically, that the early Christians bestowed upon Jesus of Nazareth the attribute "messiah"; rather, he wants to know, how it is possible in principal that this ascription can in fact be true and thus refer to an event of eschatological (eternal, unsurpassable, and world-changing) significance. Now, in my opinion Bultmann's epistemic question is nothing but a reformulation of Climacus' motto-question from the *Fragments*: "Can a historical point of departure be given for an eternal consciousness...?"[167] It should not be disregarded, however, that both the respective background of the question and the respective answer provided by the two authors are quite different. The background of Bultmann's question is not to be located in the (post-)Hegelian debate about the temporal/historical in its relation to eternal; rather, its point of departure is the purely historical or exegetical insight that in all probability Jesus did not possess any messianic self-consciousness.[168] In addition

---

[164]   See *SKS* 4, 300 / *PF*, 104: "Even if the contemporary generation had not left anything behind except these words, 'We have believed that in such and such a year the god appeared in the humble form of a servant, lived and taught among us, and then died'—this is more than enough. The contemporary generation would have done what is needful, for this little announcement, this world-historical *nota bene*, is enough to become an occasion for someone who comes later, and the most prolix report can never in all eternity become more for the person who comes later."

[165]   Bultmann, *Briefwechsel*, p. 63.

[166]   This is H. Conzelmann's formulation, affirmatively quoted by Bultmann in his famous article "Das Verhältnis der urchristlichen Christusbotschaft zum historischen Jesus." The article was originally published in 1960; I quote from the reprinted version, in Rudolf Bultmann, *Exegetica*, ed. by Erich Dinkler, Tübingen: J.C.B. Mohr 1967, pp. 445–69; the quotation is from p. 466.

[167]   *SKS* 4, 213 / *PF*, 1.

[168]   This claim is already defended at length in Bultmann's *Jesus*; it is closely related to the insight that the search for the so-called "historical Jesus," a search that caused much ink to be spilled in the nineteenth century, has largely failed.

to the varying context and background of the question, the respective answers move in a different direction, also. According to Climacus, the immediate contemporaries' act of confessing and of preaching Jesus as Christ is at any rate *sufficient* for faith to be possible; apart from referring to the actual existence of Jesus, he leaves open the question as to its *necessary* conditions, however. This is where Bultmann steps in. He suggests that the *kerygma*, that is, the particular moment and event, in which the act of preaching Jesus as Christ actually meets "the eyes and ears of faith" in the listener, is in fact the missing link. Given that Jesus did *not* actually conceive of himself as the promised Messiah, the act of bestowing this title upon him by those who became Christians precisely by performing this act can always, yet also only, be justified (and the respective attribution be true) if these Christians are trustworthy. *Are* they trustworthy? Bultmann's answer is yes. And yet, he knows, and is honest enough to admit, that the plausibility of his suggestion depends on the possibility that (a) the *kerygma* is in itself part and parcel of the very eschatological event that it bears witness to; (b) there is no belief in Christ without belief in the Church;[169] (c) the belief in the existence of Jesus is a necessary condition, the belief in certain details of his biography (his acting and teaching, in particular) merely an accidental condition for faith in Christ to be possible. Thus, on the one hand, Bultmann and Climacus are in full agreement: it is perfectly reasonable to assume that in the future, or at least in principle, we might "know" (within the limits of historical probability) a lot more about Jesus than we actually do right now; however, this additional "knowledge" is accidental at best, when it comes to determining the conditions of faith in Christ to be possible. This basic agreement notwithstanding, Bultmann's additional suggestion, though obviously inspired by Climacus, goes much further than the one Climacus himself argued for: the preaching of the Church is sufficient *and* necessary for the realization of the possibility in question; thus it participates in the very eschatological event that it continuously testifies to.

(11) A survey treating productive adaptations of Kierkegaard in some (Protestant) theologians during and after the First World War would not be complete without bringing Paul Tillich's (1886–1965) contribution into focus. Tillich's Kierkegaard reception is perhaps less sophisticated than Bultmann's; however, it is also a lot easier to localize, even in those places, where the references are of the purely implicit, perhaps even material type.[170] Interestingly enough, almost all explicit references (plus some more implicit ones) are to be found in the writings of the "American" Tillich, in other words, in his publications after 1933, when political circumstances had forced him to emigrate.[171] This notwithstanding, Tillich's pertinent utterances

---

169   See, for instance, Bultmann, "Das Verhältnis," p. 468.

170   As to Tillich's Kierkegaard reception, see, for instance, Fischer, *Die Christologie des Paradoxes*, pp. 111–29; Kjeld Holm, "Lidenskab og Livsmod," *Kierkegaardiana*, vol. 14, 1988, pp. 29–37; Kloeden, "Einfluß und Bedeutung," pp. 76–83; Schulz, "Rezeptionsgeschichtliche Brocken," pp. 411ff.

171   See Paul Tillich, *Gesammelte Werke*, vols. 1–14, ed. by Renate Albrecht, Stuttgart: Evangelisches Verlagswerk 1959–75 (some of the volumes were published in Berlin and New York: Walter de Gruyter), vol. 4 (1961), pp. 145–57 [1944]; vol. 11 (1976), pp. 96–106 [1952]; vol. 12 (1971), pp. 327–32 [1942]; see also *Systematische Theologie*, trans. by Renate Albrecht et al., vols. 1–2, 8ᵗʰ ed., Stuttgart: Evangelisches Verlagswerk 1984, vol. 2,

should not be completely omitted from the present survey. For one thing, there are distinctive traces of a Kierkegaardian impact to be found in Tillich's earlier works up to 1933; for another thing, these traces testify to the productive nature of his reception; finally, there is a striking continuity in his view of the Danish thinker—this view seems to have evolved and found its definite shape and contours already in his early German works.

Tillich discovered and was immediately captivated by Kierkegaard as early as 1905, while he was still a theology student at the University of Halle.[172] He later recalls that it "was this combination of intense piety which went into the depths of human existence and the philosophical greatness which he [sc. Kierkegaard] had received from Hegel that made him so important for us."[173] Traces of the "philosophical greatness," which impressed Tillich so much, found their way into the latter's own thinking, as is manifest in his earlier published work. Thus, in 1959 Tillich admitted in retrospect that next to Nietzsche and the German *Lebensphilosophie* it had been (Kierkegaard's) *Existenzphilosophie*, in particular, in which he discovered a most welcome inspiration for and a confirmation of his "existential" interpretation of Schelling's philosophy, as he defended it in his (second) doctoral dissertation from 1912.[174]

Even more important is the reflection of Kierkegaard's concept of the moment (as a unity of the eternal and the temporal within time[175]) in Tillich's notion of *kairos* as a symbol for the biblical "completion of time" (see Galatians 4:4), defined *"als ein Moment, in dem das Ewige in das Zeitliche einbricht, dieses erschüttert und umwendet und eine Krisis schafft im tiefsten Grunde der menschlichen Existenz."*[176] Closely connected with the idea of crisis and its function for theology is the debate (between Tillich, Karl Barth, and Friedrich Gogarten) about the idea and theological function of the *paradox*.[177] Here the main (namely epistemological) point at issue is the relation between the unconditional and the conditional. More exactly, the question is whether the essence of the absolute or unconditional can be known, believed and adequately expressed undialectically, that is, with no tinge of an entity belonging to the ontological realm of the merely conditional or relative. Tillich denies such a possibility; moreover, he concludes that the actual presence of the unconditional

---

pp. 30ff. [1957]; *A History of Christian Thought. From its Judaic and Hellenistic Origins to Existentialism*, ed. by Carl E. Braaten, 2nd ed., New York: Simon & Schuster 1968, pp. 458–76 [1963].

[172]   See Tillich, *A History*, p. 458; also *Gesammelte Werke*, vol. 13, p. 24.

[173]   Tillich, *A History*, p. 459.

[174]   See *Mystik und Schuldbewußtsein in Schellings philosophischer Entwicklung* (1912), in *Gesammelte Werke*, vol. 1, pp. 11–108; the reference to Nietzsche and the philosophy of existence is from a later preface, see ibid., p. 9. See also Kloeden, "Einfluß und Bedeutung," pp. 76–7.

[175]   See, for instance, *SKS* 4, 384–96 / *CA*, 81–93. *SKS* 4, 222 / *PF*, 13. *SKS* 4, 226 / *PF*, 18.

[176]   Tillich, *Gesammelte Werke*, vol. 6, p. 22. It must be added, though, that this "completion" takes on a more or less social utopian outlook in Tillich's further considerations. See ibid., pp. 9–28; also ibid., pp. 29–41.

[177]   The debate took place in 1923–24 and is documented in Tillich, *Gesammelte Werke*, vol. 7, pp. 216–46.

takes on, in an ever-repeating *kairos*, the form of a crisis in relation to all (as such inevitably imperfect) human conceptions and expressions of it. Thus conceived, the unconditional can also exclusively be actualized in paradoxical form: our relation to something *as* the unconditional is *in fact* a relation to the latter only if it is

> *[ein] durch das ständige radikale Nein hindurchgehendes Verhältnis zum Unbedingten.... Und gerade diejenigen Dinge und Worte, die das Paradox ausdrücken sollen, wie Religion und Bibel, Christus und Gott—und gerade Gott—sind in dauernder Gefahr, diesen götzenhaft-undialektischen Charakter zu erhalten, gegenständlich und damit bedingt zu werden.*[178]

Hence, Tillich finds it necessary at this point to take sides with "*Kierkegaard und Pascal...Luther und Augustin...Johannes und Paulus.*"[179]

By contrast, (the early) Tillich occasionally also criticized Kierkegaard, in particular the doctrine of contemporaneity:[180] "*Diejenige Theologie, die Kierkegaards Gedanken der Gleichzeitigkeit verkündet, in die wir mit Christus treten müssen, übersieht für gewöhnlich, daß die Möglichkeit dazu nur durch die historische Kontinuität gegeben ist.*"[181] Tillich raises a familiar objection here, basically the same one that we have encountered in Brunner already.[182] For any event to count as revelatory, it must, subjectively speaking (that is, with regard to the conduct of its addressee), entail a correlation between the interpretation of it as an historical fact via historical understanding and the interpretation of it as revelatory via faith. Now, although presupposing some kind of historical continuity between the understanding subject and its object (for otherwise no "understanding" in the proper sense would be possible), historical understanding itself remains this side of contemporaneity; by contrast, faith becomes truly contemporary with its object. However, just as faith presupposes historical understanding and historical understanding presupposes some kind of historical continuity, so faith also presupposes some kind of historical continuity. From this it follows, when applied to the the relation between (the possibility of) Christian faith and contemporaneity, "*dass ohne die* Konkretheit *des neutestamentlichen Bildes das Neue Sein [in Christus] eine leere Abstraktion wäre.*"[183] In order actually to be able to become Christ's contemporary, one must

---

[178]　Ibid., pp. 216–17.

[179]　Ibid., p. 216. Tillich's later doctrine of paradox defines the latter as an expression "*für eine neue Wirklichkeit*" (*Systematische Theologie*, p. 102), more specifically as the "Erscheinung des Neuen Seins [sc. in Jesus Christ] *unter den Bedingungen der Existenz, sie richtend und überwindend*" (ibid.); as to the context see *Systematische Theologie*, pp. 100ff.; also Schulz, "Rezeptionsgeschichtliche Brocken," pp. 411ff.

[180]　See, for instance, *SKS* 4, 267ff. and 285–6. / *PF*, 66ff. and 86ff.

[181]　Paul Tillich, *Dogmatik. Marburger Vorlesung von 1925*, ed. by Werner Schüßler, Düsseldorf: Patmos 1986, p. 259.

[182]　It has frequently been repeated later also, especially within theology; see, for instance, the particularly subtle version of the objection, in Carl Heinz Ratschow, *Der angefochtene Glaube. Anfangs- und Grundprobleme der Dogmatik*, 2nd ed., Gütersloh 1960, pp. 121–31.

[183]　Tillich, *Systematische Theologie*, p. 125.

understand and know more about him than the abstract claim *"daß das Neue Sein erschienen ist."*[184]

Tillich's later productive adaptions of Kierkegaardian resources can only be of marginal concern in the present context since they properly belong to his "American" phase and are, without exception, not published before 1940. I just mention in passing three major points of reference, all of which are closely connected to each other: first, the notion of existence (as an individual actualization of essential being under the self-alienating conditions of finitude[185]); secondly, the concept of anxiety (as a self-experience of human finitude, which as such has to be distinguished from mere fright[186]); finally, the doctrine of the Fall (as a symbol both for the universal and the individual human transition from essence to existence[187]).

(12) Tillich's one-time friend Emanuel Hirsch (1888–1972) is our final theological writer for examination, before we move on to some chief proponents of productive reception in contemporary philosophy. Hirsch had come across (the late) Kierkegaard before 1914 as a young student; he then heard his teacher Karl Holl lecture on him and, after delivering some reviews and scattered translations, eventually set out to write his first Kierkegaard piece in 1926.[188] The following years and decades saw him translating and publishing extensively in the field.[189] Two accomplishments stand out in this respect as the most remarkable fruits of Hirsch's life-long dedication to the Danish thinker: first, his magisterial *Kierkegaard Studien* (1930–33), secondly his translation and edition of Kierkegaard's *Gesammelte Werke* (1950–69)—a post-war project that Hirsch (who by then had almost completely gone blind) took up after prematurely retiring from his professorate at the University of Göttingen.

Not only, but also within the domain of Kierkegaard research Hirsch appears as a transitional figure, and this at least in three respects—reception-historically, typologically and politically. Let me briefly tackle the latter two aspects in turn (the historical refers to Hirsch's role in establishing an "academic" Kierkegaard appropriation in post-war Germany and will be dealt with later). Typologically speaking, Hirsch's approach lends itself to being categorized as a paradigm of the borderline type (here between receptive production and productive reception) since he both wrote extensively on Kierkegaard and picked up essential ideas from him which he reused and reworked for his own theological purposes.[190]

[184] Ibid.
[185] See Tillich, *Gesammelte Werke*, vol. 4, pp. 148ff.; *Systematische Theologie*, pp. 25–30.
[186] Tillich, *Gesammelte Werke*, vol. 11, pp. 35–8; *A History*, pp. 462–3.
[187] Tillich, *Systematische Theologie*, pp. 35ff.
[188] See Emanuel Hirsch, *Wege zu Kierkegaard*, Berlin: Die Spur 1968, p. 125. The text from 1926 ("Die Stellung von Kierkegaards Entweder-Oder in der Literatur-und Geistesgeschichte") is published here for the first time, see ibid., pp. 9–19.
[189] Emanuel Hirsch, *Kierkegaard Studien*, Gütersloh: Bertelsmann 1930–33; *Geschichte der neuern evangelischen Theologie im Zusammenhang mit der allgemeinen Bewegung des europäischen Denkens*, vols. 1–5, Gütersloh: Bertelsmann 1949–59, vol. 5 (1959), pp. 433–9; *Wege zu Kierkegaard*; *Gesammelte Werke. Kierkegaard Studien*, vol. 3: *Aufsätze und Vorträge 1926 bis 1967*, ed. by Hans M. Müller, Waltrop: Spenner 2006.
[190] Elsewhere I have tried to account for and defend the hermeneutical value of the borderline category—its categorical or referential vagueness notwithstanding: see Schulz,

To begin with, Kierkegaard clearly functioned for Hirsch as a third and perhaps as his most important *spiritus rector*—in addition, namely, to Luther and J.G. Fichte. Hence it does not come as a surprise that he argued, in terms of his overall receptive attitude, that Kierkegaard's authorship as a whole culminated in the attempt to solve a problem that was historically as well as systematically imposed upon and handed down to him already by Luther and modern Protestantism (including Pietism), on the one hand, and German idealism (especially Hegel and Schleiermacher), on the other hand. The problem can be restated as a question: is it possible to be and remain a Christian under the conditions of modernity, that is, within the restraints of a purely "human consciousness of truth" (*humanes Wahrheitsbewusstsein*) in its inexorable quest for honesty and certainty? As an affirmative answer to the question Kierkegaard suggests and provides, according to Hirsch, a theory of the "existing subject," in which the genuinely Christian expression of subjectivity (faith as a suspension of sin consciousness) appears as a genetically more profound and epistemically more complete and perfect variant of the human quest for and experience of certainty and salvation, as it is paradigmatically instantiated in the ethico-religiously essential phenomenon of conscience.

It is hardly surprising that Hirsch, who, in seeking to defend his hermeneutical approach, unanimously takes sides with Kierkegaard's pseudonymous authorship up to the *Postscript*, while simultaneously downplaying the relevance and questioning the viability of the late(r) works. He takes great pains to dispel any suspicion of an unbridgeable gap in Kierkegaard between Religiousness A and B and, consequently, between human and Christian existence. A case in point is Hirsch's reading of the *Fragments*, in which he suggests that Kierkegaard established the "*Grundlinien einer neuen Apologetik.*"[191] Emanuel Hirsch justifies his claim by calling attention to the fact that essential Kierkegaardian categories (e.g., the moment, paradox, etc.) are used in a double, namely, purely human and genuinely Christian sense

"Die theologische Rezeption," p. 228 (especially note 20). Other classical (German) instances of borderline cases include Jaspers and Adorno (see below). As to Hirsch's Kierkegaard reception in particular, see, for instance, Martin Kiefhaber, *Christentum als Korrektiv. Untersuchungen zur Theologie Søren Kierkegaards*, Mainz: Grünewald 1997, pp. 16–21 and 27–30; von Kloeden, "Einfluß und Bedeutung," pp. 64ff.; Klaus-Michael Kodalle, *Die Eroberung des Nutzlosen. Kritik des Wunschdenkens und die Zweckrationalität im Anschluß an Kierkegaard*, Paderborn: Schöningh 1988, pp. 270–80; Schulz, "Die theologische Rezeption," pp. 228–9; Schulz, "Rezeptionsgeschichtliche Brocken," pp. 414–17; Schulz, "Rezeptionsgeschichtliche Nachschrift," pp. 371–4. The most extensive treatment to date is Matthias Wilke, *Die Kierkegaard Rezeption Emanuel Hirschs. Eine Studie über die Voraussetzungen der Kommunikation christlicher Wahrheit*, Tübingen: Mohr 2005. Summing up his historical inquiry Wilke notes (p. 4), "*daß sich Hirsch sein [Kierkegaard]Bild von 1908 bis 1933 beständig weiter ausmalt und im Zuge dessen einzelne Konturen modifiziert. Nach 1933 jedoch...ändert er es nicht mehr.*"
[191]   Hirsch, *Kierkegaard Studien*, p. 671.

throughout the book[192]—and not only here.[193] This observation is taken to support
the hypothesis that Kierkegaard's major achievement lies in the incessant and
apologetically promising "*Herausarbeiten einer aller Scheidung zum Trotz sich
enthüllenden Wahlverwandtschaft des Humanen und des Christlichen,*"[194] a kinship,
which in turn allows Christianity to appear as a "*vertiefende Vollendung der humanen
Existenz.*"[195]

   The notion of *humanes Wahrheitsbewusstsein* is for Hirsch "*[der] grundlegende
Begriff seines eigenen Wirklichkeitsverständnisses.*"[196] In spelling out its historical,
epistemological, ethical, and theological implications, he primarily seeks to
address the pressing issue, if and to what extent the "Christian truth" can still be
communicated under the conditions and restraints of modernity. In trying to solve
the issue, he firmly believes, on the one hand, that he is in full agreement with
Kierkegaard; moreover, he is writing with the explicit intention in mind of helping
the reader to reach a better understanding of the latter. On the other hand, Hirsch
productively appropriates the Kierkegaardian framework in such a way as to put his
own account of the presuppositions for adequately and convincingly communicating
the Christian truth on the agenda—an account, which in part deliberately deviates
from the one Kierkegaard had given.[197] At least one important difference needs to be
mentioned here in conclusion. It bears upon the way in which Hirsch tries to cope
with the "*gesellschaftlichen Rahmenbedingungen,*"[198] which in his view determine
the particular content, strategy, and possible success of communicating the Christian
truth. Here, in an equally fatal and dangerous mixture of conservative Lutheranism and
political decisionism à la Carl Schmitt, Hirsch mistakenly transforms Kierkegaard's
insistence on the daring character of faith into the purported historical, in fact quasi-
eschatological necessity of subscribing to the truth of the Nazi-ideology in general,
and Hitler's pursuit of war in particular: "*Was Kierkegaard den 'Sprung' in den*

---

[192]   With the exception of the concept of contemporaneity; Hirsch sets out to correct this
"mistake," however, see *Kierkegaard Studien*, pp. 702–3; Schulz, "Rezeptionsgeschichtliche
Brocken," pp. 416–17.
[193]   Hirsch also draws on the *Concept of Anxiety* to make his point: see *Kierkegaard
Studien*, pp. 683–4, p. 686; pp. 693–4; pp. 699–700. The systematical importance of the
observation for Hirsch himself is evidenced by the fact that he later referred to it again by
drawing exactly the same conclusions: see Hirsch, *Geschichte*, pp. 454–60.
[194]   Hirsch, *Kierkegaard Studien*, p. 686.
[195]   Ibid., p. 688. Elsewhere I have described Hirsch's attempt to apply his hermeneutical
strategy to the dialectic of subjectivity as truth and untruth in greater detail, see Schulz,
"Rezeptionsgeschichtliche Nachschrift," pp. 371–4, especially pp. 373–4.
[196]   Arnulf von Scheliha, *Emanuel Hirsch als Dogmatiker. Zum Programm der
'Christlichen Rechenschaft' im 'Leitfaden zur christlichen Lehre,'* Berlin and New York: De
Gruyter 1991, p. 57.
[197]   Wilke sums up the main differences nicely (albeit fragmentarily), inasmuch as they
refer to the real and ideal presuppositions of communicating and thus bear upon the relation
of (a) addressee to communicator (with the key word, contemporaneity); (b) communicator to
him-/herself (with the key word, humor); (c) communicator to addressee (with the key word,
law and conscience). See Wilke, *Kierkegaard Rezeption*, pp. 536–9.
[198]   Ibid., p. 3.

Glauben nannte, wollte Hirsch als den wagenden Sprung in die geschichtsmächtige Handlung, und sei es auch der Krieg, verstanden wissen."[199] Thus, Hirsch was a transitional figure, indeed: not only in light of his constant shifting between a more receptive and a more productive perspective on Kierkegaard, but also and particularly owing to the deplorable fact that he was one of the first German theologians who "successfully" integrated ideas of the former into the framework of a Nazi-ideology—and vice versa the latter into the former.[200]

(13) In theology most of the genuinely productive adaptions of Kierkegaard during and after the First World War sprang from and more or less gravitated towards the "dialectical" school of thought. By comparison, the situation within contemporary *philosophy* appears to be much less homogenous. Thinkers of widely varying backgrounds, interests, and methodological preferences cited Kierkegaard, frequently as a source of inspiration and/or as a forerunner of their own ideas and theories.[201] Again, the impact of the *Brenner* can hardly be overestimated in terms of "spreading the news," in the first place. Thus, in 1919 a new and promising figure joined the *Brenner* circle, due to Haecker's initiative, named Ferdinand Ebner (1882–1931). Ebner, an elementary school teacher and private scholar, who like Franz Kafka died early of tuberculosis, is arguably "the earliest Catholic philosopher to recognize the importance of Kierkegaard and to be deeply influenced by him."[202] This happened around 1914, soon after he had discovered and immersed himself in some of Haecker's translations.[203] Thus, even before Martin Buber stepped onto the philosophical scene (see below), Ebner was the one to bring Kierkegaard's thinking into closer contact with what was later labelled dialogical philosophy—or perhaps it

---

[199]   Kiefhaber, *Christentum als Korrektiv*, pp. 20–1. As to Hirsch's consistent, if equally misleading "Germanizing" of Kierkegaard in his translations of the latter's works, see pp. 27ff. For a fuller account and critique of Hirsch's political views and his attempt to usurp Kierkegaard for corresponding purposes, see, for instance, Kodalle, *Die Eroberung des Nutzlosen*, pp. 270–80; in addition, Jens H. Schjørring, *Theologische Gewissensethik und politische Wirklichkeit. Das Beispiel Eduard Geismars und Emanuel Hirschs*, Göttingen: Vandenhoeck & Ruprecht 1979, pp. 56–62; pp. 159–64.

[200]   As to the German Kierkegaard reception between 1933 and 1945, see Wilfried Greve, "Kierkegaard im Dritten Reich," *Skandinavistik*, vol. 1, 1985, pp. 29–49.

[201]   As to a principal assessment of Kierkegaard's role within and significance for twentieth- century (Western) philosophy, see, for instance, Helmut Fahrenbach, "Kierkegaard und die gegenwärtige Philosophie," in *Kierkegaard und die deutsche Philosophie seiner Zeit*, ed. by H. Anz et al., Copenhagen and Munich: Fink 1980, pp. 149–69; see also Paul Ricoeur, "Philosophieren nach Kierkegaard," in *Materialien*, ed. by Theunissen and Greve, pp. 579–96.

[202]   Malik, *Receiving Kierkegaard*, pp. 386–7.

[203]   Probably he came across some of Schrempf's translations as well: compare the pertinent references in Malik, *Receiving Kierkegaard*, p. 387 (note 171). As to Ebner's Kierkegaard reception in context and in detail, see, for instance, von Kloeden, "Einfluß und Bedeutung," pp. 58–9 and pp. 71–2; Malik, *Receiving Kierkegaard*, pp. 386–7; Schulz, "Rezeptionsgeschichtliche Brocken," pp. 421–2; Theunissen and Greve, "Einleitung," pp. 60–1.

is more apt to suggest that this philosophy should be taken as, among other things, an *expression* of the former's impact.[204]

That Kierkegaard exerted in fact a great and lasting influence on Ebner is plain to see since it is widely documented in his writings: not only in his *magnum opus* (*Das Wort und die geistigen Realitäten*, 1921), but also and in particular in the numerous allusions, references, and remarks which crop up in his journals. Very often these explicit references are highly appreciative, to say the least; thus Ebner notes, for instance, that "*Kierkegaard war gewiß...einer der gewaltigsten Denker aller Zeiten.*"[205] Or, "*Was unsre Zeit braucht: Kierkegaard und nochmals Kierkegaard.*"[206] However, both in his main work and elsewhere the degree and depth of Kierkegaard's influence is in some way even more striking on a purely implicit level than in his scattered words of admiration and praise. These implicit reflections, which thus testify to the productive nature of Ebner's reception of his Danish idol, can be identified, first of all, in the organizing thought of his *magnum opus* from 1921. Ebner holds that humanity cannot be reduced to *natural* being. Rather, there is something irreducibly *spiritual* in man, or more exactly, man *is* spirit. However, the spiritual is as such "*wesentlich dadurch bestimmt, daß es von Grund auf angelegt ist auf ein Verhältnis zu etwas Geistigem* außer *ihm*, durch *das es und in dem es existiert.*"[207] For Ebner the phenomenon of language counts both as evidence and as the primary expression of this fact since language can be conceived of as the most fundamental means of relating to or addressing (and also being addressed by) the world in the sense of "some other subject." However, language, thus conceived, should not be regarded as a function or effect of human sociality *qua* intersubjectivity. On the contrary, language constitutes intersubjectivity. It constitutes both the "I" and the "You," namely as such and as (the possibility of) an ongoing mutual relationship.[208] In turn, language itself, in its capability to address part of the world as a "You," has been created by God, so that ultimately *he* appears to be the very "other," who necessarily conditions the possibility of human existence as spirit. In fact, Ebner suggests a hierarchy or an inner differential between three irreducible relations or relational levels constituting human existence: the *I–I-relation* (self-consciousness) is constituted by the *I–God-relation*; in turn, the *I–world-relation* is constituted by the I–I, and thus indirectly also by the I–God-relation. However, phenomenologically speaking, the I–God-relation is itself grounded in having a God–I-relation since the

---

[204]   Kierkegaard's overall influence and significance within the history of dialogical philosophy (which includes other German contemporary authors as well, for instance Emil Brunner, Friedrich Gogarten, and Eberhard Grisebach) is documented in detail by Shmuel H. Bergmann, *Dialogical Philosophy from Kierkegaard to Buber*, Albany, New York: State University of New York Press 1991. Ebner's and Buber's contributions, in particular, are extensively discussed in Bernhard Casper, *Das dialogische Denken: Franz Rosenzweig, Ferdinand Ebner und Martin Buber*, Freiburg: Alber 2002.

[205]   Ferdinand Ebner, *Schriften*, vols. 1–3, ed. by Franz Seyr, Munich: Kösel 1963–65, vol. 1 (1963), p. 111. The quoted passage is from Ebner's main work, *Das Wort und die geistigen Realitäten. Pneumatologische Fragmente*, see ibid., pp. 75–342.

[206]   Ibid., vol. 2, 1963, p. 527.

[207]   Ebner, *Schriften*, vol. 1, pp. 80–1.

[208]   See ibid., p. 81.

former relation is experienced by the subject as having come about and in fact been constituted by itself *as* previously having been addressed or having been spoken to by God. Correspondingly, the mundane "You" appears to have been constituted by the "I" or the experiencing subject, in that it has been approached, via language, as the subject's addressee. In conclusion, Ebner *"denkt...das menschliche Ich gleichsam als den Achsenpunkt einer Umkehrung der dialogischen Bewegung: von Gott* empfängt *das Ich—im Angesprochenwerden—das Du, dem Mitmenschen* verleiht *es—im Ansprechen—das Du."*[209]

It hardly needs mentioning that Ebner's account of man as a spiritual and thus also "dialogical" being is heavily indebted to Kierkegaard, especially his notion of spirit as self or as a "self system" comprising several relational levels and dimensions.[210] And yet, due to the special role and function, which Ebner attributes to language, it is also a highly productive and original adaptation of Kierkegaard's thought. Likewise, there are more than a few central ideas to be found in Ebner's works, which clearly (if implicitly) mirror Kierkegaard's influence.[211]

(14) Ebner's dialogical venture soon found an enthusiastic ally and follower in Martin Buber (1878–1965) who began reading the *Brenner* soon after the First World War and was therefore exposed already "in his early years not only to Ebner's philosophy but to Kierkegaard's as well."[212] Whereas the former left significant traces in *Ich und Du* (1923), in particular, the latter is (at times implicitly) present

---

[209] Michael Theunissen, *Der Andere. Studien zur Sozialontologie der Gegenwart*, Berlin: Walter de Gruyter 1965, p. 361. See also Ebner, *Schriften*, vol. 1, p. 676.

[210] See *SKS* 11, 129 / *SUD*, 13–14; in addition, Theunissen, *Der Andere*, pp. 360–1, for a brief account and critique of Ebner's adaptation of the book.

[211] See, for instance, Ebner, *Schriften,* vol. 1, pp. 443–4 (maieutic versus generative function of the word, analogous to Socratic versus Christian teaching); ibid., p. 444, pp. 557ff. (Christ as "type" and as object of unbelief versus Christ als "absolutely singularity" and as object of faith); ibid., p. 456; p. 474; p. 557 (Christ as absolute paradox and "mystery"); ibid., p. 457 ("mundane" versus "Christian faith" as faith in the word); ibid., p. 533 (the word as a genuine means of contemporaneity with Christ).

[212] Malik, *Receiving Kierkegaard*, p. 387. Buber's Kierkegaard reception is treated in Tilman Beyrich, "Kann ein Jude Trost finden in Kierkegaards Abraham? Jüdische Kierkegaard Lektüren: Buber, Fackenheim, Levinas," *Judaica*, vol. 57, 2001, pp. 20–40; James Brown, *Kierkegaard, Heidegger, Buber and Barth: Subject and Object in Modern Theology*, New York: Crowell-Collier 1962; Jacob Golomb, "Kierkegaard in Zion," *Kierkegaardiana*, vol. 19, 1998, pp. 130–7; Jacob L. Halevi, *A Critique of Martin Buber's Interpretation of Søren Kierkegaard*, Ph.D. Thesis, Hebrew Union College and Jewish Institute of Religion 1959; Robert A. Perkins, "A Philosophic Encounter with Buber," in *The Legacy and Interpretation*, pp. 243–75; Robert A. Perkins, "The Politics of Existence," in *Kierkegaard in Post/Modernity*, ed. by Martin J. Matuštík and Merold Westphal, Bloomington, Indianapolis: Indiana University Press 1995, pp. 167–81; J.W. Petras, "God, Man and Society. The Perspectives of Buber and Kierkegaard," *Journal of Religious Thought*, vol. 23, 1966, pp. 119–28; Schulz, "Rezeptionsgeschichtliche Brocken," pp. 422–3; Theunissen and Greve, "Einleitung," pp. 61–2; Jean Wahl, "Martin Buber und die Existenzphilosophie," in *Martin Buber*, ed. by Paul A. Schilpp and Maurice Friedman, Stuttgart: Kohlhammer 1963, pp. 420–47 (see especially pp. 421–8). A more recent account of Buber's philosophy in context is *New Perspectives on Martin Buber*, ed. by Michael Zank, Tübingen: J.C.B. Mohr 2006.

throughout in a later text, entitled *Die Frage an den Einzelnen* (1936).[213] In this later work Buber sets out to specify the main intentions and implications of his dialogical doctrine by distinguishing his concept of the "single individual" (in its relation to itself, God, and world) from allegedly similar conceptions in Kierkegaard and Max Stirner. In doing so, he draws on the Kierkegaardian resources in a productive way, occasionally also with the purpose of refuting what he takes to be Stirner's nominalism.[214] On the one hand, Buber obviously agrees with Kierkegaard, for he openly adopts two of the latter's basic assumptions: first, every human being is as such destined to become a "single individual." This means, first of all, that no one is *born* with such a qualification, but only with the disposition and *telos* of becoming or realizing it. Secondly, Kierkegaard rightly suggests that it is equally impossible to realize this *telos* without relating to God *and* relating to God without (precisely thereby!) becoming or having become a single individual: "*Der Einzelne entspricht Gott,*"[215] in that the individual cannot have one without the other. Accordingly, becoming oneself is tantamount to facing an unconditional task and responsibility: the responsibility of becoming and of becoming *oneself* as a single individual, precisely by relating to *God*, and by simultaneously admitting that the former cannot be had without the latter and the latter without the former. This basic agreement notwithstanding, Buber accuses Kierkegaard of a substantial misunderstanding: in order to be able to become a single individual, one has, according to the latter, to do "*wesentlich...nur mit Gott,*"[216] so that the relation to the *world* (in particular, to another human being *qua* "You") is completely kept out of the picture. Correspondingly, Kierkegaard's Christian, as such the ideal embodiment of a single individual due to its being truly contemporary with the God-man,[217] expresses and willy-nilly also promotes an "*akosmische Beziehung zu Gott.*"[218] Contrary to what Kierkegaard suggests, the single individual in fact does not meet God's demands (precisely in terms of becoming this particular individual), until he or she, as Buber puts it, "*das ihm zugereichte Stück Welt weltlich umfängt,*"[219] just like God does correspondingly, in his own *divine* way. Such an individual alone (and yet also, every such individual) "*verwirklicht das Bild [sc. Gottes], wenn er, soviel er personhaft vermag, zu den ihm umlebenden Wesen mit seinem Wesen Du sagt.*" [220]

---

[213] Both works are republished in Buber, *Dialogisches Leben. Gesammelte philosophische und pädagogische Schriften*, Zürich: Georg Müller 1947, pp. 13–128; pp. 187–255.

[214] As to Stirner's nominalism, see Buber, *Dialogisches Leben*, p. 190.

[215] Ibid., p. 200; see p. 193.

[216] Ibid., p. 206.

[217] See, for instance, *SV1*, XII, 1–2 / *PC*, 9–10.

[218] Buber, *Dialogisches Leben*, p. 208.

[219] Ibid., p. 214 (my emphasis).

[220] Ibid. Apart from this ontological or anthropological critique, Buber, in a much later work, also raised biblical and epistemological objections against Kierkegaard, and here in particular against the latter's account of Abraham's teleological suspension of the ethical in *Fear and Trembling* (see *SKS* 4, 148–59 / *FT*, 54–67). Thus, in *Gottesfinsternis. Betrachtungen zur Beziehung zwischen Religion und Philosophie*, Zürich: Manesse 1953, pp. 138–44, Buber argues that Kierkegaard did not solve, in fact did not even discuss the problem, whether it is possible unambiguously to distinguish "*ob du wirklich vom Absoluten angesprochen wirst*"

(15) To be sure, Karl Jaspers (1883–1969) may have read "*Der Brenner* in its early years"[221] and thus, in all probability, might also have stumbled upon Kierkegaard at that time. As early as 1913, however, when Jaspers published his first seminal work, *Allgemeine Psychopathologie* (Berlin and Heidelberg: Springer 1913), his later Danish idol was not yet "*im Blickfeld,*"[222] as Michael Theunissen correctly notes. On the other hand, Kierkegaard's impact on and significance for the German philosopher can hardly be overestimated; in fact, it has been rightly argued that it is possible "*das ganze Werk von Jaspers als einen einzigen Kommentar zu Kierkegaard [zu] lesen.*"[223] And even though it may be too strong a claim that in his work we find the very beginning of a Kierkegaard reception "in a stricter philosophical sense,"[224] it is certainly correct that before Jaspers no philosopher (much less any philosopher of his stature) estimated and admired Kierkegaard to such a degree that almost all of his or her writings bear witness to this fact both explicitly and implicitly. Now, although Jaspers has written quite a bit *about* his second philosophical hero (in addition to Nietzsche),[225] I would nevertheless categorize him as a genuinely productive recipient—not so much due to the originality of his Kierkegaard interpretation, but rather because of the systematical boldness and independence of assimilating and transforming the latter's ideas in correspondence to his own philosophical preferences and intentions.[226]

---

oder von einem seiner Affen" (ibid., p. 143). As to a meta-critique of Buber's objection, see Perkins, "A Philosophic Encounter," pp. 264–72; see also Abraham Sagi, "Kierkegaard and Buber on the Dilemma of Abraham in the *Akeda*," *Iyyun: A Hebrew Philosophical Quarterly*, vol. 37, 1988, pp. 248–62.

[221]   Malik, *Receiving Kierkegaard*, p. 391.

[222]   Theunissen and Greve, "Einleitung," p. 101 (note 340); see p. 64. Jaspers himself reports that he began studying Kierkegaard in 1914; see the first edition of his *Psychologie der Weltanschauungen*, Berlin: Springer 1919, p. X.

[223]   Theunissen and Greve, "Einleitung," p. 62.

[224]   See Anz, "Zur Wirkungsgeschichte Kierkegaards," pp. 20–1.

[225]   In his later years Jaspers published a number of articles and lectures exclusively devoted to Kierkegaard, for example, "Kierkegaard" (1951); "Kierkegaard. Zu seinem 100. Todestag" (1955); "Kierkegaard heute" (1964); these texts are reprinted in Karl Jaspers, *Aneignung und Polemik. Gesammelte Reden und Aufsätze zur Geschichte der Philosophie*, Munich: Pieper 1968, pp. 296–311; pp. 312–21; pp. 322–9. However, already in his earlier works Kierkegaard is mentioned and interpreted repeatedly, quite often in lengthier passages and paragraphs; see, for instance, Karl Jaspers, *Psychologie der Weltanschauungen*, 2nd ed., Berlin: Springer 1922, pp. 108–17; pp. 419–32; *Vernunft und Existenz. Fünf Vorlesungen*, 4th ed., Munich: Pieper 1987, pp. 7–34; pp. 102–20; *Von der Wahrheit*, 2nd ed., Munich: Pieper 1958, pp. 541–4; pp. 850–5; *Der philosophische Glaube angesichts der Offenbarung*, Munich: Pieper 1962, pp. 225–30; pp. 513–25.

[226]   As to Jaspers' Kierkegaard reception see, for instance, Anz, "Zur Wirkungsgeschichte Kierkegaards," pp. 20–4; István Czakó, "Das Problem des Glaubens und der Geschichte in der Philosophie Kierkegaards und Karl Jaspers,' " *Kierkegaard Studies. Yearbook*, 2000, pp. 373–82; Helmut Fahrenbach, "Kierkegaards untergründige Wirkungsgeschichte (Zur Kierkegaardrezeption bei Wittgenstein, Bloch und Marcuse)," in *Die Rezeption Søren Kierkegaards*, pp. 30–69, here pp. 42ff.; Wolfgang Janke, *Existenzphilosophie*, Berlin and New York: Walter de Gruyter 1982, pp. 162ff.; pp. 167–71; Wolfdietrich von Kloeden,

In a sense, one could sum up Jaspers' whole philosophical enterprise as an attempt to rediscover and outline the genuine possibilities, methods, objects, and cultural significance of philosophy under the anti-metaphysical and post-religious conditions and challenges of modernity. Thus, Kierkegaard's overall significance is precisely perceived and assessed by him in the light of this enterprise. Jaspers himself sums up the result of this assessment nicely in a lecture from 1955, in which he tries to determine the former's true meaning and significance over against what he takes to be a usurpation of his ideas by the then popular philosophy of existence and the so-called dialectical theology:

> *Ich halte es heute für schwer, zur philosophischen Redlichkeit zu gelangen, wenn man um Kierkegaard herumgeht. Ich halte es aber auch für unmöglich, durch ihn einen Boden zu finden. Trügerisch ist eine Existenzphilosophie, die weiß und lehrt, was das Leben tragen soll. Trügerisch ist ein christlicher Glaube, wenn er als Absurdität die Vernunft niederschlägt.*[227]

A philosophy pretending to be both capable and entitled freely to draw on Kierkegaard for the sake and with the effect of purportedly finding in him a support for a firm and certain foundation for human existence, while nonetheless feeling entitled at the same time to do away with the specifically Christian presuppositions and intentions, which in reality prove indispensable for Kierkegaard's entire thought, must be deemed illegitimate and illusory.[228] A theology, on the other hand, which—rightly—invokes Kierkegaard as testifying to and advocating a *sacrificium intellectus* as a necessary condition for Christian faith to be possible, while nonetheless pretending to be credible for the serious and honest modern philosopher also, must be considered no less illegitimate and illusory, however. This notwithstanding, there is for Jaspers a grain of truth to be found both in the contemporary philosophical and the theological endeavor: for, on the one hand, it is indeed true that philosophy is, first of all, an attempt at *"Existenzerhellung,"*[229] and hence only indirectly, namely, through this "illumination" project, also ontology and metaphysics, that is, the attempt to understand the true nature of (the possibility of a highest) being.[230] Interestingly

---

"Einfluß und Bedeutung," pp. 87–90; Schulz, "Rezeptionsgeschichtliche Brocken," pp. 423ff.; Theunissen and Greve, "Einleitung," pp. 62–6; Christo Todorov, "Das Thema des Todes als Verbindungslinie zwischen Kierkegaard und Jaspers," in *Sören Kierkegaard. Philosoph, Schriftsteller, Theologe. Vorträge des bulgarisch-dänischen Seminars, Sofia 31. März – 2. April 1992*, Sofia 1992, pp. 41–9; Sperna Weiland, *Humanitas—Christianitas. A Critical Survey of Kierkegaard's and Jaspers' Thought in Connection with Christianity*, Assen: Van Gorcum 1951.

[227]   Jaspers, *Aneignung*, p. 320.

[228]   See, for instance, Jaspers, *Vernunft*, pp. 29ff. As to the suspicion that Jaspers has in fact proved unable to escape his own verdict, see Theunissen and Greve, "Einleitung," p. 63; also Kiefhaber, *Christentum*, pp. 21ff.

[229]   Thus the title of the second volume of Jaspers' famous *magnum opus*: Karl Jaspers, *Philosophie*, 2nd ed., in one volume, Berlin and Heidelberg: Springer 1948 [1932].

[230]   See, for instance, Jaspers, *Philosophie*, p. V (my emphasis): Philosophy is *"das Wagnis, in den unbetretbaren* Grund *menschlicher* Selbstgewißheit *zu dringen...Philosophieren [ist] der* Weg des Menschen, *der, geschichtlich in seiner Zeit*, das Sein *ergreift."*

enough, the former project reveals that philosophizing (in the sense of trying to understand and become transparent to oneself in existence) is in fact part and parcel of the very existence that a philosophy, thus conceived, seeks to illuminate and describe: one cannot exist as a human being without at least trying to *understand* oneself as so existing.

Yet, on the other hand, the theological concern or agenda is also justified, at least to a certain extent since, according to Jaspers, it corresponds and can be traced back to the ineradicable human sense and, in fact, the ontologically irreducible and fully justified human desire of being related to something transcendent. However, the nature of the transcendent can no longer be conceived of as being at one's disposal through a limited stock of dogmatically fixed propositions about God or the divine. Rather, the idea of the transcendent is accessible and viable only in terms of certain codes or "ciphers" (*Chiffren*), which more or less adequately refer or merely point to it. Therefore, a philosophically viable faith is tantamout to a "philosophical faith" (*philosophischer Glaube*[231]), and in turn this faith is in full agreement, in fact even a part of what Jaspers takes to be "*echte Philosophie*"—a philosophy, in other words, which "*kennt im Grunde alle Phänomene als ihr relevant nur, sofern sie Chiffren der ihr vorhergehenden Wirklichkeit der Transzendenz sein können. Sie ergreift in ihrem Suchen die Chiffren als mögliche vestigia dei, nicht Gott selbst in seiner Verborgenheit.*"[232]

Finally, the project of "*Existenzerhellung,*" which as such takes seriously the ambivalent "ciphers" or codes of the transcendent, can only succeed by being founded upon a "*kommunikatives Philosophieren.*"[233] Neither the understanding of (oneself in) existence nor of the encoded dimension of the transcendent intimately related to it, are accessible by virtue of a philosophy *qua* "*objektives Wissen*"[234]—a knowledge, which as such would be independent of specific communicative conditions of its own genesis. Rather, just as the philosopher must always be a man of faith (even though of a purely "philosophical faith," "*ohne jede Offenbarung*"[235]), so he must, in terms of his method, always proceed indirectly, namely "appellierend *an den, der auf demselben Wege ist.*"[236]

This being said, it does not come as a surprise that Kierkegaard is of central concern for Jaspers in his attempt both to assess and to overcome the shortcomings and unacceptable ambivalences within much of contemporary philosophy (of existence) and theology. However, the impact and significance of Kierkegaard, whom Jaspers, rather tellingly, calls a "*christlicher Philosoph,*"[237] is, in the latter's opinion, equally impaired and limited, and this is due to strikingly corresponding ambivalences. Kierkegaard's major achievements are formal (indirectness as a prerequisite of proper philosophical communication), attudinal (seriousness

---

[231]   See Jaspers, *Der philosophische Glaube.*
[232]   Jaspers, *Vernunft*, p. 120.
[233]   Ibid., p. 104.
[234]   Jaspers, *Philosophie*, p. V.
[235]   Ibid.
[236]   Ibid. (my emphasis).
[237]   Jaspers, *Aneignung*, p. 297.

and sincerity as unconditional personal requirements of the philosopher) and anthropological in nature (to be human means to be transparent to or understand oneself in existence which means to reveal oneself to others in communication[238]). In all three respects Kierkegaard has established a new standard of doing philosophy, much like Nietzsche, whom Jaspers considers a hidden twin of the former in terms of their common overall philosophical attitude, method and historical significance.[239] Moreover, both Kierkegaard and Nietzsche remain fully ambivalent figures: "*Sie sind die Erhellenden und zugleich die Verführer...an ihnen ist Orientierung möglich— aber indem man sich in Distanz von ihnen hält.*"[240] In Kierkegaard's case, Jaspers feels entitled and compelled to raise an objection of principle: Kierkegaard's view of Christian faith, although fully consistent in itself, is philosophically unacceptable in that it entails the rather violent demand to submit and testify to the dogma of the God-man and, as a consequence, to imitate Christ through martyrdom.[241] By contrast, the faith of a philosopher is a genuinely philosophical faith and thus merely faith in certain "ciphers" of transcendence. Now, whereas Jesus can in fact be interpreted and experienced to this effect, the God-man cannot since he calls for being appropriated and worshipped by virtue of a violent act of will, corresponding to a complete *sacrificium intellectus.*[242] Thus conceived, Christian faith jeopardizes the very openness and communicative self-transparency of existence vis-à-vis God and the world that Kierkegaard himself—and rightly so—had emphasized in the first place. Summing up, we may say that, according to Jaspers, we need and are indebted to Kierkegaard for the present as a valuable, indeed indispensable, witness and inculcator of the proper measure or standard for all our philosophical endeavors; precisely by accepting and applying this standard, however, we are invariably led to abandon and reject as violent and rationally unacceptable certain elements of the Christian dogma that he stubbornly clings to and defends as possible, indeed unsurpassable, objects of the believing mind.[243]

(16) One of the few scattered remarks in which Martin Heidegger (1889–1976) explicitly mentions Kierkegaard's name, not only sums up his overall view of the latter's thought and significance nicely, but also bears witness to the fact that he obviously did not approve of Jasper's reading of the Danish thinker as a (Christian) philosopher in direct world-historical proximity to Nietzsche:

Die üblich gewordene, aber deshalb nicht weniger fragwürdige Zusammenstellung Nietzsches mit Kierkegaard verkennt, und zwar aus einer Verkennung des Wesens des Denkens, daß Nietzsche als metaphysischer Denker die Nähe zu Aristoteles wahrt. Diesem bleibt Kierkegaard, obwohl er ihn öfter nennt, wesenhaft fern. Denn Kierkegaard ist kein

---

[238] This latter aspect is highlighted in Jaspers' detailed account of Kierkegaard's *The Sickness unto Death*, see *Psychologie*, pp. 419–32 (especially pp. 421ff. and pp. 430ff.); see also Jaspers, *Wahrheit*, pp. 541ff.
[239] See Jaspers, *Vernunft*, pp. 11–15; also *Aneignung*, pp. 308–9.
[240] Jaspers, *Aneignung*, p. 308; p. 309; see ibid., p. 310.
[241] See, for instance, Jaspers, *Glaube*, pp. 513–26; also *Aneignung*, pp. 305–6; p. 320; p. 326.
[242] See Jaspers, *Glaube*, pp. 227–8; also *Wahrheit*, pp. 853ff.
[243] See Jaspers, *Vernunft*, p. 104.

Denker, sondern ein religiöser Schriftsteller und zwar nicht einer unter anderen, sondern der einzige dem Geschick seines Zeitalters gemäße.[244]

These utterances were written down between 1936 and 1940.[245] Roughly at the same time Heidegger warns the reader not to consider it a mere accident,

daß diese drei [sc. Hölderlin, Kierkegaard, Nietzsche]*, die je in ihrer Weise zuletzt die Entwurzelung am tiefsten durchlitten haben, der die abendländische Geschichte zugetrieben wird, und die zugleich ihre Götter am innigsten erahnt haben, frühzeitig aus der Helle ihres Tages hinweg mußten.*[246]

Contrary to what the first statement would have us expect, Heidegger here seems to suggest that at least in the sense of the history of philosophy, perhaps also in the sense of world history Kierkegaard seems to be in close kinship with Nietzsche (and Hölderlin), due to their common suffering from an "uprooting" of Western history (plus their rather untimely death). However, this slightly different accent on Kierkegaard's relation to Nietzsche leaves untouched the categorization of the former as a "religious author" instead of a "thinker" or philosopher. For Heidegger, who "subscribed to *Der Brenner* beginning in 1911"[247] and thus in all probability read Kierkegaard long before the 1920s, this categorization must have suggested itself rather early and effectively. For, some qualifications notwithstanding, it remains pretty much the same throughout his writing career; in any case, it is clearly present in his *magnum opus* from 1927, *Sein und Zeit*, which, among other things, testifies to the fact that Heidegger had sharpened his view in permanent dialogue with Jaspers, Bultmann, and others at that time already.[248]

Now, if for the time being we stick (like many scholars do[249]) to the latter work in order to unlock a few secrets of Heidegger's notoriously elusive Kierkegaard

---

[244]   Martin Heidegger, *Holzwege*, Frankfurt am Main: Klostermann 1950, p. 230.

[245]   Although first published in 1950, the lecture from which the quotation is taken was written between 1936 and 1940 already, see ibid., p. 344.

[246]   Martin Heidegger, *Beiträge zur Philosophie (Vom Ereignis)*, ed. by Friedrich-Wilhelm von Herrmann, Frankfurt am Main: Klostermann 1989 (Martin Heidegger, *Gesamtausgabe*, vol. 65), p. 204.

[247]   Malik, *Receiving Kierkegaard*, p. 391. See also John van Buren, *The Young Heidegger: Rumor of the Hidden King*, Bloomington: Indiana University Press 1994, p. 150.

[248]   See ibid., pp. 154ff.; pp. 181–2.

[249]   See, for instance, Anz, "Die Wirkungsgeschichte Kierkegaards," pp. 24–7; Patricia J. Huntington, "Heidegger's Reading of Kierkegaard Revisited: From Ontological Abstraction to Ethical Concretion," in *Kierkegaard in Post/Modernity*, pp. 43–65; Kloeden, "Einfluß und Bedeutung," pp. 83–7; Schulz, "Rezeptionsgeschichtliche Brocken," pp. 396–9; Theunissen and Greve, "Einleitung," pp. 66–73. Indispensable is van Buren's pioneering work, *The Young Heidegger*, pp. 150–4; pp. 166–76; pp. 181–98; pp. 222ff.; pp. 326–9; pp. 388–9. For a more systematic and comprehensive comparison of certain doctrines and ideas in Kierkegaard and Heidegger, see, for instance, Brown, *Kierkegaard, Heidegger*; Jörg Disse, "Philosophie der Angst: Kierkegaard und Heidegger im Vergleich," *Kierkegaardiana*, vol. 22, 2002, pp. 64–88; Günter Figal, "Verzweiflung und Uneigentlichkeit. Zum Problem von Selbstbegründung und misslingender Existenz bei Søren Kierkegaard und Martin Heidegger," in *Die Rezeption*, pp. 131–51; Knud E. Løgstrup, *Kierkegaards und Heideggers Existenzanalyse und ihr*

reception, it may seem at first sight that this reception can at best be called unproductive, typologically speaking, since Heidegger's explicit references to the Danish "religious author" are few and far between.[250] However, by taking a closer look at the three (!) infamous entries and their context in _Sein und Zeit_ where Kierkegaard is explicitly mentioned, it will quickly become clear that Heidegger's unusually brief and throughout ambivalent judgments about the former are apparently also (though not exclusively) supposed to obscure the true degree of his indebtedness to and thus also the deliberately implicit and/or material presence of Kierkegaard in his magisterial work from 1927.[251] All three entries reveal basically the same ambivalence with regard to Kierkegaard's purported merits and shortcomings: on the one hand, he described and analyzed most profoundly the "existential" (_existentielle_) dimension of a given phenomenon (anxiety, existence, temporality); on the other hand, he lacked the means to adequately account for its "existential-ontological" (_existential-ontologische_) dimension.

To begin with, let us briefly consider the famous analysis of anxiety. In _Sein und Zeit_ anxiety (rather than dread or fright) functions as a bridge between the stages of "degenerate" and "genuine existence" (_uneigentliches Existieren / Verfallenheit_ versus _eigentliches Existieren_), thereby also phenomenologically motivating the possibility of transgressing from one to the other. At this point Heidegger admits that Kierkegaard is indeed "_[a]m weitesten vorgedrungen in der Analyse_";[252] however, the significance of his analysis is restricted and impaired by its being purely psychological rather than ontological, even more so, since it is located "_im theologischen Zusammenhang...des Problems der Erbsünde._"[253] Later on (§§

Verhältnis zur Verkündigung, Berlin: Blaschker 1950; Calvin Schrag, _Existence and Freedom: Towards an Ontology of Human Finitude_, Evanston: Northwestern University Press 1961; Annemarie Vogt, _Das Problem des Selbstseins bei Heidegger und Kierkegaard_, Gießen: Lechte 1936; Michael Weston, _Kierkegaard and Modern Continental Philosophy. An Introduction_, London: Routledge 1994, pp. 33–57; Michael Wyschogrod, _Kierkegaard and Heidegger. The Ontology of Existence_, London: Routledge & Kegan Paul 1954. An interesting attempt to turn the perspective of this history of reception upside down by criticizing Heidegger from a genuinely Kierkegaardian perspective is to be found in Daniel Berthold-Bond, "A Kierkegaardian Critique of Heidegger's Concept of Authenticity," _Man and World_, vol. 24, 1991, pp. 119–42.

[250] It must be admitted, though, that no more than a handful of explicit Kierkegaard references are to be found in Heidegger's published works; see, first and foremost, Martin Heidegger, _Sein und Zeit_, 14th ed., Tübingen: Niemeyer 1977 [1927], p. 189; p. 235; p. 338 (see also the implicit allusions to _Repetition_, pp. 339; pp. 385–6); in addition _Beiträge_, p. 204; _Holzwege_, p. 230.

[251] Elsewhere I have tried to show that Heidegger's reluctance to make explicit the true extent of his indebtedness to Kierkegaard goes hand in hand with (and is perhaps motivated by) a refusal to admit the impossibility of isolating in the latter's work a purported philosophical "message," independent of and separable from certain underlying religious intentions, that is, in quintessence, the futility of any attempt to exploit (elements of) Kierkegaard's central ideas for purely philosophical purposes; see Schulz, "Rezeptionsgeschichtliche Brocken," pp. 398–9.

[252] Heideggger, _Sein und Zeit_, p. 190 (note 1).

[253] Ibid.

45ff.) we come across a corresponding reservation. Here Heidegger sets out to unveil time, or more exactly: temporality, as the root of (the sense of) being, as it is supposed to reveal itself through an ontology of existence. Now, according to Heidegger, Kierkegaard has indeed tackled the problem of existence in a rather profound way; however, only *"als ein existentielles,"*[254] so that what seems missing again in his account is the genuinely ontological perspective. Furthermore since in the latter respect Kierkegaard is and remains completely under Hegel's spell (and that of Greek philosophy, as interpreted by the latter), it seems to follow that *"von seinen 'erbaulichen' Schriften philosophisch mehr zu lernen [ist] als von den theoretischen—die Abhandlung über den Begriff der Angst ausgenommen."*[255] Heidegger moderately praises the latter treatise, not only for introducing the term "anxiety" into the anthropological debate, but also because of its attention to the phenomenon of temporality and here, in particular, to the concept of the moment (*Augenblick*). Again he inculcates the view that Kierkegaard only payed attention to *"das* existentielle *Phänomen des Augenblicks,"*[256] whereas he failed properly to grasp its existential-ontological meaning. He then goes on—wrongly[257]—to accuse the latter of having identified or confused temporality (*Zeitlichkeit*) with the mere *" 'In-der-Zeit-sein' des Menschen."*[258] Now, since, according to Heidegger such a pure being-in-time *"kennt nur das Jetzt, aber nie einen Augenblick,"*[259] we must in his opinion conclude (other than Kierkegaard himself who at this point seeks refuge in a religiously connotated notion of eternity) that within the existential (*existentiell*) experience of a moment there is *"eine ursprünglichere Zeitlichkeit, obzwar existential unausdrücklich, vorausgesetzt"*[260]—nota bene, *if* such an experience is possible.

So much for the few explicit references in *Sein und Zeit*. Now, Michael Theunissen has persuasively argued[261] that Kierkegaard's actual influence on Heidegger's book goes far beyond what these few references would have us expect, so that his implicit, if probably deliberate (and at times also misguided), presence is a lot stronger than the uninitiated reader would have thought possible in the first place. Thus conceived, Heidegger's almost monomaniacly and self-immunizably repeated distinctions between the "existential" perspective, on the one hand, and the "existential-ontological," on the other hand, between a "religious author" and a "philosophical thinker," etc. seem all too neatly drawn to be actually convincing. To undergird this claim I would like, in conclusion, to list briefly four more or less strinking

---

[254]   Ibid., p. 235 (note 1).

[255]   Ibid. Meanwhile we know, which discourses Heidegger is thinking of, in particular, the "Lilies in the Field" from 1847 (see *SKS* 8, 255–307 / *UD*, 155–212) and the discourse "At a Graveside" from 1845 (see *SKS* 5, 442–69 / *TD*, 69–102); compare van Buren, *The Young Heidegger*, pp. 193ff.; see also Theunissen and Greve, "Einleitung," p. 70.

[256]   Heideggger, *Sein und Zeit*, p. 338 (note 1).

[257]   See Theunissen and Greve, "Einleitung," p. 68; a complementary critique (here focused on the *Fragments*) is to be found in Schulz, "Rezeptionsgeschichtliche Brocken," pp. 397–8.

[258]   Ibid.

[259]   Ibid.

[260]   Ibid.

[261]   See Theunissen and Greve, "Einleitung," pp. 66–73.

parallels (three material, one methodical) between Heidegger and Kierkegaard, thereby suggesting that there is indeed a deeper connection between the two than meets the eye:[262] (a) The correlation of facticity and transcendence (in Heidegger's terms *Geworfenheit / Entwurf*) mirrors Kierkegaard's dialectic of necessity and possibility in *The Sickness unto Death*;[263] likewise (b) the "*Verfallenheit an die 'Welt'* "[264] in Heidegger's terms corresponds to the despair of finitude in the same book; (c) the idea of actualizing the "wholeness" of existence (*Dasein*) by virtue of a "*Vorlaufen zum Tode*"[265] suggests itself as being modelled after Kierkegaard's category of repetition; finally (d) Heidegger's method of analyzing the nature of "genuine existence" (*Eigentlichkeit*) as a mere "*existentielle* Modifikation *des Man als eines wesenhaften Existentials*,"[266] reflects, perhaps even imitates, Kierkegaard's "negativistic" method in *The Sickness unto Death*, according to which the true nature of the self is epistemically accessible only in indirect fashion, namely, by way of deriving it from the respective forms and structure of despair.[267] Summing up, we may say that Heidegger's Kierkegaard reception not only deserves to be called productive but also lends itself perfectly to being labelled "incognito" reception. After all, Heidegger himself was perhaps equally well aware and unwilling to admit that Jaspers prophetically got it right, when he suspected "*daß ein Philosophieren an der Hand Kierkegaards sich heimlich nährt von der christlichen Substanz, die es im Sprechen ignoriert.*"[268]

(17) Among the truly productive German recipients who (with the help of the *Brenner* and Theodor Haecker) turned into novices seeking admission to the community of ardent Kierkegaard admirers, Ludwig Wittgenstein (1889–1951) must not be left out. As is well known, Wittgenstein had financially supported a number of needy authors (such as Trakl, Rilke, Dallago, Haecker), whom he knew from their publications in Ficker's journal, just before the First World War. Later on he tried, although unsuccessfully, to talk the latter into publishing his own first book, the soon to be famous *Tractatus-Logico-Philosophicus* (1921). Now, in all probability Wittgenstein stumbled upon many of Kierkegaard's texts during those years; however,

---

[262]   For the following I am particularly indebted to Theunissen's and Greve's comprehensive account, see "Einleitung," pp. 67–71.

[263]   Compare Heidegger, *Sein und Zeit*, pp. 175–80, and *SKS* 11, 145; 153–7 / *SUD*, 29; 37–42.

[264]   Heidegger, *Sein und Zeit*, p. 175; compare *SKS* 11, 149ff. / *SUD*, 33ff.

[265]   Heidegger, *Sein und Zeit*, p. 267; as to the repercussions of Kierkegaard's notion of repetition see Theunissen and Greve, "Einleitung," p. 70.

[266]   Heidegger, *Sein und Zeit*, p. 130 (my emphasis); see also ibid., p. 179: "*[D]ie eigentliche Existenz [ist] nichts, was über der alltäglichen Verfallenheit schwebt, sondern existenzial nur ein modifiziertes Ergreifen dieser.*" If this claim does in fact have a direct parallel or model in Kierkegaard (as I think it does) we might say that, according to the latter, the self is nothing but a specific way of accepting its distortion, or that, theologically speaking, faith is tantamount to a particular way of grasping and accepting (one's own) despair.

[267]   See Theunissen and Greve, "Einleitung," pp. 70–1; also Theunissen, *Das Selbst auf dem Grund der Verzweiflung. Kierkegaards negativistische Methode*, Frankfurt am Main: Hain 1991.

[268]   Jaspers, *Vernunft und Existenz*, p. 30.

it seems almost impossible exactly to determine which ones he actually read, at what time he started reading them, and which of them left a lasting impression. Apart from very few (mostly later) explicit statements referring to Kierkegaard's *thought*, which I will return to, most of what is handed down time and again by Wittgenstein scholars are his repeated remarks of respect, admiration, and awe for Kierkegaard as a *person*, often in conversation with students or colleagues who later reported them to others. Thus, for instance, he once told Maurice Drury, one of his students, that he considered Kierkegaard "the greatest philosopher of the nineteenth century."[269] Another student reported that he always referred to the Danish thinker "with something of awe in his expression, as a 'really religious' man,"[270] etc.

Due to these few, scattered, and often second-hand remarks it does not come as a surprise that the current debate about the scope, substance, and significance of Wittgenstein's Kierkegaard reception is "a matter of much dispute and speculation."[271] Despite the rather elusive nature of this receptional attitude (in terms of its explicit expression or output), there can be no doubt that Wittgenstein profited from reading Kierkegaard in more than one and at any rate in a productive way. At least we may say that there are striking parallels to be discovered in some of their underlying convictions, intentions and overall philosophical endeavors—parallels that would deserve to be made explicit, even if it were fully evident that they are in fact *not* based on any direct Kierkegaardian influence on Wittgenstein. I just mention two of them.[272] The first touches upon the function of paradox in Wittgenstein's early philosophy. Following Frege and Russell, in particular, the *Tractatus* sketches a

---

[269]   Drury's testimony is documented in *Ludwig Wittgenstein: Personal Recollections*, ed. by Rush Rhees, Totowa: Rowman and Littlefield 1981, pp. 102–4.

[270]   Norman Malcolm, *Ludwig Wittgenstein: A Memoir*, London: Oxford University Press 1958, p. 71.

[271]   Malik, *Receiving Kierkegaard*, p. 380. As to the partly material, partly reception-historical connections between Wittgenstein and Kierkegaard see, for instance, *Essays on Kierkegaard & Wittgenstein: On Understanding the Self*, ed. by Richard H. Bell and R.E. Hustwit, Wooster, Ohio: The College of Wooster 1978; Charles L. Creegan, *Wittgenstein and Kierkegaard: Religion, Individuality, and Philosophical Method*, London: Routledge 1989; Fahrenbach, "Kierkegaards untergründige Wirkungsgeschichte," pp. 33–44; P. Gallagher, "Wittgenstein's Admiration for Kierkegaard," *The Month*, vol. 39, 1968, pp. 43–9; Jens Glebe-Møller, "Wittgenstein and Kierkegaard," *Kierkegaardiana*, vol. 15, 1991, pp. 55–68; Alastair Hannay, *Kierkegaard*, 2ⁿᵈ ed., London and New York: Routledge 1993, pp. 149–56; pp. 331ff.; Paul L. Holmer, *The Grammar of Faith*, San Francisco: Harper & Row 1978; Malik, *Receiving Kierkegaard*, pp. 380–1; Mariele Nientied, *Kierkegaard und Wittgenstein. Hineintäuschen in das Wahre*, Berlin and New York: Walter de Gruyter 2003 (*Kierkegaard Studies. Monograph Series*, vol. 7); Dewi Z. Phillips, *Wittgenstein and Religion*, 2ⁿᵈ ed., New York: St. Martin's Press 1994, pp. 200–19; Robert C. Roberts, "Kierkegaard, Wittgenstein, and a Method of 'Virtue Ethics,' " in *Kierkegaard in Post/Modernity*, pp. 142–66; Schulz, "Rezeptionsgeschichtliche Brocken," pp. 426–30.

[272]   The third one is deliberately omitted here since I have dealt with it elsewhere, on the occasion of reviewing Mariele Nientied's pertinent monograph (*Kierkegaard und Wittgenstein*); see Schulz, "Rezeptionsgeschichtliche Nachschrift," pp. 391–5. The parallel bears upon the theory and practice of method and style in both thinkers. See also Creegan, *Wittgenstein and Kierkegaard*.

semantical theory of language, which focuses on the relation between (linguistic) sign and signified. The primary function of language is to "picture" reality (that is, the world and its various elements) in the sense of determining *"was der Fall ist"*:[273] matters of fact (*Sachverhalte, Tatsachen*). Thus conceived, language does not signify or refer to things or *objects*, but rather to *"eine* Verbindung *von Gegenständen (Sachen, Dingen)."*[274]

Correspondingly, the world as a whole is coextensive with the *"Gesamtheit der Tatsachen, nicht der Dinge."*[275] Only matters of fact can be articulated or linguistically expressed in a clear and meaningful way, and only statements or propositions referring to (a part of) the world can express matters of fact. Now, according to Wittgenstein, ethical or metaphysical or religious statements ("sincerity should be pursued for its own sake"; "the world as a whole does not have a beginning or end in time"; "there exists a loving god") are supposed to tell us something about the ultimate *meaning* of the world or of life as a whole. As such they refer to some world-*transcendent* entity; for *"[d]er Sinn der Welt muß außerhalb ihrer liegen."*[276] However since clear and meaningful statements are only possible if these statements refer to some world-*immanent* state of affairs, it follows that sentences about the ultimate meaning of the world and of life as a whole can neither be clear nor meaningful. They do not convey any information about actual or at least possible states of affairs or matters of fact. Strictly speaking, these entities, though existent or real in some sense, can only be *pointed at*, but not linguistically expressed.[277] This notwithstanding since we actually use and obviously cannot cease to use language in a religious, metaphysical and/or ethical way, the conclusion can hardly be avoided that there must be an intrinsic tendency within language to "run against" its own limits and limitations, to seek to say what, strictly speaking, cannot be said, to express the unexpressable, to utter the unutterable. Now, in Wittgenstein's words, precisely this *"Anrennen...[hat] auch Kierkegaard gesehen und es sogar ganz ähnlich (als Anrennen gegen das Paradoxon)*

---

[273]   Ludwig Wittgenstein, *Tractatus logico-philosophicus/Logisch-philosophische Abhand-lung*, 15th ed., Frankfurt am Main: Suhrkamp 1980, p. 11.
[274]   Ibid.
[275]   Ibid.
[276]   Ibid., p. 111. Wittgenstein continues: *"In der Welt ist alles wie es ist und geschieht alles, wie es geschieht; es gibt in ihr keinen Wert...Darum kann es auch keine Sätze der Ethik geben... Es ist klar, dass sich die Ethik nicht aussprechen lässt."* (Ibid., pp. 111–12; see also Ludwig Wittgenstein, *Vortrag über Ethik und andere kleine Schriften*, ed. by J. Schulte, Frankfurt am Main: Suhrkamp 1989, pp. 9–19, especially pp. 12ff.; pp. 18–19.) Compare Haecker, 1913: *"Die Ethik gehört...zu den Existenzproblemen, die ohne Innerlichkeit nicht behandelt werden können, da sie objektiv, in der Natur, überhaupt nicht sind. Es gibt kein System der Ethik, auch wenn jedes Jahr ein neues geschrieben wird, es ist doch überflüssig, und gibt doch keine Erkenntnis."* (Haecker, *Innerlichkeit*, p. 52.) Did Wittgenstein know Haecker's book and did he allude to it, when he pointed out to Ficker, "that if you print Dallago, Haecker, etc., *then* you can also print *my* book?" (Letter from Wittgenstein to Ficker dated December 4, 1919; here quoted from Malik, *Receiving Kierkegaard*, p. 380 (note 142).)
[277]   Wittgenstein, *Tractatus*, p. 115 (6.522).

bezeichnet."[278] So here is our first parallel: Just as Wittgenstein calls attention to a linguistic paradox (language trying to say what cannot be said, yet without being able to let go of this attempt), so also Kierkegaard—according to Wittgenstein— calls attention to a corresponding epistemical paradox (thought trying to think what cannot be thought, yet without being able to let go of this attempt).[279]

A second parallel places us in the context of religion, as it is analyzed in Wittgenstein's later philosophy. Earlier Wittgenstein had temporarily identified religion with a speechless experience (in particular, "*das Erlebnis der absoluten Sicherheit*"[280]). In his later philosophy this experiental property merely functions as one (albeit integral) element of religion, which is conceived of as a particular "form of life." This form of life includes a variety of language games (loosely connected by certain family resemblances), going along with or accompanied by the "fundamental emotion" of feeling absolutely safe and secure: "*Die Religion ist sozusagen der tiefste ruhige Meeresgrund, wie hoch auch oben die Wellen gehen.*"[281] In the same passage faith—introduced by Wittgenstein as a synonym for religion—is characterized, with explicit reference to Kierkegaard, as a passion.[282] In its Christian variant this passion takes on some extra specifications. For one thing Christianity (here conceived of as *fides quae*) is "*nur für den, der unendliche Hilfe braucht, also nur für den, der unendliche Not fühlt.*"[283] For another thing, the believer has to take refuge, for the sake of his own consolation, in a divine promise, the exact content of which, although being witnessed to in the New Testament writings, remains rather

---

[278]   *Ludwig Wittgenstein und der Wiener Kreis. Gespräche, aufgezeichnet von Friedrich Waismann*, ed. by B.F. McGuiness, Frankfurt am Main: Suhrkamp 1984, p. 68. Probably Wittgenstein alludes to a famous passage in chapter 3 of the *Fragments* here: "The paradoxical passion of the understanding is...continuously colliding with this unknown....The understanding does not go beyond this; yet in its paradoxicality the understanding cannot stop reaching it and being engaged with it....What, then, is the unknown? It is the frontier that is continually arrived at...and therefore it is the different, the absolutely different." (*SKS* 4, 249 / *PF*, 44)

[279]   As to the scope and limit of this parallel see Fahrenbach, "Kierkegaards untergründige Wirkungsgeschichte," pp. 33–9.

[280]   Wittgenstein, *Vortrag über Ethik*, p. 14. This statement may be read as a material, hardly as a direct reception–historical reflection of Kierkegaard's notion of faith as a state of "a priori safety" or certainty, see, for instance, *SKS* 17, 247, DD:79 / *JP* 2, 1097.

[281]   Wittgenstein, *Bemerkungen über die Farben / Über Gewissheit / Zettel / Vermischte Bemerkungen*, Frankfurt am Main: Suhrkamp 1989, p. 525. This assertion will probably remind the reader of Climacus' famous formulation that faith is to be compared to a state of safety or certainty "on 70,000 fathoms of water" (*SKS* 7, 212 / *CUP1*, 232). Of course, we cannot know for sure that Wittgenstein's statement is a conscious reflection of or allusion to Kierkegaard.

[282]   Wittgenstein, *Bemerkungen*, p. 525; see also ibid., pp. 495–6. Perhaps Wittgenstein alludes to the *Fragments* here (*SKS* 4, 261 / *PF*, 59); it is also possible that this is a reference to *Fear and Trembling* (*SKS* 4, 159 / *FT*, 67).

[283]   Wittgenstein, *Bemerkungen*, p. 514. In my opinion, this "being for" includes at least three connotations: "being object for," "being destined for," and "being true for."

"*undeutlich.*"[284] Again invoking Kierkegaard,[285] Wittgenstein refuses to consider this a principal disadvantage, though:

> *Gott läßt das Leben des Gottmenschen von vier Menschen berichten, von jedem anders und widersprechend—aber kann man nicht sagen: Es ist wichtig, daß dieser Bericht nicht mehr als sehr gewöhnliche historische Wahrscheinlichkeit habe,* damit *diese nicht für das Wesentliche...gehalten werde. Damit der* Buchstabe *nicht mehr Glaube fände, als ihm gebührt und der Geist sein Recht behalte. D.h.: Was du sehen sollst, läßt sich auch durch den besten, genauesten Geschichtsschreiber nicht vermitteln; darum genügt, ja ist vorzuziehen, eine mittelmäßige Darstellung...Du SOLLST gerade nur das deutlich sehen, was auch diese Darstellung deutlich zeigt.*[286]

The context of the quoted passage clearly documents that Wittgenstein agrees with Climacus:[287] faith in the strict Christian sense is neither identical with nor solely based upon or justified by some historical truth; nevertheless it is inextricably bound up with and dependent upon a particular relation to a historical datum, namely the New Testament report(s) about Jesus Christ. This relation may be called faith, too (or perhaps more exactly, belief), in that it amounts to a relative, conditional and reversible certitude, a mere *fides historica*. By contrast, faith in a strictly Christian sense is faith "*durch dick und dünn,*"[288] an unswerving conviction of and unconditional clinging to the truth of the New Testament message, despite and vis-à-vis its vagueness and objective uncertainty.[289]

(18) Theodor W. Adorno (1903–69) started to pursue an academic and literary career after his dissertation (plus a failed attempt to get his *Habilitation* thesis accepted at the University of Frankfurt in 1927), namely with a second thesis under Paul Tillich's supervision; it was titled *Kierkegaard. Konstruktion des Ästhetischen* (submitted in 1931 and published in 1933). His *magnum opus, Ästhetische Theorie,* was published posthumously in 1970. Both titles testify to the particular role and significance not only of aesthetics, but also, as will become evident soon, of Kierkegaard for Adorno's overall thought.[290]

---

[284]   Ibid., p. 493.

[285]   Ibid., p. 494.

[286]   Ibid., pp. 493–4. As to the question, if and to what extent Wittgenstein is possibly not only drawing on, but also modifying Kierkegaard's standpoint (in the *Fragments*) here, see Schulz, "Rezeptionsgeschichtliche Brocken," p. 429 (note 160).

[287]   Wittgenstein does not say so explicity, but he probably refers to the *Fragments*, here see, *SKS* 4, 285–6 / *PF*, 86ff.

[288]   Wittgenstein, *Bemerkungen*, p. 494.

[289]   Some important (Kierkegaardian) qualifications seem to get lost in Wittgenstein's account, though, in particular the concept of paradox; see Schulz, "Rezeptionsgeschichtliche Brocken," p. 430 (note 161).

[290]   In what follows I will restrict myself to an outline of Adorno's Kierkegaard reception; other thinkers belonging (in the widest possible sense) to what has been labelled "critical theory," "critical marxism" and/or "Frankfurt School" (Herbert Marcuse, Jürgen Habermas and, though to a lesser extent, Ernst Bloch and Walter Benjamin) will thus be ignored; let me simply refer to the pertinent secondary literature at this point: Günter Figal, "Die doppelte Geschichte. Das Verhältnis Walter Benjamins zu Søren Kierkegaard," *Neue Zeitschrift für*

With the exception of Karl Jaspers (and perhaps Emanuel Hirsch in theology) Adorno may be considered one of the very few paradigmatic representatives of what I take to be genuine borderline cases between productive reception and receptive production. For apart from Kierkegaard's implicit presence in much of Adorno's work, the latter has also written and published quite a bit about the Danish thinker.[291] Moreover, it is perfectly possible that Adorno's first contact with Kierkegaard's writings was mediated, once more, by the then seemingly omnipresent Theodor Haecker, and thus indirectly or even directly by the *Brenner*; however, we do not know for sure.[292] At any rate, the largely critical stance towards Kierkegaard that Adorno adopted in his book from 1933 proved more or less consistent over the years—a certain tendency to moderate the early polemic in favor of a stronger accent on the former's philosophical merits notwithstanding.

Throughout, Adorno reads *"Kierkegaard aus dem Idealismus und den Idealismus von Kierkegaard her,"*[293] for in his opinion it is the latter who precisely by way of exaggeration betrays *"die Unwahrheit des Idealismus, seine Eingeschlossenheit in*

Systematische Theologie und Religionsphilosophie, vol. 24, 1982, pp. 277–94; Fahrenbach, "Kierkegaards untergründige Wirkungsgeschichte," pp. 44–69 (Kierkegaard in Ernst Bloch and Herbert Marcuse); Flemming Harrits, "Grammatik des Glaubens oder Zwischenspiel über den Begriff der Geschichte. Zeit und Geschichte bei Søren Kierkegaard und Walter Benjamin," *Kierkegaardiana*, vol. 18, 1996, pp. 82–99; James L. Marsh, "Kierkegaard and Critical Theory," in *Kierkegaard in Post/Modernity*, pp. 199–215; Theunissen and Greve, "Einleitung," pp. 76–80. As to the more recent signs of attention to Kierkegaard in Jürgen Habermas see, for instance, Jürgen Habermas, "Die Grenze zwischen Glauben und Wissen. Zur Wirkungsgeschichte und aktuellen Bedeutung von Kants Religionsphilosophie," in his *Zwischen Naturalismus und Religion. Philosophische Aufsätze*, Frankfurt am Main: Suhrkamp 2005, pp. 216–57, especially pp. 237–8; pp. 244–7; see also Habermas, "Kommunikative Freiheit und negative Theologie. Fragen an Michael Theunissen," in *Vom sinnlichen Eindruck zum symbolischen Ausdruck. Philosophische Essays*, Frankfurt am Main: Suhrkamp 1997, pp. 112–35.

[291]   See Theodor W. Adorno, *Kierkegaard. Konstruktion des Ästhetischen*, Tübingen: Mohr 1933; "Kierkegaards Lehre von der Liebe," in *Kierkegaard. Konstruktion des Ästhetischen. Mit einer Beilage*, 2nd ed., Frankfurt am Main: Suhrkamp 1974, pp. 267–91; "Kierkegaard noch einmal," in *Materialien*, ed. by Theunissen and Greve, pp. 557–75.

[292]   In any case, Adorno finds surprisingly respectful words for Haecker; see, for instance, *Konstruktion*, p. 23; "Kierkegaard," pp. 559–60. Normally he refers to and quotes from the Schrempf edition, however; see *Konstruktion*, p. 254.

[293]   Theunissen and Greve, "Einleitung," p. 77. Adorno's Kierkegaard reception is discussed in Jørgen K. Bukdahl, *Om Søren Kierkegaard. Artikler i udvalg*, Copenhagen: Reitzel 1981, pp. 100–23; Hermann Deuser, *Dialektische Theologie. Studien zu Adornos Metaphysik und zum Spätwerk Kierkegaards*, Munich: Kaiser 1980; Hermann Deuser, "Kierkegaard und die kritische Theorie (Korreferat)," in *Die Rezeption Søren Kierkegaards*, pp. 101–13; Helmut Fahrenbach, *Die gegenwärtige Kierkegaard Auslegung in der deutschsprachigen Literatur von 1948 bis 1962*, Tübingen: Mohr 1962 (*Philosophische Rundschau, Beiheft 3*), pp. 77–82; Hans Friemond, *Existenz in Liebe nach Sören Kierkegaard*, Salzburg and Munich: Pustet 1965, pp. 135–8; Klaus-M. Kodalle, "Kierkegaard und die kritische Theorie," in *Die Rezeption Søren Kierkegaards*, pp. 70–100; Klaus-M. Kodalle, *Die Eroberung des Nutzlosen. Kritik des Wunschdenkens und die Zweckrationalität im Anschluß an Kierkegaard*, Paderborn: Schöningh 1988, pp. 195–214 (a slightly modified version of Kodalle's earlier article); Heinrich M.

Immanenz."²⁹⁴ The keywords for understanding this "exaggeration" are "inwardness without objects" (*objektlose Innerlichkeit*), "bourgeois interior" (*bürgerliches Interieur*), and "construction of the aesthetic" (*Konstruktion des Ästhetischen*). To begin with, immanence (to use Theunissen's term) is a characteristic feature of the idealist enterprise as such. The difference of, or more exactly the purportedly unbridgeable gap between, subject and object, I and world, history and nature, mind and matter, etc. is deemed a mere appearance—and precisely as such it calls for being reconstructed as a difference *within* the cognizing and acting subject or as subject-*immanent*. However, in idealist terms this subject, which in the act or process of *realizing* itself as the unity of itself and its other simultaneously *establishes* itself as such a unity (in other words, posits itself) and cannot be identical with the "empirical I," that is, with the consciousness and activity of a particular individual. Rather, it is to be identified with the act and awareness of an "absolute I" (Fichte) or, alternatively, with the logic and phenomenology plus the natural and historical process of becoming transparent to itself *as* the absolute I (Hegel). Now, according to Adorno, Kierkegaard's project, although aimed at a radical critique and overcoming of the "phantastic" immanence of idealism, boils down, ironically enough, to a mere exaggeration and thus perpetuation of what it set out to overcome in the first place. This (*nota bene*, fully inadvertent) exaggeration comprises two aspects, for not only does the unification of subject and object take place in Kierkegaard within the empirical I,²⁹⁵ but also, the respective "objects" themselves, although dimly envisaged as the irreducible other of subjectivity, are simultaneously spiritualized and "volatilized," as it were: "*Es gibt bei Kierkegaard so wenig ein Subjekt-Objekt im Hegelschen Sinne wie seinshaltige Objekte; nur isolierte, von der dunklen Andersheit eingeschlossene Subjektivität.*"²⁹⁶ For Adorno the keyword to prove his point is inwardness, and structurally paradigmatic models of it are to be found in Kierkegaard's *The Sickness unto Death* and *Either/Or*, Part Two in particular. It is easy to see, why: according to Anti-Climacus being human is coextensive with being an existing self and as such being and acting out one's being in a specific relation. However, this relation is not to be mistaken for the relation of a subject to an object. Rather, it is a relation that exclusively (and according to Adorno, solipsistically) relates to *itself*, or relates to a relation and *in* so doing relates to itself.²⁹⁷ Likewise, Judge William states time and again that what constitutes the self is an act of choice. However, it is not some given object which suggests itself to be chosen, but rather the subject itself, *as* choosing or as having to choose: Peter becomes a self, precisely by choosing himself as having to choose (and vice versa,

Schmidinger, *Das Problem des Interesses und die Philosophie Sören Kierkegaards*, Freiburg and Munich: Alber 1983, pp. 320–4; Theunissen and Greve, "Einleitung," pp. 77ff.

²⁹⁴   Theunissen and Greve, "Einleitung," p. 77.

²⁹⁵   See Adorno, *Konstruktion*, p. 83: In Kierkegaard the dialectical method is "*nach innen geschlagen: was [für Hegel]...die Weltgeschichte, ist für Kierkegaard der einzelne Mensch.*"

²⁹⁶   Ibid., p. 31. In Kierkegaard's Christian ethics (as put forward in *Works of Love*) Adorno finds hints as to an equally abstract and thus ethically inappropriate, in fact even dangerous, inwardness; see Adorno, "Liebe."

²⁹⁷   See *SKS* 11, 129 / *SUD*, 13–14.

by choosing the inevitability of choosing as part and parcel of himself, *as* a self).[298] As seen in this light, we are, according to Adorno, entitled to speak of an inwardness without objects in Kierkegaard, an inwardness which ignores or even openly denies "*die Abhängigkeit der Person von der auswendigen Geschichte.*"[299]

Now, what does an inwardness, thus conceived, have to do with a (bourgeois) "interior"—apart from the obvious semantic proximity of both terms? Adorno's answer is: reality and thus also the epitome of what might be or become a possible object for a subject is illustrated by and is to be compared in Kierkegaard to a particular space of the "interior" (*Intérieur*[300]), namely, to what is part of and experienced inside of a—*nota bene*, bourgeois!—flat. For it is not so much the world in its natural, historical, social, political, and economic restraints, which is and appears as real in the context of such a scenery; rather, it is (as he continues to explain by invoking pertinent passages from the pseudonymous authorship) simply a *mirror*, which is and appears as real here, in other words, a medium of reflecting the world and reflecting it in such a way as to make the reflecting subject forget that what it perceives as real *is* in fact nothing but a reflection, an inverted appearance of and substitute for the real world: "*Der in den Reflexionsspiegel hineinschaut, ist der untätige, vom Produktionsprozess der Wirtschaft abgeschiedene Private. Der Reflexionsspiegel zeugt für Objektlosigkeit—nur den Schein von Dingen bringt er in die Wohnung—und private Abgeschiedenheit.*"[301]

Both ideas, inwardness without objects and the bourgeois interior as an allegory of the same inwardness as self-deceptive reflection, give us a hint as to the understanding of Kierkegaard's "construction of the aesthetical" and, consequently, of the essentially mythical character of this construction. According to Adorno, aesthetics are not to be construed in Kierkegaard as a theory of art or of producing and/or perceiving something as beautiful, but rather as a theory of the existing spirit, inasmuch as it is conceived of as a subject of desire, which, as such, always seeks enjoyment and pleasure as its highest goal. However, the subject of aesthetic desire invariably falls prey to illusion; it cannot but misunderstand itself, its object and the true nature of its own relation to the desired object. A paradigmatic case in point is the page in Mozart's opera *Figaro's Wedding,* for whom desire and desired object have not yet separated from each other, so that in him a real desire has not yet been constituted.[302] For Adorno this mythical figure of the page serves as an allegory for the truth about Kierkegaard's myth of "idealist spiritualism" as a whole: "*Die immanente Spiritualität selber ist mythisch.*"[303] Speaking and/or thinking mythically always indicates, first, an inadequate and as such necessarily self-deceptive or illusory account of the relation between subject and object; secondly, for the myth-generating subject, to be struck precisely by what is supposed to be banned or excluded by that account (in Kierkegaard's "spiritualistic" myth: to be struck by

---

[298]   See *SKS* 3, 163ff. / *EO2*, 167ff.
[299]   Adorno, *Konstruktion*, p. 35.
[300]   See ibid., pp. 44ff.
[301]   Ibid., p. 78.
[302]   *SKS* 2, 81–4 / *EO1*, 75–8.
[303]   Adorno, *Konstruktion*, p. 61.

the very power of objectivity, which belies the pretended autonomy and autarky of inwardness); finally, the impossibility of immanently separating the truth inherent to and about the myth from its mythical—and thus invariably also: poetical or narrative instead of conceptual—form, so that this truth is only expressed indirectly, hence also without philosophical self-transparency and justification. Following Adorno, we are supposed to conclude that the "musical narrative" or myth of the page in Mozart's *Figaro* (*nota bene*, a narrative about the original and most primitive form of aesthetical existence) contains the entire Kierkegaardian myth of inwardness in a nutshell!

This early polemic is only one side of the matter, however. For the genuinely productive side of Adorno's (later) Kierkegaard appropriation points to a considerably deeper and more extensive indebtedness to the latter than he would presumably have been ready to admit. This goes for Adorno's Hegel critique, in particular, as he "*entnimmt...dieser [sc. Kierkegaard's] Kritik die Grundfigur seines Philosophierens überhaupt.*"[304] Adorno's Hegel critique is supposed to make way for a "negative dialectic,"[305] aimed at a philosophical "rescue of the non-identical" (*Rettung des Nichtidentischen*). However, the non-identical, conceived of as "*die eigene Identität der Sache gegen ihre Identifikationen,*"[306] is actually

> *das im Sinne Kierkegaards Wirkliche, welches das Denken nicht mit sich zu identizieren vermag....Man kann demnach geradezu sagen, daß die Negative Dialektik [Adorno's] die Hegels so aufnimmt, wie sie durch das existenzdialektische Nein zu einer auf bloßen Identifikationen beruhenden Versöhnung berichtigt worden ist.*[307]

To a certain extent Adorno has himself admitted Kierkegaard's merits, impact, and (if only indirectly) his own indebtedness to him, and this also in *Negative Dialektik*. He writes: "*Kierkegaards Protest gegen die Philosophie war auch der gegen das verdinglichte Bewußtsein, in dem, nach seinem Wort, die Subjektivität ausgegangen ist: er nahm gegen die Philosophie auch deren Interesse wahr.*"[308] And this is precisely, what Adorno himself sets out and pretends to do: takings sides with, speaking for and preserving the true interests of the subject as an expression of the non-identical, vis-à-vis its present state of self-alienation.

(19) Speaking, on the one hand, of Adorno and the period up to the end of the Second World War, while, on the other hand, having to account for the essential aspects of a Kierkegaard reception within the field of literary studies and of belles-lettres also, it would seem natural, indeed indispensable to take a closer look at Thomas Mann (1875–1955) who is quickly put on the agenda, whenever it comes

---

[304]   Theunissen and Greve, "Einleitung," p. 78.

[305]   See Theodor W. Adorno, *Negative Dialektik*, Frankfurt am Main: Suhrkamp 1966.

[306]   Ibid., p. 162.

[307]   Theunissen and Greve, "Einleitung," p. 78.

[308]   Adorno, *Negative Dialektik*, p. 127; see also "Kierkegaard." One could even suspect that Adorno's plea for art as the only remaining medium of adequately expressing and thus also saving and preserving the non-identical under the conditions of universal delusion (see F.W. Adorno, *Ästhetische Theorie*, Frankfurt am Main: Suhrkamp 1970) has a certain Kierkegaardian ring to it; at least, if negatively, it may reflect the latter's impact.

to discussing matters like this. And in fact, on grounds of history of reception alone we cannot but take him into consideration—if only to prove that he does not, or at least not by all means, belong here! The reason for my being hesitant at this point is simple enough: while writing his allegedly pertinent and reception-historically significant works, Mann demonstrably took very little notice of Kierkegaard. Therefore, it seems we are not entitled to speak of a reception in any stricter sense, much less, *a fortiori*, of a productive reception.[309] Some might want to challenge this claim, for instance, by pointing to the undeniable fact that Thomas and his brother Heinrich Mann belonged to the "early recipients of *Der Brenner*,"[310] so that in all probability he must have come across Kierkegaard at that time already. It is also true that Mann knew Lukács' famous early essay about the Danish thinker.[311] On the other hand, it can just as little be denied that his first-hand knowledge of the Danish author came (not only "a little,"[312] but in fact) much later. This happened in the early 1940s, after his emigration to the U.S., where he met Adorno who happened to be one of his neighbors. Adorno apparently made a deep and lasting impression on Mann,[313] and this, in particular, because of the former's vast erudition in philosophy and aesthetic (especially musical) theory. A mutually fruitful collaboration began, occasioned in the first place by Mann's asking Adorno to help him come to terms with some difficult musicological issues that he was struggling with in the process of writing his masterpiece, *Doktor Faustus* (1947). Soon Adorno exerted an enormous influence on the book in general and its musicological passages in particular.[314]

---

[309]   As to Mann's Kierkegaard reception, see: Matthias Klaus, *Thomas Mann und Skandinavien. Mit zwei Aufsätzen von Thomas Mann*, Lübeck: Schmidt-Römhild 1969; Thomas Kamla, " 'Christliche Kunst mit negativem Vorzeichen': Kierkegaard and Doktor Faustus," *Neophilologus*, vol. 63, 1979, pp. 583–7; Steffen Steffensen, "Die Einwirkung Kierkegaards auf die deutschsprachige Literatur des 20. Jahrhunderts," in *Akten des VI. internationalen Germanistenkongresses Basel 1980*, ed. by H. Rupp and H.-G. Roloff, Frankfurt am Main: Peter Lang 1980, pp. 62–6. I restrict myself to Thomas Mann in the present context, although in principal it would seem worthwhile to take a closer look at some Kierkegaardian traces in authors like Hermann Broch (1856–1951), Hermann Hesse (1877–1962), Gottfried Benn (1886–1956), Alexander Döblin (1878–1957) and Robert Musil (1880–1942) also. As to the latter, see, for instance, Sebastian Hüsch, *Möglichkeit und Wirklichkeit. Eine vergleichende Studie zu Sören Kierkegaards "Entweder—Oder" und Robert Musils "Mann ohne Eigenschaften,"* Stuttgart: Ibidem-Verlag 2004; as to the rest, see the brief account in Kloeden, "Einfluß und Bedeutung," pp. 93–6.

[310]   Malik, *Receiving Kierkegaard*, p. 369. As to the available evidence for this claim, see ibid.

[311]   Ibid.

[312]   Ibid.

[313]   See Mann's own lively report of both men's first encounter, in "Die Entstehung des Doktor Faustus. *Roman eines Romans*," in Thomas Mann, *Das essayistische Werk*, ed. by H. Bürgin, vols. 1–8, Frankfurt am Main and Hamburg: Fischer 1968, vol. 3, 1968, pp. 88–205, here pp. 108–11.

[314]   Mann himself sums up Adorno's impact as follows: "*Die Darstellung der Reihen-Musik und ihre in Dialog aufgelöste Kritik, wie das XXII. Faustus-Kapitel sie bietet, gründet sich ganz und gar auf Adorno'sche Analysen, und das tun auch gewisse Bemerkungen über die Tonsprache des späten Beethoven, wie sie schon früh im Buch...vorkommen.*" ("Die

Adorno's influence went far beyond the limits of sheer music theory, though. For, among other things, he called Mann's attention to Kierkegaard. This did not happen, however, until the latter's interest had been awakened by Adorno's own book on the subject, a copy of which had been given to him as a gift by the author. Mann writes: "*Viel belehrte ich mich jetzt [sc. 1944] über Kierkegaard, sonderbarerweise bevor ich mich entschloß, ihn selbst zu lesen. Adorno hatte mir seine bedeutende Arbeit über ihn zugestellt. Ich studierte sie zusammen mit dem glänzenden Essay von [Georg] Brandes.*"[315] Keen on eventually acquiring some first-hand knowledge, he turned to Kierkegaard's own writings soon afterwards—to *Either/Or*, at any rate, which he, as he openly admits, read "*mit tiefer Aufmerksamkeit.*"[316] Especially the essay on Mozart's *Don Giovanni* [317] left a deep and lasting impression, for here Mann found most welcome support for his claim that music should be viewed as an expression of the demonic sphere of existence, which both historically and logically presupposes Christianity and the principle of spirit as opposed to sensuality. In the famous "talk with the devil" (*Teufelsgespräch*),[318] Mann refers to the Mozart essay (if only implicitly) through the mouth of the former:

> *Wenn ich nicht irre, lasest du [sc. Leverkühn] da vorhin in dem Buch des in die Ästhetik verliebten Christen? Der wußte Bescheid und verstand sich auf mein besondres Verhältnis zu dieser schönen Kunst [sc. der Musik],—der allerchristlichsten Kunst, wie er findet,—mit negativem Vorzeichen natürlich, vom Christentum zwar eingesetzt und entwickelt, aber verneint und ausgeschlossen als dämonisches [sic] Bereich.*[319]

Apparently, we have encountered some explicit evidence here that Mann's first-hand reception of Kierkegaard started in the early to mid-1940s, while he was deeply immersed in the process of writing *Doktor Faustus*, and that, furthermore, the fruits of this reception immediately found their way into the *magnum opus* itself. To a certain degree this judgment seems correct and irrefutable. It does not capture the complete picture, however, and I would rather remain hesitant about speaking of

---

Entstehung," p. 110.) That Adorno was literally omnipresent in Mann's life at this point is clearly witnessed by the numerous and often substantial references to the former in "Die Entstehung," pp. 108–11; p. 119; p. 123; p. 130; pp. 134–5; p. 139; p. 146; p. 155; pp. 163–6; p. 182; pp. 199–200. However, in a postscript to the novel itself Mann has, strangely enough, completely surpressed Adorno's influence; instead, he swears to his complete indebtedness to Arnold Schönberg (whom he also knew personally), and this precisely with reference to chapter XXII of the book! See Thomas Mann, *Doktor Faustus. Das Leben des deutschen Tonsetzers Adrian Leverkühn. Erzählt von einem Freunde*, Berlin: Aufbau 1952, p. 691.

[315]   Mann, "Die Entstehung," p. 130. The quotation is from Mann's journals, which he frequently refers to in "Die Entstehung." Given Mann gives a trustworthy report about his own reading history here, we may take it as a piece of evidence for the assumption that his earliest known reference to Kierkegaard (which dates from 1936) rests on second-hand knowledge only: see Matthias, *Thomas Mann*, p. 27.

[316]   Mann, "Die Entstehung," p. 139.

[317]   See *SKS* 2, 53–136 / *EO1*, 47–135. See Mann's reference to the essay in "Die Entstehung," p. 139.

[318]   See chapter XXV of Mann, *Doktor Faustus*, pp. 300–40.

[319]   Ibid., p. 329. In comparison, see *SKS* 2, 71 / *EO1*, 64–5.

a genuinely productive Kierkegaard reception in Mann (much less of a receptive production). It is the author himself who gives us a hint, which should alert us not to draw any rash conclusions here: *"Die Verwandtschaft des Romans mit der Ideenwelt Kierkegaards*, ohne jede Kenntnis davon, *ist äußerst merkwürdig."*[320] In other words, Mann suggests that even though he occasionally referred to Kierkegaard in his *magnum opus*, the organizing ideas, put forward in the novel, about the origin and nature of music had already been discovered and tentatively formulated by him independently of and prior to running into Kierkegaard. To be sure, Mann certainly found a welcome ally in the latter, but obviously not a primary source for generating those ideas in the first place. Therefore, if we take his word for it (and I see no reason not to do so), we are left with the conclusion that, typologically speaking, Mann's relation to Kierkegaard is one of the very rare instances of a borderline case between production without reception (= pure material reflections), a (meager) receptive production plus, finally, a few traces of a genuinely productive reception!

III. Research: The Receptive Years, 1946 and After

(1) The present essay is an attempt in reception history, not in research history. Therefore, I can and will be much briefer in its third and concluding section, as we are now entering the realm of what may be called "academic" Kierkegaard appropriation or Kierkegaard research.[321] That is to say we are entering a realm of literary production, which is more or less receptive in nature. To begin with, it does not come as a surprise that parallel to (and often as a side-effect or even mirror of)[322] the "productive" Kierkegaard appropriations, which I have sketched in the previous part of my essay as particularly significant for the period between, roughly 1910 and 1945, a considerable number of hermeneutically ambitious German secondary sources dating from the same period saw the light of day, and this especially in theology.

---

[320] Mann, "Die Entstehung," p. 139 (my emphasis).
[321] I can also be briefer here because a lot of ground has been covered already by the existing surveys of the history of research. Among these, more recent examples include: Michael Bongardt, " 'Das Kreuz, das die Philosophie nicht tragen konnte.' Zu aktuellen Auseinandersetzungen mit Kierkegaard und seinem Werk," *Theologische Revue*, no. 96, 2000, pp. 179–200; Walter Dietz, "Neuerscheinungen zur Philosophie Kierkegaards," *Allgemeine Zeitschrift für Philosophie*, vol. 3, 1993, pp. 79–88; Jochem Hennigfeld, "Denken der Existenz. Einübungen in Kierkegaard," *Philosophische Rundschau*, vol. 40, 1993, pp. 310–19; Reinhard Olschanski, "Angst—Wiederholung—Lebenslust. Zur neueren Kierkegaard Literatur," *Philosophische Rundschau*, vol. 50, 2003, pp. 141–54. Among the older surveys the following are particularly noteworthy: Wilhelm Anz, "Fragen der Kierkegaard Interpretation I/II," *Theologische Rundschau*, vol. 20, 1952, pp. 26–72; vol. 26, 1960, pp. 44–79; pp. 168–205; Fahrenbach, *Kierkegaard Auslegung*; Michael Theunissen, "Das Kierkegaard Bild in der neueren Forschung und Deutung," in *Sören Kierkegaard*, ed. by Schrey, pp. 324–84.
[322] Note, for instance, that the first monograph on Kierkegaard and Karl Barth came out as early as 1925, see Anders Gemmer and August Messer, *Sören Kierkegaard und Karl Barth*, Stuttgart: Strecker & Schroeder 1925.

More than a few of these publications turn out to be equally detailed and comprehensive accounts of Kierkegaard's thought as a whole. Thus, for some years Arnold Gilg's book[323] was widely used as a standard work on and introduction to Kierkegaard's theology in context. Although neglecting "*[s]o außerordentlich bedeutsame neutestamentliche Gedanken wie...Reichsbegriff und... Kirchengedanke,*"[324] Kierkegaard's overall theological thought is said to be of "*geradezu bestürzende[r] Aktualität*"[325] and interpreted to this effect by focusing throughout on the relation between immanent and paradoxical religion (Religiousness A and B). A few years later Friedrich Adolf Voigt published a voluminous monograph in which he outlined Kierkegaard's struggle against Romanticism, contemporary theology, and the Church in order to argue for the latter's role as a spokesman "*der inneren Opposition des [sc. neutestamentlichen] Ideales*"[326] against the confusions of an epoch suffering (especially in post-war Germany) from severe political and ideological pressures. Shortly afterwards, in 1929, Walter Ruttenbeck's book came out, the most scholarly work to date on Kierkegaard's thought.[327] For a couple of years it proved unsurpassed as a comprehensive account of the latter's theology in its historical and systematic context. Among other things the book contains lengthy passages tackling the history of reception plus the current Kierkegaard debate in Germany up to the mid 1920s. Ruttenbeck's emphasis is on Kierkegaard's significance as a theological thinker, and in his opinion this relevance lies, first and foremost, "*in der Forderung eines...existentiellen Denkens,*" a way of thinking, which Ruttenbeck defines as "*das Denken der Existenz 'vor Gott.'* "[328]

Catholic theologians jumped on the Kierkegaard bandwagon at roughly the same time, and this often with unexpected results. For instance, Alois Dempf tried to take "*Kierkegaard gegen seine eigenen Nachfolger in Schutz..., gegen die Theologen, die ihn fälschlich als Feind der christlichen Philosophie betrachten, und gegen die Philosophen, die ihn für ihre Feindschaft gegen die Theologen ausbeuten wollen.*"[329] According to Dempf, the actual historical consequences and effects of Kierkegaard's impact within the humanities of the nineteenth and early twentieth century appear ambiguous at best. On the one hand, his fight against Hegel as a "*heidnische*

---

[323]   Arnold Gilg, *Sören Kierkegaard*, Munich: Kaiser 1926.
[324]   Ibid., p. 225.
[325]   Ibid., p. VII.
[326]   Friedrich Adolf Voigt, *Sören Kierkegaard im Kampfe mit der Romantik, der Theologie und der Kirche. Zur Selbstprüfung unserer Gegenwart anbefohlen*, Berlin: Furche 1928, p. 412.
[327]   Walter Ruttenbeck, *Sören Kierkegaard. Der christliche Denker und sein Werk*, Berlin and Frankfurt (Oder): Trowitzsch 1929.
[328]   Ibid., p. 360. Walter Künneth can be mentioned here as another exemplary author drawing on Kierkegaardian resources in a modern German Protestant context and this with the explicit aim in mind of reformulating and reevaluating traditional Christian doctrines (here, the doctrine of sin) in light of these resources, see his *Die Lehre von der Sünde, dargestellt an der Lehre Sören Kierkegaards in ihrem Verhältnis zur Lehre der neuesten Theologie*, Gütersloh: Bertelsmann 1927.
[329]   Alois Dempf, *Kierkegaards Folgen*, Leipzig: Hegner 1935, p. 223.

Identitätslehre von Gott, Mensch und Welt"[330] seems to have been largely successful, and rightly so. This notwithstanding, the fight has simultaneously, if inadvertently, paved the way for a false belief in the impossibility in principle of Christian metaphysics. By unmasking this reception-historically and systematically fatal error, Dempf is quick to admit that in the end Kierkegaard's (albeit indirect) merit lies in creating a *"neue Athmosphäre für die christliche Metaphysik"*[331]—*nota bene*, a metaphysic à la Thomas Aquinas and the Catholic idea of *analogia entis*.[332]

That Kierkegaard research flourished so much in German theology during the second and third decades of the twentieth century may also be a consequence and effect of (or at least and vice versa, expressed by) the fact that the *magna opera* of two prominent Scandinavian theologians, Torsten Bohlin and Eduard Geismar, came out in German translation at roughly the same time.[333] Occasionally their presence is noticeable even in philosophy (inasmuch as the latter is concerned with Kierkegaard). Here perhaps the most remarkable contemporary accomplishment is Martin Thust's highly original, methodically sophisticated, if at times also idiosyncratic project of reconstructing Kierkegaard's thought as a "system of subjectivity."[334] According to Thust, the authorship as a whole describes and analyzes the process of becoming a self in terms of spelling out the task of actualizing three basic inner "movements": *Selbstübersteigerung* of the "immediate self," *Selbstbindung* of the "historical self," and *Selbstbezeugung* of the "true self."[335] The need to constantly shift the descriptive focus and methodical perspective from typological to systematical to historical within *each* of these self-developmental steps is vindicated by claiming that such a shift corresponds and is integral to the unfolding of the three Kierkegaardian stages of existence: for also *"[d]as Zusichselbstkommen des Menschen hat ein typologische, eine systematische und eine historische 'Seite.'"*[336]

---

[330]   Ibid.

[331]   Ibid.

[332]   See ibid., p. 14. Other contemporary German Catholics who in one way or another tried to reclaim Kierkegaard for Catholic concerns and purposes include: Erich Przywara, *Das Geheimnis Kierkegaards*, Munich and Berlin: Oldenbourg 1929; Peter Wust, *Die Dialektik des Geistes*, Augsburg: Filser 1928; see also Peter Wust, *Ungewissheit und Wagnis*, Munich: Kösel 1937.

[333]   Eduard Geismar, *Sören Kierkegaard. Seine Lebensentwicklung und seine Wirksamkeit als Schriftsteller*, trans. by E. Krüger, Göttigen: Vandenhoeck & Ruprecht 1929; Torsten Bohlin, *Kierkegaards dogmatische Anschauung in ihrem geschichtlichen Zusammenhange*, trans. by I. Meyer-Lüne, Gütersloh: Der Rufer/Evangelischer Verlag 1927. See also Bohlin's earlier pertinent works: *Sören Kierkegaard und das religiöse Denken der Gegenwart. Eine Studie*, trans. by I. Meyer-Lüne, Munich et al.: Rösl 1923; *Sören Kierkegaards Leben und Werden. Kurze Darstellung aufgrund der ersten Quellen*, trans. by P. Katz, Gütersloh: Bertelsmann 1925.

[334]   Thus the subtitle of his book: see Martin Thust, *Sören Kierkegaard. Der Dichter des Religiösen. Grundlagen eines Systems der Subjektivität*, Munich: Beck 1931.

[335]   Ibid., pp. 555–6.

[336]   Ibid., p. 559.

The theme of subjectivity (then widely debated, thanks to the impact of Heidegger, Jaspers et al.) is taken up by other contemporary authors, too,[337] frequently with special reference to the concept of despair as one of its most significant expressions in Kierkegaard's psychology.[338] Due, in particular, to the growing popularity of Freud's psychoanalysis, Kierkegaard's own "subjectivity" is tackled in a number of studies at roughly the same time, and this in terms of analyzing the latter's personality with special emphasis on some allegedly pathological character traits. Thus, Fanny Lowtzky seeks to give a psychoanalytically satisfying account of Kierkegaard's split with his fiancée. She suggests that what Kierkegaard was actually (if subconsciously) striving for

> war die Wiederholung seiner Kinderphantasie: die Mutter wie der Vater zu besitzen, mit
> ihr, wie der Vater, geschlechtlich zu verkehren....In der Identifizierung seiner Braut mit der
> Mutter, seiner selbst mit dem Vater, wollte Kierkegaard in der Ehe seine Inzestwünsche
> realisieren.[339]

However, incest is (experienced as being) strictly forbidden in Kierkegaard's view; moreover, "*[z]u dem Inzestverbot gesellt sich in der Identifizierung der Braut mit der Mutter die Übertragung der unbewußten Haßgefühle gegen sie...so war Kierkegaard gezwungen, infolge des Inzestverbotes und seiner Aggressionen gegen seine Braut die Verlobung mit ihr aufzugeben.*"[340]

---

[337]   See, for instance, Liselotte Richter, *Der Begriff der Subjektivität bei Kierkegaard. Ein Beitrag zur christlichen Existenzdarstellung*, Würzburg: Triltsch 1934. Richter defines subjectivity (in the Kierkegaardian sense) "*als der Existenzausdruck eines auf die eigne Innerlichkeit des Subjekts gerichteten Erkennens*" (ibid., p. 2); see also ibid., p. 31; pp. 34–5. See also Karl Meusers, *Der existierende Denker bei Sören Kierkegaard*, Ph.D. Thesis, University of Cologne 1926.

[338]   See Max Sack, *Die Verzweiflung. Eine Untersuchung ihres Wesens und ihrer Entstehung. Mit einem Anhang: Sören Kierkegaards 'Krankheit zum Tode,'* Erlangen: Kallmünz 1930; Bernhard Meerpohl, *Die Verzweiflung als metaphysisches Problem in der Philosophie Sören Kierkegaards*, Würzburg: C.J. Becker 1934. The concept of despair has been a matter of special concern (not only) for German Kierkegaard research up to the present, as is evident from the constantly growing number of pertinent studies; see, for instance, Bernd Heimbüchel, *Verzweiflung als Grundphänomen der menschlichen Existenz. Kierkegaards Analysen der existierenden Subjektivität*, Frankfurt am Main: Peter Lang 1983; Michael Theunissen, *Das Selbst auf dem Grund der Verzweiflung. Kierkegaards negativistische Methode*, Frankfurt am Main: Hain 1991; Theunissen, *Der Begriff Verzweiflung. Korrekturen an Kierkegaard*, Frankfurt am Main: Suhrkamp 1993; Joachim Ringleben, *Die Krankheit zum Tode von Sören Kierkegaard. Erklärung und Kommentar*, Göttingen: Vandenhoeck & Ruprecht 1995; Friedhelm Decher, *Verzweiflung. Anatomie eines Affektes*, Lüneburg: Klampen 2002; Christiane Tietz-Steiding, *Freiheit zu sich selbst. Entfaltung eines christlichen Begriffs von Selbstannahme*, Göttingen: Vandenhoeck & Ruprecht 2005 (see especially chapter II).

[339]   Fanny Lowtzky, *Sören Kierkegaard. Das subjektive Erlebnis und die religiöse Offenbarung. Eine psychoanalytische Studie einer Fast-Selbstanalyse*, Vienna: Internationaler psychoanalytischer Verlag 1935, pp. 116–17.

[340]   Ibid., p. 117. Other contemporary psychological and/or psychoanalytical accounts of Kierkegaard include: August Vetter, *Frömmigkeit als Leidenschaft. Eine Deutung Kierkegaards*, Leipzig: Insel 1928; Friedrich C. Fischer, *Die Nullpunkt-Existenz. Dargestellt*

More fruitful inspirations from Kierkegaard's authorship surface in the efforts of contemporary pedagogy and philosophy of education. A case in point is Eberhard Grisebach who repeatedly draws on Kierkegaard in his attempt to determine *Die Grenzen des Erziehers*.[341] He does so, however, without completely taking sides with the latter, who in his opinion got stuck "*in der Theorie eines Mensch-Gottverhältnisses und damit in einer prinzipiellen, nachträglich konstruierenden Dialektik, die gerade das vereinheitlicht, was ewig geschieden sein müßte, nämlich Erkenntnis und Glaube.*"[342] Grisebach holds that such a dialectical unification invariably leads (and in fact led Kierkegaard) to a "*Grenzüberschreitung des Erziehers,*"[343] which he sets out to explain and to overcome in the remainder of his book.

(2) Although most of the theological studies previously mentioned reflect the impact of and the debate about Karl Barth and/or dialectical theology at least to some extent,[344] Barth himself cannot be considererd a founder of a "school" of Kierkegaard interpretation in the proper sense of the word (a fact, which seems hardly surprising, as Barth himself took pains to establish and preserve a somewhat distanced and partly critical attitude towards Kierkegaard, especially in his later years). The most prominent of his former students who carried on his message by also incorporating certain elements of it into his own Kierkegaard approach, was Hermann Diem. In his first book[345] Diem developed a strong sense for the methodological issues looming

---

an der Lebensform Sören Kierkegaards, Munich: Beck 1933. See also Fritz H. Ryssel, *Große Kranke: Sören Kierkegaard, Vincent van Gogh, Reinhold Schneider*, Gütersloh: Mohn 1974. A purely systematic reading of certain parallels in Kierkegaard, Freud, and Lacan with special emphasis on the concept of repetition has more recently been given by Elisabeth Strowick: *Passagen der Wiederholung. Kierkegaard—Lacan—Freud*, Stuttgart: Metzler 1999. See also Jörg Disse, "Menschliche Psyche und Gottesverhältnis: Kierkegaard versus Freud," *Theologie und Philosophie*, vol. 78, 2003, pp. 509–30.

[341]   See Eberhard Grisebach, *Die Grenzen des Erziehers*, Darmstadt: Wissenschaftliche Buchgesellschaft 1966 [1924].

[342]   Ibid., p. XVI.

[343]   Ibid., p. XII. Contemporary or later efforts to draw on Kierkegaard for pedagogical purposes include: Ingrid Blanke, *Sinn und Grenze christlicher Erziehung. Kierkegaard und die Problematik christlicher Erziehung in unserer Zeit*, Frankfurt am Main: Peter Lang 1978; Michael Heymel, *Das Humane lernen: Glaube und Erziehung bei Sören Kierkegaard*, Göttingen: Vandenhoeck & Ruprecht 1988; Theoderich Kampmann, *Kierkegaard als religiöser Erzieher*, Paderborn: Schöningh 1949; Walter Rest, *Indirekte Mitteilung als bildendes Verfahren dargestellt am Leben und Werk Sören Kierkegaards*, Ph.D. Thesis, University of Münster 1937; Helmut Schaal, *Erziehung bei Kierkegaard. Das "Aufmerksammachen auf das Religiöse" als pädagogische Kategorie*, Heidelberg: Quelle & Meyer 1958; Alfred Schäfer, *Kierkegaard. Eine Grenzbestimmung des Pädagogischen*, Wiesbaden: Verlag für Sozialwissenschaften 2004. See also Otto Friedrich Bollnow, *Existenzphilosophie und Pädagogik. Versuch über unstetige Formen der Erziehung*, 5th ed., Stuttgart: Kohlhammer 1977 [1959].

[344]   As for a strongly anti-Barthian example, see Klaas Schilder, *Zur Begriffsgeschichte des 'Paradoxon.' Mit besonderer Berücksichtigung Calvins und des nach-kierkegaardschen 'Paradoxon,'* Kampen: Kok 1933.

[345]   See Hermann Diem, *Philosophie und Christentum bei Sören Kierkegaard*, Munich: Kaiser 1929. All but accidentally the book was written and published at roughly the same

large in the the former's writings. For him these issues culminated in the question, as to whether these writings could and should be called philosophical or theological in nature. Diem's answer is that they are definitely *not* theology, but rather an attempt in, indeed an impressive manifestation of, a *"christliche Philosophie"*[346] in the proper sense. As such, they testify to a deep and far-reaching coincidence or *"Übereinstimmung zwischen Philosophie und Christentum."*[347] This coincidence is based upon the fact that *"Kierkegaard [bewältigt] das ganze philosophische und christliche Denken in einer durchgehenden [Existenz-]Dialektik..., die, von der christlichen Offenbarung als Voraussetzung ausgehend, die Möglichkeiten des immanenten Denkens untersucht, um wieder bei der Offenbarung zu enden."*[348] And since this way of thinking has to be exerted *"mit denselben Mitteln des immanenten Denkens...wie...das Nachdenken über die Grenzen der Immanenz, können wir es genau so gut christliche Philosophie heißen."*[349] By contrast (as Diem suggests by exactly reproducing a leading methodological principle of the post-dialectical Barth), theology has to be conceived of as a mode of thought, which not only proceeds *"unter der* Voraussetzung *der Offenbarung...sondern das die* Offenbarung selbst denkt, um sich über die Voraussetzung klar zu werden."*[350] As such, it requires *"eine kirchliche Vollmacht,"* though, and is only possible as a genuine *"Angelegenheit der Kirche,"*[351] so that, accordingly, Kierkegaard could not claim and in fact never did claim to be a theologian.

(3) Hirsch's *Kierkegaard Studien* are certainly *not*, as Matthias Wilke has recently suggested, *"ein sprechendes Zeugnis der* Anfänge *sowohl der deutschen Kierkegaard Forschung als auch der theologischen Kierkegaard Rezeption in Deutschland."*[352] Such a claim, although clearly erring historically, is all but untypical; rather, it appears highly characteristic of authors (viewing themselves as) belonging to the very same tradition, the impact and significance of which they are about to evaluate—and thus, in

---

time as Barth had begun to recast his own theological fundaments with a special emphasis on theological method.

[346]   Ibid., p. 346.

[347]   Ibid., p. 345; p. 341.

[348]   Ibid., pp. 341–2 . For Diem, Kierkegaard's unifying methodological perspective of "existential dialectics" (*Existenzdialektik*) simultaneously secures the overall unity in the varying perspectives of his pseudonyms on the one hand and between them and Kierkegaard himself on the other hand. Since there is a basic and strategically applied *"methodische Einheit"* (ibid., p. 364) between all of them, there is no need any longer to distinguish between their and Kierkegaard's own material "views," see pp. 355–6.

[349]   Ibid., p. 346.

[350]   Ibid. (my emphasis).

[351]   Ibid., p. 347. Diem has further elaborated on the methodological implications of Kierkegaard's authorship in his later writings, see Hermann Diem, *Die Existenzdialektik von Sören Kierkegaard*, Zollikon-Zürich: Evangelischer Verlag 1950; *Sören Kierkegaard. Spion im Dienste Gottes*, Frankfurt am Main: Fischer 1957; *Sören Kierkegaard. Eine Einführung*, Göttingen: Vandenhoeck & Ruprecht 1964. The topic played an important role in his dogmatics, see also Hermann Diem, *Theologie als kirchliche Wissenschaft. Handreichung zur Einübung ihrer Probleme. Band II: Dogmatik. Ihr Weg zwischen Historismus und Existentialismus*, Munich: Kaiser 1955, see especially pp. 13–39.

[352]   Wilke, *Kierkegaard Rezeption*, p. 1 (my emphasis).

all probability, exaggerate. This notwithstanding, it can hardly be denied that Hirsch, more than others and at least within theology, proved capable of and successful in initiating something like a school or tradition of Kierkegaard research. In this respect Hayo Gerdes was arguably the first among Hirsch's former students who carried on his teacher's message. Gerdes not only completed Hirsch's project of translating Kierkegaard by adding to the former's edition of the published works a selection of journal entries in five volumes.[353] He also picked up on Hirsch's attempt to account for and assess the relevance and viability of Kierkegaard's Christology in the context of nineteenth- and twentieth-century Christology.[354] This is also Hermann Fischer's point of departure, who prior to elucidating the particular Enlightenment roots of Kierkegaard's Christology in the *Fragments*,[355] had aleady tackled the doctrine of sin in Kierkegaard (and Schleiermacher). Christology is an occasional point of reference for Joachim Ringleben's Kierkegaard reception also.[356] In addition, Ringleben is perhaps the systematically boldest and most challenging Kierkegaard reader out of Hirsch's school, in that he equally stubbornly and illuminatingly pursues the project of interpreting Kierkegaard (not only in relation to, but also) in the light of Hegel— and this repeatedly either to the disadvantage of the former or by "taking him home" into the Hegelian camp![357]

A school or tradition of thought is established at least, whenever its purported inaugurator is perceived and described as such for the first time; thus conceived, Matthias Wilke's massive study of Hirsch's Kierkegaard reception deserves to be called a reception-historical turning point, inasmuch as it bears witness to the fact that Hirsch has to be considered (not only in German Kierkegaard scholarship) a figure seriously to be reckoned with, at least for the time being. Worthy of consideration is Wilke's chief systematic claim, according to which Hirsch and Kierkegaard joined

[353]   See *Die Tagebücher*, trans. and ed. by H. Gerdes, vols. 1–5, Düsseldorf and Cologne: Diederichs 1962–74.

[354]   See Hayo Gerdes, *Das Christusbild Sören Kierkegaards. Verglichen mit der Christologie Hegels und Schleiermachers*, Düsseldorf: Diederichs 1960; *Der geschichtliche biblische Jesus und der Christus der Philosophen. Erwägungen zur Christologie Kierkegaards, Hegels und Schleiermachers*, Berlin: Die Spur 1974 (same as Gerdes 1960, see above); see also his *Sören Kierkegaards "Einübung im Christentum." Einführung und Erläuterung*, Darmstadt: Wissenschaftliche Buchgesellschaft 1982; *Sören Kierkegaard*, Berlin and New York: Walter de Gruyter 1966; finally, *Das Christusverständnis Sören Kierkegaards. Drei Arbeiten zu Kierkegaards Christologie 1960–1982*, ed. by Hayo Gerdes and Hans M. Müller, Waltrop: Spenner 2002.

[355]   See Hermann Fischer, *Subjektivität und Sünde. Kierkegaards Begriff der Sünde mit ständiger Rücksicht auf Schleiermachers Lehre von der Sünde*, Itzehoe: Die Spur 1963; *Die Christologie des Paradoxes. Zur Herkunft und Bedeutung des Christusverständnisses Sören Kierkegaards*, Göttingen: Vandenhoeck & Ruprecht 1970.

[356]   See, for instance, Joachim Ringleben, "Paradox und Dialektik. Bemerkungen zu Kierkegaards Christologie," *Kierkegaardiana*, vol. 19, 1998, p. 42.

[357]   See Joachim Ringleben, *Hegels Theorie der Sünde. Die subjektivitätslogische Konstruktion eines theologischen Begriffs*, Berlin and New York: Walter de Gruyter 1977; *Aneignung. Die spekulative Theologie Sören Kierkegaards*, Berlin and New York: Walter de Gruyter 1983; *Die Krankheit zum Tode von Sören Kierkegaard. Erklärung und Kommentar*, Göttingen: Vandenhoeck & Ruprecht 1995.

forces in trying to determine the possible and necessary "*Voraussetzungen der Kommunikation christlicher Wahrheit*"[358] under the conditions of modernity.

Interestingly enough, the repercussions of Adorno's Kierkegaard appear to be stronger in post-war theology than in philosophy. Here, Hermann Deuser's work in particular has proved instrumental for a new interest in the relation of both thinkers to arise. In trying to outline the groundwork "*einer theologischen Erkenntnislehre*,"[359] which as a genuinely "dialectical theology" seeks to do justice both to immediacy and reflection in theory and practice, Deuser draws on (the late) Kierkegaard and Adorno throughout, both of whom are located, each in his own particular way, in the " '*Destruktionsgeschichte*' *der abendländischen Metaphysik*":[360]

> *Zu je verschiedenem Zeitpunkt wird [von beiden] versucht, im Zusammenbruch der objektiv sichernden Systembildung und gegen ihren gesellschaftlichen Betrugscharakter im "Bestehenden" die humane Tradition—bei Kierkegaard die Bedingung dafür, Christ zu werden—als Konflikt gegen den Zeitgeist zu stellen, im Widerspruch ihn zur Wahrheit zu überführen.*[361]

Thus conceived, one finds in Kierkegaard and Adorno two dialectical authors, "*deren Zeitdiagnosen, Erkenntnisarbeit und Veränderungsabsicht vielfältig verschränkt sind.*"[362] A couple of other theologians (plus a few philosophers as well) have followed suit in recent years and decades, so that after all we may speak of a continuous, if comparably modest interest in the Adorno–Kierkegaard case.[363]

(4) Apart from Barth's, Hirsch's, and Adorno's influence, we barely find traces, within German post-war theology, of anything that even remotely resembles a genuine "school" or tradition of Kierkegaard reception. What we are left with, instead, is a rather lively, if more or less unorganized scene of varying themes and methodical approaches. Particularly noteworthy (both in quantity and substance) are the many publications grappling with Kierkegaard's doctrine of freedom.[364] The

---

[358]   Thus the subtitle of Wilke, *Kierkegaard Rezeption*.

[359]   Hermann Deuser, *Dialektische Theologie. Studien zu Adornos Metaphysik und zum Spätwerk Kierkegaards*, Munich: Kaiser 1980, p. 15.

[360]   Ibid., p. 16.

[361]   Ibid.

[362]   Ibid.

[363]   As to theology, see in particular, Kiefhaber, *Christentum als Korrektiv*; Kodalle, *Die Eroberung des Nutzlosen*, see especially pp. 193–233. In philosophy, compare Elke Beck, *Identität der Person. Sozialphilosophische Studien zu Kierkegaard, Adorno und Habermas*, Würzburg: Königshausen & Neumann 1991; Karin Pulmer, *Die dementierte Alternative. Gesellschaft und Geschichte in der ästhetischen Konstruktion von Kierkegaards "Entweder-Oder,"* Frankfurt am Main: Peter Lang 1982. The earliest Kierkegaard critique from an Adorno-inspired standpoint is Hermann Schweppenhäuser, *Kierkegaards Angriff auf die Spekulation. Eine Verteidigung*, Frankfurt am Main: Suhrkamp 1967.

[364]   See, for instance, Christine Axt-Piscalar, *Ohnmächtige Freiheit. Studien zum Verhältnis von Subjektivität und Sünde bei August Tholuck, Julius Müller, Sören Kierkegaard und Friedrich Schleiermacher*, Tübingen: Mohr 1996; Michael Bösch, *Søren Kierkegaard: Schicksal—Angst—Freiheit*, Paderborn: Schöningh 1994; Walter Dietz, *Sören Kierkegaard. Existenz und Freiheit*, Frankfurt am Main: Hain 1992; Dorothea Glöckner, *Kierkegaards*

numerous *contextualizing* accounts of (the use of) this category, as such primarily aimed at specifying its role and function for a Kierkegaardian anthropology and hamartiology, are worth mentioning, too,[365] likewise a number of texts treating central concepts like anxiety[366] and paradox[367] with a somewhat similar purpose in mind. Various authors inquire into the meaning and use of dogmatical categories and doctrines in Kierkegaard,[368] whereas others focus on the latter's use of the Bible

---

Begriff der Wiederholung. Eine Studie zu seinem Freiheitsverständnis, Berlin and New York: Walter de Gruyter 1998 (*Kierkegaard Monograph Series,* vol. 3). As to the philosophical debate, see, for instance, Josef L. Blass, *Die Krise der Freiheit im Denken Sören Kierkegaards. Untersuchungen zur Konstitution der Subjektivität,* Ratingen: Henn 1968; Jörg Disse, *Kierkegaards Phänomenologie der Freiheitserfahrung,* Freiburg i. Br. and Munich: Alber 1991; Günter Rohrmoser, *Emanzipation und Freiheit,* Munich: Goldmann 1990. Here and in the following I will try to document major themes and tendencies in German Kierkegaard research by listing an extensive number of representative titles in the footnotes; please note that I will stick (with very few exceptions) to: (a) monographs (b) works published after 1945.

[365]   See Anton Bösl, *Unfreiheit und Selbstverfehlung. Sören Kierkegaards existenz-dialektische Bestimmung von Schuld und Sünde,* Freiburg i. Br.: Herder 1997; Jürgen Boomgaarden, *Das verlorene Selbst. Phänomenologie und Dogmatik der Sünde,* Habilitation Thesis, University of Jena, 2004; Hermann Fischer, *Subjektivität und Sünde. Kierkegaards Begriff der Sünde mit ständiger Rücksicht auf Schleiermachers Lehre von der Sünde,* Itzehoe: Die Spur 1963; Peter Fonk, *Zwischen Sünde und Erlösung. Entstehung und Entwicklung einer christlichen Anthropologie bei Sören Kierkegaard,* Kevelaer: Butzon & Bercker 1990; Gerolf Schultzky, *Die Wahrnehmung des Menschen bei Sören Kierkegaard. Zur Wahrheitsproblematik der theologischen Anthropologie,* Göttingen: Vandenhoeck & Ruprecht 1977; Johannes Sløk, *Die Anthropologie Kierkegaards,* Copenhagen: Rosenhilde & Bagger 1954.

[366]   See, for instance, Arne Grøn, *Angst bei Sören Kierkegaard. Eine Einführung in sein Denken,* trans. by Ulrich Lincoln, Stuttgart: Klett-Cotta 1999; Arnold Künzli, *Die Angst des modernen Menschen. Sören Kierkegaards Angstexistenz als Spiegel der geistigen Krise unserer Zeit,* Ph.D. Thesis, University of Zürich, 1947; *Die Angst als abendländische Krankheit. Dargestellt am Leben und Denken Sören Kierkegaards,* Zürich: Rascher 1948; Horst Wünsche, *"Der Begriff Angst" und seine Stellung im Kierkegaardischen Philosophieren,* Ph.D. Thesis, University of Mainz, 1953.

[367]   See Hermann Deuser, *Sören Kierkegaard. Die paradoxe Dialektik des politischen Christen. Voraussetzungen bei Hegel. Die Reden von 1847/48 im Verhältnis von Politik und Ästhetik,* Munich and Mainz: Kaiser & Grünewald 1974; Henning Schröer, *Die Denkform der Paradoxalität als theologisches Problem. Eine Untersuchung zu Kierkegaard und der neueren Theologie als Beitrag zur theologischen Logik,* Göttingen: Vandenhoeck & Ruprecht 1960; Guido Schüepp, *Das Paradox des Glaubens. Kierkegaards Anstöße für die christliche Verkündigung,* Munich: Kösel 1964; Josef Steilen, *Der Begriff "Paradox." Eine Begriffsanalyse im Anschluss an Sören Kierkegaard,* Th.D. Thesis, University of Trier 1974.

[368]   As to the doctrine of God, see, for instance, Heiko Schulz, *Eschatologische Identität. Eine Untersuchung über das Verhältnis von Vorsehung, Schicksal und Zufall bei Sören Kierkegaard,* Berlin and New York: Walter de Gruyter 1994; as to Christology, see, for instance, Hermann Fischer, *Christologie;* Gerdes, *Das Christusbild;* Toshihisa Hachiya, *Paradox, Vorbild und Versöhner. S. Kierkegaards Christologie und deren Rezeption in der deutschen Theologie des 20. Jahrhunderts,* Frankfurt am Main: Peter Lang 2006.

and the hermeneutical preferences going along with it.[369] Kierkegaard's edifying literature has received modest, but steady theological attention over recent years and decades,[370] and pretty much the same can be said about his late writings from the *Kirkekamp* period.[371] A growing number of authors have pointed out more recently that a dialogue between Kierkegaard and postmodernity may yield systematically fruitful, in any case fresh and unexpected, results.[372] Finally, it is all but surprising that most, if not all of the aforementioned themes and debates recur in the pertinent writings of contemporary Catholic Kierkegaard scholars—plus some additional ones, due to the fact that a comparison between Kierkegaard and, say, Thomas Aquinas, Hans Urs von Balthasar, Romano Guardini, or Karl Rahner is less likely to be found wanting within Protestant circles.[373]

(5) Although in principle a constant bilateral crossover and cooperation between philosophy and theology, in fact a blurring at times of the boundaries between both disciplines, can be observed, whenever it comes to identifying and tackling essential themes in Kierkegaard, philosophy itself has to offer quite an impressive reservoir of

---

[369]   See, for instance, Matthias Engelke, *Kierkegaard und das Alte Testament. Zum Einfluß der alttestamentlichen Bücher auf Kierkegaards Gesamtwerk*, Rheinbach: CMZ 2001.

[370]   Deuser, *Sören Kierkegaard*; Anna Paulsen, *Menschsein heute. Analysen aus Reden Sören Kierkegaards*, Hamburg: Wittig 1973; Richard Purkarthofer, *Wider das unlebbare Leben. Studien zur Kommunikation in den "erbaulichen Reden" Sören Kierkegaards*, Ph.D. Thesis, University of Vienna 2000.

[371]   See Hinrich Buss, *Kierkegaards Angriff auf die bestehende Christenheit*, Hamburg: Reich 1970; Deuser, *Dialektische Theologie*; Kiefhaber, *Christentum als Korrektiv*.

[372]   See, for instance Tilmann Beyrich, *Ist Glauben wiederholbar? Derrida liest Kierkegaard*, Berlin and New York: Walter de Gruyter 2001 (*Kierkegaard Studies. Monograph Series*, vol. 6); Jochen Schmidt, *Vielstimmige Rede vom Unsagbaren. Dekonstruktion, Glaube und Kierkegaards pseudonyme Literatur*, Berlin and New York: Walter de Gruyter 2006 (*Kierkegaard Studies. Monograph Series*, vol. 14). See the additional inclusion of a genuinely feminist perspective in Sophie Wennerscheid, *Das Begehren nach der Wunde. Zum Wechselspiel von Schrift, Selbst und Männlichkeit im Werk Søren Kierkegaards*, Ph.D. Thesis, Humboldt-University Berlin 2006.

[373]   More recent Catholic Kierkegaard accounts include: Michael Bongardt, *Der Widerstand der Freiheit. Eine transzendentaldialogische Aneignung der Angstanalysen Kierkegaards*, Frankfurt am Main: Knecht 1995; Michael Eisenstein, *Selbstverwirklichung und Existenz—ethische Perspektiven pastoralpsychologischer Beratung unter besonderer Berücksichtigung S. Kierkegaards*, St. Ottilien: EOS 1986; Stefan Endriß, *Hans Urs von Balthasar versus Sören Kierkegaard*, Hamburg: Kovac 2006; Karl T. Kehrbach, *Der Begriff "Wahl" bei Sören Kierkegaard und Karl Rahner. Zwei Typen der Kirchenkritik*, Frankfurt am Main: Peter Lang 1992; Kiefhaber, *Christentum als Korrektiv*; Stephan Pauly, *Subjekt und Selbstwerdung. Das Subjektdenken Romano Guardinis, seine Rückbezüge auf Sören Kierkegaard und seine Einlösbarkeit in der Postmoderne*, Stuttgart: Kohlhammer 2000; Klaus Wolff, *Das Problem der Gleichzeitigkeit des Menschen mit Jesus Christus bei Sören Kierkegaard im Blick auf die Theologie Karl Rahners*, Würzburg: Echter 1991; Elisabeth Zwick, *Der Mensch als personale Existenz. Entwürfe existentialer Anthropologie und ihre pädagogischen Implikationen bei Sören Kierkegaard und Thomas von Aquin. Eine Studie über die Konstitution der Geschichtlichkeit anhand von Grundfragen zur Möglichkeit eines Dialoges zwischen Sören Kierkegaard und Thomas von Aquin*, St. Ottilien: EOS 1992.

pertinent studies on its own terms. A hermeneutical tradition in any stricter sense of the word has only been established in Germany under the auspices of Heidegger and Jaspers, however, and this at least in a twofold sense. With respect to the history of reception, that is in terms of the actual role Kierkegaard played as an inaugurator of the so-called philosophy of existence in Germany, the otherwise dubious title "father of existentialism" is certainly correct and appropriate, as a number of pertinent histories of existentialism unanimously and persuasively bear witness to.[374] On the other hand, Heidegger in particular has shaped the way in which subsequent German philosophers have read Kierkegaard to a considerable degree: not so much through passing on to them his own receptive approach, but rather by providing, in his own philosophy, a hermeneutical framework, which apparently lends itself to being put to good use in interpreting Kierkegaard also. Thus, the "hermeneutical" nature of human existence—in other words, the idea that seeking to *understand* oneself in trying to cope with the fundamental task of *having* to exist is part and parcel of existence itself—is frequently highlighted by the philosophers in question.[375]

"Kierkegaard and German idealism" has become a slogan, a second major theme and in fact a matter of much controversy among philosophically minded Kierkegaard scholars over the past fifty years or so. Here, in particular, much ink has been spilled in trying to answer the question if, and to what extent, Kierkegaard's authorship has been influenced by, belongs to the same tradition as, or at least reveals significant material and/or formal similarities with, Kant, Fichte, Schelling, also Goethe,[376]

---

[374]   See, for example, Leo Gabriel, *Existenzphilosophie: Kierkegaard, Heidegger, Jaspers, Sartre. Dialog der Positionen*, 2nd ed., Vienna and Munich: Herold 1968 [1951]; Wolfgang Janke, *Existenzphilosophie*, Berlin and New York: Walter de Gruyter 1982; Gerhard Kränzlin, *Existenzphilosophie und Panhumanismus*, Scheldorf: Brunnen 1950; Helmut Kuhn, *Begegnung mit dem Nichts. Ein Versuch über die Existenzphilosophie*, Tübingen: Mohr 1950; Jean Wahl, *Vom Nichts, vom Sein und von unserer Existenz. Versuch einer kleinen Geschichte des Existenzialismus*, trans. by Dominique Bernard, Augsburg and Basel: Verlag Die Brigg 1954; Franz Zimmermann, *Einführung in die Existenzphilosophie*, Darmstadt: Wissenschaftliche Buchgesellschaft 1977.

[375]   See, for instance, Helmut Fahrenbach, *Kierkegaards existenzdialektische Ethik*, Frankfurt am Main: Klostermann 1968; Helmut Fahrenbach, *Existenzphilosophie und Ethik*, Frankfurt am Main: Klostermann 1970; Günter Figal, *Lebensverstricktheit und Abstandnahme. "Verhalten zu sich" im Anschluß an Heidegger, Kierkegaard und Hegel*, Tübingen: Attempto 2001; Klaus Schäfer, *Hermeneutische Ontologie in den Climacus-Schriften Sören Kierkegaards*, Munich: Kösel 1968; Walter Schulz, *Philosophie in der veränderten Welt*, Pfullingen: Neske 1972; Walter Schulz, *Ich und Welt. Philosophie der Subjektivität*, Pfullingen: Neske 1979; Michael Theunissen, *Der Begriff Ernst bei Sören Kierkegaard*, Freiburg i. Br. and Munich: Alber 1958. In a certain sense even Ernst Tugendhat's analytically inspired attempt at reconstructing Kierkegaard's theory of self-reference (in *The Sickness unto Death*) as a non-reflexive relation to the facticity of existing belongs here (see his *Selbstbewusstsein und Selbstbestimmung. Sprachanalytische Interpretationen*, Frankfurt am Main: Suhrkamp 1979, pp. 158–61); for Tugendhat himself (p. 161) views Kierkegaard as an intermediary of those questions, "*bei denen Heidegger ansetzte.*"

[376]   See, in particular, Wilhelm Anz, *Kierkegaard und der deutsche Idealismus*, Tübingen: Mohr 1956; *Kierkegaard und Schelling. Freiheit, Angst und Wirklichkeit*, ed. by Jochem Hennigfeld and Jon Stewart, Berlin and New York: Walter de Gruyter 2003 (*Kierkegaard*

and especially Hegel.[377] For all we know, however, it is wrong to assume that this reception-or research-historical trend was brought about or at least initiated by one or some of the earlier philosophically influential Kierkegaard readers and scholars whom I mentioned before. This should also be kept in mind (in order, namely, to prevent rash conclusions), when it comes to explaining the comparably large number of publications dealing with Kierkegaard's aesthetics[378] and ethics, respectively. As to the latter, we may note that it is a topic of virtually permanent interest and

Studies. Monograph Series, vol. 8); Anton Hochenbleicher-Schwarz, *Das Existenzproblem bei J. G. Fichte und S. Kierkegaard*, Königstein: Athenäum 1984; Jann Holl, *Kierkegaards Konzeption des Selbst. Eine Untersuchung über die Voraussetzungen und Formen seines Denkens*, Meisenheim: Hain 1972; Ulrich Knappe, *Theory and Practice in Kant and Kierkegaard*, Berlin and New York: Walter de Gruyter 2004 (*Kierkegaard Studies. Monograph Series*, vol. 9); Anton M. Koktanek, *Schellings Seinslehre und Kierkegaard*, Munich: Oldenbourg 1962; Heinrich Schmidinger, *Das Problem des Interesses und die Philosophie Sören Kierkegaards*, Freiburg i. Br./Munich: Alber 1983; Walter Schulz, *Die Vollendung des deutschen Idealismus in der Spätphilosophie Schellings*, 2nd ed., Pfullingen: Neske 1975, see especially pp. 274–9; Walter Schulz, *Johann Gottlieb Fichte, Sören Kierkegaard*, Pfullingen: Neske 1977.

[377] See, for instance, Max Bense, *Hegel und Kierkegaard. Eine prinzipielle Untersuchung*, Cologne: Staufen 1948; Markus Kleinert, *Sich verzehrender Skeptizismus. Läuterungen bei Hegel und Kierkegaard*, Berlin and New York: Walter de Gruyter 2005 (*Kierkegaard Studies. Monograph Series*, vol. 12); Smail Rapic, *Ethische Selbstverständigung. Kierkegaards Auseinandersetzung mit der Ethik Kants und der Rechtsphilosophie Hegels*, Berlin and New York: Walter de Gruyter 2007 (*Kierkegaard Studies. Monograph Series*, vol. 16); Hans J. Strack-Goertsches, *Die Entwicklung existierender Inter-Subjektivität aus dem freien Geist. Hegels Philosophie des subjektiven Geistes mit Rücksicht auf Kierkegaard*, Ph.D. Thesis, University of Cologne 1999; Niels Thulstrup, *Kierkegaards Verhältnis zu Hegel. Forschungsgeschichte*, Stuttgart: Kohlhammer 1970; Niels Thulstrup, *Kierkegaards Verhältnis zu Hegel und zum spekulativen Idealismus 1835–1846. Historisch-analytische Untersuchung*, Stuttgart: Kohlhammer 1972.

[378] See Vagn Börge, *Kierkegaard und das Theater, mit besonderer Rücksicht auf Mozarts "Don Juan,"* Vienna: Hans Riel 1947; Peter Bürger, *Zur Kritik der idealistischen Ästhetik*, Frankfurt am Main: Suhrkamp 1983, see especially pp. 156–67; Paul T. Erne, *Lebenskunst. Aneignung ästhetischer Erfahrung. Ein theologischer Beitrag zur Ästhetik im Anschluss an Kierkegaard*, Kampen: Kok Pharos 1994; Ingeborg Frieser, *Beiträge zu ästhetischen Phänomenen bei Søren Kierkegaard mit besonderer Rücksicht auf das Theater*, Ph.D. Thesis, University of Freiburg 1950; Birgit Haustedt, *Die Kunst der Verführung. Zur Reflexion der Kunst im Motiv der Verführung bei Jean Paul, E.T.A. Hoffmann, Kierkegaard und Brentano*, Stuttgart: Verlag für Wissenschaft und Forschung 1992; Hans-Joachim Krenzke, *Ästhetik und Existenz. Eine Studie zum frühmodernen Denken unter besonderer Berücksichtigung der philosophischen Vorgeschichte der Kierkegaardschen "Diapsalmata ad se ipsum,"* Würzburg: Königshausen & Neumann 2002; Günther K. Lehmann, *Ästhetik der Utopie. Arthur Schopenhauer, Sören Kierkegaard, Georg Simmel, Max Weber, Ernst Bloch*, Stuttgart: Neske 1995; Konrad P. Liessmann, *Ästhetik der Verführung. Kierkegaards Konstruktion der Erotik aus dem Geiste der Verführung*, Frankfurt am Main: Hain 1991; Walter Rehm, *Kierkegaard und der Verführer*, Munich: Rinn 1949; Walter Schulz, *Metaphysik des Schwebens. Untersuchungen zur Geschichte der Ästhetik*, Pfullingen: Neske 1985, see especially pp. 285–91; K. Stoverock, *Die Musikästhetik Sören Kierkegaards*, Ph.D. Thesis, University of Bonn, 1995; Peter Tschuggnall, *Sören Kierkegaards Mozart-Rezeption. Analyse*

debate among philophers and theologians alike.[379] So far, much less excitement has been aroused by the quest to elucidate and assess Kierkegaard's epistemology[380] or his theory of language,[381] although the latter topic has gained some notoriety in connection with more recent accounts of Kierkegaard's rhetoric, homiletics, and theory of communication.[382] By contrast, investigations à la 'Kierkegaard and X' *do* have a long and honorable tradition in philosophy. Next to idealistic thinkers such as Fichte, Schelling, and Hegel (see above) Socrates, Lessing, Marx (and/ or Marxism), and especially Nietzsche[383] are among those who have received

---

einer philosophisch-literarischen Deutung von Musik im Kontext des Zusammenspiels der Künste, Frankfurt am Main: Peter Lang 1992.

[379]   See, for instance, *Ethik der Liebe. Studien zu Kierkegaards "Taten der Liebe,"* ed. by Ingolf U. Dalferth, Tübingen: J.C.B. Mohr 2002; Uta Eichler, *Von der Existenz zu den objektiven gesellschaftlichen Verhältnissen. Studien zur Interpretation und Kritik der Ethikauffassung Sören Kierkegaards*, Ph.D. Thesis, University of Halle 1980; Fahrenbach, *Ethik*; Fahrenbach, *Existenzphilosophie*; Hans Friemond, *Existenz in Liebe nach Sören Kierkegaard*, Salzburg and Munich: Pustet 1965; Wilfried Greve, *Kierkegaards maieutische Ethik. Von "Entweder/ Oder II" zu den "Stadien,"* Frankfurt am Main: Suhrkamp 1990; Friedrich Hauschildt, *Die Ethik Sören Kierkegaards*, Gütersloh: Gütersloher Verlagshaus 1982; Ulrich Lincoln, *Äußerung. Studien zum Handlungsbegriff in Søren Kierkegaards "Die Taten der Liebe,"* Berlin and New York: Walter de Gruyter 2000 (*Kierkegaard Studies: Monograph Series*, vol. 4); Barbara Müller, *Objektlose Nächstenliebe—Kierkegaards Verständnis der Nächstenliebe in "Der Liebe Tun,"* Ph.D. Thesis, University of Marburg 1985; Adele Schamp, *Die Ethik Sören Kierkegaards*, Ph.D. Thesis, University of Vienna 1949.

[380]   See, for instance, Stephan Ahn, *Sören Kierkegaards Ontologie der Bewusstseins-sphären. Versuch einer multidisziplinären Gegenstandsuntersuchung*, Münster: Ugarit 1997; Joachim Boldt, *Kierkegaards "Furcht und Zittern" als Bild seines ethischen Erkenntnisbegriffs*, Berlin and New York: Walter de Gruyter 2006 (*Kierkegaard Studies Monograph Series*, vol. 13); Anton Hügli, *Die Erkenntnis der Subjektivität und die Objektivität des Erkennens bei Sören Kierkegaard*, Zürich: Theologischer Verlag 1973.

[381]   See, in particular, Christa Kühnhold, *Der Begriff des Sprunges und der Weg des Sprachdenkens. Eine Einführung in Kierkegaard*, Berlin and New York: Walter de Gruyter 1975; Christa Kühnhold, *N.F.S. Grundtvigs und Sören Kierkegaards Sprachauffassung*, Stuttgart: Heinz 1986.

[382]   See Tim Hagemann, *Reden und Existieren. Kierkegaards antipersuasive Rhetorik*, Berlin and Vienna: Philo 2001; Hartmut Metzger, *Kriterien christlicher Predigt nach Sören Kierkegaard*, Göttingen: Vandenhoeck & Ruprecht 1964; Richard Purkarthofer, *Studien*; Christin Waldenfels-Goes, *Direkte und indirekte Mitteilung bei Sören Kierkegaard*, Ph.D. Thesis, University of Munich 1968.

[383]   For Socrates see, for instance, Wolfdietrich von Kloeden, *Kierkegaard und Sokrates. Sören Kierkegaards Sokratesrezeption*, Bochum: Evangelische Fachhochschule Rheinland-Westfalen-Lippe 1991. For Lessing see, for instance, André Kraus, *Kierkegaard und Lessing. Sören Aabye Kierkegaards Rekurs auf Gotthold Ephraim Lessing in den "Philosophischen Brocken" und der "Abschließenden unwissenschaftlichen Nachschrift zu den Philosophischen Brocken,"* Hamburg: Kovac 2003. For Marx see, for instance, Josef Brechtken, *Die praxisdialektische Kritik des Marxschen Atheimus. Studien zum anthropozentrisch-kritischen Wirklichkeitsbegriff vom Standpunkt der geschichtlichen Praxis und zu seinen religionsphilosophischen Konsequenzen: Hegel – Kierkegaard – Marx*, vols. 1–2, Königstein: Athenäum 1979; Wolfgang Janke, *Historische Dialektik. Destruktion*

preferential treatment here. Finally, it does not come as a surprise that philosophy, due to its natural inclination to and expertise in conceptual analysis, has always kept a keen eye on Kierkegaard's central categories and their function for the meaning and viability of the authorship as a whole: for instance, by tackling the concepts of existence, repetition, irony, history (temporality / eternity), or truth.[384]

---

dialektischer Grundformen von Kant bis Marx, Berlin and New York: Walter de Gruyter 1977; Tyong-Ho Kim, *Existentielle Dialektik und politische Praxis. Interpretationen zum Problem der Dialektik bei Hegel, Kierkegaard, Marx und Jaspers*, Ph.D. Thesis, University of Munich 1958; Hans Leisegang, *Hegel, Marx, Kierkegaard. Zum dialektischen Materialismus und zur dialektischen Theologie*, Berlin: Wissenschaftliche Editionsgesellschaft 1948. For Nietzsche see, in particular, Gerd-Günther Grau, *Die Selbstauflösung des christlichen Glaubens. Eine religionsphilosophische Studie über Kierkegaard*, Frankfurt am Main: Schulte-Bulmke 1963; *Kritik des absoluten Anspruchs. Nietzsche—Kierkegaard—Kant*, Würzburg: Königshausen & Neumann 1993; *Vernunft, Wahrheit, Glaube. Neue Studien zu Nietzsche und Kierkegaard*, Würzburg: Königshausen & Neumann 1997; Wolfgang Struve, "Die neuzeitliche Philosophie als Metaphysik der Subjektivität. Interpretationen zu Kierkegaard und Nietzsche," *Symposion. Jahrbuch für Philosophie*, no. 1, 1948, pp. 207–335. As far as I know no (German) monograph has yet been published on Kierkegaard and Schopenhauer; however, apart from having been incorporated into the history of and debate about nihilism the former has sometimes (and misleadingly) been called an advocate of pessimism and thus been considered an ally of the latter: see, for instance, Wilhelm Lütgert, *Das Ende des Idealismus im Zeitalter Bismarcks*, Gütersloh: Bertelsmann 1930, pp. 255–98, see especially pp. 286–92.

[384]   For existence see, for instance, Helmut Vetter, *Stadien der Existenz. Eine Untersuchung zum Existenzbegriff Sören Kierkegaards*, Vienna: Herder 1979; Frank-Eberhard Wilde, *Kierkegaards Verständnis der Existenz*, Copenhagen: Rosenkilde & Bagger 1969. For repetition see, for instance, Victor Guarda, *Die Wiederholung. Analysen zur Grundstruktur menschlicher Existenz im Verständnis Sören Kierkegaards*, Königstein: Athenäum 1980; Glöckner, *Wieder-holung*; Norbert Heinel, *Der Begriff der Wiederholung bei Sören Kierkegaard*, Ph.D. Thesis, University of Vienna 1975; Georg Schückler, *Die Existenzkategorie der "Wiederholung" dargestellt am Werk Sören Kierkegaards*, Ph.D. Thesis, University of Bonn 1952. For irony see, for instance, Eivind Tjönneland, *Ironie als Symptom. Eine kritische Auseinandersetzung mit Sören Kierkegaards "Über den Begriff der Ironie,"* Frankfurt am Main: Peter Lang 2004; Edo Pivcevic, *Ironie als Daseinsform bei Sören Kierkegaard*, Gütersloh: Gütersloher Verlagshaus Mohn 1960. For history see, for instance, Sören Holm, *Sören Kierkegaards Geschichtsphilosophie*, trans. by Günther Jungbluth, Stuttgart: Kohlhammer 1956; Annemarie Pieper, *Geschichte und Ewigkeit bei Sören Kierkegaard. Das Leitproblem der pseudonymen Schriften*, Meisenheim: Hain 1968; Ralph-Werner Sauer, *Ansätze zu einer Bestimmung der Geschichtlichkeit im Denken Søren Kierkegaards*, Freiburg i. Br.: Mikroreproduktionen 1953; Ferencz Tanko, *Ewigkeit in Zeit. Max Muellers Umdeutung des kierkegaardianischen Augenblicks*, Th.D. Thesis, Gregoriana University of Rome 1992; Alvaro Valls, *Der Begriff "Geschichte" in den Schriften Sören Kierkegaards. Eine Analyse der Dimensionen und Bedeutungen von "Geschichte" von "Entweder/Oder" bis zur "Abschließenden unwissenschaftlichen Nachschrift,"* Ph.D. Thesis, University of Heidelberg 1981; Kurt-Heinz Weber, *Ästhetik und Zeitlichkeit. Versuch über Kierkegaard*, Ph.D. Thesis, University of Tübingen 1976. For truth see, for instance, Mohammad R.H. Abdolhosseini, *Das subjektive und dynamische Verhältnis zur Wahrheit bei Sören Kierkegaard*, Ph.D. Thesis, University of Basel 1997; Kurt Weisshaupt, *Die Zeitlichkeit der Wahrheit. Eine Untersuchung zum Wahrheitsbegriff Sören Kierkegaards*, Freiburg i. Br. and Munich: Alber 1973.

(6) As for the field of *literary studies*, I feel entitled to take refuge in just a few bibliographical hints in passing. Of course, one could argue that some contemporary authors in the German tongue who place a focus on these studies would deserve separate treatment, and this precisely under the heading "productive reception." I have decided against such a treatment—for simple reasons: either Kierkegaard is undeniably present in and important for these authors, yet they themselves belong, as in the present case, to the *Swiss* reception and thus fall outside the scope of my article;[385] or Kierkegaard's significance remains rather elusive in the authors in question, and this would make an in-depth treatment necessary in order to be able to do full justice to its possible significance for the history of reception.[386] In this case we are facing a problem, the possible solution of which equally falls outside the scope of the present article.

Let me, as an appendix and partly as a substitute for the missing paragraph, at least provide an additional bibliography, listing the numerous *biographies and novels* which have been published to date about Kierkegaard.[387] Moreover, and in altogether

---

[385] As is the case with Friedrich Dürrenmatt (1921–90) and Max Frisch (1911–91). See Annette Mingels, *Dürrenmatt und Kierkegaard. Die Kategorie des Einzelnen als gemeinsame Denkform*, Cologne: Böhlau 2003; Roger W. Müller Farguell, "Zur Dramaturgie aporetischen Denkens. Dürrenmatt und Kierkegaard," in *Neue Perspektiven zur deutschsprachigen Literatur der Schweiz*, ed. by R. Sabalius, Amsterdam/Atlanta: Rodopi 1997, pp. 153–65. As to Frisch, see Jürgen Brummack, "Max Frisch und Kierkegaard," in *Text & Kontext*, ed. by K. Bohnen, vol. 6, Copenhagen and Munich: Fink 1978, pp. 388ff.; Christian Hoffmann, *Max Frischs Roman "Homo faber" betrachtet unter theologischem Aspekt*, Frankfurt am Main: Peter Lang 1978; Philip Manger, "Kierkegaard in Max Frisch's Novel 'Stiller,' " *German Life and Letters*, vol. 20, 1966, pp. 119–31; Theunissen and Greve, "Einleitung," pp. 56ff.

[386] This is apparently the case with Alfred Andersch (1914–80), Thomas Bernhard (1931–89), Heinrich Böll (1917–85), Wolfgang Koeppen (1906–96), and Martin Walser (1927–), respectively. See, for instance, Annette Raabe, *"Das Wort stammt von Kierkegaard." Alfred Andersch und Sören Kierkegaard*, Frankfurt am Main et al.: Peter Lang 1999; Heinrich Schmidinger, "Thomas Bernhard und Sören Kierkegaard," in *Jahrbuch der Universität Salzburg 1995–1997*, ed. by A. Buschmann, Munich 1999, pp. 29–46; Wolfgang Stemmler, *Max Frisch, Heinrich Böll und Sören Kierkegaard*, Ph.D. Thesis, University of Cologne 1972; Frank Witzel, *Die Dame im Gruppenbild als christlicher Gegenentwurf zum repressiv-asketischen Traditionsstrang des Christentums. Eruierung, Vergleich und Bewertung zweier theologisch-ethischer Konzepte. Heinrich Böll: "Gruppenbild mit Dame," Sören Kierkegaard: "Der Liebe Tun,"* Frankfurt am Main: Peter Lang 2000; Thomas Richner, *Der Tod in Rom. Eine existential-psychologische Analyse von Wolfgang Koeppens Roman*, Zürich and Munich: Artemis 1982; Siegfried Weing, "Kierkegaardian Reflections in Martin Walser's *Ein fliehendes Pferd*," *Colloquia Germanica*, vol. 25, 1992, pp. 275–88.

[387] See Albert Bärthold, *Noten zu Sören Kierkegaards Lebensgeschichte*, Halle: Fricke 1876; Hans Brøchner, *Erinnerungen an Søren Kierkegaard*, trans. and ed. by Tim Hagemann, Bodenheim: Philo 1997; Joakim Garff, *Sören Kierkegaard. Biographie*, trans. by Herbert Zeichner and Hermann Schmidt, Munich and Vienna: Hanser 2004; Edmund Hoehne, *Deutsche, Dänen und Kierkegaard. Roman*, Hamburg: Agentur des Rauhen Hauses 1948; Johannes Hohlenberg, *Søren Kierkegaard*, trans. by Maria Bachmann-Isler, Basel: Benno Schwabe 1949; Klaas Huizing, *Der letzte Dandy. Ein Kierkegaard Roman*, Munich: Albrecht Klaus Verlag 2003; Finn Jor, *Sören und Regine. Kierkegaard und seine unerfüllte Liebe*, trans. by Gabriele Haefs, Munich and Zürich: Piper 2000; Walter Lowrie, *Das Leben*

abandoning the limited perspective of any particular discipline, I would like to call attention to the fact that there also exists a vast *introductory literature* in German, either in monographic[388] or encyclopedic form[389]—provided by internationally renowned Kierkegaard scholars from various countries and fields, which supply useful information and often knowledgable commentaries for the enthusiastic Kierkegaard novice. Last, but not least, I would like to remind the reader (if need be...) of the biggest and probably most important event not only in German, but in Kierkegaard research world-wide: namely the successive publication of *Søren Kierkegaards Skrifter* (*SKS*), a new critical edition of Kierkegaard's complete writings, under the auspices of the Søren Kierkegaard Research Centre (Copenhagen). This massive editorial enterprise is not only an expression, consequence or effect of, but

---

Søren Kierkegaards, trans. by Günther Sawatzki, Düsseldorf: Diederichs 1955; Harald von Mendelssohn, *Sören Kierkegaard. Ein Genie in einer Kleinstadt*, Stuttgart: Klett-Cotta 1995; Olaf P. Monrad, *Søren Kierkegaard. Sein Leben und seine Werke*, Jena: Diederichs 1909; Anna S. Paulsen, *Sören Kierkegaard. Deuter unserer Existenz*, Hamburg: Wittig 1955; Peter P. Rohde, *Sören Kierkegaard. In Selbstzeugnissen und Bilddokumenten dargestellt*, trans. by Thyra Dohrenburg, Hamburg: Rowohlt 1955; Christoph Schrempf, *Sören Kierkegaard. Eine Biographie*, vols. 1–2, Jena: Diederichs 1927–28; Alfred O. Schwede, *Die Kierkegaards. Geschichte einer Kopenhagener Wirkwarenhändlerfamilie, insonderheit eines Vaters und seines später weltberühmten Sohnes Sören*, Berlin: Evangelische Verlagsanstalt 1989; "Sören Kierkegaards Familie und Privatleben nach den persönlichen Erinnerungen seiner Nichte K. Lund," in *Sören Kierkegaard, Ausgewählte christliche Reden*, trans. by Julie von Reincke, 2nd ed., Gießen: Töpelmann 1909 [1901], pp. 111–40; *Søren Kierkegaard 1855–1955. Zum Kierkegaard Gedenkjahr vorgelegt*, Düsseldorf: Diederichs 1955.

[388]   See, for instance, Hermann Deuser, *Kierkegaard. Die Philosophie des religiösen Schriftstellers*, Darmstadt: Wissenschaftliche Buchgesellschaft 1985; Patrick Gardiner, *Kierkegaard*, trans. by Richard Purkarthofer, 2nd ed., Wiesbaden: Panorama 2004; Grøn, *Angst*; Konrad P. Liessmann, *Sören Kierkegaard zur Einführung*, Hamburg: Junius 1993; Annemarie Pieper, *Sören Kierkegaard*, Munich: Beck 2000; Richard Purkarthofer, *Kierkegaard*, Leipzig: Reclam 2005; Johannes Sløk, *Christentum mit Leidenschaft. Ein Weg-Weiser zur Gedankenwelt Søren Kierkegaards*, trans. by Ulrich Panzer, Munich: Kaiser 1990; Tilo Wesche, *Kierkegaard. Eine philosophische Einführung*, Stuttgart: Reclam 2003.

[389]   See, for instance, Franz-Peter Burkard, "Kierkegaard," in *Großes Werklexikon der Philosophie*, ed. by Franco Volpi, vols. 1–2, Stuttgart: Kröner 2004, vol. 1, pp. 825–34; Hermann Deuser, "Kierkegaard, Søren Aabye," in *Die Religion in Geschichte und Gegenwart*, vols. 1–8, ed. by Hans Dieter Betz et al., 4th ed., Tübingen: J.C.B. Mohr 1998–2005, vol. 4, pp. 954–8; Thomas Horst, "Kierkegaard, Søren Aabye," in *Metzler-Philosophen-Lexikon. Dreihundert biographisch-werkgeschichtliche Porträts von den Vorsokratikern bis zu den Neuen Philosophen*, ed. by Bernd Lutz, Stuttgart: Metzler 1989, pp. 415–20; N.N., "Sören Aabye Kierkegaard," in *Handbuch der Geschichte der Philosophie, Bd. 5: Bibliographie 18. und 19. Jahrhundert*, ed. by Wilhelm Totok, Frankfurt am Main: Klostermann 1986, pp. 594–627; Henning Schröer, "Kierkegaard, Søren Aabye (1813–1855)," in *Theologische Realenzyklopädie*, vols. 1–36, ed. by Gerhard Müller et al., Berlin and New York: Walter de Gruyter 1976–2004, vol. 18, 1989, pp. 138–55; Heiko Schulz, "Kierkegaard, Sören Aabye (1813–55)," in *Biographisch-Bibliographisches Kirchenlexikon*, ed. by Friedrich W. Bautz, vols. 1–26, Hamm and Herzberg: T. Bautz 1990–2006, vol. 3, pp. 1466–9; Heiko Schulz, "Kierkegaard," in *Ästhetik und Kunstphilosophie von der Antike bis zur Gegenwart in Einzeldarstellungen*, ed. by Julian Nida-Rümelin and Monika Betzler, Stuttgart: Kröner 1998, pp. 460–9.

probably also a catalyst for further trends in the history of reception, or altogether new constellations. As such, it is accompanied and supplemented by numerous translation-projects drawing on the Danish sources and commentaries as a new and for the first time philologically reliable basis—among them a new German edition, the first two volumes of which have recently been published.[390]

IV. Conclusion

In the preceding sections I have proceeded along the lines of a comparably simple, perhaps simplistic historical and typological scheme or pattern. This pattern was supposed methodically to guide and structure my account, not in any *a priori* way, though. I have drawn on and made use of it, rather, as an expression of a purely *a posteriori* assumption about the major stages, phases or epochs in the history of reception—an assumption, which in turn emerged from having mustered, compared and evaluated a considerable mass of pertinent sources in terms of their quantity, distinctive features, and reception-historical type(s).

The pattern itself is a modified, in fact somewhat simplified version of an earlier proposal which suggested *four* major stages or phases in the reception instead of just three: reception without production / production without reception (ca. 1860–90); unproductive reception (ca. 1890–1910); productive reception (ca. 1910–45); receptive production (1945 and after).[391] Things look a little different to me now, owing in part to the fact that my earlier proposal was based on a more restricted perspective, as it referred to the reception of Kierkegaard in (German) *theology* only. Due to the material under inspection, I have meanwhile come to the conclusion that it is more advisable to extend the *terminus ad quem* of the first stage to the turn of the century, approximately, while, accordingly, letting the second stage begin with the year 1900 as a new (though admittedly somewhat mythical rather than purely historical) *terminus a quo*. In fact, in one of my earlier accounts I had already found it necessary to move backwards, historically speaking, from 1920 to 1910, as the point of departure for what I take to be a genuinely productive Kierkegaard reception.[392] Taught by the examples of historical key-figures like Georg Lukács and, in particular, Rudolf Kassner, I am inclined to recommend going even further now, suggesting that the turn of the century might be a more appropriate *terminus a quo*.

Moreover, it seems to make sense to condense or integrate the original three forms of reception and non-reception, respectively (reception without production, production without reception, unproductive reception), which dominated the first period (1840–99), into one single overarching type—a type that I would prefer to speak of as "pre-reception." Not only and not even primarily for didactical reasons

---

[390]   *Deutsche Søren Kierkegaard Edition (DSKE), Bd. 1: Journale und Aufzeichnungen AA–DD*, ed. by H. Deuser et al., Berlin and New York: Walter de Gruyter 2005. *Deutsche Søren Kierkegaard Edition* (DSKE), Bd. 2: *Journale und Aufzeichnungen EE–KK*, ed. by R. Purkarthofer and H. Schulz, Berlin and New York: Walter de Gruyter 2008

[391]   See Schulz, "Die theologische Rezeption," p. 234; "Rezeptionsgeschichtliche Brocken," pp. 448–9.

[392]   See Schulz, "Rezeptionsgeschichtliche Brocken," p. 449 (note 197).

(the simpler a guiding scheme or pattern, the more transparent it will be for the reader); rather, it just seems more natural to expect at the outset of an author's reception a highly *non homogenous* picture—sheer ignorance on the one hand, mixed with several disconnected and unorganized strands of reception on the other hand (reception without literary production; purely material parallels in author A's and B's work; occasional instances of unproductive reception, borderline cases). In other words, we should expect a picture to emerge exactly like the one actually found in the early traces of Kierkegaard's reception in Germany. Nevertheless, it is a *picture* that so emerges; hence my decision to summarize these several strands under one and the same typological rubric.

The decision seems advantageous in yet another respect; for it prevents giving the impression that I wanted to suggest strict historio-typological parallels here (one and the same type of reception at a given time). This impression would be utterly misleading. All I am saying is that a certain period of time *gravitates* towards a certain type of reception. Not only do we have to speak of *ideal* types, which, as such, are almost never found in pure form, so that the boundaries between them may be blurred even in one and the same author (as in Hirsch, for instance). Moreover, we are often dealing with different authors employing different receptional attitudes at exactly the same time!

To sum up, let me illustrate the results of my account of all *three* major reception-historical stages or strands (plus corresponding types and representative authors) in the following, admittedly somewhat simplifying scheme:

	ca. 1840–99	ca. 1900–45	1946 and after
Pre-reception (including mainly reception without production, production without reception and unproductive reception)	e.g., A.F. Beck, Albert Bärthold, Christoph Schrempf		
Reception (including mainly productive reception, receptive production and borderline cases)		e.g., E. Troeltsch, R. Kassner, F. Ebner, F. Kafka, K. Jaspers, T. Haecker, K. Barth, R. Bultmann, T. W. Adorno, Emanuel Hirsch	
Research (including mainly receptive production)			Hermann Diem, H. Deuser, W. Schulz, etc.

A final remark: Kierkegaard's texts are undoubtedly classics, in that they are hermeneutically inexhaustable and lend themselves to being read as a unity of form and content in Kierkegaard's own (!) terms.[393] I presume that, as such, they will be picked up time and again by readers all over the world, and this over a long period of time. This notwithstanding, my account and its schematical results, respectively, suggest no less than a reception-historical pattern or stereotype: initially, scattered, although at times also passionate interest and personal appropriation (1), sooner or later followed by systematically fruitful (if occasionally also misleading) mergings of horizons, often resulting in highly original literary productions (2); finally, academic research, drawing on and occasionally also illegitimately exploiting the sources in a more or less scholarly way (3). Now, as is well known, Kierkegaard suggests that any (essential) truth is, strictly speaking, only "true" for its original recipient. If that itself is a true suggestion, and if, furthermore, Kierkegaard's authorship as a whole deserves to be read as a manifestation of essential truth(s), then we are (in any case the German-speaking world is), on Kierkegaard's own terms, in for hard times. Thus conceived, the title of my article[394] can and should be read with due irony also.

[393]   I have elaborated on this notion of "classical" in Heiko Schulz, "Søren Kierkegaard (1813–1855)," in *Klassiker der Theologie*, vols. 1–2, ed. by F.W. Graf, Munich: Beck 2005, vol. 2, pp. 105–22, here pp. 105–6.

[394]   Which, on a hermeneutical surface level, is nothing but a generalization of Malik's following diagnosis of the history of reception, "While England, France, Italy, and Spain, in the first decade of the twentieth century, were just waking up to the importance of Kierkegaard, the German-speaking world had already been enjoying a modest head start." See Malik, *Receiving Kierkegaard*, p. 353.

Bibliography395

I. German Translations of Kierkegaard's Works

Christenthum und Kirche. "Die Gegenwart." Ein ernstes Wort an unsere Zeit, insbesondere an die evangelische Geistlichkeit, anonym. trans., Hamburg: Köbner 1861 (2nd ed., 1864).

Zur Selbstprüfung der Gegenwart empfohlen, from the 3rd Danish edition trans. and ed. by Chr. Hansen, Erlangen: Deichert 1862 (several later reprints).

Einladung und Ärgernis. Biblische Darstellung und christliche Begriffsbestimmung (excerpts from *Practice in Christianity*), trans. and ed. by Albert Bärthold, Halberstadt: Frantz 1872.

Sören Kierkegaard. Eine Verfasser-Existenz eigner Art. Aus seinen Mittheilungen zusammengestellt, trans. and ed. by Albert Bärthold, Halberstadt: Frantz 1873.

Aus und über Søren Kierkegaard. Früchte und Blätter (excerpts from *Fear and Trembling* and *Concluding Unscientific Postscript*), trans. and ed. by Albert Bärthold, Halberstadt: Frantz 1874.

Zwölf Reden von Søren Kierkegaard (excerpts from *Four Upbuilding Discourses* (1843) and *Christian Discourses*), trans. and ed. by Albert Bärthold, Halle: J. Fricke 1875 (2nd ed., 1896).

Von den Lilien auf dem Felde und den Vögeln unter dem Himmel. Drei Reden Søren Kierkegaards, trans. by A.B. [Albert Bärthold], Halberstadt: H. Meyer 1876.

Die Lilien auf dem Felde und die Vögel unter dem Himmel. Drei fromme Reden. Hoherpriester—Zöllner—Sünderin. Drei Beichtreden von Søren Kierkegaard, trans. and ed. by Albert Bärthold, Halle: J. Fricke 1877 (2nd ed., 1885; 3rd ed., 1910).

Lessing und die objective Wahrheit: aus Søren Kierkegaards Schriften, trans. and ed. by Albert Bärthold, Halle: J. Fricke 1877.

Einübung im Christentum, trans. by Albert Bärthold, Halle: J. Fricke 1878 (2nd ed., 1894).

Die Krankheit zum Tode. Eine christliche psychologische Entwicklung zur Erbauung und Erweckung, trans. by Albert Bärthold, Halle: J. Fricke 1881.

Furcht und Zittern. Dialektische Lyrik von Johannes de silentio (Søren Kierkegaard), trans. and ed. by H.C. Ketels, Erlangen: A Deichert 1882.

---

395   Substantial portions of the present bibliographical material have been compiled by Mareike Reinwald (Essen). Most welcome additions were provided by Dr. Richard Purkarthofer (Copenhagen). Part of the typing was done by Rita Lehmann (Essen). A special thanks is due to all of them.

Entweder-Oder. Ein Lebens-Fragment, trans. and ed. by Alexander Michelsen and Otto Gleiss, Leipzig: J. Lehmann 1885 (several later reprints).

Stadien auf dem Lebenswege, trans. and ed. by Albert Bärthold, Leipzig: J. Lehmann 1886 (2nd ed., Dresden: Ungelenk 1909).

Leben und Walten der Liebe, trans. and ed. by Albert Dorner, Leipzig: F. Richter 1890 (2nd ed., trans. and ed. by Albert Dorner and Christoph Schrempf, introduced by Christoph Schrempf, Jena: Diederichs 1924 (vol. 3 in Søren Kierkegaard, *Erbauliche Reden*)).

Zur Psychologie der Sünde, der Bekehrung und des Glaubens. Zwei Schriften Søren Kierkegaards (includes *The Concept of Anxiey* and *Philosophical Fragments*), trans., ed. and introduced by Christoph Schrempf, Leipzig: F. Richter 1890.

Was wir lernen von den Lilien auf dem Felde und den Vögeln unter dem Himmel. Drei Reden von Søren Kierkegaard, ed. by Alfred Puls, Gotha: C.F. Thienemann 1891 (2nd ed., Berlin 1916).

Richtet selbst! Zur Selbstprüfung der Gegenwart anbefohlen, trans. and ed. by Albert Dorner and Christoph Schrempf, Stuttgart: Frommann 1896.

Søren Kierkegaards agitatorische Schriften und Aufsätze. 1851–1855, trans. and ed. by Albert Dorner and Christoph Schrempf, Stuttgart: Frommann 1896.

" 'Zuerst Gottes Reich.' Eine Art Novelle," *Protestantische Kirchenzeitung für das evangelische Deutschland*, vol. 42, 1896, pp. 1212–13.

Ausgewählte christliche Reden von Søren Kierkegaard. Mit einem Anhang über Kierkegaard's Familie und Privatleben nach den persönlichen Erinnerungen seiner Nichte, Fräulein [Henriette] Lund, trans. and ed. by Julie von Reincke, Giessen: Ricker 1901 (2nd ed., Töpelmann 1909; 3rd ed., 1923).

Aus den Tiefen der Reflexion. Etwas für den Einzelnen aus Søren Kierkegaards Tagebüchern 1833–1855, trans. and ed. by F. Venator, Zweibrücken in Pfalz: Lehmann 1901.

Zwei ethisch-religiöse Abhandlungen von Søren Kierkegaard. 1. Darf ein Mensch sich für die Wahrheit töten lassen? 2. Über den Unterschied zwischen einem Genie und einem Apostel, trans. and ed. by Julie von Reincke, Giessen: Ricker 1902.

Das Tagebuch des Verführers, trans. and ed. by Max Dauthendey, Leipzig: Insel-Verlag 1903 (2nd ed., 1905).

Søren Kierkegaards Verhältnis zu seiner Braut. Briefe und Aufzeichnungen aus seinem Nachlaß, trans. by E. Rohr, ed. by Henriette Lund, Leipzig: Insel 1904.

Søren Kierkegaard. Buch des Richters, (journals 1833–55, in excerpts), trans. and ed. by Hermann Gottsched, Jena and Leipzig: Diederichs 1905.

Søren Kierkegaard, selected, trans., introduced, and ed. by Albert Bärthold, Hamburg: Agentur des Rauhen Hauses 1906.

Søren Kierkegaard und sein Verhältnis zu "ihr." Aus nachgelassenen Papieren, trans. and ed. by Raphael Meyer, Stuttgart: Juncker 1905.

Søren Kierkegaard. Ein unfreier Pionier der Freiheit (excerpts from *Søren Kierkegaards agitatorische Schriften und Aufsätze*), trans. and ed. by Christoph Schrempf, introduced by Harald Høffding, Frankfurt am Main: Neuer Frankfurter Verlag 1907.

Gesammelte Werke, vols. 1–12, trans. and ed. by Hermann Gottsched and Christoph Schrempf, Jena: Diederichs 1909–22.

"Kierkegaard über ästhetisches Stimmungschristentum" (excerpts from *Concluding Unscientific Postscript*), *Der Geisteskampf der Gegenwart*, vol. 9, 1911, pp. 355–6.

Tagebuch des Verführers, trans. and ed. by Richard Meienreis, Berlin: Jacobsthal & Co. 1912.

Søren Kierkegaard, selected, trans., and ed. by Edvard Lehmann, Berlin-Schöneberg: Protestantischer Schriftenvertrieb 1913.

Der Pfahl im Fleisch, trans., ed. and introduced by Theodor Haecker, Innsbruck: Brenner-Verlag 1914 (2nd ed. 1922).

Kierkegaard. Auswahl aus seinen Bekenntnissen und Gedanken, ed. by Fritz Droop, Munich: G. Müller 1914.

Kritik der Gegenwart, trans. and ed. by Theodor Haecker, Innsbruck: Brenner-Verlag 1914 (several later reprints).

"An einem Grab," trans. by Theodor Häcker, *Brenner-Jahrbuch*, vol. 5, 1915.

Eine Lobrede auf Abraham, ed. by Alfred Puls, Berlin: Furche 1916.

"Eine Schlussrede aus S.K." ("Eulogy on Abraham" from *Fear and Trembling*), *Zug ins Land. Liebesgabe deutscher Hochschüler*, vol. 7, 1916, pp. 240–50.

"Kritik der Gegenwart," *Flugblätter an die Deutsche Jugend*, vol. 15, 1916.

"Was man so einen Christen nennt" (excerpts from *The Moment*), *Flugblätter an die deutsche Jugend*, vol. 11, 1916.

Was wir lernen von den Lilien auf dem Felde und den Vögeln unter dem Himmel, trans. and ed. by Alfred Puls, Berlin: Furche 1916.

Das Tagebuch eines Verführers, trans. and ed. by Horst Broichstetten, Berlin: Borngräber 1917.

Der Begriff des Auserwählten, trans. and ed. by Theodor Haecker. Hellerau: Hegner 1917 (2nd ed. Innsbruck: Brenner-Verlag 1926)

"Staatliches Christentum," in *Geist. Die besten Essays der Weltliteratur*, ed. by Wilhelm Herzog, Berlin and Munich: Forum 1917, pp. 37–56.

"Die Sünderin," trans. by Theodor Häcker, *Der Brenner*, vol. 6, 1919, pp. 133ff.

"Die Tagebücher," selected and trans. by Theodor Häcker, *Der Brenner*, 1919, pp. 225–9; 1920, pp. 236–47, pp. 259–72; 1921, pp. 590–4.

"Gottes Unveränderlichkeit," trans. by Theodor Häcker, *Der Brenner*, 1919.

Der Verführer. Sitten-Roman. Nach dem "Tagebuch eines Verführers" von Søren Kierkegaard, trans. and ed. by O. Bernhardt, Pössneck-Berlin: Gerald-Schertling 1920.

"Die Kraft Gottes in der Schwachheit des Menschen," trans. by Theodor Häcker, in *Der Brenner*, vol. 5, 1921, pp. 734–44.

Am Fuße des Altars. Christliche Reden, trans. and ed. by Theodor Häcker, Munich: Beck 1922.

Im Kampf mit sich selbst, trans. and ed. by Christoph Schrempf. Stuttgart: Frommann 1922.

Die Krisis und eine Krisis im Leben einer Schauspielerin. Mit Tagebuchaufzeichnungen des Verfassers, trans. and ed. by Theodor Häcker, Innsbruck: Brenner-Verlag 1922.

Kierkegaard im Kampf mit sich selbst, trans. and ed. by Christoph Schrempf, Stuttgart: Frommann 1922 (2nd ed., 1924).

Religiöse Reden, trans. and ed. by Theodor Häcker, Munich: Hermann Wiechmann 1922 (2nd ed., Leipzig: Hegner 1936; 3rd ed., Munich: Kösel 1950).

Die Tagebücher, vols. 1–2, selected, trans. and ed. by Theodor Häcker, Innsbruck: Brenner-Verlag 1923 (several later reprints).

"Gottes bedürfen ist des Menschen höchste Vollkommenheit," trans. by Emanuel Hirsch, in *Zeitschrift für Systematische Theologie*, vol. 1, 1923, pp. 168–96.

"Gottes Unveränderlichkeit," trans. by Theodor Häcker, *Der Brenner*, vol. 7, 1923, pp. 26–40.

Die Reinheit des Herzens. Eine Beichtrede, trans. by Lina Geismar, Munich: Kaiser 1924 (2nd ed., 1926).

Fideles Christentum, Balingen: Verlag der Weltwende 1924.

Søren Kierkegaard: Auswahl. Erster Teil: Die Werke. Zweiter Teil: Die Tagebücher 1832–1839 (Parts 1–2 in one volume), trans. and ed. by Hermann Ulrich, Berlin: Hochweg 1925–30.

"Nachfolge Christi," *Neuwerk*, vol. 7, 1925 , pp. 41–4.

"Der Hohepriester," trans. by Emanuel Hirsch, *Zeitschrift für Systematische Theologie*, vol. 4, 1926, pp. 395–404.

Søren Kierkegaard: Schriften des Verführers, ed. by E. Guggenheim, Berlin: Bard 1926.

Aus dem Tagebuch des Verführers, Munich: Georg Müller 1927.

"Das Eine, das not tut, " *Zeitwende*, vol. 3, 1927, pp. 1–7.

Søren Kierkegaard und Regine Olsen. Briefe, Tagebuchblätter und Dokumente, selected, trans. and ed. by Gerhard Niedermeyer, Munich: Beck 1927.

"Vom inneren Bau der Oper," *Freiburger Theaterblätter*, 1927–28, p. 181.

Das Tagebuch eines Verführers, trans. and ed. by E. Th. Kauer, Berlin: Neufeld & Henius 1928.

Der Begriff der Ironie mit ständiger Rücksicht auf Sokrates, trans. and ed. by Wilhelm Kütemeyer, Munich: Kaiser 1929.

Über den Begriff der Ironie mit ständiger Rücksicht auf Sokrates, trans. and ed. by Hans Heinrich Schaeder, Munich and Berlin: Oldenburg 1929.

Søren Kierkegaard. Religion der Tat. Sein Werk in Auswahl, trans. and ed. by Eduard Geismar, Leipzig: Kröner 1930 (several later reprints).

So spricht Søren Kierkegaard. Aus seinen Tage- und Nächtebüchern, trans., ed., and introduced by Robert Dollinger, Berlin: Furche 1930.

"Søren Kierkegaard: Nachfolge und Gnade" (selections from the journals), trans. by Hermann Diem, *Zwischen den Zeiten*, vol. 9, 1931, pp. 4–8.

Das Evangelium der Leiden. Christliche Reden, trans. and ed. by Wilhelm Kütemeyer, Munich: Kaiser 1933 (2nd ed., 1936).

Von der Liebe. Zwei Lesestücke neu an den Tag gebracht, von Søren Kierkegaard und Heinrich von Kleist, ed. by Jan Thorbecke, Leipzig: Das Erbe 1933.

Der Einzelne und die Kirche. Über Luther und den Protestantismus, trans. and ed. by Wilhelm Kütemeyer, Berlin: Wolff 1934.

"Eine Meditation Kierkegaards," trans. by Emanuel Hirsch, *Deutsche Theologie*, vol. 1, 1934, p. 373.

"Katholizismus und Protestantismus. Aus nachgelassenen Tagebüchern," *Europäische Revue*, vol. 10, 1934, pp. 435–9.

Was wir lernen von den Lilien auf dem Felde und den Vögeln unter dem Himmel,
    trans. and ed. by Robert Dollinger, Berlin: Furche 1934 (2nd ed., 1936; 3rd ed.,
    Hamburg 1956).

"Worte Kierkegaards," *Nationalsozialistische Monatshefte*, vol. 5, 1934, pp. 181–7.

"Darf ein Mensch sich für die Wahrheit töten lassen?" *Neuwerk. Ein Dienst am
    Werdenden*, vol. 16, 1935, pp. 66–7.

*Wie herrlich es ist, Mensch zu sein und welche Seligkeit dem Menschen verheißen
    ist*, trans. and ed. by Robert Dollinger, Berlin: Furche 1936.

Gegen Feigheit, trans. and ed. by Robert Dollinger, Berlin: Furche 1937.

Kierkegaard Brevier, trans. and ed. by Peter Schäfer and Max Bense, Leipzig: Insel
    1937 (2nd ed., Wiesbaden: Insel 1951).

*Im Zwange des freien Gewissens. Gedanken über Gott und Mensch aus den Tage-
    und Nächtebüchern*, selected, trans. and ed. by Robert Dollinger, Berlin: Furche
    1938.

Ueber die Geduld und die Erwartung des Ewigen, trans. and ed. by Theodor Häcker,
    Leipzig: Hegner 1938.

Vom wundersamen Streit im Gebet, trans. and ed. by Robert Dollinger, Berlin: Furche
    1938.

Entweder—Oder, trans. by Christoph Schrempf, abbreviated edition by Fritz Droop,
    Leipzig: Dieterich 1939.

Gott nötig haben ist des Menschen höchste Vollkommenheit, trans. and ed. by Robert
    Dollinger, Berlin: Furche 1939.

"Abstands Religiosität und innerliche Religiosität," *Der Quäker. Monatshefte der
    deutschen Freunde*, vol. 18, 1941, p. 17.

Wahrheit, die aufbaut. Reden aus den Jahren 1834–1847, trans. and ed. by Th. W.
    Bätscher, Zürich: Zwingli 1942.

"Briefe Kierkegaards an Emil Boesen," *Cologneische Zeitung*, August 22, 1943.

Freude in der Anfechtung. Gedanken aus den Werken Søren Kierkegaards, selected
    and ed. by Erich Schick, Basel: Basler Missionsbuchhandlung 1943 (2nd ed.,
    1948).

Aus dem Tagebuch des Verführers, trans. and ed. by Fritz Droop, Munich: Zinnen
    1946.

Im Schatten des Ewigen. Ausgewählte Worte (excerpts from the journals, 1834–55),
    Stuttgart: Vita Nova-Verlag 1946.

Zur Überwindung des Nihilismus, trans. and ed. by Hermann Diem, Stuttgart: Klett
    1946.

Das verborgene Leben der Liebe und wie es an seine Früchten erkannt wird, trans.
    and ed. by Friedrich Aage Hansen-Löwe, Vienna: Amandus-Edition 1947 (2nd ed.,
    1948).

Die Lilien auf dem Felde, trans. and ed. by Friedrich Aage Hansen-Löwe, Vienna:
    Herder 1947.

Tagebücher. Eine Auswahl, selected, trans. and ed. by Elisabeth Feuersenger,
    Wiesbaden: Metropen 1947 (2nd ed., 1949).

Aus dem Tagebuch des Verführers, trans. and ed. by Fritz Droop, Munich: Zinnen-
    Verlag 1948.

Søren Kierkegaard: Das Eine, das not thut. Eine Beichtrede, trans. and ed. by Thyra Dohrenburg, Bremen: Storm 1948.

Johannes Climacus oder De omnibus dubitandum est, trans. and ed. by Wolfgang Struwe, Darmstadt: Claasen & Roether 1948.

Furcht und Zittern. Dialektische Lyrik, trans. and ed. by Helmut de Boor, Krefeld: Scherpe-Verlag 1949.

Die Krankheit zum Tode. Eine christlich-psychologische Entwicklung zur Erbauung und Erweckung, trans. by Thyra Dohrenburg, ed. by Ingeborg Frieser, Bremen: Storm 1949.

Gesammelte Werke, vols. 1–28, trans. by Emanuel Hirsch, Düsseldorf and Cologne: Diederichs 1950–69 (2nd ed., Gütersloh: Guterslöher Taschenbücher 1986–95; 3rd ed., Simmerath: Grevenberg 2004).

Philosophisch-theologische Schriften, vols. 1–4, trans. and ed. by Hermann Diem and Walter Rest, Cologne et al.: Hegner 1951ff. (2nd ed., Munich: Deutscher Taschenbuchverlag 1975–77; several later reprints).

Gebete, trans. and ed. by Walter Rest, Cologne and Olten: Hegner 1952.

Welt über Welt. Worte Søren Kierkegaards, die nicht vergessen werden dürfen, ed. by Johannes Besch, Berlin: Christlicher Zeitschriftenverlag 1952.

Die Leidenschaft des Religiösen. Eine Auswahl aus Schriften und Tagebüchern, trans. and ed. by Heinz Küpper, Stuttgart: Reclam 1953 (several later reprints).

Gott ist größer als unser Herz. Vier Beichtreden, trans. and ed. by Robert Dollinger, Hamburg: Furche 1954.

"Sören Kierkegaard. Briefe," trans. by Walter Boehlich, *Merkur. Deutsche Zeitschrift für europäisches Denken*, vol. 8, 1954, pp. 758–69.

So spricht Kierkegaard, ed. by Fritz Werle and Ursula von Mangoldt, Munich-Planegg: Barth 1954.

Briefe, selected, trans. and ed. by Walter Boehlich, Cologne and Olten: Hegner 1955 (2nd ed., Frankfurt am Main: Insel 1983).

Christliche Reden, trans. and ed. by Wilhelm Kütemeyer, Göttingen: Vandenhoeck & Ruprecht 1955 (2nd ed., 1961).

Das Gleichnis vom Kutscher (excerpts from *For Self-Examination*), trans. by Emanuel Hirsch, Düsseldorf and Cologne: Diederichs 1955.

Die Liebe deckt auch der Sünden Menge (excerpts from *Christian Discourses*), trans. and ed. by Robert Dollinger, Neuendettelsau: Freimund 1955.

Kierkegaards Verlobungsbriefe (Sept./Nov.1840), trans. by Emanuel Hirsch, Düsseldorf and Cologne: Diederichs 1955.

Existenz im Glauben. Aus Dokumenten, Briefen und Tagebüchern, trans. and ed. by Liselotte Richter, Berlin: EVA 1956.

Kierkegaard, selected, trans. and ed. by Hermann Diem, Frankfurt am Main: Fischer 1956.

Lobrede auf Abraham, trans. and ed. by Robert Dollinger, Hamburg: Furche 1956.

Mozarts Don Juan, trans. and ed. by Hermann Kiy, Zürich and Freiburg i. Br.: Atlantis 1956.

Christentum und Christenheit, selected, trans., and ed. by Eva Schlechta. Munich: Kösel 1957.

Rufe zu Gott. Gebete, trans. and ed. by Willi Reich, Zürich: Verlag der Arche 1958 (2ⁿᵈ ed., 1963).

Aber es gibt eine Macht. Eine Auswahl, selected and ed. by Eberhard Witte, Wuppertal: Emil Müller 1959 (several later reprints).

Randbemerkungen zum Evangelium, trans. and ed. by Friedrich Aage Hansen-Löwe, Munich: Kösel 1959.

Werke, vols. 1–5, trans. and ed. by Liselotte Richter, Reinbek bei Hamburg: Rowohlt 1960–64 (several later reprints).

Auswahl aus dem Gesamtwerk des Dichters, Denkers und religiösen Redners, trans. and ed. by Emanuel Hirsch, Stuttgart and Hamburg: Deutscher Bücherbund 1961 (2ⁿᵈ ed., Munich and Hamburg: Siebenstern 1969).

Der Einzelne und sein Gott, selected, trans., and ed. by Walter Rest, Freiburg i. Br.: Herder 1961.

Das Tagebuch des Verführers, trans. by Heinrich Fauteck, ed. by Hermann Diem, Cologne and Olten: Hegner 1962 (several later reprints).

Der Pfahl im Fleisch sowie Wider Feigheit und Vom Gebet, trans. and ed. by Anna Paulsen, Hamburg: Furche 1962.

Die Tagebücher, vols. 1–5, trans. and ed. by Hayo Gerdes, Düsseldorf and Cologne: Diederichs 1962–74.

Christ aus Leidenschaft. Eine Auswahl aus dem Gesamtwerk, trans. and ed. by Daniel Hoffmann, Berlin: Union Verlag 1963.

Die Gültigkeit der Ehe, trans. and ed. by Heinrich Fauteck, Cologne and Olten: Hegner 1963.

Die Lilie auf dem Felde und der Vogel unter dem Himmel, trans. and ed. by Daniel Hoffmann, Berlin: Evangelische Verlagsanstalt 1965.

Werkausgabe, vols. 1–2, trans. and ed. by Emanuel Hirsch und Hayo Gerdes, Düsseldorf and Cologne: Diederichs 1971.

Philosophische Brocken. De omnibus dubitandum est, trans. and ed. by Emanuel Hirsch, Frankfurt am Main: Suhrkamp 1975.

Über den Begriff der Ironie mit ständiger Rücksicht auf Sokrates, trans. and ed. by Emanuel Hirsch, Frankfurt am Main: Suhrkamp 1976.

Alle gute Gabe kommt von oben herab: Drei erbauliche Reden, trans. and ed. by E. Schlechta-Nordentoft, Munich: Nashorn-Verlag 1977.

Die Krankheit zum Tode. Der Hohepriester, der Zöllner, die Sünderin, trans. and ed. by Emanuel Hirsch, Gütersloh: Gütersloher Verlagshaus 1978.

Die nackte Wahrheit. Aphorismen und andere kurze Notizen. Eine Auswahl, selected, trans., and ed. by Sixtus Scholtens and Paulus Ter Doest, Kamp-Lintfort: Verlag der Karmel-Stimmen 1978.

Christenspiegel. Eine Auswahl, ed. by Wolfgang Buhne, Wuppertal: Brockhaus 1979.

Die Tagebücher. Eine Auswahl, trans. and ed. by Hayo Gerdes, Düsseldorf and Cologne: Diederichs 1980.

Tagebuch des Verführers, trans. and ed. by Helene Ritzerfeld, Frankfurt am Main: Insel 1983 (2ⁿᵈ ed., Leipzig: Insel 1997).

Der Begriff Angst, trans. and ed. by Hans Rochol, Hamburg: Meiner 1984.

"Was ihr den Geist der Zeiten heißt." Der Verführer Sören Kierkegaard. Lesestücke, ed. by Jürgen Busche, Königstein: Athenäum 1984.

Kierkegaard für Christen. Eine Herausforderung, selected, trans., and ed. by Walter Rest, Freiburg i. Br.: Herder 1987.

Kritik der Gegenwart. Der Pfahl im Fleisch, trans. and ed. by Theodor Haecker, Vienna: Karolinger 1988.

Der Augenblick. Eine Zeitschrift, trans. by Hanns Grössel, Nördlingen: Franz Greno 1988.

Sören Kierkegaard, ed. by Hans Christian Meiser, Munich: Goldmann 1988.

Philosophische Bissen, trans. and ed. by Hans Rochol, Hamburg: Meiner 1989.

Der Einzelne, trans. and ed. by Wilfried Greve, Frankfurt am Main: Hain 1990.

Begegnung mit Sören Kierkegaard, ed. by Robert van de Weyer, Gießen and Basel: Brunnen 1991.

Die unmittelbaren erotischen Stadien oder das Musikalisch-Erotische. Über Mozarts "Don Giovanni," trans. and ed. by Gisela Perlet, Berlin: Verlagsanstalt Union 1991.

Der Begriff Angst, trans. and ed. by Gisela Perlet, Stuttgart: Reclam 1992.

Tagebuch des Verführers, trans. and ed. by Gisela Perlet, Stuttgart: Reclam 1994 (2nd ed., Munich: Goldmann 1999).

Die Krankheit zum Tode, trans. and ed. by Hans Rochol, Hamburg: Meiner 1995.

Kierkegaard, selected and introduced by Boris Groys, trans. by Emanuel Hirsch, ed. by Peter Sloterdijk, Munich: Diederichs 1996 (2nd ed., Munich: Deutscher Taschenbuchverlag 1999).

Die Dialektik der ethischen und der ethisch-religiösen Mitteilung, trans. and ed. by Tim Hagemann, Bodenheim: Philo 1997.

Die Krankheit zum Tode, trans. and ed. by Gisela Perlet, Stuttgart: Reclam 1997.

Kierkegaard für Anfänger—Entweder-Oder. Eine Lese-Einführung, ed. by Asa A. Schillinger-Kind, Munich: Deutscher Taschenbuchverlag 1997.

Kierkegaard zum 18ten. Beiträge zu einer christlichen Tiefenpsychologie. Kernpassagen aus Kierkegaards Entweder-Oder, ed. by Hanne Baar, Rottendorf: Hymnus-Verlag 1997.

Die unmittelbaren erotischen Stadien oder das Musikalisch-Erotische, trans. and ed. by Gisela Perlet, Hamburg: Europäische Verlagsanstalt 1999.

Berliner Tagebücher, trans. and ed. by Tim Hagemann, Berlin and Vienna: Philo 2000.

Bewahre Deinen Fuß, wenn Du zum Haus des Herrn gehst, trans. and ed. by Tim Hagemann, Berlin and Vienna: Philo 2000.

Die Wiederholung, trans. and ed. by Hans Rochol, Hamburg: Meiner 2000.

Kierkegaard für Gestresste, trans. by Ulrich Sonnenberg, ed. by Johan de Mylius, Frankfurt am Main and Leipzig: Insel 2000.

Kierkegaard für Volljährige. Beiträge zu einer christlichen Tiefenpsychologie. Kernpassagen aus Kierkegaards Die Krankheit zum Tode, ed. by Hanne Baar, Rottendorf: Hymnus-Verlag 2000.

Entweder-Oder. Ein Buch von Katja Kuck und Jürgen Kuck. Mit Texten von Sören Kierkegaard, Berlin: Pro Business 2001.

"Sören Kierkegaards Tagebuchnotizen über Julius Müller," trans. by Tim Hagemann, in Willi, H.-P., *Unbegreifliche Sünde. "Die christliche Lehre von der Sünde" als Theorie der Freiheit bei Julius Müller*, Berlin and New York: Walter de Gruyter 2003, pp. 422–33.

Geheime Papiere, trans. and ed. by Tim Hagemann, Berlin: Eichborn 2004.

Werke der Liebe, selected and ed. by Reiner Wimmer, Stuttgart: Kohlhammer 2004.

Der Begriff Angst/Die Krankheit zum Tode, ed. by Thomas Sören Hoffmann, Wiesbaden: Marix 2005.

Der Begriff Angst/Philosophische Bissen/Die Krankheit zum Tode, vols. 1–3, trans. by Hans Rochol, special edition, Hamburg: Meiner 2005.

Deutsche Søren Kierkegaard Edition (DSKE), Bd. 1: Journale und Aufzeichnungen AA–DD, ed. by Hermann Deuser et al., Berlin and New York: Walter de Gruyter 2005.

Es gehört wahrlich Mut dazu. Gedanken über das Leben, ed. by Asa A. Schillinger-Kind, Munich: Deutscher Taschenbuchverlag 2005.

Jenseits der Angst, trans. by W. Mühs, ed. by Stefan Liesenfeld, Munich: Neue Stadt 2005.

Schriftproben, trans. and ed. by Tim Hagemann, Berlin and Vienna: Philo 2005.

II. Secondary Literature on Kierkegaard in the German-Speaking Countries

Abdolhosseini, Mohammad R.H., *Das subjektive und dynamische Verhältnis zur Wahrheit bei Sören Kierkegaard*, Ph.D. Thesis, University of Basel 1997.

Adorno, Theodor W., *Kierkegaard. Konstruktion des Ästhetischen*, vol. 2, in *Gesammelte Schriften*, vols. 1–5, ed. by Rolf Tiedemann, Frankfurt am Main: Suhrkamp 2003 [Tübingen: Mohr 1933].

Ahn, Stephan, *Sören Kierkegaards Ontologie der Bewusstseinssphären. Versuch einer multidisziplinären Gegenstandsuntersuchung*, Münster: Ugarit 1997.

Allemann, Beda, *Ironie und Dichtung*, 2nd ed., Pfullingen: Neske 1969 [1956].

Anz, Wilhelm, *Die Wiederholung der socratischen Methode durch Soeren Kierkegaard*, Ph.D. Thesis, University of Marburg 1940.

— *Kierkegaard und der deutsche Idealismus*, Tübingen: Mohr 1956.

Axt-Piscalar, Christine, *Ohnmächtige Freiheit. Studien zum Verhältnis von Subjektivität und Sünde bei August Tholuck, Julius Müller, Sören Kierkegaard und Friedrich Schleiermacher*, Tübingen: Mohr 1996.

Baas, Fritz, *Das Ästhetische bei Søren Kierkegaard in seinen Grundbestimmungen*, Ph.D. Thesis, University of Heidelberg 1923.

Bagus, Peter, *Menschliches Leiden aus der Sicht der deutschen Existenzphilosophie*, Hamburg: Kovac 1997.

Bartels, Cora, *Kierkegaard receptus. Die theologiegeschichtliche Bedeutung der Kierkegaard Rezeption Rudolf Bultmanns*, Th.D. Thesis, University of Göttingen 2004.

Balthasar, Hans Urs von, *Prometheus. Studien zur Geschichte des deutschen Idealismus*, Heidelberg: F.H. Kerle 1947.

Barth, Karl, *Der Römerbrief,* 12th ed., Zürich: Theologischer Verlag 1978 [1919, 2nd ed., 1922].

Bärthold, Albert, *Aus und über Sören Kierkegaard. Früchte und Blätter*, Halberstadt: Frantz 1874.

— *Noten zu Sören Kierkegaards Lebensgeschichte*, Halle: Fricke 1876.

— *Die Bedeutung der ästhetischen Schriften Sören Kierkegaards mit Bezug auf G. Brandes: "Søren Kierkegaard, ein literarisches Charakterbild,"* Halle: Fricke 1879.

— *Zur theologischen Bedeutung Sören Kierkegaards*, Halle: Fricke 1880.

— *Was Christentum ist. Zur Verständigung über diese Frage*, Gütersloh: Bertelsmann 1884.

— *Die Wendung zur Wahrheit in der modernen Kulturentwicklung*, Gütersloh: Bertelsmann 1885.

— *S. Kierkegaards Persönlichkeit in ihrer Verwirklichung der Ideale*, Gütersloh: Bertelsmann 1886.

— *Geleitbrief für Søren Kierkegaard: "Ein Bisschen Philosophie,"* Leipzig: Richter 1890.

Bauer, Wilhelm, *Die Ethik Sören Kierkegaards*, Ph.D. Thesis, University of Jena 1913.

Baumann, Julius, *Deutsche und außerdeutsche Philosophie der letzten Jahrzehnte dargestellt und beurteilt*, Gotha: Perthes 1903.

Beck, Elke, *Identität der Person. Sozialphilosophische Studien zu Kierkegaard, Adorno und Habermas*, Würzburg: Königshausen & Neumann 1991.

Bense, Max, *Vom Wesen deutscher Denker, oder zwischen Kritik und Imperativ*, Munich: Oldenbourg 1938.

— *Leben im Geist*, Hamburg: Hoffmann & Campe 1942.

— *Hegel und Kierkegaard. Eine prinzipielle Untersuchung*, Cologne: Staufen 1948.

Besch, Johannes, *Sprecher Gottes in unserer Zeit*, Stuttgart: Steinkopf 1919.

Beyrich, Tilman, *Ist Glauben wiederholbar? Derrida liest Kierkegaard*, Berlin and New York: Walter de Gruyter 2001 (*Kierkegaard Studies. Monograph Series*, vol. 6).

Birkenstock, Eva, *Heißt philosophieren sterben lernen? Antworten der Existenzphilosophie: Kierkegaard, Heidegger, Sartre, Rosenzweig*, Freiburg i. Br. and Munich: Alber 1997.

Blanke, Ingrid, *Sinn und Grenze christlicher Erziehung. Kierkegaard und die Problematik der christlichen Erziehung in unserer Zeit*, Frankfurt am Main: Peter Lang 1978.

Blass, Josef L., *Die Krise der Freiheit im Denken Sören Kierkegaards. Untersuchungen zur Konstitution der Subjektivität*, Ratingen: Henn 1968.

Boldt, Joachim, *Kierkegaards "Furcht und Zittern" als Bild seines ethischen Erkenntnisbegriffs*, Berlin and New York: Walter de Gruyter 2006 (*Kierkegaard Studies Monograph Series*, vol. 13).

Bollnow, Otto F., *Existenzphilosophie*, 3rd ed., Stuttgart: Kohlhammer 1949 [1942].

Bongardt, Michael, *Der Widerstand der Freiheit. Eine transzendentaldialogische Aneignung der Angstanalysen Kierkegaards*, Frankfurt am Main: Knecht 1995.

Boomgaarden, Jürgen, *Das verlorene Selbst. Phänomenologie und Dogmatik der Sünde*, Habilitation Thesis, University of Jena 2004.

Borelius, Hilma, *Die nordischen Literaturen*, Potsdam: Athenaion 1931.

Börge, Vagn, *Kierkegaard und das Theater, mit besonderer Rücksicht auf Mozarts "Don Juan,"* Vienna: Hans Riel 1947.

Bösch, Michael, *Søren Kierkegaard: Schicksal—Angst—Freiheit*, Paderborn: Schöningh 1994.

Bösl, Anton, *Unfreiheit und Selbstverfehlung. Sören Kierkegaards existenzdialektische Bestimmung von Schuld und Sünde*, Freiburg i. Br.: Herder 1997.

Braun, Günther, *Der Begriff des Humors in Søren Kierkegaards Werk und die Bedeutung des Humors für dieses*, Ph.D. Thesis, University of Mainz 1952.

Braunleder, Margot, *Selbstbestimmung, Verantwortung und die Frage nach dem sittlich Guten. Zum Begriff einer skeptischen Ethik*, Würzburg: Königshausen & Neumann 1990.

Brechtken, Josef, *Kierkegaard, Newman: Wahrheit und Existenzmitteilungen*, Meisenheim: Hain 1970.

— *Die praxisdialektische Kritik des Marxschen Atheimus. Studien zum anthropozentrisch-kritischen Wirklichkeitsbegriff vom Standpunkt der geschichtlichen Praxis und zu seinen religionsphilosophischen Konsequenzen: Hegel—Kierkegaard—Marx*, vols. 1–2, Königstein: Athenäum 1979.

Brinkschmidt, Egon, *Sören Kierkegaard und Karl Barth*, Neukirchen-Vluyn: Neukirchener 1971.

Brod, Max, *Diesseits und Jenseits*, vols. 1–2, Zürich and Winterthur: Mondial 1947.

Brunner, Emil, *Der Mensch im Widerspruch. Die christliche Lehre vom wahren und vom wirklichen Menschen*, Zürich: Zwingli 1937.

— *Offenbarung und Vernunft. Die Lehre von der christlichen Glaubenserkenntnis*, Zürich: Zwingli 1941.

— *Ein offenes Wort. Vorträge und Aufsätze 1917–1962*, Zürich: Theologischer Verlag 1981.

Buber, Martin, *Dialogisches Leben. Gesammelte philosophische und Pädagogische Schriften*, Zürich: Gregor Müller 1947.

Bürger, Peter, *Zur Kritik der idealistischen Ästhetik*, Frankfurt am Main: Suhrkamp 1983.

Buss, Hinrich, *Kierkegaards Angriff auf die bestehende Christenheit*, Hamburg: Reich 1970.

Cattepoel, Jan, *Dämonie und Gesellschaft. Søren Kierkegaard als Sozialkritiker und Kommunikationstheoretiker*, Freiburg i. Br. and Munich: Alber 1992.

Cohn, Jonas, *Die Philosophie im Zeitalter des Spezialismus*, Leipzig: Teubner 1925.

Craemer-Schroeder, Susanne, *Deklination des Autobiographischen. Goethe, Stendhal, Kierkegaard*, Berlin: Erich Schmidt 1993.

Crimmann, Ralph P., *Franz Kafka. Versuch einer kulturphilosophischen Interpretation*, Hamburg: Kovac 2004.

Daab, Anneliese, *Ironie und Humor bei Kierkegaard*, Ph.D. Thesis, University of Heidelberg 1926.

Dalferth, Ingolf U. (ed.), *Ethik der Liebe. Studien zu Kierkegaards "Taten der Liebe,"* Tübingen: J.C.B. Mohr 2002.

Dallago, Carl, *Ueber eine Schrift: Søren Kierkegaard und die Philosophie der Innerlichkeit (von Theodor Haecker)*, Innsbruck: Brenner 1914.

Decher, Friedhelm, *Verzweiflung. Anatomie eines Affektes*, Lüneburg: zu Klampen 2002.

Deiss, Erika, *Entweder-Oder? oder: Kierkegaards Rache, Einladung an die Verächter des Ästhetischen, sich fortzubilden oder fortzumachen*, Ph.D. Thesis, University of Heidelberg, 1984.

Dempf, Alois, *Kierkegaards Folgen*, Leipzig: Hegner 1935.

Dennert, Eberhard (ed.), *Klassiker der religiösen Weltanschauung*, vol. 1, *Kant, Kierkegaard, Kingsley*, Hamburg: Agentur des Rauhen Hauses 1909.

Deuser, Hermann, *Sören Kierkegaard. Die paradoxe Dialektik des politischen Christen. Voraussetzungen bei Hegel. Die Reden von 1847/48 im Verhältnis von Politik und Ästhetik*, Munich and Mainz: Kaiser & Grünewald 1974.

— *Dialektische Theologie. Studien zu Adornos Metaphysik und zum Spätwerk Kierkegaards*, Munich: Kaiser 1980.

— *Kierkegaard. Die Philosophie des religiösen Schriftstellers*, Darmstadt: Wissenschaftliche Buchgesellschaft 1985.

— *Kleine Einführung in die Systematische Theologie*, Stuttgart: Reclam 1999.

Dieckmann, Friedrich (ed.), *Die unmittelbaren erotischen Stadien oder das Musikalisch-Erotische. Über Mozarts "Don Giovanni,"* Berlin: Verlags-Anstalt Union 1991.

Diem, Hermann, *Philosophie und Christentum bei Sören Kierkegaard*, Munich: Kaiser 1929.

— *Die Existenzdialektik von Sören Kierkegaard*, Zollikon-Zürich: Evangelischer Verlag 1950.

— *Dogmatik. Ihr Weg zwischen Historismus und Existentialismus*, Munich: Kaiser 1955.

— *Sören Kierkegaard. Spion im Dienste Gottes*, Frankfurt am Main: Fischer 1957.

— *Sören Kierkegaard. Eine Einführung*, Göttingen: Vandenhoeck & Ruprecht 1964.

Dietz, Walter, *Sören Kierkegaard. Existenz und Freiheit*, Frankfurt am Main: Hain 1992.

Dischner, Gisela, *Es wagen, ein Einzelner zu sein. Versuch über Kierkegaard*, Bodenheim: Philo 1997.

Disse, Jörg, *Kierkegaards Phänomenologie der Freiheitserfahrung*, Freiburg i. Br. and Munich: Alber 1991.

Düwel, Hans, *Der Entwicklungsgedanke in Søren Kierkegaards "Entweder-Oder" und in Henrik Ibsens "Komödie der Liebe,"* Rostock: Winterberg 1920.

Ebner, Ferdinand, *Schriften*, vols. 1–3, ed. by Franz Seyr, Munich: Kösel 1963–65.

Eichler, Uta, *Von der Existenz zu den objektiven gesellschaftlichen Verhältnissen. Studien zur Interpretation und Kritik der Ethikauffassung Sören Kierkegaards*, Ph.D. Thesis, University of Halle 1980.

Eilers, Edgar, *Probleme religiöser Existenz im "Geistlichen Jahr." Die Droste und Søren Kierkegaard*, Werl: Coelde 1953.

Eisenhuth, Heinz E., *Der Begriff des Irrationalen als philosophisches Problem. Ein Beitrag zur existentialen Religionsbegründung*, Göttingen: Vandenhoeck & Ruprecht 1931.

Eisenstein, Michael, *Selbstverwirklichung und Existenz – ethische Perspektiven pastoralpsychologischer Beratung unter besonderer Berücksichtigung S. Kierkegaards*, St. Ottilien: EOS 1986.

Elert, Werner, *Der Kampf um das Christentum. Geschichte der Beziehungen zwischen dem evangelischen Christentum in Deutschland und das allgemeine Denken seit Schleiermacher und Hegel,* Hildesheim: Olms 2005 (reprint of the Munich: Beck 1921 ed.).

Endriß, Stefan, *Hans Urs von Balthasar versus Sören Kierkegaard*, Hamburg: Kovac 2006.

Engelke, Matthias, *Kierkegaard und das Alte Testament. Zum Einfluß der alttestamentlichen Bücher auf Kierkegaards Gesamtwerk*, Rheinbach: CMZ 2001.

Erne, Paul T., *Lebenskunst. Aneignung ästhetischer Erfahrung. Ein theologischer Beitrag zur Ästhetik im Anschluss an Kierkegaard*, Kampen: Kok Pharos 1994.

Esmach, Ernst, *An Søren Kierkegaard*, Leipzig: Richter 1885.

Fahrenbach, Helmut, *Kierkegaards existenzdialektische Ethik*, Frankfurt am Main: Klostermann 1968.

— *Existenzphilosophie und Ethik*, Frankfurt am Main: Klostermann 1970.

Fichtner, Ruth, *Elemente außeramerikanischer Kulturkreise in Wilders Werk*, Birkach: Ladewig 1985.

Figal, Günter, *Lebensverstricktheit und Abstandnahme. "Verhalten zu sich" im Anschluß an Heidegger, Kierkegaard und Hegel*, Tübingen: Attempto 2001.

Fink-Eitel, Hinrich, *Die Philosophie und die Wilden. Über die Bedeutung des Fremden für die europäische Geschichte*, Hamburg: Junius 1994.

Fischer, Friedrich C., *Die Nullpunkt-Existenz dargestellt an der Lebensform Sören Kierkegaards*, Munich: Beck 1933.

— *Existenz und Innerlichkeit. Eine Einführung in die Gedankenwelt Søren Kierkegaards*, Munich: Beck 1969.

Fischer, Hermann, *Subjektivität und Sünde. Kierkegaards Begriff der Sünde mit ständiger Rücksicht auf Schleiermachers Lehre von der Sünde*, Itzehoe: Die Spur 1963.

— *Die Christologie des Paradoxes. Zur Herkunft und Bedeutung des Christusverständnisses Sören Kierkegaards*, Göttingen: Vandenhoeck & Ruprecht 1970.

Fischer-Mampoteng, Friedrich C., *Menschsein als Aufgabe. Stufen der Selbstbesinnung im Leben des Einzelnen*, Heidelberg: Kampmann 1928.

Fonk, Peter, *Zwischen Sünde und Erlösung. Entstehung und Entwicklung einer christlichen Anthropologie bei Sören Kierkegaard*, Kevelaer: Butzon & Bercker 1990.

Franken, Johannes C., *Kritische Philosophie und dialektische Theologie. Prolegomena zu einer philosophischen Behandlung des Problems der christlichen Gemeinschaft*, Amsterdam: Paris 1932.

Friemond, Hans, *Existenz in Liebe nach Sören Kierkegaard*, Salzburg and Munich: Pustet 1965.

Frieser, Ingeborg, *Beiträge zu ästhetischen Phänomenen bei Søren Kierkegaard mit besonderer Rücksicht auf das Theater*, Ph.D. Thesis, University of Freiburg 1950.

Fritzsche, Helmut, *Das Problem der Gleichzeitigkeit bei Søren Kierkegaard*, Th.D. Thesis, Humboldt-University, Berlin 1962.

— *Kierkegaards Kritik an der Christenheit*, Stuttgart: Calver 1966.

Fujino, Hiroshi, *Kierkegaards "Entweder, oder." Ein "Entweder ästhetisch, oder existentiell." Versuch einer Neubewertung des Denkens Kierkegaards hinsichtlich seiner Grundkategorien des Ästhetischen, des Ethischen und des Religiösen*, Würzburg: Königshausen & Neumann 1994.

Gabriel, Leo, *Existenzphilosophie: Kierkegaard, Heidegger, Jaspers, Sartre. Dialog der Positionen*, 2nd ed., Vienna and Munich: Herold 1968 [1951].

Geismar, Eduard, *Sören Kierkegaard*, Gütersloh: Bertelsmann 1925.

— *Sören Kierkegaard. Seine Lebensentwicklung und seine Wirksamkeit als Schriftsteller*, trans. by E. Krüger and L. Geismar, Göttingen: Vandenhoeck & Ruprecht 1927–29.

Gemmer, Anders, *Sören Kierkegaard und Karl Barth*, Stuttgart: Strecker & Schroeder 1925.

Gerdes, Hayo, *Das Christusbild Sören Kierkegaards. Verglichen mit der Christologie Hegels und Schleiermachers*, Düsseldorf: Diederichs 1960 (reprinted as *Der geschichtliche biblische Jesus und der Christus der Philosophen. Erwägungen zur Christologie Kierkegaards, Hegels und Schleiermachers*, Berlin: Die Spur 1974).

— *Sören Kierkegaards "Einübung im Christentum." Einführung und Erläuterung*, Darmstadt: Wissenschaftliche Buchgesellschaft 1982.

— *Sören Kierkegaard*, Berlin and New York: Walter de Gruyter 1966.

Gerdes, Hayo and Hans M. Müller (eds.), *Das Christusverständnis Sören Kierkegaards. Drei Arbeiten zu Kierkegaards Christologie 1960–1982*, Waltrop: Spenner 2002.

Giess, Ludwig, *Liebe als Freiheit. Eine Kierkegaard Aneignung*, Temeschburg: Anwender & Sohn 1939.

Gilg, Arnold, *Sören Kierkegaard*, Munich: Kaiser 1926.

Gleiss, Otto, *Aus dem evangelischen Norden. Zeugnisse von Christo in Predigten aus der skandinavischen Kirche unserer Zeit*, Gütersloh: Bertelsmann 1882.

Glöckner, Dorothea, *Kierkegaards Begriff der Wiederholung. Eine Studie zu seinem Freiheitsverständnis*, Berlin and New York: Walter de Gruyter 1998 (*Kierkegaard Studies. Monograph Series*, vol. 3).

Görgens, Ludger, *Einfalt und Bildung bei Kierkegaard*, Ph.D. Thesis, University of Cologne 1994.

Grässe, Johann G., *Geschichte der Poesie Europas und der bedeutendsten außereuropäischen Länder vom Anfang des 16. Jahrhunderts bis auf die neueste Zeit*, 2nd ed., Leipzig: Arnold 1850 [1848].

Grau, Gerd-Günther, *Die Selbstauflösung des christlichen Glaubens. Eine religionsphilosophische Studie über Kierkegaard*, Frankfurt am Main: Schulte-Bulmke 1963.

— *Kritik des absoluten Anspruchs. Nietzsche—Kierkegaard—Kant*, Würzburg: Königshausen & Neumann 1993.

— *Vernunft, Wahrheit, Glaube. Neue Studien zu Nietzsche und Kierkegaard*, Würzburg: Königshausen & Neumann 1997.

Greve, Wilfried, *Kierkegaards maieutische Ethik. Von "Entweder/Oder II" zu den "Stadien,"* Frankfurt am Main: Suhrkamp 1990.

Grinten, Lars van der, *Verzweiflung und Leiden. Sören Kierkegaards göttliche Pädagogik*, Essen: Die Blaue Eule 2000.

Grisebach, Eberhard, *Die Grenze des Erziehers und seine Verantwortung*, 2nd ed. Darmstadt: Wissenschaftliche Buchgesellschaft 1966 (reprint of the Halle 1924 ed.).

Guarda, Victor, *Kierkegaardstudien. Mit besonderer Berücksichtigung des Verhältnisses Kierkegaards zu Hegel*, Meisenheim: Hain 1975.

— *Die Wiederholung. Analysen zur Grundstruktur menschlicher Existenz im Verständnis Sören Kierkegaards*, Königstein: Athenäum 1980.

Haecker, Theodor, *Sören Kierkegaard und die Philosophie der Innerlichkeit*, Munich: Schreiber 1913.

— *Christentum und Kultur*, 2nd ed., Munich: Kösel 1946 [1927].

— *Der Begriff der Wahrheit bei Sören Kierkegaard*, Innsbruck: Brenner 1932.

— *Der Buckel Kierkegaards,* Zürich: Thomas 1947.

— *Tag- und Nachtbücher 1939–1945*, Munich: Kösel 1949.

Hagemann, Tim, *Reden und Existieren. Kierkegaards antipersuasive Rhetorik*, Berlin and Vienna: Philo 2001.

Hagen, Eduard von, *Abstraktion und Konkretion bei Hegel und Kierkegaard*, Bonn: Bouvier 1969.

Harbsmeier, Götz, *Wer ist der Mensch? Grundtvigs Beitrag zur humanen Existenz. Alternativen zu Kierkegaard*, vols. 1–2, Göttingen: Vandenhoeck & Ruprecht 1972.

— *Unmittelbares Leben. Mozart und Kierkegaard*, Göttingen: Vandenhoeck & Ruprecht 1980.

Hauschildt, Friedrich, *Die Ethik Sören Kierkegaards*, Gütersloh: Gütersloher Verlagshaus 1982.

Haustedt, Birgit, *Die Kunst der Verführung. Zur Reflexion der Kunst im Motiv der Verführung bei Jean Paul, E.T.A. Hoffmann, Kierkegaard und Brentano*, Stuttgart: Verlag für Wissenschaft und Forschung 1992.

Heckel, Hans, *Das Don Juan-Problem in der neueren Dichtung*, Stuttgart: Metzler 1915.

Heimbüchel, Bernd, *Verzweiflung als Grundphänomen der menschlichen Existenz. Kierkegaards Analysen der existierenden Subjektivität*, Frankfurt am Main: Peter Lang 1983.

Heinel, Norbert, *Der Begriff der Wiederholung bei Sören Kierkegaard*, Ph.D. Thesis, University of Vienna 1975.

Heinemann, Fritz, *Existenzphilosophie lebendig oder tot?*, 4th ed., Stuttgart: Kohlhammer 1971 [1954].

Heiss, Robert, *Die großen Dialektiker des 19. Jahrhunderts. Hegel, Kierkegaard, Marx*, Cologne and Berlin: Kiepenheuer & Witsch 1963.

Hennigfeld, Jochem and Jon Stewart (eds.), *Kierkegaard und Schelling. Freiheit, Angst und Wirklichkeit*, Berlin and New York: Walter de Gruyter 2003 (*Kierkegaard Studies. Monograph Series*, vol. 8).

Henningsen, Bernd, *Poul Martin Møller oder die dänische Erziehung des Søren Kierkegaard. Eine kritische Monographie mit einer ersten Übersetzung seiner Abhandlung über die "Affectation,"* Frankfurt am Main: Akademische Verlagsgesellschaft 1973.

— *Die Politik des Einzelnen. Studien zur Genese der skandinavischen Ziviltheologie. Ludvig Holberg, Sören Kierkegaard, N.F.S. Grundtvig*, Göttingen: Vandenhoeck & Ruprecht 1977.

Heymel, Michael, *Das Humane lernen. Glaube und Erziehung bei Sören Kierkegaard*, Göttingen: Vandenhoeck & Ruprecht 1988.

Hirsch, Emanuel, *Kierkegaard Studien*, vols. 11–12 (2006), in *Gesammelte Werke*, vols. 1–48, ed. by Hans M. Müller, Waltrop: Spenner 1998– [Gütersloh: Bertelsmann 1930–3].

— *Der Weg der Theologie*, Stuttgart: Kohlhammer 1937.

— *Geschichte der neuern evangelischen Theologie im Zusammenhang mit der allgemeinen Bewegung des europäischen Denkens*, vols. 5–9, in *Gesammelte Werke*, vols. 1–48, ed. by Hans M. Müller, Waltrop: Spenner 1998–, Waltrop: Spenner 2006 [Gütersloh: Bertelsmann 1949–59; vol. 9, 2006 (vol. 5, 1959)].

— *Wege zu Kierkegaard*, Berlin: Die Spur 1968.

— *Kierkegaard Studien, Bd. 3: Aufsätze und Vorträge 1926 bis 1967*, ed. by Hans M. Müller, Waltrop: Spenner 2006.

Hochenbleicher-Schwarz, Anton, *Das Existenzproblem bei J. G. Fichte und S. Kierkegaard*, Königstein: Athenäum 1984.

Hofe, Gerhard vom, *Die Romantikkritik Sören Kierkegaards*, Frankfurt am Main: Athenäum 1972.

Hoffmann, Christian, *Max Frischs Roman "Homo faber" betrachtet unter theologischem Aspekt*, Frankfurt am Main: Peter Lang 1978.

Hoffmann, Karl, *Zur Literatur und Ideengeschichte. 12 Studien*, Charlottenburg: Gunther 1908.

Hoffmann, Raoul, *Kierkegaard und die religiöse Gewißheit: Biographisch-kritische Skizze*, trans. by G. Deggau, Preface by Hermann Gottsched, Göttingen: Vandenhoeck & Ruprecht 1910 (originally as *Kierkegaard et la certitude religieuse: esquisse biographique et critique*, Geneva: Romet 1907).

Hogrebe, Wolfram, *Deutsche Philosophie im XIX. Jahrhundert—Kritik der idealistischen Vernunft: Schelling, Schleiermacher, Schopenhauer, Stirner, Kierkegaard, Engels, Marx, Dilthey, Nietzsche*, Munich: Fink 1987.

Holl, Jann, *Kierkegaards Konzeption des Selbst. Eine Untersuchung über die Voraussetzungen und Formen seines Denkens*, Meisenheim: Hain 1972.

Hübner, Kurt, *Glaube und Denken. Dimensionen der Wirklichkeit*, Tübingen: J.C.B. Mohr 2001.

Hügli, Anton, *Die Erkenntnis der Subjektivität und die Objektivität des Erkennens bei Sören Kierkegaard*, Zürich: Theologischer Verlag 1973.

Hüsch, Sebastian, *Möglichkeit und Wirklichkeit. Eine vergleichende Studie zu Sören Kierkegaards "Entweder – Oder" und Robert Musils "Mann ohne Eigenschaften,"* Stuttgart: Ibidem-Verlag 2004.

Jacobs, Wilhelm G. and Fehér M. István (eds.), *Zeit und Freiheit. Schelling— Schopenhauer—Kierkegaard—Heidegger. Akten der Fachtagung der Internationalen Schelling-Gesellschaft*, Budapest 24. bis 27. April 1997, Budapest: Ethos 1999.

Janke, Wolfgang, *Historische Dialektik. Destruktion dialektischer Grundformen von Kant bis Marx*, Berlin and New York: Walter de Gruyter 1977.

— *Existenzphilosophie*, Berlin and New York: Walter de Gruyter 1982.

— *Entgegensetzungen. Studien zu Fichte-Konfrontationen von Rousseau bis Kierkegaard*, Amsterdam/Atlanta: Rodopi 1994.

— *Kritik der präzisierten Welt*, Freiburg i. Br. and Munich: Alber 1999.

Jaspers, Karl, *Psychologie der Weltanschauungen*, Berlin: Springer 1919.

— *Vernunft und Existenz. Fünf Vorlesungen*, 4th ed., Munich and Zürich: Piper 1987 [1935].

Jens, Walter and Hans Küng, *Dichtung und Religion: Pascal, Gryphius, Lessing, Hölderlin, Novalis, Kierkegaard, Dostojewski, Kafka*, 2nd ed., Munich and Zürich: Piper 1988.

Jessen, E.A.F., *Die Hauptströmungen des religiösen Lebens der Jetztzeit in Dänemark*, Gütersloh: Bertelsmann 1895.

Jörg, Josef E., *Geschichte des Protestantismus in seiner neuesten Entwicklung*, vols. 1–2, Arnheim: Witz 1862 (Freiburg: Herder 1858).

Jörgensen, Alfred T., *Sören Kierkegaard und das biblische Christentum*, Berlin-Lichterfelde: Runge 1914.

Jürgenbehring, Heinrich, *"Was will ich?—ich will Redlichkeit." Neun Versuche über Sören Kierkegaard*, Göttingen: Vandenhoeck & Ruprecht 2003.

Kampmann, Theoderich, *Kierkegaard als religiöser Erzieher*, Paderborn: Schöningh 1949.

Kassner, Rudolf, *Motive. Essays*, vol. 2 (1974, pp. 37–175), in *Sämtliche Werke*, vols. 1–10, ed. by Ernst Zinn and Klaus E. Bohnenkamp, Pfullingen: Neske 1969–91 [1906].

— *Kleine Schriften aus den Jahren 1911–1938*, vol. 6 (1982, pp. 153–444), in *Sämtliche Werke*, vols. 1–10, ed. by Ernst Zinn and Klaus E. Bohnenkamp, Pfullingen: Neske 1969–91 [1906].

— *Sören Kierkegaard*, Heidelberg: Pfeffer 1949.

— *Der goldene Drachen. Gleichnis und Essay*, vol. 10 (1991, pp. 5–304), in *Sämtliche Werke*, vols. 1–10, ed. by Ernst Zinn and Klaus E. Bohnenkamp, Pfullingen: Neske 1969–1991 [1957].

Kaufmann, Kristin, *Vom Zweifel zur Verzweiflung. Grundbegriffe der Existenzphilosophie Sören Kierkegaards*, Würzburg: Königshausen & Neumann 2002.

Kawamura, Eiko, *Das Problem des Weltbezugs bei Kierkegaard. Dargestellt am Begriff Angst*, Hamburg: Fundament Verlag 1973.

Kehrbach, Karl T., *Der Begriff "Wahl" bei Sören Kierkegaard und Karl Rahner. Zwei Typen der Kirchenkritik*, Frankfurt am Main: Peter Lang 1992.

Kiefhaber, Martin, *Christentum als Korrektiv. Untersuchungen zur Theologie Søren Kierkegaards*, Mainz: Grünewald 1997.

Kim, Tyong-Ho, *Existentielle Dialektik und politische Praxis. Interpretationen zum Problem der Dialektik bei Hegel, Kierkegaard, Marx und Jaspers*, Ph.D. Thesis, University of Munich, 1958.

King, G. Heath, *Existenz, Denken, Stil. Perspektiven einer Grundbeziehung. Dargestellt am Werk Sören Kierkegaards*, Berlin and New York: Walter de Gruyter 1986.

Kinter, Achim, *Rezeption und Existenz. Untersuchungen zu Sören Kierkegaards "Entweder-Oder,"* Frankfurt am Main: Peter Lang 1991.

Kirbach, Ernst H., *Die ethischen Grundansichten Sören Kierkegaards*, Ph.D. Thesis, University of Gießen 1927.

Klein, Ernst F., *Zeitbilder aus der Kirchengeschichte für die christliche Gemeinde*, vols. 1–4, 5th ed., Berlin: Acker 1930 [Berlin: Deutsche Evangelische Traktat-Gesellschaft 1911–27].

Kleinert, Markus, *Sich verzehrender Skeptizismus. Läuterungen bei Hegel und Kierkegaard*, Berlin and New York: Walter de Gruyter 2005 (*Kierkegaard Studies. Monograph Series*, vol. 12).

Klenke, Ulrich, *Denken und Glaube beim jungen Kierkegaard. Kritische Strukturanalyse seiner Grundlegung der dialektischen Wahrheitsbestimmungen humaner und christlicher Existenz*, Ph.D. Thesis, University of Münster 1969.

Kloeden, Wolfdietrich von, *Kierkegaard und Sokrates. Sören Kierkegaards Sokrates-rezeption*, Bochum: Evangelische Fachhochschule Rheinland – Westfalen – Lippe 1991.

Knappe, Ulrich, *Theory and Practice in Kant and Kierkegaard*, Berlin and New York: Walter de Gruyter 2004 (*Kierkegaard Studies. Monograph Series*, vol. 9).

Kodalle, Klaus-Michael, *Die Eroberung des Nutzlosen. Kritik des Wunschdenkens und die Zweckrationalität im Anschluß an Kierkegaard*, Paderborn: Schöningh 1988.

Kohlschmidt, Werner, *Die entzweite Welt. Studien zum Menschenbild in der neueren Dichtung*, Gladbeck: Freizeiten 1953.

Koktanek, Anton M., *Schellings Seinslehre und Kierkegaard*, Munich: Oldenbourg 1962.

Korff, Friedrich W., *Der komische Kierkegaard*, Stuttgart: Frommann 1982.

Krämer, Helmut, *Autorität und Erziehung als Problem der neueren Philosophie seit Søren Kierkegaard*, Hamburg: Kovac 1993.

Kränzlin, Gerhard, *Existenzphilosophie und Panhumanismus*, Scheldorf: Brunnen 1950.

Kraus, André, *Kierkegaard und Lessing. Sören Aabye Kierkegaards Rekurs auf Gotthold Ephraim Lessing in den "Philosophischen Brocken" und der "Abschließenden unwissenschaftlichen Nachschrift zu den Philosophischen Brocken,"* Hamburg: Kovac 2003.

Krauss, Stephan, *Der seelischen Konflikt. Psychologie und existentiale Bedeutung*, Stuttgart: Enke 1933.

Krenzke, Hans-Joachim, *Ästhetik und Existenz. Eine Studie zum frühmodernen Denken unter besonderer Berücksichtigung der philosophischen Vorgeschichte der Kierkegaardschen "Diapsalmata ad se ipsum,"* Würzburg: Königshausen & Neumann 2002.

Kuhn, Helmut, *Begegnung mit dem Nichts. Ein Versuch über die Existenzphilosophie*, Tübingen: Mohr 1950.

Kühnhold, Christa, *Der Begriff des Sprunges und der Weg des Sprachdenkens. Eine Einführung in Kierkegaard*, Berlin and New York: Walter de Gruyter 1975.

— *N.F.S. Grundtvigs und Sören Kierkegaards Sprachauffassung*, Stuttgart: Heinz 1986.

Künneth, Walter, *Die Lehre von der Sünde, dargestellt an der Lehre Søren Kierkegaards in ihrem Verhältnis zur Lehre der neuesten Theologie*, Gütersloh: Bertelsmann 1927.

Künzli, Arnold, *Die Angst des modernen Menschen. Sören Kierkegaards Angstexistenz als Spiegel der geistigen Krise unserer Zeit*, Ph.D. Thesis, University of Zürich 1947.

— *Die Angst als abendländische Krankheit. Dargestellt am Leben und Denken Sören Kierkegaards*, Zürich: Rascher 1948.

Lang-Grypari, Irene, *Die Enthüllung der intuitiven Reflexion durch den Aufbruch zum Subjekt der Handlung*, Lüneburg: Schmidt-Neubauer 1987.

Lehmann, Edvard, *Søren Kierkegaard*, Berlin: Protestantischer Schriften-Vertrieb 1913.

Lehmann, Günther K., *Ästhetik der Utopie. Arthur Schopenhauer, Sören Kierkegaard, Georg Simmel, Max Weber, Ernst Bloch*, Stuttgart: Neske 1995.

Leider, Kurt, *Ein die Welt revolutionierendes Philosophenquartett: Kopernikus, Bruno, Rousseau, Kierkegaard*, Lübeck: Weiland 1980.

Leisegang, Hans, *Hegel, Marx, Kierkegaard. Zum dialektischen Materialismus und zur dialektischen Theologie*, Berlin: Wissenschaftliche Editionsgesellschaft 1948.

Leverkühn, André, *Das Ethische und das Ästhetische als Kategorie des Handelns. Selbstwerdung bei Sören Aabye Kierkegaard*, Frankfurt am Main: Peter Lang 2000.

Liessmann, Konrad P., *Ästhetik der Verführung. Kierkegaards Konstruktion der Erotik aus dem Geiste der Verführung*, Frankfurt am Main: Hain 1991.

— *Sören Kierkegaard zur Einführung*, Hamburg: Junius 1993.

Lincoln, Ulrich, *Äußerung. Studien zum Handlungsbegriff in Søren Kierkegaards "Die Taten der Liebe,"* Berlin and New York: Walter de Gruyter 2000 (*Kierkegaard Studies. Monograph Series*, vol. 4).

Linde, Gesche et al. (eds.), *Theologie zwischen Pragmatismus und Existenzdenken. Festschrift für Hermann Deuser zum 60. Geburtstag*, Marburg: Elwert 2006.

Lobah, Jochen, *Das exzentrische Denken. Degression und Singularität in der Philosophie der Moderne*, Ph.D. Thesis, University of Darmstadt 2002.

Lohner, Alexander, *Der Tod im Existentialismus. Eine Analyse der fundamental-theologischen, philosophischen und theoretischen Implikationen*, Paderborn: Schöningh 1997.

Lorentz, E., *Ueber die sogenannten ästhetischen Werke Sören Kierkegaards. Versuch einer Deutung*, Leipzig: Richter 1892.

Löwith, Karl, *Kierkegaard und Nietzsche oder philosophische und theologische Überwindung des Nihilismus*, Frankfurt am Main: Klostermann 1935.

— *Aufsätze und Vorträge 1930–1970*, Stuttgart: Kohlhammer 1971.

— *Von Hegel zu Nietzsche. Der revolutionäre Bruch im Denken des 19. Jahrhunderts*, 10th ed., Hamburg: Meiner 1995 [1941].

Lowtzky, Fanny, *Sören Kierkegaard. Das subjektive Erlebnis und die religiöse Offenbarung. Eine psychoanalytische Studie einer Fast-Selbstanalyse*, Vienna: Internationaler Psychoanalytischer Verlag 1935.

Lunding, Erik, *Adalbert Stifter. Mit einem Anhang über Kierkegaard und die existentielle Literaturwissenschaft*, Copenhagen: Nyt Nordisk Forlag 1946.

Lütgert, Wilhelm, *Das Ende des Idealismus im Zeitalter Bismarcks*, Gütersloh: Bertelsmann 1930.

Lüttke, Moritz, *Kirchliche Zustände in den skandinavischen Ländern Dänemark, Norwegen, Schweden. Mitteilungen aus der Gegenwart*, Elberfeld: Friederichs 1864.

Massimo, Hermes, *Der Begriff des Wagnisses bei Sören Kierkegaard*, Ph.D. Thesis, University of Innsbruck 1948.

Matura, Ottokar, *Die Aesthetik in der Existentialphilosophie Kierkegaards*, Vienna: Selbstverlag 1933.

Meerpohl, Bernhard, *Die Verzweiflung als metaphysisches Phänomen in der Philosophie Søren Kierkegaards*, Würzburg: Becker 1934.

Metzger, Helmut, *Kriterien christlicher Predigt nach Sören Kierkegaard*, Göttingen: Vandenhoeck & Ruprecht 1964.

Meuser, Karl, *Der existierende Denker bei Sören Kierkegaard*, Ph.D. Thesis, University of Cologne 1926.

Meyer, Hans, *Systematische Philosophie*, vol. 1, *Allgemeine Wissenschaftstheorie und Erkenntnislehre*, Paderborn: Schöningh 1955.

Milech, Ursula, *Zur Dialektik von aufgegebener Existenz und vorgegebener Zeit bei Sören Kierkegaard*, Ph.D. Thesis, University of Würzburg 1980.

Mingels, Annette, *Dürrenmatt und Kierkegaard. Die Kategorie des Einzelnen als gemeinsame Denkform*, Cologne: Böhlau 2003.

Möhring, Werner, *Ibsen und Kierkegaard*, Leipzig: Mayer & Müller 1928.

Monachus (pseud.), *Relative Absoluta? Oder der Weg zur Geistesfreiheit und freien Liebe. Traumphantasien*, Leipzig: Dieter 1899.

Monrad, Marcus J., *Denkrichtungen der neueren Zeit. Eine kritische Rundschau*, Bonn: Weber 1897.

Mouty, Friedrich, *Zum Rechtsgedanken bei Kierkegaard*, Ph.D. Thesis, University of Munich 1969.

Müller, Barbara, *Objektlose Nächstenliebe – Kierkegaards Verständnis der Nächstenliebe in "Der Liebe Tun,"* Ph.D. Thesis, University of Marburg 1985.

Münch, Philipp, *Die Haupt- und Grundgedanken der Philosophie Sören Kierkegaards in kritischer Beleuchtung*, Ph.D. Thesis, University of Leipzig 1901.

— *Relative Absoluta? (Persönlichkeit Gottes? Individuelle Unsterblichkeit?). Eine Auseinandersetzung Sören Kierkegaards mit dem Geiste der Gegenwart*, Leipzigand Gotha: Wopke 1903.

Niedermeyer, Gerhard, *Sören Kierkegaards philosophischer Werdegang*, Leipzig: Quelle & Meyer 1909.

— *Sören Kierkegaard und die Romantik*, Leipzig: Quelle & Meyer 1909.

Nielsen, Christian, *Der Standpunkt Kierkegaards innerhalb der Religionspsychologie*, Ph.D. Thesis, University of Erlangen 1911.

Nientied, Mariele, *Kierkegaard und Wittgenstein: "Hineintäuschen in das Wahre,"* Berlin and New York: Walter de Gruyter 2003 (*Kierkegaard Studies. Monograph Series*, vol. 7).

Nießen, Elisabeth, *Der anthropologische Geistbegriff bei Søren Kierkegaard*, Fulda 1939 (Microfiche-Edition).

Nigg, Walter, *Religiöse Denker. Kierkegaard, Dostojewskij, Nietzsche, van Gogh*, 2nd ed., Berlin: Weiss 1952 [Bern: Haupt 1942].

— *Prophetische Denker. Löschet den Geist nicht aus*, 3rd ed., Rottweil: Verlag Das Wort 1986 [Zürich: Artemis 1957].

— *Sören Kierkegaard. Dichter, Büßer, Denker*, Zürich: Diogenes 2002.

Nussbächer, Konrad, *Psychologie und Dichtung. Über ihre Zusammenhänge im allgemeinen und bei Otto Ludwig und Kierkegaard im besonderen*, Ph.D. Thesis, University of Heidelberg 1923.

Obenauer, Karl J., *Die Problematik des ästhetischen Menschen in der deutschen Literatur*, Munich: Beck 1933.

Oehm, Heidemarie, *Subjektivität und Gattungsform im Expressionismus*, Munich: Fink 1993.

Pannenberg, Wolfhart, *Anthropologie in theologischer Perspektive*, Göttingen: Vandenhoeck & Ruprecht 1983.

— *Systematische Theologie*, vol. 2, Göttingen: Vandenhoeck & Ruprecht 1991.

— *Problemgeschichte der neueren evangelischen Theologie in Deutschland*, Göttingen: Vandenhoeck & Ruprecht 1997.

Paprotny, Thorsten, *Die philosophischen Verführer. Nachdenken über die Liebe*, Darmstadt: Wissenschaftliche Buchgesellschaft 2006.

Paulsen, Anna, *Menschsein heute. Analysen aus Reden Sören Kierkegaards*, Hamburg: Wittig 1973.

Pauly, Stephan, *Subjekt und Selbstwerdung. Das Subjektdenken Romano Guardinis, seine Rückbezüge auf Sören Kierkegaard und seine Einlösbarkeit in der Postmoderne*, Stuttgart: Kohlhammer 2000.

Perpeet, Willi, *Kierkegaard und die Frage nach einer Ästhetik der Gegenwart*, Halle and Saale: Niemeyer 1940.

Pieper, Annemarie, *Geschichte und Ewigkeit bei Sören Kierkegaard. Das Leitproblem der pseudonymen Schriften*, Meisenheim: Hain 1968.

— *Sören Kierkegaard*, Munich: Beck 2000.

Pivcevic, Edo, *Ironie als Daseinsform bei Sören Kierkegaard*, Gütersloh: Gütersloher Verlagshaus Mohn 1960.

Pfister, Oskar, *Das Christentum und die Angst*, Zürich: Artemis 1944.

Pleines, Jürgen-Eckardt, *Vom Wesen des Menschen in seiner zeitlichen Bestimmung. Ein Versuch zur Zeitanalyse des menschlichen Daseins nach Sören Aabye Kierkegaard*, Ph.D. Thesis, University of Heidelberg 1964.

Presler, Gerd, *Kierkegaard und Bischof Mynster. Auseinandersetzung zweier Theologien*, Th.D. Thesis, University of Münster 1970.

Przywara, Erich, *Das Geheimnis Kierkegaards*, Munich: Oldenburg 1929.

— *Humanitas. Der Mensch gestern und morgen*, Nürnberg: Glock & Lutz 1952.

Pulmer, Karin, *Die dementierte Alternative. Gesellschaft und Geschichte in der ästhetischen Konstruktion von Kierkegaards "Entweder-Oder,"* Frankfurt am Main: Peter Lang 1982.

Purkarthofer, Richard, *Wider das unlebbare Leben. Studien zur Kommunikation in den "erbaulichen Reden" Sören Kierkegaards*, Ph.D. Thesis, University of Vienna 2000.

— *Kierkegaard*, Leipzig: Reclam 2005.

Quehl, Ryno, *Aus Dänemark*, Berlin: Decker 1856.

Raabe, Anne, *"Das Wort stammt von Kierkegaard." Alfred Andersch und Sören Kierkegaard*, Frankfurt am Main et al.: Peter Lang 1999.

Rad, Gerhard von, *Das Opfer des Abraham. Mit Texten von Luther, Kierkegaard, Kolakowski und Bildern von Rembrandt*, Munich: Kaiser 1971.

Rapic, Smail, *Ethische Selbstverständigung. Kierkegaards Auseinandersetzung mit der Ethik Kants und der Rechtsphilosophie Hegels*, Berlin and New York: Walter de Gruyter 2007 (*Kierkegaard Studies. Monograph Series*, vol. 16).

Ratschow, Carl H., *Der angefochtene Glaube. Anfangs- und Grundprobleme der Dogmatik*, Gütersloh: Bertelsmann 1957.

Rehm, Walter, *Experimentum medietatis. Studien zur Geistes- und Literaturgeschichte des 19. Jahrhunderts*, Munich: Rinn 1947.

— *Kierkegaard und der Verführer*, Munich: Rinn 1949.

Rest, Walter, *Indirekte Mitteilung als bildendes Verfahren dargestellt am Leben und Werk Sören Kierkegaards*, Emsdetten: Lechte 1937.

Reuter, Hans, *S. Kierkegaards religionsphilosophische Gedanken im Verhältnis zu Hegels religionsphilosophischen System*, Leipzig: Quelle & Meyer 1914.

Richner, Thomas, *Der Tod in Rom. Eine existential-psychologische Analyse von Wolfgang Koeppens Roman*, Zürich and Munich: Artemis 1982.

Richter, Liselotte, *Der Begriff der Subjektivität bei Kierkegaard. Ein Beitrag zur christlichen Existenzdarstellung*, Würzburg: Triltsch 1934.

Ries, Wiebrecht, *Transzendenz als Terror. Eine religionsphilosophische Studie über Franz Kafka*, Heidelberg: Schneider 1977.

Ringleben, Joachim, *Hegels Theorie der Sünde. Die subjektivitätslogische Konstruktion eines theologischen Begriffs*, Berlin and New York: Walter de Gruyter 1977.

— *Aneignung. Die spekulative Theologie Sören Kierkegaards*, Berlin and New York: Walter de Gruyter 1983.

— *Die Krankheit zum Tode von Sören Kierkegaard. Erklärung und Kommentar*, Göttingen: Vandenhoeck & Ruprecht 1995.

Rodemann, Wilhelm, *Hamann und Kierkegaard*, Ann Arbor: University Microfilms International 1984 [1922].

Rohls, Jan, *Protestantische Theologie der Neuzeit*, vols. 1–2, Tübingen: Mohr 1997.

Rohrmoser, Günter, *Emanzipation und Freiheit*, Munich: Goldmann 1990.

Rosebrock, Cornelia, *Lektüre und Wiederholung. Zur philosophischen Deutung der Zeitkonstitution des Lesens*, Ph.D. Thesis, Kassel: Gesamthochschule 1994 (*Kasseler philosophische Schriften*, vol. 32).

Rosenau, Hartmut, *Auf der Suche nach dem gelingenden Leben. Religionsphilosophische Streifzüge*, Neukirchen: Neukirchener 2000.

Rothholz, Walter, *Die politische Kultur Norwegens. Zur Entwicklung einer wohlfahrtsstaatlichen Demokratie*, Baden-Baden: Nomos 1986.

Ruttenbeck, Walter, *Sören Kierkegaard. Der christliche Denker und sein Werk*, Berlin: Trowitzsch & Sohn 1929.

Ryssel, Fritz Heinrich, *Große Kranke: Sören Kierkegaard, Vincent van Gogh, Reinhold Schneider*, Gütersloh: Gütersloher Verlagshaus Mohn 1974.

Sack, Max, *Die Verzweiflung. Eine Untersuchung ihres Wesens und ihrer Entstehung. Mit einem Anhang: Søren Kierkegaards "Krankheit zum Tode,"* Kallmünz: Laßleben 1930.

Salomon, Gottfried, *Beitrag zur Problematik von Mystik und Glauben*, Straßburg and Leipzig: Singer 1916.

Sannwald, Adolf, *Der Begriff der "Dialektik" und die Anthropologie. Eine Untersuchung über das Ich-Verständnis in der Philosophie des deutschen Idealismus und seiner Antipoden*, Munich: Kaiser 1931.

Sauer, Ralph-Werner, *Ansätze zu einer Bestimmung der Geschichtlichkeit im Denken Søren Kierkegaards*, Freiburg i. Br.: Mikroreproduktionen 1953.

Sawatzki, Günther, *Das Problem des Dichters als Motiv in der Entwicklung Søren Kierkegaards bis 1841*, Borna and Leipzig: Noske 1935.

Schaal, Helmut, *Erziehung bei Kierkegaard. Das "Aufmerksammachen auf das Religiöse" als pädagogische Kategorie*, Heidelberg: Quelle & Meyer 1958.

Schäfer, Alfred, *Kierkegaard. Eine Grenzbestimmung des Pädagogischen*, Wiesbaden: Verlag für Sozialwissenschaften 2004.

Schäfer, Klaus, *Hermeneutische Ontologie in den Climacus-Schriften Sören Kierkegaards*, Munich: Kösel 1968.

Schamp, Adele, *Die Ethik Sören Kierkegaards*, Ph.D. Thesis, University of Vienna 1949.

Schär, Hans R., *Christliche Sokratik. Kierkegaard über den Gebrauch der Reflexion in der Christenheit*, Frankfurt am Main: Peter Lang 1977.

Scharling, Henrik, *Humanität und Christenthum in ihrer geschichtlichen Entwicklung, oder: Philosophie der Geschichte aus christlichem Gesichtspunkte*, trans. by A. Michelsen, Gütersloh: Bertelsmann 1874–75.

Scheier, Claus-Artur, *Kierkegaards Ärgernis. Die Logik der Faktizität in den "Philosophischen Bissen,"* Freiburg i. Br. and Munich: Alber 1983.

— *Ästhetik der Simulation. Formen des Produktionsdenkens im 19. Jahrhundert*, Hamburg: Meiner 2000.

Schelderup, Harald, *Geschichte der philosophischen Ideen von der Renaissance bis zur Gegenwart*, trans. by Leixner von Grünberg, Berlin and Leipzig: Walter de Gruyter 1929.

Scherer, Georg, *Sinnerfahrung und Unsterblichkeit*, Darmstadt: Wissenschaftliche Buchgesellschaft 1985.

Schilder, Klaas, *Zur Begriffsgeschichte des "Paradoxon" mit besonderer Berück-sichtigung Calvins und das nach-Kierkegaardschen "Paradoxon,"* Kampen: Kok 1933.

Schillinger-Kind, Asa A., *Kierkegaard für Anfänger—Entweder-oder. Eine Lese-Einführung*, Munich: Deutscher Taschenbuchverlag 1997.

Schjørring, Jens H., *Theologische Gewissensethik und politische Wirklichkeit. Das Beispiel Eduard Geismars und Emanuel Hirschs*, Göttingen: Vandenhoeck & Ruprecht 1979.

Schlechta, Eva, *Die Systemproblematik bei Søren Kierkegaard*, Ph.D. Thesis, University of Munich 1955.

Schmid, Heini, *Kritik der Existenz. Analysen zum Existenzdenken Sören Kierke-gaards*, Zürich: Evangelischer Verlag 1966.

Schmidinger, Heinrich, *Das Problem des Interesses und die Philosophie Sören Kierkegaards*, Freiburg i. Br. and Munich: Alber 1983.

Schmidt, Jochen, *Vielstimmige Rede vom Unsagbaren. Dekonstruktion, Glaube und Kierkegaards pseudonyme Literatur*, Berlin and New York: Walter de Gruyter 2006 (*Kierkegaard Studies. Monograph Series*, vol. 14).

Schmied-Kowarzik, Wolfdietrich, *Bruchstücke zur Dialektik der Philosophie. Studien zur Hegel-Kritik und zum Problem von Theorie und Praxis*, Ratingen: Henn 1974.

Schmitz, Victor A., *Dänische Dichter in ihrer Begegnung mit deutscher Klassik und Romantik*, Frankfurt am Main: Klostermann 1974.

Schrempf, Christoph, *Sören Kierkegaard. Ein unfreier Pionier der Freiheit*, Frankfurt am Main: Neuer Frankfurter Verlag 1907.

— *Auseinandersetzungen IV: Sören Kierkegaard. Dritter Teil: Akten zur Geschichte meines Verhältnisses mit Kierkegaard von 1884 bis 1935*, vol. 12 (1935), in *Gesammelte Werke*, vols. 1–16, Stuttgart: Frommann 1930–40.

Schrey, Heinz-Horst (ed.), *Sören Kierkegaard*, Darmstadt: Wissenschaftliche Buch-gesellschaft 1971.

Schröer, Henning, *Die Denkform der Paradoxalität als theologisches Problem. Eine Untersuchung zu Kierkegaard und der neueren Theologie als Beitrag zur theologischen Logik*, Göttingen: Vandenhoeck & Ruprecht 1960.

Schückler, Georg, *Die Existenzkategorie der "Wiederholung" dargestellt am Werk Sören Kierkegaards*, Ph.D. Thesis, University of Bonn 1952.

Schüepp, Guido, *Das Paradox des Glaubens. Kierkegaards Anstöße für die christliche Verkündigung*, Munich: Kösel 1964.

Schultzky, Gerolf, *Die Wahrnehmung des Menschen bei Søren Kierkegaard. Zur Wahrheitsproblematik der theologischen Anthropologie*, Göttingen: Vandenhoeck & Ruprecht 1977.

Schulz, Heiko, *Eschatologische Identität. Eine Untersuchung über das Verhältnis von Vorsehung, Schicksal und Zufall bei Sören Kierkegaard*, Berlin and New York: Walter de Gruyter 1994.

— *Theorie des Glaubens*, Tübingen: J.C.B. Mohr 2001.

Schulz, Walter, *Die Vollendung des deutschen Idealismus in der Spätphilosophie Schellings*, 2nd ed., Pfullingen: Neske 1975 [Stuttgart: Kohlhammer 1955].

— *Philosophie in der veränderten Welt*, Pfullingen: Neske 1972.

— *Johann Gottlieb Fichte, Sören Kierkegaard*, Pfullingen: Neske 1977.

— *Ich und Welt. Philosophie der Subjektivität*, Pfullingen: Neske 1979.

— *Metaphysik des Schwebens. Untersuchungen zur Geschichte der Ästhetik*, Pfullingen: Neske 1985.

Schweickert, Alfred, *Søren Kierkegaards Soziologie*, Ph.D. Thesis, University of Heidelberg 1924.

Schweppenhäuser, Hermann, *Kierkegaards Angriff auf die Spekulation. Eine Verteidigung*, Frankfurt am Main: Suhrkamp 1967.

Seifert, Hans, *Die Konkretion des Daseins bei Sören Kierkegaard*, Ph.D. Thesis, University of Erlangen 1929.

Seils, Martin, *Glaube*, Gütersloh: Gütersloher Verlagshaus 1996 (*Handbuch Systematischer Theologie*, vol. 13).

Sieber, Fritz, *Der Begriff der Mitteilung bei Sören Kierkegaard*, Ph.D. Thesis, University of Würzburg 1938.

Slotty, Martin, *Die Erkenntnislehre S. A. Kierkegaards. Eine Würdigung seiner Verfasser-wirksamkeit vom zentralen Gesichtspunkte aus*, Ph.D. Thesis, University of Erlangen 1915.

Sodeur, Gottlieb, *Kierkegaard und Nietzsche. Versuch einer vergleichenden Würdigung*, Tübingen: Mohr 1914.

Splett, Jörg and Herbert Frohnhofen (eds.), *"Entweder-oder." Herausgefordert durch Kierkegaard*, Frankfurt am Main: Knecht 1988.

Steilen, Josef, *Der Begriff "Paradox." Eine Begriffsanalyse im Anschluss an Sören Kierkegaard*, Th.D. Thesis, University of Trier 1974.

Stemmler, Wolfgang, *Max Frisch, Heinrich Böll und Sören Kierkegaard*, Ph.D. Thesis, University of Cologne 1972.

Stoverock, K., *Die Musikästhetik Sören Kierkegaards*, Ph.D. Thesis, University of Bonn 1995.

Strack-Goertsches, Hans J., *Die Entwicklung existierender Inter-Subjektivität aus dem freien Geist. Hegels Philosophie des subjektiven Geistes mit Rücksicht auf Kierkegaard*, Ph.D. Thesis, University of Cologne 1999.

Strodtmann, Adolf, *Das geistige Leben in Dänemark. Streifzüge aus den Gebieten der Kunst, Literatur, Politik und Journalistik des skandinavischen Nordens*, Berlin: Paetel 1873.

Strowick, Elisabeth, *Passagen der Wiederholung. Kierkegaard—Lacan—Freud*, Stuttgart: Metzler 1999.

Struve, Wolfgang, "Die neuzeitliche Philosophie als Metaphysik der Subjektivität. Interpretationen zu Kierkegaard und Nietzsche," *Symposion. Jahrbuch für Philosophie*, no. 1, 1948, pp. 207–335.

Suhr, Ingrid, *Das Problem des Leidens bei Sören Kierkegaard*, Ph.D. Thesis, University of Cologne 1985.

Tanko, Ferencz, *Ewigkeit in Zeit. Max Muellers Umdeutung des kierkegaardianischen Augenblicks*, Th.D. Thesis, Gregoriana University of Rome 1992.

Thalmann, Hans U., *Tun und Lassen. Zu Heideggers Auslegung des Handelns und der Wirklichkeit aus dem Gewissen*, Bamberg: Aku 1989.

Theunissen, Michael, *Der Begriff Ernst bei Sören Kierkegaard*, Freiburg i. Br. and Munich: Alber 1958.

— *Das Selbst auf dem Grund der Verzweiflung*, Frankfurt am Main: Hain 1991.

— *Der Begriff Verzweiflung. Korrekturen an Kierkegaard*, Frankfurt am Main: Suhrkamp 1993.

— *Vorentwürfe von Moderne. Antike Melancholie und die Acedia des Mittelalters*, Berlin and New York: Walter de Gruyter 1996.

Theunissen, Michael and Wilfried Greve (eds.), *Materialien zur Philosophie Søren Kierkegaards*, Frankfurt am Main: Suhrkamp 1979.

Thiede, Werner, *Das verheißene Lachen. Humor in theologischer Perspektive*, Göttingen: Vandenhoeck & Ruprecht 1986.

Thielicke, Helmut, *Das Verhältnis zwischen dem Ethischen und dem Ästhetischen. Eine systematische Untersuchung*, Leipzig: Meiner 1932.

— *Theologische Ethik*, vol. 3, Tübingen: J.C.B. Mohr 1964.

— *Glauben und Denken in der Neuzeit. Die großen Systeme der Theologie und Religionsphilosophie*, Tübingen: J.C.B. Mohr 1983.

Thust, Martin, *Sören Kierkegaard. Der Dichter des Religiösen. Grundlagen eines Systems der Subjektivität*, Munich: Beck 1931.

Tielsch, Elfriede, *Kierkegaards Glaube. Der Aufbruch des frühen 19. Jahrhunderts in das Zeitalter moderner, realistischer Religionsauffassung*, Göttingen: Vandenhoeck & Ruprecht 1964.

Tietz-Steiding, Christiane, *Freiheit zu sich selbst. Entfaltung eines christlichen Begriffs von Selbstannahme*, Göttingen: Vandenhoeck & Ruprecht 2005.

Tillich, Paul, *Philosophie und Schicksal. Schriften zur Erkenntnislehre und Existenzphilosophie*, Stuttgart: Evangelisches Verlagswerk 1961 (*Gesammelte Werke*, ed. by Renate Albrecht, vol. 4).

— *Begegnungen. Paul Tillich über sich selbst und andere*, Stuttgart: Evangelisches Verlagswerk 1971 (*Gesammelte Werke*, ed. by Renate Albrecht, vol. 12).

— *Vorlesungen über die Geschichte des christlichen Denkens. Teil II: Aspekte des Protestantismus im 19. und 20. Jahrhundert*, trans. by Ingeborg C. Henel, Stuttgart: Evangelisches Verlagswerk 1972 (*Ergänzungs- und Nachlassbände zu den Gesammelten Werken von Paul Tillich*, vol. 2).

Tjønneland, Eivind, *Ironie als Symptom. Eine kritische Auseinandersetzung mit Sören Kierkegaards "Über den Begriff der Ironie,"* Frankfurt am Main: Peter Lang 2004.

Treiber, Gerhard, *Philosophie der Existenz. Das Entscheidungsproblem bei Kierkegaard, Jaspers, Heidegger, Sartre, Camus. Literarische Erkundung von Kundera, Céline, Broch, Musil*, Frankfurt am Main: Peter Lang 2000.

Trojansky, Ewald, *Pessimismus und Nihilismus der romantischen Weltanschauung dargestellt am Beispiel Puškins und Lermontovs*, Frankfurt am Main: Peter Lang 1990.

Tschuggnall, Peter, *Das Abraham-Opfer als Glaubensparadox. Bibeltheologischer Befund – literarische Rezeption – Kierkegaards Deutung*, Frankfurt am Main: Peter Lang 1990.

— *Sören Kierkegaards Mozart-Rezeption. Analyse einer philosophisch-literarischen Deutung von Musik im Kontext des Zusammenspiels der Künste*, Frankfurt am Main: Peter Lang 1992.

Tugendhat, Ernst, *Selbstbewusstsein und Selbstbestimmung. Sprachanalytische Interpretationen*, Frankfurt am Main: Suhrkamp 1979.

Tzavaras, Johann, *Bewegung bei Kierkegaard*, Frankfurt am Main: Peter Lang 1978.

Uecker, Heiko and Joachim Trinkwitz, *Die Klassiker der skandinavischen Literatur. Die großen Autoren vom 18. Jahrhundert bis zur Gegenwart*, Düsseldorf: Econ 1990.

Vetter, August, *Frömmigkeit als Leidenschaft. Eine Deutung Kierkegaards*, Leipzig: Insel 1928.

Vetter, Helmuth, *Stadien der Existenz. Eine Untersuchung zum Existenzbegriff Sören Kierkegaards*, Vienna: Herder 1979.

Vogt, Annemarie, *Das Problem des Selbstseins bei Heidegger und Kierkegaard*, Gießen: Lechte 1936.

Voigt, Friedrich A., *Sören Kierkegaard im Kampfe mit der Romantik, der Theologie und der Kirche. Zur Selbstprüfung unserer Gegenwart anbefohlen*, Berlin: Furche 1928.

Waldenfels-Goes, Christin, *Direkte und indirekte Mitteilung bei Sören Kierkegaard*, Ph.D. Thesis, University of Munich 1968.

Walz, K., *Sören Kierkegaard, der Klassiker unter den Erbauungsschriftstellern des 19. Jahrhunderts. Ein Vortrag*, Gießen: Ricker 1898.

Weber, Kurt-Heinz, *Ästhetik und Zeitlichkeit. Versuch über Kierkegaard*, Ph.D. Thesis, University of Tübingen 1976.

Weimer, Ludwig, *Wo ist das Christentum? Sören Kierkegaard neu gelesen*, Bad Tölz: Urfeld 2004.

Weinberg, John R., *Der Wirklichkeitskontakt—und seine philosophischen Deutungen*, Meisenheim: Hain 1971.

Weisshaupt, Kurt, *Die Zeitlichkeit der Wahrheit. Eine Untersuchung zum Wahrheitsbegriff Sören Kierkegaards*, Freiburg i. Br. and Munich: Alber 1973.

Wennerscheid, Sophie, *Das Begehren nach der Wunde. Zum Wechselspiel von Schrift, Selbst und Männlichkeit im Werk Søren Kierkegaards*, Ph.D. Thesis, Humboldt-University Berlin 2006.

Wenzel, Fritz, *Der Einzelne und die Gemeinschaft. Ein Beitrag zur Philosophie der Kulturkrise*, Ph.D. Thesis, University of Breslau 1935.

Wesche, Tilo, *Vernunft und Erfahrung. Zur Dialektik der negativen Anthropologie Kierkegaards*, Ph.D. Thesis, University of Tübingen 2000.

— *Kierkegaard. Eine philosophische Einführung*, Stuttgart: Reclam 2003.

Weyer, Robert van de (ed.), *Begegnung mit Sören Kierkegaard*, Gießen and Basel: Brunnen 1991.

Wilde, Frank-Eberhard, *Kierkegaards Verständnis der Existenz*, Copenhagen: Rosen-kilde & Bagger 1969.

Wilke, Matthias, *Die Kierkegaard Rezeption Emanuel Hirschs. Eine Studie über die Voraussetzungen der Kommunikation christlicher Wahrheit*, Tübingen: J.C.B. Mohr 2005.

Winkel Horn, Frederik, *Geschichte der Literatur des skandinavischen Nordens von den älteren Zeiten bis auf die Gegenwart*, Leipzig: Schlicke 1880.

Witzel, Frank, *Die Dame im Gruppenbild als christlicher Gegenentwurf zum repressiv-asketischen Traditionsstrang des Christentums. Eruierung, Vergleich und Bewertung zweier theologisch-ethischer Konzepte. Heinrich Böll: "Gruppenbild mit Dame," Sören Kierkegaard: "Der Liebe Tun,"* Frankfurt am Main: Peter Lang 2000.

Wolff, Klaus, *Das Problem der Gleichzeitigkeit des Menschen mit Jesus Christus bei Sören Kierkegaard im Blick auf die Theologie Karl Rahners*, Würzburg: Echter 1991.

Wünsche, Horst, *"Der Begriff Angst" und seine Stellung im Kierkegaardischen Philosophieren*, Ph.D. Thesis, University of Mainz 1953.

Wust, Peter, *Der Mensch und die Philosophie. Einführung in die Hauptfragen der Existenzphilosophie,* Freiburg i. Br.: Waibel 1934.

— *Ungewissheit und Wagnis*, Munich: Kösel 1937.

Wüsten, Ewald, *Die Bedeutung der Subjektivität für die christliche Wahrheitsfrage. Eine Studie über Sören Kierkegaard*, Th.D. Thesis, University of Heidelberg 1924.

Zimmermann, Franz, *Das Wesen des Geistes im Werk Sören Kierkegaards*, Ph.D. Thesis, University of Munich 1969.

— *Einführung in die Existenzphilosophie*, Darmstadt: Wissenschaftliche Buchgesellschaft 1977.

Zwick, Elisabeth, *Der Mensch als personale Existenz. Entwürfe existentialer Anthropologie und ihre pädagogischen Implikationen bei Sören Kierkegaard und Thomas von Aquin. Eine Studie über die Konstitution der Geschichtlichkeit anhand von Grundfragen zur Möglichkeit eines Dialoges zwischen Sören Kierkegaard und Thomas von Aquin*, St. Ottilien: EOS 1992.

III. Secondary Literature on Kierkegaard's Reception in the German-Speaking Countries

Anz, Heinrich et al. (eds.), *Kierkegaard und die deutsche Philosophie seiner Zeit. Vorträge des Kolloquiums am 5. und 6. November 1979*, Munich and Copenhagen: Fink 1980.

— et al. (eds.), *Die Rezeption Sören Kierkegaards in der deutschen und dänischen Philosophie und Theologie. Vorträge des Kolloquiums am 22. u. 23. März 1982*, Munich and Copenhagen: Fink 1983.

Anz, Wilhelm: "Fragen der Kierkegaard Interpretation I/II," *Theologische Rundschau*, vol. 20, 1952, pp. 26–72; vol. 26, 1960, pp. 44–79 and pp. 168–205.

Bartels, Cora, *Kierkegaard receptus. Die theologiegeschichtliche Bedeutung der Kierkegaard Rezeption Rudolf Bultmanns*, Th.D. Thesis, University of Göttingen 2004.

Bell, Richard H. and Ronald E. Hustwit (eds.), *Essays on Kierkegaard and Wittgenstein: On Understanding the Self*, Wooster, Ohio: The College of Wooster 1978.

Beyrich, Tilmann, "Kann ein Jude Trost finden in Kierkegaards Abraham? Jüdische Kierkegaard Lektüren: Buber, Fackenheim, Levinas," *Judaica*, vol. 57, 2001, pp. 20–40.

Brinkschmidt, Egon, *Sören Kierkegaard und Karl Barth*, Neukirchen-Vluyn: Neukirchener 1971.

Brummack, Jürgen, "Max Frisch und Kierkegaard," in *Text & Kontext*, ed. by K. Bohnen, vol. 6, Copenhagen and Munich: Fink 1978, pp. 388ff.

Bukdahl, Jørgen K., *Om Søren Kierkegaard. Artikler i Udvalg*, Copenhagen: Reitzel 1981, pp. 100–46.

Cardinal, Clive H., "Rilke and Kierkegaard. Some Relationships between Poet and Theologian," *Bulletin of the Rocky Mountain Modern Language Association*, vol. 23, 1969, pp. 34–9.

Colette, Jacques, "Kierkegaard, Bultmann et Heidegger," *Revue des sciences philosophiques et théologiques*, vol. 49, 1965, pp. 597–608.

Creegan, Charles L., *Wittgenstein and Kierkegaard: Religion, Individuality, and Philosophical Method*, London: Routledge 1989.

Czakó, István, "Das Problem des Glaubens und der Geschichte in der Philosophie Kierkegaards und Karl Jaspers," *Kierkegaard Studies. Yearbook*, 2000, pp. 373–82.

Deuser, Hermann, *Dialektische Theologie. Studien zu Adornos Metaphysik und zum Spätwerk Kierkegaards*, Munich: Kaiser 1980, pp. 19–32.

— *Sören Kierkegaard. Die Philosophie des religiösen Schriftstellers*, Darmstadt: Wissenschaftliche Buchgesellschaft 1985.

Diem, Hermann, "Zur Psychologie der Kierkegaard Renaissance," *Zwischen den Zeiten*, vol. 10, 1932, pp. 216–47.

Disse, Jörg, "Philosophie der Angst: Kierkegaard und Heidegger im Vergleich," *Kierkegaardiana*, vol. 22, 2002, pp. 64–88.

Engebretsen, Rune A., *Kierkegaard and Poet-Existence with Special Reference to Germany and Rilke*, Ph.D. Thesis, Stanford University 1980.

Fahrenbach, Helmut, *Die gegenwärtige Kierkegaard Auslegung in der deutsch-sprachigen Literatur*, Tübingen: J.C.B. Mohr 1962.

Gallagher, Michael P., "Wittgenstein's Admiration for Kierkegaard," *The Month*, vol. 39, 1968, pp. 43–9.

Gemmer, Anders, *Sören Kierkegaard und Karl Barth*, Stuttgart: Strecker & Schroeder 1925.

Getzeny, H., "Kierkegaards Eindeutschung. Ein Beitrag zur deutschen Geistes-geschichte der letzten hundert Jahre," *Historisches Jahrbuch der Görres-Gesellschaft*, no. 76, 1957, pp. 181–92.

Glebe-Møller, Jens, "Wittgenstein and Kierkegaard," *Kierkegaardiana*, vol. 15, 1991, pp. 55–68.

Glöckner, Dorothea, " 'Furcht und Zittern' und 'Die Wiederholung' in der deutsch-sprachigen Kierkegaard Forschung. Literaturbericht," *Kierkegaard Studies. Yearbook*, 2002, pp. 330–52.

Golomb, Jacob, "Kierkegaard in Zion," *Kierkegaardiana*, vol. 19, 1998, pp. 130–7.

Greve, Wilfried, "Kierkegaard im Dritten Reich," *Skandinavistik*, vol. 1, 1985, pp. 29–49.

Halevi, Jacob L., *A Critique of Martin Buber's Interpretation of Søren Kierkegaard*, Ph.D. Thesis, Hebrew Union College and Jewish Institute of Religion 1959.

Harbsmeier, Eberhard, "Von der 'geheimen Freudigkeit des verborgnen Wohlstandes.' Zum Problem deutscher Kierkegaard Übersetzungen," *Kierkegaardiana*, vol. 17, 1994, pp. 130–41.

— "Die erbaulichen Reden Kierkegaards von 1843 bis 1845 in der deutschen Rezeption," *Kierkegaard Studies. Yearbook*, 2000, pp. 261–72.

Harrits, Flemming, "Grammatik des Glaubens oder Zwischenspiel über den Begriff der Geschichte. Zeit und Geschichte bei Søren Kierkegaard und Walter Benjamin," *Kierkegaardiana*, vol. 18, 1996, pp. 82–99.

Holm, Kjeld, "Lidenskab og livsmod—Søren Kierkegaard og Paul Tillich," *Kierkegaardiana*, vol. 14, 1988, pp. 29–37.

Janik, Allan, "Haecker, Kierkegaard, and the Early *Brenner*. A Contribution to the History of the Reception of 'Two Ages' in the German-Speaking World," in *Two Ages*, ed. by Robert L. Perkins, Macon, Georgia: Mercer University Press 1984 (*International Kierkegaard Commentary*, vol. 14), pp. 189–222.

Johnson, Thomas K., "Dialogue with Kierkegaard in Protestant Theology," *Communio viatorum*, vol. 46, 2004, pp. 284–98.

Jüngel, Eberhard, "Von der Dialektik zur Analogie. Die Schule Kierkegaards und der Einspruch Petersons" in *Barth-Studien*, Zürich: Benzinger 1982, pp. 127–79.

Kamla, Thomas, " 'Christliche Kunst mit negativem Vorzeichen': Kierkegaard and Doktor Faustus," *Neophilologus*, vol. 63, 1979, pp. 583–7.

Kiefhaber, Martin, *Christentum als Korrektiv. Untersuchungen. Zur Theologie Søren Kierkegaards*, Mainz: Grünewald 1997, pp. 14–32.

Klaus, Matthias, *Thomas Mann und Skandinavien. Mit zwei Aufsätzen von Thomas Mann*, Lübeck: Schmidt-Römhild 1969, pp. 27–8.

Kloeden, Wolfdietrich von, "Einfluß und Bedeutung im deutsch-sprachigen Denken," in *The Legacy and Interpretation of Kierkegaard*, ed. by Niels Thulstrup and Maria Mikulová Thulstrup, Copenhagen: Reitzel 1981 (*Bibliotheca Kierkegaardiana*, vol. 8), pp. 54–101.

— "Die deutschsprachige Forschung," in *Kierkegaard Research*, ed. by Niels Thulstrup and Maria Mikulová Thulstrup, Copenhagen: Reitzel 1987 (*Bibliotheca Kierkegaardiana*, vol. 15), pp. 37–108.

Kobel, Erwin, "Theodor Fontane—ein Kierkegaard Leser?" *Jahrbuch der deutschen Schillergesellschaft*, vol. 36, 1992, pp. 255–87.

Kodalle, Klaus–Michael, *Die Eroberung des Nutzlosen. Kritik des Wunschdenkens und der Zweckrationalität im Anschluß an Kierkegaard*, Paderborn: Schöningh 1988, pp. 235–90.

Kohlschmidt, Werner, "Rilke und Kierkegaard," in *Die entzweite Welt. Studien zum Menschenbild in der neueren Dichtung*, Gladbeck: Freizeiten 1953, pp. 88–97.

Lange, Wolfgang, "Über Kafkas Kierkegaard Lektüre und einige damit zusammenhängende Gegenstände," *Deutsche Vierteljahresschrift für Literaturwissenschaft und Geistesgeschichte*, vol. 60, 1986, pp. 286–308.

Lincoln, Ulrich, "Literaturbericht: 'Der Begriff Angst' in der deutschsprachigen Kierkegaard Forschung," *Kierkegaard Studies. Yearbook,* 2001, pp. 295–312.

Løgstrup, Knud E., *Kierkegaards und Heideggers Existenzanalyse und ihr Verhältnis zur Verkündigung*, Berlin: Evangelische Verlagsanstalt 1950.

— "Die Krise des Bürgertums und die Theologie unter dem Einfluß Kierkegaards," *Concilium*, vol. 5, 1979, pp. 282–302.

Malik, Habib C., *Receiving Søren Kierkegaard. The Early Impact and Transmission of his Thought*, Washington, D.C.: Catholic University of America Press 1997.

Manger, Philip, "Kierkegaard in Max Frisch's Novel 'Stiller,' " *German Life and Letters*, vol. 20, 1966, pp. 119–31.

McKinnon, Alastair, "Barths Verhältnis zu Kierkegaard," *Evangelische Theologie*, vol. 30, 1970, pp. 57–69.

Mingels, Annette, *Dürrenmatt und Kierkegaard. Die Kategorie des Einzelnen als gemeinsame Denkform*, Cologne: Böhlau 2003.

Müller Farguell, Roger W., "Zur Dramaturgie aporetischen Denkens. Dürrenmatt und Kierkegaard," in *Neue Perspektiven zur deutschsprachigen Literatur der Schweiz*, ed. by Romey Sabalius, Amsterdam and Atlanta: Rodopi 1997, pp. 153–65.

Mustard, Helen M., "Søren Kierkegaard in German Literary Periodicals 1860–1930," *The Germanic Review*, vol. 26, 1951, pp. 83–101.

Nagy, András, "The Mount and the Abyss. The Literary Reading of 'Fear and Trembling,' " *Kierkegaard Studies. Yearbook,* 2002, pp. 227–46.

Pannenberg, Wolfhart, *Problemgeschichte der neueren evangelischen Theologie in Deutschland. Von Schleiermacher bis zu Barth und Tillich*, Göttingen: Vandenhoeck & Ruprecht 1997, pp. 180–9.

Purkarthofer, Richard, "Zur deutschsprachigen Rezeptionsgeschichte von Kierkegaards Nachlass," *Kierkegaard Studies. Yearbook*, 2003, pp. 316–45.

Raabe, Anne, *Das Wort stammt von Kierkegaard. Alfred Andersch und Sören Kierkegaard*, Frankfurt am Main: Peter Lang 1999.

Roos, H., *Søren Kierkegaard og Katolicismen*, Copenhagen: Munksgaard 1952.

Ruttenbeck, Walter, *Sören Kierkegaard. Der christliche Denker und sein Werk*, Berlin: Trowitzsch & Sohn 1929, pp. 277–360.

Sagi, Abraham, "Kierkegaard and Buber on the Dilemma of Abraham in the *Akeda*," *Iyyun: A Hebrew Philosophical Quarterly*, vol. 37, 1988, pp. 248–62.

Schjørring, Jens H., *Theologische Gewissensethik und politische Wirklichkeit. Das Beispiel Eduard Geismars und Emanuel Hirschs*, Göttingen: Vandenhoeck & Ruprecht 1979.

Schmidinger, Heinrich, "Thomas Bernhard und Sören Kierkegaard" in *Jahrbuch der Universität Salzburg 1995–1997*, ed. by A. Buschmann, Munich 1999, pp. 29–46.

Schoeps, Hans-Joachim, "Über das Frühecho Sören Kierkegaards in Deutschland" in *Studien zur unbekannten Religions- und Geistesgeschichte*, Göttingen: Musterschmidt 1963, pp. 285–91.

Scholz, Frithard, "Zeuge der Wahrheit—ein anderer Kierkegaard," in *Monotheismus als politisches Problem? Erik Peterson und die Kritik der politischen Theologie*, ed. by A. Schindler, Gütersloh: Gütersloher Verlagshaus 1978, pp. 120–48.

Schrey, Heinz-Horst (ed.), *Sören Kierkegaard. Wege der Forschung*, Darmstadt: Wissenschaftliche Buchgesellschaft 1971.

Schröer, Henning, *Die Denkform der Paradoxalität als theologisches Problem. Eine Untersuchung zu Kierkegaard und der neueren Theologie als Beitrag zur theologischen Logik*, Göttingen: Vandenhoeck & Ruprecht 1960, pp. 133–91.

— "Kierkegaard, Søren Aabye (1813–1855)," in *Theologische Realenzyklopädie*, ed. by Gerhard Müller et al., Berlin and New York: Walter de Gruyter 1976–2004, vol. 18, 1989, pp. 138–55.

Schulz, Heiko, "Die theologische Rezeption Kierkegaards in Deutschland und Dänemark. Notizen zu einer historischen Typologie," *Kierkegaard Studies. Yearbook*, 1999, pp. 220–44.

— "Rezeptionsgeschichtliche Brocken oder die 'Brocken' in der deutschen Rezeption. Umrisse einer vorläufigen Bestandsaufnahme," *Kierkegaard Studies. Yearbook*, 2004, pp. 375–451.

— "Rezeptionsgeschichtliche Nachschrift oder die 'Nachschrift' in der deutschen Rezeption. Eine forschungsgeschichtliche Skizze," *Kierkegaard Studies. Yearbook*, 2005, pp. 351–99.

— "Die Welt bleibt ungefähr stets dieselbe. Grundlinien der Rezeption Kierkegaards in der Philosophie und Theologie des 19. und 20. Jahrhunderts," in Portuguese in *Revista Portuguesa Filosofia*, no. 64, 2008, pp. 511–39.

Steffensen, Steffen, "Die Einwirkung Kierkegaards auf die deutschsprachige Literatur des 20. Jahrhunderts," in *Akten des VI. internationalen Germanistenkongresses Basel 1980*, ed. by Heinz Rupp and Hans-Gert Roloff, Frankfurt am Main: Peter Lang 1980, pp. 62–6.

Stemmler, Wolfgang, *Max Frisch, Heinrich Böll und Sören Kierkegaard*, Ph.D. Thesis, University of Munich 1972.

Theunissen, Michael and Wilfried Greve (eds.), *Materialien zur Philosophie Sören Kierkegaards*, Frankfurt am Main: Suhrkamp 1979, pp. 54–83.

Thulstrup, Niels, *Kierkegaards Verhältnis zu Hegel. Forschungsgeschichte*, 2nd ed., Stuttgart: Kohlhammer 1972.

Todorov, Christo, "Das Thema des Todes als Verbindungslinie zwischen Kierkegaard und Jaspers," in *Sören Kierkegaard. Philosoph, Schriftsteller, Theologe. Vorträge des bulgarisch-dänischen Seminars, Sofia 31. März – 2. April 1992*, Sofia 1992, pp. 41–9.

Weing, Siegfried, "Kierkegaardian Reflections in Martin Walser's *Ein fliehendes Pferd*," *Colloquia Germanica*, vol. 25, 1992, pp. 275–88.

Weiland, Jan Sperna, *Humanitas—Christianitas. A Critical Survey of Kierkegaard's and Jaspers' Thought in Connection with Christianity*, Assen: Van Gorcum 1951.

Weston, Michael, *Kierkegaard and Modern Continental Philosophy. An Introduction*, London: Routledge 1994.

Wolf, H.C., *Kierkegaard and Bultmann: The Quest of the Historical Jesus*, Minneapolis: Augsburg 1965.

Wyschogrod, Michael, *Kierkegaard and Heidegger. The Ontology of Existence*, London: Routledge & Kegan Paul 1954.

France:

Kierkegaard as a Forerunner of Existentialism and Poststructuralism

Jon Stewart

When one thinks of Kierkegaard's influence in the Francophone world of letters, it is natural that one immediately thinks of the appropriation of his thought by French existentialism and poststructuralism. However, French Kierkegaard reception was far richer than this and indeed began far earlier than these movements. Today French Kierkegaard studies has developed into a specialized field with scholars who define their professional profile in terms of the Danish thinker. It can be said without hesitation that Kierkegaard research in France at present is flourishing more than at any time in the past.

I. Denmark and France: The Cultural Ties

During Kierkegaard's lifetime, many Danish scholars, writers, and artists regularly visited Paris, which ranked probably just after Berlin and Rome as a favorite destination of Golden Age intellectuals. This was no accident, for Denmark had close cultural and political ties to France. During the Napoleonic War, Denmark was allied with France, and at this time many French embassies came to Copenhagen, where they were treated virtually as celebrities. The atmosphere of these times is wonderfully portrayed in the novel *Two Ages* (1846),[1] from the pen of Thomasine Gyllembourg (1773–1856), a work reviewed positively by Kierkegaard.[2] In the eighteenth and the nineteenth centuries there were also a handful of francophone

---

I would like to express my gratitude to Katalin Nun, Darío González, Leo Stan, Nicolae Irina, and Brian Soderquist for their invaluable help with this article.

[1] Thomasine Christine Gyllembourg-Ehrensvärd, *To Tidsaldre. Novelle af Forfatteren til "En Hverdags-Historie,"* published by Johan Ludvig Heiberg. Copenhagen: C.A. Reitzel 1845.

[2] Kierkegaard, *En literair Anmeldelse. To Tidsaldre, Novelle af Forfatteren til en 'Hverdags-historie' udgiven af J.L. Heiberg.* Copenhagen: C.A. Reitzel 1846. *SKS* 8, 7–106. (English translations: *Two Ages. The Age of Revolution and the Present Age. A Literary Review by Søren Kierkegaard,* trans. by Howard V. Hong and Edna H. Hong. Princeton: Princeton University Press 1978; *A Literary Review,* trans. by Alastair Hannay. Harmondsworth: Penguin Books 2001.)

journals based in Copenhagen: *Novelles de divers Endroits* (1719–20), *Extrait des Nouvelles* (1720–22), *Gazette historique, politique et littéraire de Copenhague* (1749–76), the *Messager Français du Nord* (1825–26); also worthy of note is the journal *Jacobineren* (1796).[3] The alliance with France resulted in the British bombardment of Copenhagen in 1807. Despite the unfortunate outcome of this alliance, Denmark continued to cultivate close ties with France as it, in the course of the nineteenth century, became ever more estranged from its southern neighbors, Germany and Prussia.

Among the best-known Danes in Paris were the satirical writer and dramatist, Peter Andreas Heiberg (1758–1841), who had been exiled from the Kingdom of Denmark in 1800 due to his impertinent remarks about the established powers.[4] P.A. Heiberg lived for forty years in exile in France, where he continued to write and work as a translator, eventually becoming the secretary of the French diplomat Charles-Maurice de Talleyrand (1754–1838). His son, the poet and dramatist Johan Ludvig Heiberg (1791–1860) also lived in Paris briefly from 1819 to 1822. He was highly interested in French drama, especially the vaudevilles of the French dramatist Augustin Eugène Scribe (1791–1891). Heiberg translated and adapted Scribe's works for the Danish stage, thus introducing the Danish theater public to the latest trends in Parisian theater life. The natural scientist Hans Christian Ørsted (1777–1851) also had close ties with France. He visited Paris on several occasions, and his discovery of electromagnetism was received with great excitement among French physicists. Another significant Dane to make his way to Paris was the literary critic Peter Ludvig Møller (1814–65), who is best known for his role in the so-called *Corsair* controversy.[5] Prior to this conflict, Møller had studied different aspects of French culture. As a student, he wrote a Gold Medal treatise on French poetry. He founded a number of newspapers and reviews, which used then contemporary French journals as their model. Kierkegaard denounced Møller as being responsible for the attacks in the *Corsair*.[6] The latter left Denmark a couple of years later with a government scholarship to pursue his studies abroad. Møller journeyed throughout Germany and Prussia, ending up in Paris in 1851, where he lived for the rest of his life. Like the elder Heiberg, he earned his living by writing and translating for French newspapers and journals. During these final years, he wrote a comparative work on comedy in France and Denmark.[7]

---

[3]   See Jette D. Søllinge and Niels Thomsen, *De danske aviser 1634–1989*, vols. 1–3, Odense: Dagpressens Fond i Kommission hos Odense Universitetsforlag 1988–91, vol. 1.

[4]   See P.A. Heiberg's autobiography, *Erindinger af min politiske, selskabelige og litterære Vandel i Frankrig*, Christiania: P.J. Hoppe 1830. See also Henning Fenger, *The Heibergs*, trans. by Frederick J. Marker, New York: Twayne Publishers 1971, pp. 23–37; Povl Ingerslev-Jensen, *P.A. Heiberg. Den danske Beaumarchais*, Herning: Poul Kristensen 1964.

[5]   See Hans Hertel, "P.L. Moller and Romanticism in Danish Literature," in *Kierkegaard and His Contemporaries. The Culture of Golden Age Denmark*, ed. by Jon Stewart, Berlin and New York: Walter de Gruyter 2003 (*Kierkegaard Studies. Monograph Series*, vol. 10), pp. 356–72.

[6]   *SV1* XIII, 431 / *COR*, 46.

[7]   Peter Ludvig Møller, *Det nyere Lystspil i Frankrig og Danmark*, Copenhagen: G.E.C. Gad 1858.

There was thus a long tradition of an active exchange of culture and information between France and Denmark dating from the eighteenth century and continuing into the Danish Golden Age. It is therefore natural that French thinkers would take some interest in the cultural affairs of Denmark and the work of Søren Kierkegaard.

II. From the Earliest References to the First World War

The earliest known French reference to Kierkegaard appears in 1856 in *La Revue de Deux Mondes*.[8] The *Revue* published a series of overview articles about the political and cultural state of affairs in different countries. There in an article on Denmark, a special section is dedicated to "Religious Questions," in which the anonymous author describes the confusion surrounding the question of freedom of religion and freedom of speech in Denmark after the introduction of the Constitution in 1849. The occasion for this discussion is Kierkegaard's attack on the Danish State Church. The author is generally quite positive about Kierkegaard's actions:

> The virulent attacks of S. Kierkegaard and his followers have, it is true, bewildered many minds and troubled many weak or fearful consciences, but they have also awakened many sheep and many indolent or drowsy pastors; they have shaken or brought down many things and persons of but little importance; they have caused profound and serious souls to reflect. In brief, the Danish church, both pastors and parishioners, will doubtless emerge from this spiritual struggle more sure of themselves, more clear-sighted, in the things of faith and worship.[9]

After this general assessment of the ultimate significance and impact of Kierkegaard's attack, the author turns to a more general introduction and assessment of Kierkegaard as a writer. The text continues:

> Without ever occupying any public position, S. Kierkegaard has come to rank, during the last fifteen years or so, as one of the most productive and remarkable, and also one of the most singular, of writers in Denmark. With a lively imagination, a shrewd, caustic, and mocking mind, a far from ordinary debating talent, but bizarre in his way of writing, he has proved to be at once a speculative philosopher, an unrelenting moralist, and a merciless religious reformer. At first secretly, finally openly, he has undermined and unsettled everything; taking as his battle cries the words "freedom" and "independence," he tended to bring down everything, society and church, but without worrying about reconstruction.[10]

---

8   "Le Danemark," *Annuaire des Deux Mondes. Historie générale des divers États*, vols. 1–14, 1851–68, Paris: Revue de deux mondes, vol. 4, October 20, 1856, pp. 459–91. The relevant excerpts from this article have been translated into English in F.J. Billeskov Jansen, "The Study in France," in *Kierkegaard Research*, ed. by Marie Mikulová Thustrup, Copenhagen: C.A. Reitzel 1987 (*Bibliotheca Kierkegaardiana*, vol. 15), pp. 134–59; pp. 134–6.

9   Quoted from Billeskov Jansen, "The Study in France," p. 134.

10   Ibid., p. 135. The counterintuitive characterization of Kierkegaard as "a speculative philosopher" may be taken as an indication that P.L. Møller is the author of this piece. In the *Corsair* controversy, Møller had reproached Kierkegaard for his "barren dialectic that swirls around an infinite center" (*COR*, Supplement, p. 101) and refers to "the dialectical-critical-

Finally, the article recounts briefly Kierkegaard's death and the scandal surrounding his funeral caused by the outbreak of his nephew Henrik Lund (1825–89), who, during the ceremony, protested against the Church and the clergy. There can be little doubt that this account was written by a Dane with knowledge of French.

The first French translation of Kierkegaard was also the work of a Dane, Johannes Gøtzsche (1866–1938). In 1886 his translation *En quoi l'homme de génie diffère-t-il de l'apôtre? Traité éthique-religieux*[11] appeared in Copenhagen and Paris. It is a translation of the second of Kierkegaard's *Two Ethical-Religious Essays* (1849). The work includes a Preface by the theologian Hans-Peter Kofoed-Hansen (1813–93), which offers a brief overview of Kierkegaard's works and recommends him to the French reader. This early translation seems, however, not to have made any real impression in France.

In 1893 an article appeared entitled "Sören Kierkegaard. Le moraliste danois" in *La Nouvelle Revue*.[12] This work is from the hand of one Bernard Jeannine. The author is apparently inspired by the critical works of Georg Brandes (1842–1927), who mentions Kierkegaard in connection with Henrik Ibsen (1828–1906). In his article Jeannine portrays Kierkegaard as a central Scandinavian author, who inspired many other Danish and Norwegian writers who were to follow. His criticism of the hypocritical Christianity of his day and of petty bourgeois philistinism are mentioned, and it is in this context that he is regarded as a moralist.

By the end of the century Kierkegaard's name began appearing in French reference works. A one-paragraph article on him by Théophile Cart (1855–1931), a professor of German Studies in Paris, appears in *La Grande Encyclopédie*, which was published from 1886 to 1903.[13] Here the author summarizes Kierkegaard's thought in terms of the well-known stages:

> He [sc. Kierkegaard] declared that an unbridgeable gulf exists between science and faith and, in language that was vivid and paradoxical but of outstanding dialectical vigor, he preached renunciation of the world; a purely aesthetic conception of life, in his view, leads fatally to an egoistical search for pleasure; a purely *moral* (ethical) conception has neither foundation nor sanction; only the *religious* conception is Christian, i.e., the isolated *individual* face to face with God can stand his ground....[14]

Kierkegaard is characterized as "a rather unorthodox theologian," and no mention is made here of his philosophical or literary side.

---

analytical aspect" of his thought (*COR*, Supplement, p. 100). But more evidence would be needed to make the claim that Møller is in fact the author here.

[11]   *En quoi l'homme de génie diffère-t-il de l'apôtre? Traité éthique-religieux*, trans. by Johannes Gøtzsche, Copenhagen: Hagerup and Paris: Nilsson 1886.

[12]   B. Jeannine, "Sören Kierkegaard. Le moraliste danois," *La Nouvelle Revue*, no. 2 (November–December), 1983, pp. 578–96.

[13]   Th. C. "Kierkegaard (Soeren Aabye)," in *La Grande Encyclopédie*, vols. 1–31, Paris: H. Lamirault et Cie 1885–1902, vol. 21, p. 530. This article has also been translated into English in Billeskov Jansen, "The Study in France," pp. 136–7.

[14]   Quoted from Billeskov Jansen, "The Study in France," p. 136.

In 1897 a theological thesis on Kierkegaard for the degree of bachelor was presented to the Faculté de théologie protestante at the University of Paris. The work was by a French–Danish theologian Victor Deleuran entitled *Esquisse d'une étude sur Soeren Kierkegaard.*[15] This can be regarded as a kind of introduction to selected aspects of Kierkegaard's religious thinking. It begins with a brief biographical overview and then moves to Kierkegaard's thought. In his account of the latter, Deleuran gives a central place to the theory of the three stages. The work ends with a brief account of Kierkegaard's attack on the Church and a short concluding section. While Deleuran concedes that Kierkegaard is a passionate and controversial thinker, he insists that there is much that the attentive reader can learn from him.

In 1900 an article appeared entitled "Sören Kierkegaard. Le christianisme absolu á travers le paradox et le désespoir" in the *Revue de métaphysique et de morale.*[16] The author of the article was a psychologist by the name of Henri Delacroix (1873–1937). A highly gifted scholar, Delacroix studied at the universities of Berlin, Heidelberg, and Munich, eventually becoming a professor at the Sorbonne. The image of Kierkegaard that he presents is of a religious fanatic and cultural reactionary, who denies the importance of science and the autonomy of the individual, insisting on one's dependence on the divine. There is a certain irony in this interpretation when one considers that later Sartre would transform Kierkegaard into a champion of radical freedom.

Another article appeared in 1901 from the pen of Maurice Muret (1870–1954) entitled "Un précurseur de Henrik Ibsen. Sören Kierkegaard."[17] This work, which was published in *La Revue de Paris*, is a typical reflection of the association of Kierkegaard with Ibsen during this period. There was a wave of interest in Ibsen in France at this time since his works were being performed in Paris throughout the 1890s.[18] This article focuses primarily on Ibsen's *Brand*, which is read as an example of the Kierkegaardian demand for choice and freedom. Murat was by no means a Kierkegaard expert, and this article can be seen as a part of his attempt to make foreign literature better known to the French reader.

In 1903 an article appeared by a professor at the Sorbonne, Victor Basch (1863–1944), entitled "Un individualiste religieux: Soeren Kierkegaard."[19] This work appeared in *La Grande Revue* and presents the philosophical side of Kierkegaard. Basch praises Kierkegaard for emphasizing the individual and is sensitive to the radical nature of his religious thinking. He was among the first to recognize Kierkegaard as a forerunner of Nietzsche (1844–1900). Basch approached Kierkegaard's texts from a secular perspective and found in them tools that could be of use for his humanist

[15]   Victor Deleuran, *Esquisse d'une étude sur Soeren Kierkegaard*, Paris: Charles Noblet 1897.

[16]   Henri Delacroix, "Sören Kierkegaard. Le christianisme absolu á travers le paradox et le désespoir," *Revue de métaphysique et de morale*, vol. 8, no. 4, 1900, pp. 459–84.

[17]   Maurice Muret, "Un précurseur de Henrik Ibsen. Sören Kierkegaard," *La Revue de Paris*, vol. 8, no. 13, 1901, pp. 98–122.

[18]   See Peter Kemp, "Le précurseur de Henrik Ibsen. Quelques aspects de la découverte de Kierkegaard en France," *Les Études philosophiques*, no. 2 (April–June), 1979, pp. 139–50.

[19]   Victor Basch, "Un individualiste religieux: Soeren Kierkegaard," *La Grande Revue*, vol. 23, 1903, pp. 281–320.

program. This approach would be followed by many secular French thinkers in the twentieth century. Further, there seems to be a general consensus that, among these pioneers of French Kierkegaard studies, Basch had the best knowledge of Kierkegaard's actual texts and, unlike many of the others, did not base his opinions on second-hand accounts.

Another French-language dissertation was written at the University of Geneva, appearing in 1907 under the title *Kierkegaard et la certitude réligieuse. Esquisse biographique et critique.*[20] The author of this work, Raoul Hoffmann (1881–1972), was perhaps bilingual; he was familiar with the German Kierkegaard literature and published the work in a German translation in 1910.[21] This work focuses, among other things, on the concept of the paradox. Hoffmann did not pursue his Kierkegaard studies but instead went on to be a surgeon.

In 1914 André Bellesort (1866–1942) published an article on Kierkegaard in the *Revue de deux mondes* entitled "Le Crépuscule d'Elseneur."[22] This article portrays Kierkegaard's understanding of Christianity as typical of the dark and depressive Nordic spirit. Kierkegaard is associated with Hamlet, as a figure obsessed with anxiety. Some years later this piece was printed as an independent monograph.[23]

Since Pascal (together with Descartes) has traditionally been one of the main points of cultural orientation for French thinkers, it was natural to present Kierkegaard as a kind of Scandinavian Pascal. In 1913 the Danish philosopher Harald Hoffding (1843–1981) gave a lecture on this theme that was subsequently translated into French and published in the *Revue de métaphysique et de morale.*[24] In 1930 an article with the same title by another Danish scholar appeared in French in the *Revue d'histoire et de philosophie religieuses.*[25]

III. The Influence of the German Sources and the Russian Émigrés

Much of French Kierkegaard reception has been mediated by that of foreign sources. One of the most important of these was the body of German translations and secondary literature on Kierkegaard, which began to appear at a remarkably early period. While many French scholars could read and speak German well, Danish remained an esoteric foreign language. It was thus natural that the German-language materials played a role in pioneering French reception. Christoph Schrempf's (1860–1944) 12-volume translation of Kierkegaard's *Gesammelte Schriften* appeared in 1909–

---

[20]   Raoul Hoffmann, *Kierkegaard et la certitude réligieuse. Esquisse biographique et critique*, Geneva: Romet 1907.
[21]   Raoul Hoffmann, *Kierkegaard und die religiöse Gewißheit. Biographish-kritische Skizze*, Göttingen: Vandenhoeck & Ruprecht 1910.
[22]   André Bellesort, "Le Crépuscule d'Elseneur," *Revue de deux mondes*, no. 1, 1914, pp. 49–83.
[23]   André Bellesort, *Le Crépuscule d'Elseneur*, Paris: Perrin 1926.
[24]   Harald Høffding, "Pascal et Kierkegaard," *Revue de métaphysique et de morale*, vol. 30, no. 2, 1923, pp. 221–46.
[25]   H. Fuglsang-Damgaard, "Pascal et Kierkegaard," *Revue d'historie et de philosophie religieuses*, vol. 10, no. 3, 1930, pp. 242–63.

22,[26] with an expanded second edition following in 1922–25. This was the text that most French scholars were working with until they received translations in their own language, which began to appear in the 1930s. The early picture of Kierkegaard in France was largely shaped by German intellectuals influenced by him. Figures such as Martin Buber (1878–1965), Karl Jaspers (1883–1969), Karl Barth (1886–1968), and Martin Heidegger (1889–1976), were carefully studied and in part co-opted as the French struggled to develop their own form of existential thinking.

One key event triggered the influx of a new group of scholars into France, namely, the October Revolution in Russia. As a result of this event in 1917, a number of Russian scholars in the fields of philosophy and theology fled the country, with many of them seeking refuge in Paris.[27] Among them were thinkers such as Lev Zander (1893–1964), Ivan Tkhorzhevsky (1878–1951), and Georgy Florovsky (1893–1979), who had keen interests in Kierkegaard. The most important of these Russia exiles in Paris was Lev Isaakovich Schwazmann (1866–1938) who became known in the West as Léon Chestov or Shestov.

Shestov only began his study of Kierkegaard in the late 1920s after his arrival in Paris. It would mark the beginning of a long and highly personal struggle with his thought. At the beginning of the 1830s he was offering a course at the Department of Russian Studies at the Sorbonne with the title, "Dostoyevsky and Kierkegaard." Shestov's reputation grew as, in addition to his professional obligations, he also gave a number of public lectures, one of which was published in the well-known and widely-read journal *Les Cahiers du Sud*.[28] In connection with his lectures, Shestov was also working on his book *Kierkegaard et la philosophie existentielle*. Although this work was finished as early as 1934, due to resistance from the French communist community including André Malraux (1901–76), Shestov had difficulties publishing it. Friends of a different political persuasion, such as Nikolay Berdyaev (1874–1948) and Albert Camus (1913–60), helped him to get the book printed with a subscription plan. The work finally appeared in July 1836.[29]

In this work Kierkegaard is presented as the champion of a lived philosophy engaged in life and conscious of the demands of freedom. He is seen as a strict opponent of the corrupting influence of the rationalism or "theoretical philosophy" of much of the Western tradition. Shestov regards rationalistic thinking as a form of sin and a source of evil and corruption. Rejecting this sterile philosophy, he was interested in Kierkegaard's analysis of individual figures in real-life situations such as Job, Abraham, and Socrates. While Shestov's own relation to Christianity was a complex and changing one, he fully accepted Kierkegaard's analysis of the radical demands that faith places on the individual, and thus he was careful not to modify

---

[26]   Søren Kierkegaard, *Gesammelte Werke*, trans. and ed. by Hermann Gottsched and Christoph Schrempf, vols. 1–12, Jena: Diederichs 1909–22.

[27]   For an account of this see Darya Loungina's outstanding article "Russia: Kierkegaard's Reception through Tsarism, Communism, and Liberation" in Tome II of the present volume.

[28]   Léon Shestov, "Kierkegaard et Dostoyevski," in *Les Cahiers du Sud*, no. 18, 1936, pp. 170–200.

[29]   Léon Chestov, *Kierkegaard et la philosophie existentielle (Vox clamantis in deserto)*, Paris: J. Vrin 1936. (English translation: *Kierkegaard and the Existential Philosophy*, trans. by Elinor Hewitt, Athens: Ohio University Press 1969.)

or play down Kierkegaard's striking claims about things such as martyrdom and despair.

Shestov was reproached for writing about his own thoughts more than explicating those of Kierkegaard. This charge is, however, in a sense understandable given Shestov's existential mission to appropriate Kierkegaard's message in his own life and thinking. In any case, this book and Shestov's accompanying lectures were to be a source a great inspiration for the French existentialists. Shestov was to French Kierkegaard studies what his fellow émigré Alexandre Kojève (1902–68) was to French Hegel studies.

It has been often noted that the general mood in Europe in the wake of the First World War and the Russian Revolution was highly receptive to Kierkegaard's message. The Second World War would see this interest repeated and further intensified.

IV. Forerunners of the Existentialists

While Kierkegaard's influence on French existentialism has become a signal episode in the French reception of his thought, this influence did not appear overnight or spontaneously. The ground was made fertile for it by a handful of lesser known thinkers, who are only indirectly associated with the existentialist movement itself.

One important figure in this regard was Jean Wahl (1888–1974), a professor of philosophy at the Sorbonne. Although not a tremendously productive or original author, his didactical work was important for introducing Kierkegaard to the generation of French scholars that would made existentialism famous.[30] In addition to his influential teaching, he wrote introductions to some of the early French translations of Kierkegaard's works.[31] His essay on anxiety in Kierkegaard from 1932 may well have served as an inspiration for Sartre's later interest in this concept.[32] His many short studies of individual concepts were put together in 1938 under a single cover with the title *Études Kierkegaardiennes*.[33] His understanding of Kierkegaard was profoundly influenced by the incipient German Kierkegaard studies. In the following years this book was carefully studied by the existentialists.

Another important figure in this regard was the Romanian Benjamin Fondane (1898–1944), whose interest in Kierkegaard was inspired by Shestov. In 1936 he

---

[30]   For Wahl's importance in this regard, see Frédéric Worms, " 'La relation d'existence de Jean Wahl à Kierkegaard,' " Postface to Jean Wahl, *Kierkegaard, L'Un devant l'Autre*, Paris: Hachette Littératures 1998, pp. 275–84.

[31]   *Le Concept d'angoisse. Simple méditation psychologique pour servir d'introduction au problème dogmatique du péché originel, par Vigilius Haufniensis*, trans. by Paul-Henri Tisseau, introduced by Jean Wahl, Paris: Félix Alcan 1935. *Crainte et Tremblement. Lyrique-dialectique, par Johannes de Silentio*, trans. by Paul-Henri Tisseau, introduced by Jean Wahl, Paris: Fernand Aubier; Éditions Montaigne 1935.

[32]   Jean Wahl, "Kierkegaard: L'angoisse et l'instant," *La Nouvelle Revue Française*, vol. 20, no. 223, 1932, pp. 634–55.

[33]   Jean Wahl, *Études Kierkegaardiennes*, Paris: Aubier 1938 [2nd ed. 1949, 3rd ed. 1967].

published his *La Conscience malheureuse*, a title taken from the famous motif in Hegel's *Phenomenology of Spirit*.[34] In this work Fondane analyzes Kierkegaard together with Heidegger and Dostoevsky. Fondane's work was cut short as he ultimately fell victim to the Nazis, dying in the gas chamber in Birkenau in 1944.

A pioneering translator and interpreter of Kierkegaard, Paul Petit (1893–1944), tried to understand Kierkegaard's critique of the Danish State Church and contemporary complacency in religion as an attempt to revert to a pre-Lutheran Catholic position. Despite his attack on the public and the masses, Kierkegaard was, according to Petit, consistent with a Catholic position. In addition to a handful of articles, Petit published a translation of the *Concluding Unscientific Postscript* in 1941.[35] A posthumous translation of the *Philosophical Fragments* appeared in 1947.[36] Petit, who was active in the French resistance movement, was executed by the Germans in August 1944.

Another important French interpreter of Kierkegaard in the 1940s was the Catholic thinker Régis Jolivet (1891–1966), a professor in Lyon. In 1946 he published his much read *Introduction à Kierkegaard*.[37] Two years later he gave one of the earliest attempts at an overview of the existentialist movement, with his *Les doctrines existentialistes de Kierkegaard à J.P. Sartre*.[38] His final major work on Kierkegaard appeared in 1958 under the title *Aux sources de l'existentialisme chrétien, Kierkegaard*.[39] Jolivet gives Kierkegaard a sympathetic interpretation and, like Petit, enlists him as a defender of Catholicism.

In 1944 Henri de Lubac (1896–1991) published his *Le drame de l'humanisme athée*, which attempts to provide an overview of atheist thinking since the nineteenth century, treating primarily Feuerbach, Nietzsche, Comte, and Dostoevsky.[40] De Lubac, who was a highly influential and prolific French Catholic cardinal, examines Kierkegaard's thought and juxtaposes him to Nietzsche.[41] Despite the apparent contradiction of Nietzsche's atheism and Kierkegaard's faith, there are, according

---

[34]   Benjamin Fondane, *La conscience malheureuse*, Paris: Éditions Denoël 1936 ("Martin Heidegger sur les routes de Kierkegaard et de Dostoievski," pp. 169–98; "Soeren Kierkegaard et la catégorie du secret," pp. 199–227; "Chestov et Kierkegaard et le serpent," pp. 229–57 (with the same title originally published, *Les Cahiers du Sud*, vol. 21, August 1934, pp. 534–54)).

[35]   *Post-scriptum aux Miettes philosophiques*, trans. by Paul Petit, Paris: Mesmil 1941.

[36]   *Les miettes philosophiques*, trans. by Paul Petit, Paris: Éditions du Livre français 1947.

[37]   Régis Jolivet, *Introduction à Kierkegaard*, Paris, Abbaye Saint-Wandrille: Éditions de Fontenelle 1946.

[38]   Régis Jolivet, *Les doctrines existentialistes de Kierkegaard à J.P. Sartre*, Paris, Abbaye Saint-Wandrille: Éditions de Fontenelle 1948.

[39]   Régis Jolivet, *Aux sources de l'existentialisme chrétien Kierkegaard*, Paris: Éditions Fayard 1958.

[40]   Henri de Lubac, *Le drame de l'humanisme athée*, Paris: Éditions Spes 1944. (English translation: *The Drama of Atheist Humanisn*, trans. by Edith M. Riley, London: Sheed & Ward 1949.)

[41]   Lubac, *Le drame de l'humanisme athée*, pp. 71–113; *The Drama of Atheist Humanisn*, pp. 36–60.

to de Lubac, a number of surprising points of coincidence, including their struggle against Hegelian historicism.

The professor of philosophy Pierre Mesnard (1900–69) played a significant early role in French Kierkegaard studies. He was particularly captivated by *The Concept of Irony* and Kierkegaard's criticism of Hegel and the German Romantics. His main work is the much discussed *Le vrai visage de Kierkegaard* from 1948.⁴² This book treats Kierkegaard's main pseudonymous works, which Mesnard interprets as stages in Kierkegaard's own development. Mesnard also authored an introduction to Kierkegaard's writings in 1954 under the title *Kierkegaard. Sa vie, son oeuvre, avec un exposé de sa philosophie*.⁴³ This work also presents Kierkegaard's thought and authorship primarily in terms of the three stages. After Mesnard's own introduction, the second half of the text consists of selected extracts from Kierkegaard's writings, which are likewise organized into categories following the different stages. Sections are also dedicated to Kierkegaard's concepts of humor and irony.

Another early translator was Jean-Jacques Gateau (1887–1967) who translated some of Kierkegaard's journals and "The Diary of a Seducer," which he published as individual articles.⁴⁴ The latter text was then republished in 1929 as a monograph in the series *Le cabinet cosmopolite*, which included texts from foreign literature.⁴⁵ In the 1930s a series of translations of Kierkegaard's main pseudonymous works that Gateau made together with the Dane Knud Ferlov were published at Gallimard.⁴⁶ Finally, Gateau and Ferlov produced a five-volume selection of Kierkegaard's *Nachlaß*, which appeared from the beginning of the 1940s into the 1960s.⁴⁷ This edition, which is based on the Danish edition of the *Papirer*, remains to this day the most extensive collection of Kierkegaard's journals and notebooks in French.

The study of Kierkegaard in France was facilitated by the first systematic translation of Kierkegaard's works by Paul-Henri Tisseau (1894–1964).⁴⁸ Prior to

⁴²   Pierre Mesnard, *Le vrai visage de Kierkegaard*, Paris: Beauchesne et ses fils 1948.
⁴³   Pierre Mesnard, *Kierkegaard. Sa vie, son oeuvre, avec un exposé de sa philosophie*, Paris: Presses Universitaires de France 1954.
⁴⁴   "Fragments d'un journal," trans. by Jean J. Gateau, *Commerce*, no. 12, 1927, pp. 153–64; pp. 165–202; "Le journal du séducteur," trans. by Jean J. Gateau, *Biblioteque universelle et Revue de Genéve*, vol. 2 (December) 1929, pp. 714–43.
⁴⁵   *Le journal du séducteur*, trans. and introduced by Jean J. Gateau, Paris: Libr. Stock, Delamain & Boutelleau 1929 (*Le cabinet cosmopolite, série scandinave*, vol. 43).
⁴⁶   *Traité du désespoir. (La maladie mortelle)*, trans. by Knud Ferlov and Jean J. Gateau, Paris: Gallimard 1932; *Le concept de l'angoisse*, trans. by Jean J. Gateau and Knud Ferlov, Paris: Gallimard 1935; *Les Riens philosophiques*, trans. by Jean J. Gateau and Knud Ferlov, Paris: Gallimard 1937.
⁴⁷   *Journal. Extraits*, vols. 1–5, trans. by Jean J. Gateau and Knud Ferlov, Paris: Gallimard 1942–61.
⁴⁸   See Jacques Lafarge, "Kierkegaard dans la tradition française: Les conditions de sa réception dans les milieux philosophiques," in *Kierkegaard Revisited. Proceedings from the Conference "Kierkegaard and the Meaning of Meaning It" Copenhagen, May 5–9, 1996*, ed. by Niels Jørgen Cappelørn and Jon Stewart, Berlin and New York: Walter de Gruyter 1997 (*Kierkegaard Studies. Monograph Series*, vol. 10), pp. 274–90; especially pp. 283–4. Jacques Lafarge, "L'Édition des Oeuvres complètes de Kierkegaard en français: contexte—

Tisseau, many of the French Kierkegaard translations, like those of Gateau, were chapters or parts of larger works, such as "The Diary of a Seducer" or "In Vino Veritas," misleadingly published as Kierkegaard's signed works and as independent monographs. Tisseau wished to give the French reader a more accurate picture of Kierkegaard's writings by translating complete texts.

Tisseau had the opportunity to learn Danish since he was married to a Dane and in 1926 received an appointment as a lecturer at the University of Lund in Sweden, just across the sound from Denmark. He soon became interested in Kierkegaard and began translating individual works, without any vision of a collected edition. The first translations appeared in 1933.[49] Tisseau experienced many setbacks in his attempts. He lost his Kierkegaard books and materials when his house in Nantes was destroyed by a bomb in the Second World War. He also had difficulty finding the financial resources to support his translations. After his death in 1964, Tisseau's daughter Else-Marie Jacquet-Tisseau (1925–2003) took it upon herself to organize and supplement her father's translations in the form of a collected works edition. This was published in 20 volumes from 1966 to 1986 at the publishing house Éditions de l'Orante under the editorial supervision of Jacques Lafarge.[50] This translation used the second edition of the *Samlede Værker* as its textual basis.[51]

V. The Existentialists

There can be no doubt the many of the leading figures associated with the French existentialist movement were in some ways influenced by Kierkegaard, and some of them indeed explicitly attempted to appropriate him to their cause.[52] This appropriation has rightly or wrongly earned him the title of "the father of existentialism" and has assured the dutiful inclusion of a few excerpts from his texts in virtually every anthology of existentialist authors ever assembled. The existentialists readily identified with Kierkegaard's protest against sterile, abstract philosophy that has nothing to do with actuality as individuals experience it in their daily lives. In an age of totalitarian regimes, his emphasis on the individual and human freedom found a natural resonance. Similarly, his criticism of the masses and the public in works such as *A Literary Review of Two Ages* struck a chord in the quickly developing anonymous and spiritless modern society of the twentieth

---

historique—objectifs—conception—réalisation," *Kierkegaard Studies. Yearbook*, 2000, pp. 300–16.

[49] *La Répétition. Essai d'expérience psychologique par Constantin Constantius*, trans. by Paul-Henri Tisseau, Paris: Félix Alcan 1933; *Le Banquet (In vino veritas)*, trans. by Paul-Henri Tisseau, Paris: Félix Alcan 1933.

[50] Kierkegaard, *Oeuvres Complètes*, vols. 1–20, ed. and trans. by Paul-Henri Tisseau and Else-Marie Jacquet-Tisseau, Paris: Éditions de l'Orante 1966–86.

[51] Søren Kierkegaard, *Samlede Værker*, vols. 1–15, ed. by A.B. Drachmann, J.L. Heiberg and H.O. Lange, Copenhagen: Gyldendal 1920–36.

[52] See Ronald Grimsley, "French Existentialism," in *The Legacy and Interpretation of Kierkegaard*, ed. by Niels Thulstrup and Marie Mikulová Thustrup, Copenhagen: C.A. Reitzel 1981 (*Bibliotheca Kierkegaardiana*, vol. 8), pp. 121–34.

century. Finally, in the context of the Second World War and the German occupation of France, his profound analyses of anxiety, despair, and authenticity seemed to take on an immediate relevance and significance for many French intellectuals. They shared with him an interdisciplinary profile, often using novels and dramas instead of philosophical tracts to illustrate their ideas.

The philosopher and dramatist Gabriel Marcel (1889–1973) makes use of Kierkegaard sporadically in his long authorship.[53] Marcel refers to Kierkegaard in his book *L'Homme problématique* from 1955.[54] In this work he explores the different conditions for the self-alienation of modern human beings. In his account of the different historical diagnoses of this alienation, he dedicates a short chapter to Kierkegaard.[55] Much of this chapter is concerned with Kierkegaard's understanding of the concept of anxiety. Here Marcel treats some of the same material that inspired Sartre's theory of human freedom, but in contrast to Sartre, Marcel actually gives a reading of *The Concept of Anxiety*. Marcel agrees with Sartre that, in his rejection of abstract thinking and in his focus on the individual's relation to concrete existence, "Kierkegaard appears as the true initator of the philosophy of existence, and it is of the greatest importance to observe at the same time that this philosophy finds itself placed from the outset under the sign of anguish."[56]

Marcel, later as an old man, gave a paper on his own relation to Kierkegaard at the conference *Kierkegaard vivant* held in Paris in 1963.[57] This task was doubtless inspired by the claim, popular at the time, that Kierkegaard was the father of existentialism. Since Marcel was one of the existentialists, he felt the need to clarify this relation. At the beginning of this piece he plays down his knowledge of Kierkegaard, claiming that he did not know Kierkegaard's texts very well during the formative years of his writing. Marcel does, however, explore some connections between his own dramatic works and Kierkegaard's interest in the theater and different forms of communication. In the end he admits a more substantial influence and agrees that he and Kierkegaard belong to the same family of thinkers.

Another important thinker in this context is the Catholic philosopher Jacques Maritain (1882–1973). Kierkegaard is referred to several times in Maritain's book on the "existentialism" of Thomas Aquinas: *Court Traité de l'Existence et de l'existant* from 1947.[58] In this work Kierkegaard is taken primarily as an early representative

[53] For a useful thematic account of this relation, see J.B.L. Knox, *Gabriel Marcel. Håbets filosof, fortvivlelsens dramatiker*, Odense: Syddansk Universitetsforlag 2003, pp. 26–7; pp. 34–6; p. 72; pp. 140–2. See also Jeanne Parain-Vial, "Gabriel Marcel et Kierkegaard," in *Kierkegaard*, ed. by Jean Brun, Nyons: Borderie 1981 (special number of *Obliques*), pp. 185–91.

[54] Gabriel Marcel, *L'Homme problématique*, Paris: Aubier 1955. (English translation: *Problematic Man*, trans. by Brian Thompson, New York: Herder and Herder 1967.)

[55] Marcel, *L'Homme problématique*, pp. 126–34. (*Problematic Man*, pp. 101–6.)

[56] Marcel, *L'Homme problématique*, p. 131. (*Problematic Man*, p. 104.)

[57] Gabriel Marcel, "Kierkegaard en ma pensée," in *Kierkegaard vivant. Colloque organisé par l'Unesco à Paris du 21 au 23 avril 1964*, Paris: Gallimard 1966, pp. 64–80.

[58] Jacques Maritain, *Court Traité de l'Existence et de l'existant*, Paris: Paul Hartmann 1947. (English translation: *Existence and the Existent*, trans. by Lewis Galantiere and Gerald B. Phelan, New York: Vintage 1966.)

of existentialism.[59] Maritain also offers a criticism of Kierkegaard's separation of subjective and objective thinking:

> Kierkegaard's great error, amid all his great intuitions was to separate and oppose as two heterogeneous worlds the world of *generality*, or universal law, and that of the unique witness (unjustifiable at the bar of reason) borne by the "knight of faith." Consequently, he had to sacrifice, or at least "suspend" ethics. In reality these two worlds are in continuity; both form part of the universe of ethics, which itself is divided into typically diversified zones according to the degree of depth of moral life.[60]

Maritain insists that there is a continuity in the spheres or stages, which are conceived by Kierkegaard as being radically distinct. He also notes Kierkegaard's polemic with Hegel as follows:

> Subjectivity marks the frontier which separates the world of philosophy from the world of religion. This is what Kierkegaard felt so deeply in his polemic against Hegel. Philosophy runs against an insurmountable barrier in attempting to deal with subjectivity, because while philosophy of course knows subjects, it knows them only as objects. Philosophy is registered whole and entire in the relation of intelligence to object; whereas religion enters into the relation of subject to subject. For this reason, every philosophical religion, or every philosophy, which, like Hegel's, claims to assume and integrate religion into itself, is in the last analysis a mystification.[61]

Here Maritain seems positively disposed towards Kierkegaard's efforts to keep philosophy and religion separate.

At the end of the work Maritain makes the connection between Aquinas and existentialism by means of Kierkegaard:

> We believe that the central intuition on which the existentialism of a Kierkegaard lived was in the last analysis the same as that which lies at the heart of Thomism. We refer to the intuition of the absolutely singular value and the primacy of the act of existing, the *existentia ut exercita*. But in Kierkegaard it sprang from the depths of a faith filled with anguish, robbed of its intelligible or superintelligible structure, desperately expecting the miraculous and rejecting the mystical possession for which it thirsts; it sprang from a radically irrationalist thought which rejects and sacrifices essences and falls back upon the night of subjectivity.[62]

---

[59]   Maritain, *Court Traité de l'Existence et de l'existant*, p. 11; pp. 197–201. (*Existence and the Existent*, p. 2; pp. 123–5.)

[60]   Maritain, *Court Traité de l'Existence et de l'existant*, pp. 93–4. (*Existence and the Existent*, p. 56.)

[61]   Maritain, *Court Traité de l'Existence et de l'existant*, p. 119. (*Existence and the Existent*, p. 72.)

[62]   Maritain, *Court Traité de l'Existence et de l'existant*, pp. 208–9. (*Existence and the Existent*, pp. 130–1.) Here Maritain is actually quoting himself from a previous article.

Maritain thus finds that Kierkegaard and what he refers to as the "first existential generation"[63] kept true to this principle, while the later atheist existentialists, such as Heidegger and Sartre, betrayed it by turning it into something academic.

In 1957 Maritain authored a short essay specifically on Kierkegaard entitled "Le champion du singulier."[64] He offers a critical reading of Kierkegaard, who is again reproached for being an irrationalist who rejects any form of binding ethics. Here it seems that Kierkegaard is made to pay for the sins of Sartre, who, as we will see below, highlights Kierkegaard's thought on freedom at the expense of his thoughts on morality. Kierkegaard also plays a role in Maritain's grand work on ethics, *La Philosophie morale* from 1960.[65] In his treatment of Socrates, Maritain refers to Kierkegaard's account of Socratic irony in *The Concept of Irony.*[66] Kierkegaard is also mentioned in connection with Kant's philosophy. Maritain claims that the abstract nature of Kant's ethics was one of the factors that made Kierkegaard revolt against abstraction and the universal.[67] Kierkegaard's criticism of Hegel's understanding of religion is treated in a couple of different passages.[68] Kierkegaard is also mentioned as an important source of Sartre's existentialism.[69] Finally, Maritain compares Kierkegaard's account of the divine with that of Bergson (1859–1941).[70]

Jean-Paul Sartre (1905–80), probably the most important ideologue of the existentialist movement, apparently first read Kierkegaard during his time as a soldier in 1939–40. Sartre had already made a careful study of Husserl and Heidegger in part during a stay in Berlin in 1933–34. Sartre in fact records his reading of Kierkegaard in the so-called *War Diaries*, which he kept at this time. In his *Notebook 5*, on December 17, 1938, Sartre writes:

> If Kierkegaard is right to call "the possibility of freedom" anxiety, it's not without a touch of anxiety that I discovered once again yesterday morning that I was entirely free to break the piece of bread which the waitress had placed beside me, and free also to convey the fragments to my mouth. Nothing in the world could *stop* me from doing so, not even myself.[71]

---

[63]   Maritain, *Court Traité de l'Existence et de l'existant*, p. 213. (*Existence and the Existent*, p. 133.)

[64]   Jacques Maritain, "Le champion du singulier," *Recherches et Débats*, 1957, no. 19, pp. 14–19.

[65]   Jacques Maritain, *La Philosophie morale*, vol. 1, *Examen historique et critique des grands systèmes*, Paris: Gallimard 1960. The aforementioned essay, "Le champion du singulier," has been incorporated in his "La protestation kierkegaardienne (Médiation sur le singulier)" in his *La Philosophie morale*, vol. 1, pp. 439–59.

[66]   Maritain, *La Philosophie morale*, pp. 20–1; p. 26; p. 32.

[67]   Ibid., pp. 148–9.

[68]   Ibid., p. 232; p. 269.

[69]   Ibid., p. 464; p. 475n; p. 488.

[70]   Ibid., pp. 545–6.

[71]   Jean-Paul Sartre, *Les carnets de la drôle de guerre, Novembre 1939—Mars 1940*, Paris: Gallimard 1983, p. 158. (English translation: *The War Diaries*, trans. by Quinton Hoare, New York: Pantheon 1984, pp. 124–5.)

In a letter dated December 1, 1939 he requests to Simone de Beauvoir that she send him a copy of *The Concept of Anxiety*.[72] In the same notebook on December 19, 1939, he lists this work among the books which he has read recently.[73] This reading is reflected in some of the entries in the same journal. On December 18, he quotes the following passage from *The Concept of Anxiety*: "...the relation of anxiety to its object, to something that is nothing (linguistic usage also says pregnantly: to be anxious about nothing)...."[74] This Kierkegaard quotation and the passage quoted above can be taken as evidence that Kierkegaard is the original source of Sartre's doctrine of the anxiety in the face of the nothingness of absolute freedom.

Like many of the thinkers of his generation, Sartre was aware of Heidegger's interest in Kierkegaard. He notes this explicitly in a letter dated December 16, 1839: "I'm reading *The Concept of Anxiety*, in which there are countless things within theological terms that are obviously a bit forbidding. His influence on Heidegger is undeniable."[75] In the same notebook mentioned above, Sartre then goes on to note a similarity between the two thinkers:

> The influence upon Heidegger is clear: use of the stock phrase "to be in anxiety of nothing" is found word for word in *Sein und Zeit*. But it's true that for Heidegger anxiety is anxiety-at-Nothingness, which is not Nothing but, as Wahl says, "a cosmic fact against which existence stands out." Whereas, for Kierkegaard, it's a question of "a psychological anguish and a nothing that is in the mind." This nothing, in short, is possibility. Possibility that is nothing as yet, since man in the state of innocence does not yet know *of what* it's a possibility. But it's there, nevertheless, as a sign of freedom: "What passed by innocence as the nothing of anxiety has now entered into Adam, and here again it is a nothing—the anxious possibility of being able....as a higher form of ignorance, as a higher expression of anxiety."[76]

The last part of this passage is a quotation from *The Concept of Anxiety*.[77] The point here, with respect to Kierkegaard, is the same as in the previously quoted passages. According to Sartre, Kierkegaard's view is that there are no facts but only possibilities. We realize these possibilities by means of our freedom. But since there

---

[72]   Jean-Paul Sartre, *Lettres au Castor et à quelques autres*, vols. 1–2, ed. by Simone de Beauvoir, Paris: Gallimard 1983, vol. 1, p. 451. (English translation: *Witness to My Life. The Letters of Jean-Paul Sartre to Simone de Beauvoir 1926–1939*, trans. by Lee Fahnestock and Norman MacAfee, Harmondsworth: Penguin 1994, p. 378.)

[73]   Sartre, *Les carnets de la drôle de guerre*, p. 176; *The War Diaries*, p. 139.

[74]   *SKS* 4, 348 / *CA*, 43.

[75]   Sartre, *Lettres au Castor et à quelques autres*, vol. 1, p. 491. (*Witness to My Life*, p. 413.) See also *Lettres au Castor et à quelques autres*, vol. 1, p. 494. (*Witness to My Life*, p. 416): "I'll write to my parents and then read a bit in *The Concept of Anxiety*, which I'll send or bring back to you, and which you'll read with the greatest of interest, if only to understand Kierkegaard's influence on Heidegger and Kafka (you know that Kafka feathers his nest through that book)."

[76]   Sartre, *Les carnets de la drôle de guerre*, p. 166. (*The War Diaries*, pp. 131–2.) Translation slightly modified.

[77]   *SKS* 4, 350 / *CA*, 44–5.

are no rational criteria for choosing which ones to realize, one is left with an anxiety in the face of the manifold of equally meaningless possibilities.

Again in his journals Sartre takes up the question of moral responsibility and accountability. He writes, "the more I see that men deserve war—and deserve it more, the more they wage it. It's like the sin of Adam that each individual, according to Kierkegaard, freely adopts as his own. The declaration of war, which was the fault of certain men, we adopt as our own, with our freedom."[78] Sartre has his own account of appropriation according to which one makes the world one's own by means of one's freedom. In Sartre's extreme view, by accepting certain morally repugnant situations, one not only condones them but even makes oneself responsible for them.

Sartre's study of Kierkegaard corresponds to the period when he was writing his philosophical masterpiece *Being and Nothingness*, which was published in 1943 in occupied France.[79] This work argues for the irreducibility of human freedom and authenticity and clearly bears the stamp of some of Kierkegaard's thoughts on these subjects. Here Sartre again draws primarily on *The Concept of Anxiety* and the account of freedom given there. At the beginning of the work he writes:

> Kierkegaard describing anxiety in the face of what one lacks characterizes it as anxiety in the face of freedom. But Heidegger, whom we know to have been greatly influenced by Kierkegaard, considers anxiety instead as the apprehension of nothingness. These two descriptions of anxiety do not appear to us contradictory; on the contrary the one implies the other.[80]

This observation is an echo from his *War Diaries*, where he writes, "Anxiety as Nothingness, with Heidegger? Anxiety of freedom, with Kierkegaard? In my view it's one and the same thing, for freedom is the apparition of Nothingness in the world."[81] Sartre continues in *Being and Nothingness*: "First we must acknowledge that Kierkegaard is right; anxiety is distinguished from fear in that fear is fear of beings in the world whereas anxiety is anxiety before myself."[82] According to Sartre, for Kierkegaard there is a personal or subjective dimension of anxiety that involves a self-relation and not a relation to a genuine, objective danger in the external world. This may well be what Sartre refers to in a letter dated December 21, 1939, when he writes, in reference to *The Concept of Anxiety*, "I also found a theory of nothingness while reading Kierkegaard."[83]

---

[78] Sartre, *Les carnets de la drôle de guerre*, p. 204. (*The War Diaries*, p. 164.)
[79] Jean-Paul Sartre, *L'Être et le néant. Essai d'ontologie phénoménologique*, Paris: Gallimard 1943. (English translation: *Being and Nothingness*, trans. by Hazel E. Barnes, New York: Citadel Press 1969.)
[80] Sartre, *L'Être et le néant*, p. 66. (*Being and Nothingness*, p. 29.) Here Sartre references Wahl's *Études Kierkegaardiennes* for the connection between Kierkegaard and Heidegger.
[81] Sartre, *Les carnets de la drôle de guerre*, p. 166. (*The War Diaries*, p. 132.) Translation slightly modified.
[82] Sartre, *L'Être et le néant*, p. 66. (*Being and Nothingness*, p. 29.)
[83] Sartre, *Lettres au Castor et à quelques autres*, vol. 1, p. 500. (*Witness to My Life*, p. 421.)

In a footnote in *Being and Nothingness* Sartre refers to "the 'ambiguous' realities of Kierkegaard."[84] This is also a theme that he touched upon in his notebooks; for example, on 17 December 1839 Sartre writes, "So that ambiguity which would have been shocking to a systematic mind (and yet, I have a systematic mind)—that ambiguity which Kierkegaard calls to his aid against Hegel—first appeared to me through an experiment in physics: or, at least, this experiment in physics established *against physics* that idea of ambiguous states.)"[85] Here it is not entirely clear what in Kierkegaard Sartre has in mind; however, with the reference to the criticism of Hegel, one might infer that he is thinking of the beginning of *The Sickness unto Death*, where Kierkegaard talks about the human being as a synthesis of contradictory elements. Humans are thus ambiguous and cannot be defined straightforwardly. As we will see below, this is a motif that Simone de Beauvoir takes up. This passage might also be a reference to Kierkegaard's remarks in the Introduction to *The Concept of Anxiety* about ambiguity in relation to the sciences.

In his account of the existence of others, Sartre explains Hegel's account of lordship and bondage and the dialectic of recognition from the *Phenomenology of Spirit*. In this context, he mentions Kierkegaard as a counterweight:

> Here as everywhere we ought to oppose Hegel to Kierkegaard, who represents the claims of the individual as such. The individual claims his achievement as an individual, the recognition of his concrete being, and of the objective specification of a universal structure. Of course the *rights* which I demand from the Other posit the universality of *self*; respect of persons demands the recognition of my person as universal. But it is my concrete and individual being which flows into this universal and fills it; it is for that *being-there* that I demand rights. The particular is here the support and foundation of the universal; the universal in this case could have no meaning if it did not exist for the purpose of the individual.[86]

Sartre thus avails himself of the old cliché of Kierkegaard as the champion of the individual in the face of Hegel's unwavering claim for the lifeless universal. Finally, there is an allusion to Kierkegaard's understanding of irony,[87] but Sartre does not say enough for one to adjudicate whether or not he actually made a study of *The Concept of Irony*.

In his famous lecture from 1946, *Existentialism is a Humanism*,[88] Sartre mentions Kierkegaard explicitly as a forerunner of existentialism. Here reference is made to Kierkegaard's analysis of the story of Abraham in *Fear and Trembling*, which Sartre uses as a model for his theory of radical freedom, without reasons or excuses. He writes:

---

[84]   Sartre, *L'Être et le néant*, p. 138n. (*Being and Nothingness*, p. 94n.)

[85]   Sartre, *Les carnets de la drôle de guerre*, p. 153. (*The War Diaries*, p. 120.)

[86]   Sartre, *L'Être et le néant*, pp. 295–6. (*Being and Nothingness*, pp. 239–40.)

[87]   Sartre, *L'Être et le néant*, p. 669. (*Being and Nothingness*, p. 580.)

[88]   Jean Paul Sartre, *L'Existentialisme est un humanisme*, Paris: Les Éditions Nagel 1946. (English translation: *Existentialism and Humanism*, trans. by Philip Mairet, Brooklyn: Haskell House 1948.)

This is the anxiety that Kierkegaard called "the anxiety of Abraham." You know the story: An angel commanded Abraham to sacrifice his son: and obedience was obligatory, if it really was an angel who had appeared and said, "Thou, Abraham, shalt sacrifice thy son." But anyone in such a case would wonder, first, whether it was indeed an angel and secondly, whether I am really Abraham. Where are the proofs?....I shall never find any proof whatsoever; there will be no sign to convince me of it. If a voice speaks to me, it is still I myself who must decide whether the voice is or is not of an angel.[89]

For Sartre, the upshot of this story is that Abraham illustrates the anxiety that we feel when we realize that we are constantly in positions where we are obliged to choose, but yet we ultimately have no rational criteria by which to determine our choices. We must nonetheless accept and embrace our freedom with our choices and actions.

Kierkegaard continues to be an interest for Sartre in his later works. In *Search for a Method*, which was originally printed as an article in *Les Temps Modernes* in 1957,[90] then later as an introductory part of *Critique of Dialectical Reason*,[91] and finally as an independent monograph,[92] Sartre juxtaposes Kierkegaard to Hegel in his attempt to sketch the relation between Marxism and existentialism. Hegel is presented as the champion of knowledge and universality, while Kierkegaard is portrayed as the exponent of the individual and subjectivity. Sartre claims that in the historical development of thought, Kierkegaard represents a development:

Kierkegaard is right: grief, need, passion, the pain of men, are brute realities which can be neither surpassed nor changed by knowledge. To be sure, Kierkegaard's religious subjectivism can with good reason be taken as the very peak of idealism; but in relation to Hegel, he marks a progress toward realism, since he insists above all on the *primacy* of the specifically real over thought, that the real cannot be reduced to thought.[93]

Sartre can thus see Kierkegaard as an intermediary figure between Hegel and Marx, who also criticized Hegel's idealism and insisted on a focus on the concrete material relations. Kierkegaard is seen as anticipating Marx's emphasis on action in contrast to thinking.

There was a major conference held in Paris in 1963 organized by UNESCO on occasion of the 150-year anniversary of Kierkegaard's birth. This conference, entitled *Kierkegaard vivant*, brought together many of the major intellectuals of the period. On this occasion, Sartre presented a paper entitled "Kierkegaard: The Singular Universal."[94] This is clearly his most straightforward statement of his

[89]   Sartre, *L'Existentialisme est un humanisme*, pp. 29–30; (*Existentialism and Humanism*, pp. 31–2.)
[90]   Jean-Paul Sartre, "Questions de méthode," *Les temps modernes*, no. 139 (September), 1957, pp. 338–417; no. 140 (October), 1957, pp. 658–98. (English translation: *Search for a Method*, trans. by Hazel E. Barnes, New York: Vintage 1968 [Alfred A. Knopf 1963].)
[91]   Jean-Paul Sartre, *Critique de la raison dialectique*, vol. 1, *Théorie des ensembles pratiques*, Paris: Gallimard 1960, pp. 13–111.
[92]   Jean-Paul Sartre, *Questions de méthode*, Paris: Gallimard 1960.
[93]   Sartre, *Questions de méthode*, p. 19. (*Search for a Method*, p. 12.)
[94]   Jean-Paul Sartre, "L'Universel singulier," in *Kierkegaard vivant. Colloque organisé par l'Unesco à Paris du 21 au 23 avril 1964*, Paris: Gallimard 1966, pp. 20–63 (reprinted

understanding of Kierkegaard's thought and its significance for French philosophy at the time. Here Kierkegaard is portrayed as the proponent of the individual, who fights against all attempts to reduce people to objects and patterns of history. For Sartre, Kierkegaard should not just be "an object of knowledge" for us, but rather we must also try to understand and appropriate for ourselves "the determination of his *praxis*."[95] Sartre points out the interpretive paradox of trying to understand Kierkegaard today—a man who claimed that the interiority and subjectivity of another person is "always inaccessible to cognition in its strict sense."[96] Given this, does it even make sense to try to understand Kierkegaard, and if we do, what is it that we are really understanding?

Philosophical Fragments is the Kierkegaard text that Sartre makes the point of departure for this study. Sartre refers to the doctrines of the paradox, reduplication and contemporaneity and quotes the text directly. He outlines the problem of Hegel's all-encompassing system, which seems to swallow everything in its path. In this sense Kierkegaard was, according to Sartre, aware that he would be taken up as a moment in this universalizing system. As some authors have suggested, he represents the stage of the unhappy religious consciousness, sketched in the *Phenomenology of Spirit*. But, for Kierkegaard, this universal knowledge is not ultimately what is important. Rather, the key for the individual is the lived truth. With a quotation from the *Fragments*,[97] Sartre interprets this as a statement about freedom and autonomy:

> And so he could write, in the *Fragments*: "My own Untruth is something I can discover only by myself, since it is only when I have discovered it that it is discovered, even if the whole world knew of it before." But when it is discovered, my Untruth becomes, at least in the immediate, my Truth. So subjective truth exists. It is not knowledge but self-determination; it can be defined neither as an extrinsic relation of knowledge to being, nor as the internal imprint of a correspondence, nor as the indissoluble unity of a system. "Truth," he said, "is the act of freedom."[98]

This fits in well with Sartre's understanding of Kierkegaard as a forerunner of his own theory of radical freedom. It must, however, be said that Sartre presents this pseudonymous statement straightforwardly as Kierkegaard's own and indeed mentions nothing about the fact that this part of the text is conceived as a "thought project" in which secular Socratic knowing is sketched, only later to be contrasted to Christian knowing.

As long as Kierkegaard lived, Sartre claims, he maintained his singularity and with humor and irony resisted putting forth objective knowledge and being incorporated

---

in Jean-Paul Sartre, *Situations IX*, Paris: Gallimard 1971, pp. 152–90). (English translation: "Kierkegaard: The Singular Universal," in Jean-Paul Sartre, *Between Existentialism and Marxism*, trans. by John Mathews, New York: Pantheon Books 1974, pp. 141–69.)

[95]   Sartre, "L'Universel singulier," in *Kierkegaard vivant*, p. 21. ("Kierkegaard: The Singular Universal," p. 141.)

[96]   Sartre, "L'Universel singulier," in *Kierkegaard vivant*, p. 22. ("Kierkegaard: The Singular Universal," p. 142.)

[97]   *SKS* 4, 223 / *PF*, 15.

[98]   Sartre, "L'Universel singulier," in *Kierkegaard vivant*, pp. 26–7. ("Kierkegaard: The Singular Universal," p. 145.)

into the system. As a single individual, "he desperately wanted to designate himself as a transhistorical absolute."[99] However, this ended with his death and the destruction of his subjectivity. Then all that remained was objective knowledge for later thinkers to appropriate. His subjectivity will continue to elude us forever. Thus, Kierkegaard represents for Sartre the paradox of "the singular universal." He poses this paradox as a problem at the end of the essay.

Finally, Kierkegaard also appears briefly in Sartre's *Critique of Dialectical Reason* from 1960.[100] At the beginning of this work Sartre dwells on some methodological considerations concerning the nature of dialectical thinking and analysis. In a footnote, he refers as follows to Kierkegaard's concepts of the paradox and ambiguity:

> Theoretical psychoanalysis simultaneously employs determinism, the dialectic, and "paradox" in the Kierkegaardian sense of the term. Ambivalence, for example, cannot now be regarded as a contradiction or exactly as Kierkegaardian *ambiguity*. Given the way the concept is used, one is tempted to think of a real contradiction with interpenetrating terms or, in other words, of a contradiction without opposition. In my opinion, what psychoanalysts lack is opposition, at least in certain respects (for there is dialectical conflict between the id, the superego and the ego). They have nonetheless constructed a rationality and what might be called a logic of ambiguity—which would scandalize poor Kierkegaard.[101]

Here Sartre appeals to Kierkegaardian concepts in a criticism of psychoanalysis. By Kierkegaard's concept of ambiguity, Sartre refers to the analyses of the individual as a synthesis of contradictory elements such as infinity and finitude. This reference is quite casual, and the point that Sartre wishes to make concerns psychoanalysis and not Kierkegaard.

It is interesting that such a profoundly secular thinker as Sartre could be so keenly interested in the thought of such a profoundly religious thinker as Kierkegaard. Indeed, it is telling that Sartre effectively ignores the context of Kierkegaard's account of freedom, namely, an analysis of the concept of sin. By contrast, he is keen to exploit Kierkegaard's sense of the anxiety in the world of freedom and choice. Similarly, in his analysis of the story of Abraham and Isaac, Sartre abstracts from the very obvious religious dimension of the narrative. He is not in the least interested in the question of the obedience to a divine command or the nature of faith as Kierkegaard is; rather, for Sartre, the only real point that the story is intended to demonstrate is that Abraham has radical freedom. It is not a question about faith but rather action.

Another oddity about this appropriation is that Sartre seems to ignore the fact that Kierkegaard is an essentialist. Sartre is known for his sloganistic claim that

---

[99]   Sartre, "L'Universel singulier," in *Kierkegaard vivant*, p. 30. ("Kierkegaard: The Singular Universal," p. 147.)
[100]   Jean-Paul Sartre, *Critique de la raison dialectique*, vol. 1, *Théorie des ensembles pratiques*, Paris: Gallimard 1960. (English translation: *Critique of Dialectical Reason*, vol. 1, *Theory of Practical Ensembles*, trans. by Alan Sheridan-Smith, London: NBL, Atlantic Highlands: Humanities Press 1976.)
[101]   Sartre, *Critique de la raison dialectique*, p. 117n. (*Critique of Dialectical Reason*, pp. 17n–18n.)

"existence precedes essence" in the sense that there is no ultimate human essence, but rather our essence is fluid and mutable since we choose it freely. In *Existentialism is a Humanism* Sartre presents this as an attempt to provide a single unified doctrine that all those associated with the existentialist movement could sign on to. By contrast, while Kierkegaard does not speak of a fixed human essence as such, he does emphasize that humans are created beings subject to certain limiting factors, e.g., a dependence on God. It is thus strange that Sartre picks out Kierkegaard as a forerunner of the existentialist school given that he clearly could not agree to that school's first premise, according to Sartre's own definition of it. Finally, from these passages it is also clear that Sartre's main philosophical point of orientation is Heidegger, and his discovery of Kierkegaard came only later. Kierkegaard is thus understood by Sartre, at least in part, not on his own but rather in terms of Heidegger's universe of concepts.[102]

Albert Camus (1913–60) makes active use of Kierkegaard in his famous work *The Myth of Sisyphus* from 1942. There he avails himself of Kierkegaard's analysis of the absurd and expands it from Kierkegaard's original context as faith by virtue of the absurd to a major existential statement about the absurdity of a meaningless world. Like Sartre, Camus seems to ascribe to Kierkegaard a special role as a forerunner of the existentialist movement: "since Kierkegaard's fatal sickness 'that malady that leads to death with nothing else following it,' the significant and tormenting themes of absurd thought have followed one another."[103] Also like Sartre, Camus runs through a series of existential thinkers, giving a brief account of the contribution of each. His blurb on Kierkegaard is as follows:

> Of all perhaps the most engaging, Kierkegaard, for a part of his existence at least, does more than discover the absurd, he lives it. The man who writes: "the surest of stubborn silences is not to hold one's tongue but to talk" makes sure in the beginning that no truth is absolute or can render satisfactory an existence that is impossible in itself. Don Juan of the understanding, he multiplies pseudonyms and contradictions, writes his *Edifying Discourses* at the same time as that manual of cynical spiritualism, "The Diary of the Seducer." He refuses consolations, ethics, reliable principles. As for that thorn he feels in his heart, he is careful not to quiet its pain. On the contrary, he awakens it and, in desperate joy of a man crucified and happy to be so, he builds up piece by piece—lucidity, refusal, make-believe—a category of the man possessed. That face both tender and sneering, those pirouettes followed by a cry from the heart are the absurd spirit itself grappling with a reality beyond its comprehension. And the spiritual adventure that leads Kierkegaard to his beloved scandals begins likewise in the chaos of an experience divested of its setting and relegated to its original incoherence.[104]

Camus seems to take Kierkegaard to be a forerunner of the doctrine of the meaninglessness of the world, which is reflected both in his writings and in his

---

[102]   This has been noted before by Grimsley, "French Existentialism," pp. 121–34.

[103]   Albert Camus, *Le Mythe de Sisyphe*, Paris: Gallimard 1970 [1942]. (English translation: *The Myth of Sisyphus and Other Essays*, trans. by Justin O'Brien, New York: Vintage 1991, p. 23.)

[104]   Camus, *Le Mythe de Sisyphe*, pp. 42–3. (*The Myth of Sisyphus*, pp. 25–6.)

biography. In other words, he ascribes to Kierkegaard a doctrine quite close to that of Romantic irony that Kierkegaard was so keen to criticize in *The Concept of Irony*.

In his most substantial discussion of Kierkegaard, Camus praises him for recognizing the paradoxical nature of faith and for focusing on despair and the absurd. On this point Camus seems somewhat more sensitive to the religious dimension in Kierkegaard's thought than Sartre. However, according to Camus, Kierkegaard should have held fast with this view and not attempted to resolve it. The point is "not to be cured, but to live with one's ailments."[105] He continues, "Kierkegaard wants to be cured. To be cured is his frenzied wish, and it runs throughout his whole journal. The entire effort of his intelligence is to escape the antinomy of the human condition."[106] By embracing Christianity, Kierkegaard, according to Camus, sought an inauthentic solution to the problem of existence that he had so astutely described. Kierkegaard cannot bear the meaninglessness of existence and thus flees to an illusory comfort. Even though Kierkegaard talks about the difficulty of faith, it is still clearly a goal or ideal and what gives life meaning. By contrast, for Camus, the true existential hero is one who, like Sisyphus, can accept the absurd and the lack of meaning, and leave it at that without seeking any reconciliation. To defend his interpretation, Camus quotes extensively from Kierkegaard's journals. In a comparison of Kierkegaard with Husserl, Camus continues his critique: "The leap does not represent an extreme danger as Kierkegaard would like it to do. The danger, on the contrary, lies in the subtle instant that precedes the leap. Being able to remain on the dizzying crest—that is integrity and the rest is subterfuge."[107] Camus clearly recognizes and appreciates Kierkegaard's doctrine of offense, but he also points out passages where Kierkegaard talks of achieving reconciliation. He takes this to be a betrayal of the original principle: "Reconciliation through offense is still reconciliation."[108] One might wish to defend Kierkegaard against this charge by pointing out that, for him, faith never does reach a static point of rest but is always in a dialectic with offense, fear, and trembling. However, even if Camus has got this part wrong, what he wants to point out is that the general wish for religious reconciliation is an illusion and a self-deception for the disabused existential hero.

Camus rightly notes that "antimony and paradox become criteria of the religious."[109] Then he goes on to expand this from what Kierkegaard calls "the sphere of subjectivity" to the world in general: Kierkegaard "makes the absurd the criterion of the other world, whereas it is simply a residue of the experience of this world."[110] In other words, it is not just faith that is absurd but the entire universe. Here, however, one might object that Camus is using the word "absurd" in a way different from Kierkegaard's sense. While in Kierkegaard "absurd" refers to the doctrine of the paradox and implies the contradiction of the finite and the infinite, the eternal and the temporal, Camus takes it to imply meaninglessness or nihilism.

---

[105]   Camus, *Le Mythe de Sisyphe*, p. 58. (*The Myth of Sisyphus*, p. 38.)
[106]   Camus, *Le Mythe de Sisyphe*, p. 58. (*The Myth of Sisyphus*, pp. 38–9.)
[107]   Camus, *Le Mythe de Sisyphe*, p. 72. (*The Myth of Sisyphus*, p. 50.)
[108]   Camus, *Le Mythe de Sisyphe*, p. 59. (*The Myth of Sisyphus*, p. 39.)
[109]   Camus, *Le Mythe de Sisyphe*, p. 57. (*The Myth of Sisyphus*, p. 37.)
[110]   Camus, *Le Mythe de Sisyphe*, p. 57. (*The Myth of Sisyphus*, p. 38.)

An illuminating connection has also been suggested between Camus' novel *The Fall* from 1956 and Kierkegaard's analysis of sin in *The Concept of Anxiety* and despair in *The Sickness unto Death*.[111] Connections are also waiting to be explored between Kierkegaard's works and Camus' novel, *The Plague*, which portrays an existential struggle against a sickness, which can be understood metaphorically, in the sense of a confrontation with despair, in the way Kierkegaard suggests.

While Kierkegaard's influence on Maurice Merleau-Ponty (1908–61) seems to be less significant than that on Sartre or Camus, references to Kierkegaard's works and ideas do appear here and there in Merleau-Ponty's writings. Kierkegaard appears in the Preface to Merleau-Ponty's *magnum opus*, the *Phenomenology of Perception* from 1945. There he is counted among the first phenomenologists. Merleau-Ponty claims that "phenomenology can be...identified as a manner or style of thinking" and that "it existed as a movement before arriving at complete awareness of itself as philosophy."[112] In this sense he can identify Kierkegaard as one of its many early practitioners: "It has been long on the way, and its adherents have discovered it in every quarter, certainly in Hegel and Kierkegaard, but equally in Marx, Nietzsche and Freud."[113] In the body of the work he mentions Kierkegaard only a single time, where he refers in passing to Kierkegaard's notion of objective thinking. In describing the way in which the world emerges from our perception and experiences, Merleau-Ponty writes, "I now refer to my body only as an idea, to the universe as idea, to the idea of space and the idea of time. Thus 'objective' thought (in Kierkegaard's sense) is formed—being that of common sense and of science—which finally causes us to lose contact with perceptual experience, of which it is nevertheless the outcome and the natural sequel."[114] Here Merleau-Ponty simply refers to Kierkegaard's distinction, from the *Concluding Unscientific Postscript*, between subjective and objective thinking, intended to distinguish the sphere of science and logic from that of religious faith. Unlike Kierkegaard, who consistently insists on the absolute separation, irreducibility, and incommensurability of these two spheres, Merleau-Ponty regards them as being necessarily related and in a dialectical relation. The analogue to the religious sphere of subjective knowing in Kierkegaard would be the immediate phenomenological experience in Merleau-Ponty.

In an article entitled "The Battle over Existentialism," which appeared in *Les Temps Modernes* in 1945, Merleau-Ponty refers to Kierkegaard's conception of faith in passing. In reference to the Catholic critics of existentialism, he writes:

> Perhaps they are right in the end, when all is said and done. Perhaps the only way to sustain Christianity as theology is on the basis of Thomism, perhaps the Pascalian

[111]   Judy Gammelgaard, "The Qualitative Leap and the Call of Conscience," *Kierkegaard Studies. Yearbook*, 2001, pp. 183–98.

[112]   Maurice Merleau-Ponty, *Phénoménologie de la perception*, Paris: Gallimard 1945, p. ii. (English translation: *Phenomenology of Perception*, trans. by Colin Smith, London: Routledge & Kegan Paul and New York: The Humanities Press 1962, p. viii.)

[113]   Merleau-Ponty, *Phénoménologie de la perception*, p. ii. (*Phenomenology of Perception*, p. viii.)

[114]   Merleau-Ponty, *Phénoménologie de la perception*, p. 86. (*Phenomenology of Perception*, p. 71.)

concept of being as a blind thing and of spirit as volubility leaves room only for mystical action with no dogmatic content and for a faith which, like Kierkegaard's, is not faith in any being.[115]

As has been seen above, the comparison of Kierkegaard to Pascal is a natural one for the French researcher. In the same piece Merleau-Ponty refers to Kierkegaard and Marx as "the two halves of Hegelian posterity."[116] In both of these references, Kierkegaard is simply taken as a representative of a general movement or trend of thought, either religious or philosophical.

Similarly, Merleau-Ponty refers to Kierkegaard again in an essay called "Faith and Good Faith" from 1946.[117] There he writes: "Kierkegaard thought it impossible to say 'I am a Christian' in the way one says 'I am tall' or 'I am short,' because being a Christian means living the contradiction of good and evil, and so it also means not being a Christian."[118] To be a Christian is a subjective matter and can never be meaningfully uttered as an objective statement. Here Merleau-Ponty is also clearly attentive to Kierkegaard's account of the ineffable and the doctrine of the paradox of Christianity, which is alluded to explicitly.[119]

In his extended analysis of Marxism from 1955, entitled *Adventures of the Dialectic*, Merleau-Ponty makes a brief comparison of Kierkegaard and Marx: "When Marx said: 'I am not a Marxist,' and Kierkegaard more or less said, 'I am not a Christian,' they meant that action is too present to the person acting to admit the ostentation of a declared choice. The declared choice is nearly the proof that there has been no choice."[120] This is ultimately used as a criticism of Sartre's self-declared Marxism, which Merleau-Ponty takes to be at least in part inauthentic and even hypocritical. The reference to Kierkegaard seems to be to his statements, for example, in the attack on the Church or in *The Point of View*, where he underscores that he has never claimed to be Christian because he wishes to keep that free as an ideal. It can also be seen in connection with the aforementioned passage from Merleau-Ponty's "Faith and Good Faith," where reference is made to the subjective nature of Christian faith generally.

In his lecture "The Philosophy of Existence" from 1959, Merleau-Ponty gives a retrospective view of the development of existentialism in the twentieth century.

---

[115]   Maurice Merleau-Ponty, "La querelle de l'existentialisme," *Les Temps modernes*, no. 2, November 1945, pp. 344–56; p. 349. (English translation: "The Battle over Existentialism," in *Sense and Non-Sense*, trans. by Hubert L. Dreyfus and Patricia Allen Dreyfus, Evanston: Northwestern University Press 1964, pp. 71–82; p. 76.)

[116]   Merleau-Ponty, "La querelle de l'existentialisme," p. 353; "The Battle over Existentialism," p. 77.

[117]   Maurice Merleau-Ponty, "Foi et bonne foi," *Les Temps modernes*, no. 5, February 1946, pp. 769–82. (English translation: "Faith and Good Faith," in *Sense and Non-Sense*, pp. 172–81.)

[118]   Merleau-Ponty, "Foi et bonne foi," pp. 774–5; "Faith and Good Faith," p. 176.

[119]   Merleau-Ponty, "Foi et bonne foi," p. 775; "Faith and Good Faith," p. 176.

[120]   Maurice Merleau-Ponty, *Les Aventures de la dialectique*, Paris: Gallimard 1955, p. 266. (English translation: *Adventures of the Dialectic*, trans. by Joseph Bien, Evanston: Northwestern University Press 1973, p. 198.)

Although he deviates from Sartre's assessment in some regards, he agrees with him in ascribing to Kierkegaard the role of a forerunner of the movement. He writes:

> The term "existentialism" has come to designate almost exclusively the philosophical movement which arose in France after 1945, chiefly as a result of Sartre's investigation. In reality, this philosophical movement has its antecedents: it is tied to an entire philosophical tradition, a long and complicated tradition, since it actually begins with Kierkegaard's philosophy, and following this, is derived from philosophies such as Husserl's and Heidegger's in Germany, and in France, even before Sartre, from philosophies such as that of Gabriel Marcel.[121]

Here Merleau-Ponty seems to take it as more or less unproblematic that Kierkegaard is to be understood in line with these later thinkers. Indeed, it is so unproblematic that he offers no evidence to support this claim.

In a somewhat cryptic note from Merleau-Ponty's *Nachlaß*, dated February 1959, he associates Kierkegaard with Nietzsche and Sartre as follows:

> Start from the present: contradictions etc. ruin of philosophy—Show that that calls into question not only the classical philosophy, but also the philosophies of the dead god (Kierkegaard—Nietzsche—Sartre) in as much as they are its contrary. (and also, of course, the dialectic as a "maneuver").[122]

The reference to Kierkegaard's philosophy as a form of a "dead god" philosophy is difficult to make sense of. However, the use of "contradictions" to undermine traditional philosophy might well be understood in the context of Kierkegaard's attack on the abstract conceptual thinking of German idealism and modern rationalism generally. In any case, this passage may well be understood in the context of the previous one from "The Philosophy of Existence" since it seems to imply a family resemblance among Kierkegaard, Nietzsche, and Sartre, which could be taken to indicate their inclusion as members of a more or less continuous school of thought known as "existentialism."

Unlike Sartre and Camus, Merleau-Ponty does not enter into any analyses of particular Kierkegaard texts. Moreover, he seems not to be particularly interested in the standard set of themes in Kierkegaard, such as despair, anxiety, absurdity, and freedom, that Sartre and Camus virtually made into slogans of the existentialist movement. Kierkegaard remains a figure in the background of Merleau-Ponty's philosophical horizon.

Simone de Beauvoir (1908–86) was also keenly interested in Kierkegaard's thought. Her reading of Kierkegaard seems to date from the same period as Sartre, and indeed this is no accident given the fact that she was the one who was sending him

---

[121]   Maurice Merleau-Ponty, "La Philosophie de l'existence," *Dialogue. Revue canadienne de philosophie*, vol. 5, no. 3, 1966, pp. 307–22; p. 307. (English translation: "The Philosophy of Existence," in *Texts and Dialogues*, ed. by Hugh J. Silverman and James Barry, Jr., New Jersey and London: Humanities Press 1992, pp. 129–39; p. 129.)

[122]   Maurice Merleau-Ponty, *Le visible et l'invisible*, Paris: Gallimard 1964, p. 236. (English translation: *The Visible and the Invisible*, trans. by Alphonso Lingis, Evanston: Northwestern University Press 1968, p. 183.)

books during his time as a soldier and subsequently as a prisoner of war. In a letter dated December 21, 1840, she reports that she has "heaps of books by Kierkegaard" that she intends to read over the Christmas holidays.[123] Two days later she writes, again to Sartre, "I'm busy reading Kierkegaard and Wahl's essays on him—it really interests me."[124] On December 26, she informs Sartre that she "read *The Concept of Anxiety* at the Café de Flore."[125] Her interest in this work was doubtless awakened at least in part by Sartre's eager recommendation of it.

De Beauvoir uses Kierkegaard as a source of inspiration for her central work on ethics, *The Ethics of Ambiguity* from 1947.[126] In this work she claims that there lie a number of fundamental ambiguities in human existence, such as mind and body or rational and animal, that traditional philosophical systems have attempted to eliminate in order to arrive at a single consistent principle. In this context she hails Kierkegaard as a forerunner of existentialism for his identification of this ambiguity and his insistence on it; he resists capitulating to the urge to reduce the ambiguous terms to a single principle. She writes, "It was by affirming the irreducible character of ambiguity that Kierkegaard opposed himself to Hegel, and it is by ambiguity that, in our own generation, Sartre in *Being and Nothingness*, fundamentally defined man...."[127] Here she clearly refers to Kierkegaard's thesis of human beings as a synthesis of the eternal and the temporal, finite and infinite, etc. She has no hesitation in identifying Kierkegaard with Sartre's *magnum opus*, which was of course the defining work of the French existential movement.

Towards the end of the book she refers to Kierkegaard again by way of illustration. Like Sartre, she refers to Kierkegaard's analysis of Abraham and Isaac in *Fear and Trembling*:

> Kierkegaard has said that what distinguishes the Pharisee from the genuinely moral man is that the former considers his anguish as a sure sign of his virtue; from the fact that he asks himself, "Am I Abraham?" he concludes, "I am Abraham"; but morality resides in the painfulness of an indefinite questioning. The problem we are posing is not the same as that of Kierkegaard; the important thing to us is to know whether, in given conditions, Isaac must be killed or not. But we also think that what distinguishes the tyrant from the man of good will is that the first rests in the certainty of his aims, whereas

---

[123]   Simone de Beauvoir, *Lettres à Sartre*, vols. 1–2, ed. by Sylvie Le Bon de Beauvoir, Paris: Gallimard 1990, vol. 2, Letter 219, p. 213. (English translation: *Letters to Sartre*, trans. by Quintin Hoare, London: Vintage 1991, p. 355.)

[124]   de Beauvoir, *Lettres à Sartre*, vol. 2, Letter 220, pp. 213–14. (*Letters to Sartre*, p. 357.)

[125]   de Beauvoir *Lettres à Sartre*, vol. 2, Letter 222, p. 215. (*Letters to Sartre*, p. 358.) Her reading of Kierkegaard continued on into the new year; see *Lettres à Sartre*, vol. 2, Letter 229, p. 222; *Letters to Sartre*, p. 363.

[126]   Simone de Beauvoir, *Pour une morale de l'ambiguité*, Paris: Gallimard 1947. (English translation: *The Ethics of Ambiguity*, trans. by Bernard Frechtman, New York: Philosophical Library 1949, 1976.)

[127]   de Beauvoir, *Pour une morale de l'ambiguité*, p. 15. (*The Ethics of Ambiguity*, pp. 9–10.).

the second keeps asking himself, "Am I really working for the liberation of men? Isn't this end contested by the sacrifices through which I aim at it?"[128]

Here she refers to Kierkegaard's discussion from *Fear and Trembling* in order to illustrate the correct relation to a cause or a given end. Critical of those who wholeheartedly and without hesitation embrace nationalism or Stalinism, de Beauvoir argues that Kierkegaard has here provided us with a correct model of the proper relation to such ends; one must always seek to preserve the ambiguity, negativity, and tension involved in them and keep them present before one's eyes, always questioning and always doubting. Thus, de Beauvoir takes Kierkegaard's criticism of complacent Christianity as a model for any kind of authentic affiliation with a given end and subsequent action.

She refers to Kierkegaard several times in her classic statement of feminist theory, *The Second Sex* from 1949.[129] In her account of the "facts and myths" of women, she quotes Kierkegaard directly as follows: "To be a woman," says Kierkegaard in *Stages on Life's Way*, "is something so strange, so confused, so complicated, that no one predicate comes near expressing it and that the multiple predicates that one would like to use are so contradictory that only a woman could put up with it."[130] She refers to the beginning of Victor Eremita's speech from "In Vino Veritas."[131] Her comment on this is simply, "This comes from not regarding woman positively, such as she seems to herself to be, but negatively, such as she appears to man."[132] She uses this to begin an explanation of the concept of the woman as the Other. Kierkegaard (or his pseudonymous work) is thus used as an example of a form of sexism. She quotes from the same work in more detail later in the analysis:

> "Through woman," writes Kierkegaard in *In Vino Veritas*, "ideality enters into life, and what would man be without her? Many a man has become a genius thanks to some young girl...but none has ever become a genius thanks to the young girl who gave him her hand in marriage...." "Woman makes a man productive in ideality through a negative relation....Negative relations with woman can make us infinite...positive relations with woman make a man finite for the most part." Which is to say that woman is necessary in so far as she remains an idea into which man projects his own transcendence; but that she is inauspicious as an objective reality, existing in and for herself. Kierkegaard holds that by refusing to marry his fiancée he established the only valid relation to woman.

---

[128]   de Beauvoir, *Pour une morale de l'ambiguïté*, pp. 186–7. (*The Ethics of Ambiguity*, pp. 133–4.)

[129]   Simone de Beauvoir, *Le Deuxieme Sexe*, vol. 1, *Les Faits et Les Mythes*, vol. 2, *L'Expérience vécue*, Paris: Gallimard 1949. (English translation: *The Second Sex*, trans. by H.M. Parshley, New York: Alfred A. Knopf 1952.)

[130]   de Beauvoir, *Le Deuxieme Sexe*, vol. 1, *Les Faits et Les Mythes*, p. 236. (*The Second Sex*, p. 162.)

[131]   *SKS* 6, 57–8. / *SLW*, 56. The Hongs render this passage somewhat more favorably to Kierkegaard: "To be a woman is something so special, so mixed, so compounded that there are no predicates to describe it, and the many predicates, if they were used, contradict one another in a manner only a woman can tolerate."

[132]   de Beauvoir, *Le Deuxieme Sexe*, vol. 1, *Les Faits et Les Mythes*, p. 236. (*The Second Sex*, p. 162.)

And he is right in a sense: namely that the myth of woman set up as the infinite Other entails also its opposite.[133]

She here again refers to a passage from Victor Eremita's speech from "In Vino Veritas."[134] She connects Kierkegaard's biography more or less straightforwardly with what is said in his pseudonymous work.

De Beauvoir refers to Kierkegaard again in her insightful analysis of the "mystery" of the feminine. She writes:

> Of all these myths, none is more firmly anchored in masculine hearts than that of the feminine "mystery." It has numerous advantages. And first of all it permits an easy explanation of all that appears inexplicable: the man who "does not understand" a woman is happy to substitute an objective resistance for a subjective deficiency of mind; instead of admitting his ignorance, he perceives the presence of a "mystery" outside himself: an alibi, indeed, that flatters laziness and vanity at once. A heart smitten with love thus avoids many disappointments: if the loved one's behavior is capricious, her remarks stupid, then the mystery serves to excuse it all. And finally, thanks again to the mystery, that negative relation is perpetuated which seemed to Kierkegaard infinitely preferable to positive possession; in the company of a living enigma man remains alone—alone with his dreams, his hopes, his fears, his love, his vanity.[135]

In the absence of any textual reference, this appears to be an allusion to Kierkegaard's biography. De Beauvoir seems to ascribe to him the view that Kierkegaard found himself unable to marry Regine Olsen due to the fact that he was unable to penetrate the mystery of her person, and that he thus preferred to accept this mystery as an outward phenomenon than to ascribe to himself some role in it.

In the second volume of *The Second Sex*, she returns to *Stages on Life's Way*. In the context of a discussion of the relation of love and marriage, de Beauvoir raises the question of the possibility, raised by Kierkegaard, of ever reconciling the two. She writes:

> To reconcile marriage and love is such a *tour de force* that nothing less than divine intervention is required for success; this is the solution reached through devious ways by Kierkegaard. Love, he says, is spontaneous; marriage is a decision; the amorous inclination, however, is to be aroused by marriage or by the decision to wish to marry. Something so mysterious as to be explained only by the divine action paradoxically occurs in virtue of reflection and decision, and the whole process must be simultaneous. This is to say that to love is not to marry and that it is hard to see how love can become duty. But the paradox does not dismay Kierkegaard. He agrees that "reflection is the destroying angel of spontaneity," but says that the decision is a new spontaneity based on ethical principles; it is a "religious conception" which "should open the way to amorous inclination" and protect it from all danger. A real husband, he says, "is a miracle." As for the wife, reason is not for her, she is without "reflection"; "she passes from the

[133]   de Beauvoir, *Le Deuxieme Sexe*, vol. 1, *Les Faits et Les Mythes*, pp. 295–6. (*The Second Sex*, pp. 210–11.)
[134]   *SKS* 6, 60 / *SLW*, 59.
[135]   de Beauvoir, *Le Deuxieme Sexe*, vol. 1, *Les Faits et Les Mythes*, pp. 386–7. (*The Second Sex*, p. 289.)

immediacy of love to the immediacy of the religious." In plain language this means that a man in love decides on marriage by an act of faith in God, which should guarantee the harmony of feeling and obligations....Kierkegaard fully admits that there should be a preceding "inclination" but that this should last through life is no less miraculous.[136]

A footnote to this passage indicates that this is a loose reading of what Kierkegaard says in "In Vino Veritas" and "Some Reflections on Marriage," both from *Stages on Life's Way*.

A final reference to *Stages on Life's Way* appears in the conclusion of the work. There de Beauvoir writes, "That she is being tricked, many men have realized. 'What a misfortune to be a woman! And yet the misfortune, when one is a woman, is at bottom not to comprehend that it is one,' says Kierkegaard."[137] She continues the quotation in a footnote:

> Politeness is pleasing—essentially—to woman, and the fact that she accepts it without hesitation is explained by nature's care for the weaker, for the unfavored being and for one to whom an illusion means more than a material compensation. But this illusion, precisely, is fatal to her....To feel oneself freed from distress thanks to something imaginary, to be the dupe of something imaginary, is that not a still deeper mockery?... Woman is very far from being *verwahrlost* (neglected), but in another sense she is, since she can never free herself from the illusion that nature has used to console her.[138]

Like the other passages, this also comes from Victor Eremita's speech in "In Vino Veritas."[139] De Beauvoir seems to take this passage as evidence for her claim that women are tricked or suffer from an illusion that, despite the many disadvantages that they must endure, they are nonetheless privileged in many ways.

It is striking to compare de Beauvoir's use of Kierkegaard in this text with that of the other existentialists including her life-long companion and collaborator Sartre. While, for example, Camus and Sartre find in Kierkegaard a forerunner of existentialism and a theorist of radical freedom, anxiety, despair, and absurdity, de Beauvoir is here focused more or less exclusively on Kierkegaard's pseudonym's statements about women, love, marriage, etc. The Kierkegaard that appears in her analyses is far from being an existentialist or for that matter a thinker from whom one can gain positive insights or inspiration. In a sense he is used as just another banal example of old forms of sexism.

In 1963 Paul Ricoeur (1913–2005) published two articles on Kierkegaard in the *Revue de théologie et de philosophie*. In the first, entitled "Kierkegaard et le mal,"[140]

---

[136]　de Beauvoir, *Le Deuxieme Sexe*, vol. 2, *L'Expérience vécue*, pp. 213–14. (*The Second Sex*, pp. 489–90.)

[137]　de Beauvoir, *Le Deuxieme Sexe*, vol. 2, *L'Expérience vécue*, p. 564. (*The Second Sex*, p. 800.)

[138]　de Beauvoir, *Le Deuxieme Sexe*, vol. 2, *L'Expérience vécue*, p. 564n. (*The Second Sex*, pp. 800n–801n.)

[139]　*SKS* 6, 58–9 / *SLW*, 57.

[140]　Paul Ricoeur, "Kierkegaard et le mal," *Revue de théologie et de philosophie*, no. 4, 1963, pp. 292–302. (Reprinted in *Les Cahiers de philosophie*, nos. 8–9, Lille 1989, special issue, *Kierkegaard, Vingt-cinq etudes*, pp. 271–83.)

He gives an interpretation of Kierkegaard's account of evil in *The Concept of Anxiety* and *The Sickness unto Death*. This is a somewhat technical, text-oriented piece. Unlike Sartre, Ricoeur is sensitive to the theological dimension of Kierkegaard's thought, in particular his account of sin. At the end of this article Ricoeur raises the question of what it means to philosophize after Kierkegaard, and this is made the topic for the second article.

In this essay, "Philosopher après Kierkegaard,"[141] he explores for the first time in a more nuanced manner the complex relations between Kierkegaard's thought and the later French and German existentialists. Ricoeur was among the first to call into question Kierkegaard's association with the existentialists and the notion of a homogenous and unified school of thought called "existentialism." According to him, Kierkegaard represents an original alternative kind of philosophy, which Ricoeur refers to as a criticism of existential possibilities. With this separation of Kierkegaard from these later appropriations, Ricoeur opened the door for more independent studies of Kierkegaard on his own terms.

VI. Poststructuralism and Late Phenomenology

Kierkegaard's writings have also been claimed by the poststructuralists. Many of the features of his thought seem in different ways to anticipate some of the central themes of that movement. For example, his use of pseudonyms as a way to undermine his own authority as an author and to create a polyphony of authorial voices has been seen as an anticipation of the so-called death of the author, the deferment of meaning, and the relativity of interpretation. Moreover, Kierkegaard's interest in the concept of irony also finds resonance in a number of poststructuralist theorists. These interpreters tend to focus on the disruption of straightforward communication implied in Kierkegaard's discussion of irony. In this context, his writings become a springboard for investigations into the destabilization of meaning and the difficulty of univocal communication.

One of the leading poststructuralist theorists, Jacques Derrida (1930–2004) has long maintained an interest in Kierkegaard's writings. His most intensive encounter with Kierkegaard appears in his late work, *Donner la Mort* from 1992.[142] The third chapter of this book contains a rich analysis of the notion of sacrifice as illustrated by the analysis of Abraham and Isaac in *Fear and Trembling*. Here Derrida agrees with Kierkegaard about the ultimate incomprehensibility of the absolute and the divine, which transcends the normal sphere of ethics. This mystery of the divine other nonetheless enjoins one to act, and this is action with "fear and trembling" since one has no way to understand or justify one's actions.

---

[141]   Paul Ricoeur, "Philosopher après Kierkegaard," *Revue de théologie et de philosophie*, vol. 4, 1963, pp. 303–16. (Reprinted in *Les Cahiers de philosophie*, nos. 8–9, Lille 1989, special issue, *Kierkegaard, Vingt-cinq etudes*, pp. 285–300.)

[142]   Jacques Derrida, *Donner la Mort*, Paris: Galilée 1992. (English translation: *The Gift of Death*, trans. by David Wills, Chicago: University of Chicago Press 1995.)

The influential psychologist Jacques Lacan (1901–81) also makes use of some important Kierkegaardian themes.[143] In a handful of texts he examines Kierkegaard's concept of repetition, comparing it to the same concept in Freud.[144] In one of his seminars, after an account of "The Unconscious and Repetition," Lacan warmly recommends Kierkegaard's book to his auditors as follows: "I would ask you to re-read Kierkegaard's essay on *Repetition*, so dazzling in its lightness and ironic play, so truly Mozartian in the way, so reminiscent of Don Giovanni, it abolishes the mirages of love."[145] For Lacan, this concept in the context of psychology concerns how one is condemned to repeat certain behavioral patterns that one has learned from early on. In this context he talks about Kierkegaard's account of hereditary sin from *The Concept of Anxiety*. Each of us repeats or appropriates the sin of Adam in his or her own way. There is no exact repetition but rather always an element of difference since each person sins in his or her own unique manner. So also for Lacan the father, for example, establishes forms of behavior which the children repeat in different ways in their own lives. In another seminar Lacan appeals to Kierkegaard's distinction between recollection and repetition, again in comparision with Freud. He writes:

> Freud distinguishes two completely different structurations of human experience—one which, along with Kierkegaard, I called *ancient*, based on reminiscence, presupposing agreement, harmony between man and the world of his objects, which means that he recognizes them, because in some way, he has always known them—and, on the contrary, the conquest, the structuration of the world through the effort of labor, along the path of repetition.[146]

While Lacan is not interested in a detailed exegesis of Kierkegaard's texts, he clearly makes active use of a handful of Kierkegaardian concepts which he puts into his own psychoanalytic context.

Another Francophone philosopher to be captivated by Kierkegaard's account in *Fear and Trembling* is the Lithuanian-born Emmanuel Lévinas (1906–95).

---

[143]   For this relation, see Yves Depelsenaire, *Une Analyse avec Dieu. Le Rendez-vous de Lacan et de Kierkegaard*, Brussels: La Lettre volée 2004. Rudolphe Adam, *Lacan et Kierkegaard*, Paris: Presses Universitaires de France 2005.

[144]   See especially Jacques Lacan, *Le Séminaire. Livre XI: Les Quatre Concepts fondamentaux de la psychanalyse*, Paris: Le Seuil 1974. (English translation: *Seminar XI: The Four Fundamental Concepts of Psychoanalysis*, trans. by Alan Sheridan, New York and London: W.W. Norton 1981.) Jacques Lacan, *Le Séminaire. Livre II: Le Moi dans la théorie de Freud et dans la technique psychanalytique*, Paris: Le Seuil 1978. (English translation: *Seminar II: The Ego in Freud's Theory and in the Technique of Psychoanalysis 1954–1955*, trans. by Sylvana Tomaselli, Cambridge: Cambridge University Press 1988.)

[145]   Lacan, *Le Séminaire. Livre XI: Les Quatre Concepts fondamentaux de la psychanalyse*, p. 59. (*Seminar XI: The Four Fundamental Concepts of Psychoanalysis*, p. 61.)

[146]   Lacan, *Le Séminaire. Livre II: Le Moi dans la théorie de Freud et dans la technique psychanalytique*, pp. 124–5. (*Seminar II: The Ego in Freud's Theory and in the Technique of Psychoanalysis 1954–1955*, p. 100.)

He explores this in his essays "Á propos Kierkegaard Vivant,"[147] "Existence et éthique,"[148] and in his book *Totalité et Infini. Essai sur l'extériorité.*[149] While Lévinas lauds Kierkegaard's thesis that the individual is absolute and irreducible, he is nonetheless highly critical of Kierkegaard's ethical views, in particular the doctrine of the teological suspension of the ethical. Lévinas argues that the idea of transcending ethics in order to reach the religious sphere cannot be used as an excuse for murder. The unique and irreducible ethical quality of the individual as individual is, according to Lévinas, missing in Kierkegaard's religious stage. He claims that Kierkegaard's religious individualism precludes him from having any meaningful account of ethical relations to others.[150] He portrays Kierkegaard, with his account of the irreducibility and lack of transparency of the individual, as promoting a self-indulgent fixation on one's one inwardness and subjectivity, while at the same time eliminating all forms of intersubjectivity that can lead to a fruitful ethics and social life.

The philosopher Gilles Deleuze (1925–95) refers to Kierkegaard frequently in a number of different works, without, however, ever really entering into a detailed discussion. In his book on Nietzsche from 1962, Deleuze offers a comparison of the German thinker with Pascal, Shestov, and Kierkegaard.[151] The comparison is, however, rather brief and question-begging. Kierkegaard and his fellow "tragic philosophers" are portrayed as still being "ensnared in *ressentiment.*"[152] Kierkegaard was not a thinker who affirmed life and the will to power, but rather relied on "interiority, anguish, wailing, guilt, all the forms of dissatisfaction."[153] In *Différence et repetition* from 1968, Deleuze makes use of Kierkegaard's concept of repetition and compares him with Nietzsche.[154]

Deleuze also alludes to Kierkegaard couple of times the first volume of his work on film, *Cinéma* from 1983.[155] There he writes:

---

[147]   Emmanuel Lévinas, "À propos de 'Kierkegaard Vivant,' " in his *Noms propres*, Paris: Librairie générale française 1987 [1976], pp. 111–13. (English translation: "A Propos of 'Kierkegaard vivant,' " in his *Proper Names*, trans. by Michael B. Smith, London: Athlone Press 1996, pp. 75–9.)

[148]   Emmanuel Lévinas, "Existence et éthique" in his *Noms propres*, pp. 77–87. (English translation: "Existence and Ethics," in his *Proper Names*, pp. 66–74.)

[149]   Emmanuel Lévinas, *Totalité et Infini. Essai sur l'extériorité*, The Hague: Martinus Nijhoff 1961. (English translation: *Totality and Infinity: An Essay on Exteriority*, trans. by Alphonso Lingis, The Hague: Martinus Nijhoff 1969.)

[150]   For an account of this criticism, see Pia Søltoft, *Svimmelhedens Etik—om forholdet mellem den enkelte og den anden hos Buber, Lévinas og især Kierkegaard*, Copenhagen: Gads Forlag 2000, pp. 83–112, especially pp. 105–10.

[151]   Gilles Deleuze, *Nietzsche et la philosophie*, Paris: Presses Universitaires de France 1962, pp. 41–3. (English translation: *Nietzsche and Philosophy*, trans. by Hugh Tomlinson, New York: Columbia University Press 1983, pp. 36–8.)

[152]   Deleuze, *Nietzsche et la philosophie*, p. 42; *Nietzsche and Philosophy*, p. 36.

[153]   Ibid.

[154]   Gilles Deleuze, *Différence et répétition*, Paris: Presses Universitaires de France 1968.

[155]   Gilles Deleuze, *Cinéma*, vol. 1, *L'Image-Mouvement*, Paris: Les Éditions de Minut 1983. (English translation: *Cinema 1. The Movement-Image*, trans. by Hugh Tomlinson and

A fascinating idea was developed from Pascal to Kierkegaard: the alternative is not between terms but between modes of existence of the one who chooses. There are choices that can only be made on condition that one persuades oneself that one has no choice, sometimes by virtue of a moral necessity (good, right), sometimes by virtue of a physical necessity (the state of things, the situation), sometimes by virtue of a psychological necessity (the desire one has for something). The spiritual choice is made between the mode of existence of him who chooses on the condition of not knowing it, and the mode of existence of him who knows that it is a matter of choosing. It is as if there was a choice of choice *or* non-choice.[156]

This is the way Deleuze understands Pascal's wager and Kierkegaard's either/or. His Kierkegaard reading is here clearly influenced by Sartre, which Deleuze himself acknowledges later in the passage when he associates Kierkegaard's "alternative" with Sartre's "choice."[157] Deleuze develops this further with reference to *Fear and Trembling*:

> Kierkegaard said that true choice means that by abandoning the bride, she is restored to us by that very act; and that by sacrificing his son, Abraham rediscovers him through that very act. Agamemnon sacrifices his daughter, Iphigenia, but out of duty, duty alone, and in choosing not to have the choice. Abraham, on the contrary, sacrifices his son, whom he loves more than himself, through choice alone, and through consciousness of the choice which unites him with God, beyond good and evil: thus his son is restored to him. This is the history of lyrical abstraction.[158]

Finally, Deleuze refers to Kierkegaard's concept of repetition, which he compares with some of Nietzsche's concepts, such as the eternal return:

> The good man, the saintly man, are imprisoned in the cycle, no less than the thug and the evildoer. But is not repetition capable of breaking out in its own cycle and of "leaping" beyond good and evil? It is repetition which ruins and degrades us, but it is repetition which can save us and allow us to escape from the other repetition. Kierkegaard has already opposed a fettering, degrading repetition of the past to a repetition of faith, directed towards the future, which restored everything to us in a power which was not that of the Good but of the absurd.[159]

Generally speaking, Deleuze refers to Kierkegaard in this work to illustrate some of the points about film criticism that he wants to make, and thus he is not interested in exploring Kierkegaard's thoughts for their own sake.

The literary critic Maurice Blanchot (1907–2003) dedicates a chapter to Kierkegaard in his work *Faux Pas* from 1943.[160] This chapter in a sense represents a pioneering work since Blanchot was among the first to recognize the importance

---

Barbara Habberjam, London: Athlone Press 1986.)
[156]   Deleuze, *Cinema 1. The Movement-Image*, p. 114.
[157]   Ibid.
[158]   Deleuze, *Cinema 1. The Movement-Image*, p. 116.
[159]   Deleuze, *Cinema 1. The Movement-Image*, p. 131.
[160]   Maurice Blanchot, "Le 'Journal' de Kierkegaard," in his *Faux Pas*, Paris: Gallimard 1943, pp. 27–33.

of the *Nachlaß* for understanding Kierkegaard's thought. This chapter is thus one of the earliest to treat the journals as an independent subject of investigation. Here Blanchot touches on a number of themes regarding both the authorship, such as the pseudonyms, the theory of communication, the Kierkegaardian dialectic, and Kierkegaard's biography. With regard to the latter, Blanchot does not really get beyond the well-known clichés about Regine and Kierkegaard's relation to his father.

Blanchot returns to some of these biographical elements in *L'Espace littéraire* from 1955.[161] He takes up Kafka's interest in the story Kierkegaard's engagement, due to the former's own failed love story: "Kafka's story and the story of Kierkegaard's engagement have been compared, by Kafka himself among others. But the conflict is different. Kierkegaard can renounce Regine; he can renounce the ethical. Access to the religious level is not thereby compromised; rather it is made possible."[162] The decision to discontinue the engagement is interpreted as an act of sacrifice and compared to the Abraham and Isaac story as a test of faith. In a chapter on suicide and death, Blanchot refers in passing to Kierkegaard's title, *The Sickness unto Death*.[163]

In 1977 Sylviane Agacinski (b. 1945) published her influential work *Aparté. Conceptions et morts de Søren Kierkegaard*.[164] One of the main figures in feminist readings of Kierkegaard, Agacinski argues that Kierkegaard's mother, about whom he says nothing in his journals or published writings, represents an other, something apart. She is the secret to the authorship that Kierkegaard wishes never to be revealed. This interesting and creative reading does not pursue the matter by means of source-work research, which could potentially strengthen the argument substantially if indeed source-work evidence for it could be unearthed. This work was supplemented with a new one in 1996 under the title *Critique de l'égocentrisme: l'événement de l'autre*.[165]

The phenomenologist Michel Henry (1922–2002) was also profoundly influenced by Kierkegaard. In particular, Kierkegaard's emphasis on the individual and subjectivity was defining for Henry's work. His book *C'est moi la vérité. Pour une philosophie du christianisme* from 1996[166] shows signs of a Kierkegaardian conception of Christianity. Here he outlines the subjective nature of Christian belief in contrast to forms of objective knowing. He further explores a number of

---

[161]   Maurice Blanchot, *L'Espace littéraire*, Paris: Gallimard 1955. (English translation: *The Space of Literature*, trans. by Ann Smock, Lincoln and London: University of Nebraska Press 1982.)

[162]   Blanchot, *L'Espace littéraire*, p. 57; *The Space of Literature*, p. 61.

[163]   Blanchot, *L'Espace littéraire*, p. 103; *The Space of Literature*, p. 103.

[164]   Sylviane Agacinski, *Aparté: Conceptions et morts de Sören Kierkegaard*, Paris: Aubier, Flammarion 1977. (English translation: *Aparté: Conceptions and Deaths of Soren Kierkegaard*, trans. by Kevin Newmark, Gainsville: University Presses of Florida 1988.)

[165]   Sylviane Agacinski, *Critique de l'égocentrisme: l'événement de l'autre*, Paris: Galilée 1996.

[166]   Michel Henry, *C'est moi la vérité. Pour und philosophie du christianisme*, Paris: Éditions du Seuil 1996. (English translation: *I am the Truth: Toward a Philosophy of Christianity*, trans. by Susan Emanuel, Stanford: Stanford University Press 2003.)

paradoxes of Christianity. Henry also makes use of Kierkegaard's account of the Fall and anxiety in his *Incarnation: une philosophie de la chair* from 2000.[167]

VII. French Kierkegaard Scholarship Today

Kierkegaard studies in France have developed into a specialist field over the last few decades. In contrast to the French existentialists or postmodernists, who used Kierkegaard as a springboard in the service of a different intellectual program, the main profiles in actual French Kierkegaard scholarship have much of their intellectual identity bound up in Kierkegaard himself. While these scholars are not so well known internationally as the existentialists and postmodernists, they are, generally speaking, more thorough and careful readers of Kierkegaard's texts. They are in general more interested in understanding what Kierkegaard wrote than in appropriating his thought for another cause.

Through a series of works dating back to the 1960, Jacques Colette has for decades been one of the leading Kierkegaard experts in France. In 1964 appeared his introductory text *Kierkegaard. La difficulté d'être chrétien. Présentation et choix de textes*.[168] Four years later he published his *Kierkegaard, Chrétien incognito*.[169] While his early work focused primarily on the religious dimension of Kierkegaard's writings, Colette's later work took up Kierkegaard's philosophy. In 1972 appeared his *Histoire et absolu, essai sur Kierkegaard*,[170] which examines the relation between human existence and religious faith. Here Colette treats primarily the *Postscript* as well as the other main pseudonymous works, including *The Concept of Anxiety*, *The Sickness unto Death*, and the *Fragments*. Finally, in 1994 he published his *Kierkegaard et la non-philosophie*.[171]

The works of Nelly Viallaneix (d. 2005) have also played an important role in the French Kierkegaard research. Her most notable contributions include *L'Attente de la foi* from 1967[172] and *L'Unique devant Dieu* from 1974.[173] Also worthy of note is her two-volume *Écoute, Kierkegaard* from 1979, which was a dissertation at the Sorbonne.[174]

Another important figure in more recent Kierkegaard studies is Henri-Bernard Vergote (1931–96). The main representative of *Quellenforschung* in France, Vergote published his first main work in 1982 under the title *Sens et répétition: essai sur*

---

[167]   Michel Henry, *Incarnation: une philosophie de la chair*, Paris: Éditions du Seuil 2000, see §§ 36–9.

[168]   Jacques Colette, *Kierkegaard. La difficulté d'être chrétien. Présentation et choix de textes*, Paris: Éditions du Cerf 1964.

[169]   Jacques Colette, *Kierkegaard, Chrétien incognito*, Paris: Éditions du Cerf 1968.

[170]   Jacques Colette, *Histoire et absolu, essai sur Kierkegaard*, Paris: Éditions Desclée et Cie 1972.

[171]   Jacques Colette, *Kierkegaard et la non-philosophie*, Paris: Gallimard 1994.

[172]   Nelly Viallaneix, *L'Attente de la foi*, Geneva: Éditions Labor & Fides 1967.

[173]   Nelly Viallaneix, *L'Unique devant Dieu*, Paris: Éditions du Cerf 1974.

[174]   Nelly Viallaneix, *Écoute, Kierkegaard*, vols. 1–2, Paris: Éditions du Cerf 1979.

l'ironie kierkegaardienne.[175] This mammoth work was originally a dissertation at the University of Dijon completed in 1977. In 1993 he published an outstanding collection of primary texts from authors contemporary with Kierkegaard, such as Johan Ludvig Heiberg, Hans Lassen Martensen, Poul Martin Møller, and Frederik Christian Sibbern.[176] This collection featured his own translations as well as an extended introduction placing Kierkegaard in the context of the contemporary philosophical and theological debates of the day.

A student of Vergote, Hélène Politis continues the tradition of source-work research in France. She completed her dissertation at the University of Paris in 1993 with a long text entitled *Le discours philosophique selon Kierkegaard*.[177] This work remains unpublished. In 2002 appeared two books: *Kierkegaard* and *Le vocabulaire de Kierkegaard*.[178]

A major interpreter of Kierkegaard's theology in France is François Bousquet (b. 1947). He completed his dissertation on Kierkegaard's Christology at the University of Paris in 1996.[179] This was then substantially revised and published in 1999 under the title *Le Christ de Kierkegaard: devenir chrétien par passion d'exister, une question aux contemporains*.[180] He has also authored a three-volume work, *Temps et récit*, which appeared from 1983 to 85.[181]

One of the most prolific of the Francophone Kierkegaard scholars is André Clair (b. 1939), whose work focuses on the philosophical and literary dimension of Kierkegaard's thought. His first major work appeared in 1976 under the title *Pseudonymie et paradoxe, la pensée dialectique de Kierkegaard*.[182] This extensive work explores in detail Kierkegaard's notion of the paradox, not just in the *Fragments* but in the other pseudonymous works as well. Further, he explores the complicated constellation of problems surrounding Kierkegaard's different pseudonyms. In 1993 Clair published *Kierkegaard. Penser le singulier*,[183] which explores the notion of the single individual throughout Kierkegaard's pseudonymous writings. In 1997 he

[175]   Henri-Bernard Vergote, *Sens et répétition: essai sur l'ironie kierkegaardienne*, vols. 1–2, Paris: Éditions du Cerf 1982.
[176]   Henri-Bernard Vergote (trans. and ed.), *Lectures philosophiques de Søren Kierkegaard: Kierkegaard chez ses contemporains danois. Textes de J.L. Heiberg, H.L. Martensen, P.M. Møller*, Paris: Presses Universitaires de France 1993.
[177]   Hélène Politis, *Le discours philosophique selon Kierkegaard*, Ph.D. Thesis, Paris 1993.
[178]   Hélène Politis, *Kierkegaard*, Paris: Ellipses 2002; *Le vocabulaire de Kierkegaard*, Paris: Ellipses 2002.
[179]   François Bousquet, *Le paradoxe Jésus-Christ, Devenir chrétien par passion d'exister. Éléments pour une Christologie de Kierkegaard comme question aux contemporains*, Ph.D. Thesis, Paris 1996.
[180]   François Bousquet, *Le Christ de Kierkegaard: devenir chrétien par passion d'exister, une question aux contemporains*, Paris: Desclée 1999.
[181]   François Bousquet, *Temps et récit*, vols. 1–3, Paris: Seuil 1983–85.
[182]   André Clair, *Pseudonymie et paradoxe, la pensée dialectique de Kierkegaard*, Paris: Vrin 1976.
[183]   André Clair, *Kierkegaard. Penser le singulier*, Paris: Éditions du Cerf 1993.

published his work on Kierkegaard's ethics, *Kierkegaard. Existence et éthique.*[184] This book also explores many of Kierkegaard's most difficult concepts such as indirect communication, the paradox, and passion. Clair has recently returned to his interests in Kierkegaard's use of pseudonyms in his monograph from 2005, *Kierkegaard et autour.*[185]

Another prolific author in the Francophone literature is David Brézis (b. 1947). Since the beginning of the 1990s he has produced a series of important works on Kierkegaard's thought. In 1991 appeared his *Temps et présence: essai sur la conceptualité kierkegaardienne.*[186] Brézis is one of the main Francophone writers interested in the constellation of problems surrounding Kierkegaard and feminism. In 1999 he published *Kierkegaard et les figures de la paternité,*[187] which was followed in 2001 by *Kierkegaard et le féminin.*[188] Most recently Brézis has published a work on Kierkegaard's theory of subjectivity under the title *Kierkegaard ou la subjectivité en miroir.*[189]

Also of interest are a series of volumes of proceedings from the various conferences and seminars, which have taken place with some regularity over the past several decades. The forerunner of these more recent conferences was the aforementioned event organized by UNESCO in 1963, *Kierkegaard vivant*, which included figures such as Heidegger, Sartre, Jaspers, and Marcel.[190] From September 8 to 15, 1966, there took place in Copenhagen a conference, entitled "Kierkegaard et la Philosophie Contemporaine," which featured a number of Danish and foreign participants. The proceedings of this conference, which was hosted by the Department of Philosophy at the University of Copenhagen, were printed in the *Danish Yearbook of Philosophy* in 1971.[191] In 1997 the journal *Kairos* published a special issue with the proceedings from a joint Danish–French colloquium on Kierkegaard that took place in Toulouse from November 15 to 16, 1995.[192] Jacques Caron edited a volume of proceedings from a conference entitled *Kierkegaard aujourd'hui*, which took place at the Sorbonne in 1996.[193] From November 26 to 27, 1999, the Søren Kierkegaard Research Centre in Copenhagen hosted a Francophone seminar in Copenhagen.

---

[184]   André Clair, *Kierkegaard. Existence et éthique*, Paris: Presses Universitaires de France 1997.

[185]   André Clair, *Kierkegaard et autour*, Paris: Éditions du Cerf 2005.

[186]   David Brezis, *Temps et présence: essai sur la conceptualité kierkegaardienne*, Paris: Vrin, 1991.

[187]   David Brézis, *Kierkegaard et les figures de la paternité*, Paris: Éditions du Cerf 1999.

[188]   David Brézis, *Kierkegaard et le féminin*, Paris: Éditions du Cerf 2001.

[189]   David Brézis, *Kierkegaard ou la subjectivité en miroir*, Paris: Éditions Kimé 2004.

[190]   *Kierkegaard vivant. Colloque organisé par l'Unesco à Paris du 21 au 23 avril 1964*, Paris: Gallimard 1966.

[191]   *Kierkegaard et la Philosophie Contemporaine*, special number of *Danish Yearbook of Philosophy*, vol. 8, Copenhagen: Munksgaard 1971.

[192]   *Retour de Kierkegaard / Retour à Kierkegaard, Colloque franco-danois*, ed. by Henri-Bernard Vergote, Toulouse: Presses Universitaires du Mirail 1997 (*Kairos*, no. 10).

[193]   *Kierkegaard aujourd'hui: Actes du Colloque de la Sorbonne, 26 Octobre 1996*, ed. by Jacques Caron, Odense: Odense University Press and Grenoble 1998.

Three of the lectures from that seminar, given by Jacques Lafarge, Jacques Colette, and François Bousquet were subsequently published in the Centre's *Kierkegaard Studies. Yearbook* in 2000.[194] In 2005 there was an international colloquium, which took place at the Maison du Danemark in Paris. This event was organized by the French Kierkegaard Society and had as its theme "Kierkegaard et la critique du religieux."

Another part of the French philosophical landscape is a number of both scholarly and semi-popular intellectual journals and magazines. As the interest in Kierkegaard has increased, these journals have occasionally dedicated a special issue to him. The journal *Le Table Ronde* dedicated an issue to Kierkegaard in 1955 on the one hundredth anniversary of his death.[195] This issue contained some excerpts from Kierkegaard's journals and several articles of secondary literature. In 1963, the centennial year of Kierkegaard's birth, a special number of the Lausanne-based journal *Revue de théologie et de philosophie* was dedicated to Kierkegaard.[196] This issue included the two aforementioned articles by Ricoeur as well as three other pieces. In 1979 the journal *Les Études Philosophiques* published a special issue dedicated to Kierkegaard.[197] This work contains eight articles dedicated to Kierkegaard, three of which are authored by Danish scholars. The journal *Obliques* published another special issue in 1981.[198] It includes articles from leading French and Danish Kierkegaard scholars such as Henri-Bernard Vergote, André Clair, Henning Fenger, and Gregor Malantschuk. In 1989 there appeared a special issue of *Les Cahiers de Philosophie*, entitled *Kierkegaard: vingt-cinq études*.[199] This collection features both new and reprinted material from Danish and French scholars. In 2006 a special issue of the journal *Nordique* was dedicated to Kierkegaard's religious thinking.[200] Most recently in 2007 the popular *Magazine Litteraire* published a special issue on Kierkegaard.[201] Although this journal contains articles from recognized Kierkegaard

[194]   Jacques Lafarge, "L'Édition des Oeuvres complètes de Kierkegaard en français: contexte—historique—objectifs—conception—réalisation," *Kierkegaard Studies. Yearbook*, 2000, pp. 300–16. Jacques Colette, "Kierkegaard, L'Écrivan, vu à travers un regard particulier sur la literature française," *Kierkegaard Studies. Yearbook*, 2000, pp. 317–29. François Bousquet, "Le Motif de la foi chez Kierkegaard," *Kierkegaard Studies. Yearbook*, 2000, pp. 330–40.
[195]   *Le table ronde*, no. 95, 1955.
[196]   *Revue de théologie et de philosophie*, no. 4, 1963 (Lausanne) special issue "Soeren Kierkegaard 1813–1963."
[197]   *Les Études Philosophiques*, ed. by Pierre Aubenque, J. Brun and L. Millet, Paris: Presses Universitaires de France, April–June 1979 (special number: *Kierkegaard*).
[198]   *Kierkegaard*, ed. by Jean Brun, Nyons: Borderie 1981 (special number of *Obliques*).
[199]   *Les Cahiers de Philosophie*, nos. 8–9, 1989 (special issue: *Kierkegaard: vingt-cinq études*).
[200]   *Soren Kierkegaard et la critique du religieux*, special number of *Nordique*, vol. 10 (Spring) 2006.
[201]   *Søren Kierkegaard philosophe et dandy*, special number of *Magazine Litteraire*, April 2007 (articles by Jean-Louis Chrétien, Jacques Colette, Jacques Lafarge, and Vincent Delecroix).

scholars such as Jacques Colette and Jacques Lafarge, it regrettably continues to perpetuate the long-standing myth of Kierkegaard as a dandy.

The most recent major development in French Kierkegaard studies is the publication in 2007 of the first volume of Kierkegaard's journals and notebooks in French, *Journaux et cahiers de notes. Journaux AA–DD.*[202] This volume is the first of an ambitious and long-planned French edition of Kierkegaard's *Nachlaß*, based on the new Danish edition, *Søren Kierkegaards Skrifter*, produced by the Søren Kierkegaard Research Centre. This new French translation is the collaborative work of Else-Marie Jacquet-Tisseau and Anne-Marie Finnemann. This edition will doubtless help to open up the new Danish edition to the Francophone world, where it has until now made very little impact.

Kierkegaard studies in France represents one of the major traditions of reception, rivaling the German and Anglophone reception. In contrast to those other traditions, Kierkegaard has played a significant role in the work of many mainstream French philosophers and thinkers to this day. While there was a time when one could say this about the German reception, that period is for the most part long gone (although Kierkegaard remains important for some contemporary German philosophers such as Michael Theunissen). Kierkegaard has never been a welcome figure in mainstream Anglophone philosophy, where he has long been marginalized. Thus, one can say that Kierkegaard's writings are still very much alive in France, as they continue to inspire new generations of French thinkers.

In addition to this creative use of Kierkegaard's writings by productive French thinkers, as has been seen, there has also developed in recent years a specialized secondary literature dedicated to Kierkegaard in the Francophone world. This literature can be favorably compared with that found in other countries, such as Germany or the U.S.A., where there are strong and established traditions of Kierkegaard studies. However, in contrast to other traditions of Kierkegaard reception, where there has been a degree of international cooperation, the French reception has been more inward-looking, preferring to be in dialogue with other French scholars instead of extending their work to include German, Anglophone, or Danish scholarship. It is to be hoped that in the coming years with the growth of globalization that the French researchers will become better integrated into the larger international community of Kierkegaard scholars. The French world of Kierkegaard studies has much to teach the rest of the world, and it would itself be profoundly enriched in turn by better contacts, particularly to the Danish, German, and Anglophone research.

---

[202]   *Journaux et cahiers de notes. Journaux AA–DD*, trans. by Else-Marie Jacquet-Tisseau and Anne-Marie Finnemann, Paris: Éditions Fayard / Éditions de l'Orante 2007.

Bibliography

by Katalin Nun

I. French Translations of Kierkegaard's Works

En quoi l'homme de génie diffère-t-il de l'apôtre? Traité éthique-religieux, trans. by Johannes Gøtzsche, Copenhagen: Hagerup and Paris: Nilsson 1886.

"Fragments d'un journal," trans. by Jean J. Gateau, *Commerce*, no. 12, 1927, pp. 153–64; pp. 165–202.

"Intermèdes," trans. by Lucien Maury, *La nouvelle revue française*, no. 167, 1927, pp. 192–209.

"Le journal du séducteur," trans. by Jean J. Gateau, *Biblioteque universelle et Revue de Genéve*, vol. 2 (December) 1929, pp. 714–43.

Le journal du séducteur, trans. and introduced by Jean J. Gateau, Paris: Stock, Delamain & Boutelleau 1929 (*Le cabinet cosmopolite, série scandinave*, vol. 43).

Traité du désespoir. (La maladie mortelle), trans. by Knud Ferlov and Jean J. Gateau, Paris: Gallimard 1932 (several later editions).

In vino veritas, trans. by André Babelon and C. Lund, introduced by d'André Babelon, Paris: Éditions du Cavalier 1933 (2nd ed., 1992).

La Répétition. Essai d'expérience psychologique par Constantin Constantius, trans. by Paul-Henri Tisseau, Paris: Alcan 1933 (several later editions).

Le Banquet (In vino veritas), trans. by Paul-Henri Tisseau, Paris: Félix Alcan 1933.

"Fragments religieux," trans. by Paul-Henri Tisseau, *Le Semeur*, July 1834 and January 1935.

Le Souverain sacrificateur, le Péager, la Pécheresse, troi discours pour la communion du vendredi, trans. by Paul-Henri Tisseau, Bazoges-en-Pareds: privately published 1934.

Pour un examen de conscience, à mes contemporains, trans. by Paul-Henri Tisseau, Bazoges-en-Pareds: privately published 1934.

"Textes de Kierkegaard," trans. by Jean J. Gateau, *Foi et vie. Revue mensuelle*, no. 64 (August–September), 1934, pp. 678–94.

"Textes de Kierkegaard," Paul-Henri Tisseau, *Foi et vie. Revue mensuelle*, no. 64 (August–September), 1934, pp. 695–711.

Ce que nous apprennent les lis des champs et les oiseaux du ciel, trans. by Paul-Henri Tisseau, Paris: Félix Alcan 1935.

Crainte et Tremblement. Lyrique-dialectique, par Johannes de Silentio, trans. by Paul-Henri Tisseau, introduced by Jean Wahl, Paris: Fernand Aubier; Éditions Montaigne 1935.

Le concept de l'angoisse, trans. by Jean J. Gateau and Knud Ferlov, Paris: Gallimard 1935 (several later editions).

Le Concept d'angoisse. Simple méditation psychologique pour servir d'introduction au problème dogmatique du péché originel, par Vigilius Haufniensis, trans. by Paul–Henri Tisseau, introduced by Jean Wahl, Paris: Félix Alcan 1935.

Le Droit de mourir pour la vérité. Le Génie et l'apôtre, trans. by Paul-Henri Tisseau, Bazoges-en-Pareds: privately published 1935.

Les lis des champs et les oiseaux de ciel, trans. by Paul-Henri Tisseau, Paris: Alcan 1935.

La Pureté du coeur, trans. by Paul-Henri Tisseau, Bazoges-en-Pareds: privately published 1936.

L'Ecole du christianisme (Exercice dans le christianisme), par Anti-Climacus, trans. by Paul-Henri Tisseau, Bazoges-en-Pareds: privately published 1936.

"Existence et réalite," trans. by Paul Petit, *Mesures*, no. 4 (October), 1937, pp. 74–101.

Les Riens philosophiques, trans. by Jean J. Gateau and Knud Ferlov, Paris: Gallimard 1937 (2nd ed., 1969).

L'Evangile des souffrances, trans. by Paul-Henri Tisseau, Bazoges-en-Pareds: privately published 1937.

Prières, trans. by Paul-Henri Tisseau, Bazoges-en-Pareds: privately published 1937.

Prières et fragments sur la prière. Extraits du Journal, trans. by Paul-Henri Tisseau, Bazoges-en-Pareds: privately published 1937.

Antigone. Réflexion du tragique antique dans le tragique moderne. Un essai dans l'aspiration fragmentaire, trans. by Pierre Klossowski, Paris: Éditions "Les Nouvelles lettres" 1938.

Études kierkegaardiennes (contains extracts from the journals from 1834–39 and 1849–54), ed. by Jean Wahl, Paris: F. Aubier 1938.

"Le penseur subjectif. Sa tâche, sa forme, c'est-à-dire son style," trans. by Paul Petit, *Nouvelle revue française*, vol. 27, no. 306, 1939, pp. 412–25.

"Possibilité et réalité, esthétique et éthique," trans. by Paul Petit, *Revue de métaphysique et de morale*, vol. 46, no. 1, 1939, pp. 1–28.

L'alternative. Un fragment de vie. Publié par Victor Eremita. Deuxième partie: Contenant les papiers de B: lettres à A, trans. by Paul-Henri Tisseau, Bazoges-en-Pareds: privately published 1940.

Point de vue explicatif de mon oeuvre: communication directe, rapport historique, trans. by Paul-Henri Tisseau, Bazoges-en-Pareds: privately published 1940.

Journal. Extraits 1. 1834–1846, trans. by Jean J. Gateau and Knud Ferlov, Paris: Gallimard 1941 (2nd ed., 1963).

Post-scriptum aux Miettes philosophiques, trans. by Paul Petit, Paris: Mesmil 1941 (several later editions).

Coupable? Non coupable? Une histoire de la souffrance: expérience psychologique par Frater Taciturnus, trans. by Paul-Henri Tisseau, Bazoges-en-Pareds: P.-H. Tisseau 1942.

Journal. Extraits, vols. 1–5, trans. by Jean J. Gateau and Knud Ferlov, Paris: Gallimard 1942–61.

Ou bien...ou bien, trans. by F. Prior, O. Prior and M.H. Guignot, Paris: Gallimard 1943 (several later editions).

Vie et règne de l'amour, trans. by Pierre Villadsen, Paris: Aubier 1945.

La maladie à la mort (Le concept de désespoir), trans. by Paul-Henri Tisseau, Bazoges-en-Pareds: privately published 1947.

Les miettes philosophiques, trans. by Paul Petit, Paris: Éditions du Livre français 1947.

L'Évangile des souffrances, trans. by Paul-Henri Tisseau, Bazoges-en-Pareds: privately published 1947.

Étapes sur le chemin de la vie, trans. by F. Prior and M.H. Guignot, Paris: Gallimard 1948.

L'instant, trans. by Paul-Henri Tisseau, Bazoges-en-Pareds: privately published 1948.

Deux discours de préparation à la Saint–Cène, trans. by Paul-Henri Tisseau, Bazoges-en-Pareds: privately published 1949.

Lettres à Regine Olsen. Lettres à Emil Boesen. Fragments du journal sur les fiançailles et autres documents, trans. by Paul-Henri Tisseau, Bazoges-en-Pareds: privately published 1949.

Sur une tombe. Médiation sur la mort, trans. by Paul-Henri Tisseau, Bazoges-en-Pareds: privately published 1949.

Crainte et tremblement, trans. by Paul-Henri Tisseau, Paris: Aubier 1952.

Discours chrétiens, trans. by Paul-Henri Tisseau, Neuchâtel and Paris: Delachaux et Niestlé 1952.

Kierkegaard. Sa vie, son oeuvre, avec un exposé de sa philosophie, ed. by Pierre Mesnard, Paris: Presses Universitaires de France 1954 (*Les Philosophes*, vol. 34) (several later editions). (This work contains under "Textes choisis" various excerpts from a number of Kierkegaard's texts, pp. 41–93.)

"Pages du journal 1848–1855. Le politique," trans. by Paul-Henri Tisseau, *La Table Ronde*, no. 95, 1955, pp. 43–5.

"Pages du journal 1848–1855. La tâche à l'horizon," trans. by Paul-Henri Tisseau, *La Table Ronde*, no. 95, 1955, pp. 46–47.

Journal. Extraits 2. 1846–1849, trans. by Jean J. Gateau and Knud Ferlov, Paris: Gallimard 1954.

Journal. Extraits 3. 1849–1850, trans. by Jean J. Gateau and Knud Ferlov, Paris: Gallimard 1955.

Lettres des fiançailles, trans. by Marguerite Grimault, Paris: Falaize 1956.

Journal. Extraits 4. 1850–1853, trans. by Jean J. Gateau and Knud Ferlov, Paris: Gallimard 1957.

Journal. Extraits 5. 1854–1855, trans. by Jean J. Gateau and Knud Ferlov, Paris: Gallimard 1961.

L'Existence, trans. by Paul-Henri Tisseau, ed. by Jean Brun, Paris: Presses Universitaires de France 1962 (2nd revised ed., 1967).

Discours édifiants: La Pécheresse. De l'Immutabilité de Dieu, trans. by Jacques Colette, Paris: Desclée, de Brouwer 1962.

Kierkegaard par lui-même, ed. by Marguerite Grimault, Paris: Éditions du Seuil 1962.

Le Journal du séducteur, trans. by Jean J. Gateau, Paris: Club français du livre 1962.

Diapsalmata, trans. by Paul-Henri Tisseau, Paris: R. Morel 1963.

Kierkegaard. Présentation, choix de textes, bibliographie, trans. by Paul-Henri Tisseau, ed. by Georges Gusdorf, Paris: Seghers 1963.

L'École du christianisme, trans. by Paul-Henri Tisseau, introduced by Jean Brun, Paris: Perrin 1963.

La Difficulté d'être chrétien. Présentation et choix de textes, ed. by Jacques Colette, Paris: Éditions du Cerf 1964.

Le Journal du séducteur, trans. by F. Prior, O. Prior and Marie-Henriette Guignot, Paris: Gallimard 1965.

Oeuvres Complètes, trans. and ed. by Paul-Henri Tisseau and Else-Marie Jacquet-Tisseau, vols. 1–20, Paris: Éditions de l'Orante 1966–86:

— vol. 1, *Quatre articles. Notre littérature de presse. Des papiers d'un homme encore en vie. La lutte entre l'ancienne et la nouvelle cave à savon. Prédication de séminaire (1834–1841)* (1984).

— vol. 2, *Le Concept d'ironie constamment rapporté à Socrates. Confession publique. Johannes Climacus ou De omnibus dubitandum est (1841–1843)* (1975).

— vol. 3, *L'Alternative I (1843)* (1970).

— vol. 4, *L'Alternative II. Trois articles de Fædrelandet. Post–scriptum à l'Alternative (1843–1844)* (1970).

— vol. 5, *La Répétition. Crainte et tremblement (1843)* (1972).

— vol. 6, *Dix-huit discours édifiants. Épreuve homilétique (1843–1844)* (1979).

— vol. 7, *Miettes Philosophiques. Le Concept d'angoisse. Préfaces (1844)* (1973).

— vol. 8, *Trois discours sur des circonstances supposés. Quatre articles. Un compte rendu littéraire (1845–1846)* (1979).

— vol. 9, *Stades sur le chemin de la vie (1845)* (1978).

— vols. 10–11, *Post-scriptum définitif et non scientifique aux miettes philosophiques (1846)* (1977).

— vol. 12, *Le Livre sur Adler* (1983).

— vol. 13, *Discours édifiants à divers points de vue (1847)* (1966).

— vol. 14, *Les Oeuvres de l'amour. La dialectique de la communication éthique et éthico-religieuse* (1847) (1980).

— vol. 15, *Discours Chrétiens. La Crise et une crise dans la vie d'une actrice. Monsieur Phister (1848)* (1981).

— vol. 16, *Point de vue explicatif de mon oeuvre d'écrivain. Deux petits traités éthico-religieux. La maladie á la mort. Six discours (1848–1849)* (1971).

— vol. 17, *L'École du christianisme. La neutralité armée. Un article. Sur mon oeuvre d'écrivain (1849–1851)* (1982).

— vol. 18, *Quatre discours. Pour un examen de conscience. Jugez vous mêmes (1849–1852)* (1966).

— vol. 19, *Vingt et un articles de Faedrelandet. Cela doit être dit, Que cela soit donc dit. Comment Christ juge le christianisme officiel. L'Instant (1854–1855)* (1982).

— vol. 20, *Index terminologique. Principaux concepts de Kierkegaard* (by Gregor Malantschuk, trans. and revised by Else-Marie Jacquet-Tisseau). *Index des noms propres, chronologie, tables* (1986).

Le Stade esthétique. Le Journal du séducteur. "In vino veritas." Précédé de Kierkegaard et l'érotisme, trans. and ed. by Marguerite Grimault, Paris: Union générale d'éditions 1966.

Discours chrétiens, trans. by Paul-Henri Tisseau, Neuchâtel and Paris: Delachaux et Niestlé 1967.

L'Attente de la foi. Discours édifiant pour le Jour de l'an, trans. and ed. by Nelly Viallaneix, Genève: Éditions Labor et fides and Paris: Librairie protestante 1967.

Chrétien incognito. La Neutralité armée, trans. and by Jacques Colette, Paris: Éditions du Cerf 1968.

Hâte-toi d'écouter. Quatre Discours édifiants, trans. and by Jacques Colette, Paris: Aubier 1970.

Discours chrétiens. 3, Des Pensées qui attaquent dans le dos, trans. by Paul-Henri Tisseau, Neuchâtel and Paris: Delachaux et Niestlé 1971.

Étapes sur le chemin de la vie, trans. by F. Prior and Marie-Henriette Guignot, Paris: Gallimard 1979.

La reprise, trans. and ed. by Nelly Viallaneix, Paris: Flammarion 1990.

Ou bien, ou bien. La reprise. Stades sur le chemin de la vie. La maladie à la mort, trans. by Paul-Henri Tisseau and Else-Marie Jacquet-Tisseau, Paris: R. Laffont 1993.

Johannes Climacus ou Il faut douter de tout, trans. by Else-Marie Jacquet-Tisseau, ed. by Jacques Lafarge, Paris: Payot-Rivages 1997.

Crainte et tremblement. Lyrique dialectique de Johannès de Silentio, trans. by Charles Le Blanc, Paris: Payot & Rivages 1999.

Dieu et la pécheresse. Deux discours édifiants, trans. by Jacques Colette, Paris: Desclée de Brouwer 1999.

In vino veritas, Castelnau-le-Lez: Climats 1999.

Kierkegaard (a selection of texts), ed. by Rémy Hebding, Paris: Desclée de Brouwer 1999.

L'éternité dans le temps Six discours, trans. by Paul-Henri Tisseau and Else-Marie Jacquet-Tisseau, Paris: Les Bergers et les Mages 2000.

Correspondance, trans. by Anne-Christine Habbard, Paris: Éditions des Syrtes 2003.

La répétition. Essai de psychologie expérimentale, trans. by Jacques Privat, Paris: Payot & Rivages 2003.

La dialectique de la communication éthique et éthico-religieuse, trans. by Else-Marie Jacquet-Tisseau, ed. by Jacques Lafarge, Paris: Payot & Rivages 2004.

Diapsalmata, trans. by Paul-Henri Tisseau, revised by Else-Marie Jacquet-Tisseau, ed. by Jacques Lafarge, Paris: Éditions Allia 2005.

Post-scriptum aux Miettes philosophiques, trans. by Vincent Delecroix, Paris: Ellipses 2005.

Exercice en christianisme, trans. by Vincent Delecroix, Paris: le Félin 2006.

Journaux et cahiers de notes. Journaux AA–DD, trans. by Else-Marie Jacquet-Tisseau and Anne-Marie Finnemann, Paris: Éditions Fayard / Éditions de l'Orante 2007.

II. Selected Secondary Literature on Kierkegaard in France

Accard Couchoud, Marie-Thérèse, *Kierkegaard ou l'Instant paradoxal: Recherches sur l'instant psychotique*, Paris: Éditions du Cerf 1981.

Adam, Rodolphe, *Lacan et Kierkegaard*, Paris: Presses Universitaires de France 2005.

Agacinski, Sylviane, *Aparté: Conceptions et morts de Sören Kierkegaard*, Paris: Aubier, Flammarion 1977.

— *Critique de l'égocentrisme: l'événement de l'autre*, Paris: Galilée 1996.

Alain [i.e., E. Charlier], "Difficultés de Kierkegaard," *La Table Ronde*, no. 95, 1955, pp. 88–90.

Alexander, Ian W., "La philosophie existentialiste en France. Ses sources et ses problèmes fondamentaux," *French Studies. A Quarterly Review* (Oxford), vol. 1, no. 2, 1947, pp. 95–114.

Andersen, Georges, "Le martyre de Kierkegaard, éclairé par les flambeaux de son jubilé," *Combat*, November 10, 1955.

Anne, Chantal, *L'amour dans la pensée de Søren Kierkegaard: pseudonymie et polyonymie. Essai*, Paris: l'Harmattan 1993.

Arnou, René, "L'existentialisme à la maniére de Kierkegaard et J.P. Sartre," *Gregorianum*, vol. 27, 1946, pp. 63–88.

Avrain, Bruno, *Kierkegaard et Freud*, Paris: Éditions Alba nova 1988.

Basch, Victor, "Un individualiste religieux: Soeren Kierkegaard," *La Grande Revue*, vol. 23, 1903, pp. 281–320 (reprinted in his *Essais d'esthétique, de philosophie et de littératur*, Paris: Alcan 1934, pp. 268–315).

Bellaiche–Zacharie, Alain, *Don et retrait dans la pensée de Kierkegaard: melancholia*, Paris, Budapest and Torino: l'Harmattan 2002.

Bellesort, André, "Le Crépuscule d'Elseneur," *Revue des deux mondes*, no. 1, 1914, pp. 49–83.

— *Le Crépuscule d'Elseneur*, Paris: Perrin 1926.

Belmond, S., "Á propos de 'Philosophie existentielle,' " *Études franciscaines*, vol. 34, no. 289, 1939, pp. 676–81.

Benito Chabrier, Nathalie, *Critique, théorie et pratique de l'éducation selon Søren Kierkegaard*, Villeneuve d'Ascq: Presses Universitaires du Septentrion 2002.

Berberich, Gerta, *La notion métaphysique de la personne chez Kant et Kierkegard*, Fribourg: S. Paul 1942.

Bespaloff, Rachel, *Cheminements et carrefours. Julien Green, André Malraux, Gabriel Marcel, Kierkegaard, Chestov devant Nietzsche*, Paris: Vrin 1938, pp. 101–44 ("Notes sur 'La repetition' de Kierkegaard"); pp. 145–88 ("En marge de 'Crainte et tremblement' de Kierkegaard").

Blin, Georges, "L'alternative kierkegaardienne," *Les Temps modernes*, vol. 1, no. 4, 1946, pp. 737–50.

Blum, Jean, "Pierre-Joseph Proudhon et Søren Kierkegaard," *La Revue scandinave*, no. 4 (April), 1911, pp. 276–87.

Boisdeffre, Pierre de, "Kierkegaard et Kafka," *Revue de Paris*, no. 7, 1955, pp. 138–42.

Bosc, Jean, "La pensée protestante. Kierkegaard," *Foi et vie*, no. 80 (March), 1936, pp. 184–7.

Bousquet, François, "La vérité est de devenir sujet. La vérité comme question éthique chez Kierkegaard," in Bousquet et alii, *La vérité*, Paris: Beauchesne 1983, pp. 157–78.

— *Le paradoxe Jésus-Christ, Devenir chrétien par passion d'exister. Éléments pour une Christologie de Kierkegaard comme question aux contemporains*, Ph.D. Thesis, Paris 1996.

— *Le Christ de Kierkegaard: devenir chrétien par passion d'exister, une question aux contemporains*, Paris: Desclée 1999.

— "Le Motif de la foi chez Kierkegaard," *Kierkegaard Studies. Yearbook*, 2000, pp. 330–40.

Boutonier, Juliette, *L'Angoisse. Contribution à la psychologie et la métaphysique de l'angoisse*, Paris: Presses Universitaires de France 1945.

Boyer, Régis and Jean-Marie Paul (eds.), *Kierkegaard, la découverte de l'existence*, Nancy: Centre de recherches germaniques et scandinaves de l'Université de Nancy II 1990 (*Bibliothèque Le Texte et l'idée*, vol. 1).

Breuil, Roger, "La génie littéraire de la bible," *Réforme*, vol. 6 (December), 1947.

Brézis, David, *Temps et présence: essai sur la conceptualité kierkegaardienne*, Paris: J. Vrin 1991.

— *Kierkegaard et les figures de la paternité*, Paris: Éditions du Cerf 1999.

— *Kierkegaard et le féminin*, Paris: Éditions du Cerf 2001.

— *Kierkegaard ou la subjectivité en miroir*, Paris: Éditions Kimé 2004.

Brien, Abbé, "De l'univers de S. Thomas à l'univers de Kierkegaard," *Travaux et documents*, vol. 6 (May), 1946, pp. 47–8.

Brouillard, Henri, "La foi d'après Kierkegaard," *Bulletin de littérature ecclésiastique*, vol. 48, 1947, pp. 19–30.

Brun, Jean (ed.), *Kierkegaard* (special number of the *Obliques*), Nyons: Borderie 1981.

Burnier, André, "La pensée de Kierkegaard," *Revue de théologie et de philosophie*, vol. 31, 1943, pp. 101–13.

Caron, Jacques, *Angoisse et communication chez S. Kierkegaard*, Odense: Odense University Press 1992 (*Odense University Studies in Scandinavian Languages and Literatures*, vol. 26).

— (ed.), *Kierkegaard aujourd'hui: Actes du colloque de la Sorbonne, Paris, 26 octobre 1996*, Odense: Odense University Press and Grenoble: diff. EILUG, Université Stendhal 1998.

Cauly, Olivier, *Kierkegaard*, Paris: Presses Universitaires de France 1991 (2nd revised ed., 1996).

Chaplain, Denise, *Études sur In vivo veritas de Kierkegaard*, Paris: Les Belles Lettres 1964.

Charles, Monique, *Lettres d'amour au philosophe de ma vie*, Paris: Desclée de Brouwer 1998.

— *Kierkegaard: atmosphère d'angoisse et de passion*, Paris: l'Harmattan 2007.

Clair, André, *Pseudonymie et paradoxe, la pensée dialectique de Kierkegaard*, Paris: Vrin 1976.

— *Éthique et humanisme. Essai sur la modernité*, Paris: Éditions du Cerf 1989.

— *Kierkegaard. Penser le singulier*, Paris: Éditions du Cerf 1993.

— *Kierkegaard. Existence et éthique*, Paris: Presses Universitaires de France 1997.

— *Kierkegaard et autour*, Paris: Éditions du Cerf 2005.

Colette, Jacques, "Chronique kierkegaardienne," *Revue Nouvelle*, vol. 37, 1963, pp. 181–8.

— *Kierkegaard. La difficulté d'être chrétien. Présentation et choix de textes*, Paris: Éditions du Cerf 1964.

— *Kierkegaard, Chrétien incognito*, Paris: Éditions du Cerf 1968.

— "Bulletin d'histoire de la philosophie: Kierkegaard," *Revue des Sciences philosophiques et theologiques*, vol. 54, 1970, pp. 654–80.

— "Études kierkegaardiennes recentes, *Revue Philosophique de Louvain*, vol. 70, 1972, pp. 116–30.

— *Histoire et absolu, essai sur Kierkegaard*, Paris: Éditions Desclée et Cie 1972.

— *Kierkegaard et la non-philosophie*, Paris: Gallimard 1994.

— "Kierkegaard, L'Écrivan, vu à travers un regard particulier sur la literature française," *Kierkegaard Studies. Yearbook*, 2000, pp. 317–29.

Congar, M.J., "Bulletin d'histoire des doctrines chrétiennes: Kierkegaard," *Revue de sciences philosophiques et théologiques*, vol. 22, no. 3, 1933, pp. 551–2.

— L'actualité de Kierkegaard," *La Vie Intellectuelle*, no. 1 (November 25), 1934, pp. 9–36.

Cornu, Michel, *Kierkegaard et la communication de l'existence*, Lausanne: Éditions L'Age d'homme 1972.

Coster, Sylvain de, "La crise de l'existentialisme," *Revue internationale de philosophie* (Bruxelles), vol. 1, 1939, pp. 398–402.

Delacroix, Henri, "Søren Kierkegaard. Le christianisme absolu á travers le paradox et le désespoir," *Revue de métaphysique et de morale*, vol. 8, no. 4, 1900, pp. 459–84.

Delecroix, Vincent, *Singulière philosophie: essai sur Kierkegaard*, Paris: le Félin 2006.

Deleuran, Victor, *Esquisse d'une étude sur Soeren Kierkegaard*, Paris: Charles Noblet 1897.

Derrida, Jacques, *Donner la Mort*, Paris: Galilée 1992.

Diné, Lyliane, *Le choix de soi: les enjeux de la décision kierkegaardienne*, Nantes: Éditions Amalthée 2005.

Donier, R., " 'Crainte et Tremblement' par Søren Kierkegaard," *La Vie Intellectuelle*, no. 10, 1935, pp. 374–82.

Douchevsky, Alain, *Médiation et singularité: au seuil d'une ontologie avec Pascal et Kierkegaard*, Paris and Montreal: Éditions l'Harmattan 1997.

Dupré, Louis, "La dialectique de l'acte de foi chez Soeren Kierkegaard," *Revue philosophique de Louvain*, vol. 54, 1956, pp. 418–55.

Elsen, Claude, "La mythe du séducteur," *La Table Ronde*, no. 95, 1955, pp. 79–81.

Farago, France, *Kierkegaard: l'épreuve de soi*, Paris: Michel Houdiard 2002.

— *Comprendre Kierkegaard*, Paris: A. Colin 2005.

Fondane, Benjamin, "Héraclite le Pauvre, ou necesité de Kierkegaard," *Les Cahiers du Sud*, vol. 22 (November), 1935, pp. 757–70.

— *La conscience malheureuse*, Paris: Éditions Denoël 1936, pp. 169–98 ("Martin Heidegger sur les routes de Kierkegaard et de Dostoievski"); pp. 199–227 ("Soeren Kierkegaard et la catégorie du secret"); pp. 229–57 ("Chestov et Kierkegaard et le serpent" (with the same title originally published, *Les Cahiers du Sud*, vol. 21, August 1934, pp. 534–54).

— "Le lundi existentiel et le dimanche de l'histoire," in *L'existence. Essais par Albert Camus, Benjamin Fondane...*, Paris: Gallimard 1945, pp. 25–53.

— *Rencontres avec Léon Chestov*, Paris: Plasma 1982.

Gandillac, Maurice de, "Kierkegaard, le Pacal du Nord," *La revue universelle*, vol. 59, no. 15, 1934, pp. 371–6.

— "Kierkegaard et l'objectif," *La Nef*, vol. 2, no. 12, 1945, pp. 117–21.

Gardet, Louis, "Pour une méthode d'histoire de la philosophie. À propos d'un livre sur Kierkegaard," *Revue Thomiste*, vol. 49, no. 3, 1949, pp. 589–601.

Gateau, Jean J., "Soeren Kierkegaard (1813–1855)," *Bibliotéque universelle et Revue de Geneve*, December 1929, pp. 700–13.

Gignoux, Victor, "La philosophie de Kierkegaard," in *Cours de philosophie*, vols. 1–3, Paris: Francis Lefebvre 1947–1950, vol. 3, *La philosophie existentielle*, pp. 10–13.

Gramont, Jérôme de, *Le discours de la vie: trois essais sur Platon, Kierkegaard et Nietzsche*, Paris, Budapest and Torino: l'Harmattan 2001.

Grimault, Marguerite, *Kierkegaard par lui-même*, Paris: Éditions du Seuil 1962.

Guiraud, Paul, *Rencontre de Kierkegaard*, Ph.D. Thesis, Geneva 1942.

Gusdorf, Georges, *Kierkegaard*, Paris: Éditions Seghers 1963.

Hebding, Rémy, *Kierkegaard*, Paris: Desclée de Brouwer 1999.

Henein, Georges and Magdi Wahba (eds.), *Vues sur Kierkegaard*, Cairo: La Part du sable 1955.

Heinrich, Françoise, *Kierkegaard: le devenir chrétien: humanisme et religion*, Limoges: PULIM 1997.

Hoffmann, Raoul, *Kierkegaard et la certitude réligieuse. Esquisse biografique et critique*, Geneva: Romet 1907.

Jeannine, Bernard, "Søren Kierkegaard, le moraliste danois," *La Nouvelle Revue*, no. 2 (November–December), 1893, pp. 578–96.

Jolivet, Régis, *Introduction à Kierkegaard*, Paris, Abbaye Saint-Wandrille: Éditions de Fontenelle 1946.

— *Les doctrines existentialistes de Kierkegaard à J.P. Sartre*, Paris, Abbaye Saint-Wandrille: Éditions de Fontenelle 1948.

— "Le problème de la religion de Kierkegaard," *Revue de Philosophie de Louvain*, vol. 47, no. 13, 1949, pp. 137–42.

— "Kierkegaard et la liberté de choix," *Orbis litterarum* (Copenhagen), nos. 1–2, 1955, pp. 107–11.

— "La liberté selon Kierkegaard," *Témoignages*, no. 50, 1955, pp. 359–369.

— *Aux sources de l'existentialisme chrétien, Kierkegaard*, Paris: Éditions Fayard 1958.

Juranville, Alain, *La philosophie comme savoir de l'existence*, Paris: Presses Universitaires de France 2000.

Kierkegaard vivant. Colloque organisé par l'Unesco à Paris du 21 au 23 avril 1964, Paris: Gallimard 1966.

Kim, Jean-Jacques, "Kierkegaard et Kleist, poètes tragiques," *La Table Ronde*, no. 95, 1955, pp. 82–5.

Klossowski, Pierre, "Don Juan selon Kierkegaard," *Acéphale*, vol. 1, nos. 3–4, pp. 27–32.

— *Sade mon prochain (suivi de deux essais sur Kierkegaard et Georges Bataille)*, Paris: Éditions du Seuil 1947.

La Chesnais, P.G., "Ibsen disciple de Kierkegaard?" *Edda*, vol. 34, no. 3, 1934, pp. 355–410.

Langlois, Jean, "Essai sur 'Crainte et tremblement' de Soeren Kierkegaard," *Sciences ecclésiastiques*, vol. 6, no. 1, 1954, pp. 25–50.

Laporte, André, *Trois témoins de la liberté: Erasme de Rotterdam, Martin Luther, Sören Kierkegaard*, Thèse bach. théol, Geneva: n.p. 1949.

Lavelle, Louis, "Le vrai visage de Kierkegaard," *Le Table Ronde*, no. 95, 1955, pp. 73–5.

Le Blanc, Charles, *Kierkegaard*, Paris: les Belles lettres 1998.

Lenoir, Raymond, "Kierkegaard et la musique," *Revue d'esthétiques*, vol. 2, 1949, pp. 416–21.

Lévinas, Emmanuel, *Noms propres*, Paris: Librairie générale française 1976.

Lhote, Aude-Marie, *La Notion de pardon chez Kierkegaard ou Kierkegaard lecteur de l'Épître aux Romains*, Paris: J. Vrin 1983.

Lilienfeld, André de, *Á la rencontre de Kierkegaard*, Liège: La sixaine 1947.

Lubac, Henri de, *Le drame de l'humanisme athée*, Paris: Éditions Spes 1944.

Malaquais, Jean, *Sören Kierkegaard. Foi et Paradoxe*, Paris: Union générale d'éditions 1971.

— *La dialectique du moi absolu chez Sören Kierkegaard*, n.p. [1960].

Marchal, Georges, "Kierkegaard et le protestantisme," *Le Table Ronde*, no. 95, 1955, pp. 66–72.

Maritain, Jacques, *Court traité de l'existence et de l'existante*, Paris: Hartmann 1947.

Marquet, Jean-François, *Miroirs de l'identité. La littérature hantée par la philosophie*, Paris: Hermann 1996.

Mesnard, Pierre, *Le vrai visage de Kierkegaard*, Paris: Beauchesne et ses fils 1948.

— "Kierkegaard et l'utilisation existentielle de la figure d'Abraham," *Cahiers Sioniens*, vol. 5, no. 2, 1951, pp. 121–40.

— *Kierkegaard. Sa vie, son oeuvre avec un exposé de sa philosophie*, Paris: Presses Universitaires de France 1954.

— "Comment definir la philosophie de Kierkegaard?" *Revue d'histoire et de philosophie religieuses*, vol. 35, no. 4, 1955, pp. 393–403.

— "La catégorie de TRAGIQUE est-elle absente de l'oeuvre et de la pensée du Kierkegaard?" *Orbis litterarum* (Copenhagen), vol. 10, 1955, nos. 1–2, pp. 178–90.

Message, Jacques (ed.), *Kierkegaard. Vingi-cinq études*, Lille: Cahiers de philosophie 1989.

Mounier, Emmanuel, *Introduction aux existentialismes*, Paris: Gallimard 1962 [1947].

Muret, Maurice, "Un précurseur d'Henrik Ibsen. Sören Kierkegaard," *La Revue de Paris*, vol. 8, no. 13, 1901, pp. 98–122.

Nguyên, Joseph Van Tuyên, *Foi et existence selon S. Kierkegaard*, Paris: Aubier-Montaigne 1971.

Petit, Paul, "Fragment d'une lettre sur Kierkegaard," *Deucalion. Cahiers de philosophie*, vol. 1, 1940, pp. 245–48.

Politis, Hélène, *Le discours philosophique selon Kierkegaard*, Ph.D. Thesis, Paris 1993.

— *Kierkegaard*, Paris: Ellipses 2002.

— *Le vocabulaire de Kierkegaard*, Paris: Ellipses 2002.

Preiss, Th., "À propos de Kierkegaard," *Revue d'histoire et de philosophie religieuses*, vol. 16, no. 1, 1936, pp. 46–64.

Rennes, Jacques, *Libre humanisme. Réponse à Pascal, Kierkegaard et aux existentialistes*, St. Vaast-la-Houge: Manche 1947.

Ricoeur, Paul, "Kierkegaard et le mal," *Revue de théologie et de philosophie*, no. 4, 1963, pp. 292–302 (reprinted in *Les Cahiers de philosophie*, nos. 8–9, 1989 (special issue, *Kierkegaard, Vingt-cinq etudes*), pp. 271–283).

— "Philosopher après Kierkegaard," *Revue de théologie et de philosophie*, vol. 4, 1963, pp. 303–16 (reprinted in *Les Cahiers de philosophie*, nos. 8–9, 1989 (special issue, *Kierkegaard, Vingt-cinq etudes*), pp. 285–300).

Rilliet, Jean, "Kierkegaard et Socrate," *Revue de théologie et de philosophie*, vol. 31, 1943, pp. 114–20.

Romain, Willy-Paul, "Søren Kierkegaard et la pensée catholique," *Les Lettres*, vol. 4, no. 13, 1950, pp. 36–40.

— *Soeren Kierkegaard ou l'Esprit d'Elseneur*, Paris and Lyon: Vitte 1955.

Rougemont, Denis de, "Nécessité de Kierkegaard," *Foi et vie*, vol. 35, no. 64, 1934, pp. 605–20.

— *Les personnes du drame*, New York: Pantheon Books 1944.

Saint-Germain, Charles-Éric de, *L'avènement de la vérité: Hegel, Kierkegaard, Heidegger*, Paris, Budapest and Turin: l'Harmattan 2003.

Sipriot, Pierre (ed.), *Kierkegaard ou le Don Juan chrétien*, Monaco: Éditions du Rocher 1989.

Soren Kierkegaard et la critique du religieux, special number of *Nordique*, vol. 10 (Spring), 2006.

Søren Kierkegaard philosophe et dandy, special number of *Magazine Litteraire*, April 2007.

Soulès, Alberte Noéli, *La médicine et les médicins dans l'oeuvre de Kierkegaard*, Paris: Foulon 1949.

Sur, Françoise, *Kierkegaard, le devenir chrétien*, Paris: Éditions du Centurion 1967.

Stucki, P.-A., *Le Christianisme et l'histoire d'après Kierkegaard*, Basel: Verlag für Recht und Gesellschaft 1963.

Thibon, G., "Le drame de Kierkegaard," *Études carmélitaines*, vol. 23, April, 1938, pp. 140–50.

Tisseau, Paul-Henri, "L'Adolphe de B. Constant et la 'Répetition' de Kierkegaard," *Revue de littérature comparée*, vol. 13, no. 2, 1933, pp. 239–58.

— "Kierkegaard et l'amour," *Foi et vie*, vol. 35, no. 64, 1934, pp. 661–77.

— "La 'Confession' de Musset et le 'Banquet' de Kierkegaard," *Revue de littérature comparée*, vol. 14, no. 3, 1934, pp. 491–511.

— "Vie de Søren Kierkegaard," *La Table Ronde*, no. 95, 1955, pp. 9–17.

Vancourt, R., "Deux conceptions de la philosophie: Husserl et Kierkegaard," *Mélanges de Science Réligeuse*, vol. 2, 1945, pp. 193–234.

Vergote, Henri-Bernard, "Poul Martin Moeller et Soeren Kierkegaard," *Revue de métaphysique et de morale*, vol. 75, 1970, pp. 452–76.

— *Écoute, Kierkegaard*, vols. 1–2, Paris: Éditions de Cerf 1979.

— *Sens et répétition: essai sur l'ironie kierkegaardienne*, vols. 1–2, Paris: Éditions de Cerf 1982.

— (trans. and ed.), *Lectures philosophiques de Søren Kierkegaard: Kierkegaard chez ses contemporains danois. Textes de J.L. Heiberg, H.L. Martensen, P.M. Møller*, Paris: Presses Universitaires de France 1993.

— (ed.), *Retour de Kierkegaard / Retour à Kierkegaard, Colloque franco-danois*, Toulouse: Presses Universitaires du Mirail 1997 (*Kairos*, no. 10).

Viallaneix, Nelly, *l'Unique devant Dieu*, Paris: Éditions du Cerf 1974.

— *Écoute, Kierkegaard*, vols. 1–2, Paris: Éditions du Cerf 1979.

Waelhens, H. de, "Kierkegaard et Heidegger," in his *La Philosophie de Martin Heidegger*, Louvain: Éd. de l'institut supérieur de philosophie 1942, pp. 330–52.

Wahl, Jean, "Le mysticisme de Kierkegaard," *Hermès*, no. 1, 1930, pp. 16–23.

— "Hegel et Kierkegaard," *Revue philosophique*, vol. 56, nos. 11–12, 1931, pp. 321–80.

— "Kierkegaard: L'angoisse et l'instant," *La Nouvelle Revue Française*, vol. 20, no. 223, 1932, pp. 634–55.

— "Heidegger et Kierkegaard," *Recherches philosophiques*, vol. 2, 1932–33, pp. 349–70.

— "Sur quelques catégories kierkegaardiennes: l'Existence, l'Individu isolé, la Pensée subjective," *Recherches philosophiques*, vol. 3, 1933–34, pp. 171–202.

— "Hegel et Kierkegaard," *Verhandlungen des dritten Hegelkongresses vom 19. bis 23. April 1933 in Rom*, ed. by B. Wigersma, Tübingen: J.C.B. Mohr 1934, pp. 235–49.

— "La théorie de la croyance chez Kierkegaard," *Foi et Vie*, vol. 35, no. 64, 1934, pp. 639–60.

— "Le problème du choix, l'existence et la transcendance dans la philosophie de Jaspers," *Revue de métaphysique et de morale*, vol. 41, no. 3, 1934, pp. 405–44.

— "Søren Kierkegaard: Le paradoxe," *Revue des sciences philosophiques et théologiques*, vol. 24, no. 2, 1935, pp. 218–31.

— "Subjectivité et transcendance," *Bulletin de la Societé française de philosophie*, vol. 37, no. 5, 1937, pp. 161–3.

— *Études kierkegaardiennes*, Paris: Aubier 1938.

— *Petite histoire de "l'existentialisme" suivie de Kafka et Kierkegaard commentaires*, Paris: Limoges 1947.

— *La pensée de l'existence*, Paris: Flammarion 1951 (*Bibliotèque de philosophie scientifique*), pp. 5–58.

— *Les philosophies de l'existence*, Paris: Armand Colin 1954, p. 15; pp. 22–39 passim.

— *Kierkegaard: l'Un devant l'Autre*, Paris: Hachette Littératures 1998.

Werner, Charles, "Kierkegaard et la philosophie existentielle," in his *La philosophie moderne*, Paris: Payot 1954, pp. 282–307.

Zorgbibe, Guillaume, *Les paradoxes de la loi: Saint Augustin et Kierkegaard*, Paris, Budapest and Torino: l'Harmattan 2003.

III. Secondary Literature on Kierkegaard's Reception in France

[Anonymous], "Indications bibliographiques," *Foi et Vie*, 1934, pp. 718–20.

[Anonymous], "Kierkegaard in France," *Times Literary Supplement*, no. 34, 1935, p. 324.

[Anonymous], "Sören Kierkegaard in Frankreich," *Kölnische Zeitung*, October 29, 1936.

Billeskov Jansen, F.J., "The Study in France," in *Kierkegaard Research*, ed. by Marie Mikulová Thulstrup, Copenhagen: C.A. Reitzel 1987 (*Bibliotheca Kierkegaardiana*, vol. 15), pp. 134–59.

— "Les Études kierkegaardiennes en France," in *Kierkegaard. La découverte de l'existence*, ed. by Régis Boyer and Jean-Marie Paul, Nancy: Université de Nancy II 1990 (*Bibliothèque "Le Text et l'Idée,"* vol. 1), pp. 215–27.

Bousquet, François, "Kierkegaard. Études françaises récentes (1971–1984)," *Recherches de science religieuse*, no. 2 (April–June), 1984, pp. 243–64.

— "Kierkegaard dans la tradition théologique francophone," in *Kierkegaard Revisited. Proceedings from the Conference "Kierkegaard and the Meaning of Meaning It" Copenhagen, May 5–9, 1996*, ed. by Niels Jørgen Cappelørn and Jon Stewart, Berlin and New York: Walter de Gruyter 1997 (*Kierkegaard Studies. Monograph Series*, vol. 10), pp. 339–66 (reprinted in *Kierkegaard aujourd'hui: Actes du Colloque de la Sorbonne, 26 Octobre 1996*, ed. by Jacques Caron, Odense: Odense University Press and Grenoble 1998, pp. 91–124).

— "Note sur les études françaises concernant *Les Œuvres de l'amour* de Kierkegaard," *Kierkegaard Studies. Yearbook*, 1998, pp. 174–8.

— "Kierkegaard. Études françaises récentes (1971–1984)," *Recherches de science religieuse*, vol. 72, no. 2, 1984, pp. 243–64.

— "L'héritage morcelé: Kierkegaard chez les grands théologiens du XXe siècle," in *Retour de Kierkegaard / Retour à Kierkegaard, Colloque franco-danois*, ed. by Henri-Bernard Vergote, Toulouse: Presses Universitaires du Mirail 1997 (*Kairos*, no. 10), pp. 231–47.

Brun, Jean, "Actualité de Kierkegaard," *Foi et Vie*, 1970, no. 2, pp. 2–12.

Caron, Jacques, "Kierkegaard en France et dans quelques pays francophones," in *Le Secret de Kierkegaard*, Copenhagen: Danish Ministry of Education 1996, pp. 57–125.

— "Remarques sur la réception française de Kierkegaard," in *Kierkegaard aujourd'hui: Actes du Colloque de la Sorbonne, 26 Octobre 1996*, ed. by Jacques Caron, Odense: Odense University Press and Grenoble 1998, pp. 69–80.

Congar, M.-J., "Actualité de Kierkegaard," *La Vie Intellectuelle*, vol. 34, no. 1, 1934, pp. 9–36.

Cornu, Michel, "Actualité de Kierkegaard," *Revue de Théologie et de Philosophie*, 1971, pp. 427–38.

Depelsenaire, Yves, "La réception de Kierkegaard en France," in his *Une Analyse avec Dieu. Le Rendez-vous de Lacan et de Kierkegaard*, Brussels: La Lettre volée 2004, pp. 9–14.

Grimsley, Ronald, "French Existentialism," in *The Legacy and Interpretation of Kierkegaard*, ed. by Niels Thulstrup and Marie Mikulová Thustrup, Copenhagen: C.A. Reitzel 1981 (*Bibliotheca Kierkegaardiana*, vol. 8), pp. 121–34.

Hansen, Valdemar, "Quelques publications récentes sur Kierkegaard en Amérique et en France," *Theoria* (Gothenburg), vol. 6, 1940, pp. 83–7.

Kemp, Peter, "Le précurseur de Henrik Ibsen. Quelques aspects de la découverte de Kierkegaard en France," *Les Études philosophiques*, no. 2 (April–June), 1979, pp. 139–50.

Ladegaard Knox, Jeanette Bresson, "Some Remarks on the French Reception of *Philosophical Fragments*," *Kierkegaard Studies. Yearbook*, 2004, pp. 340–55.

Lafarge, Jacques, "Kierkegaard dans la tradition française: Les conditions de sa réception dans les milieux philosophiques," in *Kierkegaard Revisited. Proceedings from the Conference "Kierkegaard and the Meaning of Meaning It" Copenhagen, May 5–9, 1996*, ed. by Niels Jørgen Cappelørn and Jon Stewart, Berlin and New York: Walter de Gruyter 1997 (*Kierkegaard Studies. Monograph Series*, vol. 10), pp. 274–90.

— *La Diffusion éditoriale d'un oeuvre. L'oeuvre de Kierkegaard au Danemark, en Allemagne et en France (1834–1984)*, Dissertation, Université de Bordeaux, Bordeaux 1985.

— "Éditer, lire, étudier Kierkegaard," *Cahiers de Philosophie*, 1989, nos. 8–9, pp. 473–93.

— "Précisions sur la réception de Kierkegaard (reponse à J. Caron)," in *Kierkegaard aujourd'hui: Actes du Colloque de la Sorbonne, 26 Octobre 1996*, ed. by Jacques Caron, Odense: Odense University Press and Grenoble 1998, pp. 81–90.

— "L'Édition des *Oeuvres complètes* de Kierkegaard en français: contexte— historique—objectifs—conception—réalisation," *Kierkegaard Studies. Yearbook*, 2000, pp. 300–16.

Mesnard, Pierre, "Kierkegaard aux prises avec la conscience française," *Revue de Littérature Comparée*, vol. 29, no. 4, 1955, pp. 453–77 (reprinted in *Pierre Mesnard. Images de l'homme et de l'oeuvre*, Paris: Vrin 1970, pp. 212–37).

Message, Jacques, "Remarques sur la réception de *Begrebet Angest* en France (1935–1971)," *Kierkegaard Studies. Yearbook*, 2001, pp. 323–9.

Politis, Hélène, *Le Discours philosophique selon Kierkegaard*, Dissertation, Université de Paris I, 1993.

— *Kierkegaard en France au XXe siècle: archéologie d'une réception*, Paris: Éditions Kimé 2005.

Rougemont, Denis de, "Kierkegaard en France," *La Nouvelle Revue Français*, vol. 24, no. 273, 1936, pp. 971–6.

Sales, Michel, "Dix ans de publications kierkegaardiennes en langue française (1960–1971)," *Archives de philosophie*, vol. 35, 1972, pp. 649–72.

Viallaneix, Nelly, "Lectures françaises," in *The Legacy and Interpretation of Kierkegaard*, ed. by Niels Thulstrup and Marie Mikulová Thustrup, Copenhagen: C.A. Reitzel 1981 (*Bibliotheca Kierkegaardiana*, vol. 8), pp. 102–20.

Wahl, Jean, "Kierkegaard. Son influence en France," *Revue Danois. Commerciale, sociale, culturelle*, no. 1, 1951, pp. 34–6 (reprinted in his *Kierkegaard: l'Un devant l'Autre*, Paris: Hachette Littératures 1998, pp. 221–5).

Index of Persons

Bejerholm, Lars, 173, 182.
Bellesort, André (1866–1942), 426.
Berdyaev, Nikolay (1874–1948), Russian
   philosopher, 427.
van Bergen, G.G., 281, 282.
Bergson, Henri (1859–1941), French
   philosopher, 329, 434.
Bergsson, Guðbergur, 229.
Bergstedt, Harald (1877–1965), Danish
   poet, 32.
Beyer, Harald (1891–1960), Norwegian
   literary historian, 125, 158.
Billeskov Jansen, Frederik Julius (1907–
   2002), Danish literary scholar and
   author, 55, 67, 68, 70, 89, 96.
Birkedal, Wilhelm, 135.
Bjarnadóttir, Birna, 228, 229.
Bjarnason, Ágúst H., 224.
Bjørnson, Bjørnstjerne (1832–1910),
   Norwegian playwright, 126, 140–2,
   146, 149, 158.
Bjørnvig, Thorkild (1918–2004), Danish
   poet, 65.
Blackham, Harold John (1903–2009),
   British humanist and writer, 254,
   255.
Blake, William (1757–1827), English poet
   and artist, 254.
Blanchot, Maurice (1907–2003), French
   philosopher and writer, 259, 453,
   454.
Blicher, Steen Steensen (1782–1848),
   Danish author, 77.
Blixen, Karen (1885–1962), Danish author,
   96.
Blumenberg, Hans, 147.
Boas, Eduard (1815–53), German author
   and literary historian, 274.
Bocken, Inigo, 288.
Boesen, Emil (1812–81), 9.
Bohlin, Anna, 175.
Bohlin, Torsten (1889–1950), Swedish
   Protestant theologian, 22, 35, 36, 42,
   62, 173, 178, 181, 207, 371.
Bohr, Niels (1885–1962), Danish physicist, 3.
Boman, Thorleif, 159, 160.
Bomholt, Julius (1896–1969), Danish
   minister of culture, 46.
Bomstad, Johan, 130.
Bonsdorff, Max von, 208.
Borg, Stefan, 175,

Borgbjerg, F.J. (1886–1936), Danish
   politician and editor, 82.
Børsand, Grete, 161.
van den Bos, Geert, 273, 274, 276, 277.
Bousquet, François, 456, 458.
Brahe, Tycho (1546–1601), Danish
   astronomer, 242.
Bramming, Torben, 64.
Brandes, Edvard (1847–1931), Danish
   politician and author, founder of the
   newspaper *Politiken*, 12, 81.
Brandes, Georg (1842–1927), Danish author
   and literary critic, 3–8, 12–21
   passim, 30–3, 44, 50, 51, 53, 67, 82,
   83, 86, 122, 137–43 passim, 146,
   147, 150, 155–7, 164, 165, 183, 197,
   198, 242, 274, 318, 319, 368, 424.
Brandt, Frithiof (1892–1968), Danish
   literary scholar, 30, 43–6 passim,
   50–2.
Breder, Ludvig, 132.
Bremer, Fredrika (1801–65), Swedish
   author, 175, 197, 237ff.
Brézis, David, 457.
Brix, Hans (1870–1961), Danish literary
   scholar, 29, 43–5.
Broch, Hermann (1856–1951), Austrian
   novelist, 69, 328.
Brøchner, Hans (1820–75), Danish
   philosopher, 5–8, 12, 253.
Brock, Werner, 253.
Brod, Max (1884–1968), Czech-Jewish
   German language author, 332.
Brøgger, Suzanne, 69.
Brostrøm, Torben, 3.
Bruun, Christopher Arndt (1839–1909),
   Norwegian Protestant theologian,
   125, 128, 156.
Brunner, Emil (1889–1966), Swiss
   Protestant theologian, 279, 334,
   336–8, 343.
Buber, Martin (1878–1965), German
   philosopher, 91, 347, 349, 350, 427.
Buijs, Lineke, 288.
Bukdahl, Jørgen, 54, 55, 71, 73, 83, 85.
Bukdahl, Jørgen K., 83, 84.
Bull, Francis (1887–1974), Norwegian
   literary historian, 142.
Bultmann, Rudolf (1884–1976), German
   Protestant theologian, 34, 225, 334,
   338–41, 355, 386.

Jaspers, Karl (1883–1969), German
  philosopher, 247, 252, 254, 279,
  282, 351–5, 358, 363, 372, 379, 386,
  427, 457.
Jeannine, Bernard, 424.
Jensen, C.E. (1865–1927), Danish literary
  critic, 82.
Jensen, Christian (1873–1949), Danish
  pastor, 21.
Jensen, Johannes V. (1873–1950), Danish
  author, 32, 51.
Jensen, N.O., 63.
Jessen, E.A.F., 319.
Jesus, see "Christ."
Johansen, Kjell Eyvind, 162, 163.
Johansson, Gustaf (1844–1930), Finnish
  theologian, 199.
Johansson, Klara (1875–1948), 183.
John the Baptist, 248.
Johnson, Gisle (1822–94), Norwegian
  theologian, 127, 128, 130, 143.
Jolivet, Régis (1891–1966), French Catholic
  thinker, 429.
Jonker, Aart, 276.
Jonker, Gerrit, 276.
Jónsson, Kristján Jóhann, 222.
Jor, Finn, 161.
Jörg, Joseph E.J. (1819–1901), German
  historian and politician, 313.
Jørgensen, Johannes (1866–1956), Danish
  author, 32.
Juncker, Axel (1870–1952), German
  publisher, 325.

Kabell, Aage, 9, 41, 42, 50, 53, 55.
Kafka, Franz (1883–1924), Czech-Austrian
  novelist, 212, 251, 259, 331–3, 347,
  386, 454.
Kaila, Eino (1890–1958), Finnish
  philosopher, 204, 205.
Kant, Immanuel (1724–1804), German
  philosopher, 154, 225, 258, 264,
  329, 337, 379, 434.
Kassner, Rudolf (1873–1959), Austrian
  philosopher, author and critic,
  322–7, 331, 385, 386.
Kehler, Henning (1891–1979), Danish
  journalist, critic and dramatist, 32,
  51.
Ketonen, Oiva (1913–2000), Finnish
  philosopher, 204.

Kidde, Harald (1878–1918), Danish poet,
  69.
Kielland, Alexander Lange (1849–1906),
  165.
Kierkegaard, Michael Pedersen (1756–
  1838), Søren Kierkegaard's father,
  14.
Kierkegaard, Peter Christian (1805–88),
  Danish theologian, elder brother of
  Søren Kierkegaard, 4, 9, 10, 13, 29.
Kierkegaard, Søren Aabye (1813–1855),
  *The Battle between the Old and the New
    Soap-Cellars* (1837), 30.
  From the Papers of One Still Living
    (1838), 14.
  The Concept of Irony (1841), 123, 179,
    199, 310, 430, 434, 437, 442.
  *Johannes Climacus, or De omnibus
    dubitandum est* (ca. 1842–43), 62,
    78, 284, 285,
  Either/Or (1843), 14, 15, 53, 67, 68,
    123–5, 144–9, 152–4, 174, 181, 184,
    200, 201, 211, 212, 220, 222, 226,
    227, 230, 242, 245, 251, 286, 312,
    325, 332, 364, 368, 430, 431, 441.
  Repetition (1843), 19, 58, 67, 69, 163,
    212, 226–31 passim, 284, 285, 332,
    451.
  Fear and Trembling (1843), 14, 58, 67,
    91, 123, 138, 163, 174, 181, 206,
    212, 220, 222, 226, 228, 229, 231,
    259, 280, 285, 314, 327, 332, 333,
    437, 446, 447, 450, 451, 453.
  Prefaces (1844), 124.
  Upbuilding Discourses (1843–1844),
    173.
  Philosophical Fragments (1844), 22,
    35–40 passim, 58–62, 65, 66, 72,
    78, 87, 155, 159, 163, 213, 250, 283,
    286, 311, 316, 317, 336, 339, 340,
    345, 375, 429, 439, 455, 456.
  The Concept of Anxiety (1844), 35, 47,
    48, 58, 62, 67, 151–4, 163, 209, 246,
    280, 283, 286, 316, 357, 432, 435–7,
    443, 446, 449, 451, 455.
  Stages on Life's Way (1845), 15, 67, 68,
    121, 124, 154, 159, 227, 230, 286,
    431, 447, 448, 449.
  Concluding Unscientific Postscript
    (1846), 15, 34–9, 59, 64, 77, 90, 94,

486 *Kierkegaard's International Reception*

Russell, Bertrand (1872–1970), English
mathematician and philosopher, 359.
Ruttenbeck, Walter (1890–1964), German
Protestant theologian, 97, 370.

Saarikoski, Pentti (1937–83), Finnish
author, 208, 209.
Saarinen, Esa, 209, 210.
Sæmundsson, Matthías Viðar (1954–2004),
229.
Sandberg, Caspar Køhler, 131–7 passim.
Sandelin, Kalle (1893–1983; after 1936
under the name Kalle Sorainen),
Finnish Kierkegaard scholar, 56,
202–5 passim.
Saroyan, William (1908–81), American
dramatist and author, 252.
Sars, Johan Ernst (1835–1917), Norwegian
professor of history, 140.
Sartre, Jean-Paul (1905–80), French
philosopher, 209, 225, 239, 251,
252, 254, 425, 428, 429, 432–46
passim, 449, 450, 453, 457.
Savonarola, Girolamo (1452–98), Italian
religious and political reformer, 254.
Schaeder, Erich (1861–1936), German
Protestant theologian, 331.
Schelling, Friedrich Wilhelm Joseph von
(1775–1854), German philosopher,
61, 147, 342, 379, 381.
Schilder, Klaas (1890–1952), Dutch
Reformed minister, 280.
Schiødte, Andreas Ferdinand (1806–87),
Danish pastor, 8.
Schjelderup, Harald, 225.
Schleiermacher, Friedrich D.E. (1768–
1834), German Protestant
theologian, 19, 204, 248. 255, 264,
345, 375.
Schmidt, Robert (1882–1941), Danish actor,
45.
Schmitt, Carl (1888–1985), German jurist
and political theorist, 346.
Schnitzler, Arthur (1862–1931), Austrian
novelist, 331.
Scholtens, Wim, 285, 286.
Schopenhauer, Arthur (1788–1860), German
philosopher, 224.
Schousboe, Julius (1886–1960), Danish
theologian, 50.

Schrempf, Christoph (1860–1944), German
Protestant theologian, 97, 314–8
passim, 320–2, 324, 328–32, 386,
426.
Schubert, Gotthilf Heinrich von (1780–
1860), German natural scientist,
164.
Schulz, Walter (1912–2000), German
philosopher, 386.
Schwanenflügel, Hermann Heinrich (1844–
1921), Danish literary historian,
224.
Schwazmann, Lev Isaakovich (1866–1938),
Russian-French thinker, 427.
Scribe, Augustin Eugène (1791–1861),
French dramatic author, 148, 422.
Segerstedt, Torgny Karl (1876–1945),
Swedish scholar of comparative
religion, 97, 181.
Shakespeare, Steven, 258, 261.
Shakespeare, William (1564–1616), English
dramatist, 147.
Shaw, George Bernard (1856–1950), Irish
dramatist, 241.
Shestov, Lev (1866–1938), Russian-French
philosopher, 427, 428, 452.
Sibbern, Frederik Christian (1785–1872),
Danish philosopher, 19, 203, 456.
Sigurbjörnsson, Karl, 225.
Siljo, Juhani (1888–1918), Finnish author,
201.
Simonsson, Ingmar, 184.
Sjöstedt, Nils Åke, 177, 183.
Skirbekk, Gunnar, 226.
Skjervheim, Hans (1926–99), Norwegian
philosopher and essay writer, 160,
161.
Skúlason, Páll, 230.
Sløk, Johannes (1916–2001), Danish
Protestant theologian, 63, 64, 72–4,
84–6, 284.
Snellman, Johan Vilhelm (1806–81),
Finnish Hegelian philosopher, 197,
202,
Socrates, 23, 37, 49, 59, 66, 67, 78, 179,
240, 256, 278, 328, 339, 381, 427,
434.
Søe, N.H., 70, 224.
Solger, Karl Wilhelm Ferdinand (1780–
1819), German philosopher and
aesthetic theorist, 164.

Index of Subjects

freedom, 23, 71, 139, 144, 145, 161, 182,
    376, 423, 425, 427, 431–40 passim,
    445, 449.
French Revolution, 71.

God, 6, 10, 23, 38, 39, 49, 65, 66, 74, 87,
    128, 134, 177, 204, 206, 207, 211,
    220, 238, 240, 245–50 passim, 252,
    317, 327, 332, 337, 340, 348, 353,
    354, 441, 453.
God-man, 22, 59, 247, 276, 350, 354, 362.
Grace, 35, 180.
Greeks, the 49, 227.
    philosophy/thought, 6, 8, 357.
Grundtvig Academy (Copenhagen), 97.

Hamlet, 244, 426.
Hegelianism, 67, 155, 178, 203, 278.
history, 382.
Hong Kierkegaard Library at St. Olaf Col-
    lege, xi, 258.
humor, 50, 201, 205, 323, 430, 439.

idealism, 162.
immanence, 364, 374.
Incarnation, the, 221, 340.
individual, the 6, 15, 17, 94, 139, 240, 431,
    438, 454.
    the single, 178–81, 208, 272, 322, 323,
    326, 350, 440, 456.
individualism, 248, 333, 334.
infinity, 211.
inner/outer, 80, 83, 87, 200.
International Kierkegaard Commentary, xi,
    258.
intersubjectivity, 348, 452.
inward deepening, 22.
inwardness, 14f., 23, 245, 329, 336, 364–6,
    452.
irony, 49, 81, 164, 205, 209, 212, 382, 430,
    437, 439, 442, 450.
irrational, the, 19.

Job, 427.

Kierkegaardiana, x, 56, 58, 258.
Kierkegaard Studies. Monograph Series, 92.
Kierkegaard Studies. Yearbook, xi, 92, 258.

language, 348, 360, 361, 381.
leap, the, 19, 20, 128.

Lebensphilosophie, 342.
leveling, 84, 212.
life-view debate, 32.
love, 64, 65, 72, 73, 90, 177, 246, 250.

Marie Beaumarchais, 147.
marriage, 80.
martyrdom, 137, 354, 428.
Marxism, 73, 79, 181, 209, 438.
mediation, 80, 211.
melancholy, 14, 19, 24, 46, 209.
modern breakthrough, the, 4, 18, 33, 34,
    137, 140.
modernism, 79, 239, 241.
moment, the, 38, 54, 88, 94, 97, 249, 311,
    342, 345, 357.
music, 367–9.
mystery, 7, 8.
mysticism, 59, 286.
myth, 365, 366.

naturalism, 154.
nihilism, 184, 442.

offense, 40, 65, 78, 79, 155, 249, 311, 340,
    442.

paradox, the, 6–8, 14–16, 20, 22, 23, 35–40
    passim, 59, 66, 72, 78, 86–8, 94,
    144, 155, 178, 211, 221, 249, 255,
    256, 279, 280, 311, 320, 323, 333,
    342, 345, 359, 361, 377, 425, 426,
    439, 440, 442, 444, 454, 456.
passion, 15, 16, 59, 72, 155, 456.
phenomenology, 205, 282, 364, 443, 450.
philosophy, 7.
    analytic, 182, 183, 204, 209, 239, 259.
    existential, 39, 159, 205, 246, 279, 282,
    352, 379.
Pietism, 127–30, 140, 141, 145, 165, 333,
    345.
politics, 81–6.
Politiken, 83.
positivism, 154, 160, 161.
postmodernism, 79, 164, 238, 263.
poststructuralism, 421, 450.
pseudonymity, 68, 456, 457.
psychoanalysis, 73, 205, 253, 440.
psychology, 13, 19, 20, 46, 205, 209, 280,
    285, 372, 451.
recollection, 78, 155.